Love, Death and Money in the Pays d'Oc

Portrait of the abbé Jean–Baptiste Castor Fabre by the Montpellier painter Jean Coustou, 1765 (now in the collection of the Entente Bibliophile de Montpellier)

Students and External Readers	Staff & Research Students
DATE DUE FOR RETURN	**DATE OF ISSUE**
	N.B. All books must be returned for the Annual Inspection in June

Any book which you borrow remains your responsibility
until the loan slip is cancelled

LOVE, DEATH
AND MONEY
IN THE PAYS D'OC

Emmanuel Le Roy Ladurie

TRANSLATED BY ALAN SHERIDAN

SCOLAR PRESS

LONDON

First published in Great Britain in 1982 by
SCOLAR PRESS
James Price Publishing Limited
90/91 Great Russell Street
London WC1B 3PY

Originally published in France in 1980
as *L'argent, l'amour et la mort en pays d'oc*

BRITISH LIBRARY CATALOGUING IN PUBLICATION DATA

Le Roy Ladurie, Emmanuel
    Love, death and money in the pays d'oc.
    1. Faure, Jean Baptiste Castor. Istoria de
    Joan l'an-pres
    I. Title II. L'argent, l'amour et la mort
    en pays d'oc. *English*
    849'.34   PC3401.F3

ISBN 0-85967-655-2

Typeset in Great Britain by
Richard Clay (The Chaucer Press) Ltd,
Bungay, Suffolk
Set in Monophoto Ehrhardt

Printed and bound in Great Britain
at the University Press, Cambridge

Contents

Preface

For a long time, the short but highly concentrated novel *Jean-l'ont-pris* by the abbé Jean-Baptiste Castor Fabre (1727–83), the master-piece of modern Occitan literature, was regarded as a 'realistic' des-cription of village life in eighteenth-century Languedoc.[1] The present book is an attempt to re-examine this old problem.[2] I consider this great text in relation to the culture of the Midi during the *ancien régime*, the word 'culture' being understood in both the anth-ropological and literary senses. I also consider *Jean-l'ont-pris* in terms of folk literature, which belongs mainly to oral tradition. At the end of this double confrontation, we should have a clearer idea of the extent to which *Jean-l'ont-pris* is a realistic description of village life. What is more generally at stake is the thick file concerning the relations between literature and history, fiction and fact. We should not forget that in the Occitan world, where the archives of social history (notaries' records, etc.) are in French, the regional literature represents the only cultural monument in which an author can express himself in the language of the local people: in this sense, it is closer to them than the French-speaking archives, valuable as these are to historical research.

E L R L

Jean-l'ont-pris

1   One evening, as he was retiring to his castle, a nobleman of the Vaunage heard a man, some two or three hundred paces ahead of him, singing at the top of his voice and repeating every so often the words

> Good luck come my way!
> Hey! Nonny-nonny!
> Good luck come my way!

Hearing this merry air, he took the fancy to catch up with the musician and learn what good fortune made him bawl out his song on the public way. So he spurred on his horse and soon saw that the singer was a yokel dressed in black, who wore his few remaining hairs in a pigtail, with a mourning band hanging loose from a hat stuck on the back of his head.

2   'Friend,' he said, as he rode up to him, 'you are singing a refrain that scarcely befits your present attire. Would you be so kind as to explain the riddle?'

3   'Ah! my lord,' replied the Vaunajol, 'I wish you a good evening, and I am glad to see your cheek so fresh . . . The fact is, I have just buried my wife, and that, believe me, is a great relief to a man.'

4   'It may sometimes be,' replied the nobleman, 'but not always, and I would be curious to learn the mighty reasons you must have to rejoice at this circumstance, if you have time and inclination to instruct me on the matter.'

5   'One cannot refuse such a thing to gentlefolk like yourself,' replied the peasant. 'If you would keep your horse in check as far as your castle, which is on my way, I shall recount not only what you ask, but also my father's story and my own, if it so please you.'

The baron accepted the proposition, and our widower began his tale.

6   I was born, sir, at Solorgues, of a family not of the highest station, you might say, but middling in all things and among the best of the place. My father settled there and set up shop as a cobbler, with the approval of the authorities, that is to say, the magistrate, the farrier and a Capuchin friar who came every year to beg for oil. He

conducted himself with such skill and politeness, he became so well loved, so highly respected, in short, he did so well in so many things that he attained his heart's desire and married the bastard daughter of the surgeon of Calvisson. This girl had retired with her mother to Solorgues, where they lived like two young virgins. Trustworthy folk have told me that my mother looked like me, so she must have been the prettiest, most buxom wench in all the lowlands of the country. Her name was Margot, and my poor father, may he be with God, was called Truquette. Though they were not of the nobility, I enjoyed the privilege, sometimes given to sons of gentlemen, of not bearing my family name.

7 From the age of three everyone called me Jean-l'ont-pris, and that's the only name I go by.

Yet it should not be thought that this is the name of an estate, for, except for a potful of earth we had on our window-sill, in which my mother grew basil, we possessed not a single spadeful to our name. But before long I shall explain how I got this name, which has stayed with me since. Let us take things as they fell out.

8 Margot, a truly buxom wench, as I said, did not lack for lovers. There was not a mother's son in Solorgues or in the whole district who did not spend his Sundays and feast-days in her company. The whole throng devoured her with their eyes, pinched her, chased her, jostled her here and there, through fields, meadows, vineyards, hedges or ditches, taking no more account of other girls than nightingales do of bats. In the end, Truquette joined the company and, for his deserts or good fortune, was preferred above all the others. What favoured him exceedingly was that his work kept him at her side. He saw Margot the whole blessed day and every day of the week, while the others, obliged to earn their miserable livelihoods travelling the countryside, had to make shift as best they could.

9 You have to admit, my lord, that, providing he does what's expected of a man, a sharp fellow like my father, who spends six days of the seven alone with a girl, will make light work of his courtship. Margot's mother made matches, and she did not stay at home the whole day. Margot took the matches to Truquette's shop; there she cut them to the right size, tipped them with sulphur and bound them into bundles; and as she worked, she was not behindhand in doing whatever she could to arouse my father's good humour, humming the

latest song from Paris, poking him between the ribs with an awl or gently rubbing his chops with a ball of wax. My father, who did not take any of this seriously, stopped cobbling his shoes and, flinging his stirrup delicately round her neck, rode off with her. Thereupon, they frolicked about, legged it, rolled around, fell and got up again when they could, suddenly bursting into fits of laughter. All this, not to mention the fact that Truquette mended her shoes for nothing, put Margot so much in mind to love him that, on the Sundays following, all the other young men of the district found her prouder and more unyielding than the housekeeper of the *curé* of Bezouces. However, this did not stop them from singing their lovelorn nonsense at her door for a long time yet; but, whatever they did, it was to her harsher music than that of tom-cats in February, when the females have had their fill.

10   Truquette found them one evening, and just to enrage them further, he whistled as usual, pretending that he had not seen them, and bang!, there was Margot at the window. You can imagine how sheepish they all looked!

11   Another evening, as they were bawling their heads off to no avail whatsoever, Truquette walked by, sneezed, and bang!, there was Margot at the window.

Finally, another evening, when they had expended all their skills and were no further advanced in their suit, Truquette arrived, farted, and, this time, Margot appeared at the window so inflamed with desire that it was all she could do not to leap upon him. It is said that lovers recognize each other from afar; but, you have to admit, my lord, that one has to love someone pretty strongly to recognize him by a password of that sort!

12   The young greenhorns saw the success of this gallantry as an absolute discharge; they made off without a word, kept quiet night and day, and left my parents the peace that they so desired. They did feel a certain resentment, however, for in front of the other girls, they could not help saying: 'Heavens! What a pity that Margot should go and lose her head with Truquette first!' The girls, their curiosity aroused by my father's deserts, contradicted them: 'Oh yes, of course! It's an even greater pity that this Truquette should have chosen Margot.' 'Margot has taken Truquette, Truquette has taken Margot. Margot and Truquette, Truquette and Margot': for a month or more

there was no other subject of conversation throughout that Babylon of a Solorgues.

13   But at last, when enough had been said, people fell silent; my parents still loved each other despite all the what-will-they-says, and the marriage stilled the tongues of the envious.

14   Never, my lord, could there ever have been such an expensive wedding in Solorgues. However, the poor devils were to regret it later! My father, God rest his soul, saddled a couple of donkeys and went to Nîmes to fetch the food and other necessaries for the feast. He arrived back with four baskets and a sack full of things. For himself, there was a serge jacket from Cádiz, a fine pair of stockings from Saint-Marsot, a pair of grey linen knee-breeches with good, strong garters, yellow ribbons, leather gaiters and new tin buckles. For his betrothed, he brought a fine apron from Saint-Jean, a serge petticoat, a large brass cross and chain, a flannelette jacket with chamois-leather fronts and the wedding-ring, which, if it had been gold, would certainly have weighed half a pound.

15   The rest was to gorge themselves: tell me if there wasn't enough to feast all the friends and relations! Ah, my lord, look how people talk! How generous people may become when they are in love, for their damned weddings! For you have heard nothing yet of what I have still to tell you and which all Solorgues would confirm. Would you believe, my lord, that on the wedding-day, either on their way to the church or coming back or during the meal that was given, the four baskets of provisions that my father had brought back disappeared? But I'm not surprised. They cast food about in all directions, like seed. People in the street caught at least four pounds of hazelnuts, which my father threw to them, not to mention all the handfuls of hackberries that my mother threw to left and right as she raised her leg.

16   As if that were not enough, as soon as they had returned home for the feast, my wasteful grandmother – I wonder what sudden madness took hold of her, what came over the old bitch – took it into her head to stand in front of the door and throw at least twenty packets of matches into the street; and if I said twenty-two, I would certainly not be lying! Judge for yourself, my lord, judge for yourself if those who were sitting at the table would go short!

17   It is said that during the meal they consumed two large pots of

girdle-cakes, another pot full of frogs, a *roussette* weighing nine
pounds, half a dozen magpies, plus a magnificent fox that the hunter
of La Boissière had killed the night before in the Garrigue de Mus
and that he had not sold for under 12 sous without the skin. All this
was followed by four panfuls of chestnuts, sloes, cornel-berries, arbutus-berries, mulberries and the devil knows what else . . . Plus a four-
setier butt of wine. Oh, I'm sure your lordship will agree that poor
folk who give themselves such airs of greatness cannot reign. That
belongs to noblemen like yourself, and even, in the end, it would not
be a miracle to see you drowned head over heels . . .

18   The first to say that when the feast is over the fool remains
certainly knew a thing or two; he had understood what would become
of my parents' affairs, as though he had read it turning the tamis
sieve. They found themselves without bread, without wine, without
food, without leather, without sulphur, without money . . . and my
mother, nine days after the wedding, had the good grace to give forth
a fine boy who now has the honour of speaking to you. As if they
didn't have enough trouble as it was!

19   Poor Truquette, he must have had a few headaches when he saw,
on the one hand, a woman in childbed, and, on the other, a future
heir. But that numskull of a Rouergat was not so easily put out. To
get out of this pretty pickle, Truquette went off with the clothes he
had bought for his wife, sold them at half the price that anyone else
would have asked for them and brought back meat for his dear
Margot, swaddling-clothes and bed-linen for the baby, sulphur for
my grandmother, leather, wax and cheap wine for himself.

My mother, convinced that he had bought all this with money that
had been owing him for some work, thought no more about it, drank
her bowls of soup and got up after four days; but, on Sunday, when
she was going out for the first time, she sought in vain for her fine
clothes and trinkets. Not a rag remained in the cellar where they had
set up house.

20   She went through all their belongings, turning everything
upside-down. In the end, she said to Truquette:

'Tell me, my fine fellow, where are my garments?'

'Your garments?' he answered, looking more embarrassed than
surprised. 'We'll find them.'

My mother, surprised to see Truquette looking so sheepish and talking in Gavach,[1] which he did not usually do, set about him roundly:

'What are you talking about? What do you mean we'll find them? What kind of talk is that now? We'll find them, will we?'

'Yes, of course, if God so wishes,' my father added.

'Oh, yes, of course! We'll find them!' she cried, imitating my father. 'You damned Gavach! You monster! I know very well we'll find them again if you give them back to me . . .'

'Who else could have them?' said Truquette, moving towards the door.

21 Margot, at her wits' end, threw herself at the nape of his neck and, clinging to him, began to shout: 'Thief, drunkard, tobacco-pouch! Give me back my clothes, or I'll pull your hair out by the roots!' Truquette, who was not entirely at his ease, said: 'Very well! In that case, I'll give them back to you, but let me go . . .' Margot let him go, but what does that buffoon of a Truquette do then? He jumps away, grabs his stirrup and starts beating his dear wife's back with it. She, howling like a puppy getting a beating for its supper, looked around for something to defend herself with. The first object to hand was a small jug full of hot wax; she grabbed it and flung it straight at his face; needless to say, very little missed its mark.

22 My dear grandmother, who lived just opposite, jumped out of bed as soon as she heard this hullabaloo, dashed down the stairs, four steps at a time, and appeared in her night-dress, bare-headed, to restore order; it didn't take her four minutes. 'What's going on?' she said, arming herself with an awl to separate them. 'You brute! Is this the way you treat my daughter?' And without demanding further details, she set about larding Truquette's skin as well as she could.

23 The din they made in that house drew the whole of Solorgues to the shop; everyone came running to look, to listen, to find out what was happening; everyone took the side of the one he or she liked more, and, after a few minutes, the noise was four times louder outside than in.

24 As opinion was very divided, the argument became wider, more heated, and quite naturally turned into a general set-to.

25 The mother of a young man who was about to return to the fray, even though he had just provided ample proof of his words, cried: 'Come here, you fool! I hope you're not going to show yourself up in

front of those down-and-outs! Come on! Get out of there! Let them settle it among themselves!'

26 My grandmother, hearing this compliment, advanced with great nobility and composure to the cellar door and, apparelled as I have already described, turned to the old woman and said:

'Look, simpleton, down-and-outs like us are ladies and gentlemen compared with lousy tramps like you; my son-in-law and daughter have over 100 francs of their own, not to mention what they'll have from me; but great winds beat at great gates, and good fortune is not without its cares . . . Take a look at this fine lady, if you will, with her multicoloured rags! Down-and-outs in our family! A feast! Yes, certainly, all these good people saw plenty of that at my daughter's wedding! So much the worse for you. We were inside eating our fill, while you were out there, in front of our house, gnawing at the bones we threw out of the window. Down-and-outs! Idiot! Filthy old bag! Canting humbug . . .'

The other woman, seeing her in such a state, dared not stand up to her:

'Alas, good heavens!' she said to my grandmother. 'Have I angered you, my fine lady? I beg you to accept my humble apologies, and, if you will, I'll drop you a curtsy . . .'

'If you do, we will pay it back,' replied my grandmother, 'and it will be as fine as yours. Take a look at this one!'

'And you this one!'

'And you this one!'

'And you mine!'

'And you these two . . .'

'And you these two . . .'

As they said this, they each performed half a dozen curtsies, which made all the onlookers laugh and put an end to the commotion. Each went his own way, and peace was restored to our house. My father and mother were still in love, and quarrels never last long between people who find it so easy to make it up again.

27 However, they had acquired a taste for blows, and I must say that later they returned to them with considerable assiduity and haste. But, this time, things stayed as they were. They ate their meal in peace, then went to bed as though nothing had happened.

28 The following day, my grandmother called a family conference that was to have the greatest importance for us all. She began thus:

29 'Children, your wedding has caused you so much expense that your fortune is now at risk, and everything you can earn from your trade will not be enough to allow you to live according to your rank; I advise you, while you are still young, to create some capital with everything you own and set yourselves up in business. I know very well that nowadays there is no other way of getting on. In this way you can suck the public dry. I've seen I don't know how many ragamuffins, real down-and-outs, who, having chosen this path, before five or six years are out, are buying vineyards, fields, houses, castles, baronies. At first, you start in a small way; you set up as an ironmonger, a haberdasher or a muslin seller; you buy poor-quality goods cheap and sell them dear. You go out into the highways and byways, visiting stalls and fairs; there you make your purchases with a small down payment; you sell them, you accumulate money, you pocket the profit, and a good bankruptcy pays the rest. One bankruptcy, it is true, is not enough to set you up; it even turns people against you, but who cares! From the first, you go on to a second, then to a third, then to a fourth, and so on, as many times as it takes for you to be regarded as respectable, honest folk whose reputation is beyond reproach. You can then plunge your hand into the mire up to your elbow; everyone will find it perfectly clean when you pull it out. Oh, my dear Truquette, since I did you the honour of giving you my daughter in marriage, who, if it hadn't been for you, could have married a carder at least, you'll just have to make her a merchant's wife.

30 'You're a big, strong, sharp-witted fellow. A devil like you will make a fine job of the buying, while your wife and I keep the shop. What more could you wish for, my child? Do you want to spend the rest of your life as a poor cobbler, working your fingers to the bone in the path of duty? Come now, my friend, where's your sense of honour; it all depends on you whether Margot is to be a lady, Truquette a gentleman and your son a fine soldier. The little lamb!' my grandmother added, turning towards me, 'I can just see him, his hair curled in the Grecian style, with as much gold braid on his tunic as on a priest's chasuble.'

31 My father sat with his elbows on the table, his face resting on

one hand, in which he held his stirrup and wax-end, his mouth open
and his eyes turned to my grandmother, all agog at what she had just
said. I don't know whether he was seized by a taste for business from
that very moment, or whether her words merely awakened it in him;
but that very evening he sold everything he had in the shop for a total
of 10 crowns and, next day, set out for the fair at Sommières, which
was held on the day before Palm Sunday. The three days he stayed
there were, one has to admit, highly profitable. It is said that on the
night of his return – from the day he decided to become a merchant,
he never returned home before nightfall – he brought back with him
over 500 francs' worth of goods, having spent only 9 crowns and
without anyone giving him a farthing's credit. He arrived with two
donkeys, laden with goods of all kinds, and, next day, he would have
set Margot up in a shop, if he had not had special reasons to wait a
few days longer.

32   He had already gone into partnership with three other tradesmen
of his kind, who, himself apart, were the sharpest individuals the
profession has ever known. One of them, who was called Crouquet,[2]
had been a pilferer since childhood, and had brought that art to a
very high degree of perfection. Another, Jacquet by name, a very
dependable fellow, had changed his line of business so often that, in
order not to lose what he had, he took the precaution of hiding away
in his own house what belonged to others. The third, if I remember
rightly, was called Quincarlot;[3] he was blind in the right eye, which
diminished his value to some extent; but, good heavens!, fine gentleman that you are, your lordship would find it difficult to relieve him
of what he had in the purse on his left side without his knowing.
Well! Despite all their skills, these three gentlemen were simpletons
compared with my father. However, with so much intelligence and
talent, luck did not stay with them to the end. They overreached
themselves, and this cost them all their worldly goods and even no
little impaired their reputation.

33   As my father was the shrewdest of them and had provided most
of the capital, it was he who kept the stores, that is to say, his cellar,
and kept the accounts, that is to say, a double-entry system in which
he would put down only some of the receipts and a little more of the
expenditures, deducting good tithes for himself here and there. It
was also he who set out in search of the goods that the others brought

back to Solorgues, to their own gain or loss. My mother handled the retail side behind a counter, and my grandmother had nothing to do but eat, drink and look after the dear dauphin who, today, as you know, has just buried his wife.

34 The partnership prospered so well at the beginning that, before two years were up, my father bought fields, vineyards, meadows, olive-groves and the finest house in the neighbourhood.

35 Money poured in. Truquette took to wearing a wig, a jabot and lace ruffles; Margot, rings, a watch, long, hanging sleeves and lace; my grandmother, a bonnet, a fur-lined coat and slippers. As for me, I was wrapped in such a profusion of ribbons that you would have thought me a bobbin. I was so swaddled from one end to the other that no one could tell any longer who I was.

36 For about three years business continued to prosper, but then luck turned so rapidly that in twenty-four hours the whole family found itself again with nothing more than what's in the palm of your hand, and so many cares that we did not know where to turn. What lost us the game was nothing more than the envy of certain individuals, plus a few bales of wool that our partners had picked up on the highway without informing anyone of their presumed intention of paying for them. Unfortunately, they were followed as they were taking the bales to Solorgues, and the next day, alas and alack!, as the spit was turning and we sat quietly before dinner, resting from our day's labours, a band of men in blue, accompanied by the *consul* ['magistrate'] and all the riff-raff of Solorgues, burst into our house without even knocking at the door. They grabbed my father and his friends by the scruff of the neck, tied them up without so much as listening to what they had to say, got my mother to dress more quickly than a chambermaid summoned by her mistress, showed disrespect to my grandmother and, by way of letting me enjoy the cool of the evening, undressed me in such a way that you would have sworn that I had just made my entry into this base world.

37 But that was not all, my lord; those wretches cleared out the house so well that they left not so much as the plaster on the walls. They carried everything to the *consul*'s and led out the whole firm tied to the tails of their horses, and none of us ever saw my poor father again.

38 Your lordship can imagine what a state Margot must have been

in. She was quite desperate, and the next day, her heart broken and her eyes full of tears, the poor woman went off with a knife-grinder who had courted her before Truquette.

39   I was left with my grandmother, who, refusing to be cast down by so many misfortunes, went back to making matches, working herself to death and inculcating in me a knowledge of the ways of the world befitting a child of good family. My poor little grandmother! Alas! Jean-l'ont-pris will never be able to repay his debt to her!

40   But that reminds me, now that my own story is about to begin, I should tell you where that name of mine comes from, for, however bourgeois it may seem to you, I would not change it for that of Hobgoblin. You see, when the band of men in blue took away my father, I would be about three years old, and I was called Jean. In order to make me speak, the inhabitants of the village would always be saying to me: 'Jean, where's your father? Jean, where's your papa now? Jean, what became of Truquette the merchant?' And I would answer: '*Ils l'ont pris, ils l'ont pris*' ['They have taken him away']; and so the name Jean-l'ont-pris stuck.

41   But let's go back to the lessons my grandmother gave me in how a man of my station should comport himself in the world. Poor as I was, I was none the less the son of Monsieur Truquette, which meant that a certain consideration would be shown me that would not be shown, as you know, to the children of riff-raff. I won't bore you with all the sweet things my grandmother would say to me, or with all the little pet names she gave me: my chicken, my lamb, my darling, my prince, my king, my emperor; the riff-raff say such things to their children even more often than the nobility; but she taught me politeness, and the rules of elegant behaviour, which are much more important and which not everybody is capable of teaching.

'You see, my son,' she would say to me, 'if you wish to show where you come from, remember what your grandmother has taught you.

'First, you must always wear your hat at a rakish angle when you have one, and don't raise it for anyone, especially for important people, unless they have done so before you; otherwise you will be considered an incompetent who is obliged to them, whereas if you keep your hat on your head, it means: "So much for you, Jean de Paris!" You don't have to pull it down over your eyes, like a bad payer, nor straight on your head, like a bumpkin, but wear it pulled down over your right eye, like this, watch how I do it with these three packets of matches, like that, yes! No more, no less.

42 'You are still young now, so if you are in good company, and you have to blow your nose, you will raise your little gown at the front, then you will hold your pretty little nose with the shirt, you will blow as hard as you can, to get the snot out completely, and you will let your clothes drop in such a way that no one sees what has become of the jelly.

43 'When you pass the time of day with someone who is worth bothering with, you will make a loud kiss in the hollow of your hand. Then you will step back, bow, scraping the ground with both feet like a hen.

44 'If you are invited to a castle, you must put on airs, say that your pot is on the fire at home and that, thank God, you have no need of anyone else's. In this way, people will beg you to come, and will consider themselves very happy to have you in their house. If there are ladies present, don't forget to pinch their thighs and slap their knees, then drink their health, clink their glasses, put your five fingers cleanly into the salt and sprinkle their food with it. In this way you will be considered a well-brought-up young man who knows all there is to know about the customs and manners of people of fashion.'

45 I would soon send you to sleep, my lord, if I recounted all the wonderful things my grandmother told me to turn me into a respectable fellow. It may be that I am one; but all her rigmarole was never much use to me. The hat you see on my head is the first I have ever worn in my life; I always wore a cap until now. I have never had a little gown that I could lift so that I could blow my nose on my shirt; I have seen ladies in my time, but, whatever my wishes were on the matter, if I have ever eaten a morsel in their company, let it choke me. It is true that once I had occasion to sup at the Château de La Boissière, but it was in the cellar with the gamekeeper and his wife, and she was no more a lady than I'm a bishop. So you see, all my grandmother's hopes and fine words got me nowhere. Because, in her youth, she happened to have eaten, danced and even slept with people of high station, she must have imagined, I suppose, that her whole family enjoyed such a right. She took no account of the fact that Jean-l'ont-pris was not a girl and that boys, however pretty they may be, do not always enjoy such a privilege. Unfortunately, my grand-

mother was a bit hasty on this matter; but one can forgive anything in a person of that age, especially when it concerns someone one loves.

46   As soon as I was a bit older, I let her talk on and took charge of my own education.

47   She had bought me a book for 4 sous so that I could go to school. The master gave me a blow on the first day: so I exchanged my book for a good slice of egg-plant and never set foot in the school again. Nevertheless, because my grandmother wanted me to go, I would walk up to the door, perform one, two or even three pirouettes, then set off to enjoy myself in the country, where I learned everything people like us need to know.

48   First I studied how to throw stones; and I succeeded so well in that kind of exercise that even today I could hit your nose at eighty paces if it were your wish that I should take aim at it.

49   The second point of my ambition was to get a good knowledge of how to climb trees so that I could steal birds' eggs. By hard work, I achieved my aim, but anyone else would have suffered for the rest of his days if he had started in the same conditions as I. But listen to what happened to me, and you will understand better.

50   I had noticed a magpie's nest at the top of a poplar. I wanted it, and I left my cap and clogs on the ground to fetch it. Everything went quite well as long as I found thick branches; but when I was close to the top of the tree, where the nest was, the branches were thinner, they bent under my weight, and I began to swing to and fro, while the nest turned around me like a spinning-wheel. And when I managed to grasp the bough on which it was fixed, the bough cracked and broke into two pieces, though they were not entirely separated. I fell, and the ground that awaited me was so low, that looking at it, I felt dizzy; but, as luck would have it, the branches that still held – not those on which the nest was perched – got caught in my hair as I began to fall, and I found myself suspended like a lantern. My mop of hair was naturally so thick that you might have thought it a rosemary bush. Imagine how the branch was twisted into it and what pain I must have suffered! God forgive me, but I would have preferred to have fallen at once rather than find myself in such a position, without knowing how it would all end. I stayed there a good hour waving my legs about and groaning. There was nothing I could get hold of to pull myself free.

In the end the branch broke clean, and both of us fell down at the same time. I have to admit that it saved my life: as it was long, with plenty of foliage on it, it kept getting caught on its way; sometimes, to tell you the truth, it stayed rather too long in one place and nearly broke my neck. But what could be done? It was better to get hurt in one place if it saved the rest!

When I was back on the ground again, I tried to pull it free from my hair. But it wouldn't budge! That idiot of a branch was as securely fixed as a burdock twig, and I had to drag it home with me, and, to keep my grandmother quiet, I swore over and over again that I had just come from school. She found it hard to believe, and, to free me from my wool-comb, she shaved my head down to the last hair.

Next day, I could remember only one thing of all that had befallen me: the nest that I had left at the top of the poplar, and that I was in honour bound to go back and win. This I did: taking greater care this time how I did it, I managed to reach it, and my grandmother and I enjoyed the fruits of my labours. In time I was to become a past master in that difficult art.

51   As I strolled through the countryside I would sometimes meet shepherds who broke hares' paws by throwing a club at them from twenty-five paces. I was impatient to try my skill at this feat. I soon got myself a club, but hares are more difficult to find. For three months at a stretch, I saw only one that was within reach. Tired of waiting so long to try my luck, one evening, as I was looking after my grandmother's donkey, I took fifteen steps back and threw a stick at the animal's front legs. As you can imagine, the animal fell at once to the ground. But when, after a while, I saw that the poor beast was not getting up again, that it was in pain and that I had perhaps broken its legs, then, my lord, yes! – for the blood cannot lie – I fell into such a cold sweat that no one would have known whether the donkey or I had greater need of comfort. In my affliction I went up to the animal, and, tears rolling down my cheeks, I put its pretty little head on my breast. 'Come, come! my little chicken,' I said to it, using the words my grandmother had called me when I was small. 'Come, come! my son, my dear companion, my love, what's the matter, then? Did I hurt you? Forgive me; I won't do it again. Come on! Get up! Dear heart! Come on! Up you get! That's it! Take it easy!' The poor beast – I can still remember the expression on its face – looked at me

with eyes that would have broken the heart of a tax collector. However, as though it had understood, it did make an effort to get up and gently placed one of its little knees on my stomach and the other on my belly; then, a quarter of an hour later, trying again, it planted one of its feet on my chest, the other on one of my cheeks and stayed there, as though it had rented the apartment. Since I could neither move nor cry out, since it had almost crushed the life out of me with the first movement, I was forced to wait for it to decide to move again. In the end it did so, but I have to admit that if I had hurt it, it paid me back in my own kind.

52   Though I say it myself, my lord, I flatter myself that I have learned something in my life. But I have never learned anything that did not, in one way or another, cost me dearly.

53   One talent that we peasants make good use of and that, though it is not to our honour, is certainly to our profit, is that of knowing where this man's muscat grapes are to be found, that woman's figs, another's peaches and apricots and, above all, of knowing the right times to go plundering the farms.

54   I was so successful at cultivating this talent during my youth that even today, if I had to, I could go and pinch some fruit and a few chickens as skilfully as anyone. It is true that I long since gave up playing those kinds of games, at least until the opportunity presents itself; but, to get back to what I was saying, before mastering this little recreation, I managed to get at least seven or eight hundred blows on my shins. Those villains, the vineyard-keepers, either out of jealousy, or because I never had a single piastre to show them, were especially vigilant: over fifty times they put me into the situation of an *inci homme*.[4] I couldn't get into the smallest estate without them finding me; and when I thought I was safe from their attentions, and could sit down in peace and eat my fill, they were always there to disturb me.

55   Once, however, there were two of them who came to regret shaving my head. But listen on, if you will.

56   Since they always seemed to catch me, I decided in the end to get a whistle like theirs, and I went and hid behind the thickest bushes I could find; there I blew my whistle, and they, as was their wont, answered on theirs. In this way I always knew more or less where they were. When I realized that they were quite near, I went

off, without making any noise, and finished off my job somewhere else. If they were far away, it was so much labour saved, and I quietly carried out my task where I was.

57   One fine Sunday, as they were singing vespers, and it seemed unthinkable that those villains would not be there, I blew twice on my whistle and got no reply. Let's go then! I said to myself. They're at church! God be praised! Perhaps those wretches will give a thought at last to the salvation of their souls, and not come and stop you looking after the salvation of your body! Thus spurred on, I found my way into the walled orchard of a big land-owner at Langlade where there were peaches as big as your fist which their owner kept guarded like the king's body. The first thing I did was to pick a fine, velvety, tender peach. Oh, lord, the juice trickled down from my lips as fresh as hoar-frost in the month of May. But my enjoyment was short-lived; a large hand grabbed me by the scruff of the neck, and I heard myself called a thief, as though they were talking to any old yokel. However, such an insult did not prevent me from finishing my fruit; but it was extremely damaging to me, for it prevented me from taking others, and it was an affront to my honour. But since I was still nothing more than a good-for-nothing, I could not defend myself, and I had no other course but, protesting vociferously, to give myself up to the bandit who was holding me. This villain – for he was a vineyard-keeper, need I say more – this half-wit dragged me by the hair to the peach-tree and tied me to it, my hands behind my back. With a great laugh, he left me there and went off to inform the master of the orchard of his deed. If heaven had not come to my rescue, I promise you, my lord, that I would have been given a sound thrashing! As it turned out, another was regaled in my place. How the good God takes care of virtue! He never abandons me. There's nothing like honesty, be assured, to get you out of the worst scrapes.

58   That wretch of a vineyard-keeper had left one of his children in the orchard to keep watch over me until Monsieur Sestier, the land-owner, arrived. Meanwhile, the little greedy-guts took to eating the peaches with as much delight as I myself would have done if I had been allowed to continue my work; and the more peaches disappeared down his throat, the more I saw that I would have to pay for them. When he could eat no more peaches, he came up to me and said:

'Damn it! I know very well you've got a whistle that whistles loud and clear, like my father's, damn it! And I haven't got one, damn it! And I'd like to have one like yours, damn it!'

'Yes, indeed, Monsieur Dammit!' I said. 'Yes, indeed! Damn it! I'll give it to you if you untie me . . .'

'Honest? You really will give it to me?'

'I swear, honest fellow that I am, I swear on the honour of Jean-l'ont-pris, I shall give it to you.'

Whereupon the boy set about working with his fingernails and teeth with so much ardour that he soon freed me. When he had carried out his good deed, the thief asked me for my whistle, thinking that he had really got the better of me.

'Oh, my friend!' I said. 'You are quite right, but if you want to have it, you must do one more little service for me . . .'

'What? What service?'

'You must let me tie you for a while to the place I was; otherwise I won't be able to give up my whistle with a clear conscience.'

'Oh, damn it!' he said. 'Then you won't give it to me . . .'

'I won't give it to you? Idiot! Here, take it! Put it to your mouth and whistle, while I put you in the same place as I was just now.'

The poor child put the whistle between his teeth with such haste that for a moment I was afraid that he'd swallow it. Meanwhile I tied him up as best I could. When I'd finished, I said to him:

'So, little fool! You can't whistle. Give it to me, I'll show you!'

The poor innocent let the instrument go, and after saying to him, 'Look! This is how you do it!' I blew him a couple of whistles in each ear; then I took the whistle, as you might expect, gathered up the peaches that remained, left the child in my place and went to take up my post on a hillock behind the wall to avoid the scroungers, and to see how things would turn out. I heard the child calling after me for some time: 'Go! Go! You'll see what my father . . . You'll see what my grandmother and yours will do to you!' But some time later the poor lamb was singing alleluias of a quite different kind. Now, listen to this part of the story, it's worth it.

59   I hardly had a quarter of an hour to enjoy my peaches, lying in wait behind my wall, when Monsieur Sestier, alerted by the vineyard-keeper that he would find me in his orchard tied to a tree, arrived, in a furious temper, at the peach-tree, armed with a stout stick. Since he knew neither the vineyard-keeper's son nor me, he worked away with

much determination on the hide of the poor fellow he found there, without showing the slightest sign of tiredness. The boy's father, who had followed Monsieur Sestier at some distance, hastened his step when he heard his son's voice; and you can imagine his face when, instead of Jean-l'ont-pris, he found his Benjamin tied to the tree, and tanned to perfection by the master's expert hand! Without even trying to find out who was in the wrong, the great brute delivered a mighty blow between the eyes of dear Monsieur Sestier that must have given him a vision of Our Lady of Candlemas in all her magnificence. For some time, Monsieur Sestier did not seem to understand too clearly what was happening and stood there looking rather bewildered, as though he had been knocked senseless; but, man that he was, he turned round, took his guard and, stumbling slightly, retorted with a hefty blow of his stick on the keeper's cheek. The first volley was followed by several others, as when one wishes someone a Happy New Year, and if the keeper had not cried out, 'My turn!' hurling a stone at the gentleman's stomach, Monsieur Sestier would certainly have returned with all the honours of war; but that 'My turn!' did him a lot of damage. The other keeper arrived, armed with a thick branch, to come to the aid of his comrade, who had just skilfully cut himself a stout stick, and the two of them advanced boldly in the direction of Monsieur Sestier, like two Mahon cocks confronting a turkey. They had all thrown themselves into the fray, neither side wanted to give in, battle was joined. It was a battle royal: never perhaps in living memory has the Vaunage seen so many fine blows delivered as were so generously distributed on that occasion. A well-directed blow fell straight on Monsieur Sestier's skull, to which he responded subtly with two blows about his adversary's ears. But just as he was about to deliver a third, the other hit him on the head with his stick, but as he was pulling his weapon back to tear the skin, it caught only the man's wig, and, for lack of enough resistance, he fell back five or six paces into a bush. Monsieur Sestier, valiant fellow that he was, threw himself like a devil on to the clumsy keeper who had just snatched his wig and shook him like a gentleman's tapestry. If it had been given him to go on, I don't think he would have left him time to be eaten by the mites; but while he was tickling him with one hand and trying to get back his wig with the other as best he could, the man with the branch gave him a blow on the back of the neck that

made him incapable of further action. Poor Monsieur Sestier fell to
the ground, groped around for his cane, which he had let go, staggered
to his feet, then fell back like a drunkard. Then the two keepers each
threw a stone at him, which struck him on the chin and forehead, and
threw him back into a ditch at the wayside. As they thought they had
sent him to heaven and they had just caught sight of a man who knew
them, they took to their heels, without even thinking of untying the
child, whom I had installed in a much more favourable position than
the one I found myself in to observe the fight. The man whom I have
just referred to recognized them, though they had soon disappeared
from the scene, and went up to Monsieur Sestier to give what help he
could. I arrived in turn, and the two of us shook him and saw him
recover his senses.

60 'Monsieur Sestier,' said the man, 'heavens above! What
happened, then? Get your breath back! Must one get into such a state
for so little!'

'Oh,' he said, 'it's nothing, I'm just a little stunned, nothing that a
good bowl of soup won't put right. Be so kind as to fetch my cane
and my wig which must certainly be entangled together.'

I performed the service for him, and when he had his wig back on
his head, he said: 'Let's go! There isn't much damage done. I thought
it would cost me at least 6 francs to repair the damage ... The double
monsters! But tell me, gentlemen, did you see the to-do? And can
you serve as witnesses for me as need be?'

We both answered in the affirmative.

'Well, that's perfect!' he said. 'Come and have a drink with me.
Damn me, if I don't get them hanged! By the way, where's the rascal
who stole my peaches? Is he still tied to the tree?'

'Yes, he is,' I replied.

'Well, ragamuffin!' he said to me. 'Take my branch and go and
finish off the work I began. I haven't the heart to finish it, because I
haven't eaten since breakfast.'

61 I went off out of politeness; but as the apprentice-thief was less
guilty than he appeared, I decided to pardon him. I took pity on him
and sent him on his way after giving him half a dozen kicks in the
belly. For, you see, my lord, my rule has always been, which is also in
accordance with my feelings, to do as much good and as little harm as
possible.

62   As the man and I accompanied Monsieur Sestier to Langlade, we thought we would have to take our time on the road. But not at all! Monsieur Sestier walked like the fine devil he was. And he never complained of anything but the terrible hunger that afflicted him. The blows that he had been given were of no more concern to him than were the affairs of Holland. He swore to us that in his time he had sustained far heavier blows and that those he had just received were mere pinpricks compared with the thousands of others he had collected here and there. 'In my youth,' he said, 'I was a farmboy, then a shepherd, then head shepherd. People of our kind are always quarrelling among ourselves. Gradually our flesh hardens all over our bodies, and I haven't been a land-owner long enough to get soft.'

63   So we accompanied him to his house, where we dined like three pit-sawyers; *after which* our gentleman went to bed, sent for a surgeon, who visited him, without light, in the darkness, finding a thousand wounds in places where he had not been touched, dressed his wounds with cold water, drank three mugs of wine in his company on the bed and made the devil of a report.

64   The judge and clerk of La Boissière also came to hear his complaint and our statements. After which, they issued writs for the arrest of the keepers and the boy, supped with the dying man and got as drunk as grape-pickers at a wine harvest.

65   During the supper we talked business, and, since the keepers had shown themselves to be untrustworthy, Monsieur Sestier begged these gentlemen, who exercised full powers in Solorgues, to get me appointed to one of the vacant posts. A man as rich as Monsieur Sestier does not usually make requests in vain. His were carried out the next day. I went to take my oath, and I was immediately given my letters patent. You can imagine the joy I then felt, I who had no other ambition in life. For the first time, I was something in Solorgues. It was a good job, and, though it did not bring me much honour, it was not unprofitable. That year, though the harvest was not of the best, my grandmother and I did so well by ourselves that she died and I got as fat as a capon.

66   My grandmother was a Huguenot; her burial cost me only a few minutes' work with pick and shovel in a ditch, and I was undertaker, clerk and priest at once. If I tell you that I did not mourn her, my lord, I would lie, for I did mourn her. Not, perhaps, more than was

reasonable. She had left me something, but, on the other hand, she no longer brought anything in. So I mourned her as I should. When I realized that I had mourned her as much as was necessary, I laid her out in the Donkeys' Paradise, and went home for lunch.

67 On arrival I looked everywhere for something to have with my bread, and I couldn't find a single onion, shallot or clove of garlic. Yes! I thought, your poor grandmother was so prudent she seems to have scoffed everything before leaving! The damned glutton! But no, I didn't think so, she was too devout to eat so much on the day of her burial. On this last thought, which is perhaps the most Christian I've had in my life, I began to search again and found nothing. I did notice, however, an old chest, well hidden away, that I had never seen before, and which seemed to have been made out of bits of Old Father Noah's ark. I quickly pulled it out of its hiding-place, opened it, and the first thing my hands touched was a thick layer of straw. The devil! I said, if that's all it's filled with, there couldn't be much point in hiding it! However, I pushed away the straw a bit, and the first thing I found underneath was a fine piece of muslin. Good! I said, that's better than a clove of garlic. It was true; for I was so hungry that I ate my bread as though it had been soaked in good white fat.

68 Before seeing what else there was in the blessed chest, I double-locked my door. I came back and pulled out two pieces of cambric, which, certainly, were worth the trouble! I said, if this goes on, my dear little grandmother did not die in vain!

69 The inventory gave me too much pleasure for me to stop there; I went back to work with alacrity. There was a little basket made of gold and silver braid, and some twenty packets of lace of indescribable delicacy. Good! My dear grandmother! *Requiem*, my little grandmother, *requiem aeternam*, may the good God protect you up there, and give me here below as much work as it shall please him! This time heaven answered the sinner's prayer. I brought to the surface some twenty gold watches and tobacco-boxes magnificently displayed on a large piece of blue velvet. Ah! my lord, what a feast! If only it could come back ten times a week not counting Sunday! I then took out I know not how many objects of all kinds, handkerchiefs, silk stockings, all new, and, in the end, at the bottom, two dozen silver spoons and forks; and to cap it all, at the bottom of the chest,

my eyes were dazzled, St Anthony be praised, by fifty 24-franc gold pieces.

70 You see, my lord, my grandmother had collected this store when times were good, and if Truquette and his comrades had not put it there, she must have done it on her own account. Anyway, whatever happened and whatever one may think, she left the hoard to me, and that was a very good idea. A well-brought-up child does not go around trying to find out where his parents may have got what they leave him. If they got it on the right side [by fair means], so much the better for everyone; if they got it on the left side [by crooked means], so much the worse for them! When I had looked through everything, touched it and covered it with kisses, I decided to put it in a safer place: I bought a stronger chest, put everything inside it and hid it in a dark corner in the house, where no one but the rats and I would know of its existence.

71 Despite my pretty little fortune I continued to live as before, for fear that people might talk, and I said nothing to anyone, not even to Monsieur Sestier, who loved me like his own eyes. For my part, I did not love him inordinately; but he had a daughter, his only child, as fresh, buxom and good-natured as any girl you could meet, who would inherit all his wealth, and I courted them both. The daughter took a great liking to me, and it seemed that her father would have given her to me if he had not thought me a good-for-nothing.

72 A few days after my discovery I paid them a visit, and, without beating around the bush, I subtly brought the conversation round to what was on my mind: 'Heavens!' I said to Monsieur Sestier, 'she's a proud young lady, Mademoiselle Babeau! She has cheeks the colour of your clingstone peaches; teeth as white as curdled milk; eyes that could burn to ashes the coldest heart; arms, Holy Virgin!, smooth as glass, that seem to have been made in a mould; a waist, a face, a bearing to make you cry out "Help! Have pity on me! I'm on fire!" A pair of pretty feet that the queen would go to fetch in person if such pretties could be bought at the Paris meat-market; a little hand like Cupid's comb . . .'

'Well!' said Monsieur Sestier laughing, while his daughter, who was looking very pleased with herself, couldn't take her eyes off me. 'Well! My poor Jean-l'ont-pris, what do you mean by that?'

'I mean,' I replied, 'that whoever gets her will be a fool or a lucky man if he does not jump for joy! And if such good fortune came my way, I would certainly wear it around my neck at the front for ever, as I wear my pigtail behind.'

Hearing these words, Mademoiselle Babeau gave me such a tender look, and lifted her pretty chin so gracefully, that I said to myself: 'Good! Carry on! We've tickled the spot that itches!' The father, who adored her and who seemed full of friendship for me, listened to me with his mouth agape a rod wide, but, after remaining for a while in that fine state, he finally turned to me and said:

'You would not have to be a marquis or a prince or a *capitaine de santé* to have my daughter,' he said. 'If you had Truquette's money or brains, she would be yours already. But what can I do? Although your father and I were friends, and partners in the wool trade, and although he got me many a time the best goods at a price lower than that of the worst – for one has to admit the wretch had the heart of a king – although he never did me any harm and left me not a bone to gnaw in his last testament, as I feared, and however much I would like to show my gratitude to his son by giving him my daughter, you have unfortunately neither land nor talent nor fortune, and that makes it very difficult for me, as you can see.'

73 'And how much would Jean-l'ont-pris need, for example, to be able to claim her bed?'

'You see,' he said, 'I shall leave 60,000 francs to my daughter. Anyone who gets her will have to have at least that. For you, if you had only a third of that, I would give her to you with all my heart.'

'Ah, well, you see, Monsieur Sestier, I don't have 20,000 francs at the moment, in fact I'm 19,999 short; that means that I have only 40 sous in goods and money to my name; but Babeau and I are young, we can wait, if you give me a little time, like father, like son!, and heaven, perhaps, by hook or by crook, will give me the brains and the means to get what you ask.'

'And how much time do you need?' he said. 'I'm getting on, and I would like to see my daughter married, before manuring the fennel in the graveyard!'

74 'Oh!' I replied, 'you're not old yet and as stout as an oak; you have, fair and square, the teeth of a wild boar, the chest of a donkey, and you have kept, God be praised!, the stomach of a shepherd. With such tools, I don't think that three years could make you afraid. In

three years a man who has love, virtue and ambition as I have, can go a long way.'

'Well!' he said, 'I'll give you three years, if my daughter is of the same mind.'

'As far as I'm concerned, I would give him four if he needed them,' said Babeau.

'Four?' I cried, jumping for joy, 'four! That's too many. It would be the sign of misfortune if I had to keep you waiting so long!'

75   I knew that what I had in my chest amounted, more or less, to the sum that Monsieur Sestier demanded; but it was not wise to move too quickly. My memory of Truquette was still green. Monsieur Sestier, rich as he was, did not have a very high reputation, and I, I have to admit, was not regarded as the greatest saint in the Litanies. People are spiteful, suspicious and jealous, and there were very good reasons to prevent them from damning themselves, if at all possible. At Solorgues, especially, people would have talked, spread slander, made up endless stories about us, if that marriage had taken place without due preparation; and perhaps eventually they might even have found out the truth; so I was in no hurry, and in order to put the riff-raff off the track, I wanted to get everybody used to seeing me give up my rags, and rise slowly like a man who works hard and is blest by God, so that they would not be surprised by this marriage when it finally took place.

76   These precautions, which no one takes any longer and which I wished to put into practice, simpleton that I was!, brought me the greatest troubles in my life, by passing me off as a steady sort of fellow.

77   The daughter of a certain Maître Garouille, the most miserable and horrible creature that ever lived on land, sea or perhaps even in hell, a veritable knacker's yard, a hunchbacked, squint-eyed, pasty-faced animal, capable of wreaking the worst possible torments upon you at a distance of a hundred paces, and whom one could not so much as look at without feeling compelled at once to make the sign of the Cross and to recommend one's soul to God, well!, this dunghill found herself with child. It was difficult to imagine whose work this act of despair could be, for, unless Satan were the author of it, it would not have been possible for a thief, otherwise condemned to the wheel, to have dared to bring himself to perform it. Anyway, whoever

the madman was, the accursed man who had done the deed, she was with child and declared herself in my favour. Imagine, my lord, the alarm of a young man of honour and taste, with over 25,000 francs in his chest! I thought I would lose my reason before the trick that such a wretch had played on me. I went at once to share my misfortune with my good friend Monsieur Sestier and, above all, with Mademoiselle Babeau, who was even more fond of me than was her father. She wanted me to go to law; but her father shook his head and said nothing, as though he was not of the same opinion. Without beating about the bush, I said to him with all the unctuousness that the subject deserved: 'What! A boy of good family like me exposed to such dishonour! The son of Monsieur Truquette accused of an act that would shame the least of the pilgrims of St James! Could this be possible? I, betray a Mademoiselle Babeau for a Garouille! For a bitch who would scare the merest slaughterer of horses! For a stinking wretch who turns your stomach, stops your breath at half a league's distance, and who could poison the whole of Langlade however little wind was blowing from Solorgues! Do you believe that, Monsieur Sestier? Do you believe that?' He said not a word. His daughter, in tears, tried to console me; she told me to go to law, that she didn't believe a word of it, that she would wait for me as long as I wanted because she knew that she could count on me. The father, because he persisted in saying nothing, made me suspect certain things that became clearer later, and which it would be better for me to tell you now so that I can finish my story before we reach your castle. Bridle your horse a little, my lord, I beg you, he's darting about like a hobgoblin. What a spirited fellow he is! One can see you don't feed him on scraps! What I have yet to say is worth the trouble!

78   Garouille had been with child for eight months, and who would you say had committed this act of folly, that cursed work? No less a person than the honest, scrupulous Monsieur Sestier, and that was why, in order to get possession of me, he flattered me, promised me his daughter, so that he could then have me well and truly hooked. And that's what he did, the Barabbas! But, the way things turned out, I don't think he had anything to rejoice about: his little Babeau and I had arranged things our way.

79   As we talked, there entered a certain fat figure of a man like a

bundle of knavish tracks who, standing before us, frightened me as
much as if a gibbet had been set up there:

'Who is with you,' he said, 'Monsieur Jean-l'ont-pris, legitimate
and natural son of Dame Margot, bawd, and of Sieur Truquette,
former thief of Solorgues, hanged ten years ago in the market-place
at Nîmes?'

80   'He isn't here, it isn't I!' I cried, trembling throughout my body.
'Have pity! What do you want with him, then?'

On a Judas sign made him by Monsieur Sestier, he said:

'Of course you're he! You're mine. Help there!'

Immediately two other ham-stringers of his kind appeared. One
grabbed me by the scruff of the neck; the other cut the cord of my
breeches and tied my arms behind my back with string. I let them do
their work in the interests of peace. Poor Babeau wept, and Monsieur
Sestier could not contain his laughter. When I was ready, my breeches
around my knees, we set off for Solorgues. I was utterly confused to
see myself carried off in this way without knowing why. From time
to time I asked the reason, while fearing to learn it. When we were
within sight of the village, one of these gentlemen said to the others
to go on alone, for he had something to say to me in private; he would
be responsible for everything. The other two took off, and the one
who had stayed came up to me with a face like Beelzebub:

'Well! My Lord and Saviour!' I said. 'What do you want, then?'

'I want to embrace you,' he said.

'Embrace me, the devil! And why, pray?'

'Because we are related in a way; you are the son of my best friend,
and, out of gratitude, I want to do you a great service.'

'You want to untie me, then?' I said.

'Oh!' he said, 'it's something much more important to your happiness; I want to get you married . . .'

'Married! To whom?'

'To the pearl of Solorgues, beautiful young Judith Garouille.'

'The devil!' I said. 'Take her yourself if you think so highly of
her!'

'Ah!' he said, 'if I had the good fortune not to be married already,
I would jump at the opportunity. Monsieur Sestier is giving her a
dowry of 1,000 francs.'

'If she had a thousand vats full of wine, it would be out of the question,' I replied. 'But why is Monsieur Sestier giving her 1,000 francs? For her beautiful eyes . . .'

'Yes, for her beautiful eyes,' he said. 'But listen, I'm your friend, and I want you to listen to reason. Among the partners of the late Monsieur Truquette you will no doubt have heard of a certain Quincarlot. Well, here he is, before you, the very same! I had the honour and consolation of seeing your father die as if predestined. For the dear man did not want to get anyone into trouble, though he could have done so. His death so moved me that I felt quite different afterwards. The grace of God touched me thereafter. The vanities, the pleasures, the dangers of this world made me afraid: I became converted, and, in order to escape completely from sin, in order to assure my salvation, I became a sheriff's officer. Monsieur Sestier, whom I have known for a long time and who has also taken up a devout life, shared some scruples that disturbed him concerning a weakness that he had conceived for the young Garouillette. As he feared that he might make people talk, he told me that he would not refuse 1,000 francs to the girl if she wanted to put the bridle round the neck of some other man. As a good Christian I assumed responsibility for this business, and as I have great obligations towards your father, and certain others towards your mother, it is on you, my son, that my choice first alighted. By way of smoothing your path, I spoke the next day to the girl, and I must say in your honour that she immediately gave her preference to you and that she regards you most highly. At my request, she has cited you as father of her child, so, in order to pay you a good turn, I asked two vineyard-keepers to give evidence not only to prove that you had been with the girl, but also to witness that there had been some violence on your part; thus your little fortune runs with the stream; it depends on you whether you take advantage of it, and certainly happiness is for him who seeks it. Ah, my child, how people are going to envy you!'

81   If I had been untied at that moment, my lord, I'm certain that the good turn paid me by Quincarlot would have earned him a good blow on the head. 'Murderer!' I said, 'good-for-nothing! To the devil with your damned conversion! I thank you for your friendship, thief! Who asked you for it? You should have kept it for your cousin Satan, who would have paid you back in kind!'

82   Quincarlot let me rail on with a patience that disturbed me; then,

when it seemed to him that he might be able to get a word in, he launched at me the following speech, which, if it failed to inspire in me any desire for Garouille, rid me at least of some of the disgust I felt about that cursed marriage.

83 'I know,' he said, 'my dear fellow, that this girl is neither a beauty nor a virgin. But, not counting the 100 pistoles that Monsieur Sestier is giving her, Garouillette, in her present state of health, could not yield up her cargo without dying herself, which cannot be more than a month and a half from now. Her ugly body possesses the most rotten lungs in the land; more scurvy to herself than the entire English fleet at sea; a superb case of scabies that makes her gleam to her fingernails; and a pretty leg in which gangrene is spreading as though it were a blessing. So you see a girl of such merit is a treasure you must not let slip through your fingers.' The wretch was so eloquent in showing me the obvious advantages that would be mine in this punishment from heaven, that I accepted everything and married the horrible beast. It is true that it was on condition that we would never come within two hundred paces of each other. We kept our word, and my dear wife did not belie Quincarlot. Two months later, she gave birth to two kinds of water-rat, from what they tell me, but I never saw them, and yesterday she died with them in the hospital at Sommières, where I had taken them, because they would get better attention there than at Solorgues.

84 She was buried this morning: may God receive her in his Holy Paradise, for I would rather she be his than mine! You may be sure that he has taken her in: he must pay himself with all kinds of money!

85 Now I am going off with a quiet heart, I care about nothing; I have 100 pistoles more in my purse, and I'm going to tell Monsieur Sestier, if he likes, I shall take his daughter with no ill feelings. If he refuses, he is not an honourable man, for . . . But I had better hold my tongue . . .

'Finish the tale,' the baron said to him, 'it hints at some important mystery lacking in your story.'

86 'Well!' Jean-l'ont-pris said, 'since you wish to know everything, I must tell you that while Monsieur Sestier was enjoying himself at Solorgues, I was enjoying myself at Langlade, and it so happened that as a result of all that, Babeau became as round as a tennis ball.'

87 'Very well, my friend, I see . . . You have told me the life of certain people and your own in quite an amusing way; but I now see that you are worth no more than they; but I am obliged to you for confirming many of the doubts I had about the character of peasants of your kind. Miserable wretches! Who would have said that beneath that innocent exterior, they hid the most perverse morals and the most invincible malice! Finish your story if there remains anything more to be said.'

88 'Oh! There is no more, my lord,' said Jean-l'ont-pris. 'And indeed if I'd known, I would not have begun it in the first place. Here is your castle, farewell! God keep you cool in summer and warm in winter!'

89 'Stay a moment,' the baron added. 'In gratitude for the pleasure you have given me, I must share with you a few reflections that your story has suggested to me. Born of bad parents, you seem very likely to end up no better than they. Your alliance with that Sestier of Langlade, together with your own wretched inclinations, are very likely to lead you to the gibbet if you do not take care. Believe me, my child, change your ways and live as an honest man. Work, you were created for that. Seek out those to whom what you possess belongs and give it back to them. If you keep it, the least that will happen to you is that you will be unhappy and eaten up by remorse for the rest of your days.'

90 'A good sermon, my lord, really a very fine sermon! Yes, the *curé* of Nages would not have done better, even when his good angel was whispering in his ear; but to what avail? I do not understand you. Be so kind as to explain to me, for example, what you mean by remorse. Who knows! Perhaps I have it without knowing it!'

'Remorse is the reproach, the cry of conscience.'

91 'Conscience, you say! Oh! my lord, the conscience of a peasant is hoarse!'

92 'What do you mean? I don't understand . . .'

93 'I mean that the conscience of peasants has caught such a cold that it can no longer show itself, and that, if it does speak, one cannot hear it. Farewell, my lord, if you ever come to Solorgues, do me the honour of asking for Jean-l'ont-pris. We shall drink a glass of Calvisson wine together; that will stir up your conscience, you may be sure.'

Thereupon the baron reached his castle, laughing, and the vagabond continued on his way, singing

Good luck come my way!
Hey! Nonny-nonny!
Good luck come my way!

PART I

The 'Occitan Love Square'

Jean-l'ont-pris
in the Culture of the Midi

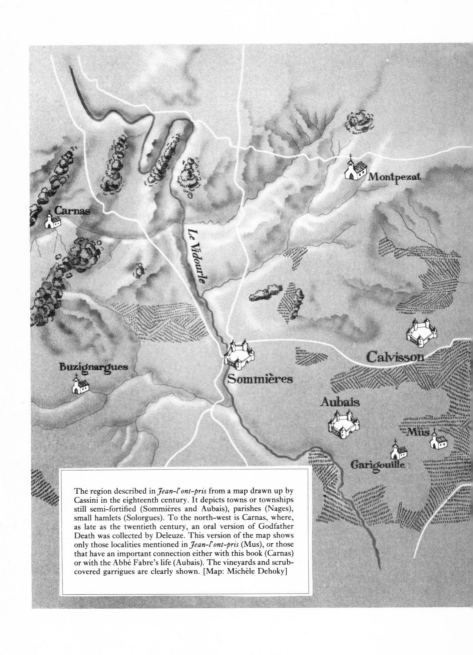

The region described in *Jean-l'ont-pris* from a map drawn up by
Cassini in the eighteenth century. It depicts towns or townships
still semi-fortified (Sommières and Aubais), parishes (Nages),
small hamlets (Solorgues). To the north-west is Carnas, where,
as late as the twentieth century, an oral version of Godfather
Death was collected by Deleuze. This version of the map shows
only those localities mentioned in *Jean-l'ont-pris* (Mus), or those
that have an important connection either with this book (Carnas)
or with the Abbé Fabre's life (Aubais). The vineyards and scrub-
covered garrigues are clearly shown. [Map: Michèle Dehoky]

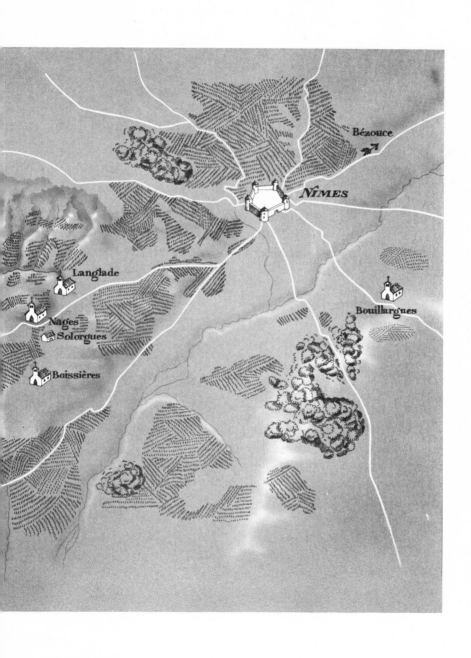

CHAPTER 1 The Abbé Fabre and the 'Love Square'

The Languedocian novel *Jean-l'ont-pris* is the principal work of the abbé Jean-Baptiste Castor Fabre (1727–83); this author, though little known to the pure French-speaking public, is one of the greatest writers of Occitan literature. I shall try to relate his novel, or rather his novella, to the Occitan stereotypes of marriage to be found in the regional literature and in the customs of the Midi; I shall also try to relate it to folk tradition. From this point of view, *Jean-l'ont-pris* is for me, at least to begin with, no more than a rather arbitrary starting-point from which I shall set out in search of a particular culture, part Occitan, part folk-tale/fairy-tale. In either case, the elements of this culture are to be found consistently, but not exclusively, among the ordinary people, below the level of the official culture of the educated élite. They occupy, as it were, the ground floor of the written language.

At this stage, it will be enough to provide a few facts about the life and work of the author of *Jean-l'ont-pris*. Thanks to the scholarly researches of Marcel Barral,[1] I can provide the following outline biography. Jean-Baptiste Castor Fabre was born at Sommières (in what is now Gard) on 28 March 1727. His father, Claude Fabre, was originally from Montpellier; at Sommières he occupied the modest post of 'regent of schools', or schoolmaster. Élizabeth Causse, Claude Fabre's wife and mother of the future ecclesiastic, was in charge of the girls' school in the same township. The couple had always moved in a quite unpretentious milieu. The people they encountered in the course of their everyday life were 'carriers' (water-carriers or chair-carriers?), masons, cobblers, agricultural workers . . . Between them, Claude and Élizabeth earned from the municipality of Sommières the princely sum of 210 *livres tournois*[2] a year. It was not much. Jean-Baptiste Castor's older brother was called Étienne. Like his father, he became a schoolmaster. In 1752, he married an illiterate woman. The sister of the two brothers was called Marie-Élizabeth. She was to become a seamstress at Montpellier. These men and women were ordinary people, but they were lacking neither in ambition nor in a certain rudimentary culture. As a younger son, Jean-Baptiste Castor had to confront the usual problems of money, or lack of it, that faced any brother who was not the eldest; according to the law of the Midi, younger sons did not inherit their father's wealth. More than one of Fabre's heroes was to be called Cadet.

Gifted, intelligent, the possessor of a fine handwriting such as one might expect of a schoolmaster's son, Jean-Baptiste Castor Fabre, author of our *Jean-l'ont-pris*, was tonsured at the age of twelve and intended by his father and mother for the priesthood. It was a traditional form of social advancement for the sons of poor, but ambitious parents – and it was a time when the parish priest had not yet become the schoolmaster's principal enemy.

After a childhood spent at Sommières, of which nothing is known, except that it was, of course, Occitan-speaking, Jean-Baptiste Castor began, at the age of eighteen, to study first philosophy, then theology, at the Jesuit college at Montpellier (1745–51). It was there that he acquired a solid grounding in classical – Latin and French – culture, which complemented his native Occitanity. In the summer of 1751, Fabre left Montpellier; at the seminary in Nîmes, he obtained the successive degrees that led him to the priesthood. He was ordained on 27 May 1752.

Thereafter, we lose trace of him for some months. But, on 20 January 1753, he took up his duties as assistant priest in the village of Aubais. He had returned to the country of the 'Vaunage', the plains and hills situated to the west of Nîmes, in which the action of *Jean-l'ont-pris* takes place.

Badly remunerated as an assistant priest, even less well than were his father and mother as schoolteachers, Fabre found a way, through his eloquence and kindness, to win the hearts of his parishioners at Aubais, whom he addressed in his sermons in the Occitan language. He preached about love of one's neighbour. He took part in the festivities of the Mardi Gras carnival, in which the local élite would meet around tables furnished with roast turkeys and shoulders of lamb. He would 'refresh' himself in the company of this élite, joining these ladies and gentlemen in taking the waters and subjecting themselves to purges. In his house at Aubais, he received visits from his sister-in-law, who lived at Nîmes: she gave birth to a fine baby, who was to become the pseudo-Chevalier de Saint-Castor, so dear to our abbé's avuncular heart. In this Vaunage parish, Fabre wrote, or at least conceived, his first play; it also forms the initial element of his *œuvre* in the Occitan language. It is called *L'Opéra d'Aubais*: its characters are local country people, and the action takes place in the poultry yard of the local castle. It is a comedy about the love of two young peasants, temporarily thwarted by old parents and lack of money.

It was at Aubais, too, that the abbé Fabre, making free use of the village traditions provided by the Vaunage, conceived *Jean-l'ont-pris*. The actual writing of the work took place from about 1756 to 1760 (the first version) and from about 1765 to 1769 (the second version).[3] It represents, in line with everything we know of the life at that time of this still young man, a total acculturation on his part, as far as the folk-tale elements and themes of popular preaching are concerned.[4]

The rest of abbé Fabre's biography is of only marginal concern to us here. Briefly, it is as follows. In 1755, Fabre left Aubais and his post. He rose in rank to become in 1755 to 1756 parish priest of Vic-la-Gardiole, a village afflicted with fevers, situated near the salt-pans that border to the south the countryside around Montpellier. The price of this advancement was a period in an unhealthy purgatory. However, the writer was favourably regarded by the bishop of Montpellier, and he did not stay long at Vic. In 1756 he was appointed parish priest of Castelnau, now in the outer suburbs of Montpellier, but at that time in a rural, wine-producing area. There, like many an eighteenth-century ecclesiastic of the Midi, he supported various members of his family: they joined him and more or less sponged off him. He fell out with the local innkeepers, who, he said, were the ruin of his parishioners. In his spare time, he made free translations of Martial and Horace, suppressing the latter's more phallic references. He wrote a second play: *Le Trésor de Substancion*. Will the rock of Substancion, near Castelnau, open, on Midsummer's Night, at the stroke of twelve, to reveal the treasure that lies hidden within it? This theme of a treasure that makes lovers rich and, therefore, their marriage possible, which he found in local folklore, recurs throughout Fabre's works; it is already to be found in *Jean-l'ont-pris*.

Living so near the university city of Montpellier, the new *curé* of Castelnau now had the leisure and opportunity to study for further examinations. In 1756 Fabre submitted a thesis in philosophy; he became *maître ès arts*, or *licencié*, as we would now say. He remained a parish priest, but, in 1762, armed with his new degree, he also took on a teaching post at the royal college of Montpellier, formerly an establishment of the Society of Jesus (the Jesuits having just been expelled from the kingdom). The departure of the Good Fathers caused a shortage of teachers; an opportunity had arisen for Fabre to try his luck and apply for a professorial chair. He was appointed to teach rhetoric, while his new colleagues took on the teaching of theology, logic, physics . . . The academic year began on 22 October 1762. A dozen students 'crowded' into our abbé's classes; under his direction they studied the Latin and French authors from Cicero to Bossuet. These young pupils belonged to a rather elevated, usually bourgeois, social milieu: their fathers were officials at the audit office, physicians and men of letters, who were also breeders of silkworms. Yet Fabre's occupancy of the chair was not to be untroubled. Against the new teachers, who, like our abbé, were secular priests, the Jesuits were not powerless; they may have been dispossessed of their college, but they still had much influence at Montpellier; they organized street demonstrations against their competitors; a hue and cry was launched, crowds rioted, stones were thrown. Fabre was a brave man, but he was not reckless; he gave up teaching, which, in fact, had brought him little money. Once again, he was able to devote himself entirely to his parish at Castelnau. The year 1765 brought a change of scenery: forever on the move, but always within strict limits, Fabre left his parish for another, the village of Le Crès, also near Montpellier. The net income of this new parish was 68 per cent higher than that at Castelnau, yet there were fewer parishioners – a bargain twice over! Fabre may have been a saintly priest, but he knew (sometimes) how to keep his feet on the ground.

From this period dates the only portrait of him to have survived. We see 'a large mouth, thick lips', dark eyes and hair, a long, Roman nose; he is wearing clerical dress, with bands, and is holding a pen; on the left is a crucifix. The portrait quietly suggests kindness and intelligence. It may have been about this time that he wrote *Le Sermon de Monsieur Sistre*, a coarse, somewhat Rabelaisian farce; with *Le Siège de Caderousse*, it was to be the abbé's most popular work in the nineteenth century; the spicy, not to say scatological, mode was one in which he felt quite at home.

The parishes in which Fabre was later to serve include Saint-

Michel de Montels, from 1769 to 1773, also on the outskirts of Montpellier, and Cournonterral, a village situated not far from that city. As we see, abbé Fabre's movements were limited in space and repetitive in time. At Cournonterral, where the income was low (240 *livres* a year, hardly more than that of Fabre's parents, and prices had risen since then), the burden of responsibility was heavy: over a thousand parishioners, 20 per cent of whom were Huguenots and, therefore, by definition, resistant to the priest's ministrations. In this village, Fabre spent his leisure writing *Le Siège de Caderousse*, a burlesque play in verse on a subject that, in itself, was far from funny: it tells the story of the struggle for grain in the Comtat Venaissin during the famine of 1709. The abbé also published some run-of-the-mill verse pieces on the opening of the aqueduct linking Les Arceaux and Montpellier; above all, he took an active interest in the future of his nephew, who had launched himself into a military career, which, like the priesthood, was a means of social advancement. Like many a young man at that time who wanted to escape his common condition, Fabre's nephew, without having the least right to it, added the aristocratic 'de' to his name and, with the further addition of a non-existent knighthood, emerged as the 'Chevalier de Saint-Castor'. His uncle had encouraged him in this direction. It was a time when, at Montpellier, or even at Versailles, one did not look too closely at claims to such a 'title'. Fabre himself Frenchified and ennobled his name; the southern *b* became a northern *v* (Favre), and a 'de' was added. The priest now called himself Favre de Saint-Castor . . .

In 1780, Fabre was made parish priest of Celleneuve, at the gates of Montpellier. This modest parish was to become a source of legal wranglings, as a result of rivalries with another priest, who had applied for the same living.

Meanwhile, the writer's nephew, the newly dubbed 'Chevalier', had married and set out for America with his young wife, leaving his young daughter, Adélaïde, with his devoted uncle. The couple were to sink without trace in the New World.

On 6 March 1783, after visiting one of his bedridden flock, though he himself had been ill for some days, Fabre caught a cold and died. He was greatly missed by his parishioners, who worshipped him for his goodness; he himself called them, none too kindly, 'those

Macassars [semi-savages] whose idol, somehow or other, I have become'. Young Adélaïde, it is said, went on to become something of a courtesan, much admired in the capital.

Thus from parish to parish, from sister to nephew, passed the life of a man who was probably the most important Occitan writer between the troubadours and Mistral. He was also, to my mind, one of the great French (Languedocian-speaking) writers of the eighteenth-century Enlightenment, a period that was not short on competition. Nevertheless, for some two hundred years, Fabre has remained almost unknown in France, except to a small band of Occitan specialists.

The abbé's *œuvre*, not all of which was published, is a considerable one. As a bilingual writer, Fabre wrote a quantity of poetry in French: lyrical poems, heroic poems (*Acidalie ou la fontaine de Montpellier*, *Amphitrite ou le pasteur maritime*, etc.); plays, such as *Théopiste ou le martyre de saint Eustache*, who was roasted inside a bronze bull; a comedy, *Le Galimatias*; 'Arabian' tales, *Les Visites de Zima*, in the style of *The Thousand and One Nights*; *Fables*, in the tradition of La Fontaine, in which Fabre attacked financiers, torture and the death penalty for theft; a burlesque funeral oration, in honour of a friend who was still alive (*Le Deuil de l'amitié*); an epistle to Sancho Panza; a poem on *Les Philosophes modernes*, which takes to task, on behalf of a pure, harsh, but informed Catholicism, such authors as Voltaire, Rousseau, Diderot, d'Holbach, Helvétius and Condillac. *Réponses précises aux questions du prétendu licencié Zapata*, in the same vein, is a refutation, argued with skill, of a short work in which Voltaire attacked point by point the veracity of biblical facts. (Marcel Barral, in his fine thesis on Fabre, compares this refutation, rather uncharitably, with a dialogue between Bournisien, a priest, and Homais, a pharmacist.) And we should not forget the *Observations morales*, in which Fabre attacked, among other things, the parasitism of noblemen who refused to lose caste. Fabre also turned into 'modern' French an earlier translation of Las Casas's *Destruction of the West Indies*, in which he reveals his hostility to the Spanish colonies. There are epigrams against this or that individual; occasional pieces or encomiums addressed to real or hoped-for protectors (king, bishop, intendant, etc.); translations of Latin poems; sometimes poems in Latin; Christmas hymns in which the angels speak French and the

shepherds Languedocian; songs, one of which at least is amicably
dedicated to the Freemasons of a local lodge; sermons in French,
which give proof of his powers as a preacher and theologian. Lastly, a
Lettre à Necker, pour les curés du diocèse de Montpellier (1780). In this
letter Fabre protested against the relative poverty of the village clergy,
with whose fate he identified. It is true that this priest, though invited
into the households of the intendant and the bishop of Montpellier
for his entertainment value, always placed himself *below* the level of
the recognized local intelligentsia, whose members were admitted into
the academy of the city.[5]

Jean-Baptiste Fabre's *œuvre* in Occitan is as vivid as his *œuvre* in
French is dead, or nearly so, because of the restrictions placed upon it
by a cold classicism. When the abbé wrote in Provençal, or, to use his
own word, in *patois*, when he gave voice in his works to the Occitan-
speaking plebs, it was, among other things, in order to amuse the
French-speaking, but more or less bilingual, aristocrats who occupied
the principal posts in the diocese and *intendance* and in the more
powerful *seigneuries*. Fabre moved freely through his world, from top
to bottom. In this way, he discovered rich seams of folk material.
Written for an aristocratic public, the works in *patois* were to enjoy in
the nineteenth century enormous popularity among the ordinary
Languedocian people, of whom the abbé, not without tenderness, had
made such fun. In the 1880s, his *Sermon de Monsieur Sistre* would be
recited as a huge joke at the lavish weddings and banquets that were
given in even the humblest strata of Occitan society. Fabre the priest
is extremely prudish when he writes in French. As soon as he turns to
his native *patois*, he uses, much to our edification today, a frank,
coarse vocabulary that veers to the scatological, sometimes even to the
overtly sexual. This should surprise no one, of course, since the rules
of French propriety cease, by definition, to be applicable in *patois*.
Can one imagine Racine crying *fil de puta* [*fille de putain*], as Fabre
does? When he writes about Antiope, seduced by the satyr Jupiter,
Fabre declares, in Occitan, that she was 'the most respectable bitch
[*salope*] in the whole of the underworld . . .' and, adds Antiope, in
Fabre's *Odyssée burlesque*, 'having twins by Jupiter is worth one's
virginity'.

Indeed, the abbé devoted a good deal of energy to adapting into

Occitan such Greek and Latin poets as Martial, Horace, Ovid, Virgil, Homer (since Fabre did not actually know Greek, he translated the *Odyssey* from a Latin or French translation). The results of these long labours carried out on the epic poems of other times take the form of *patois* versions, in the full sense of the term. Fabre's *patois* versions of the *Aeneid* and the *Odyssey* are unfaithful, burlesque translations: they aim to come as close as possible to the most carnivalesque or everyday moments in the life of the average Languedocian. Nausicaa's companions become Montpellierian washerwomen. Parody, which also underpins *Jean-l'ont-pris*, is widely used in these epics.

Another aspect of the abbé's work in Occitan involves creation, rather than translation. I am referring to the plays *L'Opéra d'Aubais*, *Le Trésor de Substancion*, *Le Galimatias* (which, unusually, is written in French); a mock-heroic poem, *Le Siège de Caderousse*; and, finally, the novella *Jean-l'ont-pris*, to which this book is devoted. Actually, I believe (and I shall return to this point in due course) that *Jean-l'ont-pris* is itself a coded, marvellously disguised 'adaptation' of a folk-tale. All these works concern the down-to-earth life of the countryside and small towns of the Midi: the Vaunage, Aubais, Caderousse, Substancion, Castelnau. They combine a mock-heroic with a seriously philosophical view of marriage.

In order to explain the plot of *Jean-l'ont-pris*, which I shall sometimes call *JLP* for short,[6] I shall follow the opposite course from that used by the abbé Fabre. He began by telling the story of the father, Truquette. I shall start my analysis with the biography of the son, Jean-l'ont-pris. Indeed, if it is compared with the other fictional works of our Languedocian priest, certain unexpected, but unquestionable facts emerge.

Jean-l'ont-pris is the son of a cobbler called Truquette, who, subsequently, becomes a swindler and ends his days at Nîmes, on the scaffold. His son belongs to the poorest section of the young peasantry of Solorgues, a hamlet in the commune of Nages, in the Vaunage (now Gard). Illiterate, he spent most of his childhood playing truant. As a young boy, and later as a youth, he is noted for his exploits involving physical skill and delinquency: stealing birds' nests from the tops of trees, felling a donkey, tying up a child, stealing poultry and fruit. Jean falls in love with Monsieur Sestier's daughter and she with him. Monsieur Sestier is a former shepherd, who has become a rich farmer, or *ménager*, as they say in Languedoc; he is in charge of flocks of sheep, fields, orchards. His daughter Babeau is pretty, or at least attractive. She has great expectations of a dowry and a fortune. She is his only daughter; her father will leave her '60,000 francs' (60,000 *livres tournois*); since Sestier has no son, the whole of his estate will go by right to Babeau.

'Sixty thousand francs' in cash, chattels and land, represents a considerable sum. Having started with very little, Monsieur Sestier is now the equal of the richest peasants and even of the bourgeois of his parish.

Sestier turns out to be intractable: in principle, Jean-l'ont-pris has no chance of marrying Babeau. But the young man has at his disposal a secret weapon, his grandmother's treasure, which he has discovered in an old chest, in his hovel, after the old woman's death. This treasure is worth 20,000 *livres*, in cash, jewellery, lace, muslin and cambric. This is more than enough to claim Babeau's hand – and to relieve the future father-in-law of 60,000 *livres*, which will make 80,000 *livres* when added to Jean-l'ont-pris's own treasure. The contents of the chest derive from the dishonest activities indulged in by the hero's grandmother. She had gradually built up the treasure by secretly deducting a portion of the stolen goods accumulated by her son-in-law, Truquette, from his escapades in the local fairs and markets, before his downfall and end on the scaffold. From this point of view, the conquest of Babeau adds a little extra spice as far as Jean-l'ont-pris is concerned, for Babeau's father had been one of Truquette's accomplices in earlier days. He got rich, just as the grandmother had done, at the expense of the former cobbler's illegal activities. By seducing the daughter, Jean kills two birds with one stone. He recovers his grandmother's family wealth, and, in time, he will put his hands on that portion of the paternal fortune misappropriated by his future father-in-law, who swindled, as well as helped, Truquette.

So far so good. But Monsieur Sestier is no innocent. He, too, has worked out a plan, in which Jean-l'ont-pris is merely a pawn. In short, Sestier has got with child the excessively ill-favoured Barbe-Garouille.[7] At the insistence of her lover, she attributes her pregnancy to Jean. He is made to 'carry the can', while Sestier, to complete the operation, indirectly greases Jean-l'ont-pris's palm by giving a dowry to Garouille. Collared by former friends of his father, the young man has no choice but to let himself be manipulated, in order to manipulate all the better. He marries Barbe-Garouille, on condition that he never approach her. As expected, she dies in the hospital, together with the twins, Sestier's children, which she has given birth to.

It is a cruel episode, during which Jean-l'ont-pris does not waste time: for his part, he has made Babeau pregnant; she has become 'round as a tennis ball'. Master of a treasure of 20,000 *livres*, which he has dangled in front of the daughter and which he will dangle in front of the future father-in-law, conqueror of Babeau's virginity, soon to be the father of a child, Jean imagines that he has left Sestier only one possible solution: will the rich farmer, for reasons involving both honour and money, be forced to give his daughter in marriage to the young man? His lordship, in the name of outraged morality, will allow himself to express *in fine* some doubts as to this happy outcome. They are legitimate enough. One may well wonder whether the marriage will really take place and whether J L P will end up, if not on the scaffold, at least in the wretched condition from which his father set out . . .

Let me try to sum up, by means of a diagram, these aspects of the plot of *Jean-l'ont-pris*. A rectangle or square will be enough. This is the 'love square', or 'marriage square', of Occitan (and other) literature.

Barbe-Garouille, the 'opponent'	Monsieur Sestier, the 'father'
Jean-l'ont-pris, the 'hero'	Babeau, the 'daughter'

———————————→

possession of a treasure by Jean-l'ont-pris, Babeau's pregnancy and Barbe-Garouille's death will serve as essential factors in a (possible) marriage between Jean-l'ont-pris and Babeau

On the right, from top to bottom, I place the father–daughter or Sestier–Babeau axis, the father being master of Babeau's wealth, body and conjugal destiny. In the bottom left-hand corner, I place the by no means bashful lover, Jean-l'ont-pris; he tries to obtain the daughter in marriage, with her semi-beauty, her potential motherhood. In the top left-hand corner is placed the obstacle, the 'opponent': in other words, the person and action that will try to thwart the love intrigue. In this case it happens to be a female 'opponent', the horrible Barbe-Garouille: her task is to 'seduce' (!) and marry Jean-l'ont-pris in order to frustrate his intentions with regard to Babeau. Lastly, at the bottom of the square, moving horizontally, like an arrow that links the young man and the girl, lies the treasure; in due course, it will enable Jean, or so he hopes, to talk to his future father-in-law as an equal, and to set up a comfortable and, therefore, valid household. At the same time Barbe-Garouille's death and the conquest of Babeau's virginity, as 'pledge' followed by pregnancy, are important factors; they contribute to the possible marriage that ought to complete the young couple's happiness.

Another, less successful, couple links Jean-l'ont-pris's father, Truquette, and his wife, Margot. The 'love square' is well represented here too:

the opponents:
Truquette's rivals   Margot's mother
for Margot's hand   (Jean-l'ont-pris's
(a knife-grinder,   grandmother)
a carder, etc.)

the hero (Truquette)   the girl (Margot)

———————————————→

Margot's pregnancy makes the
marriage inevitable in any case

On the right of the square, from bottom to top, are Margot and her lineage (her mother); in this case, the lineage can only be maternal (and not paternal, as in Babeau's case). Indeed, Margot is born of an unmarried mother; her natural father, the surgeon of Calvisson, is both fleeting and distant. On the left of the square, we have, at the bottom, the hero and, at the top, the opponents, who are here Truquette's rivals. They include a carder, a worker in taffeta and, above all, the knife-grinder, who had courted Margot before the marriage and who finally gets her, once her husband has been arrested and hanged.

What is described here is a marriage between poor people: Truquette has no treasure, no cash, no land at his disposal. Nevertheless, he has managed to acquire the irresistible trump card that assures him of the marriage: he has made Margot pregnant (she gives birth to a fine baby only a few days after the wedding). In the circumstances, it is impossible to oppose the marriage. It is a question of honour – conquered, then restored.

The theme of illegitimate and (possibly) pre-marital pregnancy is a recurrent one in *Jean-l'ont-pris*: we find it in relation to Babeau, Margot, but also Barbe-Garouille, whose marriage is not to last long, and Margot's mother, who remains unmarried.

However, the 'square' of which Jean-l'ont-pris himself forms one of the angles is exemplary in this regard. Indeed, it will be noticed that the hero, Jean, acts powerfully on the 'four corners' of the geometrical figure of which he forms part, with a view to achieving the final marriage.

First, he strengthens his own position (D) with the advantages given him by the treasure, which, via the grandmother, comes to him from his father.

Second, Jean brings Babeau (C) into his scheme, by making her 'round as a tennis ball'.

Third, he aims at becoming the heir to the wealth of his future father-in-law (B), who himself had partially stolen that wealth from Jean's father during their partnership in crime. Jean's action consists, therefore, in recovering and reuniting the paternal inheritance, formerly pillaged, on the one hand, by his grandmother and, on the other, by the unscrupulous Monsieur Sestier.

Fourth and lastly, thanks to an opportune death, which he diagnoses and prognoses without having caused it, Jean overcomes any resistance that might come from the opponent (A), Barbe-Garouille, who soon leaves the scene.

In this way Jean weakens the other three points of the square (A, B and C), while doing everything to strengthen his own (D):

$$A(-) \qquad\qquad\qquad B(-)$$

$$D(+) \qquad\qquad\qquad C(-)$$

The 'love square' drawn in this way by Jean-l'ont-pris seems to me to be highly representative of all the abbé Fabre's creative works, whether dramatic or fictional. It is also representative of an important area of Occitan literature, that which takes as its subject the social stereotypes of marriage during the seventeenth and eighteenth centuries.

The 'love square', which I have also called the 'marriage square' (depending on whether one is dealing with the period before or after the celebration of marriage), is indeed typical of all Occitan literature, from the time of Henri III to that of Louis XVI. Of course, such fiction also deals with many other subjects, but it is this particular aspect that I shall examine here.

To begin with, I shall give a wider and more comprehensive definition of this marriage square than the one I have extracted from *Jean-l'ont-pris* alone.

This new 'model', which varies very little from the previous one, will be based on the analysis of a corpus of sixty-five literary works, either printed or, in certain cases, circulated in manuscript form, between 1575 and 1790. They include a novella (*Jean-l'ont-pris* itself), fifty-nine plays, four long poems and a mock-heroic poem.[8] All these works are from the Midi; the large majority of them were written in Occitan (in Provençal, Languedocian or Limousin) or in Franco-Provençal (three cases); some were written partly, if not entirely, in French (principally ten or so plays, from the Marseille or Aix regions, belonging to the late eighteenth century). Five of the sixty-five works considered were written by the abbé Fabre himself; they also constitute the totality of his fictional work (they are *L'Opéra d'Aubais*, *Le Trésor de Substancion*, *Jean-l'ont-pris* itself, *Le Galimatias* and *Le Siège de Caderousse*). I have not used Fabre's parodies of ancient epics (the burlesque versions of the *Aeneid* and *Odyssey* in Occitan); they are of considerable interest, but their plots are dictated by their Graeco-Roman models, which owe nothing to Occitan stereotypes. The other sixty texts (especially the plays, but also the pastoral, and even epic, poems) that depict our 'marriage square' are the work of other Occitan and Franco-Provençal writers active during the two hundred or so years between 1570 and 1790. They wrote variously at Aix-en-Provence, Marseille, Avignon, Montpellier, Frontignan, Béziers, Auch, Cahors, Agen, Montélimar, even Grenoble. The corpus used is therefore fully representative of the whole of Occitan fiction; indeed, it includes (if one sets aside the religious drama) almost the whole of published fiction, plus a number of manuscripts. Moreover, this corpus of works written in the *langue d'oc* is much smaller, in terms of the number of works printed or in manuscript, than the corresponding literature written in the *langue d'oïl*; it numbers almost twelve thousand plays in the eighteenth century alone,[9] many of which, it is true, have since been lost. On the regional plane that concerns me here, this representativeness guarantees a certain view of the *cultural* stereotypes of marriage. Similarly, an examination of hundreds of thousands of notaries' contracts in the Midi, or a valid sample of these, would provide a pertinent insight into the *social* reality of marriage.

It should be noted that the year 1789/90 (our *terminus ad quem*) certainly constitutes a break; from the Revolution onwards, provincial life was transformed by the new centralism. Works of literature produced at Aix and at Marseille became animated by a new French patriotism, hints of which could already be felt in the great Provençal port from 1780 and the time of the American Revolution onwards. Lastly, the position of the 'girl's father', in the 'love square', was affected, after 1789, by new laws of inheritance that considerably reduced the father's arbitrary powers.

This being the case, the 'marriage square', already so active in *Jean-*

l'ont-pris, can now be seen as a well-established convention which lasted for over two centuries:

| the opponent or rival | the girl's father |
| the hero | the girl |

(1) In the foreground (bottom right) is placed the character whom I shall call, for the sake of simplicity, the 'girl': she is usually young and pretty, often rich and well-off; and so, because she is possessed not only of beauty, but also of a dowry, all the more desirable. She is usually in love with her future husband. But this is not an absolutely necessary condition for the marriage to take place at the end of the plot. The object rather than the subject of the action, reified much more than active, manipulated by her father and her lineage, the girl may even, like the Arlésienne, never appear on the stage at all.[10] She is, nevertheless, by definition, the nub of the whole play.

(2) A second character, whom I shall call very generally the 'father' (the girl's father). In effect, he is the individual who, in the play, or more usually in the novel, represents the girl's paternal, but also in certain cases, maternal, lineage. The father is a powerful figure in all ancient literatures or traditional societies. But he seems to be particularly strong in the Occitan region, and more generally in the Midi, where Roman law predominated (unlike the *oïl*-speaking regions, where local custom often predominated). Roman law gave the father absolute freedom to choose which of his children would succeed him as sole or privileged heir. This law brought daughters all the more under the law of their fathers. Today, with our more or less liberal views on such matters, it is difficult to imagine those thundering fathers, like so many miniature Jupiters, of the *ancien régime*. Claude Lévi-Strauss has written that a woman is always given to a man by another man; in the Occitan theatre, and probably in the real life of the Midi, too, she was 'conveyed' by her father to her future husband. In fact, this 'father' may sometimes, when he is dead, be replaced by a rich uncle or a guardian or even an older brother.[11] It is a logical substitution, since this character, in the family, already represents paternal authority.

A Provençal, non-French-speaking author like Bonnet-Bonneville, in the eighteenth century, makes masterly use of these substitutions: in his play *Ce que esperavian pas ou Jean-Pierre vengu de Brest* (1781), written in the Marseillais dialect, he depicts a heroic Provençal sailor called Jean-Pierre, who is to marry Madeleine, a peasant's daughter; the wedding takes place amid a vast festival of anchovies, peppers, wine, sardines and cod. All that matters on the bride's side is the daughter–father axis (Madeleine and her father). In the next play by the same author, again in Provençal (*Jean-Pierre venu de Mahon ou le train du Pharo*, 1782), the gallant Jean-Pierre is already a widower! But he now functions at the higher level as a symbolic 'father' for a girl who is in fact only his cousin, Babet; it is he who gives the girl the 'parental' authorization necessary for her to marry the Parisian Joseph . . .[12]

And yet Occitan fiction sometimes seems to contradict Lévi-Strauss. On several occasions, the function of the girl's father is carried out by a mother.[13] Indeed, despite its unquestionable phallo-cratism, Occitan culture accords great importance to mothers when they are also widows. Their menopause brings increased power. In such cases, their indomitable will may be as inflexible as that of the father, had he lived. Sometimes (as in the case of the Agenese legend of Françounette, a later rendering in verse by the hairdresser Jasmin of a traditional story deriving at least from the late sixteenth century), the lineal–paternal role is carried out not by a widowed mother, but by a grandmother.

In any case, it would appear that the role in question is not specifi-cally that of a father, but that of a *lineage*, paternal or maternal, the lineage of the girl, in terms of an ascending line. In another quotation, Lévi-Strauss says that women are articles to be exchanged in the same way as words and goods.[14] On this point, our traditional societies as depicted in Occitan drama corroborate the findings of anthropology. When marriage is at stake, young women are exchangeable, or at least 'conveyable'. They may be conveyed by their respective lineages to males who have proved themselves to be responsible individuals. In order to benefit from this conveyance, the males do not have to have the permission of their own lineage – at least in Occitan fiction. The previous permission of the lineage, which is obligatory for the young women, is optional for the young men. In some of the plays we have considered – those depicting the more rural patriarchal societies – the young men do require such permission. Others – those belonging to a more urban setting – omit it.

Let us return to the girl's lineage – through the father or some other representative – which plays a crucial role. In certain Occitan works, this lineage may be purely symbolic. If the girl is a servant, for example, the role of father or father–mother, in relation to her, will be carried out by her mistress – but never by her male employer, because of the obvious danger of a secondary sexual relationship between the two of them. In such a case, according to the conventions of our theatre, such a monstrous figure would seem like an incestuous father – an unlikely eventuality.

It has to be admitted, however, that in certain cases, as in the drama emanating from the Aix region in the late sixteenth, seventeenth or eighteenth centuries, the girl is a prostitute; in this case, her lineage will be represented symbolically by the procuress–mother, or 'madame', of the brothel in which she works. This may seem strange, but it is logical: the procuress is a female employer; she is, therefore, a substitute mother or widowed mother.

Lastly, the role of a girl's father may also be taken by the girl's godfather (as is the case of the godfather and police inspector in Calhol's *Les Deux Commères*, a Marseillais play of the eighteenth century).

(3) Third, we have the male, the betrothed man or future husband, who will marry the girl in the fifth act – either the role of Truquette (in relation to Margot) or of Jean-l'ont-pris (in relation to Babeau). I shall call this particular male the 'hero'.

Generally, he has a strong desire to marry the girl. But such feelings are not an absolutely indispensable condition. In certain cases, the hero is not particularly keen to marry the heroine. However, he has to make up his mind to do so by the fifth act, as a result of some vicissitude, since this happy outcome is an essential part of the game, and is the normal ending of the play.

The hero is usually young and handsome, possibly poor. However, he may be old and ugly, even rich. This is not the essential point.

As I have already suggested, this hero is often self-determined. In many cases, his paternal or maternal lineage, father or widowed mother, is not mentioned. Sometimes, however – though this is not a structural necessity – his father or widowed mother takes part in the plot; as a figure symmetrical with the indispensable character of the girl's father, he or she may be real, symbolic or a substitute. The hero's father (or mother) is more frequently mentioned in plays with a rural or patriarchal setting.[15]

If the hero is a manservant, his master is often present in the play, as the counterpart of the maidservant's mistress, the two servants being destined, in the fifth act, to marry. I leave to one side the problem of procurer as employer or symbolic father of possible male prostitutes, since these, of course, never appear in the plays we have examined. This is simply a symmetry that would be purely theoretical in relation to the case of female prostitutes, so dear to the theatre of the Aix region. It is, in fact, a false window.

In order for there to be a play or a novel or an epic, in Occitan or in any other language, something has to postpone the happy outcome until the fifth act. This 'something' that prevents the hero from marrying the girl is usually lack of money, wealth, land, connections, status and prestige; it may also, as in the case of comic manservants, be lack of honour. All the skill of the novelist or playwright is employed in remedying this lack, by means of some compensatory trick . . .

(4) There now emerges the fourth character of the square (top left), the rival; he is the ultimate ingredient, indispensable to the action. He is often, although not always, older and uglier than the hero, and usually richer. But these three characteristics are not at all necessary. This rival, obviously, is very often a male, or an old male, who claims the girl's hand. And the girl's father (or widowed mother), in view of the wealth of this additional claimant, may tend to encourage him, against the hero, who benefits from the support of the author. Sometimes, when the girl's symbolic father is in fact only her guardian, this guardian may also be the hero's rival (Gravelle's *Le Tuteur jaloux*, 1759, Marseille-Avignon).

But the rival, whom I prefer to call in a more neutral, more general way the 'opponent', is not necessarily a male. 'He' may also be a girl: she is in love with the hero; or she is driven by some intriguer (the girl's father, among others) to marry the hero. This is the case, for example, of Barbe-Garouille in *Jean-l'ont-pris*. Monsieur Sestier, the father of the charming heroine, Babeau, forces the horrible Garouille (whom he has probably made pregnant in order to be more certain of the outcome) to attribute her pregnancy to Jean, in order to force him to marry her. Thus the hero, as far as Babeau is concerned, will be set aside – so Sestier hopes.

In certain cases,[16] the 'opponent' is simply a collective entity, made up of a group of prostitutes who transmit syphilis to the hero. The girl is then disgusted and refuses to marry him. This being the case, at a time when antibiotics were not yet available, the hero has to find sufficiently convincing arguments, monetary or otherwise, to overcome the disgust of his adored one and the opposition of her lineage.

Sometimes (though not very often), the opponent may be not a rival, male or female, but simply a temporary obstacle to the conclusion and celebration of the marriage. Thus, in *Les Deux Commères*, the eighteenth-century play from Marseille already mentioned, the opponent is simply the hero's mother, a fruit-seller in the city market. She is threatened with arrest for cheating on the weight of the grapes she sells. This threat is in itself enough to prevent the marriage from taking place, since the bridegroom's mother would be unable to play her decorative and necessary role if she were in prison. The hero overcomes the difficulty by freeing his mother, after paying the police inspector, who is also the girl's godfather, the necessary financial compensation.

Now, having established our 'love square', the following question arises: how will the hero get the girl's consent? In actual fact, this is easy enough. But there is an infinitely more difficult task: how is he to win the acceptance of his future father-in-law or future mother-in-law or their symbolic equivalents?

Answer: by finding the necessary 'money', which he may then transfer to his beloved's lineage (that is to say, to herself or to one of her children). The word 'money' here may often be taken literally. But I am also using the word in a more general, perhaps too general, way to designate 'wealth' or as the material symbol of a person's 'rank' in society – it may be money, but it may also be cattle or, occasionally, land or a high social status, backed by real wealth; the hero may also improve his position, on his own account, by means of some 'trick'. This may take the form, as I have already said, of the transfer and counter-transfer of 'honour' (loss of the girl's virginity, subsequent pregnancy and 'reparation', forced or otherwise, through marriage). Magical techniques may also be used.

Another question: where and how is the hero to find this 'money', using the term in its very widest sense (land, cattle, cash, etc.)?

In actual fact, there is no choice, given the four points of the 'love square'; he can raise the capital in question in only four ways:

(1) from his own property or that of his lineage, or from his own industry and cunning;

(2) from the property of the rival or 'opponent';

(3) from the property of the girl's father or lineage (in ascending line);

(4) from the girl herself.

He has, I repeat, only four possibilities; they are not mutually exclusive. In these works of fiction, one remains within the *logical* framework of the Occitan 'love square'.

CHAPTER 11 The Lineal Treasure of the Hero

Let us consider to begin with the case in which the hero (like Jean-l'ont-pris when he is planning to use his grandmother's treasure) uses for display or to raise more money certain capital of his own or of his lineage; this capital will be the decisive argument that will bring about the marriage with the heroine.

In this respect one might cite a Languedocian play, *Daphnis et Alcimadure*, which is exactly contemporary with *Jean-l'ont-pris*.

It is a so-called pastoral opera. Written in Languedocian by Mondonville (born at Narbonne), it was played before the king in 1754. The shepherd Daphnis, in love with the beautiful Alcimadure, is rejected by her. Jeannet, the girl's older brother, is a village 'Monsieur' [*Moussu*]; in relation to his young sister, he plays the 'paternal' role of family head. He decides to test the sincerity of Daphnis's feelings; he is not necessarily favourable to the young man as a potential brother-in-law. So he presents himself to the lovesick shepherd as the girl's betrothed. In short, he plays the role of lucky rival. Daphnis reacts as he should to this test. He displays sincere despair; he goes on to save Alcimadure from a wolf, but, when he believes all his hopes of marrying his beloved are lost, he announces that there is nothing left for him to do but die. Chivalrous to the end, he takes the opportunity of letting everyone know that he is leaving his inheritance, his flock and even his dog to Alcimadure! Daphnis's father will arrange all the details of the gift after his son's funeral. In fact, Daphnis does not die (he was not really expected to do so). A final stratagem throws him alive and vigorous into Alcimadure's arms. The two young people marry.[1]

This cleverly written play reproduces the classical 'square' in a rather original way: Jeannet, the head of the family; the girl; the lover; and, lastly, the 'preventer' (who is none other than the head of the family, temporarily duplicated, Jeannet II). Here, the circulation of the 'treasure' is the transfer by Daphnis of his paternal inheritance to Alcimadure.

Jeannet II, pseudo-betrothed	Jeannet, Alcimadure's older brother and 'symbolic father'
Daphnis, the heroine's lover	Alcimadure, the heroine

→

transfer of Daphnis's inheritance

The use of his own property, in this case livestock, by the hero who wants to marry a girl is a very ancient and popular theme in the Languedocian pastoral. Take, for example, *Les Amours de Damon et de Lucrèce*, published at Béziers in 1657, and performed on the public square, during the annual *charités* for Ascension Day, which, in that town, represented the high point of popular celebration.

As a result of these *Amours*, the old mother has a daughter, Lucresso, the shepherdess (Lucrèce). Lucrèce loves the shepherd Damon, who also loves her. A drunken old soldier wants to marry the girl. The mother hesitates between these two possible sons-in-law. With the help of his armed troops, the soldier carries Lucrèce off by force. Damon promises to go with his shepherd companions to free her; he will carry out this sacred mission, 'even if he has to sell his whole flock of sheep to pay for the expedition'. In fact, he does not have to sacrifice this capital, which will fortunately be preserved for his marriage . . . Lucrèce manages to escape captivity in a way that is never made clear; she even saves her virginity, reserved in advance for Damon, from the soldier's attacks. The two young people will marry, under the tearful eye of the old woman.

the soldier	the old woman
the shepherd Damon	Lucrèce

→

the possible sacrifice, by Damon, of his entire flock

In short, the marital appetite of the young shepherdess is certainly whetted by the shepherd's well-fed flock – a commonplace of the theatre, but also a stereotype used by Frontignan in his *Chanson pastorale* (seventeenth century).[2] A shepherdess, after tumbling in the hay on several occasions with a shepherd, and *after accepting a lamb from him as a present*, refuses to marry him and finally goes home to her mother. That, indeed, is a scandal; and it shocked the seventeenth-century Montauban poet Jean de Valès, himself a writer of pastorals and, like the abbé Fabre, the author of an *Énéide burlesque*.[3]

It is not only the shepherd who is at issue here; the young Limousin peasant Capiote, in the early-seventeenth-century, north Occitan play of the same name, makes great show of his credits (30 *livres*), his cattle, his expectations in terms of inheritance (80 *livres*) in order to win the hand and dowry of the beautiful Hauzanne, daughter of the rich farmer Rougeau. This dowry consists of 250 *livres*, plus a bed worth 20 *livres*, napkins, linen, etc. As there is no serious rival in view, the marriage could have been concluded in the first act. In order to spin out the plot, the playwright invents (in addition to a few visits by soldiers) an opponent, and a plausible enough one at that: the young peasant girl loves Capiote, but she is sexually afraid of her betrothed's member. This exorbitant organ is therefore promoted to the role of obstacle to the marriage. It takes five acts for Capiote to tame his beloved with dances, kisses and a good deal of fine talk. The play ends in the bed on the wedding-night; Hauzanne declares that she is fully convinced. Next morning, an onion soup, brought in by the girl's parents, will restore the strength of the young couple, exhausted by their triumphal night.

physiological obstacle	Rougeau, Hauzanne's father
Capiote	Hauzanne

$$\longrightarrow$$

Capiote's capital will make the marriage possible, once the fear of the 'physiological obstacle' has been lifted

Without having to resort to the term 'realism', in the limited sense, it is obvious that the problem of the husband's contribution, whether in the form of treasure, sheep or cash, was as much the concern of the Languedocian notaries of the time as it was of the Occitan play-wrights.[4] But the notaries put greater stress on the bride's dowry; the literature of the Midi, on the other hand, emphasized the pro-spective husband's contribution.

A number of plays depict variations on this theme, while maintain-ing the notion of the transfer of goods from the young male. The farmer's daughter remains herself, but her lover, the hero of the play, becomes mythically the son of the ruler of Morocco – which makes him all the more generous ... Let us examine for a moment *L'Empereur du Maroc* (a play in Provençal, performed at Tarascon in 1646).[5] The author is a certain Séguin, a local 'captain' in his spare time.

Cibel, the legitimate heir to the throne of Morocco, expelled from his country by a usurper, lives in exile in the 'island', in fact in the Comtat Venaissin, where he works as a shepherd. He falls in love with Driotte, daughter of the rich farmer Lésimar (in Provençal, as in French, this name suggests *lésine*, 'avarice'), and she returns his love. In relation to Cibel, the grotesque Gloujou functions as an unlucky rival, who claims Driotte's hand. Lésimar does not like unknown strangers who have neither family nor patrimony; he fears that the honour of his house will be in jeopardy if Cibel sticks his dibble into his daughter's flowerpot, and so makes her swell up in nine months' time. Driotte's family wants her to marry a rich, healthy man of good stock (good lineage). The false-shepherd–true-prince decides, there-fore, to reveal his treasure. He gives a first instalment to Driotte in the form of pearls, diamonds, sapphires, rubies and emeralds. The girl has a whole apronful (these precious stones are what is left of Cibel's Moroccan fortune). Is Driotte so dazzled by them that she will sacrifice her virginity? In any case, after a first attempt on Cibel's part to carry her off, she is caught, *in flagrante delicto*, with her lover, by the authorities of the island; they are both condemned to death. As luck would have it, the Moroccans are ridding themselves at that moment of the usurper; so they send their delegate, called, naturally enough, Ramadan, to persuade Cibel to return home to his lawful throne and empire. Ramadan stops the execution. Cibel, recognized in his true identity, triumphs; he sets out for Morocco in the company of Driotte, who will become the empress of her new country. Before leaving, the good-hearted Cibel endows the island, Driotte's collective progenitor, with millions of sequins and thousands of oriental pearls, taken from the inexhaustible treasure now in his hands as the new emperor of Morocco. Usually fertile in treasure of all kinds (compare *Jean-l'ont-pris*), Occitan literature has never proved so generous. Beaten in the marriage stakes, Gloujou will remain a shepherd; by way of compensation, Cibel gives him the sheep from the flock of the former shepherd (Cibel himself) who is now to become a monarch and will, therefore, have no further use for his 'woolly cattle'. The 'marriage square' functions perfectly.

Gloujou	Lésimar, Driotte's father
Cibel	Driotte

Cibel's Moroccan treasure →

These various plays set out from the well-founded notion that the hero is rich to start with; he has therefore only to reveal his wealth to win the girl's hand and, by the same token, her dowry.

Occitan literature, however, has not always been so 'fixist'. It accepts that the lover may himself become rich in order that, at the end of this process of individual promotion, he will be in a position to seduce his beloved's lineage. This acquisition of wealth may take place, quite simply, through theft; once he has accumulated enough wealth, the thief is in a position to marry his beloved. Take, for instance, *L'Histoire pastorale représentée dans Béziers sur le théâtre des marchands le jour de l'Ascension* (1633).[6]

The shepherd Sirène and the shepherdess Diane live in the countryside around Béziers. A Parisian gentleman, Riolan, pays court to Diane, who does not take it seriously; but Sirène becomes jealous. The people have just emerged from a time of civil war (the Protestant war around Rohan, in the Cévennes, and the recent revolt at Montmorency). The villagers hate the looting soldiers and take reprisals against them. Sirène, who is poor, gets rich by attacking with other peasants the soldier Polacre and relieving him of valuables worth over 4,000 ducats. In the end, the gentleman and the soldier leave the district. The young lovers can now look forward to marriage. Once again, everything takes place under the tearful eye of the old woman, who conveniently completes the canonical square.

Riolan   (the old woman)

the shepherd Sirène   Diane, the shepherdess

————————————————————————→

with the 4,000 ducats he has stolen, Sirène becomes *ipso facto* a suitable partner for Diane

This play is all the more interesting in that it enacts in an explicit way certain 'social' themes that underpin the usual love rivalries: among these themes, one can observe the peasants' resistance to the soldiery; and the frustration of provincial commoners at the sight of Parisian noblemen seducing the local women at the expense of the local bloods, who, because they live outside the capital and are of low birth, might suppose that they have less chance of attracting the available girls.

The presence of the soldiery, with its consequent looting and counter-looting, was a familiar feature of the Languedoc during the war-torn Richelieu period. In Provence, individual enrichment, which provides the key to a good marriage, may take a legitimate, commercial form. The hero wishes to attract the lady of his choice. Poor as he is, he manages to get rich by means of a well-run apothecary shop: this is the plot of Brueys's *Comédie à onze personnages* (late sixteenth century), published in the *Jardin des Muses provençales*.[7]

Bourgau, who is poor, loves Angelo (Angèle), who loves him. But Angèle's father does not care for younger sons with no fortune; so he marries his daughter to Matériau; this individual is certainly rich, but lacking in wit, as his 'materialist' name suggests. Left to his own devices, Bourgau has all kinds of far-fetched amorous adventures; he seduces a married woman, moves in with her and sets up, with her money, a highly lucrative apothecary shop. He earns huge sums of money, which take him far from his original poverty. But he does not forget his old love: on the pretext of treating, as an apothecary, Angèle's womb – she is now married to Matériau – he sleeps with this lady, practically on stage. In the end, Matériau dies, and Bourgau can marry Angèle; he is rich; she a widow and free of her father's authority.

Matériau	Angèle's father
Bourgau	Angèle

———————————————————————————→

Bourgau becomes an apothecary and gets rich; Matériau dies; previous, complete seduction of Angèle by Bourgau

At Marseille, in the eighteenth century, the character of the sailor, who may or may not have got rich, wins female hearts and upsets agreements between lineages. *Le Marché de Marseille ou les deux Commères*,[8] a charming play by J. Calhol, is very telling in this respect. The sailor, Jeannet, who comes back rich from a voyage, is the son of Embanado, a Marseille gossip and picturesque retailer of fruit; he wants to marry Jeannette, goddaughter of the inspector of police. But Embanado has cheated her customers on the price and weight of the grapes she sells. The marriage will be prevented, temporarily at least, because of the imminent imprisonment of Embanado, the bridegroom's mother. Fortunately, the young man saves the situation by giving 6 francs to the inspector (who will hand the money back to Embanado's victims and so refrain from having the old woman imprisoned). The hero, then, has used his own resources or recent acquisitions to obtain a much larger sum of money from his beloved's symbolic lineage (the godfather–police inspector). In return, the inspector will give his goddaughter a symbolic dowry, since he will, in fact, pay the wedding expenses.

Embanado, Jeannet's mother, threatened with imprisonment	the police inspector, Jeannette's godfather or 'symbolic father'
	Jeannette,
Jeannet	his goddaughter

→

money raised from the hero's earnings at sea, transferred to the girl's symbolic lineage, allows the marriage to take place

Marseille is a special case; elsewhere, in a stagnant Occitania, growth is not such that a self-made man, if the cultural stereotypes are to be believed, can expect much in the way of sudden wealth.

According to the Occitan dramatic tradition, therefore, it falls to the hero's lineage to make possible the display or raising of capital: it is his own family that will help the hero gain access, through marriage, to his beloved's lineage. This, of course, is the case of Jean-l'ont-pris: he obtains his treasure both from his paternal lineage (his father's illicit gains) and from his maternal lineage (the secret hoarding of these gains by his maternal grandmother). Indeed, the abbé Fabre repeated the same theme in an unpublished play, entitled *Le Galimatias*.[9]

The beautiful young heroine, Lucinde, nicknamed Colette, is the daughter of an authoritarian marquise, who does not hesitate to wear a periwig in order to display her virago's 'virility'. Clitandre is in love with Lucinde; he is the son of a viscount who previously disinherited him, but through a theatrical trick, Clitandre has managed to obtain his father's wealth, having already rid himself of the comic suitors who claimed Lucinde's hand. With a huge fortune suddenly at his disposal, Clitandre can now exert enough pressure to achieve his desires. He gets the consent of the viscount and marquise to his marriage to Lucinde. The play also involves an intelligent tutor (modelled on Fabre himself, or on his father), who is contrasted with the stupid nobles and peasants who indulge in an 'antifeudal' class struggle against one another.

The rectangle is a classic one:

various suitors   the marquise,
                                                   Lucinde's mother

Clitandre   Lucinde

$$\longrightarrow$$

the obtaining and use of Clitandre's
paternal wealth in order to get the
families' assent, which is indispensable
to the marriage

Before becoming a revolutionary, Collot d'Herbois was well known as a Provençal playwright. In his *Nouveau Nostradamus*[10] he, too, used his hero's paternal wealth to win, on stage, assent to a marriage.

Canzonin, a musician and a lover of the troubadours, has a daughter, Joséphine; she is sixteen and pretty. He has promised her to Captain Tribord, a Provençal, *patois*-speaking, well-off ship's master. But Alexis, son of Dastrimon, a village worthy and, incidentally, a passionate dabbler in astrology, loves Joséphine. Dastrimon kills two birds with one stone: he buys his son, Alexis, a legal office, thus strengthening his material and moral prestige; and he declares that astrologically the conjunction of Virgo (Joséphine) and Libra (Alexis, who will become a judge) is in accordance with the attraction of the planets required at that moment. Captain Tribord gallantly steps down, since, as a sailor, he needs a woman in every port. Unable to marry them all, he will marry none. This being the case, he could not do right by Joséphine in marrying her. Hence the happy ending for Joséphine and Alexis, arranged under the fatherly eye of Canzonin. (In a similar situation, however, the sea captain Louragan, rival of the hero in Gravelle's *La Marseillaise* [Avignon, 1760], kicks up a hell of a fuss when he is out-manoeuvred by the hero; in the end, the police are forced to incarcerate the irascible and well-named Louragan [*ouragan*, 'hurricane'].)

Collot d'Herbois's play follows tradition in stressing the dual, irresistible influence exercised by lineage (the hero's), first, by raising money to buy a legal office and, second, by magico-astrological prediction. Here magic, which we shall come back to, shows the cloven hoof.

Tribord, sea captain	Canzonin, the 'troubadour', Joséphine's father
Alexis	Joséphine

→

decisive influence of the wealth of Alexis's father, assisted by astrological predictions

What is involved in this type of play is the problem of the husband's financial contribution to his own marriage; or – a variant that is of particular interest to us here – that of the contribution of the bride-groom's parents and, in particular, the contribution of the young man's *father*. Here the theatre reflects real life, as far as the classes favoured by fortune are concerned: on 5 July 1720, Noble Lambert Fargeon, son of a judge at the court of aids at Montpellier, married Marie-Louise de Valette, of noble family. The intended wife's dowry: 30,000 *livres*. The father of the intended husband gave his son the sum or the equivalent of 200,000 *livres*, including a post as judge at the audit office (65,000 *livres*), a house (35,000 *livres*) and the rest in the form of an annual income. In the world of master craftsmen, the sums involved were by comparison modest enough (for example, 1,000 *livres* in dowry from the girl's family, 2,500 *livres* from the betrothed man's father), but the principles involved are the same.[11]

The theatrical (but not legal) rule according to which it is first the *hero* (not the heroine) who provides the financial contribution of his own lineage towards the wedding expenses is never violated in our Occitan literature, either in the theatre or in fiction. There is, however, one exception: François de Cortète's *Ramounet*,[12] which is so eloquent on the problems presented to the Occitan lands by the bellicose activities of soldiers in the early seventeenth century.

At the end of a complicated plot, Ramounet, a former soldier, now a deserter, is to be hanged on the orders of his superior officers,

despite the supplications of his mother, Leno. A 'young man' called
Carlin reveals that, in fact, 'he' ('Carlin') is a young peasant girl
(temporarily disguised as a man) called Charlotte. At the same time,
Charlotte announces that she is in love with Ramounet. She brings
with her 1,000 *livres tournois*, taken from the inheritance of her peasant
father. This money will constitute the ransom that will allow
Ramounet to escape the scaffold. Ramounet will therefore marry
Carlin/Charlotte, who has saved him from imminent death. For him,
she abandons a charming girl, Philippo, who previously loved Carlin/
Charlotte when he or she was still regarded as a male; Philippo will,
therefore, be given in marriage to another soldier, called Dulaurie.

Philippo   Leno, Ramounet's mother

Carlin/Charlotte   Ramounet

———————————————————————→

1,000 *livres* from Carlin/Charlotte's
paternal lineage

For once, the raising of money in order to facilitate marriage is
carried out by a girl, and not by a man. But, of course, this girl is
'virile'. She had previously disguised herself as a boy. The golden
rule by which a spouse is 'bought' by the future husband or his
lineage is therefore only partly violated; hardly violated at all.

It took a feminist novelist from outside the Midi, George Sand (*La
Petite Fadette*, Ch. XXXIII), to overthrow completely the system
that François de Cortète had only partly disturbed. In Sand's story,
Fadette, an orphan and therefore independent, discovers the treasure
(40,000 francs) of her dead grandmother, who was something of a
magician; thanks to this discovery, she is able to win the consent of
the father of the boy (one of two twins) she loves. The plot offered
on this question by George Sand is all the more original in that the
novelist took as her inspiration an Occitan text (Jasmin's *Les Deux
Frères jumeaux*, Agen, 1846), the story of which is, in effect, super-
ficially reproduced in *Fadette*. But the energetic contribution of

female capital made by the heroine of Sand's story certainly derives from an original initiative on the great novelist's part.[13] No Occitan writer of the seventeenth and eighteenth centuries would have been capable of such an idea; not even François de Cortète, who got closest to it in his *Ramounet*. Would this be, among other things, because there was not a single woman among the important authors of Occitan fiction between 1580 and 1790? Male writers are obsessed by the problems that concern the search for a wife and the indispensable obtaining of male capital, intended to serve as a basis for setting up house. These gentlemen do not pose the other question, which certainly preoccupied Occitan women: namely, the problem of the girl's search (symmetrical with the previous one) for a dowry that will influence the family of the man she loves. In this sense, Occitan fiction in the classical age is rather a reflection of the financial obsession of men than an accurate description of ·social reality, on both sides of the barrier that separates the sexes.[14]

Let us go back, then, to this male money that is certainly central as far as the cultural stereotypes of the Midi are concerned; it may come not from the hero's real lineage, but from his symbolic lineage. Thus the manservant who is about to marry the maidservant of a certain mistress may obtain from his master enough money to set him up, which, for the girl, compensates for the fact that the betrothed man is afflicted with a venereal disease – this is one of the sub-plots of Pierre Rousset's *Le Jaloux attrapé* (Sarlat, 1645).

Zeloto forces his manservant Grizoulet to marry Morgui, the maidservant of Callisto, Zeloto's wife. For the ancillary marriage, Zeloto will provide the initial funds required. Morgui then agrees to this marriage, which she previously rejected on the grounds that Grizoulet was and is still diseased.

Morgui's competitor-rivals, who have diseased Grizoulet	Callisto, Morgui's mistress and Zeloto's wife
Grizoulet, Zeloto's manservant	Morgui, Callisto's maid

$\longrightarrow$

Zeloto's money, paid out to Grizoulet to set up house

If the hero is a soldier of low rank, his symbolic, and generous, lineage will be logically represented by a high-ranking soldier, as in *La Bienfaisance de Louis XVI ou les fêtes de la paix* (in Provençal) by Matthieu Blanc-Gilli (Marseille, 1783).

Margarido, a seamstress and daughter of Maître Cauvin, owner of a fishing boat, saves the life of her lover, the sailor Tounin, dangerously wounded in the left arm during a sea-fight with the English. He will become a sardine fisherman in turn . . . However, the colonel, who has seen many a fight at sea between marines, is moved to tears at the sight of these good Provençals (*how simple these people are, how interesting!*); he gives a purse to Tounin. This will be the young man's 'dowry'. And Tounin hastens to reconvey it to the girl he is going to marry.

the English enemy, who nearly made Tounin unavailable	Maître Cauvin, Margarido's father
Tounin	Margarido

$\longrightarrow$

transfer of the purse [*bourse*], given by the colonel, who functions as the hero's 'symbolic lineage'

In short, Tounin makes a suitable husband, because he is promoted, at the end of the story, to the rank of 'bursar' [*boursier*] of the French army and navy.

*

Of course, if the hero is a peasant, his symbolic lineage may consist quite simply of the lord whose tenant he is. Bonnet-Bonneville's *Les Vœux satisfaits ou le Roumavagi*, in Provençal (Aix, 1788), was played during the festivities to celebrate the re-establishment of the *parlement* of Provence. It was written expressly to the glory of the noble *parlementaires* of the province. In *Les Vœux satisfaits*, Suzon persuades her great-grandfather, Cyprien, during a feast of cod and eel soup, to allow her to marry her lover, Jean-Louis. The count, the local lord of the manor, will pay 'the wedding expenses and the dowry'.

Cyprien,
Suzon's great-grandfather

Jean-Louis   Suzon

————————————————————→

the financing of the marriage by the count

These symbolic lineages or fathers that set up a young man with enough money to enable him to get a wife are to be found not only in Occitan fiction, but also in the real life of the French Midi, as notaries' deeds show. 'Absolutely outside the actual family,' writes Pierre Lamaison, who at this point is particularly interested in symbolic kinship, 'it sometimes happened that a poor man, completely devoid of any means himself, is given by some paternally-minded benefactor a gift of money that enables him to marry; thanks to the will of a priest at Ribennes (a village in the Lozère), several marriages were made possible in the years following the good priest's death. In one of these, a Jean Souchon married a Louise Gibelin on 28 July 1745, with a dowry of 100 *livres* left him by the recently deceased priest: being well over thirty years of age, Jean Souchon had not previously been able to accumulate enough money himself to claim a woman's hand in marriage.'[15]

The theme of the symbolic lineage derives prosaically enough from social reality; but through fiction, it may also set off on a crazy course towards the epic and the burlesque. In the abbé Fabre's epic, *Le Siège de Caderousse*, the symbolic lineage that provides the hero with the pre-marital means required is nothing less than the city of Avignon itself.

Le Siège de Caderousse, written by the abbé Fabre between May and September 1774,[16] is based on a real event. The long, severe winter of 1709 ruined the crops and caused acute shortages of food. This, in turn, led to black-market speculation and stockpiling of grain. The city of Avignon was hungry. However, the tiny, semi-rural township of Caderousse (two or three thousand inhabitants)[17] had considerable stocks of wheat. Under the direction of the vice-legate, who represented for them, living in a papal zone, the supreme pontiff, the people of Avignon decided to requisition the cereals. An initial expedition of a hundred men was organized to carry this out. It was repulsed before fighting ever began by the threats and insults screamed at the Avignonnais by the Caderoussian women and, on the ground, by the Caderoussian men, armed with axes and roasting spits. A second, larger expedition was then planned: two cannon and carts laden with pickaxes for the siege and spoons for the soup accompanied it. The cavalcade appeared under the walls of Caderousse. The terrified inhabitants immediately handed over the keys of the town to these 'papal' soldiers. The town was invaded by the soldiery and moderately looted, without shedding of blood.

This real incident was simply a violent conflict over provisions, and of a particular kind. Fabre had read the printed account, and it was on this that he based his mock-heroic epic, *Le Siège de Caderousse*.[18] The work is structured on the relationship between Avignon/hunger and Caderousse/food. The contrast was one of the keys to *Jean-l'ont-pris*: Jean-l'ont-pris's family, called *les meurt-de-faim* ['down-and-outs', but literally, 'die-of-hunger'], is symbolically contrasted with Sestier-le-Goinfre ['greedy-guts']. Again, if the hungry man of Avignon is to get his hands on food and a woman, he must use cunning or violence and give up something in favour of the 'axis' of the opposite side, thus operating the exchange.

The famine of 1709 is raging at Avignon, Fabre writes: 'It keeps the monks' assholes tight . . . No more shit. Everything is as clean as your hands, for lack of food. The bourgeois fry their shoes, the rich devour their cats, the poor chase the rats . . . the canons see their bands hang loose . . . their bellies stick to their backs . . .' Meanwhile, the news is spreading through the city that Caderousse, a small town, has just taken in four hundred cartloads of grain. This town was dominated at the time (according to Fabre's fiction) by the strong personality of a farrier, Lafeuillade, whose wife is called Louise and their daughter, Françounette. The surname and Christian name are larded with various allusions and references: Louis(e) and Françoise (Françounette) are 'French' Christian names, the first monarchical and the second national; they suggest the Gallican resistance of Caderousse to the 'papal' intentions of Avignon. The trade of farrier, in the abbé's fiction, accompanies a situation involving a comic 'notable' in some tiny locality. At Solorgues, too, the most important local worthies are, if *Jean-l'ont-pris* is to be believed, 'the magistrate, the farrier and a Capuchin' . . . Margot, the heroine of the novella *JLP*, is the (bastard) daughter of a 'surgeon', the local physician. Françounette, the heroine of *Le Siège*, is the daughter of a farrier, also the local veterinary surgeon. I shall come back in the second part of my book to these important homologies.

I spoke, a moment ago, of Gallicanism. We shall not take too seriously our abbé writer's patriotism. The farrier [*maréchal-ferrant*] Lafeuillade, of Caderousse, is certainly a grotesque substitute for a particular marshal of France, but one who was also among the more contemptible and ridiculous in French history. I am referring to the Maréchal Louis de la Feuillade (1673–1725), who was responsible for the ignominious failure of the siege of Turin, and son of the Maréchal François de la Feuillade (who died in 1691). We shall note in passing that this Louis and this François correspond point by point to the Louise and Françoise Lafeuillade of *Le Siège*.

But there is more to it than that. At Caderousse, the Lafeuillade/ father–Françounette/daughter axis corresponds point by point to the Sestier–Babeau axis at Solorgues. Caderousse is certainly on the side of Babeau (or of Françounette), on the side of the girl whom the lover must try to win.

The Avignonnais, in Fabre's version, set out against Caderousse. Their 'crusade', advocated by a fanatical Dominican who in other times would have roasted Albigensians, forms 'the army of hunger', made of up tailors, apothecaries, masons. It is commanded by a certain Boiardo-Pantalon-Octave. This name embodies the mock-heroic epic, the comic *pantalonnade* ['farce'] and the juvenile lead of *plaisanterie* ['comedy'].[19] In the imaginary setting of *Le Siège*, he will play the role that Jean-l'ont-pris is to play in the Solorgues tale. Jean-l'ont-pris's grandmother promised her grandson, son of a newly rich, former cobbler, a future as a *marquis-mirliflor* ['fop', 'dandy']. At the instance of the vice-legate of Avignon, Boiardo has already been made 'marquis of here, duke of there, prince of I-know-not-where . . .' The military equipment of Boiardo/Jean-l'ont-pris, in the procession of carts, is made up of 'fifteen or sixteen cartloads of spoons, forks, pots, dishes . . . to cook and guzzle the food'. The battle takes place under the walls of Caderousse in Homeric style. Lafeuillade proves to be as expert in giving and taking blows as was his counterpart Sestier in the story of Jean-l'ont-pris. The apothecaries of Avignon form one of the besieging companies; they bombard the Caderoussians with purges, causing fits of diarrhoea.

Caderousse has no alternative but to submit to the law of the victor. But Françounette, daughter of Lafeuillade, leader of the besieged town, looks after her compatriots' interests. She invites Boiardo/Jean-l'ont-pris to come and drink a glass of wine with her. An attractive and opulent Judith, she does not cut off the head of her Holofernes. She gets him drunk and stuffs him with food; they decide to marry there and then by mutual consent, since the opposition of the father, Lafeuillade, has now been lifted. A priest–notary has them sign the marriage contract, accompanied by a few splashings of holy water. During the first night, the marriage remains unconsummated. Boiardo, too drunk to act, sleeps like a log. On the morning of the pseudo-'wedding-night', the serious business begins. Boiardo is assured of the (self-interested) love of Françounette. Avignon/male owes it to himself to seduce in turn Caderousse/female, but now by peaceful means. The military equipment of the Avignon people, the treasure that always circulates in the work of Fabre and other Occitan writers in the opposite direction from that taken by the women, is therefore handed over to the Caderoussians: it consists of the fifteen cartloads of dishes, pots and soup-spoons which the 'crusade' had brought from Avignon.[20] In return, the compatriots of Lafeuillade and Françounette hand over to the hungry people of Avignon, as though they were making a dowry, half their stored food, that is, two hundred cartloads of wheat out of the four hundred stored away by Caderousse. The gift of half the food, already envisaged in passing in Fabre's *L'Opéra d'Aubais*, was a usual practice among Languedocian notaries, in the relationships between the old parental couple and the young couple . . . After this exchange of pots for wheat, the aforementioned crusade, now a gigantic wedding procession for Boiardo and Françounette, takes the road back to Avignon. Behind the soldiers, behind the two hundred cartloads of grain snatched 'at treasure point' from the hands of the father-in-law Lafeuillade, come the two love-birds, with full stomachs.

The mock-heroic epic obeys, of course, quite different laws from those that govern the novel or the comic play. It involves certain characters, but also certain heroic entities; among these figure the respective peoples of Avignon and Caderousse, both on a war footing. Nevertheless, the usual structures in which the abbé Fabre's inventiveness takes shape also appear in *Le Siège*, as they had already done in other works (such as *Jean-l'ont-pris*, *L'Opéra d'Aubais*, *Le Trésor de Substancion* and *Le Galimatias*).

the Caderoussians, defenders of the walls and potential claimants to Françounette's hand	Lafeuillade, master of the wheat of Caderousse and Françounette's father
Boiardo, head of the army from Avignon	Françounette

$$\longrightarrow$$

the cartloads of kitchen equipment from Avignon are handed over to Caderousse in exchange for the girl who will marry Boiardo and the wheat that will feed Avignon

These plots, in which the hero (or his real or symbolic lineage) raises or simply displays capital, are very simple indeed as far as their underlying principle is concerned; because of this, they can often run out of steam. The old or new strings that are pulled in the Marseille theatre (and others), such as the unexpected arrival of a large inheritance that makes the hero 'attractive' to his future father-in-law, can do little to save the more run-of-the-mill plays.[21] The Occitan playwright uses more or less sophisticated procedures so that the play can 'hold up' during the mandatory five acts. An example: the hero wishes to show that he is a worthy applicant for the girl's hand; to do this he must prove that his lineage is rich, which leads him to refute the abominable calumnies, propagated by the girl's father, according to which the said lineage is so poor that its members scarcely own the clothes on their backs. The launching of the big lies in question and their refutation alone can easily take up three or four acts ... In this case, the problem boils down to how the lover, who was undervalued by error and spite, can be 'revalued' or 'rehabilitated'. A good example of this is Michalhe's *Les Mariages rhabillés, pastorale représentée dans Béziers sur le théâtre des caritadiers mages de ladite ville, pour l'Ascension de 1647.*[22]

A double marriage is being arranged, between, on the one hand, an old couple – the widower Policart, a grazier from Béziers, and the rich widow Donne Coucoune, from Colombiers (a nearby village) – and, on the other hand, a young couple – the shepherdess Sérane, Policart's daughter, and the shepherd Alimon, Coucoune's son. What we have, then, at the outset of the play, is the same situation with which the abbé Fabre's *L'Opéra d'Aubais* ends: it is understood that the two couples will live under the same roof, sharing expenses, etc. This was a classic notary's solution in the Languedoc. However, it is also shown that the young couple are in love.

Nevertheless, Cascavel, a shepherd, discontent with the low wages and blows given him by his true-to-life employer, Policart, plays the role of the preventer-opponent (but not the rival). He spreads calumnies about both families; he claims (among other things) that the old woman Coucoune 'is as poor as Job', which disqualifies Alimon, her son, henceforth regarded as too poor to be a son-in-law in Policart's family.

Fortunately, Cascavel's lies are exposed. The double marriage will take place at the end, under the auspices of the notary Poupou and to the great joy of the two lovers.

Cascavel   Policart, Sérane's father

Alimon, Coucoune's son   Sérane

$$\longrightarrow$$

refutation of the lie that Alimon is
poor

As we see, the catalyst that allows the pretty Sérane to be transferred to her shepherd derives from a symbolic and 'financial' transfer
in the opposite direction: all calumnies having been refuted, the fifth
act makes it quite clear that Alimon is a rich heir; he has, therefore,
expectations of a fortune; they will allow the common household of
the double marriage to prosper, first under the patriarchal reign of
Policart, then, after his death, under Alimon's management.

With less verve than Michalhe, the Grenoble playwright Jean Millet,
in his *La Bourgeoisie de Grenoble* (a play in Franco-Provençal, a language very close to Occitan),[23] sets up a plot that is similar to the one
just summarized.

At the beginning of *La Bourgeoisie de Grenoble* (1665), Marciane, a
woman of substance in Grenoble and a widow, praises to her daughter,
Diane, the wealth of old Rochinion and his son, Cassore: a large
income from oil, wine, fruit and meat; credits that bring in interest;
kitchen furniture, a good table, a fire of six logs in the chimney in
winter . . . What more could one want? Diane is delighted, since she
loves Cassore, and he loves her. But the two old people have a taste for
young flesh and want to marry the youngsters themselves (a similar
plot to that of Fabre's *L'Opéra d'Aubais*). Thrown into despair by the
extravagant plans of his father, Cassore 'abandons his inheritance'
for a time and becomes a pilgrim. Fortunately, after all kinds of
vicissitudes, some of them quite pointless, the fairies of Grenoble
remove the obstacle and miraculously make the two old people fall in
love with each other; the normal marriage of the young people can
then take place, since Rochinion is no longer the rival or opponent of
his son Cassore.

Rochinion, old and rich	Marciane, a widowed bourgeoise, Diane's mother
Cassore, Rochinion's son	Diane, Marciane's daughter

Cassore's family fortune, once freed from parental intrigue, makes the young man a perfect match for Diane, now that he has hopes of a large inheritance

Like *La Bourgeoisie de Grenoble*, *Les Mariages rhabillés* is particularly interesting for its juridico-social analysis of Occitan or Franco-Provençal marriage customs. Both works, in effect, concern a double marriage that regroups two parents, a widower and a widow, each therefore free to remarry, and brings together their respective children. It is the situation that the abbé Fabre will describe once again in *L'Opéra d'Aubais*. But in the Béziers comedy, an incredible degree of refinement is achieved. Let us suppose that Dame Coucoune, as is her duty, conveys a dowry, say of 500 *livres*, to her new husband, Policart, who has simply to reconvey the same sum to his daughter, Sérane, who will use it in turn as the dowry that will go to her young husband, Alimon, who simply has to deposit the 500 *livres* with his own mother, Coucoune, once they have set up the new household in which they will all live; thus the 500 *livres*, initially conveyed to Policart, returns to Coucoune. In other words, Coucoune will not even have to take out this money, since in any case it will come back to her.

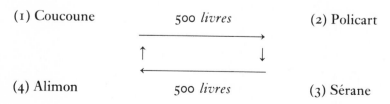

(1) Coucoune	500 *livres*	(2) Policart
(4) Alimon	500 *livres*	(3) Sérane

Is such a financial 'pirouette' purely theoretical? Not at all. The Languedocian notaries commonly used this device of 'interlinked alliances' with even more mastery than the playwrights. Let us examine a few fascinating cases that occurred in reality in northern Languedoc. In a village in the Lozère (the 'Gévaudan'), on 30 January 1728, three marriages took place simultaneously. I shall summarize Pierre Lamaison's subtle analysis: André Pascal, widower of Marie Arsalier, marries Catherine Trousselier, widow of Pierre Farnier; at the same time, the two children of André Pascal, Pierre and Antoinette, marry two of Catherine Trousselier's children, Catherine and Pierre Farnier, junior. On the one side, Pierre Pascal is heir (to the entire inheritance of André Pascal); on the other, it is Pierre Farnier, junior, who gets the entire inheritance of his widowed mother, Catherine Trousselier, Farnier's ex-wife. The older couple, André Pascal and Catherine Trousselier, will live under the same roof as the household formed by Pierre Pascal and Catherine Farnier; the latter conveys as dowry 200 *livres*, which her husband, Pierre Pascal, reconveys to his father, André Pascal, as is the practice whenever this type of union is arranged. Thanks to this dowry, André Pascal is able to provide his daughter, Antoinette Pascal, with a dowry of 200 *livres*, which Antoinette Pascal's husband, Pierre Farnier, junior, conveys to his mother, Catherine Trousselier-Farnier, in exchange for her wealth, which he himself has received in the form of usufruct. The loop is therefore looped without any actual money changing hands – Catherine Farnier, junior, had in fact received the dowry of 200 *livres* in the first instance from her own mother, who is none other than Catherine Trousselier-Farnier, senior, who recovers the 200 *livres* once again at the other end of the chain. What extraordinary subtlety! The whole situation can be studied at a glance in Pierre Lamaison's schema, shown below, in which the dowry turns through E, G, H, A, C, D, and back to E, anti-clockwise! Certainly peasants are not the 'strange animals' or semi-gorillas they are depicted as being in the defamatory writings of such authors as Maupassant. Though it is true that it must have taken a notary of some genius to work out the circuit.

A   André Pascal, widower of

B   the late Marie Arsalier

E   Catherine Trousselier, widow of

F   Pierre Farnier, senior

D   Pierre Farnier, junior, his son and *heir* of Catherine Trousselier, marries

C   Antoinette Pascal, daughter of André Pascal

G   Catherine Farnier, junior, daughter of the late Pierre Farnier, senior, marries

H   Pierre Pascal, son and *heir* of André Pascal

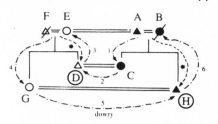

The course of the dowry of 200 *livres* is circular, and therefore fictitious, since the loop is looped in an anti-clockwise direction.

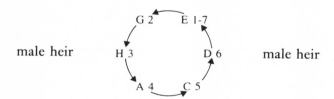

In other words, the mother (E) reconveys the dowry to her daughter (G), who reconveys it to her husband (H), who reconveys it to his father (A), who reconveys it to his daughter (C), who reconveys it to her husband (D), who reconveys it to his mother (E). End of cycle.

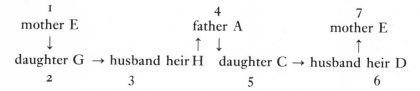

The (female) dowry forms the (mobile) woof, but the male inheritance constitutes the (fixed) warp of the socio-marital material. The two male heirs, Pierre Pascal and Pierre Farnier, junior, who hold (in the case of D6) or will hold (in the case of H3) the inheritances, in the younger generation, are the two pillars of the system; their contributions of male capital, which are almost actual in the case of D6, the father's orphan son, and consist principally of well-founded hopes of an inheritance in the case of H3, are the bait with which the circulating dowry will be trapped – it is temporarily caught, like a fly in the calyx of some carnivorous flower. It is in this that reality and fiction are one. In the seventeenth and eighteenth centuries, the social structure is re-enacted: it is transported on to the stage and into the fiction of the Midi.

By the same token, simultaneous marriages between relations belonging to two successive generations are also to be found frequently in notaries' records. Barthélemy Cruvellier and Isabeau Bessière, for example, both widowed, married on 1 June 1684, at the same time as Étienne Itier, son of the first marriage of Isabeau Bessière, whose sole heir he is, and Marie Cruvellier, Barthélemy's daughter, who receives a dowry of 350 *livres*. 'All will live under the same roof, which again makes it possible to postpone the payment of any dowry.'[24] The principle of *L'Opéra d'Aubais*, *La Bourgeoisie de Grenoble* and *Les Mariages rhabillés* is already contained in its entirety, in real life, in these 'remarkable marriages'.

I should like to mention, in passing, another incident: the play *Les Mariages rhabillés*, mentioned above, is described by its author as a 'pastoral'. It would be tempting to see it and several other plays of its kind as deriving quite simply from contemporary or earlier pastorals found in France, Italy, Spain, Portugal, etc.: I am thinking of Racan's *Les Bergeries*, Tasso's *Aminta*, Mairet's *Sylvie*, etc., and even, two thousand years earlier, Theocritus's admirable *Cyclops*. In fact, certain names of shepherd–heroes, Licidas, Crisante, etc., found in the plays from Béziers, are borrowed from French or Italian literary works. But the story of the Italian *Aminta* or of the French *Sylvie*, with their slender plots, intended for the edification of noblemen and courtiers, has little in common with the heavily materialistic and patrimonial concerns of the shepherds in our Occitan theatre. Mairet's and Racan's heroes are courtiers disguised as shepherds. The characters of our Occitan plays, though bearing names borrowed from literature, possess the authentic, healthy smell of farm manure; their tirades in Occitan are versified notaries' contracts.[25]

Having made this point clear, let us return to our plays from Béziers. In discussing *Les Mariages rhabillés*, I have referred to the dramatic revaluation of a lover's lineage, which, owing to the successful machinations of calumny, is regarded as poor; another theatrical procedure might be called 'self-revaluation' of the hero's or claimant's market value. The latter is a fairly poor man. But the region is attacked by plague, which kills off the majority of available males. Suddenly, with the scarcity of possible husbands, the hero's value or 'price' rises on the market and he is able to marry the rich, beautiful girl. This is precisely the plot of *L'Histoire du mauvais traitement fait par ceux de Villeneuve à la ville de Béziers pendant la contagion: représentée sur le théâtre des marchands de Béziers le jour de l'Ascension de 1632*.[26]

It is 1632. The plague, which arrived in 1628, has been depopulating Béziers for several years; the peasants of Villeneuve, a rural locality near Béziers, refuse entry to their fortified township to the inhabitants of the plague-ridden town. In the same way, in the next century, in 1709, Caderousse will refuse its grain supplies to the starving city of Avignon. A beautiful young girl from Béziers, Florinde, has taken refuge at Villeneuve since the onset of the plague. She is desperately unhappy; her father, who is of a miserly disposition, insists that his daughter's husband should be a rich man, and refuses to give her to the heroic soldier Filène, whom she loves. (We are again with the Languedocian militarism of the 1630s.) However, this Filène comes back to Villeneuve after three years' absence. He is more than ever in love with his Florinde. The peasants of Villeneuve who stand guard at the gates (against the danger of contagion) refuse the soldier entry into their village. A violent scuffle gains the hero access at the first gate. A large tip, given by Filène, silences the scruples of the guard at the second gate, which in turn is opened to the soldier, who is at last able to enter the village. Florinde and Filène are reunited. They express their rapturous passion for each other. The town of Béziers, represented by an actress, overcomes the resistance of Florinde's recalcitrant father, who abandons his insistence that his daughter marry only a rich husband. In the name of demographic patriotism, it is right, say Filène and the town in unison, to repopulate the town of Béziers, which has lost so many men to the plague. The paternal consent is therefore wrenched from Florinde's father, with the help of the whole community. Filène and Florinde will marry; they will have many children to make up the breach made in the population by the plague.

We see that the plot, in its earlier stages, offers certain parallels with that of the later *Siège de Caderousse*. The tip given by Filène to enter Villeneuve is reminiscent of the fifteen cartloads of jugs and pots from Avignon – the gift of which finally encourages the Caderoussians to hand over half their wheat to the people of Avignon. But from a certain point, the plots diverge: Filène will marry Florinde, not because he finds and presents a treasure, but because he himself has *become* a treasure. The extermination by the plague at Béziers between 1630 and 1632 made husbands scarce and, therefore, dear. Before the epidemic, Filène represented for the well-off girls of the town simply one potential husband among many, and even, from a financial point of view, not one of the most attractive. Suddenly, following the genocide at Béziers, he is transformed into a personage of high price for the girls who survived the plague by moving away. Florinde's father will therefore need little persuasion to give his approval to the wedding, which is further justified by Filène's fine qualities as a soldier.

a rich man as Florinde's possible husband

an avaricious father

Filène

Florinde, his daughter

→

revaluation of Filène as a fit match thanks to the demographic disaster of the plague

One finds different procedures of self-revaluation when marriage is at stake. They consist, for example, in exorcizing the threat of a trial that might swallow up the capital of the hero's lineage.[27] Or a clever use will be made of the techniques of local folklore: the lover or hero will oust his rich rivals from other towns by organizing a charivari against them. In this way, by implementing a protectionist policy opposed to the free trade of partners, he restricts to his own town the matrimonial market of available males. Certainly, the hero is regarded as a nonentity at the regional level. But according to the limited criteria of his small urban community, he may be regarded as well off. He may, therefore, after the charivari, marry the girl of his dreams.

This schema is employed in G. Zerbin's *La Comédie à sept person-nages*:[28] the lover (from Aix) loves and wants to marry a young lady (also from Aix) called Catherine, daughter of Monsieur Paulian. A rival from another town, a rich old man, pot-bellied and dull-witted, offers himself: he is Tacan, who would like to oust the lover and win Catherine's hand.

The lover knows very well that once he is married, he will have to maintain Catherine in the position, for him extremely costly, required by her rank and dowry. It is a problem of 'fortune', as the young man's father, Monsieur Rancussi, rightly puts it. In the end, the girl's father decides to marry her off to the higher bidder, that is, to Tacan. The girl is desperate. To thwart this plan, the young lover organizes with his friends a charivari outside Monsieur Paulian's house, which is all the more justified because old Tacan is a stranger to the town; he is particularly liable to this kind of disturbance, since he has come to Aix specifically to get for himself a girl who would normally be married to a young man of her own city. Catherine takes advantage of the disturbance to escape from her father's clutches and to her lover. Old Tacan gives in, for he realizes that, in the circumstances, Catherine will simply make him a cuckold if she is forced to marry him.

In fact, the endogamic strategy of the charivari underpins the lover's victory: Catherine's father specifically wants his daughter to marry a (rich) stranger; this enables him to raise the bidding, with the result that the young men of Aix, who are lacking in money in comparison with the Marseillais (for example), will be ousted. The charivari violently limits the matrimonial market to the territory of Aix-en-Provence, and revaluates the lover, who is well situated as far as his local rivals are concerned, but who is inadequately endowed

with money in comparison with rich strangers, who will fortunately
be set aside after the charivari.

Tacan, the rich old man	Monsieur Paulian, Catherine's father
the lover	Catherine

→

the lover, 'revaluated' as a result of the
strategy of the charivari, may claim
Catherine's hand

Again a revaluation, after an earlier devaluation. The young hero
in love with the girl was well off thanks to his work as a blacksmith.
Is it bad luck that has thrown up a rival? The hero's arm weakens; he
can no longer strike the hammer on the anvil. In the end the arm
is cured, material prosperity returns to the hero, and constitutes
one of the factors that will enable him to marry the girl he loves. All
that remains is to rid him of the sorcery that seems to prevent the
marriage . . .

This plot was to constitute one of the themes of Jasmin's
Françounette, published under Louis Philippe[29] but based on a legend
dating from the late sixteenth century. During the wars of religion,
the poor, young and attractive farrier Pascal loves Françounette, and
she loves him. The soldier Marcel, rival of the hero–farrier, fights with
him over certain kisses exchanged with the girl; Pascal is wounded in
the arm, which reduces him to idleness and poverty. However, the
arm eventually heals, and he is able to resume his lucrative trade. But
certain problems remain. Marcel uses the services of the terrifying
witch of the Black Wood; he accuses Françounette of being a
Huguenot and therefore in the pay of Satan;[30] she has the evil eye,
and, indeed, a second young man, who tries to pay court to
Françounette, is wounded in the arm, like Pascal. Even Françounette's
grandmother now advises the girl to marry the soldier Marcel.
Gradually something of a witch-hunt surrounds these two women,
the old woman and her granddaughter. The people want to kill them.
Françounette is fortunately saved by the combined efforts of Pascal,

inspired by his passion for her, and of Marcel, regenerated by his unfortunate but sincere love. The marriage of Pascal and Françounette takes place, with a distribution of pieces of garter the day after the wedding-night. Marcel, overcome with remorse, confesses to his past dealings with the witch. He then goes off to war.

Marcel	Françounette's grandmother
Pascal	Françounette

--→

after the episode of (pseudo-) black magic, the return of material prosperity, through the agency of love, makes the marriage of hero and heroine possible

In the various hypotheses considered so far, money conforms to the wishes of love, and in the end the reverse is also the case. However, the Occitan authors are aware of the social realities of their time; they have to admit that often money is stronger than love (whereas the absolute opposite is never true, at least in their plays: when love is victorious it must always have found some base, in the form of financing or valuation of capital, put at the hero's disposal; no *pure* love is ever victorious).

In cases where the male's wealth alone provides the marital solution, we see, for example, a girl blithely accept a marriage with a wealthy man, simply because of his wealth. In one such case, the girl breaks off a previous relationship with a boy whom she really loves for just such an offer. This is what happens in Routtier's *Lou Mariagi de Margarido* (Marseille, 1781).

Margarido, daughter of a *métayer* ['share-cropper'], loves a young peasant, who loves her. But the owner of the *métairie*, of which the girl's father is a mere tenant, has arranged for an inheritance. He wants to take advantage of this in order to grant a favour to his *embalaire* ['packer'], a young illiterate artisan. If Margarido will marry the *embalaire*, the landlord will give 500 *livres* to set up house, which, once she is married, will enable Margarido, or so she believes, to play the lady; she will no longer have to wash the dishes, and she will have a husband who wears a periwig. Seduced by this tempting prospect, Margarido drops her lover. Simply out of a desire for money, 'which tames the proudest', she allows herself to be 'carried away' [emballer] by the embalaire, whom she will marry.

Here the provider of money represents the betrothed man's symbolic lineage (in effect, the landlord–benefactor regards this young man as his personal embalaire). Moreover, this play breaks the usual framework of our model: most unusually, money wins a decisive victory over love. It goes well beyond the solution of a mere compromise between these two factors.

the peasant,   the métayer
Margarido's lover

the embalaire   Margarido,
                                               the métayer's daughter

_____→

the money of the landlord, the embalaire's patron, excludes the lover and leads to the marriage between the embalaire and Margarido

A collection of Occitan poems of the early seventeenth century, Bertrand Larade's La Margalide gasconne,[31] presents the same situation as Routtier's Mariagi. But it has already been achieved, for the marriage for money has taken place before the poem was written; the versified lamentations come after the event.

Bertrand Larade loved Margalide (Marguerite). But it was a love based on social inequality. Another man, a certain Vulcain, 'richard comme le cul', has married this adorable girl, who, in fact, is a grasping mistress. Whoever manages to marry her has crowns in his purse, no water in his codpiece and straw in his head . . . He is an instrument of Pluto, god of wealth . . .

To come back to Routtier's play, it is not without a certain cynicism to be found already in the previous century. Zerbin, one of the better seventeenth-century playwrights working in the Aix region, was equally cynical where marriage was concerned. In his *Seconde Comédie provençale à six personnages*,[32] he depicts the subsequent misadventures of two young women whose fathers married them against their will to rich and repulsive husbands. They soon turn to systematic procuring and cuckoldry.

We have just examined cases in which the hero, who in himself is hardly attractive, uses his money to marry the girl he desires.

However, there are certain situations in Occitan literature in which the hero's money (such is its power!) brings about a marriage *against* the will of the hero himself. This, for example, is the plot of Zerbin's *Comédie provençale à cinq personnages*.[33]

Old Brandin desires – but not for marriage – the attractive Dardarino, a woman of loose morals. He wants only to sleep with her, for one does not marry a woman who is known to be immoral. Alas, his meanness gets the better of him! At the last minute he refuses to give up the bag of crowns that would get the girl's consent. A stratagem thought up by the procuress Pinatelle (who represents the prostitute's *symbolic lineage*) takes our man well beyond the point he wished to go. Dardarino's parents (in other words, her real lineage), with the girl's complicity, trick the old man: they surprise him in bed with the girl and force him to marry her. Brandin's money, which Dardarino and her family coveted, has formed the basis of their marriage.

Dardarino's clients (who in principle have destroyed her honour, and ought to have deprived her of any hope of marrying)	Dardarino's parents (who arrange to surprise the rich old man in bed with their daughter and so force him to marry her)
the rich old man	Dardarino, the 'loose' woman

the trick to extract the old man's money, this 'extraction' taking place by means of a forced marriage between him and the courtesan Dardarino

A structurally similar, if less comic, plot is to be found in *Marra*, a play by the Provençal playwright Jean de Cabannes.[34] Here, too, money makes a marriage, despite the wishes of its male possessor.

Marra, a rich, sixty-eight-year-old bourgeois, originally of peasant stock, is besotted with the noble, young and attractive Mademoiselle Lascaris and allows himself to be trapped into marriage with her. He has signed a paper: in exchange for an expected promise of marriage, this paper hands over control of his vast fortune to the Lascarises, mother and daughter. When he learns that the two women are planning to rob him of his wealth, once the marriage has taken place, Marra wants to withdraw. But Mademoiselle Lascaris's mother is firm; the members of this noble family threaten Marra with death. He feigns madness. The trick misfires. The duke and governor of the city is a devoted friend of the Lascarises, with whom his family has been connected since 1323! He sends Marra to the lunatic asylum, hands over administration of the so-called madman's wealth to Mademoiselle Lascaris and decrees that the two 'love-birds' should marry as soon as Marra has recovered his wits. Marra, who is afraid of the lunatic asylum, drops his feigned madness and agrees to the marriage.

men of honour who, according to the girl, might court her	Madame Lascaris, the girl's mother
Marra	the daughter, ('Mademoiselle')

$\longrightarrow$

Marra's money makes the marriage possible, thanks to the future mother-in-law's initiative, against the will and despite the tricks of Marra himself

In some Provençal plays the symbolic equivalent of money, as a force that enables the hero to 'cross the threshold' of marriage, is constituted by the possession of such cultural advantages as a knowledge of French. Take, for example, M. Mayer's *Lou Retour doou Martegaou* (Marseille, 1775).

Young Janet is the son of a Provençal, *patois*-speaking, comfortably off *métayer*. The young man has just returned from a journey to Paris, where he saw the king and queen and learned to speak French, though with a strong southern accent. Puffed up with pride, he now refuses to marry his local betrothed, charming, but Occitan-speaking Margarido; she is the daughter of Louis le *Derata* (Louis le Dératé, in other words, the 'Alert' or the 'Quick'). Janet now wants to marry the French-speaking Julie; she is the daughter of a rich bourgeois who acts as sub-delegate. Unfortunately for Janet, Julie is too highly placed on the social ladder. By means of a trick, concocted by a third party, Janet will finally marry Margarido. Curtain.

Julie, *grande bourgeoise*, Margarido's 'rival' or 'opponent'	Louis le Dératé, Margarido's father
Janet	Margarido

→

the symbolic capital at Janet's disposal, his knowledge of French, raises him somewhat above his honourable peasant origins, which make him absolutely worthy of marrying a pretty, young peasant girl, and, indeed, he will marry her; on the other hand, this cultural, and other, capital remains too small to qualify him for a more ambitious marriage with a French-speaking girl born into the *haute bourgeoisie*

This play, then, is a hymn to the joys of socio-professional and cultural homogamy, laced with feminine hypergamy.

The hero's capital, in terms of money, land and education, may also give him a higher socio-economic status, which is clear enough at the beginning and is finally revealed at the end of the play. Such a status gives the lover an exalted, irresistible position. It enables the male character and future husband to marry without difficulty a girl of a lower socio-economic status, such as a maid, a farm-girl[35] or a prostitute. The potential difference is, in effect, so great between him and her that, as soon as a serious contract has been drawn up between them, the girl has no alternative but to accept his proposal and throw herself gratefully into the arms of a man who, for reasons that the play has carefully brought out, has had the immense kindness to ask for the hand of this humble girl in marriage. Such a mechanism is irresistible: Claude Brueys's *Première Comédie à sept personnages* (Provence, late sixteenth century) is based on such a structure.

At the end of this *Comédie*, the rich aristocrat Carlin marries Nicolette, Pauline's maid. A number of episodes have, in fact, excluded Pauline, with whom Carlin was at first in love; for this young mistress has dishonoured herself by sleeping with a carter just for the pleasure of it. Also excluded, after four acts, is Pelegrin (Carlin's manservant), who had been pursuing Nicolette in the coarsest way. Pelegrin, of course, has to give way before the irresistible financial and social prestige of his master, Carlin. During the first few acts a 'false scent' has concealed the functioning of our 'love square', or 'marriage square'; Carlin was supposed to be courting Pauline and not to be interested in Nicolette, the maid, whom he will eventually marry. It should be added that Carlin's social prestige is such that, apart from his own wedding, he is able to force the lady Pauline (to punish her for her misconduct) to marry the manservant Pelegrin; as a further punishment, he even forces the super-virile and over-attentive carter to marry an old procuress, who is delighted with the arrangement.

Pelegrin	Pauline, Nicolette's mistress
Carlin	Nicolette, maid

———————————————————→

irresistible power of the financial and
social prestige of Carlin, who will
marry Nicolette without difficulty

It will be noticed that, in this play, Pauline, who provides much of the 'false scent' of the plot, also constitutes the symbolic lineage of her maid, Nicolette.

What goes for the maid also goes for the prostitute, who cannot refuse marriage to a man who is in love with her and whose social status is considerably higher than hers. This is the 'lesson' that emerges from *Liseto amouroso*,[36] by the Provençal Jean de Cabannes (1653–1717).

The delightful Lisette (Liseto), fresh of face and sweet of mouth, has become a courtesan in order to earn money and so save her parents from poverty. All very touching! She has been practising this new profession, with its *parties carrées* ['foursomes'], for only a short time; she does not yet (?) deserve to be called a prostitute. Dono Viano, a good-hearted procuress, serves as Lisette's symbolic father and mother. Lisette is in love with Pelagi, rich and newly ennobled; he loves her. But he recoils, on grounds of honour, before marriage to a prostitute. The procuress responds by calling him a Turk, a barbarian, a Judas . . . In the end, after a whole series of episodes and reversals that prolong the play, Pelagi decides, in the fifth act, to marry Lisette in order to console her for her disappointment. Dono Viano has turned the wheel. The social difference between the two young people is such that, as soon as *he* has made up his mind, *she* cannot but feel overwhelmed with happiness and fly to the altar with him; the higher status that he enjoys enables him to choose any wife he likes from among the women of lower status than himself. Of course, on marrying, Lisette will give up prostitution. It's the least she can do.

Lisette's lovers and clients   Dono Viano, the mother–procuress

Pelagi   Lisette, courtesan

⟶

influence in the direction of marriage of Pelagi's higher social status

The various situations described in this chapter, according to which the future husband contributes to the marriage capital that is his own or that has come from his lineage, corresponds in real life to three hypotheses that were meticulously recorded by Provençal and

Languedocian notaries when they were working in a traditional milieu.

(1) The young man is an orphan; just before his marriage contract is signed, he provides male wealth from his inheritance. This could be the case of Jean-l'ont-pris himself, if the marriage is concluded, as one might expect it to be, after the young man's narration.

(2) The young man's parents – or at least one of them – are still alive. He will be the sole and privileged heir and will live with them in their house and on their estate. He is able to enter marriage, therefore, with *hopes of inheritance*, which are sufficient to tempt the future father-in-law; in such circumstances, the father-in-law agrees to cede to the boy not only his daughter, but also the whole of her dowry. Daughter and dowry will pass to the young man's household, which he will also share with his own parents. Indeed, in certain cases, the young man's parents, who are already old, even hand over their patrimony to him in exchange for a retirement pension. In such circumstances, he becomes all the more attractive to a future father-in-law.[37] One often reads that the young couple will live *à feu et à pot* ['under the same roof'] with the husband's old parents.

(3) The young man is a younger son; he has no right to the inheritance that one day will be left by his parents, who are still alive. In such a case, the parents nevertheless provide him with a modest quantity of money, furniture or land. In view of this gift of capital, another father will decide (or not, as the case may be) to give his daughter and dowry to the young man in question. If a girl's father decides favourably, the boy may set up house (armed with his own capital) with his new wife in her father's house, which one day he will be called upon to manage in turn, when his parents-in-law die or become incapacitated.[38]

In all three cases, Occitan fiction, so revealing of cultural stereotypes, takes little interest in the female dowries. These are certainly important,[39] but they are regarded as a non-theatrical *donné*. Under the authority of her father (and later of her husband), the girl, with her dowry, 'is not free to act as she will'.[40] She is not, therefore, a completely theatrical character – nor is her dowry, however important it may be from a financial point of view. The really dramatic moment of the pre-marital action is when the negotiations between the girl's father and the hero take place with a view to deciding whether the capital displayed by the hero is sufficient, together with the girl's dowry, to lay the foundation for a marriage. It is not as easy as that to get one's hands on a dowry. These negotiations, which will remain uncompleted, are also carried out in Fabre's novella between the rich Sestier and Jean-l'ont-pris, himself secretly armed with his treasure.

CHAPTER III Jean-l'ont-pris Financed by Sestier: Extraction of Capital from the Lineage of the Future Father-in-law

The 'love square' consists of four poles or characters. The problem facing the hero is always how to arrange a display or even a transfer of capital, with a view to obtaining the girl's hand in marriage. This capital may be provided, as we have seen, out of the hero's own fortune (as in the case of our Jean-l'ont-pris), duly produced, or by the wealth of his lineage, real or symbolic.

And yet . . . Where there is a lack of wealth, whether personal or lineal, might not the hero turn to his future father-in-law or to the girl's lineage in general? Why could he not obtain the necessary capital from this source? As we shall see, Occitan drama and fiction of the seventeenth and eighteenth centuries thoroughly explored the possibility offered by a future father-in-law: to begin with, one might mention two comedies by Fabre himself, *Le Trésor de Substancion* and *L'Opéra d'Aubais*, as well as his novella, *Jean-l'ont-pris*.

Le Trésor de Substancion is a comedy especially conceived for the village theatre. It was written by the abbé Fabre about 1765, some ten years after *Jean-l'ont-pris*. The action takes place at Castelnau, the village of which Fabre was the parish priest at the time of writing. The rock of Substancion, which gives the work its title, is situated within this locality, now a suburb of Montpellier. The name of the rock corresponds to that of an old Gallo-Roman township, Sextatio, which flourished at a time when Montpellier did not yet exist. It was situated on the Via Domitia, a Roman road that linked Spain to Italy along the coast of Languedoc. The whole region is rich in folk tradition.

The plot of the play is simple enough: Maître Nicol is a fairly well-off farmer [*ménager*] at Castelnau, as was Monsieur Sestier in the Vaunage. Maître Nicol has several daughters, among whom are to be counted Jeanneton, who will be the principal heroine, and Babeau, of whom little is said and who is there simply to remind the author and the reader or spectator of the 'paternal' equivalence between the

Nicol of the *Trésor* and the Sestier of *Jean-l'ont-pris*, both of whom have a daughter named Babeau. But, in fact, the structural equivalence of the daughters is set up between the Babeau of *Jean-l'ont-pris* and the Jeanneton of the *Trésor*.

Cadet, the son of Maître Pascau, is in love with Jeanneton. Like Jean-l'ont-pris, he is poor. As if we needed to be reminded, his very name indicates that he does not occupy the position of eldest son, who was generally sole heir to the family fortune; for, whether or not they were enshrined in written laws, the ancient customs of the Languedoc often followed the rule of primogeniture. It was, there-fore, an overdetermined poverty. Not only was he a younger son, he also came from outside the village (Maître Pascau, Cadet's father, was not a native of the locality of Castelnau). Similarly, his structural homologue, Truquette, Jean-l'ont-pris's future father, is not from Solorgues, the village in which his son is to live, but from Rouergue and, as such, is a victim of anti-Aveyronnais discrimination. In *Le Siège de Caderousse*, Boiardo-Pantalon-Octave also bears in his name the mark of an Italian origin, whether theatrical or real.

Having fallen in love with Jeanneton, Cadet will need a treasure if he is to obtain his beloved's hand in marriage. The obstacle to his plans for a 'seduction with a view to marriage' is real enough – it is constituted by Toni, a lumpish, but rich young fellow. Toni's mother is the odious Dona Rancurela, who is as repulsive as Barbe-Garouille; it is she who is urging her son to marry Jeanneton. In this, Rancurela finds an ally in Maître Nicol: he does not want as his son-in-law a good-for-nothing like Cadet, who, he predicts, will end up in the workhouse. He prefers Toni; he may be stupid, but he has money and land, and that is what counts when one is settling the future of a daughter who, like Jeanneton, has both wealth and beauty.

The 'treasure' element intervenes at this point. It will, of course, bring about the eventual victory of Cadet/Jean-l'ont-pris.

The folk tradition of Castelnau-Substancion was well known to Fabre, a *patois*-speaking priest who lived at close quarters with his flock. According to this tradition, which dates back to the beginnings of Christianity in the Gallo-Roman period, the rock of Substancion opens at the stroke of twelve on Midsummer's Night (June 23/4). Is not this the dark hour when rivers part their waters? Thus the Montpellierian river Lez, which flows around the foot of the rock, divides on that very midnight, leaving its bed dry. An opening appears there. From then on, one is able to penetrate into that haunt, at the bottom of which, in solid rock, at the end of a long path, is a cave filled to overflowing with gold and silver. Providing one takes certain precautions as to the time and route, one has only to help oneself to the treasure. A spirit, allied to the devil, undertakes to guide and possibly ensnare the treasure-seeker.[1]

Cadet reveals to his beloved Jeanneton one of the possible solutions; if the legend is true, the young man will go into the opening, accompanied by his father, Pascau. They will seek out the treasure and come back laden with *louis-d'or* and crowns. Cadet will thus be able to overcome Nicol's objections, supplant Toni and marry Jeanneton. But, of course, Nicol himself will also find his way into the celebrated cave, so reminiscent of Ali Baba's. But since he will go in alone (Toni being too timid to go with him), his booty will be half that of the Pascau–Cadet 'binomial'. Nicol will be unable to resist Cadet's superior wealth and be forced to accept him as his future son-in-law. According to this hypothesis, it will be, as in the previous chapter, the hero's lineage (in other words, his father and himself) who will provide the 'sinews of war' indispensable to the marriage.

However, there is a second possibility: the legend may be an old wives' tale. The magic cave may never open, may not even exist. Hence the second variant of the Pascau–Cadet plan. Pascau is not from Castelnau; he is an 'outsider'. Like the abbé Fabre, but for quite different reasons, he does not believe in the local legends, to which natives like Nicol cling so fiercely. So Pascau wagers his meagre fortune against Nicol's very substantial one. That is what is at stake in the wager, on this Midsummer's Night – the sceptic Pascau refuses to admit the existence of the opening cave and its treasure, while the believer Nicol is equally convinced that the cave will open at midnight and bring him untold wealth.

The twelve strokes sound. The rock does not open. Nicol has lost his wager and all his wealth. His house and lands are, in principle, transferred to Pascau. As a result, the miserly Rancurela refuses to make Jeanneton her daughter-in-law; the girl, now without a dowry, has no more than the clothes she stands up in. She is no longer of any interest to Toni, the old woman's son. Pascau, however, proves to be magnanimous. He gives his wealth back to Nicol, on condition that

Nicol accept Cadet as his son-in-law. So Cadet goes to live under the same roof as his new father-in-law, with Jeanneton and Nicol. As it turns out, he will inherit, through his wife, the old man's wealth and enjoy usufruct of it during the latter's lifetime, according to the ancient customs codified by the Languedocian notaries. The transfer of Nicol's fortune to Cadet thus becomes possible and bearable; it will then be returned to its first owner in exchange for a daughter, a dowry and a share in the working of the land . . . The treasure has moved from hand to hand in one direction, and the daughter in the opposite direction. In this case, the operation has been carried out at the expense of the future father-in-law.

The schema on which *Le Trésor de Substancion* is based is very similar to that of *Jean-l'ont-pris*, except that the money comes from the future father-in-law and not from the father or the maternal grandmother.

However, certain transformations from the one to the other may be noted. On the diagonal A C, we still find a shrew in A (Rancurela/ Barbe-Garouille) and a desirable daughter in C (Jeanneton/Babeau). But along the diagonal B D, certain changes may be noted: in B, Sestier was a cunning individual; Nicol is a fool. In D, Jean-l'ont-pris and Truquette were swindlers; Cadet and Pascau are both very honest – hence the vivacity of the novella in comparison with the insipidity of the play. With good sentiments, one makes less good literature.

A Rancurela and her son, Toni	B Nicol, Jeanneton's father
D Cadet, assisted by his father, Pascau	C Jeanneton

———————————————→

having gained possession of the wealth of his future father-in-law, Nicol, Cadet may claim Jeanneton's hand

In Fabre's *L' Opéra d'Aubais*, the hero also obtains the capital he needs from his beloved's family; but this time it is at the expense of the future mother-in-law and not of the future father-in-law.

L'Opéra d'Aubais was written by Fabre shortly before 1755, at about the same time as *Jean-l'ont-pris*. Again, though in the form of an opera, it is a light-hearted village comedy interspersed with charmingly written songs. It concerns characters living in the township of Aubais, which was well known to Fabre, since he had served there as assistant priest. Aubais is only a few kilometres from Solorgues, where *Jean-l'ont-pris* takes place. We are still in the Vaunage district.

At the beginning of *L'Opéra d'Aubais*, young Pierrot (Pierrotta, in Occitan) is in love with the charming Jaquette (or Jaquetta). However, the girl is held on a tight leash by her mother, the elderly, unattractive Couderta, a widow. There is also another problem: the amorous desires of Pierrot, who is presented to us as a mere labourer, are being thwarted by the designs of his own father, a rich farmer [*ménager*] of Aubais, Maître Reinau, a widower. (The son, Pierrot, can pass from the status of labourer to that of *ménager* only by succeeding his father.) Now the old fellow has a fondness for young flesh and wants to marry Jaquetta himself. It is just too bad if this brings him into competition with his son. In order to win Jaquetta, Reinau agrees to an exchange with the ageing Couderta, who, moreover, happens to be his former mistress: the old woman will marry Pierrot, who, of course, wants nothing to do with such an ill-matched union, and she will hand over her daughter to Reinau. However, Pierrot frustrates the plot worked out by his elders, who are hell bent on marrying the young people of their choice. He entices Couderta to hand over to him, under the supervision of a notary, all her wealth: by divesting herself of her property, the old woman hopes to force Pierrot to marry her. For her part, Jaquetta does as much with Reinau. The old man takes some persuading and is willing to offer, according to current practice, only half his wealth (of which, of course, he would keep the usufruct). But Jaquetta, at Pierrot's instigation, rejects this half-and-half proposal and tells Reinau straight: 'It's all your wealth or nothing!' And she adds: 'It seems to me that when a rich old man *buys a girl* [*sic*], he does not buy her too dear in giving her all he has. What I shall gain from it is not worth the pleasure I shall lose.'

So the old parents give up all their wealth in favour of the two youngsters whose favours they hope to obtain; indeed, they expect, through marriage, to recover if not the property itself, at least the usufruct of the wealth that they have given up. However, there is a hitch! Once the property has been transferred in the presence of a notary, the two youngsters refuse to marry Couderta and Maître Reinau. At this point, another young man, named Cadet, comes on the scene; he is a friend of Pierrot and acts as his spokesman. Emotionally close to the hero Pierrot, he is the junior counterpart of the Cadet/Jean-l'ont-pris of *Le Trésor de Substancion*. It is he who proposes the solution: the two elders will marry each other, leaving the two youngsters free to do the same, following the dictates of their hearts. All four will live under the same roof as a joint estate. The two love-birds will remain the legal owners of the total wealth of the foursome. But the young couple will leave to their two elders, for as long as they live, the usufruct and virtual control of the wealth of which the two elders have been theoretically divested. This is exactly one of the technical solutions adopted by Languedocian notaries at this time, when they formulated, in a registered document, the structures of a joint estate enlarged to include an old and a young couple.

Comparing *Jean-l'ont-pris* with other works by the abbé Fabre, we find again our canonical schema.

On the right is the generational axis BC, B being the parental element, in this case the mother, Couderta. Her daughter, the beautiful Jaquetta, is in C. Young Pierrot occupies D. In A is the preventer-rival, in this case the hero's father, Maître Reinau, whose matrimonial plans compete with those of his son. The transfer of wealth from Couderta to Pierrot gives the young man's love the necessary weight to enable him to marry Jaquetta. In any case, this wealth will return to Couderta in the form of usufruct, by means of the common life that she intends to lead with Pierrot and Jaquetta, once these two have been united in marriage. Maître Reinau's wealth follows a symmetrical course, but in the opposite direction.

A	B
Maître Reinau	Couderta, Jaquetta's mother
D	C
Pierrot	Jaquetta

$\longrightarrow$

transfer of wealth from Couderta to Pierrot, then its return to Couderta, via Jaquetta

In Claude Brueys's *Seconde Comédie à sept personnages*, the extraction of capital effected by the hero at the expense of his future mother-in-law is depicted with all the richness of colour, all the deliciously bawdy humour that we associate with late-sixteenth-century Provençal literature.

Luquet, Tristan's young manservant, desires the pretty Raguino, who repulses his rather straightforward advances. Raguino is the daughter of the bawd Fourgonno. Now this elderly procuress – she is getting on for seventy – has received, as the price of her usual professional services, 50 crowns from a local worthy, Roulin, who is one of her clients. So the old woman offers this bag of 50 crowns (which is to circulate like a cheque) to Luquet in order to encourage him to sleep with her, despite the repugnance he feels for such an adventure, given the disparity in their ages. However, Luquet agrees to accommodate the procuress. Then, having earned his 50 crowns, he offers them to young Raguino in order to persuade her in turn to sleep with him. She accedes to his demands. She becomes pregnant. Tristan, Luquet's master, forces his manservant, the young 'paying stud', to marry Raguino.

In this conjuncture, old Fourgonno occupies the two upper points of the rectangle: on the one hand, she is the parent of the beautiful Raguino; on the other, she is her rival and, in so far as she is Luquet's temporary, lucrative mistress, an obstacle to the love of the two young people. The money (50 crowns) travels round the rectangle anti-clockwise: it originates with Fourgonno, the girl's mother; the old procuress receives it, then spends it; it then passes from the same Fourgonno, *qua* Luquet's elderly mistress; this money then passes to

Luquet, the kept lover, then to Raguino, the corruptible mistress; it thus serves as a link between the two young people, who are further united by Raguino's deflowering, followed by her pregnancy. Everything culminates in their marriage, with which the play ends. It is not out of the question that the money thus put into circulation might one day return to Fourgonno (to its source); all that would be required would be for the new, young couple to agree to live as part of an extended family in the procuress's maternal and maternal-in-law brothel-home.

Fourgonno, as Luquet's mistress	Fourgonno, as procuress and as Raguino's mother
Luquet	Raguino

———————————————————————————➔

the 50 crowns originating with Fourgonno and Luquet's purchase of Raguino's virginity, resulting in pregnancy, lead in the end to marriage

Again it is the girl's lineage that is in question: the future father-in-law may be led, by means of some intrigue, to finance the career of his prospective son-in-law. This is one of the themes of *Le Jaloux attrapé* (1645), a play in the Périgord dialect by Pierre Rousset, of Sarlat.[2]

The jealous Zeloto imagines that his wife, Callisto, is being unfaithful to him. A plot is worked out to disabuse him of this opinion: fortunately, he is made to realize in the end that the couple that he has been spying on at night, weapons in hand, and that he thought he recognized as his wife and her lover, are in fact two young lovers, the boy Floridor and the girl Olympo, thwarted in their love by the girl's father, Filémon. Delighted at being reassured of his wife's fidelity, Zeloto persuades Filémon to allow his daughter Olympo to marry Floridor. By the same token, Filémon gives up any intention of forcing his daughter into a lucrative marriage with a rich *officier* ['magistrate']. What is more, Filémon, who is extremely well off, even agrees to buy on behalf of his son-in-law, from the financiers of the town, a number of offices (presidial court judge, seneschal, administrator of an *élection*, receiver of tithes, inspector . . .). There is no longer any obstacle to the marriage since Floridor is now rich, thanks to his father-in-law's money, which will now be transformed into prestigious offices.

a rich magistrate   Filémon, Olympo's father

    Floridor   Olympo

$$\longrightarrow$$

the father-in-law's money, transformed into offices for Floridor, makes the marriage desirable and possible

Another (theatrical) way of extracting capital from one's future father-in-law, so that the hero may become in his eyes a presentable son-in-law, consists in making available wealth that this father-in-law possesses but does not control. In Féau's *Comédie de l'intérêt ou de la ressemblance*, taken from the *Jardin des muses provençales* (1665), a magical theme is added to the usual theme of money.

Maître Gounin has a daughter of marriageable age called Flaminte. He also has, in his garden, treasure, which he is prevented from enjoying by goblins. Gounin promises that the man who succeeds in recapturing this treasure will also have his daughter in marriage. A rich braggart, Captain Fricasse (Fricasso), assisted by his manservant, has the poet, who is also in love with Flaminte and is therefore the captain's unhappy rival, put to death. (The poet had previously disguised himself as a wizard in a vain attempt to exorcize the goblins.) Fricasse, however, succeeds in expelling the goblins; he therefore obtains the treasure and Flaminte's hand. Gounin, *qua* father and father-in-law, gives his blessing to the marriage of the two youngsters, Flaminte and Fricasse. But the poet's ghost comes back from hell and puts an end to the marriage, which has only just been concluded: Flaminte dies of fear. Fricasse is dragged down to hell by the poet's ghost. Leaving aside this melodramatic, Don Juanesque ending, the marriage schema is a classic one.

the poet	Maître Gounin, Flaminte's father
Captain Fricasse	Flaminte

→

the hero seizes the father-in-law's treasure and may therefore marry Flaminte

As well as working *in favour of the father-in-law* (in which case he willingly divests himself of his property in favour of his future son-in-law), the magical theme may work *against him*. Either way it amounts to the same thing: the hero walks off (in this instance, by main force) with the father-in-law's fortune. Let us look at Fescais de La Tour's *Le Loup Garou* (1783).[3]

The rich farmer Pierre Leblon hopes to marry off his daughter Antoinette, without a dowry, to the rich, stupid and lovesick shepherd Jacques Ledoux. But the handsome peasant Mathurin is also in love with Antoinette, who loves him. Following the advice of a witch, Mathurin disguises himself as a devilish bogey, surrounded by flames; in this way he forces the terrified Leblon to give him his daughter. In order to rid himself of the bogey, Leblon must also give up to Antoinette, as a dowry, half his vast fortune.

the shepherd Jacques Ledoux	Leblon, the father
the handsome, but poor peasant Mathurin	Antoinette, Leblon's daughter

→

by divesting, through magic, the future father-in-law of half his wealth, the hero succeeds in marrying the heroine

Along the same lines (the extraction of a fortune from the girl's lineage), a clever trick is for the future (theatrical) son-in-law to get himself soundly thrashed by his future mother-in-law. In this way, she owes him something, as compensation for the physical damage she has inflicted on his body. She can repay this debt only by giving him her daughter's hand. In this case, the future son-in-law has succeeded in his marriage plans: he has tapped for his own benefit a purely fiduciary circulation of wealth; it comes, in the first instance, from the future mother-in-law. Such are the miracles of credit recorded in *L'Opéra de Frontignan* (1679).

This pastoral is the work of Nicolas Fizes (1648–1718).[4] An educated man, highly skilled in astronomy and mathematics, Fizes nevertheless had a perfect command of the local idiom of his native Frontignan. He knew Tasso's *Aminta*, but his own pastoral derives from Languedocian traditions, which are in no way an imitation of the Italian model.

L'Opéra de Frontignan was written during the winter of 1678/9, after the celebrations that marked the Peace of Nijmegen. Like the works of the abbé Fabre, Fizes's *Opéra* concerns characters drawn from the lower or middle classes of a small township; nevertheless, such works found admirers among the most important figures in the province. The intendant of Languedoc was to receive the abbé Fabre at his table in the 1770s. In 1679, M. de Joubert, syndic of the Estates of Languedoc, took a personal interest in the printing and proof-correcting of this comedy from Frontignan.

To summarize the said 'opera': Micoulauo, a poor apprentice or student, is one of the best dancers and fiddlers in Frontignan. He loves, and is loved by, Françoun (Françounette), daughter of Dona Tognia; mother and daughter are also from Frontignan. Tognia, who is crippled with debts, wants to give her daughter in marriage to an old gentleman who is little more than 'warmed-up soup'. In this way, she hopes to regild her inheritance, since, as she says, 'Micoulaou's fiddling doesn't fill your belly.' A number of vicissitudes (including the scheming of Janeta, Françoun's rival for Micoulaou's affections) temporarily separate the two lovers. They are reconciled when they learn that Janeta worked out her scheming precisely to separate them. In the midst of the lovers' reunion, old Tognia arrives. She is furious when she sees that her daughter's love affair has resumed its course. She strikes Micoulaou with a large stone and makes a hole in his head. However, the young man comes out of the faint that ensues. Threatened with a serious charge against her, old Tognia becomes, so to speak, Micoulaou's debtor and owes him reparation in the form of a heavy penalty (including money), imposed on Tognia by the court. Possessing this 'credit' over his adversary, Micoulaou circulates the said credit as a bill of exchange; he turns against Tognia and requires her daughter's hand in exchange for dropping the charge that he can now bring against her. Tognia is forced to accept him. In short, Micoulaou has repaid the counter-value of his wife to his prospective mother-in-law with the lien he holds over her wealth and liberty.

the old man ('warmed-up soup')	Tognia, Françounette's mother
Micoulaou	Françounette

→

Micoulaou's 'credit' over Tognia makes the marriage possible

If the money required for the marriage by the prospective son-in-law is not provided (as a result of the hero's machinations) by the father-in-law or the mother-in-law, it may be provided by the girl's paternal or maternal uncle. In such a case, the capital still comes from within the girl's lineage. Take *Lou Novy parat*, by the Provençal J.-B. Coye (eighteenth century), a rather conventional and 'literary' play in Occitan.

M. Griffou wants his pretty daughter Nouradou to marry the rich old Casteouroux. But Tourvillou elopes with Nouradou in a ship (we are at Arles), then saves her from shipwreck. The name of this saviour, Occitanized from the *oïl* name of the famous Admiral Tourville, suggests adventures at sea ... Casteouroux, furious, realizes that if he marries Nouradou he will be cuckolded. So he takes back the money that he had invested in the business of his former future father-in-law, M. Griffou. In these circumstances, Griffou readily consents to his daughter's marriage to young Tourvillou. M. Pistachou, whose name suggests well-being and 'butter in the spinach', then enters; he is Griffou's brother-in-law, the girl's uncle, and will duly play the role of 'American uncle'. Not content with promising his inheritance to his niece, he immediately gives 1,000 crowns to the young couple, who can now look forward to setting up a well-provided household.

Casteouroux   M. Griffou
                                                     (and Pistachou)

Tourvillou   Nouradou

————————————————————————→

              withdrawal of the rival's money; con-
              tribution, to the future couple, of the
              money of Pistachou, the girl's uncle, as
              reward for Tourvillou's good deed

We also meet the character of the indulgent uncle who, though belonging to the daughter's lineage, finances his niece's future husband, in two plays from Marseille: *Pierre et Perrette* (1758) and *Le Taciturne* (1778).[5]

Le Taciturne: The noble, but poor Valère loves Angélique, and she loves him. But Madame Argante, Angélique's mother, wants to give her daughter in marriage to Ariste, rich in 'bills to pay the bearer' and land, who is willing to take Angélique without a dowry. Fortunately, the will of Angélique's paternal uncle transforms Valère into an immensely rich heir. The girl's mother consents, therefore, to the marriage with Valère, who has now become a suitable son-in-law.

Ariste   Madame Argante,
                                                     Angélique's mother

Valère   Angélique

————————————————————————→

              the wealth from Angélique's lineage, in
              other words, from her maternal uncle,
              turns Valère into a suitable heir and
              son-in-law

Pierre et Perrette: Pierre, a nobleman's son disguised as a gardener's boy, begins and ends a pseudo-idyll with Perrette, the young wife of the head gardener at the castle. The young man is, in fact, to marry the marquise – the charming, but widowed, lady of the manor. On condition that she agree to this marriage, the marquise receives from her future husband the promise of a large inheritance, from *her* uncle, a rich baron. Naturally enough, she says yes. What else could she do?

Perrette, the gardener's young wife	the rich baron, the marquise's uncle
the nobleman's son	the marquise

$$\longrightarrow$$

the marriage is made possible by the baron's inheritance, transmitted via the nobleman's son

Another, less expensive, trick might be called 'devaluing the future father-in-law'. The basic idea is the same in this case as in the earlier ones: it amounts to saying that the prospective son-in-law must be *adjusted* to the capital of the girl's father. The two fortunes must be brought to a compatible, comparable level. If one aspires to a girl's hand and is unable to prove that one is rich, one can always try the opposite course, that is, prove that the future father-in-law is poor. In this way, if one is oneself poor, one is no less worthy to marry his daughter. It amounts to paying or displaying less capital, thanks to the fact that one has previously devalued the future father-in-law's expectations. One acts on his character not by extracting anything from his fortune, as in earlier cases, but by reducing it in reputation. *Lou Groulié bel esprit* ('The Cobbler'), whose author was a Toulon stage-setter, Étienne Pelabon, enjoyed great success from 1790 onwards, at a time when egalitarian tendencies were already modifying various mythical notions about matrimonial strategies, while falling short of actually disturbing a certain conservatism in society.

Lou Groulié: The cobbler Maniclo, who has quite unjustified social pretensions since he has become a syndic of his corporation, wants to marry his daughter Suzeto (Suzette) to Trotoir, a 'rich', toothless old man, a dealer in rabbit skins. The sailor Tribor, who is in love with

Suzette, and she with him, has a fight with Trotoir, who immediately gives up any idea of marrying the girl out of fear of a trial and being made a cuckold in the future. Maniclo is aware of the fact that the very modesty of his station as a cobbler does not allow him to choose a son-in-law as 'rich' as Trotoir; so he is willing to give his daughter to Tribor. The moral, as Maniclo says at the end, is that one should not take on airs; and where marriage is concerned, whatever one's age or rank, one should remain in the 'estate', or social level, in which one was born.

Trotoir	Maniclo, Suzeto's father
Tribor	Suzeto (Suzette)

→

in the last act, the sailor Tribor shows that he has enough in relation to the social level of the cobbler Maniclo, whom he brings down to his true level

The extraction of capital by the hero from the future father-in-law's wealth represents a literary fiction, sustained by Occitan culture. However, this fiction is not totally unfounded. It derives from two procedures practised by the notaries of the Midi where marriage contracts were concerned. The first, a frequent, though not universal one, is as follows: a father and mother have no son. They would, therefore, like a young man to come into their own house to marry their daughter and to succeed them in the management of the family household and lands. So they give to their newly married daughter, that is to say, to the new couple, that is to say, *in fact*, to their young son-in-law (who now holds the legal authority in marriage), the usufruct and soon the semi-ownership of half of or all their wealth. In this way, the potentially poor son-in-law that fate has brought them becomes rich from what is a *de facto* extraction; Occitan fiction glorifies this practice by so arranging things that the husband takes possession of a portion of his father-in-law's wealth *de jure*.[6]

The second practice, which is subjacent to the fictional notion of the 'despoiling of the father-in-law by the son-in-law', concerns the very forms of the transfer of the dowry. In theory, the dowry continues to belong to the wife, who receives it from her father on signature of the marriage contract. In fact, the dowry is given *directly* by the girl's father to the man who is to become his son-in-law. The girl possesses it only temporarily and theoretically. The husband gains real possession of the dowry from his wife. Cases of separation of the partners in which the woman succeeds in leaving her husband, with her dowry, are extremely rare. That is the second reason why it is easy for Occitan fiction to transform the poor young man (who succeeds in getting a large dowry from his wife's family) into a sort of hero who has literally *despoiled his father-in-law*.[7]

It should be added that we also find in notaries' records gifts by the girl's uncle (paternal or maternal) with a view to her marriage. The true beneficiary of such generosity, once again, is not the girl, who is the theoretical owner of these presents, but her husband, who becomes their effective owner. It is clear how our Occitan fiction, as we have seen in such cases as that of good uncle Pistachou, made the best of an indulgent uncle's generosity.[8]

To return to our basic text, the hero Jean-l'ont-pris succeeds, once at least, in extracting capital from his future father-in-law, Sestier: in effect, he receives indirectly from Sestier a female dowry of 1,000 *livres*, which encourages him to marry Garouille, who will soon die, leaving her husband a widower and henceforth in a position to marry Babeau, Sestier's daughter. By conveying a dowry of 1,000 *livres* to Garouille, Sestier had previously financed Jean-l'ont-pris, who was later to dupe his future father-in-law.

CHAPTER IV Margot's Mother, Margot Herself,
Garouille and Babeau: All Four Pregnant
Before Marriage

The general hypothesis examined in the previous chapter was the
following: the hero extracts for his own profit a portion of the capital
belonging to the girl's father (or mother); or he devalues this capital
in such a way as to raise his own fortune, in some way or other, to
their level, thus making the marriage possible. This may be called
'acting on the capital of the girl's lineage'. Let us pose a crude, but
conceivable variant: we might imagine that the hero actually takes
money straight from the girl's pocket, in such a way as to raise his
own financial level and to make himself financially worthy of her
with a view to marriage.

One has only to think about it to realize how absurd it would be.
To begin with, the girl does not have a 'pocket'. It is her father who
at the last moment conveys the dowry. Yves Castan [1] has shown that
the Languedocian women of the *ancien régime* had no control over the
family's money, which remained entirely in the hands of the father,
the brother (or the husband). They did not even have 'pocket-money'
on them.

Second, the attraction of the girl, as far as the hero is concerned,
lies not only in her beauty, but also in her dowry, to which her lineage
holds the key. To take any portion of her money, supposing that such
a thing were possible, would be to diminish her dowry, to make the
girl less desirable, and so diminish his interest in the proposed marriage. The play could never get to the fifth act, which would be a
dramatic catastrophe!

In fact, the only capital that a boy can extract from a girl in order
to make the marriage inevitable is her virginity, her 'honour'. The ideal,
which is not always achieved in our Occitan fiction, is obviously that
the deflowered girl should become pregnant, in which case marriage
is the only way by which the boy can restore the symbolic capital that
he has stolen; in this way, a counter-transfer of honour, in the opposite
direction from the previous one, can take place. These marital res-
torations may occur with or without the willing co-operation of the
'guilty' man. The main point is that they should take place.

Situations of this kind are to be found in *L'Histoire du valet Guillaume et de la chambrière Antoigne*, a play written at Béziers, for performance at the popular festivities of the Ascension, some time between 1620 and 1650.[2] A summary of the plot is as follows: the manservant Guillaume and the chambermaid Antoigne (Antoinette) are struck by Cupid's unavoidable arrows. After a few misunderstandings, the two lovers are drawn irresistibly to each other, their sensuality *heating up like an oven*. They exchange kisses of *sugar and honey*. Guillaume kisses Antoigne's feet: *so that my kisses may rise to her knees, to her belly*. For a year, the two servants, who adore each other, go to bed over thirty times. Antoigne is soon pregnant. After their initial anger has subsided, their respective employers, Monsieur and Mademoiselle, decide to arrange their marriage. Of course, the lovers are as poor as Job, but never mind! The maid has lost her honour, and only Guillaume, in the legitimate intercourse of a wedding-night, will be able to restore this capital. Only contact with Achille's spear, Monsieur remarks, was capable of curing the wound that this weapon had caused the hero Telephs. Similarly, Guillaume will restore Antoigne's honour by the application of the same organ – but this time, legitimized – that had earlier occasioned the girl's dishonour and illegitimate pregnancy.

Guillaume has no money, but, thanks to his unscrupulous effrontery as a lover, he possesses stolen capital, Antoigne's honour, which he alone can give back to her, through marriage.

It will be noticed, however, that Guillaume is confronted by exceptionally easy circumstances:

(1) He has no competitor. The place of the rival-preventer in the 'marriage square' remains empty. The stakes, therefore, remain very low. (But Monsieur, his master, as a possible seducer of the maid Antoigne, is the potential preventer. The play refers to the danger of subsidiary loves, but Monsieur is regarded as too old to be a fornicator.)

(2) The maid Antoigne is without a dowry. She has honour, but no money; a mistress, but no visible father on the horizon. The mere seizing of a pledge, the girl's virginity, followed by an unwanted pregnancy, is enough to allow the man to obtain the girl's hand. The abbé Fabre (in his *Le Galimatias*) is pessimistic about this

kind of marriage. 'At first it will be happy because they love one another, but they will be poor and poverty sustains neither love nor virtue.'

The 'love square' is as follows:

Monsieur, possible candidate for Antoinette's subsidiary favours	Mademoiselle, Antoinette's mistress
Guillaume, manservant	Antoinette, maid

marriage as restoration of honour as capital, after the deflowering and pregnancy of Antoinette

We should note in passing that the authoritarian implementation of the maid's marriage under the auspices of her symbolic lineage, in other words, her employers, is an old tradition in the Occitan theatre; a good example is *La Tasse*, by the Comte d'Aulbe, alias Claude Bonet or Benoet du Lac (sixteenth century).[3] At the end of the play, the maid Georgette is ordered by her employer to marry (she is quite happy to do so) the manservant Bertrand (who has the same employer).

Similar, subsidiary, pre-nuptial developments are to be found in Brueys's *Comédie à onze personnages*,[4] except that, in this play, no pregnancy is involved. There is simply pre-nuptial fornication with loss of honour and later restitution of the same in marriage.

At the end of the plot of this *Comédie à onze personnages*, Brilletto, Perlino's maid, marries Fouquet, Farlin's manservant; Fouquet had, in fact, become her lover only a short time before, the complete seduction having taken place practically on stage. Previously, Farlin and his friend Bourgau had both obtained Brilletto's favours during a *partie à trois*. Coming third, Fouquet may claim Brilletto's hand with some success, since he has already had the rest of her, and since in any case this simple girl does not belong to the marriage market that would be likely to interest the girl's two previous lovers.

Bourgau and Farlin   Perlino,
                                      Brilletto's mistress

Fouquet   Brilletto

———————————————————————→

Fouquet is in possession of Brilletto's
'honour'; he is also capable of restoring
it to her through marriage, her other
two lovers being too highly placed

It will be noted that in the drama from Aix-en-Provence and
Béziers, it is the servants who embody ardent sensuality, in opposition
to the more restrained world of the masters and mistresses. This
sensuality is not necessarily a negative characteristic. It is as much a
matter of the heart as of sex. The vital but tender bawdiness of the
Occitan theatre, especially at Béziers, Aix, Avignon and in Limousin,
is a delightful feature of the sixteenth and seventeenth centuries; it
was to be lost after 1700, under the influence of an irresistible pru-
dery imported from French culture and from a Jansenist-influenced
Catholicism.

It was to be lost except in the abbé Fabre's fiction. Indeed, *Jean-
l'ont-pris* is full of stories that, like those just examined, are really
about pre-marital or illegitimate pregnancy. But the social milieu
described at Solorgues involves poor villagers — and they are not
subsidiary characters. For example, Truquette marries the girl whom he
had previously made pregnant. In this case, marriage follows as a
matter of course; it does not matter whether the hero (Truquette)
does or does not want the marriage.

the knife-grinder,   Margot's mother
who courted Margot

Truquette   Margot

———————————————————————→

marriage after the onset of pregnancy

One could say the same for Jean-l'ont-pris himself: he consciously makes Babeau pregnant in order to make the marriage inevitable.

Barbe-Garouille, temporary preventer of marriage between Jean-l'ont-pris and Babeau	Monsieur Sestier, Babeau's father
Jean-l'ont-pris	Babeau

———————————————→

Babeau's pregnancy and Jean-l'ont-pris's treasure will make the marriage possible – or so one hopes . . .

Even the affair with Barbe-Garouille involves a pre-marital conception. But this episode belongs to the next chapter, which concerns the self-eviction of the 'rival' (Monsieur Sestier, who has made Barbe-Garouille pregnant) to the 'advantage' (?) of the hero, Jean-l'ont-pris.

As for Jean-l'ont-pris's grandmother, she was the mother of an illegitimate child, Margot. If it had depended only on this future grandmother, would her bastard daughter have been born legitimate after a pre-marital conception? But the lover–surgeon was probably already married. It was therefore impossible to marry this gentleman.

The abbé Fabre has skilfully calculated his effects where these four episodes are concerned. There is a negative version: pregnant, the future grandmother of J L P will not marry her lover, the surgeon of Calvisson. Two versions are positive: Truquette marries Margot, who is pregnant; Jean-l'ont-pris marries Barbe-Garouille, who is also pregnant. Lastly, there is an 'interrogative' version: will Jean-l'ont-pris marry, as everyone hopes, Babeau, whom he has made pregnant?

The theme of deflowering as a prelude to the indispensable marriage was also treated by Jean de Cabannes, writing during the reign of Louis XIV, in his Provençal play *Lou Jugi avare*.[5]

The 'young lady' – pretty, sixteen years old, poor, but of a good Brignolles family, 'of one of the best known' lineages in the area – has been seduced by a 'fairly rich' young man, who promises marriage. The seducer then reneges on his promise.

It is true that, in order to justify his detestable behaviour, the lover claims that the young lady has had other lovers before him . . . The girl, supported by the general feeling of the play, declares that this is a calumny. She therefore institutes an action in law to force him into marriage. Unfortunately, the magistrate is himself a corrupt and immoral individual. First he tries to seduce the girl in exchange for a promise that he will then, by judicial sentence, force the seducer to marry her. He therefore takes his place as a potential lover in the gallery of the girl's so-called lovers. But the young man (the seducer) is very rich; he sets about greasing the magistrate's palm with 50 *louis-d'or*. The magistrate abandons any notion of seducing the girl and decides to accept the money from the seducer. In exchange for this, he will dismiss the girl's claim to marriage and send her to the 'Refuge' (an asylum for fallen women); he will therefore put an end to the girl's prospects of marriage, which would have made the girl well off. By doing so, the magistrate ceases to play the role of prospective lover and takes up the symbolic place of a terrible father who, in the classic way, refuses to defer to his daughter's wishes. Fortunately, this magistrate will be brought down by his own corruption: he is arrested by agents of the king; his honest successor reinstates the order forcing the unchivalrous seducer to marry the deflowered girl.

Everything is as it should be: honour is restored to the girl; the young man's money will go, whether he likes it or not, towards setting up the new household.

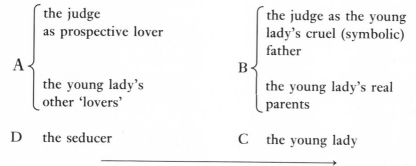

A ⎰ the judge
⎱ as prospective lover

    the young lady's
    other 'lovers'

B ⎰ the judge as the young
⎱ lady's cruel (symbolic)
    father

    the young lady's real
    parents

D   the seducer   C   the young lady

after various vicissitudes, the de-flowering of the girl and the seducer's well-placed position make the marriage desirable and possible

The obligation to marry would have been all the stronger if a girl of quality (from Aix) were seduced by a young man 'of little substance', a younger son: *If the daughter of a gentleman from Aix went to law against a local younger son* [for making her pregnant], *this young man would have to marry her, on pain of death*, says the wife of the corrupt judge in Jean de Cabannes's play.

Outside the strictly Occitan area, in the 'Franco-Provençal' zone of the Dauphiné – which is already part of the Midi and which is thus close, linguistically, to Languedoc, or Provence – the theme of virginity as capital that is transferred when marriage is in prospect, marriage thus becoming obligatory, was also a very common one from the seventeenth century onwards. Take the *Pastorale de la constance de Philin et Margoton*, written by the Grenoble playwright Jean Millet. Published at Grenoble in 1635, it is written in Franco-Provençal.

The poor shepherd Philin loves the shepherdess Margoton, daughter of the peasant Diguo, and she loves him. Moreover, Philin has saved Margoton's virginity from an attempted rape perpetrated by soldiers; as a reward, therefore, she must yield up her 'flower' to this lover, in a legitimate marriage. She is more than happy to do so. The rumour runs through the village that Philin has already taken an advance payment and has already deflowered Margoton, without her making the slightest objection. Unfortunately, all kinds of obstacles (which last through the duration of the play) are erected against the proposed marriage. The girl's father is against the marriage, for he hates the young man's family, which he regards as a race of vipers. A shepherd–competitor also tries to get Margoton's hand; then he gives up. Then the local lady of the manor comes on the scene; she falls in love with Philin and tries to win him from Margoton, but he refuses. Thus thwarted, the lady puts Philin into the manorial prison. Fortunately, everything works out for the best. A (diabolical) cat, while walking on the roof of the lady's castle, dislodges a tile, which 'knocks the lady's brains into her mouth' and kills her. The king of France arrives, has Philin freed and gives him Margoton's hand, with the consent, more or less forced, of the girl's father. The two lovers tenderly embrace and run off to get married.

{ a shepherd, Philin's rival,   Diguo,
  and a noble lady,   Margoton's father
  Margoton's rival

Philin   Margoton

——————————————————→

Philin saves Margoton from rape by
soldiers, then conquers her virginity,
thus ensuring for himself, after various
vicissitudes, Margoton's hand in marriage

Without conceding the preponderance of a flat realism, one has to
admit that on this point the Franco-Provençal or Occitan playwrights
and the novelist Fabre were largely inspired by the reality around
them. 'Pre-marital conceptions' (pregnancies before marriage,
followed by births during the first eight months of marriage) were
frequent in the Languedoc: 10 per cent of the total of first births in a
village in Lozère, and rates of 12 per cent, 20 per cent and 40 per cent
in various villages in the present-day departments of Hérault and
Pyrénées-Atlantiques.[6] In this respect, the work of the Occitan writers
was directly inspired by social truth (and by the fantasies of male
Languedocians).

CHAPTER V The Lover Financed by the Rival

A fourth solution, for the hero, lies in taking the capital he needs to turn himself into a good match directly from his rival, the fourth usable pole of the 'love square'. Such an operation may be carried out in several ways: the simplest is humiliating the rival, thus causing a fight with him, beating him and seizing his possessions. In this way, the potential difference between the hero and the rival is reversed to the advantage of the former. Enriched by his adversary's spoils, the hero becomes a 'good match' and marries the girl.

This theme is illustrated in the *Pastorale du berger Silvestre et de la bergère Esquibo, composée par Michalhe et représentée dans Béziers pour l'Ascension de 1650.*[1]

The shepherd Silvestre and the shepherdess Esquibo are in love with each other. Esquibo's mother, an old innkeeper–grazier in the Béziers village of Saint-Genieys, is a miser: *her whole body burns with avarice, right down to her pisshole.* The old woman, who is called Donne Baudeto, wants her daughter to marry a gentleman, the Seigneur de Puechevez; he is a customer at Donne Baudeto's inn and is reputed to be immensely rich. The shepherd Silvestre, assisted by the *pillart* (a local word meaning 'assistant shepherd'),[2] attacks the gentleman and disarms him. The two attackers take the Seigneur de Puechevez's sword, his belongings and above all his money; they go through his pockets so well that this noble 'aristocrat' cannot even pay his bill to the old innkeeper, who, therefore, gives her assent to the marriage of the two lovers.

<table>
<tr><td>the gentleman</td><td>the old innkeeper,
Esquibo's mother</td></tr>
<tr><td>Silvestre</td><td>Esquibo</td></tr>
</table>

→

annulment of the gentleman–rival's financial superiority in relation to the shepherd–hero

Esquibo's mother specifically hoped that the gentleman would pay the debts that she had already contracted once he was married to her daughter. He possessed, therefore, the possibility of a future credit over the old woman. By robbing the gentleman, the shepherd Silvestre acts as though he were annulling this credit in advance, as though he were demonstrating, by theft if necessary, that Puechevez would always be incapable of being the creditor-financier of Esquibo's mother. Esquibo's mother thus becomes indebted to the shepherd, the agent of this anticipated 'repayment'; so she gives him her daughter in marriage to balance the accounts between him and herself. Incidentally, this play also embodies, a hundred years before the French Revolution, the notion of anti-aristocratic struggle.

Other authors from the Midi also make use of the devaluation of a rival's possessions, but achieved by gentler means than those employed by Silvestre; such a devaluation may result, for example, in the rival suffering a mere reversal of fortune.[3] Or, again, in *Moussu Jus* (1784), it proceeds from the orders of the local lord: he forbids the hero's rival to marry the girl in question and the self-financing of the marriage by this rival; however, this lord finances the young peasant hero's marriage to the heroine, the daughter of one of his tenants living in the Provençal *seigneurie* in question.[4] Another method is to devalue the rival's symbolic capital. To achieve this, one has to expose the true commoner beneath the mask of pseudo-nobility; he is shown to be an imposter, and, to punish him, he is sent to work the fields as a bachelor. Even in this case, however, the hero will have to trick the rival out of his inheritance in order to marry the heroine.[5]

Objectively, the mechanism that marries Jean-l'ont-pris to Barbe-Garouille is of the same type as the one encountered in the *Pastorale du berger Silvestre*, even though the motivations of the protagonists in Fabre's novella are the reverse of those in Michalhe's play. Barbe-Garouille was Monsieur Sestier's mistress. This gentleman loses a large sum of money, Garouille's dowry, of which Jean-l'ont-pris will have the usufruct; thanks to this sum, J L P agrees to marry Garouille.

Sestier   Maître Garouille,
Barbe-Garouille's father

Jean-l'ont-pris   Barbe-Garouille

⟶

having obtained Sestier's money, Jean-
l'ont-pris marries Barbe-Garouille

The difference is that in the *Pastorale du berger Silvestre*, woman and money were *violently seized* from the rival third party (the Seigneur de Puechevez) by the hero. In the abbé Fabre's novella, on the contrary, woman and money are *voluntarily ceded* by the third party (Sestier) to the hero. But the double transfer, financial and female, operates in exactly the same direction in both works. From the point of view of the economic story, which is indifferent to feelings, it amounts to the same thing. The theme of the rival who drops out (not dishonestly, like Sestier, but graciously) and who even goes so far as to finance most generously the hero's wedding was treated, again during the reign of Louis XVI, in two (unpublished) plays by Fescais de La Tour, a Provençal, but French-speaking, author.[6]

In *Jean-l'ont-pris* this double transfer, financial and female, even becomes quadrupled, since it also concerns two additional entities: the honour of Barbe-Garouille, who was made pregnant and therefore dishonoured by Sestier; and the *progeniture* (twins) that she finally gives birth to. The honour of which Sestier has robbed Barbe-Garouille by making her pregnant is transferred to Jean-l'ont-pris, who is finally entrusted with the task of restoring this capital to its legitimate owner – by marrying her. JLP thus becomes, for a very short time, the functional father of Barbe-Garouille's stillborn twins.

This case of transfer and restoration of female honour by an interposed accomplice is unique, to my knowledge, at least in the Occitan theatre of the *ancien régime*, if not in real life.[7] However, its counterpart is to be found in an English pastoral of the Elizabethan period. An English eclogue by Francis Sabie, a minor poet, dating from 1595, has the following plot: 'A shepherd (Tityre) lives with his parents as a confirmed bachelor. Suddenly he falls madly in love with

Phillida (who, however, is not very beautiful; she is cross-eyed); she likes dancing with Alexis. Tityre, rejected by the girl, falls ill. His mother plies him with sweetmeats, and his father proposes to go and see Phillida's father and explain to him that the boy's family is not as poor as that. But to no avail. In the end, circumstances resolve the situation, in the most melodramatic fashion. Phillida sleeps with a most unscrupulous boy, who makes her pregnant and abandons her. She then agrees to marry Tityre, who passes over this incident and transfers all his affection to the child of which he is not the father.'[8]

The methods used, at Béziers in the *Pastorale du berger Silvestre*, and in other plays from the Midi, are violent, or at least crude: simply to rob the rival. There are also other, more sophisticated techniques for transferring the rival's capital to the girl's lineage and so facilitating her marriage to the hero. Take *La Miramoundo*, by François de Cortète, Sieur de Prades, in which not only is the rival's capital transferred to the heroine, but the rival himself is transferred to a sister of the heroine, thus satisfying the girl's lineage and enabling the hero to marry the heroine.

A noble of the Agenais, a good Christian (like the abbé Fabre), linked through his family to the magistrature and consulate of Agen, François de Cortète (1586–1667) wrote a five-act pastoral, *La Miramounda*. Its theme concerns directly the cultural and Occitan conception of marriage. It depicts, in a strictly peasant environment of graziers and wine-growers near Agen, various characters, among whom we find our four canonical figures: the beautiful girl; the girl's father, a well-off, but miserly farmer; the girl's lover; and the fairly rich rival-preventer. Other plots, apart from the central one referred to here, are developed throughout the play, which has been cleverly analysed by Robert Lafont.[9]

Of the beautiful girl, Miramoundo the shepherdess, there is not a great deal to be said, except that she is endowed with all the graces of her sex; moreover, she has some hope of a dowry and a fortune from her father. She has a sister, Bertrando (Bertrande, in French), who will play a role in engineering the happy ending.

Guilhot, Miramoundo's father, is particularly authoritarian; he governs his *ostal* (the Occitan word means both 'house' and 'family') along strict military lines. He has his wife and two daughters well under control. He yells and shouts and goes out himself to buy, in the neighbouring town of Agen, his daughter's wedding trousseau: dresses, hose, shoes and all the rest ... Master of the fields, distributor of female lingerie, he carries out roles that, in our time, are no longer regarded as masculine. Guilhot himself defines his essential values quite explicitly: 'Wife, honour and *ostal*.' How are we to interpret this trinity?

The lover is called Roubert. He is an attractive shepherd: his enemies claim that he gets up late, is lazy and even, from time to time, drinks. But he is a good fighter, an excellent dancer, and for Miramoundo, whom he adores, he makes spears, swings and traps for small birds.

Peirot, Roubert's preventer-rival, is a good worker, a sort of dim-witted Hercules, son of a rich (but mean) father who owns vines, flocks, houses and fields. Peirot himself is skilled at reaping, digging, cutting the vines, ploughing. He represents the pole of 'goods' or 'the good' (in other words, property), which is so ubiquitous in our rural texts; he leaves to Roubert the pole and the role of passionate seduction.

The problem for Roubert is always the same: how can he get rid of his rival; and how, at the same time, can he transfer some of the 'goods of this world' to Guilhot, Miramoundo's father, in order to obtain the girl's hand in marriage. As always, it is a question of transferring this capital to the daughter's lineage. The solution invented by de Cortète is particularly elegant: Roubert marries Miramoundo in secret, with the complicity of the girl's mother, Peyrouno (Pierrette). Peyrouno is an indulgent mother where her daughter's feelings are concerned. Then Roubert palms off Peirot, his rich rival, on to his new father-in-law, Guilhot! Peirot will therefore marry, whether he likes it or not, the kindly Bertrando, Guilhot's other daughter, Miramoundo's sister. As it happens, Bertrando is not entirely pleased at the idea of marrying Peirot. But how can she refuse such a brilliant combination! Apparently old Guilhot has no son; the new son-in-law Peirot will therefore live in his father-in-law's house. He will, in any case, play the role of treasure, enriching the father-in-law's *ostal*. Thus the Peirot–Bertrando marriage removes the obstacle that still stood in the way of the final declaration of the new union between the lovers, Roubert and Miramoundo.

Peirot   Guilhot,
Miramoundo's father

Roubert   Miramoundo

$\longrightarrow$

Peirot's wedding and his contribution in wealth to Miramoundo's lineage, socially legitimating, by ricochet, the marriage between Roubert and Miramoundo

The same solution is used, quite independently, by Captain Séguin de Tarascon in his *Dardin*,[10] a five-act Provençal tragicomedy of the seventeenth century.

The shepherd Amidor, who has mysteriously disappeared after a battle with a giant, loved the beautiful Melindo, and she loved him. Melindo is the daughter of the rich farmer-grazier Calidon; she is also the sister of the pretty Bersino, Calidon's other daughter. The attractive Melindo is beloved by many other shepherds ('I tremble like a pig pissing,' cries the shepherd Janon when he speaks of his passion for this girl). As an authoritarian father (*my daughter has no voice in the chapter*), Calidon intends Melindo for the shepherd Sillan, who is also in love with her. This shepherd interests the father all the more because Monsieur Guillen, a rich wine-dealer, has made him a gift of all his wealth after his death, which is imminent. Everything works out in the end: Amidor reappears to marry Melindo; Sillan reconciles himself to marrying Bersino, Melindo's sister. Maître Calidon, who apparently has only daughters, will therefore enjoy the satisfaction of having a rich son-in-law (Sillan) to succeed him in his household. This enables Melindo to follow the desires of her heart in marrying Amidor.

Sillan	Calidon, Melindo's father
Amidor	Melindo

$\longrightarrow$

granting of another son-in-law (Sillan),
who is rich, to the future father-in-law
in exchange for the hand of his daughter Melindo, who is given to Amidor

The strategy of 'palming off' a rival on to another sister, so that the hero may marry the girl who interests him, has some real foundation in the practice of notaries. In the records of the Languedocian notaries, we find, in effect, a fairly large number of marriage contracts in which the son-in-law, suitably endowed, comes with his small or large fortune under his arm to take up residence in the home of his parents-in-law because they have no son; he will live with them and with the daughter who has become his wife. He will provide the common household of both couples, the old and the young, with the strength of his arms, and also the contribution of his capital (money, cattle, land, etc.). It is understandable that parents who have no sons would wish to recruit a well-off son-in-law of this calibre.[11] The hero, too, if he has the means, may fulfil these parental desires in order to get the girl he loves; to do so, he will have to get rid of any possible rival by deflecting him towards the girl's sister, and therefore the position of resident son-in-law. This is what happens in *La Miramoundo* and in *Dardin*. In this case, Occitan literature becomes bogged down in a gaping possibility, which forms one of the gaps that open up in the practices of the notaries of this period.

In most of the methods used so far to obtain a girl's hand in marriage, the hero organizes a display or an export of capital in the direction of the girl's lineage. This capital is sometimes constituted by honour, but more usually by money or wealth of some kind. This is particularly so when the hero extracts this capital from his rival, or when he directly switches this rival's wealth towards the girl's lineage, with a view to getting this girl by way of compensation. Such a strategy oriented towards the rival, however, necessitates some very special tactics, which have scarcely anything to do with the obtaining of capital, followed by its transfer. They consist of the use of magic or counter-magic. We are then confronted with a very archaic mental stratum: it surfaces from time to time in the drama of this period, but it has never more than a subsidiary importance.[12]

One of the methods used is that of presenting the rival as a disreputable magician who is trying (in vain) to attack the hero's genital area and the love of the girl for the hero. In these circumstances, the victorious riposte lies to hand: the hero and more generally the playwright have merely to demonstrate that the rival is both guilty of witchcraft and inefficient in this dubious activity. This is the theme proposed by *La Fausse Magie découverte* (Béziers, 1635).

The beautiful Olimpe loves Crisante, and he loves her. The shepherd Rosidor, who loves Olimpe without success, tries to disturb by various magic tricks the happy, mutual passion of the two lovers. These spells fail or turn against him. Olimpe and Crisante will marry.

In this case the rival is deprived of his wealth by the hero or by some other person (the magician Clidaman, who organizes the attempted sorcery, refuses Rosidor's offers of money); this rival is simply dishonoured and ridiculed, 'devalued' by his unsuccessful contacts with 'hell'. Similarly, in *Jean-l'ont-pris*, Barbe-Garouille, the opponent-preventer, is presented as a demonic creature.

In fact, the magical technique used in this comedy from Béziers is basically an *aiguillette*: Rosidor (disguised as a magician) takes Olimpe's wedding-ring and puts it for a few moments in his own mouth while speaking a spell. The *aiguillette* was an old castration rite used by the witches of the seventeenth century in both the north and the south of France.[13] It was performed by confiscating the betrothed's sex, symbolized by coins representing the testicles, and confiscating the girl's sex, symbolized by the ring or by some circular space (the keyhole of a church), in order to hand over these – symbolic – objects to a rival who wants to possess the girl.

The specific technique of taking possession of the ring (the vagina) may take the forms of urinating through this ring or of pouring a jet of white wine through it, thus reproducing ejaculation.[14] Magical techniques of this kind are also to be found in plays emanating from the Béziers region: they are implemented by a rival trying to gain possession of a girl betrothed to another; they usually take the form of the girl imbibing white wine.

Twenty years after *La Fausse Magie découverte* from Béziers, a play written in the Franco-Provençal dialect of Grenoble dealt with similar themes: this is the *Pastorale et Tragi-comédie de Janin* by Jean Millet (published at Grenoble in 1633).

The beautiful shepherdess Lhauda, daughter of two well-off peasants (Piero and Thievena), has long been courted by a rich shepherd-farmer, Janin; his farm, with four pairs of cows and three pairs of oxen, plus land, would be more than enough to feed a family. Unfortunately, Janin is too impatient; he wants to seduce Lhauda and 'stick his peg in her hole'. The virtuous Lhauda is furious and encourages the intentions of the gentleman Amidor, one of the great lords of the Grésivaudan. Thievena, Lhauda's mother, an ambitious peasant woman, is delighted at the idea that her daughter will become a lady, exchange her old cloth for new satin and eat white bread at every meal. But old Piero, the heroine's father, reacts along class lines, as a peasant. He does not care for the idea of having a noble son-in-law, whom he despises. A stratagem is worked out to overcome the old man's vigilance. Amidor and Lhauda marry before a notary with the consent of the girl's parents. This contract is dated 1633. Amidor brings all his considerable wealth as male contribution to the marriage; moreover, he promises the entire inheritance from his own father, who is already dead, plus 500 gold crowns, to his future wife (as life insurance) in case he dies first – this is the counterpart of the dowry. The rival Janin, advised by a witch, has tried to practise the *aiguillette* on the future spouses, at the very moment the marriage was being consecrated, so that Amidor would become impotent or, as he puts it, so that 'Amidor's bow can no longer shoot its arrow'. But, a frequent trick in this kind of situation, the young people, who expected as much, brought forward the time of their wedding, and Janin arrives too late at the church. He dies by throwing himself into a precipice.

Janin

Piero and Thievena,
Lhauda's parents

Amidor

Lhauda

————————————————————→

Amidor's noble birth and great wealth,
plus the failure of the sorcery practised
by Janin, make the marriage of the two
lovers possible

This crude, socially cynical play is situated at the intersection of
themes that were examined in Chapter II (the hero's contribution of
capital, in terms of money and honour) and that are also considered
in this chapter (symbolic devaluation of the rival, who is unmasked as
a pitiful witch, inefficiently practising the *aiguillette*).

In 1629, an Occitan play written for the festival drama at Béziers
had intertwined these two themes in a similar way: *La Pastorale du
berger Célidor et de Florimonde sa bergère* (Béziers, Ascension 1629).

Célidor and Florimonde love each other. The rich Spaniard Don
Bravaste wants to marry Florimonde. She rejects him because, she
says, 'money is a metal that gives mechanical and brutal pleasure'.
Doctor Potingue relieves Bravaste of 100 crowns by selling him a
magic beverage that will make Florimonde love him. This beverage
is, in fact, white wine. Florimonde, who has drunk it, remains pas-
sionately faithful to Célidor, whom she will marry. Don Bravaste is
ridiculed.

This play, within the context of the cultural stereotypes of Occitan
marriage, is partially classified under the heading 'picking the rival's
pockets' (in order to make him equal or inferior to the true lover).
However, the magical element (which is in fact ridiculed) brings it
closer to the 'fantastic' category of pastoral which has just been
examined.

The hero may ridicule his rival by unmasking him as a 'failed
magician' and pseudo-witch. But he may also attack him or get him
attacked magically – not by exposing him as a sorcerer (a pitiful one
at that), but by practising sorcery on him. This is the solution chosen
by Jean de Cabannes in his *Paysan astrologue*.[15]

The baron, in love with the princess, runs the risk of opposing the wishes of the duke (her father), who wants to give her in marriage to the prince, Cléanthe. So the baron uses the services of a peasant, a pseudo-soothsayer, who, after proving the efficacy of his magic, accuses Cléanthe of being interested only in the fortune of his future father-in-law, the duke; he also accuses Cléanthe of being impotent, of not possessing the 'oil' that will allow him to eat the princess 'in a salad'. Convinced by the peasant, the duke now believes in Cléanthe's impotence. So he decides to give his daughter's hand to the baron, who has shown great generosity to the rural soothsayer by giving him a purse of *louis-d'or*. In the end, the peasant will be unmasked as a false soothsayer, but the duke, faithful to his promise (the great keep their word!), will nevertheless give his daughter's hand to the baron. The concept of wealth is therefore discreetly suggested: as the bidding rises, it is accepted that the *giving* baron will win over Cléanthe, the *taking* prince, who wants to extract his share of the duke's wealth. Yet the essential theme remains 'magic': the baron–hero uses the services of a soothsayer in order to weaken the sexual and financial reputation of his prince–rival.

Magic and, more generally, the Marvellous, which I shall return to in relation to *Jean-l'ont-pris* and the grandmother's 'magic', nevertheless play only a marginal, quasi-residual role in these social and cultural stereotypes of marriage in the Midi. The *aiguillette* loses its importance after 1600 or 1650. In the seventeenth and eighteenth centuries the important problem is always to reconcile love and money – or, more widely, let us say, passion and capital. Moreover, is not the act of dishonouring one's rival by showing that he is a sorcerer and, what is more, an inefficacious one, also a way of devaluing him, of diminishing the symbolic capital possessed by this rival? By acting in this way, one kills two birds with one stone; one also increases, along the scale of relative value, the symbolic capital that gives value to the lover–hero, the serious candidate for marriage.

Beyond these vicissitudes, the essential stress is on the male side of the couple: the young man may love, be loved; he must *also* acquire (or show that he possessed previously) some form of capital, if not money, at least honour. This acquisition, or this demonstration, corresponds to the development of the plot; in this way, the hero will at last be transformed, in accordance with the wishes of his beloved's lineage, into a suitable aspiring son-in-law. This is the model. It involves an alternative. Either the hero prevails by his superiority or by his financial and social worthiness, and marries without difficulty at his own level or below it (the normal situation of social homogamy and social hypogamy), or he must find capital to marry higher than himself, and thus achieve social ascension or hypergamy. In either case, he must be armed (in advance) or arm himself (along the way) with capital, real or symbolic.

To conclude these four chapters let us say that Occitan literature, or more particularly the Occitan fiction and drama of the seventeenth and eighteenth centuries, with *Jean-l'ont-pris*, with Fabre's work and with that of other Occitan writers, made marriage or the preparations for marriage its 'ontological site'. There are two series of reasons, negative and positive, for this.

Negatively: Occitan literature, as Greimas would say,[16] is a culture of 'social contract' and not of 'class struggle'; it emanates from geographical areas that are without their own state. Moreover, they have no calling to be a state, at least in this period. Of the two great human passions defined by Pascal, love and ambition, Occitan literature concerned itself above all with the first. It is on the side of Goldoni rather than of Shakespeare; Occitan drama is interested in love, but it is hardly ever oriented towards tragedy in the strict sense of the term: is this because 'tragedy' is 'politics'? In the seventeenth and eighteenth centuries, Occitan literature tends towards apoliticism.

Positively: Marriage is not only the result (in theory) of love; it is not only the essential mode of reproduction of society. Marriage also represents for the man, *for the male* (and the Occitan literature of the two centuries in question was written entirely by men), the mark of accession to a status. For example, it is by marrying that the young farmer, who now sets himself up as master or semi-master in the household of his parents or parents-in-law, finally achieves the status of tenant farmer, or, as they say in the Midi, *ménager*.[17]

Again, the 'love square', which the literature of the Midi in general and *Jean-l'ont-pris* in particular have enabled me to analyse in terms of its four sides, is in no way a monopoly of the Occitan world (see Goldoni, Molière . . .). But the Occitan culture of the seventeenth and eighteenth centuries, in Occitan *and* in French, being totally divorced from politics and public life, gave this 'marriage square', so typical of private life, an extraordinary importance. The limited number of the Occitan literary works available (just over sixty in two centuries) gives the historian an opportunity of making a more or less exhaustive reading of them; in any case, let us say that such a reading is broadly representative. A similar work on French drama generally from 1576 to 1790 would be an almost impossible task (there are more than twelve thousand works for the eighteenth century alone, though, of course, not all of them have been preserved). And how would it be, on top of all that, if one wanted to read all the French novels produced under the *ancien régime*! In fact, one would have to employ the techniques of sampling, which are themselves open to question. The very smallness of the dimensions of Occitan literature represents, paradoxically, an opportunity for the historian of societies. Occitania is a window on the world: it becomes, from this point of view, a metaphor of Western marriage, though a metaphor charged with original, regional features.

CHAPTER VI

Chronology of a Model

When, then, did the socio-literary model of the Occitan 'love square' originate? The abbé Fabre made enormous use of it, but he found it already in existence. The earliest Occitan plays or verse to use the model date from the late sixteenth century. Oral tradition (in the limited sense of being *known*) does not carry it much further back: Jasmin's *Françounette*, which uses it in the 1840s, takes as its starting-point a legend from the Agen region, dating precisely from the military interventions of Blaise du Montluc in the south-west of France (1560–75).

In the Middle Ages, on the contrary, Occitan literature was hardly concerned at all with the model that so obsessed it in the seventeenth and eighteenth centuries. The troubadours of the twelfth and thirteenth centuries were often obsessed by their poverty. But their love (as, for example, in the poems by Bernart de Ventadour) was addressed to a noble, and often rich lady, who was already *married*.[1] This left no room for marriage as a clever reconciliation between love and money after the initial problem of poverty had been overcome. However, all the later literary works that I have analysed end in marriage.

The model that concerns us was developed, therefore, in the Occitan world from the end of the sixteenth century, at a time when the religious drama that had flourished during the late medieval period and the Renaissance was beginning to be duplicated by a profane drama; it was also duplicated by works of fiction (epics, novellas, poems), which in thematic terms proved to be parallel with that theatre. This expansion of the profane drama in the Midi during the second half of the sixteenth century is evident enough when one compares the two 'notebooks' of the brothers Platter,[2] Felix (about 1550) and Thomas (the 1590s). Between 1550 and 1590, our model, in the Midi, emerged in the drama, at least at the level of the literary works preserved by printing. The earliest example of the 'square', though incomplete (it lacks the 'rival'), is to be found in a rustic play in dialect, performed at Montélimar in 1576 and printed at Lyon in 1580; it is situated, linguistically, on the frontiers of Franco-Provençal and Occitan. It is the *Comédie de*

Seigne Peyre et Seigne Joan, 'played by peasants from Montélimar' in 1576. To summarize:

There is a temporary respite from the wars of religion. People imagine (wrongly) that the recent truce will last. The moment seems to have come to talk about marriage. Seigne Peyre (Maître Pierre), a small peasant, has a young son, André, a good worker, who will be 'the staff of his old age'. He suggests to Seigne Joan (Maître Jean), another small farmer of similar rank, that André marry his daughter Catherine. The text implies that the young couple will live in Peyre's cottage, as an extended family, with Peyre himself; the young couple will also en-joy Peyre's lands, hives and rights in the collection of acorns, which are, in fact, ridiculously modest (this is the main source of comedy in the play: his property produces two *setiers* of wheat and rye, two measures of acorns, etc.). Seigne Joan agrees and gives as his daughter's dowry (in addition to a dress, some linen and corn) a 'large' (?) plot of land, which yields – one measure of peas! The wealth of both sides com-bined is still comically small. The rule of the male gift and female counter-gift is thus stressed all the more. This play was actually per-formed by peasants (even if it was probably written by an unknown bour-geois). The theme is an authentically rural one: thus it presents on the stage, not only the girl's father, but also the young man's father;[3] on the other hand, in this decidedly agrarian and patriarchal society, the young couple, like the Arlésienne later, hardly appears at all. Boys and girls are supposed, in this case, to be under their parents' control.

Seigne Joan,
Catherine's father

André,   Catherine
Seigne Peyre's son

the compatibility of (ridiculously small) 'fortunes' will facilitate the marriage, concocted by the fathers[4]

Of course, this play from Montélimar is not the first of its kind. J. Chocheyras tells us that at Toulon in the late fifteenth century there was a comedy entitled *La Fille et l'Amoureux*, of which only the title has survived. The literary monuments that have survived from 1576 onwards, and especially since 1600, follow an older tradition, unknown to us.

Before raising the problem of the specific 'roots' of this model – literary or real, ideological or social – I shall raise the question of its decline: when did the model disappear within an Occitan culture that itself continued to survive? When did it come to be regarded as stupid, or simply ignored?

From a purely realist, non-literary, point of view, it has to be admitted that the Occitan 'love square' was doomed, most of the time, to failure. Outside the theatre, in everyday life, it was rare for a young man to find among his dead grandmother's chattels a treasure that would transform him into a suitable son-in-law in the eyes of the rich father of the girl he loved. In ordinary life, the failure of this kind of enterprise was so frequent that, in the seventeenth century, an Occitan writer decided to face up to the fact in a play. This play, *Scatabronda*, was written by an author whose identity will no doubt be discovered in the course of new research.[5]

It is an audacious, even somewhat cynically 'feminist', play for the period: Jacques Berrié, alias Scatabronda, graduate, doctor and lawyer, is a professor at the University of Cahors. He is rich and miserly. His only daughter, Jeanneton, is the mistress and confidante of a priest, the abbé Coton. Perhaps to give a decent cover to this liaison, Jeanneton thinks of marrying the poor doctor, Romiguière: *I shall dominate him and you will be my master*, Jeanneton says to the priest Coton (whom she loves) when she proposes the idea of such a marriage. Romiguière doesn't love Jeanneton much; in any case, he regards her as neither beautiful nor healthy. But he wants to marry her all the same, for he covets the bags of crowns that will come to him from the future father-in-law, first in the form of a dowry, then as an inheritance. Unfortunately, the rich Scatabronda is furious with the doubly calculating plot being hatched between the girl and the doctor. To put an end to it, he sends Jeanneton to a convent; but Romiguière succeeds in gaining access to her. The ultimate, definitive spectacle occurs when Scatabronda draws up a will, a fine piece of notarial writing, Occitan and baroque, in which he sets up his daughter

Jeanneton as sole heir, on condition that she never marry Romiguière, on pain of being disinherited. In these circumstances, the marriage will not take place for two reasons: Romiguière has not found the money (the possible treasure) that would enable him to cross the threshold; and Jeanneton for her part has no longer anything to gain from marrying the doctor. Were she to do so, she would lose any hope of her own inheritance. It is preferable for her to continue, as an unmarried girl, her secret liaison with the abbé Coton, who will 'caress' her all the more. 'For a girl, one shot in secret is worth more than a hundred when she's married,' says Louison, the heroine's friend. If Jeanneton becomes pregnant, there will always be time to marry Romiguière . . .

As we see, the classic square has broken down and is working in the wrong way. The game has not been brought to its expected conclusion in marriage even if the rules that govern it are strictly respected; nevertheless, they are handled in a highly original way. The rival wins over the chosen candidate for marriage; but he does not marry the girl – for professional reasons, since the priest is confined to celibacy.

the abbé Coton   Professor Scatabronda,
                                            Jeanneton's rich father

Romiguière,   Jeanneton
the doctor–claimant

——————————————————————————————→

                    no marriage

The claimant fails to obtain the money or social status that would bring him to the required level. He does not, therefore, contrary to custom, form the link between the 'future spouses', who will probably remain unmarried. Romiguière is still poor; if Jeanneton married him, she would be deprived of her father's fortune. The abbé Coton will continue to 'caress' the heroine, but remaining himself, that is, unmarried. At the end of the play, Jeanneton and her accomplice Louison exalt the celibacy of girls: to marry, they say, is to produce children who cry all night and to have breasts that will soon droop. This play is a decidedly eccentric, non-conformist one. Written in

1697 at Cahors, it was supposedly printed at Rotterdam; it bears a dedication and a seal of clerical approval that certainly seem fake. Was there something underground about it? In any case, Jeanneton refuses to 'enter the system'. She does not play the classic game of the Occitan 'love square'; everywhere else it would be 'crowned' by a marriage in the fifth act. Through his mistress, the abbé Coton wishes to assume full ecclesiastical celibacy, with all its amatory possibilities. Compared with Fabre de Saint-Castor, the so-called Fabre de Thémines (?) showed less talent, but more audacity.[6]

Scatabronda remains an exception throughout the seventeenth and eighteenth centuries. After 1850, however, it seems that the model that had functioned so well throughout the classical period finally comes apart at the seams. Proof of this is to be found in a handful of masterpieces, in Occitan or French, emanating from the Midi.

To begin with, there is Frédéric Mistral's *Mireille* (1859). At the outset, the Occitan 'love square' is fully laid out in this masterpiece of Provençal literature. First there is the *girl*, Mireille herself, young, beautiful, charming and rich. It goes without saying that she has an authoritarian *father*, Maître Ramon, a rich peasant, who owns and works a large farm in the Camargue. The *hero*, Vincent, is a poor but attractive basket-maker. There are several *opponents* or *rivals*, who, like Vincent, claim the girl's hand. One of them is the rich shepherd, owner of migrating flocks of sheep. The second breeds horses. The third, Ourrias, is a bull-tamer. One senses that Ourrias will have an uphill struggle. It is an opportunity for Mistral to introduce his readers to the different agricultural activities of the lower Rhône, each of which takes on, symbolically, some aspect of Provençal love-lore. The mulberry bushes are full of *jeunes filles en fleur*, who collect the leaves; the breeding of silkworms is linked by Mistral, who depicts local traditions, to female activities and to the laborious games of love: here, love blossoms between Mireille and Vincent among the mulberry bushes. The production of wheat in these huge plains is related to the power exercised by Ramon, *father* of the girl and master of the farm, over both his fields and his family. The raising of sheep, bulls and horses introduces the three *rivals* of the young man, Vincent, beloved of the heroine. Lastly, moving four by four over the various sides of the 'love square', Mistral evokes basket-making and the crafts, which introduce the noble figure of the *hero* himself. *Mireille* then emerges as a veritable handbook of village life and the working of the land. Everything should work out well: the happy ending is not far off.

Unfortunately, things do not turn out like that. Despite the efforts of those concerned, the model refuses to function. The rich owner does not give his consent to the proposed marriage between his daughter and the young hero; in fact, this strict father has every reason to behave as he does, since the hero in question is irremediably poor. Mireille herself dies of sunstroke during a pilgrimage to Saintes-Maries-de-la-Mer, which she had joined in the vain hope that the saints would help her to marry Vincent. But we are in the nineteenth century, and the effect of Voltaire is still felt; the time has passed when the saints in heaven, death or the devil can produce a treasure that would make a poor lover, with money problems, a suitable match for a rich man's daughter. There is, it is true, an element of magic in Mistral's poem. But it intervenes in only a subsidiary way, in the curing of Vincent and the drowning of Ourrias.

In the end, the hero embraces the mortal remains of his beloved. An empty wedding! He could not marry Mireille because he had no money. He cannot even make her pregnant since she is no more.

Ourrias, and Vincent's other rivals	Maître Ramon, patriarch of the farm and Mireille's father
Vincent	Mireille

⟶

no marriage, because Vincent has no money; death of the heroine

The collapse of the old model is also exemplified in Eugène Le Roy's *Jacquou le Croquant*, another masterpiece of southern literature, published in 1899. A French-speaking author, Le Roy remains the honest writer of Occitan Périgord. He wrote in French, but he had a perfect knowledge of the language, culture and life of the inhabitants of Périgord. Through his decisive orientation towards the national language and towards the left, he smothers the Occitan 'love square' in beauty.[7]

In Le Roy's novel, the hero, Jacquou, is a poor, young, attractive peasant. It would seem that he has some chance of attracting and even marrying Galiote, the charming daughter of the abominable Comte de Nansac, the local lord of the manor. But he has more or less lost his father's wealth, which makes him, in principle, less interesting. All the same, he still has the fortune that derives from his mother's dowry. It should be added that the hero, Jacquou, was actually the leader of the peasants' revolt during which the family mansion of the Nansacs went up in flames. It is understandable, therefore, that he does not seem a very presentable son-in-law to the count! Second, Jacquou might be able to obtain the capital which, in the 'love square', constitutes the necessary condition for a young man to marry a girl from such a family. A kindly priest, the abbé Bonal, has left Jacquou his patrimony. But the novelist, with quasi-perverse meticulousness, has arranged for the priest's will not to be dated. It is, says the notary, an invalid document. So Jacquou remains as poor as Job, which disqualifies him once again as a possible Nansac son-in-law. Not to mention the fact that he has burnt down the castle of his potential father-in-law. Lastly, Jacquou belongs to the left, to that new left that became so potent a force in the Périgord of the nineteenth century. This means that the young man cannot decently renege on his political opinions and desert his class by marrying an aristocratic girl, who belongs by birth to the right. In the eighteenth century, Jean-l'ont-pris, who was as apolitical as he was rural, did not have to confront problems of this kind when he was thinking of marrying Babeau. In the end, Jacquou marries Bertrille, Galiote's rival. This Bertrille is a kindly, not very attractive, poor peasant girl, and Jacquou does not love her. They have a lot of children, followed by grand-children, who help to repopulate the Périgord countryside, the real object of Eugène Le Roy's attentions.

Bertrille   Comte de Nansac,
                                             Galiote's father

Jacquou   Galiote

$\longrightarrow$

the model breaks down; Jacquou
marries Bertrille, the poor and unattractive rival of the girl he loves

It would be easy to give other examples of the collapse of the
model. I am thinking in particular of Daudet's *L'Arlésienne* (1872).
Modern Occitanists do not care for Alphonse Daudet; they accuse
him, sometimes quite rightly, of having defamed the Midi with his
exaggerations. Yet he had a good knowledge of the life and mentality
of the Midi. His *L'Arlésienne*, which began as a short story and was
then turned into a play, set on a Provençal farm, might, in another
period, have developed like the plays of the abbé Fabre or of Cassanea
de Mondonville; having done so, it would have ended in marriage,
which itself would have been made possible by the conquest or display
of capital on the part of the male. However, this play, which was
based on the tragic death of one of Mistral's friends, ends with the
jealous hero's suicide, even though the hero's rival does not manage to
marry the girl, though he has slept with her. Daudet, Mistral and Le
Roy belong, therefore, to the decline of a great Occitan fantasy about
marriage, of which the abbé Fabre was one of the paragons. The
fantasy certainly survived into the nineteenth century in a vast sentimental literature, but it was no longer to be found in works of the
same quality as those it had inspired under the *ancien régime*.

CHAPTER VII Cultural Stereotypes and Social History

The collapse of the model is of only marginal concern here. Let us return to the model itself: it underpins *Jean-l'ont-pris* and over sixty other works that represent the whole of extant Occitan literature of the seventeenth and eighteenth centuries.

To begin with, a few words on the structure of the model itself. It exemplifies the categories isolated by such analysts as Souriau, Greimas or Propp.

First opposition of categories: *subject* in relation to *object*. The hero is the subject. The girl is the object. The problem is to transfer the object to the subject, to give the girl in marriage to the hero. In the sample of Occitan literature that I have studied here, the object is always the hero's beloved. In this, the sample is highly representative of Occitan literature in general. In literature originating in other cultures,[1] the object may be God and the salvation of the soul (*Polyeucte*), the liberty of Florence (*Lorenzaccio*), an asylum to die in peace (*Œdipus at Colonus*), the Grail (*Parsifal*), the crown (*Macbeth*). But Occitan culture, which is not centred on a national state, is unaware of political objects; its attention is directed solely to love objects. (However, there did exist in Occitania, in the fifteenth and sixteenth centuries and even later, a religious drama. The object of the plot was, by definition, celestial and divine; but such a drama does not concern this book.)

Second opposition: *giver* in relation to *receiver*, or *sender* in relation to *recipient*. In our 'love square', the girl's father (Monsieur Sestier in Fabre, or Maître Ramon in Mistral) is obviously the giver or sender; indeed, he directs the destiny of the girl, as an owner controls the transfer of goods. The hero, on the other hand, plays the role of receiver or recipient. At the end of the work, he has only to open his arms to receive the girl, sent to him by her father or lineage. The hero, then, combines the functions of subject and receiver. (He may sometimes be a receiver in spite of himself, as in the case of the rich old man who is forced, after being surprised with the girl, a prostitute, to marry her.)

Third opposition: the *auxiliary* in relation to the *opponent*. Here the opponent is the rival in the top-left corner of the love square; a rival who may compete either with the girl (Barbe-Garouille is a 'rival' of this type) or with the hero himself (Peirot in *La Miramoundo*). It is essential that this 'opponent' delay the marriage for a time, though generally the marriage takes place at the end of the play. In certain cases the opponent may be a mere object, for example, the hero's sex organ, regarded as too large by the girl in *La Capiote* (from Limoges) or in another culture (French) it may be the nose that is the obstacle, as in Rostand's *Cyrano*.[2]

The auxiliary, or 'rescuer', in Occitan literature is the person who finds the capital needed by the hero. This capital may, of course, be land, money, cattle or honour; wealth actually transferred to the girl's lineage by the hero or simply exhibited by him with a view to impressing his future father-in-law; real or fiduciary wealth, or merely expectations of an inheritance; or wealth signified implicitly, from the fact that the hero possesses a high social status. We have seen that the auxiliary may, according to the particular case, move to any of the four corners of the love square: he may be identified with the hero himself or with his lineage; he may coincide with the future father-in-law; he may be identified with the deflowered and pregnant girl, when she is deprived of virginity and places her honour at the hero's disposal; he may be identified with the opponent or rival when the hero uses him, at the end of some scheme, as an involuntary ally and as an additional provider of capital for the heroine's lineage.

In the structures of real life, among the societies of the *ancien régime*, one also meets, as in the literature, the transfer of a daughter conveyed by a father to a man, against the wishes of a rival-opponent and with the help of some ally or auxiliary. The question now arises as to how the cultural and real structures are linked. Are the two love squares, that of literature and that of life, the same? The problem cannot be reduced to a trivial equivalence according to which literary or popular culture is the 'reflection' or a mere copy of life. The anthropologists take a more subtle view; they have accustomed us to the idea that certain correspondences exist between mythical (or literary) structures and the elementary structures of kinship. Cultural and functional are correlated. Why should what is true for the American Indians not also be true for the mechanisms of conjugal alliances between two lineages in Occitan literature and society?

At first sight, however, the situation appears, from this point of view, to be desperate. In Occitan literature, it seems, to put it simply, that the hero 'buys the girl' from her father, after paying or at least displaying the required capital. Now, in the social reality of the Midi it would seem, on the contrary, again simplifying, that it is the girl or the girl's lineage that 'buys the boy': the dowry that she derives from her father enables her, in effect, to get a husband conforming to her rank and wishes. Failing this, it is the girl's lineage that takes on the task of providing the necessary wealth by means of the dowry.

Are we to conclude, then, that in the Occitan-speaking regions, in the seventeenth and eighteenth centuries, fiction was simply the reverse image of social reality?

Before pursuing this point, one question should be raised: what does the popular expression (which is even to be found in Occitan drama)[3] *to buy a wife* mean? Can one legitimately link this verb and this complement?

In fact, the anthropologists who have studied such customs among the various populations of Africa, the East Indies and Asia[4] speak not of the buying of the wife or the price of the wife (brideprice), but of the wife as wealth (bridewealth). This 'wealth' is transferred by the betrothed man to his future wife or lineage in the form of various services, or of gifts of cattle, goats, beer, hoes, spears, pearly shells, pigs, feathers of rare birds, camels, horses, guns and, in our day, money. For the man who is going to become a husband, it is not only a question of 'buying a wife', but of demonstrating, by means of material or financial allowances, his marital rights over her. Moreover, he thus contributes to the upkeep and food of his young wife; he may also assist in the working and defence of his father-in-law's land. Thanks to the deliveries in kind or in money that he has arranged, he establishes his unchallengeable rights over the children who will be born from the marriage that he has contracted with the woman of his choice.

In Europe, where the dowry seems to be thrown out like a lasso, from the girl to the man, the structures seem to function quite differently. And yet . . . Lucy Mair notes, in her study of marriage, that 'among Greek peasants (including Cypriots), given the recognition of a general principle that a woman should be endowed by her parents when she marries, there is a balance between the material value of the endowment and the social or prestige value of the husband'.[5] 'Prestige' in the rural world, in Greece as elsewhere, is largely a matter of land ownership. What does this amount to if not that in this case, money goes to money or, to be more precise, female wealth goes to male wealth; the female dowry is to the male inheritance what interest is to capital. The Mediterranean peasant, whether he is Greek or Occitan, real or theatrical, must organize a display of capital, make known the existence of the 'treasure' he possesses, before being accepted as a suitable husband for a well-endowed girl. From this point of view, then, our Occitan literature should be taken seriously; it goes beyond reality – by modelling itself on it in its own way.

In the mountainous region of Béarn, as a result of the traditional character of the local agriculture, the old Occitano-Gascon practices were preserved longer than elsewhere; Pierre Bourdieu has made a brilliant analysis of life in that province between 1900 and 1920. These practices were locally conservative, retaining an archaic eighteenth-century character that had long disappeared in the lowlands of Aquitaine.

For Bourdieu[6] female remuneration, in an agrarian society, goes to male capital ('one only lends to the rich'), and marriages are made between families of the same rank: 'A younger son of lower rank does not ask a big peasant's daughter to dance at the ball. Farm servants may sometimes dance with heiresses, but it is rare.' Before marrying X, a young farmer, a girl 'looks in at the door' of the young man's family farmhouse, hoping to see signs of luxury and to assure herself at least that X is comfortably off. The girl looks for a husband more highly placed than herself; 'a small *household* would do anything to get its daughter married to a rich elder son'; 'an elder son of good family can easily marry a younger daughter of a small family', whereas, conversely, 'an elder son of small family cannot marry a younger daughter of a big family'. However, the boy's mother will oppose her son 'marrying a woman of too high a condition, because she is afraid of being looked down on and tyrannized by her daughter-in-law'. 'Dissymmetries (of money and prestige) that favour the heir-ess' would give her the right to wear the trousers, which would worry the young husband's family. On the contrary, a young man who comes 'as son-in-law' into a family of the same rank as his own 'and who brings with him a good *adot* [a good financial gift or 'male contribu-tion' from his own lineage] . . . is honoured and treated as a veritable master'. A thrifty servant, before 1914, 'might hope to buy a house with ten to twelve years' wages'; by marrying late (at thirty-one) 'and with the help of a girl's dowry, he could acquire a farmhouse and land'.

As far as the young man is concerned, such practices place him in the position of having to provide or display his contribution in money or land with a view to marriage; this will enable him to contract 'a fine marriage'. Nevertheless, such a marriage will tend not to link the young husband to a family more highly placed than his own. We see that in this sense the lessons of our Occitan literature from the *ancien régime*, with their insistence on the male contribution, which is more stressed than the female dowry, were not entirely lost. They were to preserve their relevance in the backward Béarn for a century or more. The young Béarnais of the 1900s still interiorized these finan-cial requirements of their autochthonous culture sufficiently for love to conform very often to the demands of the social structures: as an heir, one loved the rich younger daughter whom economic destiny sent you; one did not 'buy' her, but one procured her, together with her dowry, by revealing or mirroring, on the male side, an adequate fortune and the enormous expectation of an inheritance to come. If one were a mere farm-servant, one aimed distinctly lower: one would marry a maid or a poor younger daughter. The rural group func-tioned in the manner of the court of Louis XIV as described by Saint-Simon; it operated according to the principles of a hierarchical society [*société de rangs*].

The very improbabilities of Occitan literature tend in the last analysis to strengthen the social structure. Beggars do not marry princesses; and if Occitan fiction tells us that the beggar has found a treasure in the garbage that allows him to marry the princess, it merely goes to show that, in real life, things do not happen like that, since one marries according to one's rank, fortune and prestige – never much higher or much lower. This 'never' has, of course, a statistical rather than an absolute value.

Occitan literature stressed the principle of a society of rank, in so far as it required that the husband be possessed of sufficient capital to obtain from the father of a well-endowed girl the right to marry her. This is what Pierre Lamaison, in his computer study of marriages in north-east Languedoc (Gévaudan/Lozère) in the eighteenth century, has called socio-occupational homogamy or, a very much more valuable expression, class endogamy – which, in simple language, means that one marries *within one's own milieu*, or, better still, *at one's own level* (of fortune, prestige, etc.). 'It is the nobles, the bourgeois, the artisans and the peasants,' writes Lamaison,[7] 'who are the most endogamic [the most skilful practitioners of a society of rank]. Journeymen and weavers form their alliances within their social class without specific reference to socio-occupational homogamy.' (In effect, such young people, boys and girls, are concerned not so much to marry according to their specific *occupation* or 'estate', as to marry someone, for lack of anything better, *within their social class*; in this way they situate themselves in a general way at the simple 'lower' level, which includes *both* weavers and journeymen.) 'For example, male weavers marry female weavers in 25% of cases, but they also marry peasant girls (30.6% of their marriages), or daughters of small shopkeepers (5.6%) or artisans' daughters (5.6%). The journeymen act in a similar way, though they apparently prefer to marry journeymen's daughters (52.5% do so), that is to say, daughters of modest condition. When they reach marriageable age, weavers and journeymen frequent shepherdesses, cowgirls, maidservants rather than daughters of shopkeepers. Following patrimonial imperatives, they marry within their social class a girl of their own condition, even if she is not of their estate.'[8]

'Class endogamy rather than socio-occupational homogamy[9] ... importance of patrimony in the choice of spouse ... Among the peasants, 65.6% marry peasant girls; 4.7%, bourgeois girls; in this way they form unions within their class or slightly above. The latter (marriages of certain peasants with bourgeois girls) can only be marriages contracted by heirs (by relatively well-off peasants), whereas on the contrary the 17.2% of marriages contracted by peasants with journeymen's daughters, and the 10.9% of marriages between peasants and weavers' daughters, undoubtedly involved poor, younger sons of peasants, possessing just a male "dowry" and not an inheritance, and lacking in any considerable wealth.' It will be noted that at this point in his study, Pierre Lamaison uses the important notion of *heir*, or heiress, and *inheritance* – in opposition to that of *younger* son or daughter and *dowry*, which is female or in certain circumstances male. It should be remembered that the Languedoc is a country of primogeniture among commoners, or at least one in which the inheritance of parents is transmitted to *one* of the children, generally the eldest male, who is the heir; this single transmission sometimes operates to the benefit of a daughter who, in such a case, is made the heiress. From this point of view, under the *ancien régime*, the Occitan countries differ enormously from northern France, where, in varying degrees, the inheritance is divided among several children. In literature and in reality, the problem of how the future husband is to display capital is presented in different ways according to whether the males are of rich or poor parents; *within the same family* this problem is presented differently between 'eldest' or 'inheriting' children and younger children, who are only poorly endowed, instead of being, as in the case of the heir, put in possession of the very patrimony of the parents or of expectations of this patrimony.

The abbé Fabre, who was himself a younger son – which may be why his parents destined him for the priesthood – was well aware of this problem. He gave the name Cadet to several of his characters, in particular to the hero of *Le Trésor de Substancion*; he placed these poor *cadets* ['younger sons'] in the situation, for them logical enough, in which they have to find outside their own lineage some treasure or large gift in order to marry the girl they love.

I shall now return to Pierre Lamaison's description of the social difference of rank and level in Lozère: 'The same goes for the poor journeymen,' Lamaison writes. 'The 27.5% of them who marry a peasant girl (in principle, better off than they) *apparently* achieve a union above their condition (as poor men). It may involve the union of two younger children (that is, relatively lacking in money, which is equivalent to a marriage between two persons economically poor and, therefore, well suited to each other). In this case the girl (despite the title "peasant girl", which places her *in theory* above the daughters of journeymen) belongs to a family of peasants with little money (who are *in fact* at the level of the journeymen, of the poor). But it may also happen that the boy (a journeyman and, therefore, theoretically poor) manages in fact to build up, through work, an additional male dowry, which places him above his own condition.' (In this case, the reverse of the situation described earlier, it is not the girl who marries below her, but the boy who, through his work, manages like a salmon to leap one or two levels of the waterfall, in order to raise himself to the girl's level.) 'But generally speaking,' Lamaison continues, on the subject of these marriages between (theoretically poor) *journeymen* and theoretically well-off *peasant girls*, 'it concerns a marriage between a journeyman who is also an *heir* (therefore relatively well-off, despite his low socio-occupational title) and a *younger* daughter of a farmer' (therefore relatively poor, despite the status implied by the description of the girl's father as *laboureur* ['farmer']; from this point of view, we see that the boy is more highly placed than expected, and the girl less well placed than expected, which harmonizes their conjugal adjustment, in accordance with the *practical* rule of the structures of real society and also with the *mythical* rules of Occitan literature).

On this matter, Lamaison stresses that what we have here are pre-conjugal adjustments to social class; moreover, even within the same class, other pre-conjugal adjustments take account of subtle, but nevertheless substantial, differences introduced into each family by the respective positions of the older and younger children. 'The *heir* (unlike the *younger* son) of a (rather poor) artisan who marries the daughter of a rather well-off farmer seems to be forming a union above his class, whereas in reality if this girl is a younger child the contrary is the case.' (She was, in fact, *below* him, and she had to 'play hard to get' in order to get him; one recognizes here the tendency, which was to remain dear to the peasants of Béarn and which Bourdieu refers to, by which it is desirable that the husband's socio-occupational status be slightly higher than that of the wife, so that the 'normal' rules concerning the distribution of power within the household be respected – and so that the wife does not 'wear the trousers'. Hence the importance of marriage involving an heir and a younger daughter, which was once thought to provide a perfect harmony between the 'plus' element of the male and the 'minus' element of the female.) 'Class endogamy,' Lamaison concludes (p. 100), 'makes more sense here therefore than strict socio-occupational homogamy; but this proposition is valid only if one remembers that the occupation and the "estate" of an individual do not *in themselves* indicate to which class he belongs, even if the historian knows the financial position of this individual's father.' In fact, one must also know whether the candidate for marriage is an *heir* or a *younger* son.

When analysing the profound reasons for 'class endogamy', which expresses a hierarchy among households, and various levels within this hierarchy, Pierre Lamaison introduces what he calls the principle of reciprocity:[10] every (well-off) household which, in marrying one of its daughters into another well-off family, has to provide a large dowry, will expect one day to recover an equivalent dowry by marrying one of its sons into a similarly well-off family. The same reasoning goes for poor households: they do not, after all, have the same interest in obtaining large dowries for their sons, for they would then have to provide a large dowry, with consequent ruin to themselves, by marrying a daughter into an equivalent level. Consequently, in general, the rich marry the rich and the poor, the poor. Hence the stress that our theory of marriage, as it finds expression in Occitan literature, places on the need for a large male contribution, as soon as this can be 'remunerated', through marriage, by means of a large female dowry. Let us return for the moment to the apparently hopeless question of realism: our Occitan literature does not provide a *model of* (of real life), but a *model in order to*[11] (in order to propose certain desirable rules for real life). These rules are not necessarily imitative of actual experience. They are intended to be normative, for social life as it ought to be lived.

Lamaison's analysis of Lozère is confirmed by that of Molinier on the populations of the Gulf of Lions, Delbos on Quercy, Collomp on the valley of the Verdon, Sentou on Toulouse, Carrière on Marseille and Durand on the wine-growers of Beaujolais.[12] When a young man plans to marry a girl with a dowry, he must exhibit capital proportionate to the said dowry, in the form of a contribution to the marriage and expectations of an inheritance.[13] If he has no capital, he will not marry the girl, at least in real life: patrimony and matrimony will not converge. If the situation is a literary one, the playwright or novelist takes care to arrange things differently: in the space of five acts or a couple of chapters, he will obtain for the unfortunate young man the necessary capital for his marriage. But these imaginary arrangements are simply intended to demonstrate, in terms of fantasy, that, in

By means of sometimes incredible contortions, the Occitan drama tries to harmonize the capital of the future husband with the dowry of the future wife. Traditional society succeeded in this quite spontaneously among the wine-growers of Beaujolais (see the excellent thesis by G. Durand, p. 353) in the eighteenth century (the coefficient of correlation is 0.86, which is very high, between the respective contributions of husband and wife, at the marriage, calculated in *livres tournois*).

Traditional society succeeded in a similar way from the fifteenth century (1437) among married couples in Arles (Louis Stouff's thesis on Arles in

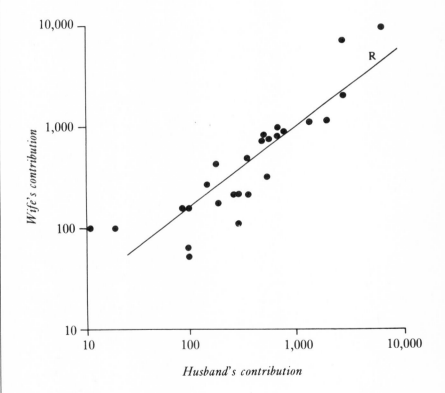

Correlation between the respective contributions of husband and wife, according to marriage contracts in Beaujolais (1750–80)
Logarithmic scale. Coefficient of correlation between the two series of contributions: R = 0.86.

the late Middle Ages). We see, for example, at the top of the line in Louis Stouff's remarkable graph, that the large fortunes of the husbands (over 100 florins and over 500 florins) closely correspond to the large dowries of their wives (over 500 florins) and so on: small male fortunes were matched by small female dowries (bottom of the line).

DOWRIES IN ARLES

WIVES' DOWRIES AND HUSBANDS' FORTUNES

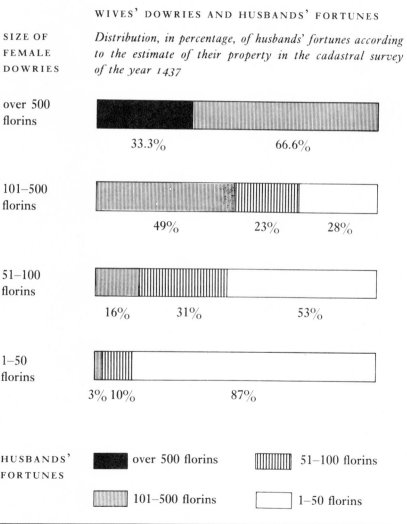

| SIZE OF FEMALE DOWRIES | Distribution, in percentage, of husbands' fortunes according to the estimate of their property in the cadastral survey of the year 1437 |

over 500 florins
33.3%   66.6%

101–500 florins
49%   23%   28%

51–100 florins
16%   31%   53%

1–50 florins
3% 10%   87%

HUSBANDS' FORTUNES

over 500 florins   51–100 florins

101–500 florins   1–50 florins

terms of actual life, the boy was defeated in advance. It is in this respect that literature is not imitative of social life, but normative in relation to it and correlative with it. This correlation, which may go as far as inversion, is the essential characteristic of the discipline known as *histoire des mentalités*.

The display of capital by the candidate for marriage is accompanied by the symbolic or real presenting of money so dear to literature, but also to be found in folklore. At the beginning of the nineteenth century, the Comte de Villeneuve,[14] a good observer of Provence, noticed this practice: 'When the date of a marriage is finally fixed, the future husband is eager to present his betrothed with the *lioureio* (a Provençal word synonymous with the French *livrée* ["livery"]; in accepting the present, the betrothed girl is supposed to take on her future husband's livery). The *lioureio* consists of the wedding basket, containing jewels, the wedding dress, etc.' The buying of the *lioureio* is ritualized and therefore emphatic: 'In the villages, the future husband arrives, on a horse or mule, to fetch his betrothed. She mounts behind him; escorted by other members of the family they go into the neighbouring town to buy the *lioureio*. This present (the purchase of which is thus carried out in the presence of witnesses) is always given to the betrothed in front of witnesses (which solemnizes the event). The acceptance of these preliminary gifts may be regarded as a betrothal ... In the region of Arles in the Camargue, the farmers spend extraordinarily large amounts of money on their weddings. They buy their betrothed valuable jewellery, and any man who on such an occasion spends only ten to twelve thousand francs is regarded as excessively thrifty, even mean ...' We must not forget, of course, that the future husband will also give his betrothed, apart from the *lioureio*, his name: that is to say, a capital of prestige and honour. In Savoie, the boy who asks for the hand of a girl in marriage symbolically gives her a crown piece.[15]

In Spain, in the twentieth as well as in the sixteenth century, folklore has preserved certain customs reminiscent of what is called rather simplistically the 'buying of the bride'. On the wedding-day, the bride is given thirteen blest coins or an orange stuffed with small silver coins or just an orange or an apple. 'This is a reminiscence,' Noël Salomon writes boldly but interestingly, 'of an old marriage tradition proper to certain Visigothic tribes, among whom it was the custom for the husband, during the wedding ceremony, to give his future wife a gold or silver coin (as the price of the wife, who was thus actually bought).'[16]

The male display of capital is referred to, then, both in the regional, dialectal literature and in folklore. It also appears in innumerable notaries' records. 'In the eighteenth century,' says Henri Michel, a specialist in the social history of Montpellier, 'marriage contracts drawn up by notaries make increasing mention of the financial contributions of both husband and wife; and sometimes the former are greater than the latter. Perhaps because in the seventeenth century, the husband's parents were already dead, whereas in the eighteenth century they tended to survive. The wife's parents could not, therefore, be content simply with expectations of an inheritance that their future son-in-law would one day enjoy; instead they asked the husband to obtain from his family a considerable initial advance on the patrimony to be included in the marriage contract itself . . . To this was added, always provided by the young man, the *augment de dot* . . . this amounted to less, of course, than the dowry itself (which came from the girl), but it could be substantial, the equivalent even of 10,000 *livres tournois* in the more important contracts. This *augment de dot* was a life insurance that the husband gave his wife to cover the eventuality of his dying first. Similarly, there was a *contre-augment de dot*, paid by the wife to the husband . . . But this *contre-augment* of female provenance was less than half the *augment de dot* provided by the male.'[17] Moreover, the male contribution was linked to very strong traditions in the Occitan regions, at least among the nobility, about which, in earlier periods, we know more than about the rest of society: *out of honour, out of love and for thy beauty, I have given thee a part of my inheritance*, says a noble from Bigorre to his future wife, in a marriage contract dating from the eleventh century.[18]

What emerges from all this is a certain philosophy of the female dowry. It would seem that in Occitania, and in the West more generally, it is not central, but peripheral to the institution of marriage itself. Using a different image, one might say that the female dowry is the glorious or visible part of the iceberg, of which the male contributions are the decisive mass; this male mass is usually, if not always, to be found in the notaries' records, in which it is sometimes concealed in so far as it may take the form of mere expectations of inheritances, these being self-evident and therefore not explicitly mentioned as such in the marriage contract. However, this male mass is heavily stressed, as we have seen, in the regional, dialectal literature, which was so close to the people.

At this point of the argument, perhaps, we should stand back somewhat and look at these questions from the point of view of comparative anthropology, which may help us to understand more clearly, in various contexts, the respective roles and contributions of the husband and wife. In her book *Woman's Role in Economic Development*, Ester Boserup sums up her argument on the function of women (and, in a complementary way, that of men) in traditional communities. She distinguishes between two types of societies in the Africano–Eurasiatic space: 'The first type is found in regions where shifting cultivation predominates . . . [and] the major part of agricultural work is done by women. In such communities . . . bridewealth is paid to the girl's family by the future husband or his family. The women are hard working . . . The second group is found where plough cultivation predominates and where women do less agricultural work than men. In such communities we may expect to find that . . . a dowry is usually paid by the girl's family; that a wife is entirely dependent upon her husband for economic support; and that the husband has an obligation to support his wife and children, at least as long as the marriage is in force. We find the first type of rural community in Africa south of the Sahara, in many parts of South East Asia and in tribal regions in many parts of the world.'[19] The second type (female dowry) is, among others, Western.

Boserup's remarks have remarkable implications for this study. In its most essential structures, the female dowry appears to be the marginal complement of a male patrimony, land, which is worked by the man. This patrimony will provide the woman and any subsequent children with their principal source of subsistence; the dowry being intended, in the final analysis, only to oil the cogs of a male patrimonial machine, without which it would scarcely have any substance at all.

In this sense, our Occitan literature of the classical period, with its insistence on the display of male capital,[20] is much more faithful to the deeper reality of Occitan marriage than are the notaries' records, obsessed as they are, in their 'superstructural' way, with the legal niceties of the female dowry.[21]

From an existential point of view, the Occitan love square is based on one side (the right-hand one) on the vertical father–daughter axis, the latter being strictly subordinate to the former; on the other side (bottom left) on a certain independence possessed by the young man, the hero: by displaying his patrimony, he deals as an equal with the girl's lineage, in other words, with her father. The father–future son-in-law, or Sestier–Jean-l'ont-pris, relationship is a fundamental one.

Is it one that was to be found in real life and not only in literature? On this particular point, we do not have the data of everyday Occitan life. But Nicolas Rétif's Burgundy offers comparisons: this was, in effect, almost as much as the Languedoc, a region in which paternal power, in terms of decisions and questions of inheritance, was very strong, owing to the local infiltration of Roman law, which arrived there from the southern provinces in the late Middle Ages.[22]

Rétif's account of the amatory and pre-marital customs of Burgundy is a rigid one: it involves a preliminary flirtation of the boy with the girl, which leads to rivalries among young men. But very soon the boy is confronted by the girl's parents, in particular her father, who approves or rejects the claimant, in terms of a positive or negative *diktat*, which is both summary and final. Of course, the boy may discuss the details with his own father, but it is always he, the young man, who is in charge of the negotiations; it is he who comes with the proposals for a marriage treaty; he discusses them at the summit, not with the girl, but with the father or father-substitute.[23]

There is a secondary reason why the hero, and not his lineage, is dramatically confronted with the girl's lineage, and not with the girl herself. This reason concerns the age structure of the couple: the girl who is at the centre of the intrigue is always supposed to be desirable, and therefore in the power of her father, mother, godfather, elder brother, mistress or procuress. The play may also involve the marriage of an elderly widow, but these secondary marriages are merely an incidental element in the plot; they are never central to it. What counts, in theatrical terms, is the marriage of the *young* woman.

The hero's age, on the other hand, is generally unimportant, though in fact in most of the plays we have considered he is young. He need only be a sexual adult, 'anything from 17 to 77'. Structurally speaking, he is not under his father's or mother's authority, even if, occasionally, an older relation of the hero appears in a particular novel or play, especially in a highly patriarchal, rural setting.

However, there is an intriguing question here: traditional society was based on the tutelage of the daughter by the father, on respect for social rank, on matrimonial strategies and on the essential role of the male patrimony as far as marriages were concerned; this society existed well before the seventeenth century, even, for example, in the late Middle Ages.[24] Why, then, did Occitan literature, which burst forth on the archipelago of small towns, become interested in the question only from the 1570s onwards and become most preoccupied with it in the period of the abbé Fabre? Is it because an attitude of capitalistic financial calculation, directed towards the quantitative adjustment of the male and female contributions to marriage, spread with the beginning of the modern age? Perhaps. But nevertheless a hierarchical society, with all the questions that it raises, existed long before the first massive spread of capitalism and even of the market economy, in the forms they have taken from the Renaissance onwards.

In fact, the answer to our earlier question has already been given in this book: the troubadours of the twelfth and thirteenth centuries wrote for the aristocratic public they served and for the married women they loved. They cared little, therefore, for marriage, in its popular or bourgeois forms. Later (in the fifteenth and sixteenth centuries), Occitan literature returned to a greater extent to religious considerations (the mystery plays, etc.). From the second part of the sixteenth century, for various reasons, in plays written in dialect by bourgeois and performed in the public squares before a popular audience, the regional culture turned at last to the problems of ordinary people and to the central question of marriage. Only then, in the south of France and in other Mediterranean or Continental cultures, did the problem of the 'love square', with its displays of patrimony, carried out by the hero in the direction of the girl, unfold in all its banal splendour. In this area, Occitan literature provides solutions that are often wrapped in mystery or at least, with Fabre to the fore, to be found at the centre of a wonderfully complicated plot.

*

However, there still remains the question as to why the model that we have examined in some detail in *Jean-l'ont-pris*, in other works by the abbé Fabre and in some sixty other literary pieces – which cover practically all the works published in Occitan at the time – should lose its value, collapse or in any case no longer be taken seriously after 1850. Let us look at *Mireille, Jacquou le Croquant, L'Arlésienne*, etc.

I shall make only the beginning or a summary of an answer to this riddle. I believe that the hierarchical society that culminated in the seventeenth and eighteenth centuries lost its vigour after the mid-nineteenth century. The possibilities of social advancement had always existed, with or without marriage; Occitan literature had dealt with them more than once. But, after the period from 1789 to 1850, which brought the *ancien régime* to an end, they became much more important. Marriage itself now offered a more likely career: economically more accessible and less dangerous. Moreover, men managed to marry younger and have fewer children,[25] which diminished the risk for the couple of increasing poverty. In such circumstances, the tricks, the feeble little tricks (such as the discovery of a treasure, a present arriving from some rich benefactor, etc.) that our authors invented so readily to enable the poor hero to marry the rich girl, those techniques suddenly seemed ridiculous. The world had lost its magic. Such dramatic inventions were no longer to be taken seriously. They were now seen as little more than a fantastic justification for an earlier social rigidity that was now at an end. It would be better for the hero to kill himself (*L'Arlésienne*) or to become a revolutionary (*Jacquou*), or for the heroine to perish from sunstroke (*Mireille*), than to have recourse to subsidiary, pre-marital tricks that no longer amused anyone or that seemed trivial to serious people. If one was to rise in society, one would do it rationally, in literature as in reality, without recourse to happy endings – or to the string-pulling of an earlier, simpler age.

CHAPTER VIII

A Theme in Folklore?

The theme of the boy who wins a girl from her father (or from her mother) by means of a 'treasure', against a rival, is a widespread one in Occitan literature of the seventeenth and eighteenth centuries.

Is it also a theme in folklore? The very character of the Occitan literature of the classical age, at least that which concerns us here, developed by dialect-speaking bourgeois for a plebeian, or even peasant, theatrical public, would lead one to think so. If this is the case, one should find some trace of this theme in the folk-tales and fairy-tales told by grandmothers on dark winter evenings or by professional story-tellers, of which there were then so many in that part of the world, to audiences of adults or children. A brief investigation would seem to be all the more appropriate in that the abbé Fabre himself showed a great interest in fairy-tales.[1] Certainly, he introduced into his writings, in both Occitan and French, some elements that belong strictly speaking to the fairy-tale. One thinks, for example, of the fabulous, if temporary, enrichment of poverty-stricken Truquette; the quasi-miraculous circumstances in which Jean-l'ont-pris finds the treasure-chest of his dead grandmother; the allusion, if ironic, to the nocturnal miracles of the rock of Substancion; and, lastly, the parody in another work (*Zima*) of *The Thousand and One Nights*. It does not matter that Fabre should sometimes change this fairy-tale element into burlesque. In any case, Fabre wrote in a period of extraordinary vitality when oral traditions were still being handed down, without interruption, from earliest times and which, at the same time, looked toward the future.

Let us confine ourselves, for purposes of this research, to the Languedocian and Provençal regions, stretching from Ariège to the Hautes-Alpes, via Aude and Hérault – that in which our authors lived and wrote.

Very close to certain basic themes of the writings of Jean-Baptiste Fabre is the folk-tale from Hérault called *Le Mariage de la princesse*.[2] Collected about 1900 and published in 1901, it dates, like many such tales, from a much earlier period. In it reference is made to *dîmes* ['tithes'], which existed before the French Revolution and which would date the story from at least the eighteenth century. In fact, it would seem that this tale is a distant oral adaptation of *Jean de Paris*, a famous chivalric romance dating from the late Middle Ages and to which the grandmother refers in *Jean-l'ont-pris*, in order to give an example to her grandson.[3]

The plot of *Le Mariage de la princesse* may be summarized as follows: René, king of the kingdom of Pampélibournes (in fact, a mere farm), is the father of a pretty 'princess' named Doucinelle. In the hope of obtaining the girl's hand in marriage, a number of characters, from the outset of the plot, shower the king with 'gifts': cartloads of wheat, velvet robes, silk coats . . . On the advice of the fairy Ermelinde, Doucinelle's godmother, King René organizes a tourney, in which the various candidates for his daughter's hand will compete. A variety of men turn up: blacksmiths who can split an anvil with a sword; ploughmen and reapers, experts in ploughing a furrow and binding sheaves. Then two giants arrive, one of whom, like Ourrias in *Mireille*, is a tamer of bulls; these two wrestle to the death to win Doucinelle's heart. One of them has his head crushed in; the other loses an arm. These two are followed by a fiddler, who, to great applause, charms the birds, the butterflies and the lovers. Lastly comes a merchant, Cousudor, not at first sight a very attractive character. But he casts off his carnival finery to reveal, at the last moment, his wagons, filled with pearls, diamonds, gold coins and spangled silks. His servants empty, at the princess's feet, bags filled with precious stones. René, the king–farmer, though dubious at first, is overcome with joy: *you will be my son-in-law*. Doucinelle, overcome with happiness, throws her arms around Cousudor's neck and marries him.

various pretenders   the 'king',
                                      Doucinelle's father

Cousudor   Doucinelle

　　　　────────────────────────────→

the treasure of the chosen pretender
makes the marriage possible

Undoubtedly, this tale tells the story of a man who wins a girl from her father by dominating his rivals with his wealth. The story is told in a rather crude way. But there are other similar, subtler tales.

There is the story of the hundred rabbits, which was collected by Jean Guilaine in the valley of the Lanquet in Aude.[4] It is one of the Languedocian versions (adapted to local taste) of a 'type' that was very widespread throughout Europe. According to this version from the Midi, there was once a father who had three sons, all coal-merchants. They learn that the king's daughter is to be married to the man who will bring him the three finest pears.

The first son, who takes his basket of three fruits to the royal palace, meets on the way an old fairy who asks him what he has in his basket. He replies insolently: 'Shit!' When the king opens the basket, what does he find? Instead of the three pears, there are three turds. The young man is thrown into prison! A similar misadventure happens to the second son, except that, this time, the fairy turns the pears into rats. The third son, however, believes that honesty pays: he tells the fairy that he is taking three pears to the king in order to compete for the princess's hand in marriage. Suddenly the old woman becomes kindly and changes the fruit into three golden pears. The king has no alternative but to promise his daughter to the coal-merchant's third son. However, he imposes additional trials on his future son-in-law. One of these is to keep one hundred rabbits without losing a single one. The trial is rather difficult, but the boy succeeds. It is to be found in various European versions of the tale, which derives from the task its generic code-name – *The Tale of the Hundred Rabbits* – in Aarne and Thompson's international classification.[5] The Languedocian version also includes, after the treasure of the 'golden pears', another 'financial' episode: a scheme worked out by the royal accountant enables the future son-in-law to increase his capital by winning 50,000 francs. In the end, after various tribulations, he marries the princess. In a version of the story from Aude, collected in 1902, the three pears taken to the royal palace are ordinary fruits that have not been turned into gold; but the third young man – the one who is to marry the princess – previously recovers three diamonds for the king.[6]

The same could be said, in the Provençal region, of the story of *The Platinum Flower*. Collected in the Hautes-Alpes, it tells of a boy who kills the seven-headed monster: this allows the hero to recover a bunch of flowers made of precious metals (gold, silver, platinum). He brings this treasure to the king, who at once gives him his daughter in marriage. This Occitan tale derives from type number 317 of the tale (in the French classification of Delarue).[7]

A tale from Quercy also offers the theme of a young man made rich: by obtaining treasure, this character is able to win the assent of his future father-in-law to the marriage with his daughter, which at first had been refused him. The scene is set in the village of Faycelles: Maître Guillaume, the local miller, produces exquisite flour, owing, very largely, to the quasi-magical services of his assistant *farinier* ['flour-maker'], in local dialect, the *farinel*.[8] The *farinel* is in love with Jeannette, Maître Guillaume's younger daughter, and she with him. But the master miller refuses to give his daughter's hand to a mere worker. On the contrary, he intends her to marry a local noble. Thrown at first into despair, the *farinel* goes off for a long period to Spain (as a great many emigrants from Quercy once did). He returns after seven years, having made his fortune in business. Jeannette has been faithfully waiting for him, refusing to marry anyone else. His objections overcome by the bucket of gold and silver coins that the *farinel* has brought back with him from Spain, Maître Guillaume agrees to give his daughter to him in marriage.

Jean-l'ont-pris and the works parallel to it sprang, therefore, from a favourable soil of popular culture, which was certainly older than the eighteenth century. But a more interesting – indeed, fascinating – question for anyone interested in this masterpiece of Occitan literature now arises: is not *Jean-l'ont-pris* based directly on a particular folk-tale?

The question has never so far been raised. My thesis, which is radically new in the historiography of Occitan literature, is that *Jean-l'ont-pris* is not only one of many expressions of the cultural stereotypes relating to the theories of marriage in the Occitan region. In my opinion, Fabre's novel also derives, very specifically, from a fairy-tale entitled *Death's Godson*, or *Godfather Death*; this primitive text carries the number 332 in Aarne and Thompson's international classification of folk-tales (AT). To simplify matters, then, I shall refer to it as AT 332/*Godfather Death* or, quite simply, as AT 332.

So dogmatic a statement requires detailed demonstration. I would apologize, therefore, for the sometimes technical and not always rhetorical character of the argument that follows. Fabre himself hinted that his tale was a *parable* filled with *riddles*.[9]

I think I have deciphered, 'cracked the code', of this enigmatic parable. My demonstration will rest on the evidence of a *community of structure* between *Jean-l'ont-pris* and the regional versions from Languedoc and Provence of AT 332, themselves flanked by earlier known versions of the same tale (prior to 1756). It will also rest on an analysis that is not only general (like the demonstration of this community of structure), but also *detailed*; it being understood that, following the golden rule of structural research, the similarity of a particular detail in *JLP* and in some other version of AT 332 is of value only on two conditions:

(1) this particular detail must be set in a strategically homologous site of the structural chain of the narrative, comparing the two narratives, *JLP* and the other one;

(2) any comparison with an earlier version of AT 332 (German, Italian, Breton, in short, non-Occitan) must involve, in one way or another, *regional* evidence, derived from strictly Occitan (or Catalan) versions of the tale, and *historical* evidence, derived from the oldest versions (prior to 1756, the year in which *JLP* was written).

PART 2

Death, Money, Love

A New Interpretation of
Jean-l'ont-pris

CHAPTER IX The Life of Truquette

To begin with, here is my own summary of the Languedocian version of the tale AT 332/*Godfather Death*, which is structurally and geographically (with *Galdric*, see Chapter XV) closest to *Jean-l'ont-pris*. The hero of this Occitan version (from Narbonne) is called Jean-de-trop.[1] His family biography, as in the fictional work of the abbé Fabre, might be divided into two parts, and each part into several segments.

Childhood of Jean-de-trop and story of his parents

A man was as poor as a church rat.[2] He had five children and was hard put to feed them, when his wife gave birth to a boy! 'What shall we call this one?' the husband asked his wife.

And she replied that they had better call him Jean-de-trop.

So the father and mother set out to look for a godfather for the child's baptism. Everyone – relations, friends and neighbours – refused to be his godfather. In the end, a poor man (in fact, it was 'Our Lord Jesus Christ', no less), to whom the couple had given a piece of bread out of charity, agreed to be the godfather. He undertook to find a godmother and the provisions for the feast.

Next morning, donkey-loads of bread, wine, meats, poultry arrived one after another. When the relations, friends and neighbours saw so many provisions, they came to see the new mother and her husband, in the hope of giving a little help with their teeth or jaws. The mother and her husband, who were kindly folk and whom all this food had put into good humour, invited them all to the baptism.

On the table, arranged for the meal that the couple gave for the occasion, there were, among much else, large bottles of old wine and fruits of all kinds; on the fire was a great pot for the soup, a tart as big as a tamis sieve, a turkey and two capons on a spit, which was turned by the eldest child.

When the baptism bell rang, the poor, old godfather arrived in a coach and four and helped the godmother out: it was Death, a skeleton of bones as white as snow. Terrified, the guests fled. 'Have no fear,' said Death to Jean-de-trop's family, 'I am your friend. All the members of your family will live for two hundred years without ever falling ill, and I shall teach my godson a secret that will make him the richest man on earth.'

Death covered herself with a cloak and a thick veil, and everyone went off to have the child baptized.

When they got back from the church, Our Lord said: 'Death and I have no need to eat. Sit down and eat your fill.'

The husband, wife and children ate and drank, and they had enough food left over for another week. They all prospered thereafter and never went short of anything.

Jean-de-trop without his parents: apprenticeship and various exploits

Jean-de-trop went to school. When he had learned to read, write and count, his godmother came to him and said:

'Jean, you are eighteen years old; it is time you learned a trade.'

'I haven't thought about it yet, godmother. I shall do as you wish.'

'You must become a physician.'

'You are making fun of me, godmother. The doctor who comes into our village knows Latin and many other things that I do not know. How could I become a physician?'

'You don't have to know anything. I shall make you a physician within the hour. When you go to a patient, if you see me at the head of the bed, you will say to the parents that they can call the notary and the priest. If you see me at the foot of the bed, you will give them a phial of liquorice water: you will tell them to place three drops in a glass of water, and the patient will be cured. No one but you will see me.'

'How can I cure the sick with liquorice water, godmother?'

'Simpleton, you won't cure them. When I am at the head of the bed, the patient will die. When I am at the foot of the bed, he will live. Off you go, you must start your new profession: when the doctor comes to this village, you will also pretend to go and see the patient. When the doctor is gone, you will say: "The patient will not live" or "He'll come to no harm with my phial".'

Jean-de-trop did as his godmother told him.

At first, seeing that he was so young and that he had not studied medicine, people did not want to believe him. However, as he was never wrong,[3] his reputation spread. It reached the neighbouring town, then travelled from town to town as far as Paris. All the rich folk of France sent for Jean-de-trop when they were ill, and he was never wrong.

One day, the king's daughter fell ill. All the doctors of Paris declared that she would die. The king's cook, who was from the same village as Jean-de-trop, told the king of his skill and assured him that if the princess could be cured, Jean would do it.

The king sent his coach to fetch Jean. When he arrived, he asked where the king's daughter was. He was led to the princess's bed-chamber. As he entered, he saw his godmother at the foot of the bed. Jean then took the father to one side and said:

'What will you give me if I cure your daughter?'

'I'll give you a cartload of silver.'

'That is not enough.'

'I shall give you one of my provinces . . . half my crown . . .' Each time Jean-de-trop replied: 'That is not enough.' In the end, he said: 'You must give me the hand of your daughter in marriage.'

'I shall,' replied the king, 'providing she agrees to marry you.'

The princess was a beautiful girl of nineteen; Jean a handsome lad of twenty-two. The princess found him attractive and said:

'If he cures me, I shall marry him.'

In two weeks, with his phial of liquorice water, Jean had cured the princess.

They married. There was a month of feasting. They loved each other dearly. But Jean, to whom Death had promised two hundred years of life, was concerned at the idea that one day he would be separated from his wife by her death.

He asked his godmother to give his wife as long a life as his own. After repeated requests, Death still refused.

'I now see that you do not have as much power as you say,' said Jean.

Jean had a small gourd in which he kept brandy for his travels. As a joke, he said to his godmother that she did not have enough power.

In order to get his godmother to prove this power, he dared her to enter the gourd. The godmother fell into the trap, made herself as small as a cricket and climbed into the bottle. Immediately Jean screwed on the stopper. He said to Death:

'I will not let you out until you have granted my wife as much life as I have.'

For a whole week, Death remained shut up in the tiny gourd. For a whole week, no one throughout the whole world died. The devil was astonished to see no damned souls arrive.

In the end, on the eighth day of her confinement, seeing that her work was behind, Death granted her godson's wife a life as long as his.

In this version from Narbonne of *Death's Godson*, the unfolding of events is very similar, even in detail, to that found in other versions of the same tale deriving from the Midi, Ariège, Catalonia, Roussillon, even Nevers, Brittany and the German-speaking lands. It should be noted, however, that the Narbonne version, collected by a folklore specialist from a plebeian from Aude about 1880, has a happy ending, whereas 'normally' the tale (number 332 in the Aarne and Thompson classification) ends in a 'cave with lights': Death, who always has the last word, takes his physician godson into a cave or cellar in which millions of candles and lamps of all kinds are burning. (Later, I shall come back to the question of the grandmother's matches in *Jean-l'ont-pris*.) Death shows the hero his own 'light of life', which, of course, is about to go out; he then twists the young man's neck. Curtain.

I shall now divide up this Narbonne version of *Jean-de-trop*, which I shall abbreviate as *JDT*,[4] into a number of segments; these correspond, point by point, with homologous segments of *Jean-l'ont-pris*. I shall then comment on this comparison. To begin with, Table 1 briefly summarizes this double segmentation.

It goes without saying that by tracing these two narratives in parallel I am in no way claiming that one derives literally from the other. It is easy to demonstrate that *JDT* belongs precisely to a whole family of versions, from the Midi, Brittany and even Germany, of AT 332.

For its part, *Jean-l'ont-pris* derives from one or several oral versions of AT 332 that also belong to this 'family', which includes an archaic *JDT* of the eighteenth century. These versions came originally (from a very distant origin) from Germany; they underwent a transition in Switzerland and other frontier regions; they had long been perfectly Occitanized; they were circulating throughout the Midi during the

Table 1

COMPARISON OF *JEAN-DE-TROP* AND *JEAN-L'ONT-PRIS*

A = *JDT*	B = *JLP*
A1: Marriage of a poor couple.	B1: Nothing.
A2: This couple, already parents of five children, conceive a sixth and last one.	B2: Truquette and Margot, a poor couple, conceive a first and last child.
A3: Birth of this child, Jean-de-trop, and the search for a god-father.	B3: Nothing.
A4: She-asses bring provisions for the festivities.	B4: Asses bring provisions for the festivities.
A5: Nothing.	B5: Marriage of the poor couple (Truquette and Margot).
A6: Banquet long after the wedding and just before the baptism.	B6: Banquet just after the wedding and shortly before the baptism: a menu homologous with that of A6.
A7: Nothing.	B7: Birth of Jean-l'ont-pris.
A8: Just as everyone is setting out for the church, Death, the godmother, alights naked from her coach outside JDT's house.	B8: Just as Margot is about to go out for the first time since giving birth, the grandmother comes down bare-headed from her apartment opposite JLP's house.
A9: She causes a scandal among the neighbours.	B9: She causes a scandal among the neighbours.
A10: She promises, in all seriousness, that the couple will make their own fortune.	B10: She promises, jokingly, that the couple will make their fortune.
A11: After a while, she tells the couple how they are to make their fortune.	B11: After a while, she tells the couple how they are to make their fortune.

A12: The couple, JDT's parents, make their fortune, described in general terms.	B12: The couple, JLP's parents, make their fortune, described in detail.
A13: JDT's parents disappear discreetly from the narrative.	B13: JLP's parents disappear from the narrative in spectacular fashion.
A14: Death becomes JDT's teacher.	B14: The grandmother becomes JLP's teacher.
A15: JDT accepts Death's lessons.	B15: JLP rejects his grandmother's lessons.
A16: Thanks to Death's gifts, JDT marries the king's daughter.	B16: JLP outwits the forces of death in general, after outwitting his grandmother in particular, and gets a treasure from her.
A17: JDT outwits Death and wins concessions from her that will prolong his marriage to the king's daughter.	B17: Thanks to this treasure, JLP seems to be able or obliged to marry the rich peasant's daughter, whom he has recently made pregnant.

youth of the abbé Fabre from about 1730 to 1760. These versions, which have since either disappeared or been forgotten as such, are the common source both of Fabre's literary reworking of the tale, *Jean-l'ont-pris*, and of *Jean-de-trop* (collected before 1885), a version from the Midi of AT 332, passed down orally from generation to generation in the Languedocian region, and, more particularly, in the area around Narbonne; this took place between 1750 and 1880. These versions also gave rise to the tale of *Galdric* from Roussillon (see Chapter XV).

We shall now take each of the episodes or 'segments' as numbered in Table 1:

A1: *Marriage of Jean-de-trop's parents.*
B1: *Nothing.*

The marriage of Jean-l'ont-pris's parents enters the sequence only at B5 of Table 1, whereas that of Jean-de-trop's parents occurs earlier in relation to the Narbonne narrative.

A2: *The poor couple conceive JDT: their sixth and last child.*
B2: *Truquette and Margot, also poor, conceive JLP, their first and last child (pre-marital conception).*

In short, the Narbonne tale characterizes the poverty of Jean-de-trop's parents by lack of food: 'They already had great difficulty feeding their five children.' Similarly, Jean-l'ont-pris's parents are nicknamed *meurt-de-faim* [25, 26].[5] The adjective used (Occitan *poure* = *pauvre*) is the same in the homologous sequences at the beginning of both texts: *l'homme pauvre* ['the poor man', *JDT*]; *mon pauvre père* ['my poor father', *JLP*, 6].

But Fabre's narrative went beyond the initial status of a folk-tale and became a completed literary work: the author embodies his hero in the first person, whereas a simple folk-tale never says 'I'. Fabre broke open the constraining framework of the folk-tale, which in his hands became a long 'novella'; as a result, many other, more precise details are provided about the poverty of Jean-l'ont-pris's parents. His mother was a bastard – indeed, an illegitimate birth is generally associated with the poverty of persons afflicted with this so-called taint. Moreover, Jean-l'ont-pris's mother and father are in no way land-owners; they do not own a single spadeful of earth. Furthermore, Truquette is a migrant worker, from Rouergue, and therefore *a priori* a victim of poverty and discrimination.[6] However, he does have the advantages of a trade: he is a cobbler. Indeed, this trade competes with some others (woodman, peasant . . .) in several of the versions of AT 332 from the Midi, France, Italy, Switzerland, etc.

Truquette's courting of Margot is described at some length by the abbé Fabre, and it culminates in a pre-marital conception. In most of the French and other versions of AT 332 that have been collected by folklore specialists in the nineteenth and twentieth centuries, the child who is to become 'Death's godson', or the hero of the tale, is born quite normally after nine months or more of marriage. Does this mean that the abbé Fabre was himself responsible for altering this element? Did he quite simply invent this 'pregnancy before marriage' in order to make his narrative more picaresque? I don't think so. A

very old version of AT 332, collected and versified by the German
dramatist Ayrer, who died in 1605, also has 'Death's godson' conceived well before marriage.[7] Now the version of AT 332 presented
by Fabre about 1755 is, together with Geuellette's *Mille et Un Quarts
d'heure* of 1712, the first to emerge in written literature in France.
The chronology of the old versions leads one to believe, therefore,
that AT 332 arrived in France (see Chapter XIV) at a relatively late
date (after 1500?) from Germany, the archaic epicentre of the tale.
Thus it is possible that Fabre was able to use as a source an early,
oral, French version of AT 332 that was still closer to the models that
had come directly from Germany: in this version, as in those of Ayrer
and Wolff, the hero may well have been conceived before marriage.
Furthermore, it is a fact (see the end of this chapter) that Fabre *also*
used an Occitanized version that had unquestionably come from
German-speaking Switzerland. It should not be forgotten that for
our abbé, as for other Christian authors of this kind who did so much
to spread the moralizing aspect of AT 332, one aim was to show that
peasants 'of this kind' as depicted by the tale [87] are *not* good
Christians.[8] It is a short step from this to say that their first child
is conceived before marriage – a step that is rapidly crossed by both
Ayrer and Jean-Baptiste Fabre.

A3: *Birth of the child, Jean-de-trop, and the search for a godfather.*
B3: *Nothing.*

The birth of Jean-l'ont-pris will be related *after* the marriage of his
parents: at this stage of the narrative, the wedding has not yet taken
place, despite Margot's pregnancy. Fabre therefore shifts this nuptial
episode; it takes place later, in segment B7 of *Jean-l'ont-pris* (Table
1), instead of in segment A3, as in *Jean-de-trop*. This is why B3 in
Table 1 bears the word 'nothing'.
However, the similarity at the beginning of the two narratives will
be noted: Jean-de-trop's parents want to find a name for their son at
once, and they decide, in the third sentence of the Narbonne story, to
call this boy Jean-de-trop. Similarly, in *Jean-l'ont-pris*, Fabre's hero
mentions first his parents' poor background; then, in the same breath,
at the very beginning of his narration, he tells us that his name,
followed by a nickname (a nickname which, moreover, will be given

to him fully only three years later), is Jean-l'ont-pris (Jean-l'an-près, in Occitan). In each case, Jean-de-trop and Jean-l'ont-pris bear, as Fabre emphasizes, 'a name [a nickname] which is not that of their father'. The trisyllabic and consonantal resemblance between the two names Jean-l'ont-pris and Jean-de-trop is an additional clue to the kinship of the two stories. This clue is insufficient in itself, but it becomes significant when linked to other innumerable similarities in overall structure, individual detail and sequence of incident to be found from beginning to end in both texts.

Segment A3 of *Jean-de-trop*, which I have summarized above, tells at some length of the search for a godfather [9] for the newborn child: this search takes up over thirty sentences in the Narbonne version of *JDT*. In this it conforms perfectly to the general structure of AT 332 to be found in the most geographically dispersed versions of the tale throughout the Christian world of Europe and America.

The search for a godfather in these various versions, from the earliest to the most recent, raises two problems.

(1) First, he must be a 'just' godfather. That is why, in many variants of AT 332, a number of candidatures are rejected in turn, including those of Our Lord Jesus Christ, the Good God, the devil, St Peter, a king, etc.: these various characters are *unjust* in varying degrees. One refuses entry into paradise to certain people, creates a world that is unjust or makes the young die before the old;[10] or, again, in the case of the devil, he is reproached with the terrible injustices of hell, over which he presides. Death, on the contrary, is just, since he takes everybody without distinction – the great and the small, the rich and the poor. Therefore Death will be chosen as godfather of the baby of the two poor parents.[11]

This solution is satisfactory from the point of view of the various finalities offered by AT 332. This tale is intended to flatter a certain popular egalitarianism. By 1755, thanks to Jean-Jacques Rousseau, notions of secular egalitarianism had become widespread; but before that date, the ideology of equality was above all a religious egalitarianism before death. The medieval Dance of Death, in which rich and poor took part in the saraband of skeletons, was a particularly strong expression of this ideology, and it was one that survived into later centuries.

However, it should not be thought that by exalting death (as equitable) and by attacking Christ (as unjust), A T 332 has an anti-Christian function. In fact, Christianity has always maintained that justice is not of this world. To affirm the injustice of creation and the fact that only death is equitable is not, therefore, in contradiction with Christian apologetics; on the contrary, such a notion is at the heart of A T 332, in its predicatory and theatrical forms, throughout the late medieval and baroque periods.

(2) Nevertheless, the very serious question of the sex of Death arises in the version of A T 332 to be found in the Latin countries. In German-speaking regions there is no problem: *der Tod* ['death'] is masculine. 'He' becomes, therefore, the boy's godfather without any difficulty. If various specialists, basing their conclusions on precise texts, are to be believed, the point of departure of A T 332, in its definitive structure, is a pun on *der Tod* ['death'] and *der Tod* (a word which, in Franconian dialect, means 'godfather').[12] Thus, in terms of other texts (see Chapter XIV), the Franconian origins of A T 332 in its classic form would appear to be situated about 1300.

In Latin countries, the word 'death' [*la mort*] is feminine. How could a feminine entity be a god*father*? The earliest French versions of A T 332, which preserve direct traces of its importation from beyond the Rhine, did not hesitate to overcome this difficulty by simply imitating their models. A number of versions of A T 332, even ones from the Midi, involve, therefore, *une Mort* who is a god*father*. Others, more meticulous (in particular, in Ariège), say that Death is *both* godfather and godmother. Versions from Aquitaine use a male Death, flanked by his major-domo or lord high executioner, to whom he delegates his work on several occasions; he, too, is male.[13]

The Narbonne version of *Jean-de-trop*, which is otherwise so close to the precise texture of the other French versions of A T 332, invented, on this point, a highly original solution: it begins, following the primitive Germanic and French models of the story, by initiating a quest for the *godfather*[14] by the hero's father. In order to do this, it makes use of the character of *Our Lord* [*Nostre-Segne*], who is not blamed for injustice as he is in other versions of A T 332; instead, it sets up 'Our Lord Jesus Christ' in a condition of semi-companionship with Death. Christ, therefore, becomes quite naturally the godfather of the child Jean-de-trop; and Death, as in other Occitan versions (that of Maugard, from Ariège, for example), as also in the

Italian, Catalan, Castilian – in short, Latin – versions, becomes the godmother, a kind of 'eternal feminine'.

In writing *Jean-l'ont-pris*, the abbé Fabre simplified these problems of 'looking for a godfather' which we have examined in *Jean-de-trop*. In effect, he has transformed Death, from the godmother that she was, into a grandmother (moreover, this transformation of godmother into grandmother may already have been carried out in the original versions from the Midi that Fabre used to construct his *Jean-l'ont-pris*). It should be noted that by acting as he did, he in no way did violence to the initial text that was his raw material: the word *pepin* – *pepi* in Occitan, and especially in Ariège, and included in one particular version of A T 332 (*Almanach de l'Ariège*, 1895) – means both 'grandfather' *and* 'godfather';[15] while in traditional France, both north and south, from the sixteenth to the nineteenth century, the grandmother, if still alive at the time, was a natural choice to serve as her grandson's godmother.[16] This is why the Occitan term *meirino*, from the Tarn to the Var, corresponds to the French *marraine* ['god-mother'], but also to *grand-mère* and, more generally, to the eldest woman in the household; the synonyms being *grand* (*grand-mère*) and *meirino*.[17] In this way, J L P's 'grandmother' is certainly the homo-logue of Jean-de-trop's *meirino*.

Furthermore, on this conceptual identity – in any case desirable, if not always achieved – between the functions of grandfather or grand-mother and godfather or godmother there is no shortage of recent documents; they confirm what we already knew about the period from the sixteenth to the early nineteenth century. In northern France (Argonne), the abbé Lallement,[18] who possessed an excellent knowledge of local tradition, noted in 1914 that 'in earlier times the honour of godfatherhood, especially where the eldest child [our J L P] was concerned, was reserved for the grandparents, but this custom is disappearing [in the twentieth century]'. It may be objected that this may apply to northern France, but there is plenty of evidence in the south to confirm it. In addition to the observation (already quoted in a note) of the Comte de Villeneuve concerning the region of the lower Rhône in the 1880s, we have the decisive example of Ariège (comté de Foix), with the equivalence, noted earlier, of the words *pepi* and *pepin*. In Périgord, an indisputably Occitan province, Eugène Le Roy and the abbé Rocal confirmed, quite independently of each other, in the 1890s and again in 1920, that 'the grandparents are honoured for their functions as godparents. They even take on the title when they have not actually held their grandson over the baptismal font.'[19] So the situation is exactly the same in Ariège and Périgord, which stresses the unanimous reactions of the culture of the Midi on this question: grandfather and grandmother are godfather and godmother *unofficially* even when they do not carry the official title. So the abbé Fabre had no difficulty in shifting the function of godmother, as it exists in tale AT 332, to that of grandmother in his novella, since the two roles largely overlap, even at the popular linguistic level. The same confusion of roles exists in Armagnac (an Occitan-speaking region) and in Savoie (a Franco-Provençal region).[20]

So Jean-l'ont-pris is both his grandmother's grandson and her godson. He is Death's godson. Indeed, it is his grandmother who brings him up, as a godmother should (and as does Jean-de-trop's godmother), after his parents' disappearance.[21]

It was useless, at the beginning of *Jean-l'ont-pris*, to look for a godmother, since she was already appointed in the person of the grandmother (Margot's mother). However, one finds in *Jean-l'ont-pris* an equivalent of the *Christ–Death* or *godfather–godmother* couples that are to characterize the earlier versions of *Jean-de-trop*. This is the unmarried couple, surgeon–Death or surgeon–grandmother. This couple functions as godfather–godmother in relation to the hero Jean-l'ont-pris, since, according to Franco-Occitan tradition, the grandfather was a godfather already available to the newborn child. It should be remembered that the future 'grandmother' had initially conceived the bastard Margot, Jean-l'ont-pris's mother, after an illegitimate affair with a local surgeon. This surgeon, by virtue of his profession, has the further advantage of stressing the medical vocation of his grandson and functional godson, Jean-l'ont-pris, who, through his structural role within AT 332, is in effect Death's godson; he is also (in the spirit of the physician Death's godson in AT 332) something of an amateur physician himself. I shall come back to this.

A4: *She-asses bring back provisions for the festivities.*
B4: *Asses bring back provisions for the festivities.*

In *Jean-de-trop*, it is she-asses [*saumos*], commandeered by the supernatural godfather, that bring the 'provisions' [*provisieus*] for the baptismal festivities: bread, wine, meat, poultry. In *Jean-l'ont-pris*, in which the supernatural is subjacent but masked, it is two asses that bring back from Nîmes the 'provisions' [*provisiouns*, 14 and 15], together with wedding garments for the two betrotheds, Truquette and Margot. The parallelism of the two segments (A4 and B4) of *Jean-de-trop* and *Jean-l'ont-pris* is carried far, since Fabre writes [15] about the provisions carried on the backs of asses: 'The rest was to gorge themselves: tell me if there wasn't enough to feast all the *friends and relations*!' While *Jean-de-trop* tells us: 'When the *relations, friends* and neighbours saw so many provisions, they came to see the new mother and her husband, in the hope of giving a little help with their teeth.' It is remarkable that the same sentence (friends, relations and 'gorging'), and the word 'provisions', should feature in the same structural position in both *Jean-l'ont-pris* and *Jean-de-trop*. This is a way of saying, or rather confirming, that these two texts are closely related. Another clue: on the subject of the invitation given to these people, the same word, for the same scene, occurs in *JLP* (*convidats*, 'guests'), in *JDT*[22] (*convideroun . . ., convidats*, pp. 187 and 188) and in the Catalan version of A T 322 (*convit* in Amades, 1950, p. 244; *convidats* in Caseponce [Roussillon], 1907, p. 74).

A5: *Nothing.*
B5: *Marriage of the poor couple.*

The marriage of two poor people has already taken place in *Jean-de-trop* in segment A1 of Table 1. Segment A5 is therefore 'nothing'. By contrast, B5 sees the marriage of the poor couple Margot and Truquette in *Jean-l'ont-pris*, which had led up to the girl's pregnancy and the sending of the asses to Nîmes to fetch provisions for the festivities. The ceremony of the wedding is briefly mentioned in a half sentence of *Jean-l'ont-pris*: 'Would you believe, my lord, that on the wedding-day, either on their way to the church or coming back . . .' [15].

A6: *Banquet: sometime after the wedding (at the church) and just before JDT's baptism.*

B6: *Banquet: just after the wedding of Margot and Truquette and just before the birth and baptism of JLP.*

Structurally, and by means of a simple correction, the position of this banquet may be compared in both texts (A6 and B6 of Table 1). In *Jean-l'ont-pris* the banquet occurs immediately after the parents' marriage and some time (thirteen days) before Jean-l'ont-pris's baptism. In *Jean-de-trop*, the banquet occurs some time (about thirteen years)[23] after the parents' marriage and immediately before the baptism of the hero JDT.

This banquet is treated in the two narratives in a strictly similar way. Taking *Jean-l'ont-pris* first, Fabre's novella announces [14] the wedding festivities that *pave the way* for the birth (in a few days) of the baby JLP with the following words: 'Never, my lord, could there ever have been such an expensive wedding in Solorgues.' Then this text suggests [17], immediately after the complete description of the feast, the following conclusion: 'Oh, I'm sure your lordship will agree that poor folk who give themselves such airs of greatness cannot *reign*. That belongs to noblemen like yourself, and even, in the end, it would not be a miracle to see you drowned head over heels.'

In *Jean-de-trop*, the corresponding comment on the festivities, which occur after the birth of the hero, is: '*Never* had a *king*'s son had such a baptism' (*JDT*, p. 188).

In both cases, then, we find the same type of dithyrambic praise beginning with the word 'never'. We also find the identical reference, which is burlesque in the first case, serious in the second, to the *royal* pretensions of such a feast. Jean-de-trop is literally compared to a 'king's son'; later, far from home, and quite independently of this judgement, he is to become a king's son-in-law. Similarly, Truquette and Jean-l'ont-pris are compared on several occasions in the course of the narration, the first to a king, the second, implicitly, to a king's son, and, explicitly, to 'my prince, my king, my emperor' [41]; this comparison, in turn, is independent of the fact that Jean-l'ont-pris is to become the son-in-law of a notable, Sestier. Pursuing this series of similarities, the resemblances between the *menus* of the two banquets are essential: in *JDT*, after the non-meat food (bread, creams, fruit, girdle-cakes, soup, tart), the climax of the meal is reached with the poultry, which form the main course ('a turkey and two capons on a

spit, which was turned by the eldest child'). In the second version of
Jean-l'ont-pris the meal proceeds in a similar way, even if no child has
yet been born to turn the spit: non-meat foods (pastries, followed by
various kinds of fish) are served first; then, as a culmination, *half a
dozen magpies, a good pair of crows turning on the spit*. The very
similarity of the verb in the imperfect (*virar*, in Occitan, 'to turn')
underlines the homology of the two lists of birds:

Jean-de-trop	*Jean-l'ont-pris*
Register of tamed poultry:	Register of wild birds:
a turkey	half a dozen magpies
two capons turned [*viravo*] on a spit by the eldest son[24]	a good pair of crows turning [*viravoun*] on the spit

It will be noted that in *Jean-de-trop* the verb 'to turn' (the spit)
implies the action of a person (the eldest son, already born). In *Jean-l'ont-pris*, it is the food that turns (in the passive); it is moved by a
person who remains anonymous in the story, since there is no eldest
son before the birth of the baby JLP.

We can ignore in passing a few obvious similarities:[25] kitchen
equipment (cooking pots, grill, bottles and cask) is present in both
JDT and *JLP*; libations of wine are mentioned on both occasions;
pots of *farinette* [girdle-cakes] of traditional Languedocian cooking in
the eighteenth century, in *Jean-l'ont-pris*, are replaced by *Jean-de-trop's white bread*, since this tale was adapted, partially at least, to the
tastes of the day by the peasant narrators of the nineteenth century –
the characters, therefore, eat white bread, according to the habits that
had reached the countryside from the cities after the Revolution. We
should note the common mention of the tamis sieve. In *Jean-de-trop*
the banquet includes a tart as big as a *tamis* for sieving flour. In *Jean-l'ont-pris*, the paragraph that *immediately* follows the list of victuals
for the banquet states that one could guess the coming ruin of the
young couple, as if one were reading it while turning[26] a *tamis* sieve –
this 'turning of the sieve',[27] a way of playing with the wheel of
fortune or 'roulette', was a mode of divination currently practised in
Languedoc. The essential difference between the two banquets is
obviously to be found in the opposition between civilized food (*Jean-*

de-trop: turkey, capons) and wild food (*Jean-l'ont-pris*: magpies, crows). In *Jean-de-trop*, the listing of the dishes places the meal unquestionably in the category of mouth-watering *haute cuisine*: white table-cloth, a large bottle of old wine, snow-white bread, creams, various fruits, girdle-cakes, soup, tarts, turkey, capons. In *Jean-l'ont-pris* the dishes consist of wild or flesh-eating animals: frogs, *roussette* [a kind of small shark], *plus a magnificent fox that the hunter of La Boissière had killed the night before in the Garrigue de Mus . . .* not to mention, of course, the crows and half a dozen magpies, the latter being associated with misfortune[28] and one of the favourite dishes [50] of the grandmother Death, if not of her grandson. To these wild and/or flesh-eating animals is added, in *JLP*, an extraordinary enumeration of wild fruits from the forest or scrubland that are not part of normal cultivation: cornel-berries, arbutus-berries, mulberries, sloes, chestnuts, hazelnuts, hackberries – which Margot throws under her leg – sorb apples, etc. Such food, offered here to wedding guests, would normally be given to cattle, not to humans.

It should be noted that other versions of AT 332 from the Midi also stress, as does *Jean-l'ont-pris* in the case of the wedding breakfast, the poverty-stricken character of the baptismal meal whenever Death is present at it: the meal consists entirely of grilled sardines; in two versions, the meal is spread on an ordinary food basket, which is simply turned upside-down, etc. This basket or *banasta* is reminiscent indeed of the *banastadas* of provisions [15] that are eaten at Truquette's feast at an exactly homologous place in the narrative.[29]

The essential opposition, in relation to this poverty-stricken character of the meal, is still that set up between *Jean-l'ont-pris* and *Jean-de-trop*: at Jean-de-trop's baptismal banquet, Death had not yet appeared in the narrative. She arrives on the scene only in the next paragraph. On the occasion of the gastronomic celebration, the food had been provided in miraculous abundance by the godfather, Christ himself; it was only to be expected, therefore, that the food would be rich and luxurious. At the banquet to celebrate Jean-l'ont-pris's baptism, however, the grandmother Death was already present. She had symbolically thrown in front of the threshold of the house where the feast was to be held her twenty-two packets of matches, the significance of which deserves analysis. In the circumstances, one could hardly expect luxury and refinement! So macabre a banquet had to be wild in character, that is, in harmony with the particular characteristics of Death, as they are perceived in innumerable versions of AT 332. Among these versions, by far the most important (until the establishment of the German epicentre in the sixteenth century) is a fine Icelandic text of the fourteenth century. This was followed in the fifteenth century by an English version, in the sixteenth century by an Italian and in the early eighteenth century by a French. The various versions are quite categorical: Death makes an appearance in them at the moment of confrontation with the hero (Death's godson, or father of this godson) as a *wild* character who lives in the forest, near a large tree, on moorland, in the desert or in some wild area – that is to say, on land that either has never been cultivated or has returned to its wild state. Fabre had an intimate knowledge of the extraordinarily vivid folklore of his native Languedoc. He laid great stress on the wild environment surrounding the grandmother Death; hence the menu of the feast that she honours with her presence: flesh-eating animals, wild berries or fruit from trees grown in the forest (chestnuts). Very interesting from this point of view is the allusion to the fox *that the hunter of La Boissière had killed . . . in the Garrigue de Mus.* La Boissière is, in fact, a village quite close to Solorgues: there is a large castle there (see Cassini's map), whose owner, the local baron, enjoyed the privilege of maintaining a professional hunter. This domestic had the task of exterminating the wild animals, foxes included, which were then sold. Given that there was no real forest around La Boissière, the wild woodlands outside the cultivated agricultural lands, from which the Death of AT 332 is supposed to originate, are represented above all in Fabre's reference to the *garrigue* de Mus. It is there that the hunter, who provides the wild fauna for the banquet given by the grandmother, killed the fox. Ecologically, the *garrigue* is a remnant of the original forest lands of the Mediterranean countries, ruined by the grazing of cattle and by the fires started by shepherds. In it, the bushes, which yield wild berries, have replaced trees as such. Later, Jean-l'ont-pris is to throw himself into a determined revolt against his grandmother Death. Suddenly he is associated, no longer with the *hunter*[30] of the castle at La Boissière, but with the most antithetical opponent of this Nimrod,

who is none other than the *gamekeeper* [45] of the castle at La
Boissière,[31] who, like the other officers of this manor (see Chapter
XI), proves to be hostile to the forces of death.

Moreover, by means of the correlations of which Fabre has the
secret and which are dotted throughout his work like so many keys,
our author has specifically associated this fox, eaten at the wedding
feast of Truquette and Margot, with the grandmother Death. On the
whole, the abbé's lists of provisions, at the wedding feast, take the
form of multiples of two: four *setiers* of wine, four pounds of hazelnuts, a pair of capons, etc. In the case of the fox, however, Fabre
takes great care, in the second version of his tale, to use an odd
number; he warns us that the flesh of this animal 'is not worth more
than eleven sous without the skin'. This links us to that multiple of
eleven, which is quite close to the text (a few lines before), concerning
the twenty-two packets of matches (twice times eleven) which the
'wasteful grandmother' [16] throws in front of the door of the house
at the moment when the guests are about to sit down at the table
placed outside the house.[32] Here Fabre plays with almost diabolical
subtlety on a reference in the second version of his tale to the first.

These apparently innocent matches play a crucial role in the biography of the grandmother, and even of Margot and Truquette.
Their manufacture (by the grandmother, assisted by Margot) and the
buying of the sulphur required in their making are mentioned on a
number of occasions at the beginning of the novella. Later the grandmother is to use them in order to erect on her own head a sort of
tripod or combustible hat that will conceal her right eye and reveal
her left, 'the evil eye'; she will present this head-covering during the
lessons on polite behaviour that she gives Jean-l'ont-pris, when the
boy is finally deprived of both father and mother. Lastly, it is under
a pile of these same matches that J L P discovers at the crucial moment
his dead grandmother's treasure.

These matches are constantly associated with our grandmother
Death at almost each of her appearances in the narrative. They are
the equivalent of the candles and oil-lamps, so many lights of life, to
be found in most of the Occitan and French, European and Europeo-
American versions of A T 332. We know that these lights go out in
turn, at the very moment of each person's death, and that they are
placed under the constant surveillance of Death (in this case, of

grandmother Death). The Occitan and Catalan word *lumet*, which means 'little light' or 'small lamp', and which is used in the Catalan versions of AT 332 when referring to the cellar of lights,[33] establishes a very plausible association of ideas between the lights of AT 332 and Fabre's matches. In his novella Fabre used the Occitan word *brouquéttas*, but, speaking French as perfectly as he did, he was well aware that the French translation of this word *brouquétta* is *allumette*.

It may be objected that Fabre's tale differs radically from AT 332 on the question of these lights of life: they appear *at the end* of most of the versions of AT 332, at the moment when Death finally takes the hero into the cellar, where he will die; this cellar is filled with thousands or millions of candles, lamps, etc. However, the matches of the grandmother/Death appear essentially at the beginning of Fabre's story.

I shall suggest two answers to this objection:

(1) The matches are also to be found in *Jean-l'ont-pris*, just as in AT 332, in a final episode, the death of the principal character, here the grandmother/Death: she leaves behind her treasure buried under matches.

(2) Certain French versions of AT 332, several of which are Occitan and one Breton, possess a remarkable peculiarity: in them Death offers the light of life (a candle or two candles, depending on the case) as a present at the beginning of the tale. This is what happens in the version from Ariège collected by Joisten (1965, p. 62). The versions of AT 332 from Ariège are particularly valuable to us because in overall structure and in considerable detail they are often the closest to the 'Audois' *JDT* and the 'Gardois' *JLP*. In Joisten's version, Death, who is both godfather and godmother, is talking after the baptism with the father of the child who has just been baptized. The father wants this child, who has just been christened Juste (like his godfather, Death), to become a doctor. 'So Death said to the father: "Ask of me whatever you will. But if you see me behind the door, he [the future doctor] must not insist on wanting to cure the patient, for he will die in any case." And Death gave a candle to the father and said to him: "As long as this candle burns, your son will be in good health; but the day he disobeys me, the candle will go out and that will be the end of him . . ." ' (There follows an account of the successful career of the young doctor up to his death, which is brought

about because he deceives Death himself.) In Arnaudin's *Contes popu-laires de la Grande Lande*[34] (a version from the Lande, and therefore an Occitan version of AT 332) Death acts in a similar way towards the father who is looking for a godfather for his child; but, this time, Death gives him two candles [*candelouns*] of life, one for the son, the second for another man whose identity is not specified. Versions of AT 332 of the same type (an initial gift of two candles by Death to the hero) must have existed in Spain, the nearest neighbour to our Occitania, since such versions have been rediscovered in those re-positories of ancient Castilian culture represented by the Spanish-speaking Mexican isolates of the south-west region of the United States.[35] Lastly, to return to the French zone in Brittany (another country of a linguistic or peripheral minority, which functions like Occitania as a repository of AT 332), we also know of two versions of *Godfather Death* in which the lights of life appear at the beginning of the tale. One of these is by F. Gueriff:[36] in the course of the action that takes place in a vague, but not too distant past, approximately in the sixteenth or seventeenth century, Ankou (Death) gives a candle to the mother of a child whose godfather Death has agreed to become. This candle, given at the beginning of the narrative, has been taken, moreover, from the candles burning on the high altar of the church; it represents the child's light of life. In another Breton version of AT 332, that from Ille-et-Vilaine published by Adolphe Orain in 1901 (pp. 211ff.), the lights of life, which are those of all the local inhabi-tants and which burn in thousands at night on the *lande* ['moor'], also appear to the doctor at the beginning of the tale even before he makes his fortune on their account; even before he makes his fortune, more exactly, thanks to the diagnostic abilities concerning the survival or death of a particular patient that are conferred upon him by a know-ledge of these lights.

In the version collected by Orain, the supernatural entity who gives the doctor his powers is not Death himself, but the devil (this 'dia-bolical' variant is also to be found in several versions of AT 332, in the minority in France and abroad; it is also to be found – I shall come back to this in *JLP* – in the character of Quincarlot/Cancrelas).

To sum up, then, various versions of AT 332 have circulated throughout French territory; some of them possess a remarkable peculiarity, unknown in versions of AT 332 to be found in countries east of France. The candles of life appear *at the beginning of the tale*;

they are neither given as presents nor displayed, for the benefit of the hero or other mortals, by Death, or even by the devil, whether a single candle, a pair of candles or even thousands of candles are involved. These phenomena beyond the Death who uses them are linked both to the divine (church candles) and to the diabolical (lights on the moors). These versions are old ones: Gueriff's makes specific reference to an episode that occurred at least before 1750 or 1780; that from the Landes (Arnaudin) contains a final episode in which the hero, in order to escape Death, refuses to bite into an apple. Now this episode has entirely disappeared from the other French versions of AT 332; it is to be found as such only in versions deriving from Quebec, which obviously represent an earlier version of the tale, contemporary with the period before 1763, when Quebec would be constantly replenished, culturally, from France itself – which was no longer the case after 1763, when Canada was lost to France.

The grandmother's matches certainly belong to this schema, even if, as matches, slightly different from the candles of the original tale that served as their model, they represent a literary innovation, due to abbé Fabre's cunning imagination. Like the candles given by Death in Ariège or in the Grande Lande, they represent a *gift* given to the inhabitants of Solorgues by the *spendthrift* or wasteful grandmother [16]. They cannot be given by the grandmother to the hero J L P, who will only be born a few days later; but they are distributed nevertheless (in the Occitano-Landaise and Breton versions) to no one in particular, to the other 'mortals' of the region (*the riff-raff dancing in front of the door*, as Fabre puts it in the second version of his tale). There are hundreds, perhaps thousands, of these matches, since they are distributed in whole packets – just as there are thousands of candles on the moor or in Death's cellar. But the memory of two candles or of the pair of lights of life to be found in other Occitano-Landais, Breton, Spanish and Armenian versions are to be found in Fabre's tale in the form of the *twenty* or *twenty-two* packets of matches (a multiple of two in each case) which the wasteful grandmother distributes liberally. These matches have something diabolical about them: they are specifically tipped with sulphur; Margot also makes large quantities of them for her mother. But like the candles in the Gueriff version, they preserve a link with the church, since it is after the return from the religious ceremony at the church that the grandmother throws them in all directions in front of the door of the house. Among these innumerable sulphur-tipped sticks, there is certainly one that will represent the hero's light of life. It is desirable that it is not used; that is why this hero will have the opportunity of rediscovering much later a whole pile of unused matches, with a magnificent treasure underneath, after the providential death of his grandmother Death. They are certainly lights of life! They do not yet announce death, but, on the contrary, life and happiness, because no one has had the idea or the means, for the moment, of lighting them.[37]

Fabre stresses that the grandmother throws the matches *in front of the door* of the house, that is to say, towards the outside, towards the street; the text of the second version is quite clear about this: 'and just as she was about to sit down at the table inside the house, she threw into the midst of the riff-raff dancing in front of the door twenty packets of matches . . .' Later, in both versions of *JLP* [26], the grandmother brings out this opposition between the 'inside' of the house, where the lucky guests 'eat their fill', and the 'outside' in the street, where the village riff-raff 'gnawed at the bones we threw out of the window'. It is remarkable, therefore, that in both *Jean-l'ont-pris* and *Jean-de-trop*, at the moment she arrives at the feast (post-nuptial, pre-baptismal in *JLP* and also post-nuptial, pre-baptismal in *JDT*), Death is placed initially and explicitly, coming from the outside, in front of the door (the outside door that opens on to the room where the meal is taking place). *Davans la pôrta*, says the Occitan version of *Jean-de-trop* (p. 187) . . . *Davant la pôrta*, says the Occitan version of *Jean-l'ont-pris* [16].

It is a crucial position! There are, indeed, eleven versions of AT 332 – seven of which derive from southern France, one from central France (Nevers), one from Venice and one each from Germany and Catalonia – which, with a greater or lesser degree of elaboration, unequivocally stress the two contrasted positions of Death.[38]

When Death is *in front of the door* (and has, therefore, not yet entered the house), he is not dangerous: he is in any case outside the house; he may even be perceived at this point as a dispenser of favours, candles or lights of life that are not yet consumed; he therefore promises long life and prosperity to the interested parties. However, when Death is *behind the door*, in the house,[39] possibly at the bedside of the patient or near him, then he is deadly for the patient, or deadly even for the ageing hero–doctor who for so long has been his lucky protégé.

Of the eight French versions, three are from Ariège (Perbosc and Cézerac manuscripts, tale 39; Mir and Delample, 1948, p. 109; Joisten, 1965, p. 62); one is Catalano-Roussillonnais,[40] and very close to both *JDT* and *JLP*; one, the most detailed in this respect, is from the Landes: it also possesses certain remarkable archaic features (Arnaudin, pp. 578 and 586); two are Languedocian (*JDT* and *JLP*); one is from Nevers (Millien and Delarue manuscripts, A T 332, version D, collected about 1880, same details as in Arnaudin, p. 578). To which one should add a Breton version (Sébillot, 1885, p. 429) and a Spanish version (Busk, 1870, p. 129), in both of which Death moves from in front of to *behind* the door, from the outside to the inside of the hero's house through the keyhole (Brittany) or by creeping under the door (Spain), in order to kill the doctor who has tricked Death or become too old; in the case of the Spanish version, this hero–doctor is called John the Hungry. This is reminiscent of the fact that our *Jean-l'ont-pris* is born of a family of *meurt-de-faim*.

Let us return to *JLP*: when she gratuitously throws in the direction of the crowd outside and in front of the door her twenty-two packets of unused matches, the grandmother establishes herself in the early stages of the novella in the role of Death as initially a source of prosperity; this role characterizes the character of Death in the earlier stages of A T 332, before this character becomes, towards the end of the tale, identified once again with its strictly lethal vocation, when men's lights of life go out.

Later (see Chapter XII), J L P is to barricade himself *behind his door* in order to prevent, among other perils, the 'ghost' of his dead grandmother coming to disturb him behind this door as he draws up a list of the treasure that she has left him [68] . . .

Let us return to the rest of Table 1.

A7: *Nothing.*
B7: *Birth of the child Jean-l'ont-pris.*

Let us return in fact to Table 1 and compare the two columns. The stagger-effect between the births of the two heroes is identical to that between the weddings of their parents. The marriage of Jean-de-trop's parents takes place in A1; that of Jean-l'ont-pris's parents in B5: the stagger consists, therefore, of four sections. The birth of JDT occurs in A3; that of JLP in B7: again, a 'drop' of four sections. A simple slide downwards, in relation to two levels of the grid (marriage and birth), was operated in Fabre's narrative in relation to the canonical structures of AT 332, as represented in *JDT*. This slide fully respects the compartmentalization or general composition of the whole, which remains the same in *JDT* and *JLP*. As far as Jean-de-trop is concerned, his birth intervenes quite normally nine months after conception. In *JLP*, the hero's birth occurs nine days after the wedding. In *JDT*, the banquet is pre-baptismal and is situated just after the child's birth. In *JLP*, the banquet is also pre-baptismal and is situated *just before the child's birth*, which results, it will be remembered, from a conception that took place well before the marriage. Indeed, Fabre's tale slides directly and without transition from a meditation on the festivities to the brief announcement of JLP's birth, which, by definition, precedes a baptism.

> A8: *As everyone is about to set off for the church, Death, having become the godmother, alights, bare-headed and in* déshabillé, *from her coach to meet JDT's parents and their child.*
>
> B8: *On the first Sunday that her daughter has left her house since the birth of her child, the grandmother/godmother dashes down the stairs of her apartment, bare-headed and wearing her night-dress, to meet JLP's parents and their child.*

A8: 'When the bell rings,' recounts the narrator of *Jean-de-trop* (he is referring to the church bell that summons the guests at the banquet to the church for the baptism), a coach and four arrives;[41] the 'coach' stops in front of the door, and the poor old man gets out. (He is 'Our Lord Jesus Christ', who, as we saw at the beginning of Jean-de-trop's narrative, has himself offered to be the child's godfather.) Then the godmother, Death, alights from the vehicle: it is her first appearance in the narrative of *Jean-de-trop*. She is a naked skeleton, whose snow-white bones are further emphasized in the text by the well-combed white beard of the godfather, Jesus. The coach in which Death arrives is sometimes referred to as a coach (on two occasions in the Occitan text of *JDT*); sometimes as a cabriolet or carriage (in similar versions of AT 332, deriving from central France and Germany); sometimes as a death-cart driven by Ankou, a being who personifies death in Brittany (in the Breton version of AT 332, which is also the closest to *JDT*).[42] By contrast, the theme of the death-cart, which, however, was not unknown to old Languedocian folklore (see the end of my *Montaillou*), appears only fleetingly in *JLP* [second version]: when the hero takes his (first) dying wife to the hospital at Sommières, *where she croaks on arrival* [*sic*], he puts her and the twins, who are also dying, on to a cart. The three criminal accomplices of Death in *JLP* are also, *par excellence*, users of carts.

Let us pause for a while at line A8–B8 of Table 1. In both cases (*JDT* and *JLP*), Death performs the action of alighting. In *JDT* this 'descent' is from a coach, which has stopped just outside the hero's house. The same descent takes place from an apartment, in *JLP*: leaping from her bed, the grandmother Death of Fabre's hero bounds down the stairs. This apartment, like the coach of Death in *JDT*, is situated, literally, just opposite the hero's house. The impression of sudden descent is all the stronger in *JLP* in that the old woman descends from her first- or second-storey apartment to the cellar where Truquette and Margot live and work. We see that Fabre, who had given little space to Death's coach in his narrative, has replaced it by another, highly elegant solution: the garret at the top of the building opposite. In fact, the Death of AT 332, when he appears opposite the hero in order to manipulate him first for good, then for evil ends, appears to him from above: either he descends from a tree or from the sky (an Andalusian version of AT 332, known as *Juan Holgado*); or he alights from a coach or cart or from horseback (*JDT*, and versions from Nevers and Brittany); or he dominates the hero by his height, etc.[43]

The details concerning the way Death is dressed are parallel in both cases. In *JDT*, she is naked, her bones exposed, with neither cloak nor hat (veil). She puts on her 'cloak and a thick veil' only in the following sequence, when she goes to the baptism. In *JLP* [22], the grandmother Death is also, during this episode, without either cloak or hat, in other words, 'in her shirt and bare-headed'. Indeed, there is a detail here that is frequently to be found at precisely this strategic point of AT 332 also outside Languedoc: in Brittany, in a version of AT 332 that is very close to *JDT*, Ankou (Death) in his cart as he is about to meet his future godson is 'dressed in a sheet that hardly hides his fleshless bones' (Cadic, 1908, p. 8). In a German version of AT 332, Death 'takes off his cloak in order to be recognized by his future co-sponsor' (Vernaleken, 1884).

> A9: *Godmother Death causes a scandal with the neighbours.*
> B9: *Grandmother Death causes a scandal with the neighbours.*

A9: In *JDT*, the appearance of Death in *déshabillé*, alighting from the coach, is brief, terrifying and scandalous: *seeing her, all the guests who had been invited fled. Only the father, the mother and the children remained in the house . . .*

B9: In *JLP*, the first oral intervention of the grandmother Death is also scandalous. Indeed, the situation takes a turn for the worse when this lady dashes down the stairs to her son-in-law's house. What *Jean-de-trop*, a popular tale, dispatched in a sentence becomes, in *Jean-l'ont-pris*, a literary work, a whole episode: Truquette's fight with Margot (a fight that is, in fact, already to be found in that other source of *JLP*, the 'Swiss tale' [see the end of this chapter]); then the intervention of the old woman, who 'pricks' her son-in-law's 'rind' with an awl; the arrival of the neighbours; the final counter-offensive of the grandmother Death during which a young man, who belongs to a family that are the sworn enemies of the old woman's lineage, is scalped; finally, the departure of the neighbours. Fabre has inserted into this long paragraph certain details which, apart from the fundamental fact of the very position of the episode (see my commentary on the chronological location of the 'interval' in line A11–B11 of Table 1), fully confirm (according to the numbering of Table 1) the kinship of this segment B9-*JLP* with the segment A9-*JDT*. A detail to begin with: in his second version, the abbé Fabre presents this fight as *a carillon that became greater outside than in.* This 'carillon' in *JLP* immediately suggests the bell-ringing in *JDT*: this church clock, situated in effect 'outside' the hero's house and not 'inside', announces the ceremonies of baptism, but it also rings at the stage of the narrative, as a prelude to the triggering of the scandalous panic, that is homologous in *JLP* and *JDT*.[44]

Another remarkable detail: the end of the fight is marked by the same words in *Jean-l'ont-pris* and in *Jean-de-trop*. In *JLP*, 'each went his own way [the neighbours went off to their own homes], and peace was restored *to our house. My father and mother* were still in love . . . [*dins l'oustâou. Moun païre ét ma maïre . . .*]' (26]. In *JDT*, the neighbours, relations and friends 'fled in all directions. There remained *in the house only the father, the mother* and the two children [*dins l'oustal que la maïre, lou païre*]'. The identity of the Occitan words in this phrase ('in the house', 'father' and 'mother'), at the same strategic and tactical point in the two narratives, is an additional clue, among many others: Fabre, in 1756, and the story-teller from Narbonne, about 1880, were each inspired by oral versions of A T 332 that were similar even down to the detail of the 'little phrase'. These versions circulated in lower Languedoc in the eighteenth century. They thus came directly to the knowledge of the abbé. Subsequently, they spread in the Narbonnais dialect until the Third Republic, until L. Lambert collected one of these versions and published it in 1885 in the *Revue des langues romanes*.

Nevertheless, this episode in *Jean-l'ont-pris* is original in relation to the segment of *Jean-de-trop*. In *Jean-l'ont-pris*, at this stage of the narrative [19–21], a Homeric fight between Truquette and his young wife is described first, a battle that immediately follows the end of the banquet: 'When the feast is over the fool remains', as *JLP* puts it. 'When the feast was over . . . [*Acabada la festassa . . .*]', a Catalan version of A T 332 observes in a similar vein, at this very point in the narrative (Amades, tale 99, p. 245). Again, the version from Roussillon of A T 332 collected by the abbé Caseponce (1907, p. 48; see Chapter XV) uses almost identical words at this point [*El festill acabat*]. Is not this theme of the fight between husband and wife inspired by 'the real life of the peasants', as Fabre's commentators, including E.-G. Léonard, have somewhat crudely put it? At the level of the tale, in any case, it also has its source in another version of A T 332: this version circulated in the eighteenth century on the highways that led from the German-speaking world to the Occitan world, from Switzerland to Languedoc. I shall consider this version later in the chapter. However, the grandmother takes part in this marital row, and, quite naturally, she flies to the help of her daughter against her son-in-law. The old woman picks up a cobbler's awl, which lies to hand among Truquette's tools in the cellar that serves him as workshop, kitchen and bedroom. The theme of godfather Death or godmother Death, grandmother Death in this case, armed with an awl, a needle, an arrow or some other pointed instrument is also to be found in another version of AT 332, one from Provence, collected and published by Mistral in 1876 (and also in a very old version of the tale dating from the late seventeenth century). In this version from Provence,[45] which is quite close geographically to the Gard and the Vaunage of *Jean-l'ont-pris*, Death is the child's godfather.

And at the baptismal meal, there was a dish of lentils and Death ate them by pricking them with the point of a needle. Then the man [the child's father] *said to him:*

'*How is it, Death, that you eat lentils with a needle?*'

'*My fine fellow,*' *said Death,* '*I am a man of patience. I may be slow, but I have all the time in the world. The young, the strong and the happy take no account of me and laugh at Death; but I am waiting for them in the pit* [*trou*, 'hole', in French; *trau*, in Occitan]. *Not one escapes me.*'

The 'pit' or 'hole' in question is a reference, of course, to the digging of a grave. However, this *trou* has a double meaning; it is 'polyvalent' or 'polysemic'; it is also related to the 'hole' made by the needle or sharp tool with which Death kills all. In *Jean-l'ont-pris*, too, grandmother Death uses the awl to 'lard the rind' [*tràouquilhar la coudéna*] of her son-in-law and *compère* ['co-sponsor'] [22]. The needle–hole link is thus clear in both southern versions of AT 332, in the course of which Death towards the beginning of the narrative is dangerously armed with a sharp instrument.

This sequence of *Jean-l'ont-pris* is specific, however, in relation to the general corpus of the versions of AT 332; Margot is Truquette's wife and the hero's mother; but she is also the *daughter of Death*. She is not only Death's *commère*[46] ['co-sponsor'], as is the mother of Death's godson in most of the versions of AT 332. This close kinship, which goes exceptionally far, between Margot and Death, enables the abbé Fabre to identify to some extent the first with the second – the daughter with the mother – and even to fuse them, in a slip, or a pseudo-slip [9].

We have just seen how the grandmother, in B9-*JLP* (Table 1), 'lards' her son-in-law's skin with an awl. Indeed, we are told later, on the subject of the matches or lights of life, that this old woman liked to 'work herself to death' [*travailler à crève-corps*] [39]. In a double sense, of course. She 'works herself to death' [*se crève*], but she also 'bursts', 'kills off' bodies [*crève les corps*]. Now, from the beginning of the narrative, in B2-*JLP* of Table 1, Margot, during Truquette's persistent courtship of her, which is to end with her pregnancy, pricked her lover's ribs, or 'poked him between the ribs with an awl' [9]. In short, Margot amusingly pre-figures the homicidal action of her mother, a few sequences later, against the cobbler.[47] This compares with the Provençal version of AT 332, in which Death displays his dangerously sharp needle during the baptismal meal. In *Jean-l'ont-pris*, the cobbler's awl, with which the grandmother Death pierces Truquette's skin, is introduced just before the Sunday outing that ought to take the form immediately of the hero's baptism. Am I, in stressing the comparison between Margot and her mother, forcing the text? The sceptical reader has only to refer to the two key passages in *JLP*: [9] and [21]. In the first, Margot pokes Truquette playfully with an *awl*, and the cobbler replies by giving her a close caress with his *stirrup*. In the second, the order is reversed, but the actors and the tools are basically the same: Truquette beats his wife with his *stirrup*, and the grandmother Death (of whom her daughter Margot is the deadly double) pricks the cobbler's skin with an *awl*.

A close comparison of the two episodes (Margot's initial courtship by Truquette, and Margot's and her mother's attack on Truquette) manages to demonstrate the profound structural kinship of these two events. It also has the effect of establishing the identification of the respective roles of the aggressive Margot and her mother Death.

In the workshop of the cobbler Truquette

A Margot's flirtation with Truquette [9]	B Margot's and her mother's attack on Truquette [21–22]
(1) Margot pokes Truquette in the ribs with an *awl*.	(1) Truquette beats Margot on the back with a *stirrup*.
(2) She rubs *wax* on his mouth.	(2) She throws a pot of boiling *wax* at his jaw.
(3) He puts his *stirrup* round her neck.	(3) The grandmother pricks her son-in-law's skin with an *awl*.

Since attack is in principle the opposite of a courtship, the order of the factors is simply inverted in the right-hand column (B) in relation to the left-hand column (A).

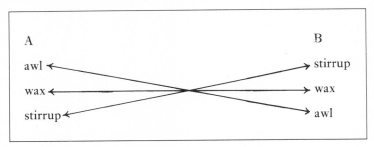

The identification between Margot and her mother is carried still further: the two women have collaborated very closely in the making of the dangerous matches. So much so that in a remarkable slip at the beginning of his narrative, in both versions of his text, Fabre has completely fused, at least for the space of a sentence [9, the opening of the paragraph], daughter and mother.[48] Furthermore, Truquette's *basement* shop (cellar shop [19, 26]) has become, in paragraph 9 of the text, the cellar with lights of AT 332, in which Margot makes matches or lights of life for her mother and in which the hero Truquette, later, will meet his end.

It should be added that at the moment of the fight with Truquette, Margot threatens at one point to strangle her husband, at another to scalp him (to tear off his 'mane'). According to this second hypothesis, she even links gesture to words; she seizes Truquette's hair and sets light to his beard [21]. Now the young woman, in this case, merely imitates the methods of her mother Death, in other words, the grandmother Death, who is a specialist in techniques for scalping and pulling out hair: the old woman uses such methods when meeting young men, whether Jean-l'ont-pris himself or another village boy [50]. It is also she who, *qua* general killer of mankind, will strangle Truquette to death (on the scaffold). The oldest and most original versions of AT 332, in Germany, Flanders and elsewhere, from the sixteenth and seventeenth centuries, prefer the methods of strangling or of twisting the neck, when the hero is killed by the godfather Death.[49] From this point of view, then, Fabre has simply conformed to the oral traditions that provided him with the raw material of his narrative. Margot, like her mother, tries to strangle her victim.

Lastly, while we are picking up all the available similarities, perhaps it should be noted that Margot, at the time of the fight, as she leaps out of bed, is *en négligé*, while the grandmother is *en chemise*, having leapt from her bed and dashed down the stairs without dressing. Margot, a fatal portent, will also be wearing her night-shirt when her husband is arrested some time later [36].

In short, Margot is presented by Fabre as a close accomplice of her mother Death and also as her double. By marrying her, the unfortunate Truquette has become at once the son-in-law and, in a sense, the husband of this personified Death. This is certainly enough to ruin him! Though, of course, it does not prevent the young woman, divided against herself, at the time of her honeymoon, from feeling genuine love for her cobbler husband. This complicity on the part of Margot with the forces of death and this ambivalence in love seem to me, in any case, to explain a remarkable detail that apparently has never attracted the attention of Fabre's commentators. At the beginning of his narrative, Jean-l'ont-pris observes that *except for a potful of earth we had on our window-sill, in which my mother grew basil, we possessed not a single spadeful to our name.* It might be pointed out that the spadeful of earth is not only that of the farmer, but also that of the gravedigger. More important, however, the pot of basil is a highly suggestive detail for anyone who knows Mediterranean literature and folklore, and it is surprising that an object so charged with meaning should have remained for so long unnoticed by Fabre's commentators. Of course, the reference in the abbé's narrative may be quite simply to a pot of flowers or a purely decorative green plant; but the hypothesis of a symbolic value attached to this basil cannot be excluded, *a priori*, from any interpretation of this passage.

The first reference, which is both traditional and detailed, to the theme of the pot of basil is to be found in the fifth novella of the fourth day of Boccaccio's *Decameron*. Lisabetta no longer has any parents, but lives under the guardianship of her three brothers, merchants at Messina, who tend to watch jealously over the fragile virtue of their sister. Nevertheless, a lover, Lorenzo, succeeds in seducing Lisabetta. The brothers secretly kill and bury him. The young woman manages to learn the truth; she recovers her lover's corpse and takes away the head; she then buries the head in a pot of basil, which she installs in her bedchamber and waters with her tears. This basil grows into a magnificent plant. Lisabetta does not denounce her brothers to the authorities, but later dies of a broken heart. Popular Sicilian songs, in Boccaccio's time, were devoted to this edifying story of the girl and the pot of basil, which was very popular both in the north and south of the peninsula.

Later, the tale was to evolve in oral tradition; it survived into the twentieth century along the Gulf of Lions: Piedmont, Liguria, Catalonia, Corsica. It told of a girl who watered her pot of basil or who watered (according to other versions) the basil in her garden; after various episodes, the girl goes into the bedchamber of the prince who is in love with her 'and pretends that she is *Death*, to the great terror of this young man'.[50]

The abbé Fabre, whose reading was wide and deep, certainly knew Boccaccio;[51] and he was something of an expert on the living folklore of the coasts of the north-east Mediterranean and would have had the opportunity of hearing oral versions of the tale, subsequent to Boccaccio's work. The mention of the 'pot of basil' was the equivalent, on the abbé's part, of a wink to the reader; it was a way of linking Margot in person to the release of a deadly force that was to bring the unfortunate Truquette to his ruin. Either the young woman, as in the oral versions of *The Girl and the Basil*, momentarily identifies herself with Death (in this case, with her own mother), who will shortly bring about Truquette's death, or Margot (if the abbé places himself in direct succession to Boccaccio) is regarded as an accomplice in the death of the man she loves, simply by virtue of the fact that, after the event, she keeps silent on the matter. By definition, it is, in effect, Death, in other words, Margot's mother, who will kill Truquette, using the hangman as an intermediary at the end of the first part of *Jean-l'ont-pris*. While watering her pot of basil, Margot keeps as silent on the deadly activities of her mother that have made her a widow as Boccaccio's Lisabetta on the violent death of her lover at the hands of her three brothers. Whichever point of view one may adopt, deriving from folklore or from Boccaccio, the pot of basil *accuses* Margot.

The close collaboration that is established, under the aegis of Death, between the (dominant) grandmother and her daughter, Margot (subordinate-docile), also throws light on another detail in Fabre's narrative. Let us return to the preceding paragraphs. As the people are leaving the church in which the wedding has just taken place, and at the moment (immediately following) when they enter the banqueting room, the grandmother performs a number of actions (for the time being benevolent ones) that emphasize her nature as godmother Death: she hands out matches to all and sundry, an action similar to the distribution by Death of the lights of life (candles) at the beginning of various versions of A T 332, one of which is Breton and several Occitan. What is more, the old woman places herself *in front of the door* of the house, a highly stressed action. According to many regional versions of A T 332, this means that she is in a beneficent mood, and that she is not yet disposed to kill, but, for the moment, disposed to cure; she is temporarily ready to dispense prosperity to those whom she has decided to protect. The grandmother Death is to take part in the banquet of wild food (service-berries, hackberries, etc.), by which she suggests, in passing, her affinities with uncultivated nature and, more particularly, with the forest or (in Languedoc) with the *garrigue*.

However, one action is missing that is to be found in the oldest versions of A T 332, collected as such from oral tradition: I am referring to the *German* version collected by the brothers Grimm (tale 44) and the *French* version collected by Jacob Grimm in the early nineteenth century.[52] Just before Death reveals herself as the godmother (the ceremonial feast), Death, according to these two versions, reveals herself by 'showing her dry leg', which she does by opening her cloak. Now, if we admit that Margot functions at the highest point as the double or subordinate of her mother, in other words, of the grandmother Death, it is important to characterize Margot's behaviour at the moment before her arrival in the banqueting room: she distributes to all and sundry the woodland fruits (hackberries). This flow of fruits derives directly and literally from this strategic position in the narrative (I shall return to this in Chapter XV) of an old Occitano-Roussillonnais version of A T 332. It is interesting to point out, therefore, with Fabre, that Margot throws these hackberries *while raising her leg*, that is, necessarily, *while showing her leg*. As always in Fabre, there is a double meaning: in this case, to show one's leg is to declare oneself (for the initiated) to be Death's double; it is also, for everybody, to present oneself as a 'loose woman'. Similarly, later [38], when Margot, after leaving Truquette, who has been thrown into prison, 'runs off' with a knife-grinder who had courted her before her marriage, and becomes a *coureuse*, the equivocation is once again cleverly maintained. To be a *coureuse* in this instance is to sleep around. But it is also to travel around in the company of the knife-grinder, who spends his days sharpening highly dangerous knives: the *coureuse* will show that she, like her deadly mother, will know how to use these blades.

We now come to line 10 (A10 and B10) of Table 1.

> A10: *Death seriously declares that the young couple will make their fortune.*
>
> B10: *The grandmother jokingly declares that the young couple will make their fortune.*

There is (for the moment) a contrast, in Table 1, between the *seriousness* of A10-*JDT* and the *humour* of B10-*JLP*: the first, on this point, is strong; the second, weak. This opposition will later change into its opposite.

In *Jean-de-trop*, as indeed in the overwhelming majority of the hundreds of versions of AT 332, from throughout the world, the strength of Death's promises is unequivocal: the scandal caused to 'neighbours, relations and friends' ends only with their terrified flight; the macabre visitor is then able to tell Jean-de-trop's parents: *Have no fear, I am your friend. All the members of your family will live for two hundred years without ever falling ill, and I shall teach my godson a secret that will make him the richest man on earth.* In *Jean-l'ont-pris*, the promises of prosperity made by the grandmother, though real enough as the story eventually shows, are presented at this point as rather unconvincing tall tales: 'down-and-outs like us are ladies and gentlemen compared with lousy tramps like you; my son-in-law and daughter have over 100 francs of their own, *not to mention what they'll have from me* . . .' We should not forget that the grandmother will indeed leave on her death a treasure that she has built up from her son-in-law's thefts, which were originally carried out at her instigation.

A11: *After a while, Death shows the young couple how to get rich.*

B11: *After a while, the grandmother shows the young couple how to get rich.*

In *Jean-de-trop*, this gap in time corresponds to the moment when, once the scandalous entry has ended, and Death has delivered her first declarations, she throws off her cloak and veil to reveal her skeletal nakedness; she immediately sets off for the church to which the bell calls her, in the company of the family, for the child's baptism. It is perhaps worth noting that, in the versions of AT 332 that mention the day of the week when this baptism takes place, it is always a *Sunday*.[53] The departure of godfather Death or godmother Death and the child and his father, on a Sunday walk from the father's house to the church where the baptism will take place, is an absolutely canonical[54] and ritually situated moment of AT 332.

In *Jean-l'ont-pris*, it is precisely on the occasion of Margot's first outing, on the first available *Sunday*, that the scandalous row takes place, followed by the humorous suggestion as to how the couple are to make their fortune. Here, too, then, it is a question of going to the church, very probably to baptize the child. According to Sauzet,[55] the baptism would have taken place in the diocese of Nîmes, in the eighteenth century, four or five days after the birth; and the husband and wife, Truquette (by birth) and Margot (at least since her marriage), are undoubtedly 'Catholics'.[56] In any case, Fabre says no more about this much-heralded outing. The interval that separates, in Table 1, the first advice as to how to get rich (A10–B10) from the second (A11–B11) corresponds in *Jean-de-trop* to a journey from the house to the church for a baptism and vice versa; and, in *Jean-l'ont-pris*, to the fact that a first Sunday outing (necessarily to the church, if only to go to mass) is envisaged, this fact being followed by a night of reflection that brings advice.

There is then the *second* piece of advice on how to get rich. The first was weak in *Jean-l'ont-pris*, strong in *Jean-de-trop*. In the case of the second, the reverse applies: it is weak in *Jean-de-trop*, strong in *Jean-l'ont-pris*.

In *Jean-de-trop*, Death, as far as this second 'rain of blessings' that is to fall on the young parents of the child is concerned, confines herself to serving as an auxiliary of Our Lord Jesus Christ, who had already provided the victuals for the baptismal banquet and who simply declares that these victuals will last, thank God, much longer than expected. So, he says to the parents, *sit down and feast yourselves*[57] *at your ease.* In fact, what we have here is a Gospel-type miracle such as the marriage feast at Cana or the multiplication of loaves and fishes. The victuals last eight days. Later, the affairs of JDT's parents go from strength to strength, increasing and multiplying miraculously until the parents themselves disappear.

In *Jean-l'ont-pris*, the second intervention of the grandmother by way of advice is much 'stronger'. To begin with, the old woman does not leave to another the task of acting as leader (in *Jean-de-trop*, the function of this more eloquent 'other' was taken by 'Our Lord'). She immediately takes things in hand herself. She does not confine herself, as does Death in *Jean-de-trop*, to suggesting how to use the 'leftovers', in other words, miraculous prolongation of the wedding feast, by multiplication of loaves and fishes, during the following week. In fact, the grandmother dangles before the young couple's eyes the prospect of untold riches. She advises her son-in-law to set up in business and, by swindling, to make his fortune. Obviously fascinated, 'bewitched' says the second version, caught in the trap by magic, Truquette accepts; it brings him immediate good fortune, and ultimate disaster.

A12: *JDT's parents become rich, described in a general way.*
B12: *JLP's parents become rich, described in detail.*

At this point, the *Jean-de-trop* version is 'weak'. There is a brief remark: *from then on, their business* [that of JDT's parents] *prospered more and more. They were never short of anything in the house.* It is simply noted, then, that the couple has passed from a state of poverty (at the beginning of the narrative) to a situation of wealth (in this new stage of the narration). It is specified that this wealth affects the *house* of the hero's father.

In *Jean-l'ont-pris*, the change is exactly of the same type, but it is described, in considerably more than a mere sentence, in a number of powerful details, over several paragraphs.

So Truquette becomes, as far as one can judge, a swindler. He creates capital with goods that he appears to have stolen at the fairs that took place on the Saturday before Palm Sunday, at Sommières, a small urban Protestant centre of the Vaunage. He makes so much profit that he can then buy whatever he wants. Indeed, it is here that Fabre's text assumes, quite frankly, the appearance of a fairy story: *before two years were up, my father bought fields, vineyards, meadows, olive-groves and the finest house in the neighbourhood. Money poured in. Truquette took to wearing a wig, a jabot and lace ruffles; Margot, rings, a watch, long, hanging sleeves and lace; my grandmother, a bonnet, a fur-lined coat and slippers. As for me, I was wrapped in such a profusion of ribbons that you would have thought me a bobbin* . . . [34–35].[58] Indeed, the grandmother had already predicted this magical acquisition of a fortune in her second 'harangue': *I advise you*, she tells her son-in-law, . . . *to set yourselves up in business* . . . *I've seen I don't know how many ragamuffins, real down-and-outs, who, having chosen this path, before five or six years are out, are buying vineyards, fields, houses, castles, baronies* . . . [29].

In any case, this prosperity affects the splendidly furnished *house* in *JDT*, and the *house* bought for a princely sum in *JLP*. It is remarkable that the very terms in which Truquette's recent wealth is described (the buying of a fine house, land, etc.), as predicted by the grandmother or achieved later in the story, appear more or less word for word in a number of versions of AT 332 that are very close, geographically, to this Occitan version, implied in *Jean-l'ont-pris*: I would mention in this respect, among others, two versions from the Midi and another, more distant one, from Brittany.[59]

Noteworthy, too, as far as Truquette's swindling is concerned, is the description given by the abbé Fabre of the three accomplices. It is Truquette's business partners [32] who are to become guilty of his death [36]; we are also told that the grandmother Death belongs to the partnership [70]. One of them, in the second version, is called the Renaoûvi, which, in Languedocian, means a 'widower who has married a widow'.[60] Another, called Quincarlot or Cancrelas, 'was blind in the *right* eye, which diminished his value to some extent; but, good heavens!, fine gentleman that you are [says Jean-l'ont-pris to the baron], your lordship would find it difficult to relieve him of what he had in the purse on his left side without his knowing' [32]. Later, Fabre tells us that this character has a face like Beelzebub's. In the

198 LOVE, DEATH AND MONEY IN THE PAYS D'OC

second version, he notes that the three swindlers (four with Truquette, who has now joined their gang) *could have given advice to the entire synagogue of Avignon*. Such anti-Semitic sentiments do not show Fabre in a particularly good light, but at least they tell us that this gang, since it is compared to a synagogue, is hardly Catholic, in short, that it has something maleficent about it (despite the presence in its ranks of Truquette, a papist turned swindler). This 'synagogue' goes well enough with the grandmother's Huguenot beliefs, of which Fabre makes much.

The fact that Quincarlot has lost his right eye, and that he has a well-filled purse 'on his left side', is in itself interesting. When the left eye alone is open, it is the evil eye, that of the ghost, of the dead person who is not really dead and who comes back, moving among the living, like a ghost, to drive them to death. On this question, Breton folklore coincides with that of Languedoc. In Brittany, 'if the left eye of a dead man does not close, one of his close relations is threatened with imminent death'.[61] This evil eye of friend Quincarlot does indeed bring misfortune to Truquette, who is a relation (at least through marriage) of this one-eyed individual and his best friend [80], and who will soon end his days on the scaffold. Blindness in the right eye suggests death – and also the grandmother: she has a liking for 'blindness' in the right eye, and she presents it as a model to follow, or at least to imitate in one's dress. Take the advice she gives her grandson, whom she would like to turn into another Quincarlot: *You don't have to pull it down over your eyes, like a bad payer, or straight on your head, like a bumpkin, but wear it pulled down over your right eye, like this, watch how I do it with these three packets of matches, like that, yes! No more, no less* [41]. Generally speaking, Fabre is well aware that the left brings bad luck, if not at once, at least in the long run,[62] and the right, good luck (which is why he conceals, blinds or eliminates the right eye in this case). *A well-brought-up child does not go around trying to find out where his parents may have got what they leave him. If they got it on the right side* [by fair means], *so much the better for everyone; if they got it on the left side* [by crooked means], *so much the worse for them!* [70] In the second version, the casket that is at the bottom of the dead grandmother's treasure-chest is placed on the left. The hat that smells of sulphur, and seems to blind the grandmother's right eye, is (among others) one way for Fabre to indicate the complicity, at once macabre and diabolical, between the old woman and Quincarlot. As Fabre put it, *if Truquette and his comrades had not put it there, she must have done it on her own account.* So much so that she had accumulated, by secretly concealing some of the proceeds of Truquette's great thefts, the treasure that was later to bring fortune and happiness to Jean-l'ont-pris. During her son-in-law's lifetime, the grandmother belongs to the team, together with the three swindlers, who helped Truquette while betraying him: she collaborates with the Renaoûvi, the widower who marries a widow; with Quincarlot, the man blind in the right eye; and with their comrade Carcanas, in other words, the buzzard or the bird that eats flesh whether it is alive or dead. Similarly, Death, according to Fabre, is one of these three Fates. *Inexorable Death*, writes Fabre in another work, which takes the form of necrological parody, *your scythe has cut off the precious days of my friend. Odious fate, your infernal scissors have cut the thread that was the glory of your bobbins ...* [63]

A13: *JDT's parents disappear discreetly from the narrative.*
B13: *JLP's parents disappear from the narrative in a spectacular fashion.*

After the sentence 'thereafter their affairs continued to prosper; nothing was lacking in the house', there is no further mention of Jean-de-trop's parents. This break in the narrative corresponds to one found in a number of other versions of AT 332, German, French,[64] etc.: after the story and death (mentioned or not) of Death's *compère* (the hero's father and, in Fabre's tale, Truquette), there begins canonically the biography of his son, Death's godson – in other words, the hero himself (JLP or JDT).

I know of only a single case in which the story is treated in the opposite sense: in the Italian novella by Forteguerri (about 1550), which contains one of the oldest known versions[65] of AT 332/ *Godfather Death*, the parents, called Hatred and Envy, have a child, who becomes, at the baptism, Death's godson. This child dies at the age of twelve; from then on, the narrative immediately takes up again the story of this godson's parents, in other words, Death's fellow-sponsors, who become *par excellence* the bearers of the classic plot of

AT 332. What one has, then, is a 'going back over' the narrative, towards the older generation beyond this break, itself due to the death of a young person. The Forteguerri version may thus be read: Death of Death's godson ⟶ Adventures of Death's *compère*.

But this initiative of Forteguerri's was not, as far as we know, followed; in general, the break moves from the old to the young, with the 'descent' of the narrative:

Death or disappearance ⟶ Adventures of
of Death's *compère* Death's godson

In *JDT*, this break is simply noted with the resumption of the name 'Jean-de-trop', which had been mentioned only once since we were informed, at the beginning of the narrative, that the poor parents had just called their newborn child 'Jean-de-trop'.

So, after the final mention of JDT's parents, we set off again, with this name, which is mentioned twice:

Jean-de-trop went to school . . .

There is exactly the same procedure in Fabre's narrative. The name of Jean-l'ont-pris surfaced once, at the beginning of the text, and it was associated quite naturally with the initial mention of the hero's parents. It occurs a second time, as in *Jean-de-trop*, at the time of the 'break' constituted by the disappearance of the parents; or, rather, immediately after this disappearance.

'I was *left* with my grandmother [deprived as I now was of my father and mother] . . . My poor little grandmother! Alas! Jean-l'ont-pris will never be able to repay his debt to her' [39]! And the hero then explains where the nickname Jean-l'ont-pris comes from; while still a small child, he used to say constantly *ils l'ont pris* ['they have taken him away'], or the authorities (and death by hanging) *have taken my father*.[66] This explanation can come only at this precise stage in the text, since by definition it follows the capture of the father by the constabulary of Solorgues, who intervene only in line B13 (Table 1). The expression 'Jean-de-trop' does not even have to be explained: it is self-evident at the beginning of the narrative. That particular Jean was indeed *de trop* in relation to the five brothers and sisters who preceded him.

Table 2 (see also Table 1)

FOUR EPISODES...

... in *JDT*   ... in *JLP*

A10: *strong* Serious prediction of fortune	B10: *weak* Joking prediction of fortune
A11: *weak* Incidental, indirect encouragement to make their fortune	B11: *strong* Strong, detailed encouragement to make their fortune
A12: *weak* Prosperity, generally defined	B12: *strong* Prosperity, specifically defined
A13: *weak* Discreet disappearance of parents	B13: *strong* Spectacular disappearance of parents

However, we should comment directly on the episode of line B13-*JLP* (Table 1), which, incidentally, will force me to go back to an earlier point.

I have observed that in comparison with the story of Jean-de-trop's parents, the adventure of Truquette and Margot included a weak episode (B10 of Table 1), followed by three strong and well-stocked episodes (B11, B12 and B13).

The story of Truquette is certainly homologous with that of Jean-de-trop's father. But the first is clearly fuller than the second. A question, therefore, arises: is there not, in the enormous corpus of the versions of AT 332, a source other than the version that was *JDT*'s ancestor, which would be responsible for precise details that, taken together, form structurally in *JLP* the very original career of Truquette? The investigation of this matter may be focused on the versions that took root in the Occitan and Franco-Provençal Midi,[67] and also on versions that circulated along the southern margins of the German-speaking

world (which is the birthplace of AT 332) – in particular, in
Switzerland, whose commercial and religious contacts with the southern half of France were so important in the later Middle Ages and
throughout the entire modern period. We should think, for example,
of the merchants and innumerable Huguenots who travelled between
the region around Nîmes and Switzerland, from the sixteenth to the
eighteenth century. In fact, I have found among the Swiss versions
of AT 332 a very precise model for our Truquette: his story, through
oral transmission and translation, could not fail to circulate towards
southern France. It gave rise, during the seventeenth and eighteenth
centuries, to a southern French version that has since been lost, but
which could easily, at this time, have reached the ears of the abbé
Fabre: he drew his inspiration from it. Here, in any case, is the Swiss
model that engendered the southern 'pre-Truquette', who in turn
gave form and substance, in Fabre, to our Truquette, the father of
Jean-l'ont-pris.[68]

A poor cobbler had thirteen children in his little shop, and nothing
to eat. His wife, who had just given birth again, lay in bed, sick. The
cobbler went in search of a godfather for his newborn child. In a
wood, he first met God [*Seigneur Dieu*].

He refused, of course, to choose him as godfather, since God
is unjust. While still in the forest, the poor man then met a
hunter wearing a fine green jacket, in the Tyrolean manner; he had
a bunch of flowers stuck smartly in his little green hat. The
cobbler explained his problem to this individual. They came to an
agreement:

'I shall be your child's godfather,' said the Green Man, 'and if you
do as I wish, you will have enough money; every week I shall bring
you a full purse. And here is a root, give it to your wife and it will
cure her; and the two of you will never lack for anything.'

'Well,' replied the poor man, 'if I do not have to do anything
wicked, then I shall give him to you [I shall give you my son as
godson].'

'Over there,' replied the Green Man, 'there is a miserly tailor. Go
and kill him – he deserves no better – and take his money.'

The cobbler refused. He did not want to be a murderer.

'Very well,' the Green Man continued, 'over there, there is a miserly peasant. He has buried a pile of money under the stairs. Go and take if off him. I shall make sure that no one shall know about it.'

'No I shall not.' [The cobbler did not wish to be a thief!]

'Very well,' continued the Green Man, 'then go to the inn. Go and drink a mug [*une chopine*; *Scheppli*, in dialect; *Schöpplein*, in German] of good wine. And here is the root to cure your wife.'

The cobbler saw nothing wrong in drinking a mug of wine; he took the money and the root; he went home, making a detour to the inn, where he drank, as ordered, his mug of wine. When he got back to the house, his wife complained of her husband's long absence. He calmed his wife and showed her the large sum of money that the Green Man had given him. He gave her the root: his wife recovered rapidly.

The mug of wine had whetted the cobbler's appetite. As he now had money, he went every day to the inn. He did not stop at a single mug a day and began to drink like a Templar. Soon it was two, three mugs a day and more. He began to gamble and be drunk for weeks on end. His wife complained, but he replied: 'It's my money, mind your own business.' Peace no longer reigned in the home. The woman, who, like all women, wanted to have the first and last word, was beaten by her husband, and in the end killed by him. The man ended his days on the scaffold. In this way the Green Man achieved his aim.[69]

German folklore specialists[70] have very logically classified this tale in the Swiss subsection of the more general group of the various versions of AT 332 in the German languages. It is a reasonable classification: the outline of the narrative conforms to the general schema of *Godfather Death* except that the supernatural character who comes on the scene is not Death, but the devil. This, however, does not matter, since the devil is actually godfather or at least protector in the various versions[71] of AT 332. The structure of the 'Swiss tale' is very typical of AT 332:

(1) the search by a poor man for a godfather for his child;

(2) the rejection of the first candidate (God) and the acceptance of the second (the devil);

(3) magical gifts, which are given by this godfather to the child's father, the hero of the narrative;

(4) the eventual murder of this hero, by the supernatural character,

Table 3

THE 'SWISS TALE' AND 'TRUQUETTE'

C 'Swiss tale'	D 'Truquette' (in *JLP*)
C1: A poor cobbler becomes the father of a newborn child.*	D1: A poor cobbler becomes the father of a newborn child.
C2: His wife, who has just given birth, is in bed.	D2: His wife, Margot, who has just given birth, is in bed.
C3: The Green Man (the devil) will become the godfather.	D3: The grandmother will become the godmother.
C4: The Green Man promises that the cobbler will make his fortune.	D4: Nothing.
C5: He asks him to become a swindler at the expense of a tailor; the cobbler refuses.	D5: Nothing.
C6: The cobbler drinks a *chopine*, then another and so forth.	D6: The cobbler is called 'Chopine' (Truquette, in Occitan). His wife calls him a drunkard after he has drunk a lot of wine.
C7: The cobbler gets his wife up by giving her a root to eat.	D7: The cobbler gets his wife up by giving her soup to drink.
C8: The cobbler often fights with his wife and, in the end, kills her.	D8: The cobbler often fights with his wife but, in the end, does not kill her.
C9: Nothing.	D9: The grandmother promises that the cobbler will make his fortune.
C10: Nothing.	D10: She asks him to become a swindler; he agrees and operates in textiles.
C11: The cobbler is condemned to death and executed.	D11: The cobbler is condemned to death and executed.

who uses for his purposes one of his collaborators, in this case, the executioner.

All the more remarkable are the profound resemblances between the Swiss narrative and the 'Truquette' episode of our *Jean-l'ont-pris*.

Let us compare the two, using a synchronic table of the ordering of the homologous episodes of the two texts, which I shall call respectively C and D.

A brief summary of the different sections of Table 3: lines 1, 2 and 3 (that is, C1, C2, C3 and D1, D2, D3: poor cobbler, wife giving birth to new child, quest for a godfather) correspond in Fabre's text to the whole of the narrative up to the point when Margot gets out of bed; they also correspond, more briefly, to the very exposition of the narrative of *Jean-l'ont-pris*, in the course of which the young man rapidly presents (to his listener and also to the reader) his father (D1), his mother (D2) and his grandmother (D3).

There follow sections C4 and C5: the Green Man promises a fortune to the cobbler (C4). He then asks him to become a swindler (C5). Sections D4 and D5 are empty ('nothing') in Truquette's biography, since this whole section (the promise of fortune [C4] and the request to become a swindler [D5]) is also dropped five sections in the right-hand column of Table 3, concerning Truquette's fate. We find the two sections as such in the right-hand column in D9 and D10; and we shall discuss them, in terms of the two columns – the 'Swiss tale' and 'Truquette' – when my analysis reaches this particular stage of the biography of the Languedocian cobbler.

So we come to C6: in C6, the Swiss cobbler obeys the injunctions of the Green Man, who finances his drinking; he drinks mug after mug of wine. In D6, the Languedocian narrator, Jean-l'ont-pris, after presenting the various members of his family to us, tells us[72] his father's name, Truquette, which specifically means *chopine* ['mug of wine'] in the Occitan dialects of the Rhône valley, and especially in

---

* The hero of AT 332 practises the trade of cobbler in the 'life of Truquette' (*JLP*) and in the 'Swiss tale', and also in Italian and Castilian versions of AT 332 (L. and F. Ricci, *Crispino e la comare* [c. 1840]; A. M. Espinosa, *Cuentos populares de Castilla*, . . . [n.d.], p. 78), but not in certain German and Swiss versions (L. Mackensen, *Handwörterbuch des deutschen Märchens* [1934–40], vol. II, p. 617).

Gard. To be precise, the word *truquette*, in this area, indicates a small measure of wine that is the equivalent of a *chopine*. So much so that Fabre's first translator in the nineteenth century, Roumieux, an excellent dialect specialist, translated *Truquette* by *chopine*, a word that corresponds exactly to the *Schöpplein* and *Scheppli* of the 'Swiss tale'. Marcel Barral has also suggested this translation.[73]

However, the Switzerland–Languedoc distinction, from the seventeenth century onwards, is seen as a contrast between a country of wine-drinkers threatened by alcoholism and drunkenness (German-speaking Switzerland) and a region of reasonable soberness (Languedoc), in which the inhabitants, who are often wine-growers, drink extremely moderately and almost never sink into drunkenness.[74]

This contrast is extremely important if we are to understand the genealogy of our Languedocian tale: the Swiss cobbler, in the local version of AT 332 collected by the folklore specialist Müller, was quite naturally a member of that vast corporation of drunks who proved so numerous in his country. When this 'Swiss tale', at an indeterminate time in the modern period (a period in any case well before the 1750s, when *Jean-l'ont-pris* was written), reached, from Switzerland, first the Franco-Provençal, then Provençal-Languedocian regions, it quite naturally lost these references to drunkenness; they did not correspond to the new context in which it now took root. The cobbler–hero, a great downer of mugs of wine in his native Germany or Switzerland, nevertheless preserves in the Midi the name or nickname of *Chopine* (Truquette), now devoid of any deep meaning. In *JLP* this name is simply a 'de-semanticized' survival; it now functions for us as a mere marker. However, Fabre's narrative preserves some memories of the oral tale from which it sprang, and in which the prototype hero Truquette appeared as an excessive drinker: during the fight with her young husband, Margot calls Truquette a drunk and a *tabateur*, that is, a man who abuses wine and tobacco [21]. Truquette, of course, does to some extent deserve this insult, since just prior to the row in question, not content with having drunk a large amount of wine during the wedding, he bought for himself a quantity of *vinette* [*vinet*, 19], or cheap wine. *Vinette* is here the diminutive of *vin* ['wine'], just as in the 'Swiss tale', *Schöpplein* (literally, *chopinette*) is the diminutive of the German

Schöppen [*chope*, 'pint']. It should be noted in passing that a *chopinette* (*Schöpplein*) is a fraction of a pint, just as a *truquette* is (see Frédéric Mistral's *Trésor . . .* on this word). As for the abuse of tobacco on the part of the hero, this too is to be found, at exactly the same point in the narrative, in the version from Roussillon of AT 332, entitled *Galdric*, which is so close to our *JLP* (see Chapter XV).

C7: *The cobbler of the 'Swiss tale' gets his wife (who has only just given birth) out of bed*, and gives her a medicinal root that the Green Man has supernaturally given him; it hastens her recovery.

D7: *The cobbler Truquette gets his wife (who has just given birth) out of bed*, and brings her food (in particular, meat), with which she makes soup that helps to put her on her feet. This meat comes from the sale of the wedding garments that Truquette had brought back on his asses from Nîmes (the Huguenot and magico-maleficent city).[75] We now know, through the comparison with *Jean-de-trop*, that the asses laden with clothes and provisions functioned by virtue of the supernatural powers that served as Jean-de-trop's godparents (Jesus Christ and Death), and that served as Jean-l'ont-pris's godmother (the redoubtable and macabre grandmother). The 'root' in the 'Swiss tale' and the 'meat soup' in *Jean-l'ont-pris* have, therefore, the same 'non-prosaic' source, beyond the cobbler who provided them. In any case, the root, on the one hand, and the meat soup, on the other, were given by the cobbler to his wife, who was recovering from childbirth; they have on her the same curative effect at the same structural point in the two narrations, which further corroborates the kinship of the two episodes. This root–soup dichotomy corresponds, moreover, to the great dichotomy in the versions of AT 332 themselves in which the curing placebo used by the doctor (Death's godson) is sometimes a root or a herb and sometimes a liquid (see Chapter XI).

C8: *The cobbler in the 'Swiss tale' often fights with his wife and, in the end, kills her.*

D8: *The cobbler in* Jean-l'ont-pris *often fights with his wife but, in the end, does not kill her.*

Before passing to the final difference, we should emphasize the profound resemblances that unite these two homologous segments.

In both cases, it is after certain excesses in the way of food that the wife, who sees her husband wasting money, gets angry: in the 'Swiss tale', this female anger is turned against the cobbler's endlessly repeated *chopines*. In *Jean-l'ont-pris*, it is turned against the ruinous and rather drunken banquet, which gets Truquette, who bought cheap wine for himself, called a 'drunk' by his wife. The Swiss wife is presented to us as verbally quarrelsome: she always wants to have the first and the last word ('Swiss tale'); and indeed Margot in the first row (before the couple actually come to blows) has the first and last word with Truquette. Following this, the Swiss wife, and Margot, are immediately and soundly beaten by their husbands [27]. There is an important difference, however: the Swiss wife is killed after a particularly violent row. But Margot is not. This is because, in the 'Swiss tale', the cobbler is first ordered to become a murderer, then a thief. Confronted by these orders, the tradesman agreed in fact (after a polite refusal) to the first injunction (he will murder his wife), but refused the second (he does not become a swindler). By contrast, it is as though Truquette had refused the first order (he does beat his wife, but he does not kill her), only to obey the second (he does indeed become a swindler – in textiles). The two heroes, then, are inversely symmetrical: where one accepted, the other refused and vice versa.

The Swiss cobbler	The Languedocian cobbler (Truquette)
— He *refuses to rob* a tailor.	+ He *agrees to steal* textiles.
+ He beats and *kills* his wife.	— He beats his wife *but does not kill her*.

C9 and C10: *Nothing.*

D9: *The grandmother promises the cobbler that he will make his fortune.*

D10: *She asks him to become a swindler; he agrees and operates in textiles.*

These two segments of *Jean-l'ont-pris*, D9 and D10, represent, as we have seen, the same division as C4 and C5 in the 'Swiss tale'; but this segment, in *Jean-l'ont-pris*, is shifted downwards. That is why sections C9 and C10 are 'nothing' in the 'Swiss tale'; they no longer have any reason to be there (by virtue of C4 and C5, earlier).

About D9 (the promises made by the grandmother/godmother to the cobbler Truquette after his fight with Margot that he will make his fortune), there is not a great deal to say, except that, in view of a drop of five segments (right-hand column), this segment D9 corresponds exactly to the promises made to the Swiss cobbler by the Green Man godfather in C4. These promises are ritual and normal in all the versions of the tale A T 332/*Godfather Death* at this precise point in the plot.

On the other hand, the parallel between C5 and D10 is a remarkable one: in C5, the Green Man suggests that the Swiss cobbler become a thief, at the expense in particular of a tailor. The Swiss cobbler refuses to agree to this request, since a little later he will become the murderer of his wife, which will be quite enough to put him in the 'dock'. In D10, the grandmother suggests that the Languedocian cobbler become a swindler, in particular in muslin and haberdashery. He agrees, since he has not killed his wife during the earlier fight with her; his criminal activities in the rag trade will be enough to justify his final condemnation. We now come to episodes C11 and D11, which are fundamentally the same in both tales.

C11: *The Swiss cobbler is condemned to death and executed.*

D11: *The cobbler Truquette is condemned to death and executed.*

Yet there is a difference: in the 'Swiss tale', in C11, the cobbler is killed by the executioner's sword. Beheading is, in fact, an ancient method of capital punishment.[76] Moreover, we find this execution by sword, but only in the form of a threat to the hero, in the oldest version of A T 332, the one collected by Jacob Grimm in the early nineteenth century.[77] In *Jean-l'ont-pris*, the grandmother, who is the functional equivalent of the Death of A T 332, also attacks her son-in-law Truquette with a blunt tool (an awl). But Truquette survives. In the end, death will come to this son-in-law through hanging, a technique which the grandmother or Death (or their accomplices) also uses, in various ways, in the course of the abbé Fabre's narrative; it is also one that Death uses (in the form of strangling or twisting the neck) in the oldest versions of A T 332.[78]

The detailed comparison of *Jean-l'ont-pris* and the 'Swiss tale' seems to me to have a further interest: by means of an additional homology, it links *Jean-l'ont-pris* more securely still to the Germanic and southern French cycle of AT 332.

Lastly, it will be recalled that the final disappearance, at the end of the first part of the novella, of J L P's father and mother affects the parents differently: Truquette, as a thief, ends on the scaffold. Before meeting Truquette, Margot might have married a carder or a journeyman taffeta-maker; these two trades are, in the Nîmes region, strongly linked to Protestantism.[79] Once her husband Truquette is arrested, she swings more clearly still to the side of her mother, the old woman; she is a Huguenot, of course, but, 'worse than that', she represents Death. Margot will now travel the world and enjoy a perfect love affair with a knife-grinder, who will willingly sharpen cutting and pointed blades for his deadly mistress.[80] Perhaps we should add that the word *Margot*, in Occitan, is not only the diminutive of the Christian name Marguerite. It also means 'magpie' (a bird of ill-omen) and even, quite simply, 'death'.[81] Once more, Margot, the girl with the basil, appears as a deadly partner of her mother, who herself represents Death.

CHAPTER X

The Forces of Death Attack
Jean-l'ont-pris

At the end of the 'life of Truquette', we left J L P as naked as on the
day of his birth [36], undressed by the constabulary who had come to
arrest his father. The hero is therefore ready for a new departure, for
a second cycle of his romance.

So we come to the second part of the abbé Fabre's tale. This is no
longer the life of Truquette, but that of Jean-l'ont-pris; no longer the
father, but the son. On this point the parallel between *Jean-de-trop*
and various versions of A T 332 is a precise one; they, too, recount first
the life of the father, Death's *compère*, then that of the son, Death's
godson. Generally speaking, every version of A T 332, whether
German, Spanish-American or French, which deals with Death's godson
(J L P) begins by evoking, however briefly, the life of the father of
this godson and *compère* of Death, in other words, our Truquette.

Let us come back to this son: in A14 of Table I (*Jean-de-trop*),
Death becomes the young man's teacher. In B14 of the same table
(*Jean-l'ont-pris*), the grandmother becomes Jean-l'ont-pris's teacher.
Again, there is a homology. But in the next sentence, in A15 and B15,
respectively, the narratives diverge: J D T in A15 accepts Death's
teaching. J L P, in B15, on the other hand, rejects his grandmother's
teaching. These two sequences A14–A15 and B14–B15 (Table I) are
worthy of examination.

Death's teaching (A14) is presented at the same crucial stage of the
narrative in almost all the known versions of A T 332, from the first
texts – Icelandic, German, Anglo-Latin, Italian and French,[1] from
the fourteenth to the eighteenth century – right up to the innumerable
popular versions of the tale, collected in the nineteenth and the twentieth centuries in various parts of the Christian world, from western
and southern France, from Europe and America. (Indeed, it should
be remembered that despite a few local 'openings' of A T 332 towards
European or Eastern Judaism, and towards Turkish Anatolia, this is
a tale deeply rooted in Christianity, since it is based on the institution
of godfatherhood at the time of baptism. There is no A T 332 in
Chinese folklore, and for a very good reason: the Chinese do not
baptize their children).

Death's teaching, in *JDT*, rests on the classic themes of the A T 332 tale type: in the context of family prosperity that was previously brought about by godmother Death, the young man (J D T) is sent to school, taught to read and write; however, he manages not to learn Latin. His macabre godmother tells him, now eighteen years of age, that he should take up medicine; in other words, he will be endowed with supernatural powers in this domain: he will predict that the patient will die when Death, visible to him alone, stands at the *head* of the sick-bed. In A T 332 in general, as in *Jean-l'ont-pris* in particular, Death attacks the patient's upper extremities: the hair, the neck and, of course, the 'head' in general. If Death stands at the foot of the bed, however, the patient will survive, and Jean-de-trop need only administer a glass of water, containing a few drops of liquorice water; in this way he will be able to take credit for the cure – and make a fortune from the magnificent fees that will fall into his lap.

In certain versions of A T 332, German, French and others, however, a reversal takes place: Death is mortal when he stands at the foot of the bed, and not mortal when he stands at the head of the patient. This inversion does not in any way change the development of the plot. *Jean-de-trop* conforms to the canonical German, French, etc., schema of A T 332, right down to the smallest detail: the placebo of cold water or phial of water, with or without the addition of liquorice water, that is supposed to cure the patient. (In some versions of A T 332, this phial of water is replaced by a magic herb or root.)

Quite specifically, Death's teaching (*JDT* in A14 of Table 1) belongs to the second stage of the structural and canonical schema of A T 332, which is valid for some three hundred versions of the tale, collected in various countries. Perhaps therefore, we ought, briefly, to recall this schema, which has been perfectly defined by Bolte and Polivka, whose analyses were later to be taken up by Aarne and Thompson.[2]

The schema of AT 332

First stage: *Death is godfather*, or godmother. He becomes, therefore, the *compère* or *commère* of the poor father of the child whom he will hold over the baptismal font.

Second stage: *Death's gifts*. 'Death', write Aarne and Thompson, '*gives* the father (or the child when he has grown up) the power of predicting the outcome of an illness, depending on whether Death stands at the head or the foot of the bed . . .' It is specifically at the beginning of this second stage, called 'Death's gifts', that the pedagogical episode that interests me for the moment is situated: Death *teaches*, or announces to the beneficiary, the medical gifts that he will now have at his disposal. It should be noted, however, that in certain versions of AT 332, Death's gifts may consist simply in the granting of prosperity to his family or of a rewarding future, with the help of diabolical powers, as a swindler – the medical reference being in such cases scarcely visible. This is so, for example, in the 'Swiss tale' and in the 'Truquette' episode of *Jean-l'ont-pris*. Even according to this hypothesis, the pedagogical phase is still heavily stressed by the narrative: take the advice given by the Green Man to the Swiss cobbler, and that given to Truquette by the grandmother, who gives her son-in-law certain lessons in how to make his fortune through swindling [30]. It should be added that the medical allusion, even in this apparently non-medical context, never completely disappears: in the 'Swiss tale', the cobbler is given a root by the Green Man that will enable him to *cure* his wife, who is sick and bedridden after childbirth. As far as Truquette's good acts are concerned, these consist of the soup and meat, bought by him with what is left of his splendid wedding garments, which will enable Margot, also in bed after childbirth, to get on her feet again, that is, to be cured, after the morbid fatigue of parturition that produced the child Jean-l'ont-pris. I shall speak, in the next chapter, of the medical actions in which JLP himself takes part, including the curing of Sestier and the failure to cure Barbe-Garouille.[3]

Third stage: *Death is betrayed*. The doctor, previously showered with gifts by Death, deceives Death and saves a patient threatened with death. In order to do this, he turns, from end to end, instantaneously (on castors, and with the help of four strong men) the bed on which his patient lies; he therefore, *ipso facto*, changes the strategic site of Death. Having stood at the patient's head, the position in which he announced death, Death is now, without having moved, at the foot of the bed, the position that announces a cure. So the man is safe and sound. There is another trick, which sometimes occurs alone or sometimes immediately after the previous one: the doctor, whom

Death wishes to punish for betraying him and who normally succeeds in doing so at the end of his life, arranges for his *own* bed to be turned or to turn himself 180 degrees in his bed in order to escape Death, who is at his head;[4] or he manages never to end the prayer for the dying that he was reciting on his own account, the *Pater Noster*, for example;[5] or he does not finish an apple that he has begun to eat, etc. His own death is thus indefinitely postponed. Or, again, by trickery, he encloses Death in a bottle, a chest, a cask of Languedoc wine or a barrel of Scandinavian beer. The doctor Death's godson then buries the bottle, throws it out to sea, etc. Temporarily, at least, Death can no longer do anything against him, or even against mankind in general. For some time, nobody dies . . .

Fourth stage: *Death takes his revenge.* He emerges from his barrel or bottle, or whatever it was that he was enclosed in. He then puts out the doctor's light of life, in the cellar in which all men's lights of life are to be found, in the form of candles, oil-lamps, torches, etc. He kills his godson by strangling him or striking him. He first has to trick him into stopping the interminable prayer that he is saying, lest in the end, despite a violent death, he dies with his soul at peace.

It should be noted that the versions of AT 332 that I have so far commented on comply faithfully with this four-part schema, in its logically linear development; and this is so even when one of the links may be missing, thus mutilating the whole sequence, though without in any way destroying it. Thus in 'Truquette', we have stage 1 (the grandmother/godmother), stage 2 (the grandmother's gifts to her son-in-law—*compère*, which bring unlawful prosperity to Truquette) and stage 4 (the disappearance of the hero, attacked and punished by Death, herself identified elsewhere with the grandmother).[6] However, stage 3 (Truquette betrays Death, alias the grandmother) is missing, except in a highly vestigial and implicit way. Truquette is too generally a born 'loser' to 'trick' Death.

As far as *Jean-de-trop* is concerned, the first three stages are perfectly identified:

(1) *Death* is the child's *godmother.*

(2) *Death's gifts* go first, in the form of prosperity, to Jean-de-trop's parents in the course of an initial repetition of the complete

development of AT 332; they then go a second time to Jean-de-trop himself, during the pedagogical episode (and subsequently) that will soon transform the young man into a famous doctor.

(3) Jean-de-trop *betrays Death* in order to obtain from her an additional favour that was not envisaged in the original agreement: he tricks her into entering a gourd, in which he then shuts her up until she accedes to his request.

(4) But stage 4 is missing. Death *does not take revenge* on Jean-de-trop. He triumphs insolently. He will die, it is true, but only in two hundred years (though this may be seen as Death's final revenge). It will be noticed that this happy ending is to be found in several versions of AT 332, in particular those in which the hero is the bearer of a characteristic that eludes Death by definition: those in which he is called *Penury*, *Falseness*, *Hatred*, *Envy* or *Dearth*. In such cases, Death's inability to take revenge, through murder, for the tricks that the hero who bears this predestined name has played on him, can mean only one thing: *Falseness* (Anglo-Latin version of AT 332, about 1450) or *Dearth* (versions from Quebec, imported from France into Canada between 1633 and 1763) or *Penury* (many French versions, going back at least to the eighteenth century) or *Hatred* and *Envy* (an Italian version of 1550, and a nineteenth-century Flemish version) are immortal.[7] These unsympathetic beings will always remain on earth, and for very good reason. Popular wisdom, of a rather pessimistic turn, is borne out here. In this case the happy ending is ambiguous: the victory over Death benefits some lying, poverty-stricken – in short, evil – entity. Nevertheless, the happy ending does exist in these specific cases. It concerns very old and authentic versions of AT 332 that were often contaminated by tales of other types (in particular, by the very popular AT 330 concerning *Bonhomme Misère*, or *Hodge*, as he is known in English). The happy ending thus proposed contradicts, in an exception that proves the rule, the general law of AT 332, according to which this tale is one of the few folk-tales or fairy-tales to end unhappily; in most cases, Death kills the doctor–hero in the end. There is nothing surprising about this general rule: AT 332 implies the active, personal intervention of Death; most of the heroes are all-powerful, except against Death, who is stronger than they. Truquette follows the general rule and is subjected to an unhappy ending; this is not, however, the case for Jean-l'ont-pris himself or

for Jean-de-trop, who both escape, at least temporarily, at the end of
the tale, from Death's attacks. Just as, in other versions, *Falseness*,
Penury and *Dearth* also escape him; indeed, the first of these is reminiscent of Jean-l'ont-pris himself, the swindler; and the other two
of Jean-de-trop, who was poor, and of Jean-l'ont-pris's parents, who
were *meurt-de-faim*. We should add that it was easier for Fabre,
having transformed Death into a mortal grandmother, to protect his
young hero from her ultimate attacks; through the death of this
grandmother, these attacks cease to be fatal, despite the final intervention of other substitute characters embodying the forces of death
(the one-eyed Quincarlot and the baron).

The first part of Fabre's tale, concerning Truquette, respected, as
does *Jean-de-trop*, the four-part development of A T 332, despite particular gaps that do not, however, undermine the overall structure.
Can the same be said of *Jean-l'ont-pris*, in the strict sense, that is the
second part (= *JLP 2*) of the abbé Fabre's tale, the part concerning
Truquette's son?

The answer, it would appear, is in the negative. In this second part,
Fabre seems to innovate in a rather radical way. Of course, he has
every right to do so, since as a writer, his only obligation is to write
well. Is not the status of *Jean-l'ont-pris*, a literary work, different
from that of folk-tales or fairy-tales as such, where the narrator
confines himself to transmitting from generation to generation a
certain canonical structure? The most he does is to alter it with small
touches of local or general inversions; in any case, whatever he does,
the structure always falls on its feet in the end, unless irreparable
deterioration has set in. For his part, Fabre overthrows, without any
apparent hesitation,[8] from the second part of his text onwards, the
raw material that folklore had provided him. Perhaps this is a round-
about way of coming back in the end, through total inversion, to the
deepest structures of the tale, the substance of which he has borrowed
and modified. I shall come back to this point.

In any case, where Truquette's son is concerned, Fabre has not
played the canonical game of A T 332. He tells us that, on his emergence
from childhood, this boy refuses Death's teaching, or, let us say, his
grandmother's teaching. He has decided that Jean-l'ont-pris will
betray the old woman as soon as his adventures begin.

At the end of his personal adventure, Truquette was dead, having followed the teachings of his mother-in-law; she had promised him the earth; she had guaranteed him prosperity through fraudulent bankruptcies. As a result, after some apparently happy, deceitful years, the scaffold had caught the dishonest cobbler. The lesson was not lost on the son: from the outset, he is to be the opposite of his father, success instead of failure, an anti-Truquette.[9] So he rejects the lessons in polite behaviour offered him by the old woman whose aim above all, expounded in a long speech [41–45], is that he frequent the rich and great. In fact, these lessons come straight from various southern French versions of AT 332: in at least four versions (*JDT* from Languedoc and others from Gascony, Aude and Catalonia), the tale insists at the beginning of its four-part cycle on the importance, for the hero, of connections with people of a higher social rank than his own. In her first speech in Jean-l'ont-pris's personal cycle, the grandmother, a character developed in written literature, sounds exactly like those models that came to the abbé from oral literature. 'One likes frequenting the rich – there is honour and profit in it; frequenting the poor brings nothing but displeasure,' says the Gibert and Maugard version of AT 332 at the point at which the first adventures of the hero, Death's godson, are about to be introduced. Similarly, the problem that bothers the poor woodcutter, who is soon to become a doctor protected by Death, in the Gascon AT 332 (Bédat de Monlaur, 1943, pp. 57–8) is how to get to eat with the rich, in other words, the precise theme of the grandmother's speech to her grandson J L P. At the beginning of *Jean-de-trop*, which derives as we know from what was one of the closest models of *JLP*, the theme of the hero's deplorable lack of rich connections is also treated with some vehemence; J D T's father, in effect, goes to his friends to ask them, in vain, if they would be so kind as to be godfather to his male child: *There were not many of them, because he was poor.* The aim of the hero or of the hero's father at the beginning of the cycle of *Godfather Death* is to persuade, if possible, some important people to come to the baptismal banquet, 'a banquet of grandees', as Amades's Catalan version puts it (tale 99, p. 244). We know what a fundamental role patronage and friendship, especially with the great, played in pre-industrial societies. We saw that Jean-l'ont-pris goes on to reproduce, but with greater success, the life adventure of his father, who was first protected by mother-in-law Death, until dismissed and later killed by the forces of death. Now, the initial banquet that introduced the Truquette cycle was intended, in a burlesque manner, of course, to be a feast for gourmets, with the 'riff-raff' left in the streets, outside the dining-room. It is hardly surprising, then, from the point of view of fidelity to the canonical beginnings of the tale *Godfather Death* (from the Midi), or from the point of view of repetition, with J L P beginning in the same way as his father, that the grandmother in her inaugural harangue treats of the fundamental theme of *the fellowship or conviviality that comes with wealth*. This theme, at this particular point in A T 332, is a ritual one. It is insepar-able from the motif of apprenticeship in 'politeness and the ways of the great world' [*JLP*, second version] or in 'good manners' (Cadic, 1908, p. 6) by the hero, under the auspices of the Languedocian grandmother Death or of the Breton godfather Death.

The grandmother also wants J L P to go to *primary* school [47]. In fact, the hero of A T 332, in this precise position, at the beginning of his career, is often educated in the context of the pedagogical under-taking of godfather Death.[10] But J L P has his own ideas on primary education. *I let her talk on and took charge of my own education* [first version]; *I listened to her while I was still small, but when I had grown up I took no notice* [second version]. In most of the versions of A T 332, Death transforms her godson's father, and then this godson himself, into a doctor – or in some cases she transforms him into a rich swindler, who is prosperous for a time (the case of Truquette and of the hero of the 'Swiss tale'). More elliptical and more allusive, Jean-l'ont-pris's grandmother touches on the 'medical' subject only indi-rectly by 'parables' and 'prophecies'. She does no more than suggest that she would like to turn her grandson into someone of *importance*, a skilful man.

The desire to make him a doctor does operate, however, in the form of an incomplete allusion and a half-attained fulfilment. Jean-l'ont-pris is, in effect, the functional equivalent of the physician-godson in A T 332. Now the relations between this young Languedocian and medicine, or at least the healing art, are unquestionable, if ambivalent. To begin with, he is of a medical, or paramedical, lineage: he is the grandson, by the left hand, of the surgeon of Calvisson, who was the lover of the future grandmother and the father of the bastard Margot, the hero's mother. Second, Fabre hints (by means of a joke that must be taken seriously) that not only the illegitimate grandfather, but also Jean-l'ont-pris's father belongs in some way to the medical profession. 'As for me,' Jean-l'ont-pris recounts in the second version, speaking of his infancy, 'they wrapped me in such a bundle of lace and ribbons that you would have taken me for the son of the king of Majorca or for the bastard son of a *capitaine de santé*.'

These two terms (*king of Majorca* and *capitaine de santé*) are redolent of 'folklore', in the most valuable sense of that abused word. In the Middle Ages, the kings of Majorca exercised their sovereignty over the region around Montpellier, so close to the abbé Fabre's Vaunage. They lost this local power to the kings of France after 1349.[11] The *capitaine de santé* was an official, a sort of medical dictator in the community, appointed in the southern towns and townships during the plagues of the sixteenth and seventeenth centuries; to be more precise, between 1530 and 1640.[12] They are, therefore, terms that were archaic in 1755, when Fabre wrote *Jean-l'ont-pris*. The abbé did not draw them from his personal stock of raw material. Did he draw them, then, from the oral folk-tale itself, in other words, from those versions of AT 332 that reached Languedoc and Catalonia (then under the suzerainty of Majorca) well before 1750? They then became adapted and modified, while retaining the deep structure; in the end, they provided the novelist–priest with his raw material, set in the hamlet of Solorgues, which had become largely Protestant since 1560.

The son of a *surgeon's* bastard daughter, who is himself compared to the bastard of a *capitaine de santé*, Jean-l'ont-pris actually has fantasies of personal identification with the double profession of apothecary and (again) of *capitaine de santé*. The boy is a scarcely concealed Aesculapius; he hints, on three occasions, each concerning one of three generations, at his vocation for the healing art! In the first version of *Jean-l'ont-pris*, Monsieur Sestier tells the young hero, Truquette's son, quite plainly: 'You would not have to be a marquis or a prince or a *capitaine de santé* to have my daughter. If you had Truquette's money or brains, she would be yours already . . .' [72]. The term *capitaine de santé*, then, has moved downstream a generation. One joke, quoted above, attributed this quasi-medical title to the hero's father. The second joking reference, made this time by Monsieur Sestier, proposes a similar title for the son; it seems a burlesque one, and yet it turns out to be particularly relevant when one delves into the depths of the narrative. In the second version, as if to leave no doubt on the matter, Fabre wanted to stress this point more. In this second version, the abbé took up a position, therefore, at the same strategic point in the plot as previously, when Jean-l'ont-pris asks Sestier for his daughter's hand: 'You see,' the young Languedocian says to the rich farmer, 'if I were a prince, a duke, an *apothecary*, instead of just a miserable down-and-out, I'd come and throw myself at your feet to ask for your daughter's hand.' To which Sestier replies with the same words as used in the first version. Nevertheless, he brings to these words certain systematic, significant attenuations: 'My child,' he says to Jean-l'ont-pris, 'you would not need to be a count or a marquis or a *wigmaker* to have my daughter, if you had *half* Truquette's money or only a *quarter* of his brains . . .' These attenuations amount, in fact, to a social, even an arithmetical, descent in the terms used: from the first version to the second, the marquis becomes a count; the prince, a marquis; the *capitaine de santé*, a wigmaker; and Truquette's 'money or brains' is transformed into 'half Truquette's money or only a quarter of his brains'. Simple divisions by two or four . . . They in no way alter the general meaning of the sentence, which remains as it was in this 'descent', but they enable us to understand Fabre's intentions more clearly. There is nothing mysterious about the decline from 'prince' to 'marquis', from 'money' to 'half his money'. What, however, is one to make of the rhetorical decline from *capitaine de santé* to wigmaker? The second term denotes a humble profession, possessing less prestige than the first, which implies the quasi-medical dictatorship practised by a *capitaine* over a plague-infested town. But why a *wigmaker* rather than some other, possibly different term that would also stress the humble nature of his profession? Fabre's mind, in this case, functioned by association of ideas, either 'free association' or conscious reasoning. From prince to marquis, the decline of a hierarchy functions within an aristocratic milieu . . . But what profession, on the great social scale, would indicate the next stage below a *capitaine de santé*? Physician is excluded for two reasons: first, this profession, as such, is banned from Fabre's tale. Certainly, Fabre kept very close to A T 332, but, by a kind of 'inferiorization' of the narrative, he shifted all values downwards. Second, the prestige possessed by a physician, a university graduate, is higher than that of a *capitaine de santé*, who, though a powerful figure of authority, is not even a qualified doctor. In fact, the term that is the next stage down from that of the *capitaine de santé* of the first version ought, normally, in the second version, to have been 'surgeon'. One would then have:

$$\frac{\text{prince}}{\text{marquis}} = \frac{\textit{capitaine de santé}}{\text{surgeon}}$$

Surgeon or, to be more precise, surgeon-barber: these two professions, both quite humble, that involve the knights of the lancet and razor, were, as we know, linked under the same title during the *ancien régime*. The brilliant surgeons of our own day, the equals of filmstars and playboys, had not yet arrived on the scene. Yet Fabre could not, at this point in his text, use the term 'surgeon'. For he had already used this term on two occasions in *Jean-l'ont-pris*: on the first occasion to designate the hero's grandfather [6]; on the second, to describe the individual who treats Monsieur Sestier's wounds [63]. He could do this twice – a third time would be too much. So Fabre finds, in the field of professional titles closest to that of 'surgeon-barber', the approximate or at least associative equivalent of this term. This equivalent, which refers to specialists in hair, is obviously 'wigmaker': so, in the second version, he replaces the term 'surgeon-barber', or 'surgeon', *qua* degraded substitution of *capitaine de santé*, so dear to the first version.

Lastly, we should note another association, or 'connotation': it concerns the remarks already quoted, made by Jean-l'ont-pris, when, in the second version, he describes the luxurious nature of his infantile clothing: 'you would have taken me . . . for the *bastard* son of a *capitaine de santé*'. Marcel Barral, the painstaking editor of Fabre's novel, has rightly reminded us of a line from Racine, a comic author on this occasion, in *Les Plaideurs*: 'Sir, I am your *apothecary's bastard*.' It is a very pertinent allusion: Fabre was a highly cultivated man who knew his classics; this line from Racine was part of the stock of available memories that would suggest themselves to him when writing about the bastard son of an individual working in the health services.

We can now arrange in a table Jean-l'ont-pris's paramedical aura:

	Fabre's text	Surrounding evocations or connotations
Ancestors	JLP is the grandson, through a bastard mother, of a *surgeon* (first generation). He compares himself to 'the bastard son of a *capitaine de santé*' (second generation).	→ Which evokes 'your *apothecary*'s bastard' (Racine, *Les Plaideurs*) (second generation).
JLP himself	JLP compares himself to a *capitaine de santé* (third generation). In the first version, Monsieur Sestier compares him to an *apothecary* (third generation).	In the second version (same passage), the evocation of a → wigmaker by Monsieur Sestier in relation to JLP is linked by association to the semantic field of the *surgeon*-barber (third generation).

In this table, the *apothecary/capitaine de santé/surgeon* triptych occurs twice: once in relation to Jean-l'ont-pris's forebears, grand-father and father (first and second generation) and, second, in relation to the hero himself (third generation). Jean-l'ont-pris is therefore anchored on all sides, in his real or humorous genealogy and in his own person, to a triple paramedical base; it concerns the preparation of remedies (apothecary), the mending of limbs (surgeon) and the control of the sick (*capitaine de santé*). At the same time, Fabre's text, examined from this point of view, takes away with one hand what it gives with the other: to present Jean-l'ont-pris as an apothecary/sur-geon/*capitaine de santé* is to declare *ipso facto* that he is *not* a doctor. The three professions involved here certainly have a worthy place in the healing art. They cannot, however, claim the supreme eminence that is possessed by the medical profession itself.

Whether seriously or in a burlesque way, Jean-l'ont-pris is no more than a medical assistant and not a fully qualified doctor; hence the novel treatment that Fabre is to give to two themes originally deriving from AT 332: the complete cure of a sick individual and the infallible prediction of a death. The first instance concerns the JLP–Sestier relationship and the second the JLP–Barbe-Garouille relationship. I shall come back to this.

In any case, Jean-l'ont-pris's undoubtedly paramedical vocation forces us to look more closely at certain passages [44] in the grandmother's speech to her grandson: 'If you are invited to a castle . . . if there are ladies present, don't forget to pinch their thighs and slap their knees, then drink their health . . . put your five fingers cleanly into the salt and sprinkle their food with it' [44]. In the second version, the 'five fingers' to take the salt become 'the *two* fingers like this'.

It will be noted that the educational speech delivered by the godmother Death or godfather Death of AT 332 in general refers, according to the canons, to the hero's future vocation as a doctor or *health* officer; now in this harangue (the homologue of this speech), delivered by the grandmother at the same strategic point in the tale, the only passage in which there is any mention of *health* is precisely that just quoted. It deserves, therefore, to be studied more closely and compared, if possible, with other available versions of AT 332.

I am thinking in particular of the version collected at a very early date by J. W. Wolf, published in 1851.[13] However, this comparison can be productive only when we have further advanced in the complete analysis of Jean-l'ont-pris's biography. I would therefore ask the reader to be patient (see Chapter XVI).

In any case, the shift downwards in the career of the hero JLP in relation to that of a fully qualified doctor proves illuminating: it throws light on certain procedures of composition that Fabre initiated in his treatment of the folklore type (AT 332) that provided him with his raw materal.

In fact, a double shift has taken place: *JLP* is based on an old medieval tale, transformed in the baroque period and orally transmitted to Fabre, in which Death is the godfather of a character whom he turns into a doctor. But Fabre transformed Death into a grandmother, and the doctor into a young village ruffian. This double gap allows the author certain divergences from his model. Death, having been secularized into 'grandmother', can be made to die in

JLP all the more easily. It is a highly ambivalent way of saying that she is herself and nothing more. As Death, she ought in principle to be immortal. However, being nothing more than an old woman, she finally dies [65] of indigestion brought on by an excess of grapes and other fruit, this being regarded as a true sign of poverty [67]. In the vast majority of the canonical versions of AT 332, Death triumphs at the end of the narrative: he carries off the hero to the cave filled with millions of candles or oil-lamps. There he dies just as his own light of life is put out. This final episode is encountered in a number of the very old German, French and especially southern French versions of AT 332. There is no doubt that Fabre knew this; but he had transformed Death into a mere old woman, doomed to die. He could not, therefore, allow her a final triumph, or give the godson a fatal apotheosis in the cave. Nevertheless, he kept the tiny means of light, so dear to the old woman in the form of matches. Conforming to the general schema of AT 332, he brought them in at the end of the old woman's narrative career; but they are also present at the beginning of this career, for Fabre, following certain Occitan versions of the tale, had the right to proceed in this way (see Chapter IX).

The gap between the grandmother, then, and the Death of folklore that served as the model for Fabre's literary character, is a modest one. But we should also note a gap between the young JLP and the doctor/Death's godson, of AT 332, from whom he derives: JLP is crypto-medical or paramedical, and yet not a doctor. Some of the things said by the grandmother in her speech to JLP [41–45] stress this dissonance. Let us look at what the grandmother says: she suggests to her grandson, in order to make him her accomplice, that he wear his dress and hat in a certain way. But, although the young man nods his assent, he in fact refuses to follow her advice. On this matter JLP is quite adamant that for a very long time, and quite deliberately, he wore neither hat nor gown [45].

This refusal takes place in a whole context of negations, by means of which JLP takes up a position in direct contradiction to the old woman's commandments: in fact, what he wants above all else is to avoid becoming the underling that this shrew had made of his father, a state that had brought him to the scaffold; he wants to avoid being 'strangled' (as was Truquette) by assuming the social ambitions she proposes (see paragraph 45, where this refusal to be strangled is quite clearly stated). For example, in the comments that JLP throws out from time to time concerning his grandmother's advice, he emphasizes quite strongly that, contrary to the old woman's orders, he has never frequented the rich and powerful; that his only contact with lords of the manor was through the gamekeeper of the Château de La Boissière, a quite unimportant, friendly individual with whom he has occasionally dined [45]. Now this professional predecessor of poachers is quite simply the precise antithesis of the *hunter of La Boissière*, mentioned on the occasion of Truquette's wedding [17], presided over by the dangerous grandmother, some twenty years before.

Let us look more closely at the hat and at the way the grandmother insists that it should be worn. (However, when the forces of death attack JLP, they try, with the grandmother to the fore, to uncover his head by shaving it, pulling out the hairs, etc.)

By ordering JLP to wear diabolical headgear in the form of a tripod of matches, *pulled down over the right eye*, and herself showing him how (*Death shuts one eye*, Grimm observes at the same point of AT 332),[14] the grandmother wants to transform her grandson into a macabre and temporarily lucky accomplice of herself or of Death; an accomplice like Quincarlot, who wore his purse on the left and was blind in the right eye, in other words, a carrier of the *evil eye* (or sole surviving left eye).[15] It is understandable that JLP should refuse this poisoned proposition, since he wants above all to avoid the lucrative, but in the end fatal enterprises of his dangerous stepmother and grandmother. So the hero will wear a child's cap for some time [45], but not a hat. Much time will have to elapse after the old woman's death before he will agree to covering his head. Even then he will wear his hat on the back of his head, carefully pulled down, completely *exposing* his forehead and eyes . . . [1]. There is no question of pulling it down over the right eye.

This refusal of a hat or of a particular way of wearing it is in general a rejection of his grandmother, whose respectful, obedient grandson – and therefore doomed to a violent death – he refuses to be. But it is also, implicitly, and taking into account the overall structures of the master narrative of AT 332, a specific refusal to become Death's godson doctor, or the grandmother's grandson doctor. The southern French versions of AT 332, which are often very close to our *JLP*, lay considerable stress on the fact that the hero, who follows the instructions of godmother Death, is transformed into a doctor, and henceforth wears the cap and gown that are characteristic of his medical status.[16] JLP, however, rebels against his grandmother. He refuses to be and to appear a medical individual and therefore to wear the gown and hat that for him would be the external signs of medicine. He wears the peasant child's cap [17] and not the hat of a notable [45]. Jean-l'ont-pris is in a situation of refusal. As soon as his grandmother's speech is over [45–7], he has made his secret choice. He will say no. He will not go to school, but play truant: instead of making bows, he will turn somersaults; he will get rid of the schoolbook that the old woman bought for him, exchanging it for a slice of egg-plant [47]. This love of fine fruit and vegetables continues to inspire the young man in the next phases of the narrative: he devours [53] the fine plump clingstone peaches in Monsieur Sestier's orchard. A little later he is seduced by the velvety cheeks of the desirable Babeau, which are 'the colour of clingstone peaches' [72].

JLP's youthful refusal of his grandmother's discipline is severely punished, 'countered', as soon as it appears. This brings us to the following episode of *JLP*: the hero learns to throw stones, climb trees and fight a donkey. Fabre obtained these details from versions of a tale closely related to AT 332, then current in southern and western France. This tale is *Jean-lou-pec* (*Jean-le-sot*); with its initials ('JLP') and general sound, its title is very close to our *Jean-l'an-près* [Jean-l'ont-pris, in Occitan]. It is also close as far as the meaning of the words is concerned: Jean-l'ont-pris (*l'an-près*, but also *l'emprès*) means (among other puns on his name) not only Jean-*ils l'ont pris* ['they have taken him away'], but also Jean *l'empoté* ['the clumsy'], *l'entrepris* ['the senseless'], *le nigaud* ['the fool'] – in short, Jean-le-sot ['the stupid'], alias 'Jean-lou-pec'.[18]

However, the essential proximity of the two texts (*Jean-l'ont-pris* and *Jean-le-sot*) derive in the first instance from the common contents of the narrative.

Before examining this link between Fabre's work and *Jean-lou-pec*, we should first clarify the relationship between *Jean-lou-pec* and AT 332. On this point I would mention an illuminating Breton version of *Godfather Death*. This version has nothing specifically Celtic about it. It simply corresponds to the concrete form, which remained faithful to the original structures, that tale type 332 assumed when it arrived from central Europe and took root in southern or western France, and therefore in Brittany. A T 332 became naturalized without difficulty in the Breton peninsula: the originally male, because German, character of Death [*der Tod*, in German] was identified easily enough with the Breton Ankou,19 a local personification of death who also happened to be masculine. In the Latin countries, in which the word 'death' is linguistically feminine, a whole gymnastics was necessary to transpose, by means of a variety of transitions, the godfather Death of the countries beyond the Rhine into what eventually became the godmother Death of A T 332 in its French, Italian, Castilian, Portuguese or Spanish-Mexican forms.

I shall now summarize one of the versions collected by F.-M. Luzel in his *Légendes chrétiennes de la Basse-Bretagne*20 under the title *Ankou and His Compère*.

A poor man is looking for a godfather for his newborn child. A stranger (Ankou) offers his services. The baptism takes place, followed either by a frugal or by a sumptuous meal. Ankou gives the child's father the gift of being a physician, in other words, of predicting the patient's death or survival, depending on whether Ankou is at the head or the foot of the bed. Suddenly dubbed 'doctor', the hitherto poor man gives cold water as a pseudo-remedy when the prognosis is favourable; as a result, his ability to foresee the future is considered by people to be a miraculous pharmaceutical technique. The new physician rapidly acquires the reputation of being more efficacious than his colleagues, whether they owe their titles to the university or are mere quacks: they use herbs [*louzou*] that do not cure. The new doctor, from the outset, decides to trick Ankou, who has the fatal habit of standing at the head of the bed of the patients visited: the trick consists in getting the bed completely turned round (or as we would say in geometry 'pi over 2', $\frac{\pi}{2}$) by a couple of strong fellows; in this way Death finds himself automatically at the feet of the patient, who, for that reason, is cured and who attributes this cure to the cold water imbibed on the doctor's orders. In this way our hero brings two great lords back to health; he becomes rich, thanks to the magnificent fees that these two gentlemen have paid him. He cares not a fig that Death is furious with him, and he continues on his triumphant career. He decides to go and 'cure' the king of France, who is ill. He takes the road for Paris and goes to visit His Majesty. During the journey, he crosses a forest in which he meets Ankou, who, as always, haunts woods and forests. Ankou threatens him. He shrugs his shoulders and continues on his way. He arrives at his destination, and overcomes the resistance of the porter at the royal palace, who calls him 'a poor Breton bone-setter' and threatens to set the dogs on him to prevent him from entering that august place. However, he gains access to the king's bedside. The usual scenario takes place – the trick of the turned bed, Death's anger, the placebo of cold water – and the sovereign is cured. The doctor returns to his own country, showered with presents and accompanied by four mules laden with money. He buys farms and woods and has a magnificent castle built. He is nicknamed Trompe-la-Mort ['Trick Death']. But everything comes to an end. In one of the two versions of this Breton narrative, the shorter one, the rich physician follows the classic procedure of being taken by Death/Ankou into the cellar of lights, and he dies, with the extinction of his own light of life. In the other version, the doctor lends his assistance to Ankou, who has become a carter, in order to cure one of the horses of the 'death-cart', a horse suffering from wind and diarrhoea. So the physician picks up a stone from the road and sticks it as a bung firmly into the horse's anus. But the animal summons up its strength and, with a well-calculated fart, expels the stone. The physician is struck on the forehead and falls down dead. Ankou has won. His revenge is complete. (We should also note that in Brittany, another tale, collected by Sébillot,[21] describes the fart of a priest, particularly given to this kind of thing, who with a well-calculated fart sends a deadly turnip into the midst of his congregation: this takes place, of course, during the celebration of the mass in the old style, when the priest had his back to the faithful for most of the service.)

The Breton hero of the narrative collected by Luzel has many common features – and there is nothing surprising in this resemblance – with the first hero of *JLP*, Truquette, and also with Jean-de-trop. The baptismal meal is sometimes sumptuous (white bread), sometimes frugal (buckwheat pancakes), depending on the versions.

sumptuous meal	first version of Breton tale	Jean-de-trop
frugal meal	second version	Jean-l'ont-pris

The Breton hero, we are told, is fond of his *chopine*, as is Truquette [*chopine*] and the Swiss archetype of Truquette [*Schöpplein*]. The beginning of the Breton tale describes the hero, walking-stick in hand, meeting Death, just as Truquette, the Rouergat immigrant, sticks his pilgrim's staff [second version of *JLP*], at the beginning of the narrative,[22] in the ground where he is to meet grandmother Death. Like Jean-de-trop, the Breton doctor goes to Paris to cure the king of France. The hero's wealth, possibly obtained at the outset by Death or by the old woman, is transported on donkeys laden with food in *JDT* or *JLP*, on four mules laden with money in the Breton tale. The supernatural prosperity of the same character is marked by the buying of various lands, vineyards, olive-groves 'and the finest house in the neighbourhood' (*JLP*), or by 'the buying of farms, woods and the building of a magnificent castle' (Luzel, 1881); indeed, this acquisition of property often occurs, at the same strategic link, in the French and Spanish versions of A T 332. The correspondence, feature by feature, between *Jean-de-trop* and the Breton text derives, of course, from their connection with common ancestors, in other words, from archetypal versions of A T 332 that reached France some centuries before and which bifurcated in the direction of either Brittany or Occitania.

Also of great importance is the kinship between *Jean-le-sot*, an episodic tale disseminated from Poitou to Languedoc and from Normandy to Provence, and A T 332, which reached the west and south of France. (I would reject as too facile any hypercritical view that *Jean-le-sot* is an invention of the nineteenth century, dating after the abbé Fabre; in fact, *Jean-le-sot* already existed on French territory before 1763, or, to put it more simply, before 1756 and Fabre's *JLP*, since it is still to be found in many parts of Quebec as a fossil of the cultural imports that arrived from France before the treaty of Paris [1763], during the reigns of Louis XIV and Louis XV.)[23]

The episode of the horse's fatal fart, in the Breton tale, is also to be found at the end of the Occitan version[24] of *Jean-lou-pec* (Jean-le-sot, or John the Fool). This version was collected in the early 1880s by J.-F. Bladé in Gascony. A character who represents Death or at least Death's messenger informs Jean-lou-pec that he will die under the impact of his donkey's third fart. After this redoubtable animal's first two farts, which begin to fulfil this prophecy and which are the equivalent of the diarrhoea, mentioned earlier, suffered by Death's horse, an anxious Jean-lou-pec sets about stuffing a strong, sharp stake up the animal's anus. In order to drive this 'bung' in more securely, he gives it a few blows with a hammer (in the Breton narrative, the doctor struck the stone, which served as a bung, with another stone). But in Bladé's version the donkey swells up; it makes a great effort and, with a gigantic fart, expels the stake – which goes right through Jean-lou-pec. The prediction of Death's messenger is thus fulfilled; just as, in the Breton narrative, Ankou finally rubs his hands, delighted at having foreseen and arranged his *compère*'s death by means of his horse's fart.

So the tale of *Jean-lou-pec* is related or 'anastomosed', by means of its conclusions (identical to those of *Ankou and His Compère*), to the cycle of AT 332, in western and southern France. A version from Ariège of AT 332, collected by G. Maugard, also preserves the (attentuated) memory of the same episode. In it we see, in effect, that the physician–hero has tricked Death into a barrel; when the bung is inadvertently taken out, the horrible shrew leaves the barrel through the opening, like a violent wind, and nearly knocks out anyone who happens to be in the way. In a German version of AT 332 (Aurbacher, 1879, p. 121), a strong, cold wind comes in through the window and blows out the physician's light of life, which Death was holding; in this way the seriously sick doctor, who had previously thought he could trick Death by turning his bed round in the usual way, meets his own death.

It is, in any case, interesting and certainly legitimate to compare *Jean-lou-pec* and *Jean-l'ont-pris*.

It is no accident that there are strong structural resemblances (together with logical transformations that further emphasize the structure by respecting it) in the way a particularly crucial episode is treated in these two narratives; they are an effect of the kinship shared by both *Jean-lou-pec* and *Jean-l'ont-pris* with the southern cycle of AT 332.

To begin with, I offer a brief analysis of the 'common trunk' of our two stories; it corresponds to the episode described in paragraphs 48 to 51 of the Occitan version of *Jean-l'ont-pris*. In the case of *Jean-lou-pec*, I shall first give a summary of Bladé's Occitan version collected and published in the nineteenth century. It circulated here and there well after that time, and, in 1958, Daniel Fabre collected further important fragments, purely oral in origin, from a family of storytellers in the Minervois.[25]

After various adventures of a peculiar or stupid kind, Jean-lou-pec (John the idiot) attacks the statue of a saint, which he reproaches with dishonesty. He strikes the statue with a stick, breaks open an alms-box at the foot of the statue and seizes the money. He then climbs a tree and with a hatchet cuts off the branch on which he is sitting! A passer-by tells him that he will fall, and, in fact, he does so. The man then predicts that he will die from a fart from his donkey . . . The end of the narrative then follows (I have already summarized the version collected by Bladé: the death of Jean-lou-pec, killed by a stake ejected by the donkey's fart).

Table 4 shows the comparison of this large final portion of *Jean-lou-pec* with a corresponding episode in *Jean-l'ont-pris*.

The abbés Fabre was well acquainted with a number of versions of *Jean-lou-pec*: they circulated throughout the Occitan world and in the west of France; they reached the Vaunage; he made free use of them in order to construct the triple episode *JLP* summarized in the right-hand column of Table 4. Working in this way, Fabre respected the structures of the folk-tale that provided him with his raw material. But he systematically *weakened* them – or he may have borrowed (from oral tradition) an already existing weak version that subsequently disappeared without any other trace but in his own work, so that nineteenth- and twentieth-century folklore specialists were able to collect only *strong* versions of the tale.

Whatever the case, a new table, summarizing Table 4, brings out at every level the effects of this 'weakening', in the version borrowed or rewritten by Fabre (see Table 4a).

We should also note other movements away from the oral tale to the written novel. Jean-lou-pec is always holding some weapon that he uses stupidly and clumsily, in a direct, violent, crude way: a club to smash the statue of the saint (Table 4, F1), a hatchet to cut the branch on which he is sitting (F2), a sharpened stake which he stupidly

Table 4

Jean-lou-pec (collected by Blade, 1886)	*Jean-l'ont-pris* [48–51]
F1: Jean-lou-pec, who goes around breaking things, strikes the statue of a saint with a stick.	G1: Jean-l'ont-pris, an expert stone-thrower, claims that he could hit the baron's nose at a distance of eighty paces [48].
F2: Jean-lou-pec cuts the branch of a tree on which he is sitting. He falls to the ground.	G2: JLP climbs to the top of a high tree to get a bird's nest. The branch on which he is sitting snaps, and he falls to the ground in danger of his life [49–50].
F3: Jean-lou-pec sticks a stake up his donkey's *behind*. The donkey then farts and ejects the stake, which goes right through Jean-lou-pec's body and *kills* him. In other versions of the tale (see D. Fabre, Millien and Delarue, etc.), Jean-lou-pec *revives* after this 'death', which is then shown to have been shammed.	G3: JLP throws a stick at the *front* legs of his grand-mother's donkey. The donkey counter-attacks by placing its legs on JLP's head and belly, crushing, but not quite *killing* him. In the end JLP *gets up*, somewhat bruised [51].

(and vainly) knocks into the donkey's anus (F3). Contrasted with this stupid individual is Jean-l'ont-pris, his brother in folklore. He is cunning. He is a skilful huntsman who can fight an enemy at a considerable distance; at eighty paces [48], he can throw a stone that will hit the nose of a human target (Table 4, G1); in order to catch magpies that are out of reach, he skilfully and dangerously climbs to

Table 4a: Summary of Table 4	
Jean-lou-pec	*Jean-l'ont-pris*
F1: Real aggression (= *strong*)	G1: Symbolic aggression (= *weak*)
F2: Quasi-suicidal accident (= *strong*)	G2: Genuine accident (= *weak*)
F3: The donkey kills the hero (= *strong*)	G3: A dangerous, but not fatal, ordeal imposed on the hero by the donkey (= *weak*)

the top of a tree (G2). At fifteen paces, he throws a stick to break the legs of a hare or a donkey (G3). It is a weaker version of the tale; a cleverer character. A double translation, therefore, is involved. And yet the abbé respected the threefold development of the tale that served as his raw material: aggression, tree, donkey.

Now to the details: Jean-lou-pec's real aggression against the statue of the saint is directed against a character who is supposedly *dishonest* (the saint has tricked him, the idiot believes, as to the price of a piece of cloth that the idiot has sold him). This aggression is also directed against a *rich* character: at the feet of the saint lies an alms-box full of money. The baron, who is the object of the symbolic aggression that Jean-l'ont-pris claims to be capable of (a stone thrown at a distance of eighty paces could smash the lordly nose of the nobleman in question, J L P tells him . . .), is also depicted as *rich*. He owns a castle; he could, says J L P, finance a great festival, at the risk of getting drowned head over heels [17]; above all he is described, like the saint, as possibly dishonest, capable of stealing the purse of one of Truquette's accomplices [32]. Moreover, the said Quincarlot, whom J L P, a little later, also thinks of treating to a stone in the face [81], is in turn an outstanding symbol of dishonesty; he is even called 'bundle of knavish tricks' [79].

In G3 of Table 4, Fabre also begins with a similarity (the donkey), but he carries it to the point of inversion in order to mark the distance, the opposition even, that separates Jean-l'ont-pris and his homologue Jean-lou-pec. So the donkey turns 180 degrees, the classic 'pi over 2' that is later to be found canonically used: the hero no longer attacks this donkey at close quarters, between the back legs, or by stopping the anus with a stake. He attacks the animal from a distance, and from the front; he throws a club across the two front legs. Leaving this animal's rear orifice, the hero, regretting his action, gives the animal (which he has brought to the ground) a hundred kisses on the mouth and eyes [51]. By way of reply, the animal gives the young man, instead of a fart that would pierce his chest, a look that would have pierced the soul of a tax collector [51]. The piercing eye has certainly replaced the anus capable of emitting piercing farts.[26] Does this transformation or horizontal rotation from back to front represent, on the abbé's part, some moral delicacy, an attempt to suppress the scatalogical aspects of the story by a shift from the donkey's anus to its eye? It is rather, I would repeat, a way of indicating a distancing or an inversion. It is also a way, as far as JLP's destiny is concerned, of avoiding the hero's death at the 'hands' of the donkey's fatal fart; the best way of making sure of this is, of course, by confronting the animal from the front and not from behind. It is not yet time, as it will never be time, in *JLP*, to kill the hero; by definition, this hero escapes death, at least during the entire development of the tale.[27] JLP will never, therefore, be pierced by a stake delivered by a fart. At most he will be 'crushed' [51], but not in a fatal way, by the weight of the donkey's head and legs. JLP's symbolic death or 'crushing', followed by his resurrection, has its equivalent in many versions of *Jean-le-sot* in northern and southern France: at the end of these versions, the young hero revives after the donkey has inflicted on him a 'death' that is merely a pseudo-death. We should also note that in both cases the aggression from the donkey is aimed at the hero's chest: *Jean-l'ont-pris* expressly mentions this fact [51]; in the oral, Languedocian version of *Jean-lou-pec* collected by Daniel Fabre, the story-teller also stresses that it is the young man's chest that is pierced by the 'donkey's kick', or by the stake that is expelled from the animal's anus. This stake pierces right through the boy's body.

I should like to say a few words now about the donkey itself, the author of a counter-offensive in which JLP's body is 'flattened' or 'crushed'. Does the place occupied at the successive stages of Fabre's novella by this animal throw any light for us on its precise role? Let us follow the thread: from the first pages of Truquette's biography, a couple of donkeys are laden with food for the post-nuptial, pre-baptismal feast [14]; then another couple of donkeys, or the same ones, are laden, again by Truquette, with goods stolen by him in accordance with the evil advice given by the grandmother [31]. These pairs of animals are the homologues of the donkeys laden with provisions for Jean-de-trop's pre-baptismal feast that were guided by the supernatural powers of the tale. In *JLP*, they function as miraculous agents that assist, first in providing the sumptuous feast, then in Truquette's professional life; just as, in *JDT*, they assist in the prosperity of Jean-de-trop's father (see, also, in the Breton version of AT 332,[28] the mules laden with money; they symbolize the recent wealth of the physician–hero, who, like Truquette, uses it to buy land, a fine house, etc.). Each in his own tale and on his own account, Truquette and Jean-de-trop's father use them or benefit from them, but they are not the real owners of these beasts of burden; their true 'inspirer' (Death? the grandmother?) remains veiled in mysterious, but easily exposed anonymity. At a later stage of the plot, the grand-mother's donkey, which JLP nearly kills, behaves as a maleficent power, capable of killing the young hero [51]. In *Jean-lou-pec*, the same donkey is unequivocally fatal. Death's messenger in *Jean-lou-pec* dots the *i* on this point. In the following episode, JLP's grand-mother, a Huguenot, and therefore a heretic, is to go after her death to the *Donkeys' Paradise* [66]. In the second version, JLP replaces this expression with another: *with a pick and shovel, I made her a hole to get to paradise*. This is a way of saying that the grandmother, because she was a Huguenot, was not buried in sanctified ground but in the donkeys' cemetery or knacker's yard, together with suicides and pagans. A little later, Barbe-Garouille, also a Huguenot, a macabre and disgusting individual (who dies shortly after concluding a forced marriage with Jean-l'ont-pris, her reluctant spouse), is presented to us by her momentary husband as the image of death among the donkeys; Garouille's body, that is, is only just good enough to be left to the knackers [77]. Again, when the grandmother, for her own evil ends, pours forth her torrent of eloquence, she speaks as though she were addressing *all the donkeys of the lowlands*. The community of Solorgues, that Huguenot Babylon given over to the forces of evil, is a *herd of donkeys*. The donkey, as featured in various passages of *JLP*, is remarkable, therefore, not only for its stupidity, an attribute with which it has remained synonymous to our own day. The donkey also belongs, in various ways, to the camp of fatal or diabolical forces that have trapped Truquette and which will later, unsuccessfully, try to eliminate JLP. The donkey is at once stupid and evil, even on the supernatural plane, where its good-heartedness (as a bearer of provisions and of stolen goods) paves the way for a final catastrophe. It signifies the forces of death; this signification sometimes spreads to other related quadrupeds [57]: the vineyard-keeper, who is the undoubted agent of these deadly forces, is called a *bardot* ('hinny', a mule born of a she-ass, sired by a stallion) and a *double horse* [second version]. In short, he is first called a half-horse, then a double horse. Not entirely an ass, but not really a horse.

A monograph on the theme of the ass in Fabre's novella does not, however, entirely solve the problem of the comparisons between *Jean-l'ont-pris* and *Jean-le-sot*. Nor can one refer once and for all, as far as the latter is concerned, solely to the version collected by Bladé in Gascony. In fact, it is the entire French cycle, from north to south, of *Jean-le-sot* that must be referred to (briefly). This cycle enjoyed a remarkable circulation in many different regions: the Midi, Languedoc, Gascony, the Basque country, Provence, Franche-Comté, Nivernais, Poitou, French- and Celt-speaking Brittany, Normandy, not to mention Quebec. These disseminated versions are structurally, and even in detail, very close to one another. At the time when they were collected by folklore specialists in the nineteenth and twentieth centuries, they represented the remains of a tale to which Fabre had had access, during the eighteenth century, in a more vivid form, because of the extraordinary wealth of oral traditions in the Languedoc; these various versions were in contact through a multiple transmission with those of southern France and, by various relays, with those of northern France, at a very early period.[29] Indeed, the same can be said of some regional versions of AT 332 that reached Fabre's ears: they belonged to the general proliferation of *Godfather Death* in its various forms, which had spread throughout France and the neighbouring countries.

Take, for example, the version of *Jean-le-sot* collected by Daniel Fabre in the Minervois. We find two of the three essential elements, which I have already noted in the episode in *JLP* and in Bladé's Gascon *Jean-le-sot*: first the hero's fall from a tree [49–50]; then J L P's attack on the donkey [51], itself followed by the animal's counter-attack. There is, however, a remarkable fact: in order to unify these two elements still more closely, the tale from the Minervois followed an earlier version, which makes the hero a *woodcutter*. An organic link is thus created that remains only subjacent in *JLP*. The Minervois hero in effect (Jean-le-sot), by virtue of his trade, takes his ass into the forest to load it with wood; he then falls from the tree by cutting the branch on which he is sitting, and with which he had intended to load the ass. Lastly, he is a victim of this ass's evil ways: the animal's blocked-up anus emits the third fart, which is either fatal or pseudo-fatal. This personification of Jean-le-sot as a woodcutter or wood-gatherer, provided with an ass, certainly goes back to old versions of the tale *Jean-le-sot* that were sources of later ramifications: indeed, we also find it in Provence, in Nivernais, in French-speaking Brittany – that is to say, in that part of Brittany most open to the influences from the French provinces to the east – finally, in the Basque country, where of course it is an imported tale.[30]

In the context of the sequence of elements common to *Jean-le-sot* and the episode [48–51] in *Jean-l'ont-pris*, a particular sub-episode strikes me as being of special interest: it concerns a character possessing supernatural or divinatory powers. In most versions of the tale, this individual appears between moments in which the hero falls or is about to fall from the tree, and those in which the donkey is about to land the hero with the fatal fart or fatal kick. More specifically, this character first predicts that the young man will fall from the tree, which goes without saying. Then, having made himself credible, as a prophet, to the mind of the simpleton, he predicts a less obvious calamity, which is later fulfilled; he predicts that he will perish (in reality or fictitiously) from some evil act (a fart or something else) on the part of his donkey. This sub-episode of the 'soothsayer', which is always inserted at the same canonical point in the tale, appears in practically all the detailed versions of *Jean-le-sot*: those from Gascony, Nivernais, the Basque country, Franche-Comté, Normandy and French-speaking Brittany.[31]

The 'soothsayer' in question may be a man, or sometimes an old witch. He or she functions, in any case, as the messenger of Death who transmits to the hero an intimation of his forthcoming death. Moreover, in the episode from lower Brittany already mentioned (Luzel, 1881), it is Death himself (Ankou) who assumes this task.

In our *JLP*, between the hero's fall from the tree and his near-fatal fight with the donkey, a sub-episode is also inserted. But it differs from its homologue, as I have just described it on the basis of the various versions of *Jean-le-sot*. In *JLP*, between the hero's fall and fight, the grandmother shaves her grandson's head under the pretext of freeing him from the twigs matted in his hair. In doing so, is the old woman concerned with anything more than hygiene? Or, knowing the grandmother as we do, as a character functionally related to Death, must we not consider that, in fact, she may be indulging in a symbolic aggression that is a portent or threat of death, a threat that the hero, moreover, will later successfully outwit? The very precise place of this sub-episode in the structure of the narrative, as well as the usual behaviour of the grandmother and of the individuals who are her accomplices, all of them 'shavers', force us to ask this question, which will be given an answer a little later in this book, when dealing with the problem of 'tonsures'.

A still more general comparison between the southern cycle of *Jean-le-sot* and the northern cycle, with reference to *Jean-l'ont-pris*, is highly illuminating. In this respect, I shall mention, on the northern side, the Norman version of the tale, in which the Jean-le-sot figure is locally called 'Jean-Bart'.[32]

Young Jean-Bart is a simpleton, as are all the citizens of his village. (This location of the hero of the cycle of *Jean-le-sot* in a village whose inhabitants are regarded as stupid by the surrounding population appears frequently in various versions[33] of the *Jean-le-sot* tale – for example, in Provence, in relation to the 'stupid' communities of Cagny, Six-Fours and Martigues; and in Franche-Comté, in relation to the village of Goux.) I hasten to add that this Norman 'Jean-Bart' is merely a facetious homonym for the famous sailor. Again, we find the usual presence of the first name Jean for the central character of the *Jean-le-sot* cycle: *Jean*-lou-pec and, incidentally, our *Jean*-l'ont-pris in the Occitan regions; *Jean*-Colas in Nivernais;[34] *Jean*-Bart in Normandy, etc.

The action of this *Jean-Bart* takes place in the following phases:

(1) He finds treasure at the foot of an oak-tree.

(2) He climbs a tree and, at the very top of this tree, tries to reach, with outstretched arms, a magpie's nest placed at the end of a branch. In the end, he falls to the ground without managing to obtain the contents of this nest.

(3) After he has risen, he finally 'dies' when his donkey emits three farts. The third fatal explosion dispatches to Jean-Bart's jaw the bung that the hero had stuck in the animal's anus after the second fart, in the vain hope of avoiding a third. Moreover, Jean-Bart, apparently knocked out and 'killed' in this way, soon recovers his senses.

A chain of continuous kinships connects this Norman *Jean-Bart* with the other versions of *Jean-le-sot* to be found in Brittany, Poitou and Nivernais; and with those of the wider, more varied world of Occitania: a term-by-term comparison between *Jean-Bart* from Normandy, *Jean-lou-pec* from the south-west and the relevant episode of our *Jean-l'ont-pris* [48–51] from the south-east suggests structures that echo one another, derived as they are from a common source (see Table 4b).

The kinship of this particular episode of *JLP* with the structure of the narrative of *Jean-le-sot* certainly explains what might otherwise appear as an anomaly in Fabre's narrative: JLP first toys with the idea of throwing stones (at the baron's face); then he recounts his climbing a tree and the fall that followed; lastly, he describes his way of throwing sticks at hares and (in the absence of these animals) at a donkey. In the abbé's version, one would expect the throwing of sticks to be included in a single paragraph relating to the 'throwing' of fatal objects; such a regrouping would have occurred after (or before) the episode of the tree, which concerns a very different physical action.

But, in fact, what counts in Fabre's narrative is that it is inspired directly, in this triple episode, by the profound structure or canonical succession that characterizes *Jean-le-sot*. In itself, the act of throwing the stone or stick is unimportant; what matters is, in the following order:

(1) the attack on the face or body (the baron's in *JLP* and the saint's in *Jean-le-sot*);

(2) the episode of the tree (derived from *Jean-le-sot*);

(3) the episode of the donkey (derived from *Jean-le-sot*).

Table 4b

JEAN-L'ONT-PRIS AND *JEAN-LE-SOT*

		Jean-Bart (Normandy)	*Jean-lou-pec* (Gascony)	*Jean-l'ont-pris* (Languedoc)
I	A		Jean-lou-pec demolishes the statue of a saint hitherto the object of much alms-giving.*	Jean-l'ont-pris threatens to throw stones at a rich lord [48].
	B	Jean-Bart discovers treasure at the foot of an oak-tree.	Jean-lou-pec discovers treasure at the foot of the statue of this saint.	
II		Jean-Bart falls from the top of a tree, trying to reach a magpie's nest.	Jean-lou-pec falls from a tree by cutting the branch on which he is sitting.	Jean-l'ont-pris falls from the top of a tree, trying to reach a magpie's nest [49–50].
III		Jean-Bart dies symbolically after the counter-attack of a donkey that he had previously attacked.	Jean-lou-pec actually dies after the counter-attack of a donkey that he had previously attacked.	Jean-l'ont-pris is symbolically 'crushed' by the counter-attack of a donkey that he had previously attacked [51].

*This 'motif' is also to be found in two versions of the *Jean-le-sot* cycle from Quebec (kindly provided by Mme Maranda): *La Pièce d'étoffe* (coll. C. Laforte, recorded 6 September 1954) and *Un sou le poil* (C.-M. Barbeau, coll. MS. no. 89). This gives further weight to a dating of the tale *Jean-le-sot* prior to 1763.

Hence the apparently paradoxical development of the abbé's text at this point; this development can be explained only by the use of a folklore source, unquoted but subjacent.

The three narratives certainly belong to the same family, to the French cycle, north and south, of *Jean-le-sot*. The episode of the magpie's nest, in particular [*JLP*, 49–50], is not a gratuitous invention on Fabre's part. It is inserted by the author at its correct place in the development of a narration that is freely, but faithfully, inspired by the models that came to him from oral literature.

The versions of *Jean-le-sot* from Franche-Comté deploy similar structures to those just described (fall from the tree, attack by the donkey). Furthermore, interesting coincidences of detail bring them close to our *Jean-l'ont-pris*; these occur – an essential fact for a structural analysis – at the same strategic points of the narrative in both cases. For example, the Jean-le-sot from Franche-Comté, in accordance with the tale of which he is the hero, falls from the tree. Is this, as in the Gascon *Jean-lou-pec* and in many other versions, because he has cut the branch on which he was sitting? Not at all;[35] in the version from Franche-Comté another variant is used, in which the hero climbs a tree, to the small, fragile branch almost at the very top, from which, as a result of an almost inevitable accident, he falls to the ground. Now it is this variant (available, among others, in a number of versions of the tale long current in northern and southern France) that was used by both the Languedocian *Jean-l'ont-pris* and the Norman *Jean-Bart*.

A final remark: our *Languedocian* Jean-l'ont-pris is soon to become the accomplice, not without a degree of culpability, of his grandmother's death. Now the Jean-le-sot from *Poitou* (who, incidentally, marries a king's daughter) is confronted, as is Jean-lou-pec, with the statue of a saint. Later, like Jean-l'ont-pris, he becomes guilty of the murder of his grandmother.[36] The *Basque* Jean-le-sot also falls from a tree; he is attacked almost fatally by his donkey; he is confronted by the statue of a dishonest saint. Finally, he kills not his grandmother, but his elderly mother, which amounts to the same thing.[37] Another Jean-le-sot, also Basque,[38] begins by killing his very old mother, then goes off to see the witches in the wood, where he has the opportunity of treating *the king's daughter*. Later he marries her. Another Basque counterpart of this character falls dangerously from a tree.[39]

We shall soon return to the question of Jean-l'ont-pris as a para-medical agent connected to the 'royal family', first by 'curing' the 'king's' daughter, then by marrying her. I shall show that the rich farmer, Monsieur Sestier, the hero's (possible) future father-in-law, occupies in Fabre's novella the same position as that of the 'king', or rich peasant, in the many Occitan and other European versions of AT 332/*Godfather Death*. We have to admit, in any case, that the abbé Fabre *also* drew, and very widely, on the *Jean-le-sot* cycle in order to provide one of the episodes of his novella. He did not find this at all difficult: this cycle and that of AT 332 (*Godfather Death*, which provided the overall inspiration for *JLP*) were already closely related and interpenetrated in the ancient French folklore of north and south. The raw material had already been prepared for Fabre. All he had to do was use it.

Up to this point in the tale *JLP*, it seems that the abbé Fabre drew his inspiration very closely from at least two oral versions (then well known in the Languedoc) of tale AT 332: the version (since lost) from which was to come, through successive generations, the tale *Jean-de-trop*, collected in Languedoc at the end of the nine-teenth century; and the version (also since lost) of a tale (itself re-lated to AT 332) that had reached Languedoc from its German or Swiss place of origin, through German-speaking Switzerland and down the Rhône. (An extant offshoot was collected in Switzerland itself, about 1920.) Fabre also used the tale *Jean-le-sot*, which lent itself all the more to this use in that it was connected by certain affinities or 'anastomoses', Occitan and Breton, to this French ver-sion of AT 332.

However, from the episode of the donkey crushing the hero [51] onwards, the tale *JLP* moves into less charted ground. Certainly, the reader will be aware of a large number of similarities with AT 332 in general and with *Jean-de-trop* in particular. For example, Monsieur Sestier, a rich farmer and Jean-l'ont-pris's future father-in-law, occupies the exact site, narrative and functional, of the *king* who, in *Jean-de-trop*, gives his daughter in marriage to the young hero, during the second part of the narrative.

This 'regality' possessed by Sestier, who thus becomes the homo-logue of the *king of France* or *king of Paris* in *Jean-de-trop* and in other French versions of AT 332,[40] is indicated, moreover, in several passages of Fabre's novella: Sestier has his peaches guarded as though they were *the king's body* [57]; his daughter, Babeau, has a 'pair of pretty feet that the queen would go to fetch in person if such pretties could be bought at the Paris meat-market' [72]. In a more general way, Sestier does not *really* seem to have sprung from the village of Langlade (Gard), in which Fabre, for his own practical reasons, has placed the vast estate of which this gentleman is owner.[41] He is a fictional character. Sestier is, in general, the functional equivalent of the powerful individual, whether or not a king, whose daughter the physician Death's godson (or Death's *compère*) in various versions of AT 332 marries, after curing the king or his daughter of a fatal illness. This marriage is presented as the supreme reward given to the doctor for the miraculous cure that he has effected.

Of course, this equivalence is embodied in a particular way in Fabre's novella: the hero JLP, as we have seen, is not a physician, but only a 'paramedical' figure. This peculiarity gives a special flavour to the narrative, but it does not alter its structures. Two medical (or paramedical, we should say) actions that are perfectly typical of AT 332 are performed by the hero himself or by one of his accomplices in the remainder of the text.

The very assimilation of Monsieur Sestier to 'the rich and powerful father of the girl who will marry Death's godson' presents no difficulties. Indeed, this rich, powerful father is actually referred to as a king in certain versions of AT 332, but in many other cases, and especially in the older 'archetypal' versions of this tale, deriving from the sixteenth and seventeenth centuries, he is simply a rich peasant or a rich merchant (Strobl, in the 1690s);[42] elsewhere, and especially in Occitania and Brittany, right up to several versions that have been collected in recent years, this character may be a rich lord, a provincial intendant during the last century of the *ancien régime* or quite simply a rich farmer of the Sestier type,[43] and not necessarily a king, though in many recent versions he often appears as a king.

The story-tellers who transmitted and interpreted AT 332 from generation to generation must have felt that what mattered most about the character in question was not whether he bore the title of king, but his wealth and power. In an Irish version of AT 332, the great figure who is to become the father-in-law of Death's godson at the end of the tale is not a king, but a *duke*. In Mexico, he naturally becomes a *cacique* (or simply a rich man), after the tale, Spanish in origin, took root on the other side of the Atlantic.[44] Anyway, the abbé Fabre makes this figure a rich peasant. By doing so, the writer obeyed not only the letter of the tale, in its oldest forms, but also its more durable logic: it stresses above all the character's power and importance, rather than his possible royalty.

The identification of *Monsieur Sestier* with the *king* in *Jean-de-trop* or with the *rich and powerful man* of AT 332 in general does not, I repeat, prevent the appearance of a certain autonomy in the last part of *JLP* (from paragraph 47 onwards) in relation to the tale type on which it was modelled up to this point. This being the case, the best procedure would be to summarize and analyse the last part. In this way we shall see whether it does not represent, through possible transformations, a true structural kinship with AT 332, with *Jean-de-trop* and with other southern versions that were originally related to *Godfather Death*.

Here, then, are this summary and this analysis: to begin with, *the forces of death, some of which are explicitly connected with the grandmother, attack the hero.*

From the first moment that the hero (JLP) wanted to deceive his grandmother by playing truant, a number of attacks, which might have proved fatal, were levelled at him as punishment for actions regarded as incorrect. The aggressive series began even before the decision to give up school: the schoolmaster to whom the grandmother had entrusted the child also struck him. Then JLP falls from the top of a tree that very nearly scalps him. He then has his head totally shaved by his grandmother. Then his grandmother's donkey almost 'crushes' him to death. It was undoubtedly *Jean-le-sot* that provided the abbé with the theme of the aggressive attacks by the forces of death.

From the outset, the situation is quite clear to the hero. Each conquest that he makes brings with it reprisals in the opposite direction: *I have to admit that if I had hurt it* [the donkey], *it paid me back in my own kind. Though I say it myself, my lord, I flatter myself that I have learned something in my life. But I have never learned anything that did not, in one way or another, cost me dearly* [51–52]. An eye for an eye and a tooth for a tooth. One does not trifle with the forces of death.

The hero then wishes to continue his wild, untutored life as an eater of fruit. He has exchanged the schoolbook given by his grandmother for a slice of egg-plant. He now throws himself into the battle against the prohibitions concerning uncontrolled fruit-picking, expressed by the orchard-owners, supported by the vineyard-keepers appointed by the municipality of Solorgues.[45] And so, inside the rich men's enclosures, he picks the grapes, which it will later be his task to protect when he in turn becomes a vineyard-keeper; they are the same grapes that, shortly afterwards, kill his grandmother with indigestion. He also steals Monsieur Sestier's clingstone peaches, the velvety skins of which are explicitly compared to the peach-like cheeks of Babeau, the rich farmer's daughter, who will be promised to him at the end of the tale. Lastly, by logical and metaphorical conclusion, he steals ladies' figs [53]. Not to mention the chickens, which he also gets away with. As a punishment for these thefts, one of the vineyard-keepers takes the hero by the scruff of the neck and ties him to a tree. The hero uses his whistle in a cunning trick to get himself freed by the vineyard-keeper's young son. He then ties this boy to the tree as a substitute for himself. The boy realizes that he is being tricked and explicitly announces that JLP's grandmother will punish her grandson for this deed.

Let us take a quick look at this episode of the 'fight'. One is surprised at first by the evil, even diabolical, attitude adopted towards the hero (and, before him, towards his father) by the vineyard-keepers of Solorgues and by the municipality or community of this village in general. One particular fact lies behind this: Solorgues was an essentially Protestant locality.[46] It belongs, therefore, to the camp of evil reprobates on whom the Catholic priest Jean-Baptiste Fabre had spent his life pronouncing the curses that are to be found implicitly in his narrative. Solorgues, the abbé is saying under cover of his narrator, is a *Babylon* [12]. The wind blowing from it, through the medium of the abject Garouille the Huguenot, poisons the village of Langlade situated to the north [77], just as the malarial marshes [*garouilles*] of the Languedocian coast contaminate the more northerly inland villages, through disease-bearing sea breezes. In other words, Solorgues represents the human group (*Babylon*) held in execration by the pious Jews of the Old Testament, whose opinion was valued by the papists. Furthermore, the community of Solorgues is a *troop of donkeys* [second version], which is hardly a flattering description in view of the defamatory and even diabolical views expressed in *Jean-l'ont-pris* of these animals. The first appearance, in the narrative, of the community-municipality of Solorgues is catastrophic for the hero's family: the magistrate of Solorgues arrives in person, followed by *all the riff-raff of Solorgues* and by the *men in blue* (the ushers, sergeants, local constabulary); they have come to arrest Truquette, J L P's father, with a view to taking him to prison, which he will leave only to end his life on the scaffold in the market-place at Nîmes – another Protestant community. This intervention on the part of the *men in blue* who have taken [*ont pris*] Truquette is said to be the cause [36–40] of the hero's luckless nickname. The municipality of Solorgues intervenes for a second time in the appearance of the village *schoolmaster* (who functioned at that time as a municipal officer, and not, as in the twentieth century, as a functionary of the national state). This schoolmaster is an accomplice and even a pedagogical double of grandmother Death. From his first appearance, he sets up a conflict with the hero, whom he strikes, to which J L P responds by contravening his grandmother's wishes and selling the schoolbook she had given him: he can thus devote himself to the conquest of the fine fruit (egg-plants, peaches, apricots, grapes, figs, Babeau's cheeks) that will make his fortune. One is reminded (see Chapter XIV) of the story of Hans-with-the-goitre, the hero of an Austrian version of AT 332 which is particularly close to *Jean-de-trop* and, therefore, to *Jean-l'ont-pris*. Death, after lavishing his advice on Hans-with-the-goitre that he should become a physician, and after practically inciting him to betray him, launches him on the career that lies before him – by landing him a mighty blow (Vernaleken, 1864, p. 229).

The third intrusion on the part of the municipality [54] is in the persons of the vineyard-keepers appointed by the community of Solorgues. They attack the hero to the point of making him an *inci homme*, in other words a Christ-figure, bleeding from the scourging inflicted on him.[47] They behave towards him, then, like the 'wicked Jews' of the New Testament, who tortured the Saviour: Solorgues is both a Babylon as seen by the pious Israelites of the Old Testament and the locality most hostile to the New Testament Christ of the Passion. The village lies under a double curse!

The vineyard-keepers are specifically described by Fabre as wicked. More particularly, because they belong to Solorgues, a Protestant locality, they are Huguenots. They do not go to vespers on Sunday or attend to the salvation of their souls [57]. They are villains and half-wits [57], wretches [58] and brutes [59]. Their highly explicit villainy brings them close to the diabolical and fatal Quincarlot, himself described as a bundle of knavish tricks [79]. Furthermore, the Protestant colouring of the vineyard-keepers is referred to by Monsieur Sestier, who declares that the blows they had given him were of no more concern to him than were *the affairs of Holland* [62]. Now *Holland*, like *England* and the *convict-prison at Toulon* (where Huguenots were sent), functions in Fabre's prose as a Protestant marker: see also the cambric [*toiles de Hollande*, 68] found in the treasure-chest of the dead Huguenot grandmother, the accomplice of the vineyard-keepers. Or take the Huguenot Judith Garouille's scurvy, which is compared in turn to *the entire English fleet at sea* [83] and to that of the *convicts of Toulon* [second version]. Judith Garouille, the Huguenot, is thus connoted in each of the two versions of the tale by a different geographical allusion: *England* in the first version, the *convict-prison of Toulon* in the second. She is given, therefore, two Protestant markers, of different kinds. At the same time, Holland, as Protestant toponym, serves twice to characterize a double series of Huguenot or Huguenot-linked characters: the grandmother, on the one hand, and the vineyard-keepers, on the other.

To conclude, these vineyard-keepers, whose practices smell of Dutch Calvinism, are regarded by JLP as untrustworthy [65]. The municipal revolution that is to bring about JLP's change of fortune will consist precisely in his being appointed vineyard-keeper in their place. For this post is a particularly 'juicy' one (as we shall see), especially as it has been occupied so far by dishonest persons.

Later, the wicked vineyard-keepers of Solorgues spring out like jack-in-the-boxes to attack JLP once again. In this, they are the direct accomplices of Quincarlot [80], a macabre individual, blind in the right eye, whose *evil eye* the grandmother had once tried to inculcate in JLP. Quincarlot, let us not forget, is a devil, a Beelzebub, a Satan [81]. The municipality of Solorgues is the macabre, Huguenot, diabolical condensation of a perverted peasantry.[48]

I should like to say one more thing about the Huguenot community of Solorgues, whose bases of municipal power, beginning with the vineyard-keepers, are necessarily heretical, noxious and harmful in the eyes of an abbé Fabre, who functions in this business, quite literally, as a *Catholic novelist*.[49] Solorgues, *ipso facto*, appears as 'non-Catholic' in Fabre's eyes, as in those of his readers or listeners. They know that Nages-et-Solorgues, a merged community of which Solorgues was a part, was 80 to 90 per cent Huguenot. This community, in the shape of a 'double star', was made up of a principal town (Nages) and a neighbouring village (Solorgues). Solorgues elected its own particular *consul* ['magistrate'], who belonged (with other colleagues bearing the same title) in the consulate, unique because twinned, of Nages-et-Solorgues. The ultimate sign of hostility to the Roman Catholic, Apostolic Church was that whereas Nages, the chief town of this 'binary group', had at least one parish priest, Solorgues did not have a parish priest of its own, but had to content itself with the services of the priest in Nages. Though Fabre's text does not appear to touch on this problem, it does stress the total negativity of Solorgues on the question of local clergy: *Jean-l'ont-pris* mentions in passing the *curé of Bezouces*; this toponym, Bezouces,[50] designates a large (ultra-Catholic) village in the region of Nîmes, not far from Fabre's own. Margot's rejected lovers, Fabre tells us, all natives of the Protestant Solorgues, found this ex-Huguenot, when flirting with the papist Truquette, *prouder and more unyielding than the housekeeper of the curé of Bezouces* [9]. At the end of *Jean-l'ont-pris*, the *curé of Nages* himself is mentioned [90]. The author certainly emphasizes the distressing spiritual situation of Solorgues, distressing in the eyes of a writer of the Roman religion: he tells us that the only priest to visit the locality is a rapacious *Capuchin* friar; this individual comes to Solorgues once a year, not to inculcate the great truths of religion, but to collect the tithes due in olive oil [6]. It is hardly surprising, then, if Solorgues appears to be under the joint sovereignty of Calvin and Satan; there is nothing there to act as a counter-weight, to support the cause of the Church of Rome.

This Capuchin friar, who comes begging for oil, and his entourage merit a little closer attention; it might provide us with a few additional clues to the position of the community of Solorgues and of various characters, in terms of the constellation of forces at work in the plot erected by Fabre. Take the meaning of the 'triad' referred to in the first sentences of the novella: 'My father settled there [at Solorgues] and set up shop as a cobbler, with the approval of the *authorities*, that is to say, *the magistrate, the farrier and a Capuchin friar who came every year to beg for oil*' [6]. Why this association of the magistrate, farrier and friar in the specific context of the relations set up between the community (dominated or defined by these three individuals) and the other characters of the narrative? A comparative study of Fabre's works enables us to solve this riddle, which would be impossible to solve on the basis of a reading of *Jean-l'ont-pris* alone. The key text, in this case, is *Le Siège de Caderousse*, in its own way a homologue of *JLP*. We have seen [51] how the township of Caderousse had stockpiled wheat during the famine of 1709; this wheat was then seized by an armed 'crusade' organized by the people of Avignon; in this way they managed to feed the starving bellies of the papal city. With *Caderousse* (completed in 1774), Fabre transforms into a (mock) epic an actual event that took place in 1709. In *JLP*, written eighteen years earlier, he had followed the same course, but in the opposite direction. He had transformed a folk-tale (AT 332/*Godfather Death*) into a realistic or pseudo-realistic novella. *Caderousse* moves from reality to fiction. *JLP* descends from the second to the first. At the intersection of these two trajectories, we meet, at least on the particular ground of this 'triad', a common structure.

Solorgues, then, is a Protestant community, a Babylon reeking of heresy, a 'dung pit' from the Catholic point of view. [52] Caderousse is a township of the Comtat-Venaissin or present-day Vaucluse; it is six kilometres from Orange, the capital city of a principality in which the Protestants, originally supported by the princes of Orange, exercised a vast influence. The clergy in Fabre's epic of the *Siège* declare, in fact, that the people of Caderousse are heretical (*Siège*, 1876 edition, p. 77). This same text adds, quite explicitly, that the practices of the Inquisition and the anti-Cathar crusade *to fricassee the Albigensians* (*Siège*, 1876 edition, p. 76) should be implemented against this people. Of course, Caderousse (like Solorgues) has a *consul* or 'first consul' ['magistrate']; as a kind of second in command, the informal leader of Caderousse is a *maréchal-ferrant* ['farrier'], the picturesque Lafeuillade. He is the homologue of that other farrier who, according to Fabre, was the second most important citizen of Solorgues, after the *consul*. We also find, in both cases, the Capuchin friar who does not belong to the community itself, but who visits each year to collect the tithes on a basic agricultural product. At Solorgues this takes the form of the collection of olive oil [6]. At Caderousse, we are told of a friar (Franciscan or Capuchin) who comes to collect the tithes in wheat (*Siège*, 1876 edition, p. 17); he then takes back with him a quantity of this wheat to his starving priory in Avignon, the year being 1709. The rest of the Caderoussian epic lays great stress on the importance of these Capuchin friars. Furthermore, in the two narratives, the conquest and conflicts are arranged in the same way. At Solorgues, the down-and-out cobbler Truquette-*chopine*, armed with his awl and stirrup, is an immigrant: he has come into the community from the outside. He literally puts his hands on a beautiful young village girl, Margot. Once he is married to this Dulcinea, the cobbler has his skin pricked [22] by his mother-in-law, during a squabble between husband and wife that degenerates into a family row and eventually involves the whole village. He then becomes a rich merchant who swindles and steals, carrying his goods by donkey. It is hoped that he will become, through a series of bankruptcies, a rich gentleman, the founder of a line of barons. Meanwhile, his activities as a dishonest merchant are compared by Fabre to those of the Jews of the Avignon 'synagogue', in accordance with anti-Semitic feelings that are no less unpleasant for being so widely held at the time.

Now let us turn to Caderousse: a ragged army has conquered the community from the outside in order to seize grain and a beautiful girl; the first detachment of these troops is repulsed by the inhabitants of Caderousse, who prick the skins of the soldiers from Avignon. This 'army' includes cobblers, also explicitly armed with awls and stirrups. It also includes a group of merchants riding donkeys and waving a placard that reads: *Take courage, get rich, another* [bankruptcy] *will make you a marquis.* They are accompanied by an 'Israelite' from Avignon, whose task is to symbolize their mercantile vocation, just as the 'synagogue' of Avignon connoted the merchant Truquette. It will be noted that, in both cases, Fabre has used religious expressions ('Israelite', 'synagogue') and not the brutally ethnic term ('Jew'). The head of the Avignon army, called Boiardo-Pantalon-Octave, is a pseudo-duke, marquis, count; more rational than Truquette-*chopine*, he loves wine so much that he gets drunk.

There are, therefore, in both cases, the enumeration of a certain number of roles, objects and situations:

(1) 'immigrant' cobbler, with awl and stirrup;

(2) 'skin pricking' inflicted on the intruder or immigrant by an inhabitant or inhabitants of the community;

(3) a merchant, a loaded donkey, wealth through bankruptcy, comparison with the Jews of Avignon;

(4) the possibility of fraudulent acquisition of titles, alcoholism;

(5) the seizure of the local girl by the hero, an outsider.

These various items are quite simply fused, at Solorgues, in the character of Truquette; at Caderousse, they are collectively gathered together in Boiardo-Pantalon's army. Indeed, Boiardo-Pantalon himself is made to stand for the whole at the end of the story (as Truquette had already done), when we come to his marriage. Boiardo, in turn, grabs the beautiful Françoise (Françounette), the daughter of the farrier, Lafeuillade, who plays the role of collective emanation of the community of Caderousse. A marriage follows.

In each case, we have a community regarded as heretical; in the charge of a *consul* and a *farrier*; and visited by a mendicant friar or *Capuchin*, begging for food. This triad is articulated, also in both cases, on the marriage between an attractive local girl and an outsider, who is himself the bearer of certain characteristics that are either concentrated in his own person (Truquette) or diffused in the group that he directs (Boiardo).

Certainly, from Solorgues to Caderousse, there is a logical transformation of structure: Margot is the daughter of an inhabitant of Solorgues and of a surgeon of Calvisson (of whom little more is said). Her marriage to Truquette ends *badly*, in line with her initial illegitimacy. Françounette is the legitimate daughter of an inhabitant of Caderousse and of the farrier Lafeuillade. Her marriage to Boiardo ends *well*, in line with her initial legitimacy. These differences, which are logically based in each case, stress all the more the closeness of the two girls and their mothers to the respective communities of Solorgues and Caderousse. The *consul*–farrier–Capuchin triad functions for us, in each case, as an indicator. It confirms certain profound similarities in the arrangement of forces active at Solorgues and Caderousse.

It indicates even more strongly the unshakable alliance that binds Margot and her mother to the leaders of the heretico-delinquent community at Solorgues, and to the employees of that village: from the magistrates to the vineyard-keepers, they were all united against the unfortunate Truquette; they then renew this alliance against his son, Jean-l'ont-pris.

The way in which the vineyard-keepers of the Huguenot Solorgues and their kind act, or, rather, the way they attack, is also worthy of interest. What we have is the whole problem of attacks against the victim's *neck* (strangling, hanging) and *hair* (attempts to scalp or shave) – attacks, generally speaking, against the head. These attacks are unleashed by the aggressors and the forces of death, including the grandmother, throughout Fabre's novella. It is worth enumerating these offensive acts in turn.

In *JLP*, aggression seems to be oriented, at the beginning of the narrative, towards the use of sharp instruments. In her playful flirtation with Truquette, Margot *pricks* him with a cobbler's awl [9]; the mother then uses the same awl to prick the skin of the same young man, now her son-in-law [22]. The second action is typical of the woman's evil nature. However, the awl is again only a way of *marking* Truquette for the fate that awaits him on the scaffold. The fundamental procedures of aggression are of another kind. Margot inaugurates these during her row with Truquette, some days after marrying him: *Margot, at her wits' end, threw herself at the nape of his neck and, clinging to him, began to shout: 'Thief . . . give me back my clothes, or I'll pull your hair out by the roots!'* [21]. The violence of Margot's language to her husband becomes, in the second version of *JLP*: *Margot, clinging to the back of Truquette's neck shouted: '. . . give me back my clothes or I'll strangle you.' She seized a pot full of glue and threw it straight at his jaw . . . As he tried to wipe it off, Truquette pulled out the hairs of his beard, and even the skin of his chin. He swore like a damned soul and returned to the fight.*

Thus from the first battle, Margot, the praying mantis, daughter and double of the suspect grandmother, lays down the two possibilities open to those threatened by the forces of death from Solorgues, among the first rank of which are Margot and, above all, her mother. They have the choice, which may turn into both together, of being scalped [first version] or being strangled [second version]. The first possibility (scalping) takes the form of pulling hairs out of the beard [second version] and, more particularly, of pulling out the hairs of the head [first version]. The rest of the narrative will remain faithful to these double premises. To take strangling first. Truquette, conforming to the canonical schema of *Godfather Death*, is successful at first, then unsuccessful and finally dies; at the end of a supernatural cycle of prosperity, he eventually ends up strangled according to the favourite method of the tale type 332: he is hanged, as a thief, in the market-place at Nîmes. This follows the authentic tradition of AT 332: the oldest versions of the tale (German, sixteenth and seventeenth centuries) tells us that the hero dies when Death *twists his neck*. This tradition reached France; it is to be found in the final stifling of the hero in the version of AT 332 from the Nivernais, which is so close in many ways to our Languedocian versions.[53] Truquette's fate, moreover, threatens to encompass his son. Jean-l'ont-pris, who plays in the second part of Fabre's tale a remake of AT 332, is to feel, in turn, threatened by the same fate, which he is fortunate enough to escape. Quincarlot, the diabolical bearer of the evil eye and the grandmother's former accomplice, had seen Truquette hanged (*I had the honour and consolation of seeing your father die*, he declares to JLP [80]). It will be noticed that it is to Quincarlot in person that Fabre entrusts the task of announcing for the first time in the narrative [79] that Truquette died on the scaffold. This announcement occurs many years after the actual event [37], which for a long time remained shrouded in mystery. Quincarlot is, therefore, if not the executioner himself, at least his 'visual' witness and his messenger after the event [79]. It is hardly surprising if JLP calls him 'murderer' [*bourreau*, 'executioner'; 81]. This Quincarlot is merely a walking gibbet! When Jean-l'ont-pris, who is about to be arrested by him, sees him, *he frightened me as if he had set up a gibbet there* [79]. Quincarlot's first accomplice was called Crouquet, that is, a hook at the end of which the fish is *hung*. The second accomplice is Jacquet, which rhymes with Crouquet-the-hanging-hook, and who in the second version becomes Carcanas, the buzzard that feeds on the flesh of corpses at the foot of gibbets [32]. In fact, there is a risk that JLP's own life will end badly, through the usual strangling, since Quincarlot comes to arrest JLP. The hero in fact is freed, but in the last lines of the novella, the baron hints at a possible ending on the scaffold [89].

After the strangling (which, in the particular case of Truquette's son, remains no more than a terrifying possibility) there is another method, particularly dear to Margot, her mother and family: pulling out the hairs from the victim's head or chin, scalping or, at best, shaving the head. On this point, Fabre's text is particularly rich. Margot, as we have seen, pulls out her husband's hairs and burns his beard. Later, the row between Truquette, his mother-in-law and his wife is transformed into a battle involving the whole village. The party favourable to J L P's grandmother, or perhaps the grandmother herself, takes the opportunity of scalping a third of the hair of a boy whose family belongs to the local clan that opposes the old woman [second version]. Some years later, Truquette is arrested: he is not 'taken by the hair', it is true; but, by an inversion of the usual process, he is tied to the tail of the horses belonging to the constabulary that is taking him away [37]. 'Scalping' is resorted to again during J L P's misadventures with his friend–enemy Sestier; both are victims of various attacks and accidents, bound up with relations with the grandmother and later with the sinister practices of the vineyard-keepers.

Scalping and complete shaving of the head: Jean-l'ont-pris climbs a tree, against the orders of his grandmother, who does not want him to play truant. Punishment is not slow in coming: the hero falls and is nearly killed [50]. However, a broken branch gets stuck in his mass of matted hair, almost pulling it out; this branch temporarily and painfully suspends our young hero in the air like a twisting lantern. In order to rid him of the twigs embedded in his hair, the suspicious and angry grandmother shaves her grandson's head right down to the last hair [50]. The hero has managed to perform the *tour de force* of playing successively the roles of two biblical characters, Absalom and Samson! Absalom, bearer of an enormously heavy head of hair, from which he is left hanging from the branch of a tree; Samson, who loses all his strength when a treacherous woman cuts off his hair.[54]

He really is unlucky; after this complete shaving at the hands of the grandmother, the hero's mop of hair grows again, only to be the victim of attack once more. J L P steals peaches in an orchard. A vineyard-keeper who treacherously attacks him from behind, catches him by the nape of the neck and drags him by the hair to the very peach-tree whose fruit JLP has stolen [57]. There he is tied to the trunk of the tree, his hands bound behind his back. This does not prevent the hero, while the villain is pulling at his hair from behind, from continuing to sink his fine teeth into the peach: *such an insult did not prevent me from finishing my fruit.* Fabre is quite specific on the methods used by the vineyard-keepers: they certainly wanted to subject the hero to a symbolic shaving of the head [*tondre*, in French; *toundre*, in Occitan; 55]. Moreover, JLP declares on this occasion that he was only a poor *pelaout* [57].[55] In the second version, Fabre replaces *pele* with *boullarot*, which means in Occitan 'little gudgeon' or 'little man'. Like all fish, of course, gudgeon are by definition hairless.

In the second version of *JLP*, Fabre explains the symbolic shaving of the head carried out by one of the vineyard-keepers on the hero. Indeed, whereas the relevant sentence in the first version reads, 'there were two of them [vineyard-keepers] who came to regret shaving my head' [55], the verb used in the second version is not *tondre*, but *écornifler*. Etymologically, this verb is related to *écorner*: 'to remove the horns from the head', in other words, to scalp; in this case, to deprive someone of his vigour, as a bull is deprived of his strength when he arrives in the ring without horns. It should be noticed that the Occitan verbs that correspond in current usage to *écorner* and *écornifler* are *escornar* 1, which means, in the figurative sense, 'to eat into some possession or sum of money'; and *escornar* 2, which means 'to affront, to insult someone'. Lastly, we should mention *escorniolar*: 'to strangle'.[56] The French verb *écornifler*, which has more or less fallen into disuse and which provided Fabre with his burlesque *escournifla*, means 'to be a parasite; to get money or a good meal out of someone'; in other words, to pinch, to scrounge, to fleece someone . . . The battery of meanings is thus organized around the 'Occitan' verb *escournifla*, which in the midst of the same sentence appears in the second version of *JLP* as the symbolic equivalent of shaving in the first version. It is a 'battery' of three possible ideas:

(1) to insult, to attack the hero's honour;
(2) to seize his modest possessions;
(3) possibly to strangle him.

The third meaning (*escorniolar*) refers us, then, to the idea of strangling: this act represents, in combination with the pulling out of hair, one of the two great forms of aggression practised in *Jean-l'ont-pris* by the forces of death (that is, the grandmother, Margot, the vineyard-keepers and the municipality of Solorgues). The first two meanings imply that the fact of symbolically shaving [first version] and, which amounts to the same thing, the fact of *écornifler* [second version] lead in any case to a diminishing of material capital or wealth (*escornar* 1) and to a diminishing of moral capital or honour (*escornar* 2), which are both possessed by the hero. This double attack on the material and moral integrity of the person is made perfectly clear in comments made by the hero himself [57]. Describing the attacks of the vineyard-keeper who takes him by the scruff of the neck, J L P declares: *this insult ... was extremely damaging to me, for it prevented me from taking others* [other peaches, a material injury], *and it was an affront to my honour* [moral injury].

Later, indeed, the hero declares that the possession of a good head of hair is not only the symbol of a certain material wealth and moral prestige for a man; [57] it also refers to the fact that one is the fortunate possessor, maritally and sexually, of a beloved woman. *If I were fortunate enough to have and to marry Babeau*, says J L P to Sestier in the second version, *I would always wear her round my neck in front as I wear my little pigtail behind*. And in fact, from the beginning of the narrative, the hero, who is about to recount his life and who already possesses Babeau, now pregnant, proudly wears his hair pulled down behind his head. This is an explicit way of saying: *I have buried my wife whom I did not love. I am going to marry Babeau, whom I adore, and who will make me rich*. Margot, hostile to the hero's father, clung to Truquette's hair from behind in order to pull it out [21]. Babeau, well disposed to the hero, functions symbolically in the reverse way, as an entity who will be worn at the front – which is equivalent, says Fabre, to J L P's precious pigtail which Margot wanted to destroy by eradication. Babeau is the anti-Margot.

It will be noticed that the vineyard-keepers' first attack on J L P echoes the attack made earlier by Margot, the hero's mother, on her husband Truquette, the hero's father, some days after their marriage; both episodes take place specifically on a Sunday. [58] Margot first attacked her husband from behind, throwing herself at the nape of his neck [36]. Similarly, an anonymous hand (that of one of the vineyard-keepers) grabs J L P [57] by the scruff of the neck. Then

Margot threatens to pull out her victim's hair; this is made all the
easier by the fact that Margot is actually hanging from the nape of
his neck, that is, from his pigtail. The vineyard-keeper also drags
JLP 'by the hair' towards the trunk of the peach-tree, to which he
ties him. In both cases, the insult used by the attacker is the same:
Truquette and JLP are each called 'thief', by Margot and by the
vineyard-keeper respectively. It is true, in both cases, that the victims

Table 5

ATTACK ON HAIR

	'Truquette' episode	'JLP' episode
Attacker	Margot	the vineyard-keeper
Victim	Truquette	JLP
Day of attack	Sunday	Sunday
Direction of attack	from behind	from behind
'Organ' attacked or threatened	nape of neck hair	scruff of neck hair
Insult used by attacker	'thief'	'thief'
Type of behaviour implied and punished by the attacker	'drunkenness' (excessive imbibing of the fermented juice of the grape)	excessive eating of peaches or muscat-grapes

have seized objects on which the aggressors exercise in principle a right of possession or protection.

There is, therefore, an equivalence or homology in the aggressive roles played, respectively, by the evil Margot and by the evil vineyard-keeper, both agents of the forces of death. By one of those winks to the reader (or to the author, that is, to himself) in which he specializes, Fabre stresses this equivalence of functions between the hero's mother and the municipal police. He does this by a geographical indication that he has repeated twice, with the lightest of touches.

J L P describes the vineyard-keepers who have attacked him and who then attack Monsieur Sestier as two Mahon cocks confronting a turkey [59]. In the second version, Margot is depicted as wearing 'a hat à la Mahonne'. Thus *Mahon*, in the masculine, refers to cockscombs; *Mahonne*, in the feminine, to a woman's hat. The reference to Mahon, the principal town of the island of Minorca (Balearic Islands), is both a reference to a certain breed of poultry and a certain feminine fashion. This geographical code puts on the same level, dichotomized into the strong sex and the weak sex, the wicked vineyard-keepers who attack Jean-l'ont-pris and Sestier, on the one hand, and Margot, Truquette's wicked assailant, on the other. The vineyard-keepers and Margot, under the superior direction of the grandmother, both belong to the forces of death.

Thus this geographical code materializes a parallel and a complicity. It also indicates an opposition and even an antagonism: Margot, comically decked out in a hat à la Mahonne, is connected with Minorca (Balearic Islands); she is thus contrasted with her husband,[59] adversary and victim, Truquette, who is compared in a burlesque way, probably deriving from folklore, to the king of *Majorca*. The opposition of the two principal Balearic Islands, Majorca and Minorca, has no interest in itself in the novella (except, perhaps, in a 'folkloric' reminiscence of the Montpellierian kings of Majorca and to the possible Catalan importation of A T 332). It serves above all, in Fabre's hands, to encode and to place the characters: Margot *against* Truquette; Margot *with* the vineyard-keepers, they and she bound together, under the forces of death, themselves dominated by the grandmother and unified by the community of Solorgues.

The vineyard-keepers' seizure of J L P by the hair is reminiscent, point by point and detail by detail, of the similar attack made by

Table 6				
THE MAJORCA–MINORCA CODE				
Nature of forces involved	'Balearic' code		horizontally: community and complicity	
Forces of death ('*minor*') embodied in Margot and the vineyard-keepers	*Minorca* (Mahon)	*vertically: contrast and aggression*	Margot with her hat *à la Mahonne* (= Minorca)	The vineyard-keepers as two *Mahon* cocks (= Minorca)
Forces of life ('*major*') embodied in the hero's father and in the hero himself; they are threatened by the forces of death, which kill the father and endanger the son	*Majorca*		Truquette compared to the king of *Majorca*, and attacked by Margot	JLP compared to the son of the king of *Majorca*, and attacked by the vineyard-keepers

Margot on Truquette in the first part of the novella. Similarly, there takes place, a little later, the snatching of Sestier's wig, again by the vineyard-keepers; this snatching is effected by means of a large branch in which the threads of the wig have accidentally become entangled. The blow was originally intended to knock Sestier out, not to 'scalp' him. The second scene refers specifically to the previous sub-episode during which a branch, again accidentally, gets entangled in J L P's mop of hair as he falls from the tree. The final solution is of precisely the same order in both adventures, even if the technical means employed differ to some extent from the one to the other: in both cases, it is all the hair (J L P) or all the wig (Sestier) that is lifted from the head of its rightful owner; there is no alternative, since it is irremediably entangled in the fatal branch. There is only one solution: to detach the wig (the act of the vineyard-keeper); or to shave the young man's head (the act of the grandmother). We should note in passing that the same verb is used by the narrator in the two unsuccessful attempts that precede the total scalping: the vineyard-keeper tries at first, in vain, to *pull* the branch from Sestier's wig; Jean-l'ont-pris tries, equally unsuccessfully, to *pull* the branch from his thick hair. The double failure of these 'pullings' leads to the ultimate scalping.

There are two couples of 'shavers', or 'attackers on the hair', who may be individualized in the following way.

First 'couple': grandmother–vineyard-keepers. The grandmother shaved J L P's head [50]; similarly, the vineyard-keepers shave Monsieur Sestier's head [59]. The two episodes resemble each other in even the smallest details.

Second 'couple': Margot–vineyard-keepers. Margot clung to Truquette's hair; the vineyard-keepers drag J L P by the hair. The development of the two actions also provides a succession of similar 'strong points'.

Let us symbolize these two respective couples, who are basically in a relationship of contagious imitation, in a table marked by two vertical arrows (A to C, B to D).

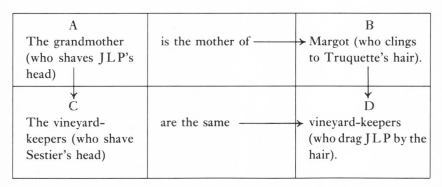

A The grandmother (who shaves J L P's head)	is the mother of ⟶	B Margot (who clings to Truquette's hair).
C The vineyard-keepers (who shave Sestier's head)	are the same ⟶	D vineyard-keepers (who drag J L P by the hair).

Two horizontal arrows at the top and bottom of the table remind us that the whole group is interdependent – from top to bottom, of course, but also from left to right. On the top line, the grandmother (on the left, in A) is simply the mother of Margot (on the right, in B); these two women, continuously linked, have never lacked fidelity to each other, this fidelity implying subordination of the second person (B) to the first (A). On the lower line, the vineyard-keepers who 'undressed' Sestier's scalp (in C) are the very same who attacked JLP's hair (in D). Moreover, the four episodes, which all come under the heading of what, to simplify matters, I shall call the 'scalp', maintain between themselves, in the table above, links that are not only horizontal, but vertical. The attack (A) in the form of total shaving, carried out by the grandmother on meeting her grandson, completes a very similar situation (C) that brings the vineyard-keepers into contact with Sestier's wig. But this same offensive on the part of the grandmother is *also* reminiscent of Margot's attack on Truquette's hair (B).

Similar horizontal links are depicted in the lower line of the preceding table: in seizing JLP first by the scruff of the neck, then by the hair, the vineyard-keepers attack his *honour* [57] and emphasize that he is a *good-for-nothing*. A little later, they rob Monsieur Sestier of his wig, which, in the Vaunage, is a mark of social prestige.[60] In inflicting this defeat on him, they deprive him of the 'honours of war' [59] that would normally have been his if he had managed to maintain the superiority that he had enjoyed at the outset, when still in possession of his wig, in his fight against the two municipal employees.

In short, the grandmother, her daughter and the two vineyard-keepers, all united under the banner of the community of Solorgues, form a nest of vipers – all too capable of delivering a deadly sting. Truquette's tragic end is sufficient illustration of their lethal powers. The redoubtable grandmother dominates this group of aggressors.

All these 'scalpings' are not situated, so to speak, at the same level. Truquette nearly loses his hair, and in the end he does not save his skin. Jean-l'ont-pris loses his hair once and almost has it pulled out a second time. The shadow of the scaffold is always over him, even if, at the end of the novella, he is lucky enough to escape its clutches, at least for the time being. The attacks on the hair of father and son are, therefore, *strong* episodes: they are inserted into the narrative in accordance with the canonical development of the tale closely inspired by AT 332; they endanger the hero, father and son, who is temporarily protected from death by Death, but who in the end is threatened, if not actually defeated, by Death.

Sestier is not endangered as far as his *real* hair is concerned. All he has to lose is his wig. This episode is, therefore, a *weak* one in comparison with the similar misadventures of Jean-l'ont-pris and his father. The relative 'weakness' of this episode does not prevent it from being highly dramatic and from contributing to the development of the plot.

Let us examine for a moment the misfortunes, whether or not connected with their hair, that befall Truquette and his son. They amount, as we have seen, to two essential techniques:

(1) attacks on the neck – strangling, hanging;

(2) attacks on the hair – shaving or pulling of the hair, possibly of a wig.

The first technique (strangling or hanging, in other words, asphyxiation and breaking of the cervical vertebrae) follows the strictest tradition of AT 332, the tale in which Death, as often as not, strangles the hero or twists his neck at the end of the plot. In fact, Truquette, who has already been threatened with suffocation by the old woman's daughter, ends on the scaffold. Her son feels the threat of strangling or of having his neck twisted when the heavy hand of the vineyard-keeper takes him by the scruff of the neck [57]. In the end, it is true, this hand merely pulls his hair. But twice in succession, the perspective of the gibbet rises before him: once in flesh and blood, in the form of Quincarlot, 'Death's chamberlain',[61] *who, standing before us, frightened me as much as if he had set up a gibbet there* [79]. Second, at the conclusion of Fabre's novella, in the baron's final speech, in which he takes the young man to task: *Born of bad parents, you seem very likely to end up no better than they. Your alliance with that Sestier of Langlade, together with your own wretched inclinations, are very likely to lead you to the gibbet if you do not take care* [89]. It was worth referring,[62] therefore, to the pertinent theme of suffocation/strangulation/twisting of the neck in the various versions of AT 332.

It may be objected that in *JLP* the grandmother, who occupies functionally and specifically the role of Death in AT 332, does not herself take on the job of strangling or suffocating her son-in-law, Truquette. It is, if I may say so, Death in person and not the grandmother who carries out this macabre duty, by means of the hangman at Nîmes, at the end of the first part of Fabre's tale. By arranging his narrative in this way, the abbé was indeed answering in advance the objection that I have just suggested. In fact, he is not unfaithful to the general schema of *Godfather Death*. He simply uses the version of this tale type that was one of his models and that was to survive elsewhere up to the twentieth century in the form of the 'Swiss tale'. We have seen that in the Swiss model of AT 332, versions of which had reached Languedoc, the supernatural and diabolical being (the equivalent of our grandmother) who made the hero rich for a time, then delegates to the local Swiss hangman (the equivalent of the hangman at Nîmes) the task of killing his protégé.

If the strangling and, more generally, the attack against the hero's larynx, trachaea and cervical vertebrae are related to the great tradition of AT 332 in its oldest versions, what are we to make of what might be called in general 'the attack on the hero's hair'?

To begin with, these attacks, unlike strangling or hanging, are not intended – though one could be forgiven for believing the contrary! – to bring about directly the death of the victim. They are rather a portent of that death. They are 'messages of death'. They concern the two central heroes of the tale: Truquette and his son, Jean-l'ont-pris, who takes over from his dead father. Other 'portents of death' may concern less important characters in our narrative: thus Quincarlot, 'Death's chamberlain', announces in advance the imminent death of Barbe-Garouille, on the basis of the external signs that make up the unfortunate woman's ill health, including scurvy. He compares Garouille to such cursed heretics as *the entire English fleet at sea* [83] and *the convicts of Toulon*: the sick woman has certainly lost, as a result of this disease, most of her teeth. She is to die shortly afterwards from her disease, reinforced by scabies, gangrene and tuberculosis. Is there in the AT 332 cycle a similar tradition of attacks on the hair or teeth of the hero (Death's *compère* or godson) that function as portents of death? If so, the attacks on the hair on which Fabre lays such stress in his narrative belong to a more general and remarkably limiting logic.

On this subject, I would like to mention a Spanish (Andalusian) version of AT 322, entitled *Juan Holgado and Death*.

Juan Holgado (John the Idle), a poor man, sees Death standing before him at the foot of a tree from which she has just fallen.[63] She calls him a physician, because of the benefits that she has received from him. As usual, he will infallibly prognosticate the death of the patient if Death is at the head of the bed, and cure if she is at the foot. In the second case, things take place exactly as in *Jean-de-trop* and *Jean-l'ont-pris* and as in so many other German, French, etc., versions of AT 332: Juan Holgado gives a placebo (water in this case) in order to complete the illusion of a miraculous cure.[64] The first reaction of the poor man, when he sees himself made a doctor by Death, is literally the same as that of Jean-de-trop and several others: *how can I be a physician when I do not even know Latin?* Death, of course, brushes aside this objection, as she does in the other stories. The usual advice given by Death (the very same that J L P rejected) is enough to qualify this Andalusian hero of AT 332 as a doctor.

As she leaves the newly created physician, the macabre, supernatural apparition tells him that she will come back to take him – that is, to kill him – if ever he allows his house to collapse. Juan Holgado soon becomes a rich and famous doctor whose children are promised the greatest titles. He installs a resident mason in his house in order to keep it in good condition, and thus deflect the threats made by Death. Unfortunately, his prosperity does not last forever: he becomes old, very old; first his *hair*, then his *teeth* fall out. Death, who has announced herself in this way, then sends him a bat and an illness; then a screech-owl and a cold; and lastly a dog and an emission of blood.[65] Finally, Death appears before Juan's perfectly barricaded house and manages to slip in through a crack. The doctor protests: 'My house is not crumbling, I was not expecting you.' But Death cuts him short: 'It is your body that is your house! It has crumbled! Have you not lost your hair and your teeth?' And she kills him.

Bolte and Polivka,[66] in their famous *Anmerkungen* (commentaries on Grimm's tale 177, p. 296), were the first to notice that this *Juan Holgado* from Spain is a fusion of two tale types which, in northern Europe, remain separate: these are AT 332/*Godfather Death*, to the schema of which, despite certain original aspects, *Juan Holgado* remains faithful, and AT 335 (Grimm's tale 177), *Death's Messengers*. The theme of the second tale was often used by story-tellers (who influenced Hans Sachs or Grimm) and preachers in the medieval and baroque periods: a man complains that he has to die; Death reminds him that she has sent him many a warning; he has sent him premonitory signs, such as the whitening of his hair, the loss of sight and memory. He did not understand the messages and continued to live happily. So much the worse for him! *Juan Holgado* (and before it a southern Mediterranean cycle of AT 332 plus AT 335, since lost, which inspired it) makes a double innovation in this respect: it introduces the theme of the loss of hair (and not only its turning white) as a message of Death; and it is the first to graft the plot of AT 335 on to the longer, more complex plot of AT 332/*Godfather Death*.

Juan Holgado and many other Spanish versions of AT 332 travelled at a very early date to Mexico, and from there to other parts of Spanish and Portuguese America. There they perpetuated, in transformed, but perfectly recognizable forms, the essential structure and strategic nodal points of the tale type, as it had once flourished in the Iberian Peninsula before its departure for the New World. The theme of hair loss as a prelude to death was to remain of crucial importance in the American versions, despite or because of the tricks used at this particular point by the hero of AT 332, doomed to the death that he tries in vain to avoid. In various Mexican, Central American, New Mexican and even Brazilian versions of AT 332, the doctor–hero tricks Death, who is standing at the head of the patient's bed, by turning the bed round, much to Death's fury. Certain of the punishment that now awaits him, the doctor decides to make himself unrecognizable by completely shaving his head. Death arrives, seeking revenge, and is disappointed not to find her former protégé, whom she wished to punish by ending his life. So she throws herself upon the first 'totally bald' individual she encounters and kills him. Of course, the unfortunate individual is none other than the hero himself: by disposing of his hair, he had fixed on his completely naked skull the clearest of messages, or portents, of death.[67] This motif, which became particularly associated with the Latin American versions, is certainly of European origin, more particularly of Iberian and Mediterranean origin, since it is also to be found in the Greek version of AT 332:[68] it therefore crossed the Atlantic from east to west and the Mediterranean from west to east (or the reverse?).

The Iberian tradition is quite close to that of our Languedoc. Given the ease and frequency of communication by sea, assisted by the close Latinity of the languages involved, the Pyrenees had little effect in obstructing relations between Occitans, Catalans, Andalusians, Gascons, Aragonese and Castilians. It is hardly surprising, then, if Fabre gave such an important role in his novels, which were so largely inspired by the oral and plebeian literature of the Latin populations, to the portents of death. The triple Iberian theme (fused with AT 332) of the messages of death – loss of hair, total shaving and loss of teeth – already occurred with extraordinary frequency, in the area immediately to the north of the Pyrenees, in *Jean-l'ont-pris*.

All the characters in Fabre's narrative who are threatened with death (Sestier, Jean-l'ont-pris) or who are in fact struck down by death (Truquette, Barbe-Garouille) are given their due 'ration' of portents concerning their hair. The man and woman who die (Truquette and Garouille) are, moreover, the objects of an earlier attack on their teeth, which makes the signs all the more premonitory. The next two characters, father and son, Truquette and J L P, who occupy in succession the place of the central hero of AT 332 in the narrative, are particularly subject to these macabre messages, as were Juan Holgado and similar heroes in Spanish, Latin American and Greek versions. The forces of death – which of course include the grandmother, but also her daughter Margot, who carries out much of her mother's work, and the vineyard-keepers, also her assistants, and Quincarlot, the chamberlain of Death – take delight in carrying out or threatening these attacks on hair and teeth. I have listed them in detail, and I can now give a more systematic summary of them.

(1) *Attacks on both hair and teeth, followed by strangling:* The grandmother, her daughter and the faction that supports her in Solorgues attack Truquette, who is grabbed by the hair and almost strangled; then, in the commotion, these individuals shave about a third of the head of a young man of the opposite faction.[69] Furthermore, Truquette gets a pot of hot glue thrown in his teeth by Margot.[70] He ends on the scaffold.

(2) *Attack on the hair and total shaving:* J L P's hair is almost torn out by a branch, after the young man has disobeyed his grandmother; as a result, he has his head shaven by the same grandmother. He is then threatened twice with the scaffold, the second occasion being in the last lines of the novella.

(3) *Attack on the hair and an operation equivalent to total shaving:* The vineyard-keepers, continually agents of the forces of death, attack J L P's hair. Then, warming to their task, they repeat in their own way the previous scene described above in (2); using a branch, they lift

off Monsieur Sestier's wig and bare his cranium. The victim is left for dead (he revives).

(4) *Attack on the teeth:* Quincarlot, Death's chamberlain, tells us that the unfortunate and frightful Barbe-Garouille has lost all her teeth as a result of scurvy, which has Protestant associations: she cannot, therefore, live long. (See also the attack on Truquette's teeth in (1).)

Lastly, the body/house equivalent, which is clearly stated in *Juan Holgado*, is also to be found, at the corresponding point, in *JLP*; this occurs in the episode in which the magistrates and 'riff-raff' of Solorgues come to arrest Truquette. His body, already marked by repeated attacks by the two harpies – his mother-in-law and his wife – is handed over to the scaffold. The magistrates no longer even have any need to seize their victim by the hair. They confine themselves to tying him to the tails of their horses. Since they have respected his body, and especially his hair, all that is left for them to do, logically, is to seize his house, which they ransack so thoroughly that 'they left not so much as the plaster on the walls' [37]. Their actions, then, are both symmetrical with and the inverse of those of Death in *Juan Holgado*. Death, in the Spanish tale, pretended to threaten the house of its owner, but in the end she attacked Juan's body, that house of flesh, while respecting the dwelling of stone, bricks and plaster. The Solorgues magistrates operate in the opposite direction, even if the final result is similar: they temporarily respect the body and also the hair of their prisoner Truquette, who has nothing to lose by waiting, but reduce his house of stone and plaster to ruin.

JLP is a full member of this Iberian and Occitan group of versions of A T 332, in which the hero always has the same Christian name: Jean-l'ont-pris, Jean-de-trop, Jean de Carnas, Juan Holgado, etc. This particular Christian name, which is often to be found elsewhere in other tale types (Jean-le-sot, from Normandy to Provence and Languedoc), introduces, as far as A T 332 is concerned, a specifically southern or Mediterranean element; indeed, the Germanic or northern French heroes of *Godfather Death* do not for the most part have a Christian name.[71] Is it surprising, then, that, among these Ibero-Occitan versions of the Jeans and Juans of *Godfather Death*, one constantly meets, in *JLP* and in several Iberian versions, a complete fusion between *Godfather Death* and *Death's Messengers*, A T 332 plus

AT 335, the synthesis operating around the central theme of an attack on hair? Contrariwise, this synthesis was non-existent farther north. The abbé Fabre was certainly successful in achieving single-handedly a fusion of two tales, which a Spanish narrator seems to have reinvented in his own way. However, the repetitive profusion of attacks on hair, as portents or threats of death in *JLP*, tend to remind one that here, too, Fabre found this theme ready made in the oral literature of his region, of which he had an intimate knowledge. It played the same role for him as it did for the Spanish story-teller – that of raw material.

Hence the close similarities (even in certain precise details, strategically placed at similar points in the narrative) between *Jean-l'ont-pris*, *Juan Holgado* and other Iberian versions of AT 332.

CHAPTER XI

Jean-l'ont-pris Tricks the Forces of Death

We now come to what might be called the first 'medical' action specifically described in *JLP*. This action concerns the apparently burlesque 'cure' of Monsieur Sestier, left for dead after a pitched battle between the unequal forces of the vineyard-keepers and himself: *they thought they had sent him to heaven*, Fabre adds [59]. After an amusing 'self-resurrection', the victim of this 'pseudo-murder' subjects himself all the same to the usual formalities; he is given medical treatment, which is described in detail: *after which, our gentleman went to bed, sent for a surgeon, who visited him, without light, in the darkness, finding a thousand wounds in places where he had not been touched, dressed his wounds with cold water, drank three mugs of wine in his company on the bed and made the devil of a report* [63].[1] This episode in Fabre's novella is a systematic comparison with tale type A T 332, concerning the *physician* Death's godson (or Death's *compère*), and therefore an important one.

Nevertheless, the question does arise: who is 'Monsieur Sestier'? The answer is easy enough: he occupies exactly the same place as does the king in *Jean-de-trop* and in many versions, northern or southern, French or not, of A T 332. This character may actually be a king of France, a German king, a king of somewhere else or of nowhere in particular; or a provincial intendant of Gascony, an Irish duke or a German duchess;[2] or, in earlier stages of this narrative type, a rich, powerful peasant of the Sestier type;[3] or even a Mexican *cacique*, when the tale ends its long migration in Latin America. It does not matter: the constant fact is that this powerful or royal individual functions in the tale as the rich future father-in-law of the hero J D T, Death's godson. Similarly, Sestier becomes the future father-in-law of the hero J L P, grandson of grandmother Death.

By way of example, Table 7 compares Sestier in *Jean-l'ont-pris* with his royal homologue in *Jean-de-trop*, the two tales being in many respects, as we have seen, closely related.

Note the geographical gap: J D T's native village is far from the (northern) locality in which the king of France resides; this is seen by the story-teller to be not 'Versailles', but Paris. Similarly in *Jean-*

Table 7	
Plot of *Jean-l'ont-pris*	Plot of *Jean-de-trop*
Truquette and Margot	JDT's father and mother
inhabitants of the Languedocian village of Solorgues	inhabitants of a Languedocian village
have a son	have a son
called Jean-l'ont-pris; he is the grandmother's grandson; the grandmother acts as his god-mother, and she embodies death	called Jean-de-trop; he is Death's godson
he will soon be (or so he hopes) the son-in-law of the rich and powerful Monsieur Sestier, a big farmer in the village of Langlade, north of Solorgues.	he will soon be the son-in-law of the king of France, previously treated by the doctors of Paris, north of JDT's native village.

l'ont-pris: the hero's native village (Solorgues) is at some distance from the more northerly village of Langlade, where the powerful Sestier lives. This is simply one among the great many homologies, in general structure and in detail, between *JLP* and *JDT*.[4]

Incidentally, I have noted that the story-tellers of AT 332 in southern France are entirely ignorant of Versailles, which became the royal residence after 1680. Indeed, in versions of the tale that go back through successive generations to the eighteenth century, at least, and even to the seventeenth, the king of France is seen as residing in Paris (*JDT*) or, which amounts to the same thing, in the Louvre (Bédat de Monlaur's Gascon version, 1936 or 1943).

But to return to the problem of 'medical' treatment. Whether we are dealing with the 'rich man cured on meeting Death' or the 'king cured on meeting Death', as they are found in the old versions of AT

332, which are more relevant to our concerns here, the procedure is generally identical: the hero–physician Death's godson (or Death's *compère*), in the standard plot of the tale, cures the bedridden king (normally doomed to die, since Death stands at the head of his bed). In order to operate this change, the hero turns the bed right round, so that Death is now at the patient's feet. *Jean-de-trop*, which derives from a particular, very old version on which the *Jean-l'ont-pris* of 1755 is based, but which was not collected as such until the end of the nineteenth century, has the enormous advantage of being the first 'marker' to provide the key to Fabre's novella. Nevertheless, this *Jean-de-trop*, collected at a late date (in the 1880s), shifts the medical attention from the king himself to his daughter, whom the physician–hero twice cures and brings back to health. However, the French versions of A T 332, known to us directly or indirectly *in their eighteenth-century form* (which is not the case with *Jean-de-trop*), are definitely concerned, as is *Jean-l'ont-pris*, with the cure of the king (or rich peasant), and not of his daughter. These very old versions (which follow on this point the old German versions of A T 332, those of the sixteenth, seventeenth and eighteenth centuries) were made available to us through Geuellette's collection, published in France in 1712 (see Bibliography), and through other collections recently made in Quebec. Indeed, no one can deny that the six versions of A T 332 collected in this vast province on the other side of the Atlantic are the result of a later development, but one stemming from a version of the tale that arrived from France *before 1763*. This date marks the cutting, by the English, of the umbilical cord that bound French Canada to the mother country; this break affected folklore as it did everything else. Of course, A T 332 was later to develop in its own way in French-speaking North America (though no Indian element has surfaced in the French-Canadian versions of this tale). At least it has remained completely free of the distortions and transformations that A T 332 underwent in France between 1763 and 1950. Indeed, the sheer archaism of the Quebec versions is proved by the fact that they always speak of a *godfather* Death, in accordance with the German origin of A T 332 (*Gevatter Tod*, in the masculine); they never mention any *godmother* Death. This late feminization takes place in the Latin countries in the versions collected during the nineteenth and twentieth centuries; it was gradually to adapt the tale in the non-German zone to the feminine gender that characterizes in France, Italy, etc., the words *mort*, *morte*, etc.

The Quebec versions, like that of Gueullette, authenticate an ancient state of the tale in the French-speaking zone. They all speak of the cure of the *king*, brought about against Death's wishes; they do not mention, *in the first instance*, any cure of the king's daughter, snatched from Death by deception. Fabre, like Gueullette and the Quebec story-tellers, and like the earlier Germans, concentrates the first truly medical episode of his narrative on the treatment, preceded by a trick, that brings Monsieur Sestier, who occupies the place of the king or 'rich peasant' of AT 332, completely back to life. In this respect, then, Fabre remained completely faithful to the oral traditions concerning this matter, as they were available to him in his time. These traditions certainly envisaged the curing of the king's daughter, but they placed in the forefront of attention the restoration to health of the king himself.

Fabre may have decided on the transformation of the 'king' of AT 332 into a 'rich peasant' or into the 'Sestier' of *Jean-l'ont-pris* on his own initiative. But one cannot exclude the possibility that he found such a transformation ready made. Very old versions of *Godfather Death* from a time well before Fabre already referred to a rich farmer or a rich notable [5] (and not to a king) as the double beneficiary of the first medical action and of the tricking of Death, both carried out by the hero, and characteristic of the narrative. In the vast area of his oral culture, Fabre may well have known a Languedocian version that has since disappeared which was similar to those very old versions and which may have derived from them, through a distant importation from beyond the Rhine and beyond the Rhône.

In any case, Fabre did not simply use *as such* in his narrative the function of the notable subjected in the plot of AT 332 to medical treatment. The abbé enriched this role. He extended it in a number of ways that have no equivalent in the existing versions of AT 332, whether old ones or ones recently collected, which confine themselves, in accordance with the tradition of the oral tale, to reducing the 'rich farmer' or 'king' to the sum of his precise actions in the narrative, spiced with a few suggestions as to his royal magnificence. In his novella, however, Fabre makes full use of the sovereign rights of the creative writer, as opposed to the simple oral story-teller. Fabre's

Sestier is strongly marked by the theme of social climbing [62]; this, on the contrary, is totally ignored in the corresponding character (rich peasant, king, intendant, great lord) in all the versions of AT 332. From this point of view, Sestier leaves his mark on the other characters depicted in the novella; indeed, he has points in common with Truquette (the hero of an exercise in social climbing that ends in disaster) and with Jean-l'ont-pris (the hero of a similar exercise that, for the time being at least, seems plausible). These similarities between Sestier and two other male characters constitute an addition that the author inserts in his own narrative over and above the canonical schema of AT 332; they are normal in Fabre's work if we take into account the importance that the theme of ascending social mobility had for the abbé, both in his own life and in his writings.

Another characteristic of Sestier which also distinguishes him from the similar character of 'king' of AT 332 is his physical strength: *stout as an oak . . . the teeth of a wild boar, the chest of a donkey . . . the stomach of a shepherd* [74]. This strength allows him to withstand the blows showered upon him [62]; it also assists him in his vigorous social ascent from shepherd to rich farmer. From this point of view, Sestier has again left his mark on Truquette, or vice versa. Truquette is also physically strong, and keen on self-betterment, despite his eventual failure. *You're a big, strong, sharp-witted fellow*, his mother-in-law tells him [30]. This physical strength, the old woman adds in the second version, must help you to become 'a gentleman, turn Margot into a lady, and young Jean into a soldier . . .' The Sestier–Truquette comparison extends from this point of view to vocabulary. In particular, Fabre tells us that Sestier has *the strength of a bull* [second version]. Truquette, too, gives the same impression of bovine or taurean strength.

The similarities between Sestier and Truquette are very extensive, since the big farmer has collaborated with the former cobbler and the group of riff-raff that surrounded him, in a piece of dishonest commerce involving the reselling of wool that had not been bought or paid for [72].

In a way, Sestier and Truquette, who are heroes – the first of a successful social ascent, the second of a social success that begins brilliantly, then fails – both belong to 'ethnic minorities'. The first is regarded, at least in terms of the insults paid him, as something of a gypsy (the children he begets with Garouille are 'Bohemian remnants', in the words of the second version). The second is a Rouergat, that is to say, a member of a group of people regarded as more or less 'wild' by the rest of Languedoc; they were discriminated against in much the same way as gypsies still are. This emerges in the first part of the novel in the anti-Rouergat and anti-Gavach insults thrown at her husband by Margot [20].

Lastly, Sestier's profound dishonesty, his sexual and other kinds of double-dealing put him on the same footing as JLP. Sestier, the rich peasant or 'king' of the narrative, thus appears to us as an individual who leaves a deep mark on the other characters of the plot, and vice versa. He is not simply bound to them by functional and mechanical relationships that derive from his origin in the cycle of AT 332.

Sestier's 'regality' flows, however, from this functional position, which derives from the original structures of the tale type used as model. Sestier suggests this royalty discreetly enough: he has his peaches guarded as though they were *the king's body* [57]; his daughter has the feet of a queen [72]; he is a man of great influence, he can 'do what he likes' with the men in power in Solorgues. But there, too, as previously, Sestier does not leave others unaffected: these royal characteristics extend by a sort of sympathetic magic from Sestier to Truquette and JLP.

The former cobbler Truquette possesses, in effect, 'the heart of a king'. He is compared in a humorous way to the 'king of Majorca'. Jean-l'ont-pris himself is described as a *dauphin* [33]; he is therefore the son of 'King' Truquette, until such time as he may become King Sestier's son-in-law. Elsewhere, the hero of the narrative (JLP) masquerades, as a joke, as the *Grand roi quatorze* (Louis XIV).

However, there is a certain gradation in this 'regality': Sestier possesses the *body* of the king, an essential, and even exhaustive part of the royal person. He is actually *the* king. Truquette, less well divided, possesses by only partial participation the 'heart' of the king, a mere organ, which, though certainly very important, is not a complete 'body'. Jean-l'ont-pris, though, as Truquette's son and above all the prospective (?) son-in-law of 'King Sestier', has the finest future ahead of him; he is referred to as 'prince', 'king', 'emperor' [41], *Roi quatorze* or Louis XIV, which, one has to admit, is a considerable list of titles. We should also note that if Sestier's symbolic 'regality' derives directly from one of the forms of the original tale type of AT 332, the regality of Truquette and of Jean-l'ont-pris *also* derives from a subsidiary source, namely, the brief encounter that is to take place a little later in Fabre's narrative between an episode of the plot and the tale of the *Cinderella* type or, more specifically, Mme d'Aulnoy's 'Finette-Cendron'. I shall return to this connection shortly.

So Sestier is connected with the other characters and has an effect on them. His and their positions may be mutually defined in terms of various 'encodings' that Fabre has dropped at certain points in his text. These are the diabolical, Christian and discriminatory codes.

To take the diabolical code first. On several occasions, certain characters in the plot of the novella are compared to 'devils'; actually this single word corresponds to different Occitan words, with varying significations.

The first 'devil' is Truquette, to whom the grandmother (his mother-in-law) delivers the little speech that is to turn him into a dishonest merchant and a rich man: *A devil like you will make a fine job of the buying, while your wife and I keep the shop* [30]. 'Devil', which refers here to the idea of hard and somewhat dishonest work, is translated from the Occitan *dragas*, which itself is linked to *drac* and 'dragon'. These two terms suggest pagan monsters, winged serpents or mere goblins, preserved for whatever purpose they may serve by Occitan folklore;[6] they are very different from the traditional, infernal 'devil' of Christian theology. This distinction between the *dragas* of pagan folklore and the Christian devil or *diablatz* is very old in Occitan: it is to be found in the most popular expressions of the Occitan language from the beginning of the fourteenth century.[7]

Sestier is also compared to a *dragas*. He throws himself like a *dragas* [59] on the vineyard-keepers who have just removed his wig; later, when the fight is over, he *walked like the fine devil he was. And he never complained of anything but the terrible hunger that afflicted him* [62]. The word *dragas*, used twice of Sestier, conveys the man's superabundant, somewhat supernatural energy. Showered with blows, left for dead by the vineyard-keepers, the *dragas* Sestier bounces back to life; he sets off like a madman to walk from Solorgues to Langlade, with no other idea in his head but to satisfy his ravenous appetite.[8]

Lastly, the grandmother herself functions as a *dragas*. Immediately after the imprisonment of Truquette, who will soon be hanged, and after Margot's flight, the old woman went back like a *dragas* to making matches [second version]. The manufacture of these sulphur-tipped sticks, which suggest the lights of life (and of death) of AT 332, certainly has something diabolical about it. But the *dragas* or female dragon to whom the grandmother is compared also refers directly, in Fabre, to the functions of death that are carried out by this old woman, in so far as she is the equivalent of the character of godfather Death in AT 332. Indeed, in the first version of *JLP*, Fabre did not write, as he did in the second, 'she went back *like a dragas* to making matches', but quite simply, she 'went back to making matches, *working herself to death*' [39]. This is an allusion to the fact that the old woman works extremely hard at this task. But it also suggests her fatal powers; the grandmother uses not only matches, but also needles and awls. Armed with these pointed implements, she is certainly skilled in pricking skin, beginning with her son-in-law's [22].

Lastly, Jean-l'ont-pris himself has his own arsenal of names deriving from folklore. Indeed, he suggests that his name, Jean-l'ont-pris, might be exchanged (but he is not keen on the idea) for that of Hobgoblin [40]. In other words, 'little devil'; once more, this word must be understood in its pagan, folkloric sense, and not in the truly infernal sense given it by Christianity.

To sum up, Truquette is once called a dragon [*dragas*]; Sestier, twice, and the grandmother, once, are treated to the same name. JLP is once called a hobgoblin. In other words, from the first half or two-thirds of Fabre's text we are immersed, not without humour, in a fairy story, deriving in this case from AT 332/*Godfather Death*.

In the last part of the narrative, things change. We enter quite decisively, without leaving the field of the tale, into a world of infernal diabolism, though of course Fabre's humour does not desert him.

The Occitan word *diâblé* ['devil'], which signifies not a dragon of folklore, but a true creature of hell, appears for the first time when Sestier is being treated in bed: the surgeon, whose action, in fact, does have something supernatural about it, later writes up 'the devil of a report' [*un rapport de tous les diables*, 63]. Shortly afterwards, when he is discovering his grandmother's treasure, which also has something very strange about it, Jean-l'ont-pris cries out: 'The devil' [*Aou diâouqua*, 67]. He twice uses, when referring to his grandmother's legacy or offspring, the Occitan word *diâouqua* (the equivalent of the modern French *diantre*, 'deuce', a euphemistic form of 'devil' whose weakened, familiar significations are still nevertheless diabolical). In the second version, the precautions taken by JLP to hide his grandmother's treasure are called *diaoucas*; the ceremony uniting Truquette with the daughter of this same grandmother is referred to by the hero as a 'damned wedding' [*diaouqou dé mariâgé*, 15].⁹ By means of this word *diauco*, a slight diabolization of the grandmother's legacy is effected, and yet the grandmother had first functioned as a harmless dragon [*dragas*] of folklore.

However, a true devil is now about to appear. The one-eyed Cancrelas/Quincarlot comes on the scene for the second time, in the last episodes of the novella. (We first met this individual during Truquette's lifetime.) Since then things have certainly taken a turn for the worse. His hole for a right eye and his macabre connotations generally made him already suspect. Now diabolism will return whenever his victim, none other than our unfortunate JLP, addresses him: 'The devil [*Aôu Diâblé*] . . .' [80]. And again [81]: 'To the devil [*Diâblé*] with your damned conversion! I thank you for your friendship . . . You should have kept it for your cousin Satan, who would have paid you back in kind!'

In the rest of the text, Cancrelas/Quincarlot is no longer Satan's cousin, but Satan or 'Beelzebub' in person. 'As we talked, there entered a certain fat figure of a man like a bundle of knavish tricks who, standing before us, frightened me as much as if a gibbet had been set up there.' Here the terrifying but comic Quincarlot functions both as a messenger of death (setting up a gibbet) and as a Beelzebub, and therefore a particularly evil devil. He operates – I shall come back to this – as a satanic attendant of Death. Moreover, he is related to grandmother Death.¹⁰ The services he renders are those of a devil [*Diâblé*] and deserve no more payment than 'a good blow on the head'.

Also connected with Satan in some way, a damned soul in any case, a victim of hell, if not its executioner, is Barbe-Garouille (in Occitan, a *garouille* is a swamp or swampy ground): 'the most miserable and horrible creature that ever lived on land, sea, or perhaps even *in hell*, a veritable knacker's yard, a hunchbacked, squint-eyed, pasty-faced animal, capable of wreaking the worst possible torments upon you at a distance of a hundred paces, and whom one could not so much as look at without being compelled at once *to make the sign of the Cross*[11] *and to recommend one's soul to God*, ... this dunghill found herself with child. It was difficult to imagine whose work this act of despair could be, for, unless Satan were the author of it, it would not have been possible for a thief, otherwise condemned to the wheel, to have dared to bring himself to perform it...' [77]. This passage takes cognizance of Garouille's infernal associations; but it also implies a modest diabolization of Monsieur Sestier himself. Hitherto compared, quite simply, to a dragon of folklore [*dragas*], now, as the exposed lover of Barbe-Garouille, he is regarded as a *Satan*, capable of getting Garouille pregnant.

In a more general way, we move, in the course of the narrative, from characters who are mere *dragas* of folklore (Truquette and Jean-l'ont-pris/Hobgoblin), to roles which become gradually more diabolical (Sestier), culminating in a frankly infernal personality (Barbe-Garouille) or even entirely diabolical (Quincarlot, whose diabolism, for all its comedy, is unquestionable).

There is a second code, which might be called Christian or 'Christic'; it is centred, more specifically, in Fabre's narrative, on the Passion, the face, the family, the friends and the enemies of Jesus Christ.

The central character here is Jean-l'ont-pris himself. After his first rough handling by the vineyard-keepers, he declares [54] that the same men, after seven or eight hundred blows on the shins, left him in the condition of an *inci homme*, an Occitan deformation of *Ecce homo*: it was in these words that Pilate presented the scourged Christ, crowned with thorns (John 19:5). This identification with the Christ of the Passion is discreetly suggested a second time when, discovering his grandmother's treasure, Jean-l'ont-pris addresses the Almighty thus: *Your will be done* [second version], an obvious paraphrase of Jesus's words on the Mount of Olives (Luke 22:42).[12]

If a burlesque J L P is compared in this way to the suffering Jesus, Monsieur Sestier, on account of a number of evil deeds with which the hero reproaches him, is explicitly compared to a *Barabbas of the Passion* [78] and to a *Judas* [80]. He is not, therefore, placed directly among JLP's persecutors or among the enemies of this 'Christ-figure'; Sestier belongs rather among those who, apostles like Judas or prisoners like Barabbas, possess certain affinities as friend–enemy with the Christ-like image of the hero, who is himself compared to Jesus, when imprisoned and scourged. It goes without saying that the Judas/Barabbas of this type is quite capable of harming the hero, either because he is a criminal (the case of Sestier/'Barabbas') or because he will betray the young man (Sestier/'Judas'). The same applies, of course, to the ambiguous relations between the powerful man of AT 332 and the hero of that tale in general, and to the relations between Sestier and JLP in particular: in relation to the hero or to JLP, this powerful man or Sestier is a friend (future father-in-law); at the same time, he is an adversary, at least temporarily, since he rejects at first this role of future father-in-law. In the oldest specifically oral version of AT 332, collected in France in the early nineteenth century by Jacob Grimm, this ambiguity of the king, or powerful man, as friend–enemy of the hero is quite clear.[13] See also the Austro-baroque version of *Hans-with-the-Goitre* (AT 332), so close to our *Jean-de-trop*: there is the conflict between the hero Hans (homologue of JLP) and the king's constabulary (homologue of Sestier), whereas the king's daughter (homologue of Babeau) supports the hero's cause (Vernaleken, 1864, p. 224).

Against the hero, who functions as a kind of tragicomic Christ, against his friends–enemies of the Sestier/Judas/Barabbas type, there are always the true satanic devils, who are in complete contrast to the 'Christ' model. Quincarlot was Beelzebub in the first coding, and he remains so in this one. Indeed, the name of Beelzebub is given to him by the narrator at a very precise point in the text: JLP has just defined Sestier as 'Barabbas' [78] and almost in the same breath calls the same individual 'Judas' [80], who by a sign[14] betrayed Christ, identified in Fabre's narrative with JLP. The comparison between Quincarlot and Beelzebub stands between this Barabbas and this Judas.

So Quincarlot/Beelzebub, flanked by his infernal Garouille, is, in the scale of evil, even more repulsive than Judas and Barabbas; Quincarlot/Beelzebub belongs systematically to a gallery of portraits organized at a greater or lesser distance, favourable or unfavourable, from the central figure of the 'Christ'–hero.

Where does the grandmother stand in terms of this 'Christic' encoding? Unquestionably, in the network of the 'Holy Family' of *JLP*, the old woman is identified with the Virgin Mary, but, of course, she is a macabre Mary, who tends to represent Death; such a tendency is in accordance with the traditional role of J L P's grandmother, since she is the functional equivalent of the godfather Death of A T 332.

Let us take in turn the 'virginal-marial' references contained in *Jean-l'ont-pris*. There are four of them, three of which are directly linked to the grandmother, while the last refers to a situation of quasi-death.

(1) 'Good heavens!' a woman says to the grandmother during a village fight, 'have I angered you, my fine lady of mercy [*ma belle dame de miséricorde*]? I beg you to accept my humble apologies . . .' [26, second version].

(2) As J L P goes through his grandmother's treasure he exclaims: '*Holy Virgin*, pray to your son that it should go on . . .' [69, second version].

(3) At the beginning of the narrative, the grandmother and her daughter, Margot, who have retired to Solorgues, are compared to *two young virgins* [6].

(4) Early on in the fight between Sestier and the two vineyard-keepers, one of them 'delivered a mighty blow between the eyes of dear Monsieur Sestier *that must have given him a vision of Our Lady of Candlemas*'. Sestier, knocked half senseless, recovers all the same to take part in a fight to the death, itself followed by a resurrection [59].

(5) We should perhaps add, by way of reminder, that Garouille is described as not being a *virgin* [83]. This term is technically correct; it has the additional advantage of contrasting the unfortunate death's head of Garouille with the 'burlesque virginal' figure of the grandmother.

Let us examine these various 'virginal' aspects, one by one:

(1) The grandmother is comically compared to the 'Lady of Mercy'. The cult of the Virgin of Mercy, or Lady of Mercy, or Virgin with the Cloak, is of medieval and perhaps Byzantine origin.

During the Middle Ages and the Renaissance, this theme was widely disseminated by and among the religious orders: Cistercians, Dominicans, Carthusians, not to mention, at a later date, Jesuits; and among women, Carmelites. Indeed, in 1563, St Teresa of Avila saw (in the manner of visionary monks and nuns) the Virgin wearing a white cloak of the kind worn by all Carmelite nuns. The confraternities of penitents, especially in the Midi, diffused this theme in the secular world: the huge cloak of the giant Virgin was a shield; it protected all those who hid in its folds against the arrows of the plague. The epidemic deaths of the fourteenth century did much to popularize this image. The Virgin appears as even more powerful against Death than St Sebastian or St Roch, the traditional anti-plague saints. Up to the seventeenth century, painters like Zurbaran and Simon Vouet demonstrated the importance of the theme. They depicted the Virgin of Mercy, protecting with her cloak Jesuits and Carthusians.

In the eighteenth century, Jansenism, through its theory of predestination, denied or diminished the favourable influence of intercession through the Virgin and the saints; the cult of the Lady of Mercy suffered a corresponding setback. 'Predestination kills intercession.' This particular cult of Mary remained alive, however, among the people: the plague of 1630, at Nancy and at Aix, brought something of a revival of the cult. There were a large number of altarpieces of the Lady with the Cloak in the churches of southern France; they made it possible for this devotion to continue unhindered, despite the hostility of the new theological thinking that had taken root among the élite. In the 1630s, when the plague was over, a girl from Aix-en-Provence, Madeleine Martin, founded the religious order of Our Lady of Mercy, which was to have a great future. The Lady of Mercy appeared, moreover, in person to a Provençal priest, 'and showed him, at a glance, that she held under her cloak all the Novices who were to take the habit in that New Monastery, as a certain mark that she would take them under her special protection' (Alexander of Arles, p. 40). As a result, this priest, inspired by the Virgin, persuaded Madeleine Martin to establish a convent of Mercy at Arles.[15] This cult was to remain alive until the eighteenth century: several houses and altarpieces of Mercy with the Cloak still survive in the Midi and elsewhere.

To return to *JLP*, the grandmother has no cloak; she is in her night-dress [22]. This rather special 'Lady of Mercy' is, therefore, quite unable to protect her followers in the shield of her vast cloak; on the contrary, there is a sense in which she brings down the arrows of death upon them. One can appreciate the irony of the woman who gives this pious name to the scrawny, semi-naked body of the grandmother. She is a funny kind of virgin, or *viergette*, to use Fabre's own word. There is nothing surprising in the fact that the abbé, in what is after all, as so often with him, a burlesque mode, should have chosen that particular 'Mary' to symbolize a character (the old woman) who occupies functionally (in the narrative *JLP*) the role that was that of Death in the tale type that served as a model for his novella.

(2) The exclamation *Holy Virgin* used by J L P when discovering the treasure of his recently dead grandmother does not require much commentary: it is linked, again, and in a very close way, to the old woman herself. We should also note that such an interjection occurs in the period immediately after the grandmother's death, in other words, in the precise context of the death of Death, or Death squared; we know that the grandmother occupies functionally in *JLP* the role of Death in AT 332.

(3) The use, at the beginning of the narrative, of the expression 'two young virgins' about the grandmother and her daughter, Margot, has never been seriously studied until now by Fabre's commentators. Anatomically, the term has no meaning: Margot is certainly a virgin at the time, but her mother, an unmarried mother, is no longer a virgin. Everything becomes clear, however, if we admit that in this case, it is a question not of physical anatomy, but of one of the codes used by Fabre: this basically Christic code centred on the figure of the hero becomes, as we have already seen in previous examples, 'virginal-marial' in the case of the old woman. Nevertheless, in accordance with the techniques of displacement used over and over again by Fabre (for example, his treatment of Jean-l'ont-pris, a young man who is a doctor without being one, a mere *capitaine de santé*, etc.), the grandmother is not a true Virgin Mary, but a quasi- or semi-Virgin, a *viergette*. As for Margot, who is always so deeply implicated in her mother's doing, she is included, like her mother, under the common term of *viergette*. This term is all the more legitimate in her case, since she is indeed, at the time, a virgin and young [*viergette*]. The two

women, moreover, will have a maternal relationship (like the Holy Virgin) to J L P/Christ; the old woman will function in relation to him as a godmother, and soon as a teacher (after Margot's departure). Margot herself will be the mother of this pseudo-'Jesus'. On the other hand, it is stressed that Barbe-Garouille is not a virgin [83].

(4) We now come to the vineyard-keepers, who, knocking Sestier senseless, give him a vision of *Our Lady of Candlemas in all her magnificence*. The commentators have often remarked that this is a comically religious equivalent of the secular expression 'seeing thirty-six candles' when one is being knocked out. However, the term used by Fabre refers to the marial cult (Our Lady) and to a feast (Candlemas), which requires some explanation.

In the liturgical calendar Candlemas is 'a feast celebrated on 2 February of each year with blessing of candles and procession, to commemorate the presentation of the Christ child in the temple at Jerusalem', and also to commemorate the legal purification of Mary forty days after the birth of her son. Though originally Christological, 'this feast has taken on a marial character: this is apparent in the texts read at the offices of that day'.[16]

However, folklore studies complement this purely theological point of view: it appears, in fact, that even as late as the early part of this century in Catholic countries, and, for example, in both northern and southern France, the candles blessed for the Candlemas of the current year were lit around deathbeds. By extension, this practice was also applied during serious illnesses. In certain southern villages, the choirboy who accompanied the priest carrying the viaticum to the dying held a lit Candlemas candle belonging to the family of the sick individual.

In the early nineteenth century, these practices were still alive: in the Provençal region, Candlemas represented, for the faithful, a preparation involving prayers and candles for a death that might occur during the year. In the Occitan-speaking region, there is evidence from the fourteenth century of the use of candles held near or over the dying.[17]

By showing Sestier *Our Lady of Candlemas in all her magnificence*, the vineyard-keeper who had delivered him a mighty blow between the eyes was offering him, in no uncertain terms, the thirty-six blessed candles of his deathbed. So the farmer lay as if dead on the ground:

his subsequent resurrection is unexpected, almost miraculous. Our Lady of Candlemas functions here as a brilliantly illuminated goddess of Death, in short, of the final moments of life, or at least those presumed to be so.

What we find here, by intersection, is a familiar, fundamental theme of AT 332. At the end of the tale, in its classic versions from Germany and France, Death leads the hero into the cave with the millions of candles; he shows him his own candle, his light of life, doomed soon to be extinguished.

Fabre did not use this 'motif' of the candles of life *directly*. In this case he followed perhaps the oral version of AT 332 that served as model for his novella. Yet the abbé does allude to these lights in the form of matches: the grandmother (Death) makes these matches all her life and distributes them to various individuals, and they lie in large piles near her at her own death.

Fabre also transposed the theme of the lights of life that shine for the last time during the final moments of life when he made Sestier see *Our Lady of Candlemas in all her magnificence*, at the moment of being knocked senseless by the vineyard-keeper. The fact that Sestier recovers does not contradict the point I am making: in one version of AT 332, the hero sees his candle of life, then escapes Death, while the light also escapes the fatal extinction that threatens it.[18]

Elsewhere, in two southern or Occitan versions of AT 332, one from the Nîmes-Montpellier region (*Jean de Carnas*, Dezeuze, 1953) and the other from Limoges (*Lemouzi*, 1911), the king of the tale, unusually, changes function. He is no longer the sick notable treated by the physician–hero, but one of the characters (certainly notables) who are suggested at the beginning of the narrative (before Death herself is proposed) as the hero's godfather. He is no longer threatened by Death, but he becomes a possible substitute for Death – not *against her*, but *on the same footing as her*. In these circumstances, the theme of the thirty-six candles, possibly deriving from Our Lady of Candlemas, is completely switched: the king is no longer, as was Sestier, he who *sees*, when stunned, the thirty-six candles of the deathbed that awaits him, even if he recovers a little later. On the contrary, the king has become a full member of Death's gallery (Dezeuze, 1953, p. 69), carries the thirty-six candles on his hat, dazzling those who see him, and especially the hero. This is reminiscent of the cloak covered with dazzling stars worn by the Virgin Mary, also presented in this particular case as a possible substitute for Death (since she is a candidate for the role of godmother) in the oldest French oral version of AT 332, collected in the early nineteenth century.[19] She is also, incidentally, or rather specifically, a Virgin of Mercy, the wearer of the cloak, and close to Death.

Leaving aside the theme of candles and Candlemas, let us return to the 'marian' theme. It would appear that in *JLP*, the four relevant references – *Our Lady of Mercy, two young virgins, Holy Virgin* and *Our Lady of Candlemas in all her magnificence* – are linked, or at least three of them are, to the character of the grandmother, herself the equivalent of Death; and, in the case of the fourth, to a potentially fatal action, involving an allusion to the lights of life.

Still more specifically, the two *detailed* 'invocations' to the Virgin, as Our Lady of Mercy and as Our Lady of Candlemas, are associated by Fabre, in a burlesque way, with functions of the Virgin Mary through which she is temporarily concerned:

(1) *either with the danger of sudden death*, against which the Virgin of Mercy is supposed to deploy her protective cloak (but, in the case of *JLP*, the grandmother/Lady of Mercy/mother of Christ is bareheaded, wearing a night-dress, and has no cloak; she can therefore only facilitate the action of sudden death; this grandmother behaves as a cruel stepmother; she is literally a Virgin of Death);

(2) *or with situations in which death is imminent*, in the case of Our Lady of Candlemas. There, too, she is a Virgin of Death. (In a more general way, the association of Mary with Death is a basic element in the religion of our predecessors: of the four great Catholic prayers, the *Pater Noster*, the *Ave Maria*, the *Credo*, the *Confiteor*, only one explicitly refers to the inevitable death, attended by Mary, of the person praying, and that is the *Ave Maria*.)

The association of 'Our Lady' with grandmother Death and with death itself in *JLP* seems therefore quite clear. Moreover, it is not entirely an innovation as far as the Languedocian cycle of AT 332 is concerned: after all, in *Jean-de-trop*, too, the godmother Death of the future physician is on the best of terms with Our Lord (Jesus), the godfather of the same child. She is not absolutely diabolical: she may be regarded quite simply as a holy person whose only wrong is to be somewhat macabre; in short, a sort of Our Lady of Death.

On this question, one may look at things from a somewhat higher level and wonder what, fundamentally, is the theological status of Death in A T 332. To what extent does this status bring him closer to a *negative* supernatural character (the devil), or to a *positive* supernatural character, a role that functions on terms of friendship with God and that, in Latin countries, because of the feminine gender of the word 'death', may be approximated to the functions of a Virgin Mary possessing associations with death?

A T 332 appears for the first time in 1350 in the German-speaking lands; in England, the first accounts of the tale date from the fifteenth century; in Germany again and in Italy, from the sixteenth century; in France, from 1712. In every case, the oral versions, unknown to us as such (they were not to be collected until the nineteenth century), pre-date to a greater or lesser degree the texts that the generally obscure writers left on both sides of the Rhine, the Channel and the Alps between 1350 and 1712. The initial dates are not open to question: undoubtedly (I shall come back to this), the tale was a popular preaching theme in the fifteenth century; it spread rapidly in the rich soil provided by the taste for the macabre so characteristic of the later Middle Ages and of the baroque period. Such a taste derives from the monastic meditations on death as a sign of contempt for the world. It was diffused after 1300 among lay people through the sermons preached by the mendicant friars. The deaths from the plague of 1348 and of the next hundred years, which killed half the population of Western Europe, provided a sounding-board that gave to the macabre, between 1350 and 1500, an immense, sinister popularity. It is against this background that A T 332/*Godfather Death* developed, an example among so many others of the use made, in this period, of a personification of death.

The Death of this late medieval period is an ambiguous character. Under the impetus of the notions, themselves ambivalent, that were forged about her in the twelfth and thirteenth centuries, she was regarded sometimes as a loving mother, sometimes as a pleasant Franciscan *sister*,[20] since she also opened the gates of eternal salvation to the soul of the dead person – she snatches it from our corrupt or corrupting world. Sometimes she is regarded as a diabolical entity, an accomplice of Satan and an abominable stepmother who cruelly attacks the living. Fabre, heir to a long tradition, sensed this old ambivalence of Death: mother, wicked stepmother; on the side of God, on the side of the devil; happiness for the saved soul, horror for the survivors. Take the funeral oration for Renaud de Villeneuve, bishop of Montpellier, written and spoken by Fabre himself in 1766: *O Death, thy shafts are swift ... O Death, for the holy prelate thou art but the peaceful sleep of the just, for us thou wilt be an awakening full of bitterness and terror.*[21] The celestial–demoniacal ambiguity of Death is also apparent in the versions of AT 332 that Fabre used, derivatives of which have reached us elsewhere in the nineteenth and twentieth centuries in the form of *Jean-de-trop* and the 'Swiss tale'. In the first of these two, Death is a close friend of Jesus, and therefore of divine essence. She is a 'dependant of God'. And yet, even in this instance, she is not innocent; her imprisonment in the bottle at the end of *JDT* will please God, for this episode will temporarily deprive Satan of the daily supply of damned souls which, thanks to Death, he usually receives. In the second text ('Swiss tale'), the role of the Death of AT 332 is carried out by a semi-diabolical character, the Green Man.[22] So, in writing *JLP*, Fabre divided into two a character that represents Death without actually saying so. In one of the later parts of the narrative, Death will be Quincarlot, a sort of Satan/Beelzebub; he will laugh diabolically, minus his right eye. However, during the 'Truquette' episode and the beginnings of the 'JLP' episode itself, Death was the grandmother; her role was far from being an agreeable one. There was a whiff of sulphur about her, as about her matches, and she covered her right eye, as did Quincarlot. But, as a non-demoniacal dragon of folklore, she could become quite naturally, when encoded into Christian or Christic language, a kind of macabre *Holy Virgin*, while Quincarlot will be seen as both demoniacal and burlesque. The problem will be to pass from the folklorico-marian image of (grandmother) Death to her satanico-risible representation (Quincarlot). To do this, the grandmother has previously to be killed off. We shall come back to this.

Lastly, Fabre uses in *JLP* a third code, which might be called the 'discriminatory' code. It consists in marking a particular individual by means of a label that places him among the outcasts of the religious system: those being presented as non-Catholic (Protestants) or even non-Christian ('Jews'). I put the word 'Jew' in inverted commas. When this concept is used in *JLP*, it is simply in order to stigmatize a particular individual who *in fact* is either a Catholic or a Protestant, but who is supposed to behave according to the dishonest practices of a hostile and for us unpleasant stereotype attributed, at that time, to the Jews. Fabre, in fact, simply uses as a metaphor for this taboo term the words 'synagogue of Avignon' [second version].

The Protestants of the narrative are true Huguenots. We know that they were very numerous, in any case, in that part of the Vaunage around Nîmes. These anti-Semitic and anti-Protestant prejudices, which are quite rare in the abbé's books as a whole, are not, of course, the pleasantest aspects of his work. But the analysis of his text is forced to make use of these 'markers', even if they shock, and rightly so, our contemporary sensibilities.

Protestants: first, the grandmother is explicitly indicated as such [66];[23] second, Judith Garouille, or Barbe-Garouille, is presented in several ways as a Protestant:

(1) Her first name, Judith, is biblical and Huguenot, absolutely not Catholic, according to the Languedocian traditions of the period. Moreover, people make the sign of the Cross when they see this unfortunate woman: in his thesis, Sauzet has shown to what extent in the Vaunage the Cross marked the hostile reaction of a Catholic to a Huguenot. Similarly, there is the gift of a brass cross [14] given by the Rouergat (and therefore Catholic) Truquette to his future wife, Margot, the daughter of a Protestant, when taking her to the wedding at a papist church that will finally cleanse her (or so he hopes!) of her family's Huguenot associations.

(2) Barbe-Garouille is compared successively, because of the execrable smell that she gives off, to 'the entire *English* [83] fleet at sea' (England is Protestant) and to the inmates of *the convict-prison at Toulon* (which, typically, would contain a large proportion of Huguenot deportees). (See on this subject the *Histoire de Toulon*, recently published by Privat at Toulouse.)

(3) Lastly, Garouille is presented as entirely repugnant and unpleasant, which of course proves nothing in itself, but accords well, in view of her generally Huguenot characteristics, with the anti-Protestant prejudices that Fabre has mobilized against her.

'Jewish' characters, or at least those compared metaphorically to the synagogue of Avignon, even if they are, in real life, Christians or non-circumcised: these include the swindler Quincarlot and his two accomplices (who quickly disappear from the narrative) and finally the 'merchant' Truquette.

These terms (Protestant and 'Jew') are used by Fabre to mark the forces of death. They are also used to mark those who are to be victims of these forces of death, that is, those who will die.

Forces of death: the grandmother, who is a *Protestant*. Quincarlot, who is a 'Jew'.[24]

Victims of death: the 'Jew' Truquette, marked for death by his *Protestant* mother-in-law, who takes the role of Death during the first two-thirds of the novella. In fact, Truquette is executed by hanging. Another victim of death is Barbe-Garouille, a *Protestant*, whose death, which actually takes place, is announced in advance with some force by Quincarlot, the 'Jew'.[25] To sum up, then, we have:

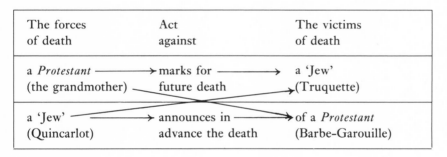

The forces of death	Act against	The victims of death
a *Protestant* (the grandmother)	marks for future death	a 'Jew' (Truquette)
a 'Jew' (Quincarlot)	announces in advance the death	of a *Protestant* (Barbe-Garouille)

In this table of death given or received, Fabre, then, has played on the terms with a certain mastery, which is not, it is true, to our taste.

It will be noticed that this table may be read either horizontally or vertically (in columns): in either case, 'Jew' goes further, more intensely, than *Protestant*. On the left, moving from bottom to top, the 'Jew' Quincarlot is a stronger and more satanic figure than the *Protestant* grandmother. On the right, from top to bottom, the 'Jew' Truquette, the central hero, in the first instance, of AT 332, is a stronger figure than the *Protestant* Garouille, a minor character whom Fabre, as we shall see, has adapted in order to furnish the end of his plot. In order to blacken still more the 'bad' image of Truquette, Fabre insinuates not only that he has a 'Jewish' mentality, in inverted commas, but also that, although a Catholic and a Rouergat from birth, and married in church [15], this unfortunate Truquette displays Jansenist tendencies! He dies 'as a predestined' [80], Quincarlot is to say of him. Now whoever speaks of predestination in about 1750, where a non-Protestant is concerned, implies *ipso facto* Augustinism and Jansenism.[26] Quincarlot himself is also blessed with a kind of burlesque 'grace of God' that suggests Jansenism [80].

It will be noticed that the other heroes of the novella, who are neither forces of death nor victims of death, are scrupulously left free of these marks of heterodoxy – whether Jewish, Protestant or Jansenist. Jean-l'ont-pris is the son of a Rouergat father, therefore of papist origin, and a mother (herself born of a Protestant mother) whose husband, with little success, had tried to Catholicize by marrying her in the church and by giving her a brass *cross*.[27] The young hero JLP, therefore, is, in principle, a Catholic; he has absolutely no Huguenot tendencies, and, indeed, he is married by a priest. The 'religion' of Monsieur Sestier is none too clear. But it will be remembered that Holland, in Fabre's novella and in geographical reality, functions as a Protestant marker. (I am thinking in particular of the cambric [*toiles de Hollande*, 68] found in the Huguenot grandmother's treasure.) Take Sestier's reaction to the vineyard-keepers (who themselves are depicted as wicked villains, inhabitants of the Huguenot Solorgues and placed, with the Huguenot grandmother, in the 'camp of Death'). On the subject of this reaction, the narrator declares: 'The blows that he had been given were of no more concern to him than were the affairs of Holland' [62], in other words, 'he didn't care a fig for them'. This expression is a way of distancing the farmer from the Protestantism of the vineyard-keepers.[28] It is a way of saying that Sestier, who is, of course, Jewish neither literally nor metaphorically, functions as a non-Protestant and implicitly as a Catholic. However, for all that, the farmer does not become 'the greatest saint in the Litanies'.

Let us now try to link the three codes – folklorico-diabolic, Christian-Christic and discriminatory.

Turning to Table 8, we have, on the far right, Quincarlot, the black or negative character *par excellence*. He is satanico-diabolic, Beelzebub and, a significant term in the context of the discriminatory mentality of the period, a 'Jew'. In these circumstances, it is hardly

Table 8

THE CODES

A	B	C	D	E	F	G
1 Axis of Fabre's narrative →	Truquette	Jean-l'ont-pris	Monsieur Sestier	Grandmother	Barbe-Garouille	Quincarlot
	Narrative	at first folkloric →		then diabolization of the plot		
2 Folklorico-diabolic code	dragon	hobgoblin and little dragon	dragon, then Satan or *diantre*	dragon, then a *diantre*, or burlesque semi-devil	unfortunate damned soul, victim of hell	Satan
3 Christian-Christic code		Jesus Christ in his Passion	Judas or Barabbas	macabre Virgin Mary or 'Our Lady of Death'		Beelzebub-the-gibbet
4 Discrimina-tory code	'Jew' victim of E4	not discrimin-ated against (= explicitly Catholic)	not discrimin-ated against (= probably Catholic)	Protestant	Protestant victim of G4	'Jew'
5 Axis of tale type AT 332	first hero (sacrificed), who is father of second hero (survives)	second hero, son of first, who seems suc-cessful, at least temporarily	'king', funda-mentally ally and second-arily the enemy of the hero	godfather Death; or, in Latin countries, godmother Death		devil as substitute for godfather Death in certain ver-sions of AT 332

292 LOVE, DEATH AND MONEY IN THE PAYS D'OC

surprising that the last part of *JLP*, in which Quincarlot plays an important role, follows certain versions of AT 332, in which Death is replaced partly or entirely by the devil.[29]

Barbe-Garouille is also an infernal, or rather a 'damned' creature. But she is a victim, not a killer. According to the discriminatory code, she is regarded as a Protestant ('non-Catholic'), and not as a 'Jew' (that is to say, non-Christian, which would be 'worse'). She is, therefore, less negative than Quincarlot.

In the folklorico-diabolic code the grandmother is a dragon, which has nothing infernal about it, or a *diantre*, a devil with semi-demoniac tendencies who must not however be taken too seriously. She does not go as far as the complete satanism of Quincarlot. Also, in the Christian-Christic code she is resolutely placed at a distance from hell. She is in no way a satanic creature. In fact, she is placed (at least at the beginning of her descent to earth) much higher in the heavens; she functions, in effect, as a macabre Virgin Mary, or Our Lady of Death. Indeed, she escapes, characteristically, the worst discriminatory marks: she is not a 'Jew', but simply a Protestant. She shares, therefore, the ambivalence of Death, as he appears in the classic versions of AT 332 that are more numerous in the group referred to here. In these versions, Death is certainly a formidable creature, but one who in the last analysis derives from God before going to the devil: in any case, he 'descends' from above, from the heavens above, into a subterranean hell; in short, from God to devil.[30]

Monsieur Sestier is depicted as a dragon of folklore; there is also a touch of the *diantre* or devil about him. But he is very far removed from the total satanism of Quincarlot. Basically, he functions in the Christian-Christic code as one of the figures closest to the Christ–hero, though certainly a delinquent or traitorous figure of the *Barabbas* or *Judas* type. In other words, he is a friend–enemy of the hero; much more than a complete and utter enemy who, in this case, would be described as a 100 per cent Satan/Beelzebub. As the classic king of AT 332, Sestier is quite capable of playing nasty tricks on the hero. However, he remains a highly placed accomplice: in any case, just before the end of the tale, the hero in question becomes the king's son-in-law; and in the case of JLP, he certainly hopes to become Sestier's future son-in-law.

Where Jean-l'ont-pris himself is concerned it should be stressed that he is in no sense whatsoever satanic or diabolical. On the level of folklore, the young man functions simply as a little dragon, a kindly hobgoblin. On the level of the Christian code, Jean-l'ont-pris operates as a *Christ of the Passion*. This role is eminently positive, even if it is treated, in the general spirit of Fabre's novella, in a burlesque style. As the son of a Rouergat[31] who by definition is a papist, Jean-l'ont-pris is, in any case, implicitly Catholic; father and son are both married in church by a priest [15]. This young man is certainly not 'the greatest saint in the Litanies', but he is certainly not a Protestant or a 'Jew' (even if it is only a matter of a pseudo-Judaism expressed in the form of an insult). Jean-l'ont-pris is wholly and entirely the positive hero of AT 332, someone who, one may hope, will triumph, temporarily at least, at his future or possible marriage, over Death.

Truquette is the unfortunate hero of the 'first cycle' of AT 332/ *JLP*, the cycle of 'Death's *compère*'. The poor fellow is, therefore, a 'dragon-*dragas*', without any trace of the diabolical. He is the victim of Death (whom his son, in contrast, will have some success in avoiding), and he shows a number of chinks in his armour. These are enough to earn him the description of 'Jew', on the grounds of a discriminatory stereotype of the supposedly dishonest trader. It is also suggested that he is implicitly a Jansenist: his mother-in-law marked him with an awl, as though to make him *predestined* to an early death.

The preceding analysis and Table 8 enable us to situate the roles of the characters in the novella, Monsieur Sestier in particular, by means of the positions that these individuals occupy in the respective networks defined by the different codes used by Fabre in his narrative. Let us come back now, by logical continuation, to the first medical action of the novella, the one that concerns the curing of Sestier.

I shall compare this episode with the classic medical episode found so often in the various versions of AT 332. First let us recall the outlines of this medical episode.

The physician–hero is called to a patient's bedside. In the versions collected in the nineteenth and twentieth centuries, this patient may be a king or some other powerful individual or the king's daughter, who by way of reward will be given in marriage to the hero. In the versions explicitly prior to 1763, and which correspond to those known to the abbé Fabre, it is always the king or the powerful man (whose daughter the hero will possibly marry) who is the patient. What we have in such cases is the functional equivalent of our Monsieur Sestier. By means of the gift of medical clairvoyance given him by his macabre godfather, the hero sees this godfather, Death, at the *head* of the patient's bed. This, as we know, means that the patient will shortly die.

Violating the pact that binds him to Death, the hero then decides to operate a permutation of 180 degrees, or $\frac{\pi}{2}$. Following his instructions, four strong men suddenly turn the bed. Death, who was at the head of the patient, is now *ipso facto* at the patient's feet, thus enabling him to survive. What counts in this matter is not the actual movement from head/death to feet/health, but the rotation of 180 degrees on the horizontal plane. Indeed, in a number of versions of AT 332, French and others, the usual schema is reversed: Death at the patient's feet signifies death; at his head, health. In this case, too, the semicircular permutation takes place. Sometimes it is the physician–hero himself who is threatened by Death, whom he sees beside his head. He then arranges to have his own bed rotated at 180 degrees.[32] Whatever variants are used, Death is always furious at being tricked in this way.

Once Death has been tricked, the curing of the powerful individual, who, up until this moment, was dying, follows quite logically. In any case, he already feels better. In order to establish his own reputation as an infallible curer on a firmer footing, the physician gives the patient a placebo that is supposed to bring about a complete cure, but which in fact is quite ineffective. It is the turning of the bed that is responsible for everything. This placebo may consist of herbs or roots; but more often, in the various regions of Europe, including southern France, it takes the form of cold water, with the possible addition of liquorice, etc.

In all versions of AT 332, the cure or quasi-resurrection of the powerful individual, with the help of the liquid placebo, is effected immediately after a process that comprises two essential phases:

(1) the powerful individual, in his sick-bed, is regarded as lost, or more or less dead;

(2) a trick is performed by the physician–hero on Death.

As soon as he had to implement this succession, which was available at Fabre's time in the written and oral versions of AT 332 then circulating in France,[33] the abbé was presented with certain delicate problems. As the author of a hyper-realistic parody of a fairy-tale, bordering on caricature,[34] Fabre has turned the grandmother into a Death who is not Death; as for the hero, who in the original tale was a physician, he has transformed him into a paramedical figure who is not entirely a doctor. As a result, Fabre cannot really save the classic scenario of AT 332. How can he bring together at the bedside of the dying individual a semi-Death and a quarter doctor? With his usual dexterity, the author has inverted the order of the two essential sequences of the episode in question.

The previous procedure by which *the cure of the powerful man* was achieved in two phases, (1) *quasi-death of the powerful man* and (2) *Death tricked*, is taken up therefore by Fabre, but by reversing the order: *the cure of the powerful man*, according to this new arrangement, is achieved after the two successive phases (1) *Death tricked* and (2) *quasi-death of the powerful man*.

First sequence: 'Death tricked' or rather *the forces of death tricked*. It was logical to introduce this initial segment of the episode in the development of the overall narrative. Generally speaking, in fact, this segment corresponds to the stage in progress, in the general structures that Fabre gave to the personal biography of Jean-l'ont-pris, which forms the second part of his novella. (On these general structures, which *reverse* the classic, four-part schema of AT 332, see the end of Chapter XIII.) More specifically, Jean-l'ont-pris, from the beginning of his own career, in other words, from the time that he is orphaned by the loss of both parents, finds himself exposed, under the malevolent auspices of his grandmother, to attacks from the forces of death: the grandmother herself, the tree, the donkey, the municipality of Solorgues represented by the teacher and the vineyard-keepers. After killing his father, they strike at him, pull his hair, grab him by the scruff of the neck, shave his head, beat him, etc. It is time for the young man to defend himself and, in his turn, decide to fight the forces of death;[35] to begin with, he sets out to trick Death. To do so he uses the classic trick taken from AT 332, the permutation of 180 degrees. But he is not *lying* on a bed, as the sick man, the physician–hero himself of AT 332, sometimes is, who swings his own bed round in order to escape his godfather Death (Wolf, 1851; Aurbacher, 1879).

JLP operates from a standing position, tied as he is to the peach-tree or 'torture post' to which the vineyard-keepers, the 'municipal emissaries and allies of the forces of death', have tied him. In short, a displacement in time of the 'Death tricked' sequence, from position (1) to position (2), is accompanied by a displacement in space, the hero moving from the lying position to the standing position. There is nothing surprising in that: he is not ill, and therefore has no reason to be lying down.

AT 332	JLP
180° ⟮ feet ↖ ⟯ 180° head ← Death turning round of the bed	vineyard-keeper's son 180° ⟮ ◯ ↖ ⟯ 180° ◯ forces JLP ← of death tying to the torture post and switching with the vineyard-keeper's son

At the end of the permutation of 180 degrees, JLP, using a trick [58], changes place with the vineyard-keeper's young son, whom he ties to the same peach-tree or torture post, this post being the target aimed at by the forces of death, who expected to attack the hero's head. In fact, thanks to this trick, JLP will literally put himself in the child's place; he will place himself in the position where a few moments before this child, the vineyard-keeper's son, was placed; by doing so, he will subject the boy to several ordeals.

Moreover, not content with changing place in this way with the vineyard-keeper's son, JLP, a few paragraphs later, plans to take over the post of vineyard-keeper himself, thanks to the support of Sestier [65]. There is, in fact, permutation all along the line.

We should note in passing the use, in this episode of *JLP*, of the whistle. It is this whistle that, thanks to a trick invented by the hero, makes possible the semicircular permutation with the vineyard-keeper's son. In a version from central France, the hero of AT 332, thanks to godfather Death, at the decisive moment of the 'turning of the bed', is also endowed with a magic instrument that he sticks under his tongue.[36] Above all, the use of whistling accompanies, in the case of both Truquette and JLP, the decisive moment when the hero enters the magic game of the grandmother and Death – no longer a passive, suffering or neutral character, but an active force, determined to achieve victory, followed by catastrophe (Truquette) or a less conditional success (JLP).

In fact, Truquette threw himself into the game seducing Margot, the daughter of grandmother Death, a seduction that will be the guarantee of his future fortune ('crowned', of course, by a disaster). What did the cobbler first do to ensure that he won the big prize that Margot represented? He whistled, then sneezed, then farted and 'bang', on each occasion, there was Margot at the window, ready to respond to the desires of her lover [10–11].

Similarly, when JLP, before and during the 'permutation of 180 degrees', wants to bring the vineyard-keeper's son (son of a municipal agent of Death, just as Margot was the daughter of grandmother Death) into his scheme, what does the young hero do? In order to win over the boy [58], he uses the power of attraction and the strident sound of his whistle. In both cases, the father Truquette and the son JLP are equally brilliant in the way they use their whistling to launch themselves, with varying success, on the careers that will enable them to manipulate the forces of death or, which amounts to the same thing in this case, the children (daughter or son) of the same, to their own advantage.

Death is always furious at being tricked in this way. This is true in innumerable Occitan and other versions of AT 332. It is also true in *JLP*, as far as the reactions attributed to grandmother Death are concerned, tricked as are the forces of death in general by the permutation of 180 degrees operated by the hero. *Go! Go! You'll see what my father . . . You'll see what my grandmother and yours will do to you!* the child cries to JLP from his torture post [58]. This cry thus unites, in conjoined threat, the legitimate fury of the two forces of death that consider themselves tricked: the first a principal one (the grandmother of the over-cunning hero); the other, secondary (the vineyard-keeper). Both versions of the novella are unanimous on this point.

In the classic versions of AT 332, the trick played on Death *was brought about* by the desperate situation of the powerful man, who found himself *in bed* close to death. In order to save his patient, the doctor had no other choice but to trick Death by turning the bed at an angle of 180 degrees. Here it is exactly the reverse: it is the initial trick played on Death that is *to bring about* the temporary incapacitation of the powerful man, *laid out* or *put to bed* as a result of the blows given him by the vineyard-keepers/forces of death. This reversal of the structures of the tale is due to the very particular constitution of the story of Jean-l'ont-pris himself. In all the versions of AT 332, including Truquette's biography, the hero's complicity with Death occurs first; the conflict with Death occurs only in the second and even third act. In the story of Jean-l'ont-pris himself, on the contrary, the conflict between the young hero and grandmother Death comes first, during his childhood; this conflict very soon arouses in JLP the irrepressible need to deceive his so-called protectress, who for him is in fact no more than an oppressive force. Beginning with this basic fact, Fabre has turned the quasi-death agony of the powerful man into a fact that is not primary, but secondary, in relation to the tricking of Death; the quasi-death agony is no longer the *cause*, but the *result* of the trick played on Death. In the classic versions of AT 332, the physician saves the powerful man before saving himself. In the personal autobiography of JLP, in which the four-part schema of AT 332 is reversed, the hero saves himself before saving the powerful man Sestier.

In most of the *ad hoc* versions of AT 332, the hero finds the powerful man lying close to death, in his bed, and he treats him by tricking Death. Here the problem is reversed, since the two sequences are placed in reverse order. The fact of tricking Death must, therefore, produce a situation in which the powerful man, who is in perfectly good health, is 'put to bed' or more exactly laid out, knocked senseless by the forces of death. He is thus temporarily 'sent to heaven' or regarded as 'dying' [59, 64].

Fabre found an elegant solution to the technical difficulties involved in this reversal of the sequences. J L P tricked the vineyard-keepers; in his place he tied the son of one of them to the peach-tree or torture post. This trick creates the misunderstanding that leads to the attack on the powerful man (Sestier), who beats the vineyard-keeper's son, thinking him to be J L P. He therefore gets attacked in turn by the child's father and the father's fellow vineyard-keeper. These forces of death, as in A T 332, stand 'at the patient's head'. In short, they had sent Monsieur Sestier 'to heaven' (had killed him). 'I arrived in turn, and the two of us shook him and saw him recover his senses' [59]. However, there is no question in *JLP* (as in the second sequence of the same episode in A T 332) of tricking Death in order to achieve this resurrection (immediately after the trickery). In fact, in *JLP*, as we have just seen, Death *has already been tricked* in the first sequence of the episode in question. It is understandable that, having been so thoroughly tricked, Death did not find the necessary energy to kill Monsieur Sestier completely: he therefore revives without much difficulty, since the forces that should have killed him, having been thwarted at the outset (with the permutation of 180 degrees around the peach-tree), are now in no state to deprive him fully of life. Emerging very quickly from his comatose state, Sestier revives unaided, so to speak. This is attributable – or at least he attributes it – to the prodigious, elephantine hardness of his skin, acquired during his years as a shepherd, before he became a rich farmer. What we see here is the reappearance of the theme of social ascent, so dear to Jean-Baptiste Fabre. Sestier also displays, on this occasion, a gargantuan appetite, stuffing the food between his jaws, which, it is later said, are 'a rod wide' [72]. It is true that the theme of the gigantic appetite of the powerful man was at least suggested in *Jean-de-trop* (which is the folkloric counterpart of *JLP* on the side of A T 332): it is, indeed, the *cook* of the powerful man (of the 'king', in this case) who summons Jean-de-trop to the royal palace to exercise his medical talents. In any case, there is more than a hint of the tale A T 332 in the very fine scene of the placebo, situated in this final sequence, that of the cure. 'So we accompanied him [Sestier] to his house, where we dined like three pit-sawyers; *after which* our gentleman went to bed, sent for a surgeon, who visited him, without light, in the darkness, finding a thousand wounds in places where he had not been touched, dressed his wounds with cold water, drank three mugs [*chopines*][37] of wine in his company on the bed and made the devil of a report' [63].

This passage clearly states the useless, pitiful character, which is burlesqued here, of the final pseudo-treatment; it arrives on the scene when no longer required. It occurs after the tricking of Death and after the real cure, which follow directly Sestier's last 'agony'. The surgeon, therefore, has to invent fictitious wounds on the rich farmer's body; and he locates them in total darkness and 'dresses' them with a placebo of cold water, to be found in so many versions of AT 332 at the same strategic and tactical point in the narrative.[38]

In one Occitan version (Bédat de Monlaur), this technique is basically the same as in *JLP*: the physician–hero has actually cured the powerful man (or his daughter) thanks to the trickery effected at the expense of Death; he then pretends to achieve this cure (in fact already guaranteed) by the use of the placebo. But whereas this placebo is administered *internally* in AT 332, it is applied *externally* in *JLP*: as a result of the particular structure that he gives to this episode, Fabre subjects his powerful man to wounds inflicted from the outside.

We should also note in *JLP* the reintroduction, at the moment when the placebo is about to be applied, of the bed, so characteristic of this group of tales [63]. Sestier had no need of a bed, since he was already completely cured: in fact, he had walked several miles home. But no sooner is he about to subject himself to a sprinkling of cold water in the darkness than Sestier lies down for the first time on a bed. The only point of this piece of furniture is to evoke the typical powerful man of AT 332, the homologue of the specific Monsieur Sestier.

It is true that the notion of 'physician–hero', which remains unified throughout the duration of a 'normal' AT 332, in particular while the medical actions are being performed, tend, by contrast, to be divided into two during the medical action of *JLP*.

Indeed, at the beginning of this 'action', in Fabre's novella, it is the hero himself (JLP) who tricks the forces of death, during the scene of the permutation of 180 degrees around the 'torture post' (the peach-tree). It is also he [59] who first treats the powerful man (Sestier), victim of an attack and a quasi-death. But since JLP is not a doctor or even a paramedical, further 'treatment' must be given by someone else during the rest of the scene. So he confines himself to the role of a mere witness, while a surgeon called in from outside takes it upon himself to administer the remedy or placebo of cold water [63] that JLP, because of his inadequate qualifications, does not have the right to give the patient. Death had made the hero of AT 332 a doctor in the full sense of the term. The grandmother in *JLP*, who is really no more than a semi-Death, was unable to transform her grandson into a fully qualified doctor. However, the two of them – Jean-l'ont-pris, who gives the initial treatment, and the surgeon, who applies the placebo (himself only half a doctor since he is 'only' a surgeon) – constitute together a complete physician in two parts.

With his usual lightness of touch, Fabre suggests, moreover, the incomplete character of the radical inadequacy of Jean-l'ont-pris's 'medical' (in fact, paramedical) aptitudes. Once again, the comparison provides certain keys. In *Jean-de-trop*, a significant expression is used: the story-teller stresses (p. 190) the medical *savoir-faire* of the hero Jean-de-trop, the physician Death's godson, summoned to the royal palace to exercise his remarkable talent. In his novella, on the other hand, Fabre insists essentially on the *savoir-vivre* [39] that might have characterized his hero JLP if he had listened to his grandmother. There is no question for JLP of a specifically medical *savoir-faire*, since JLP does not, by virtue of the deviant orientation given by Fabre to his own narrative in relation to the original model of the tale type, possess the art and diagnostic capacities of a fully qualified doctor. On the other hand, Truquette's *savoir-faire* is fully recognized: he has, in effect, carried out, and fortunately for him, the career of a swindler who soon becomes rich (then equally quickly hanged!) canonically assigned to him by the first part of the tale. At the same time, the narrative stresses that his son, JLP, is far from possessing even 'a quarter' of his father's *savoir-faire*. This can be summed up in a table (see Table 9).

In short, Jean-l'ont-pris is lacking in *savoir-faire* because he is 'neither count, marquis, nor wigmaker', nor a true *surgeon*-barber, nor a doctor – at most he is a kind of emergency nurse [59], but possessed, as we shall see, with a rare ability to trick Death.

Despite this inadequacy on the part of the hero himself, the strictly medical action, in the biography of a JLP who is not himself medically

Table 9

PROBLEM OF *SAVOIR-FAIRE*

COMPARISON OF *JDT* AND *JLP*

	JDT	*JLP*
The fathers	JDT's father, Death's *compère: no information*. It is true that his undeniable prosperity in the tale *JDT* is merely a 'gift of Death' without any specific modality.	Truquette, JLP's father and grandmother Death's son-in-law *compère*, is a swindler in accordance with the canons of A T 332 (see, in particular, the 'Swiss tale'). He possesses *savoir-faire* explicitly.
The sons	JDT, wholly and entirely Death's godson/physician, in accordance with the canons of A T 332, possesses *savoir-faire explicitly*.	JLP, grandson and functionally godson of grandmother Death (but paramedical at most, by virtue of Fabre's particular arrangements), *does not possess savoir-faire*, which is normally possessed by the physician Death's godson in the canonical versions of A T 332.

qualified, is inserted in the heart of the narrative, in the second part; just as in the first part (the biography of the hero's father) is inserted the action by which Truquette seduces Margot, then becomes a temporarily lucky swindler. In both cases, the problem is similar, even if there is a final failure on Truquette's part and, on the other hand, a final success, or appearance of success, on the part of JLP. It is still for the hero (first father, then son) a question of manipulating to his own ends the forces of death, by obtaining from them love, marriage and fortune (Truquette), and by tricking them and thus winning the albeit ambivalent friendship of Sestier, the rich father and possessor of the desirable Babeau (Jean-l'ont-pris). Things turn out badly for Truquette because he imagines himself to be cleverer than he is: for it is he in reality who is manipulated and finally crushed by the forces of death (the old woman, her daughter Margot, the municipality of Solorgues and the hangman of Nîmes). Jean-l'ont-pris, however, knows how to remain temporarily master of the situation. In the end, he even manages to bury the old woman.

Moreover, the chronological boundaries of this action–manipulation are marked in both cases. This begins with a whistle: Truquette whistles for Margot [10] at the moment when, having previously been aroused by her, he begins to take seriously the prospect of marrying her. Jean-l'ont-pris in turn [56, 57 and 58] whistles at the vineyard-keepers, and then at the son of one of these vineyard-keepers: in fact, he uses the boy to manipulate and trick the forces of death, who include the vineyard-keepers personally, as municipal officers of Solorgues. The *whistle* begins things. *Night* ends them. Night of mystery and of dark deeds: it is at night that the heroes' first more or less ephemeral triumphs take place. It is *at night* [31] that Truquette comes home with his donkeys laden with mysterious goods stolen or not paid for. Later, in the second part of the novel, it is *without light, in the darkness* [63] that the surgeon dresses the pseudo-wounds of Monsieur Sestier, who, to show his gratitude, will become the benefactor of his nurse J L P. Between *Whistling* and *Nocturne*, the heroes try to master their destinies, dominated by a supernatural force, Death, which they try, with or without success, to bend to their advantage.

The next stage: Jean-l'ont-pris has to continue his tricking of Death, or his grandmother, to the very end. In *Jean-de-trop*, derived from an archetype on which *JLP* is also based, and which is therefore a 'homologue' of *JLP*, this trickery is achieved on a single occasion, in the second and final segment of the second and last part of the tale. The young Jean-de-trop wants to get godmother Death to grant him a very special favour, namely, two hundred years of additional life *for his wife* (he has already obtained *for himself* the guarantee of these two hundred years). Godmother Death is reluctant to grant this wish. So J D T traps her into accepting a stupid bet: he challenges her to enter his little brandy gourd. Accepting the bet, she makes herself as tiny as a cricket (in a version from Quebec, Death makes himself 'as small as a fly')[39]. She then enters the gourd, which JDT quickly seals with a tight cork. Death struggles in vain. After eight days of 'confinement', she is forced to grant JDT the two hundred years of life that he has demanded for his wife. He can then free Death. God harbours no resentment against JDT for neutralizing Death in this way for eight days; he knows that he is a good, devout boy.

This fragment of plot is connected to a motif or even to a tale type that folklore specialists have gathered here and there and which they call *The Spirit in the Bottle*, or AT 331.

In southern, central and western France and in Quebec, this short narrative often forms part of *Godfather Death* (AT 332), exactly as it does in *JDT*. From this point of view, the Occitan versions are the most interesting. In Ariège,[40] in a local version of AT 332, godfather Death is shut up by his physician godson in a wine gourd, from which he will emerge only after two hundred years. In this way the physician obtains a safe life for himself for that period of time. There are two features in this version from Ariège that vouch for its antiquity: Death is a *godfather*, thus indicating an archaic state of the tale, before the complete feminization and Latinization of the supernatural character; the gourd is used for *wine*, the age-old drink of the Midi (and not for brandy, as in the version that we possess of *JDT*; this presence of brandy, a later drink produced by distillation, became widespread among the people of central Languedoc about 1660 to 1680, and thus suggests a modification of a detail in the narrative, itself later in date, during the oral transmission of *JDT*).[41]

In the Aude, where *Jean-de-trop* was collected, another version of AT 332 also uses the theme of 'Death shut up in a wine receptacle'. The hero–physician Death's godson wants to save his seriously ill mother from Death.[42] Fortunately, godmother Death is thirsty. She would like a cool drink. So the hero shuts her up in a wine barrel, which, apparently, is empty; this barrel has a tap and a vent secured by a peg. The hero carefully replaces the peg in the hole through which Death has slipped by making herself as thin as an eel. Unfortunately, the young man's father comes to check the state of his casks; he pulls out the peg. Death flies out of the barrel like a violent gust of wind, almost knocking the father over (compare the fatal fart of the donkey or priest, both sacred characters, maleficent or beneficent, in the *Jean-le-sot* cycle, which is related, as we have seen, to *Godfather Death*). Of course, the first thing that Death does is to go and kill her godson.

In Brittany, Death is enclosed in a kneading trough. However, the 'bottle prison' as such occurs in AT 332 in Catalonia, in central France (Nivernais) and in Brittany. In Scandinavia, where wine is rare and where alcoholic drinks are made with cereals, Death is shut up in an empty beer barrel. In Quebec, where the French versions of AT 332 emigrated before 1763, the local story-tellers have transmitted the same theme for over two hundred years: Death walks up and down in the bottle in which he has been enclosed, a scythe over his shoulder. This bottle is itself placed by the prudent physician Death's godson in a formidable construction of wooden boxes, one inside another, like Russian dolls, the whole measuring four square feet.[43]

However, as the folklore specialists have shown, the theme of 'the spirit in the bottle' is not irremediably linked to AT 332. It may quite simply occur *alone*, in which case Death may be replaced by the devil. A fine example, from the Occitan Midi, concerns the struggle between Punch and the devil, himself called Ratapon.[44] Through a trick involving a bet, Punch shuts the devil up in a bottle. He will let him out only if this Ratapon gives him a treasure worth 100,000 francs and a woman (the original reward for the winner of the bet). In Grimm (tale number 99), the hero gets from the devil, whom he has enclosed in the bottle, a treasure in the form of money and also the ability to become a physician. The tale *The Spirit in the Bottle* is an old one, older than the known appearances of *Godfather Death*, which has been traced back to 1300 and in its quasi-definitive form to 1450. The 'Genie in a Jar' was already found in *The Thousand and One Nights* (tenth century); in the West, we meet the same narrative in the legends of the Middle Ages and the Renaissance, in the German, Latin and French languages. Virgil lets the devil out of a bottle, on condition that he initiate him in magic. Paracelsus (1493–1541) uses the same method to obtain a drug that will cure any disease and a tincture that will change anything into gold.[45] After an attentive reading of *JLP* (as we shall see), there is, therefore, every reason to suppose that the versions of AT 332 known to Fabre by word of mouth and which he used, did contain this very old theme of 'Death in the bottle', since we find this theme in the *Jean-de-trop* from

Narbonne, derived from the same version; in the oldest French versions of A T 332 (which travelled to Quebec before 1763); and in many another Occitan or Catalan version of *Godfather Death* or of *Punch and Ratapon*. According to these texts, Death, or the supernatural entity, was forced when trapped in this way to grant the hero certain wishes: treasure; medical or simply paramedical abilities; a woman; the hand of the great man's daughter; survival for the hero himself or for his young wife, etc.

In these circumstances, what does Fabre do? Let us follow the thread: we left the hero (J L P) at the point at which his participation in the quasi-miraculous treatment that cures Sestier the powerful man is completed. The cure is achieved according to the classic prescriptions of A T 332, inverted by Fabre, and accommodated by him to the requirements of a hyper-realistic parody. Death was tricked by a permutation of 180 degress. A placebo of cold water is administered to the previously dying man – and Sestier is put on his feet again. This rich farmer, therefore, is to do what the powerful man or king of A T 332 always does with regard to the hero–physician Death's godson, in this case with regard to J L P, hero–paramedical grandson and godson of grandmother Death. He will reward the young man. To begin with, he will make him a vineyard-keeper of Solorgues, a highly lucrative job. Sestier's 'royalty' reaches Solorgues from Langlade, just as that of the king of France reaches the Languedoc of *JDT* or of Bédat de Monlaur from the Louvre or from Paris. Through intermediaries, the rich farmer can do 'anything' [65] in Solorgues, which facilitates the appointment of Truquette's son as vineyard-keeper. At the same time this will be a new defeat for the forces of death, more thoroughly defeated than ever. The former vineyard-keepers have been sacked for bad conduct in order to make room for J L P. Now, they were agents and active participants of the forces of death, as docile executants of the municipality of Solorgues, which was, together with the grandmother, responsible for Truquette's arrest and death.[46] So much so that in order to rid himself legally of the old team of vineyard-keepers, Sestier short-circuits the municipality, about which he is under no illusions; in order to carry out the sacking of this team, he uses, on a higher level, the secular arm of the *seigneurie* of La Boissière, in the persons of its judge and clerk [64–65]. This *seigneurie* is already opposed to the grandmother's camp with its diabolical and woodland associations: see above [17, 45] the contrast between the hunter of La Boissière, who provided (more or less by poaching) wild forest animals for Margot's wedding banquet, and the *gamekeeper* of La Boissière, a friend of JLP and a natural enemy of this hunter.

So JLP has become the new vineyard-keeper. He thus receives the first gifts or benefits from the powerful man, by way of reward for his paramedical attentions. Thanks to this newly acquired position, the hero will finally be able to *trap* his grandmother. The Languedocian archives of the villages and even the abbé Fabre's novella throw light on the normal activity of the vineyard-keepers: they were supposed to protect the produce, grapes and other fruit, in particular against theft by children, dogs, girls and thieves of any kind.[47] But there is no better poacher than an active gamekeeper. The dishonest vineyard-keepers stuff themselves with grapes and other fruit, and they keep their children and relations, etc., abundantly supplied. The new vineyard-keeper JLP, therefore, gets as fat as a capon fed on grapes. His grandmother actually dies of an excess of the fruit.

He gets fat. She dies of a sort of swelling up, due to excessive eating of grapes, before the harvest. In any case, the text of *JLP* stresses these phenomena of swelling up. Immediately before being raised to the rank of vineyard-keeper and before the death of his grandmother, JLP notes, before there is any question of the old woman's excessive eating: *they . . . got as drunk as grape-pickers at a wine harvest* [64]. On this occasion JLP and Sestier refrain from wine, but the 'grape-pickers' stuff themselves with grapes the day before the harvest, just as the grandmother is going to do: the reference is premonitory. Jean-l'ont-pris himself was quite used to it: he was eating muscat-grapes and peaches from Sestier's orchards just before the Homeric fight with the vineyard-keepers; this took place no more than a few days before he in turn became the official guardian and therefore unofficial thief of that fruit.

The notion, explicitly stated by the hero, of a grandmother with a voracious love of grapes, filled to bursting point and beyond, will recur, in fact, a second and third time, after the old woman's death. The treasure-chest that she leaves her grandson is a 'Noah's ark' (we know that Noah got so drunk that he dishonoured himself before his children). The grandmother's capacity for food is then referred to by her grandson. He finds nothing to eat after the death of the old woman, who, it seems, had devoured everything: *On arrival I looked everywhere for something to have with my bread, and I couldn't find a single onion, shallot or clove of garlic* [67]. (In fact, these three vegetables, of the bulb type, are harvested in summer; their consumption occurs at the very time described by Fabre, that immediately preceding the wine harvest: in Languedoc the wine harvest takes place in September and often in the first weeks of that month.) The old woman is implicitly accused by her grandson, therefore, of stuffing herself with fruit – albergo peaches, unripe green grapes and muscat dessert grapes, so common in Languedoc. She had also explicitly devoured the seasonal 'bulbs'. Since everything had been stolen from the estate on which her grandson worked as vineyard-keeper, he is, in a sense, responsible for the old woman's death, with, it is true, her own stupid and gluttonous co-operation. *Your poor grandmother was so prudent she seems to have scoffed everything before leaving! the unmitigated glutton!*

The sentence 'I looked everywhere for something [*pitanco*, in Occitan; *pitance*, in French] to have with my bread [*pan*], and I couldn't find a single onion . . . [*l'y trouvêré pas soulamént úna sébba, . . .*]' [67] is worthy of consideration. It is, in fact, an exact repetition of the phrase that occurs in the first half of the novella, that devoted to Truquette, at the strategically homologous point of the narrative [18, 19]; there is a point-by-point comparison between the lives of Truquette and JLP. The point in question is that which immediately precedes, at the time of maximum poverty, the canonical phase of 'Death's gifts'. 'My parents,' JLP relates, 'found themselves [*se trouvéroun*] without bread [*pan*], without wine, without food [*pitança*] . . . without money' . . . Margot 'sought in vain for her fine clothes and trinkets. Not a rag remained . . . [*n'en trouvêt pas soulamént un pétas . . .*]'. In the first instance (life of Truquette), it is the whole family, the grandmother included, who gorged themselves at the wedding meal and who were left with no money and nothing to eat. This gives grandmother Death the opportunity of 'giving a treasure' to the members of 'Truquette's family', so that they will become prosperous again; but in order to become so Truquette must put himself in the old woman's hands, agree to become a swindler under her direction, bound hand and foot to her. In the second case (the life of JLP himself), it is only the grandmother who eats everything; but, by a just reversal of fortune, it is now she who is tricked – stuffed with grapes, she will now disgorge treasure, which will go to her grandson. The second version of *JLP* adds, moreover, to the words 'I couldn't find a single onion, shallot or clove of garlic', the phrase 'not even a dried sardine [*arencâda*]'. Now the dried sardine, the Languedocian dish of the poor, in various Occitan versions of AT 332[48] illustrates precisely under the name of *arencâda* the poverty-stricken nature of the meal eaten by the poor tradesman or peasant who is to become Death's *compère* and who will soon be given, by way of contrast and as part of a dangerous contract, a prosperous future. The lack of even this pitiful *arencâda* or dried sardine on the menu provided to Death's godson or grandson (JLP) symbolizes the difficulties, where food is concerned, facing the young hero at the moment when at last he is about to reverse the situation; at the moment when at last he will be able to *manipulate* grandmother Death's wealth and treasure to his own advantage. These difficulties of subsistence were previously felt, at the homologous starting-point of a similar adventure, by the young man's father, at the moment when, like a sort of farcical turkeycock, he was to be manipulated to his own detriment by his mother-in-law Death or *commère* Death.[49]

At the climax of Death tricked (AT 332), we have two comparable scenes in AT 332 and in *JLP*: (1) the passing of the diminished body of Death through the 'hole' [*trauc*] of a wine-holding receptacle, 'bottle, gourd or barrel' (this is the motif generally called 'the spirit in the bottle') (AT 332/*JDT*); and (2) the placing of the paralysed body, stuffed with grapes, of grandmother Death in the hole [*trauc*] of a burial ditch (*JLP*). These two operations are carried out by the hero himself. In the versions of AT 332 that we are examining here, and that originate in southern and central France, the hero always plays the role of Death's godson (and not of his or her *compère*); or he is the grandson/godson of grandmother Death, who herself acts as godmother (in the case of JLP). The similarity, therefore, is carried very far.

Table 10 will make it possible to measure this homology in AT 332

Table 10

DEATH IS TRICKED OR TRAPPED AFTER PASSING THROUGH AN ORIFICE

	AT 332/*Godfather Death*: mainly *JDT*, but also GM, AA and other southern French versions of AT 332 that are relevant to this episode.	*JLP* [65–70].
Sources		
Period of the yearly cycle when the episode takes place (if specified)	'In August' (before the wine-harvest) (GM).*	'Before the wine harvest' (September, a critical time for the vineyard-keepers) [*JLP*, 65].
A First sequence	Action on Death's body.	Action on the body of grandmother Death.
B Second sequence	The passing of the body, thus prepared, through a hole [*trauc*].	The passing of the body, thus prepared, through a hole [*tràou*].
C Third sequence	After this 'passing through', the setting aside of this body in a receptacle, which later may itself be buried or thrown into a well.	After this 'passing through', the putting away of this body in a mortuary ditch.
D Fourth sequence	The hero locks up this body, previously	The hero covers with earth the buried body

	JDT	JLP
E Fifth sequence	The hero (JDT) begins a *dialogue* with this body.	The hero (JLP) begins a *monologue* addressed to this body; this monologue is homologous with the dialogue opposite.
F Sixth sequence	The religious character of this situation is stressed in a serious way (*JDT*).	The religious character of this situation is stressed in a burlesque way (*JLP*).
G Seventh sequence	Body continues to be locked up (following action in line D).	The hero locks the door of the house against an *external* danger (see line D, left-hand column).
H Eighth sequence	Death, now powerless, grants the hero considerable advantages: cure of his mother (GM); two hundred years of life for the powerful man's daughter, now his wife (*JDT*), etc.	Grandmother Death, now powerless, grants the hero considerable advantages: in this case, treasure that will enable him to possess, perhaps even to marry, the powerful man's healthy daughter.
I Ninth sequence	Death's body finally emerges from the 'prison' and resumes its lethal activities.	Another macabre character (Quincarlot) replaces grandmother Death, who has been finally 'put away'.

* G. Maugard, *Contes de Pyrénées* (1955), p. 118, translates: 'At the *beginning* of August'. In fact, the original Occitan text collected by U. Gibert states simply: 'in the month of August [*als mes agest*]'. For *JLP*, see [65].

in its Occitan or other forms and in *JLP*, which is the literary descendant of this tale type. Of course I want to speak of those versions of *Godfather Death*, Occitan or other, that include the episode known as 'the spirit in the bottle'. We know that many versions of AT 332 do not in fact include this episode. For them, therefore, Table 10, and the paragraphs concerning it, do not apply.

To begin with, let us say what the basic data of Table 10 are: on the left, we have the versions of the master tale (AT 332); on the right, the narrative that derives from it (*JLP*). The type of narrative is, therefore, supernatural on the left, hyper-realistic on the right: I have already said that Fabre, among other accomplishments, tries to transform the supernatural symbolism of folklore (godfather Death) into hyper-realistic, even caricatural visions. As far as the abbé is concerned, in short, his aim is to transform 'the all too intemporal beauties of the fairy-tale' into 'the outrageous ugliness of the contemporary village'.[50]

The sources of Table 10 confront *JLP* with three versions in Occitan of AT 332: these were collected respectively in the 1880s, 1890s and 1920s, from much older traditions. Two of these versions come from Aude, a department which, in Narbonnais and in Corbières, constituted until the Third Republic a good oral conservatory of the Occitan eighteenth century. These are the versions *Jean-de-trop* (*JDT*) and Gibert and Maugard (GM); the region of Aude, especially with *JDT*, is valuable for the comparisons it provides with *JLP*. The third version (also in the Occitan language) is from Ariège. It is derived from the *Almanach de l'Ariège* of 1895 (AA).

In the analysis of Table 10 that now follows, and in the interests of a wider comparison, I shall also use, once the first links have been established on Occitan soil, the various versions from Catalonia, southern, central and western France, and Quebec within which the motif of 'the spirit in the bottle' is inserted into AT 332 or even, occasionally, occurs independently. It is useless to repeat how valuable to this enterprise are the versions surviving from isolation in Quebec, despite their distance: they are direct evidence of the old state of the tale in France, in its emergence in the eighteenth century in versions that were contemporary with or prior to *JLP*.

The first line of the table concerns the period of the episode in the annual cycle of viticulture: this is specified in one of the versions of the tale from Aude (GM) and in *JLP*. This period – August – precedes the wine harvest (GM); or, in the same way, it is the period immediately before the grape harvest, 'supervised' by the new vineyard-keeper, JLP [65]. Grapes, verjuice, wine, then barrel or gourd of wine or brandy play an important role in this episode.

In the first sequence (line A of the table) an action is performed, with the participation of the hero, on the body of Death: in AT 332 (*JDT* and other southern and northern French versions, etc.), the hero, by means of a provocative bet, urges Death to reduce her body or, at least, to make it thinner, so that she may enter a narrow orifice in the wine receptacle (gourd, bottle, barrel), in which the hero hopes to keep her prisoner. We are now in the supernatural register of the fairy-tale: everything is possible, including the spectacular reduction of an adult body. At the end of such a process, this body must be capable of being substituted for the usual contents, which will later be kept in the bottle or barrel, which happens to be empty at the time of year in question.[51] This bottle or barrel will be capable, therefore, of containing the trapped body of Death without difficulty, instead of being filled, as it would normally be after the wine harvest. The reduction of the body is sometimes carried to extraordinary lengths: Death makes herself 'as tiny as a cricket', says the *JDT* from Narbonne. He becomes 'as small as a fly' in the Quebec versions.[52]

But Fabre is working in a hyper-realistic mode. He cannot, therefore, allow one of his characters such a spectacular reduction in size. He, too, will work on the grandmother's body, but he will remain within the realm of possibility. In *JLP*, therefore, grandmother Death will become the providential victim of paralysis due to old age (*she was old, she could no longer walk* [second version]). What a contrast with the alacrity of the same person twenty years earlier descending the staircase of her house in Solorgues four steps at a time! Second, grandmother Death will eat her share of the fruit surreptitiously obtained by the hero as vineyard-keeper, and swell up accordingly. She, too, therefore, will become a substitute for the contents of a wine bottle. Not, as was the case of Death in AT 332, because her body had been reduced to allow herself to enter a gourd. The grandmother had so stuffed herself with grapes that she had become like a sackful of fruit at harvest time, when the contents are about to be thrown into the vat. Without over-emphasizing this 'viticultural' parallel, Fabre turns at last in a third movement of this first sequence (which corresponds to line A in Table 10) to the theme of the paralysis of the grandmother's body, already mentioned in the first movement. This paralysis is a result, after the excessive consumption of grapes, of the nefarious actions of the hero on this body; she is no longer merely senile, as in the first movement; she finally takes on the rigidity of a corpse. With her ungovernable taste for grapes, the old woman has devoured so much of her favourite fruit, stolen by her grandson, that she 'bursts' [*crève*], that is, dies. Line A as a whole (right-hand column) covers three movements: the old age and paralysis of the grandmother's body; her swelling up with grapes; her death.

We now come to the second sequence, or line B, of Table 10.

This is the theme of the hole, or orifice of the receptacle, in which Death will be imprisoned. As the version from Aude (GM) puts it: ' "You think you can slip in everywhere," said Death's godson to his godmother, "then get into the hole [*trauc*] of the vent of the barrel and see if there's any wine left . . ." No sooner said than done.' When Death re-emerges from this barrel, she travels along the same path: 'September came and with it the wine harvest. The father of the hero went to look at the barrels. He pulled out the pegs and put his nose into the hole [*trauc*] to see if they smelled stale. Heavens above! As he pulled the peg out of one barrel, a gust of wind came out so strong that the poor man nearly fell over. It was Death [free at last] and she went back to her work.' Sometimes the hole is referred to, as it were, by ricochet: 'I shall follow you everywhere even if I have to pass through the hole [*trauc*] of a needle,' says Death to his physician godson (AA, p. 56). Thereupon, the physician challenges Death to enter the neck of a wine gourd on the table. The challenge is accepted: Death enters the gourd. In *Punch and Ratapon* (Perbosc and Cézarac, 1954, p. 103), Punch bets that he can get through the hole of a cat-door. The devil Ratapon, not to be outdone, claims that he could get through the eye of a needle; in the end, Punch successfully urges him to climb into a bottle. In Nivernais (Millien and Delarue, version A), Death appears to his physician godson, who has previously blocked all the holes in the house except the keyhole: 'How did you get in?' he asks – 'Through the key*hole*,' he replies – 'Since you are so clever, get into this bottle.' No sooner said than done . . . Sébillot's Breton tales always refer specifically to the 'hole' when Death gets into the bottle, but they too use a slight displacement of the word, if not of the thing. The physician–hero blocks the 'hole' that he digs in the garden.[53] The Quebec tales are doubly important to us by virtue of their literal transcription and their congenital archaism; nor are they lacking in information on these points: ' "So make yourself really tiny," says the physician godson to his godfather, "so that you can get through a nail hole, or a key*hole*." There was an empty bottle standing there. He said: "Then make yourself small enough to get through a nail hole." So Death made himself very small, then the physician grabbed him and put him in his bottle.'[54] As in western France (Sébillot), so in Quebec, the hole in the ground is the alternative to the keyhole or nail hole, which itself foreshadows the neck of the bottle. In the Quebec tale recorded in 1966, Death, reduced to the size of a fly, is soon imprisoned in the bottle. Then the physician, Death's *compère* from AT 332, put the cork back in the bottle, 'then he went to a mountain far from there, where no one had ever been and there he dug a *hole*, then he buried the bottle . . .' The Catalan versions of AT 332, almost twins of the Languedocian versions, are, as always, of crucial importance: 'I have heard tell,' declares Death's physician in one of these versions, 'that you can make yourself so small that you can get through tiny holes . . . Could you get inside this wine gourd?' Death answers, of course, that she can and is imprisoned in the bottle (J. Amades, 1950, number 202, p. 492).[55] In these texts the hole for Death has a certain autonomy in relation to the neck of the bottle.

Coming to the second sequence (line B) of our table, Fabre's narrative also confronts the problem of the 'hole' through which the reduced body of Death must pass (here the body of grandmother Death). In any case, the grandmother's body having been 'transformed' by old age and by the hero to the point that it is little more than a corpse, there will be no question here of a bottle, gourd or barrel, but quite simply of a burial rite. 'The burial of my grandmother cost me nothing,' Jean-l'ont-pris tells us. 'With a pick and shovel I made a *hole* for her to pass into paradise, then I went and had lunch' [second version]. The first version provides a few additional details: 'My grandmother was a Huguenot; her burial cost me only a few minutes' work with pick and shovel in a ditch . . . I laid her out in the Donkeys' Paradise, and went home for lunch' [66].

Let us look more closely at this incident: it refers to a hole in a ditch, and therefore a doubly deep orifice, a 'hole squared'. This hole is also a *passage*. On this point, Fabre has taken up the Occitan verb *passar*: 'a hole to pass [*per passa*] into paradise'. This verb *passar* and this preposition *per* are also to be found in the version from Ariège of 1895, in which Death flatters himself that he can *passer par un trou d'aiguille* ['pass through the eye of a needle'].[56] They are also to be found in the Catalan versions in which Death can make herself small enough *per passa pels forats* ['to get through holes']. Lastly, it is to be found in the Gascon version of *The Devil in the Bottle* or *The Spirit in the Bottle*: Punch and the devil Ratapon contemplate in turn passing 'through the cat-door', passing 'through the eye of a needle', passing 'through the neck of a bottle' (Perbosc and Cézavac, 1954, p. 103).

However, those who have transmitted to us the versions from Aude that we call *Jean-de-trop* and Gibert and Maugard have followed on this point an oral tradition that differs slightly from the earlier one: they both use, not the verb *passer* or *passar*, but the Occitan verb *dintrar* ['to enter'] (the gourd or barrel). The *Almanach de l'Ariège* uses first *passar* than *dintrar*. Generally speaking, these various verbs (meaning 'to pass through' or 'to enter' an orifice) refer to the notion that Death is always capable of 'slipping' through any slit, either to kill someone or, as here, to get trapped by someone cleverer than her (by J D T, J L P . . .). The first idea (to kill someone) is particularly well expressed in Sébillot's Breton version (1900, p. 251) and in the Andalusian version of A T 332, *Juan Holgado* (F. Caballero, 1861, p. 88), in which Death 'slips in through a slit in a wall' [*se colo por una rendija*] in order to kill her physician protégé.

Line C of Table 10 (third sequence) presents few problems. In the left-hand column (canonical version of A T 332), the body of Death, still alive, prisoner in the 'wine receptacle', is simply *put away*: the barrel that encloses Death remains in its place in the cellar (G M); or the gourd is placed on the chimney (A A); or it is placed 'in a corner where no one will ever find it' (Amades's Catalan version, 1950, number 202). In the Nivernais versions, a little more to the north than ours, the bottle containing Death is hidden on the surface of the ground, in a pile of sand, for example.[57] In Quebec (item 51 of the Maranda file, 1966), this pile of sand becomes a mountain, but the principle remains identical, since the mountain is itself raised in relation to the flat country around it. Another way of leaving the bottle 'on the surface' is to hide it in a bush: this solution is found in Nivernais (version D) and in one of Grimm's tales (tale 99), in which the receptacle lies, a little lower, among the roots of an oak-tree. Lastly, it is also tempting to let the receptacle float on water; a fisherman or river-dweller might easily find it. This was the solution of *The Thousand and One Nights*; it is also a solution found in Ireland, Lithuania and Quebec. We should note that in the Gascon version of *The Devil in the Bottle*, Ratapon, the devil imprisoned in his receptacle, also embarks on an aquatic adventure, but in this case it is holy water, enough to burn the skin of that burlesque, infernal creature.[58] While we are about it, mention should perhaps be made of a remarkable Flemish solution: the bottle containing Death is placed not 'on the surface of the ground', but actually above it, left hanging from the ceiling of a hut and thus hidden among the cobwebs, until the daughters of the house accidentally knock it off with a broom; it then falls and breaks. Death escapes and returns to his work of mowing down the living, etc.[59]

However, it should not be thought that the bottle containing the supernatural entity must necessarily be placed on the surface of the ground or above it. There are other, different solutions: in the fine Austro-baroque version of AT 332 (astonishingly close to our Languedocian *Jean-de-trop*), the bottle, once the hero has trapped the supernatural being in it, is thrown (again by the hero) into the depths of a precipice, never to be seen again (Vernaleken, 1864, end of the tale).

In both Flemish versions,[60] matters are expedited even more swiftly; the father of the hero—physician Death's godson, in order to protect his son from Death's threats, tricks him into allowing himself to be thrown into a well, which is then carefully blocked up with small rocks, earth and a stone lid. (Death re-emerges and takes up his killing again when newcomers, ninety-nine years later, have the unfortunate idea of unblocking the well, with a view to using it.) To sum up, then, there exist in the French and more generally 'Latin' world (Nivernais, Quebec), on the borders of this world (Austria, Flanders) and even in the depths of Germany (Grimm), a fairly large number of versions that use *Godfather Death* combined with *The Spirit in the*

Bottle, or, occasionally, *The Spirit in the Bottle* alone, in which Death or the supernatural entity, with or without the wine receptacle to contain him or her, is buried deep down or on the surface, temporarily or permanently, at a stage in the tale that corresponds to line C (third sequence) of the table. Fabre was able to reinvent this theme, in order to furnish the third *ad hoc* sequence of this episode in his own tale. But the very fact that this theme of burial is encountered in both Quebec versions of AT 332 (chronologically so close to our eighteenth-century fairy-tales) and in both versions from Nivernais (geographically so close to our Languedocian version of the *JDT* type) leads one to think that Fabre was quite capable of deriving this theme from one or another of the many versions of AT 332 then current in Languedoc. The hero, then, goes to bury grandmother Death in the hole that he himself has dug in a ditch [*dins un valat*]; there he lays out the corpse. One will remember that it was also in a ditch [*dins un valat*] that Monsieur Sestier, knocked senseless, had been left as dead by the two vineyard-keepers, full members of the forces of death [59]. It is just retribution, therefore: J L P has simply to pay back grandmother Death, who belongs to the same party as the vineyard-keepers, in her own kind. It is pointless to leave the corpse of grandmother Death on the surface (unlike the Death imprisoned in a bottle, as in 'AT 332 combined with AT 331'), since her corpse does not have to be used again in the narrative. We should not forget that Fabre is working in a hyper-realistic mode, and not in that of a self-evident fairy-tale. The diabolical-macabre Quincarlot will, therefore, be given the task, by way of replacement, of embodying the forces of death, just as his old accomplice,[61] the grandmother, now dead and buried,[62] had once done.

Let us examine line D, or the fourth sequence. In the left-hand column, which concerns *Jean-de-trop* and the other southern (and non-southern) versions of AT 332 combined with AT 331, the moment of the locking needs no comment. If Death is kept alive in a bottle or in a gourd, etc., or at the bottom of a well, the important thing is to prevent him or her from coming out. *Jean-de-trop immediately shut her up with a tight cork.* Absolutely all the versions of AT 332/*Godfather Death* that are combined with AT 331/*The Spirit in the Bottle* refer explicitly to this act of quickly sealing the receptacle, once Death is trapped in it: we are even told that the gourd is 'locked' with a cork (*JDT* and AA, in Occitania; Amades, in Catalonia; etc.); or of locking the barrel with the peg (GM, in Corbières); or of the well locked by blocking it with large stones (Flanders, version mentioned above; etc.). Of course, the same goes for the 'isolated' versions of *The Spirit in the Bottle*, those unconnected with *Godfather Death* (*The Thousand and One Nights*, in the version mentioned; Grimm, tale 99; devil Ratapon, 'locked' in this way in the Gascon version of AT 331 of Perbosc; etc.).

As far as Fabre is concerned (right-hand column of Table 10, line D), his task as an author of fiction is different; he adopts a realistic, rather than a fantastic point of view. In his narrative grandmother Death, once buried, has no real chance of emerging from her grave, since she has become quite simply a corpse. In fact, the forces of death reappear later in the tale, but in the guise of a different charac-ter: Cancrelas/Quincarlot. The operations of locking, in Fabre, are reduced therefore to a strict minimum; this minimum is so obvious that it is not even mentioned in the narrative. The hero (JLP) fills in with earth the ditch in which he has just buried his grandmother; then he goes back to the house for lunch. In fact, the operation of 'locking' remains, so to speak, available for a later phase in the nar-rative. Fabre, as we shall see, uses it in line G of Table 10, in the right-hand column. This is the single, slight twist that he allowed himself in relation to the canonical development of the episode that he had derived from oral tradition, as it is deployed in nine sequences, in the left-hand column of Table 10.

Line E, or the fifth sequence: in the left-hand column, a dialogue in many versions in which *Godfather Death* (AT 332) is combined with *The Spirit in the Bottle* (AT 331). In Sébillot's Breton version Death is shut up in a bread-bin, then in a bottle, and each time Death talks with his *compère* physician–jailer. Pleas, mockery, threats and promises alternate and fuse throughout (Sébillot, *Archivio . . .*, vol. V, 1886, pp. 428–9). This type of dialogue also occurs in the Occitan versions. They sometimes indicate it in only an embryonic way, as in the Gibert and Maugard version (in Occitan) from Corbières: 'Death begged her godson to let her out [of the barrel]. But he went away . . .' In *Jean-de-trop* (p. 193), a direct homologue of our *JLP*, the dialogue is fully developed: 'Jean!' cried Death, 'let me out.' – 'No, godmother,' Jean-de-trop replied, 'I love you dearly, for you have made me happy: but I also dearly love my wife; I will not let you out [of the gourd] till you have given my wife as much life as you have given to me.'

In a version from Quebec, the element of dialogue features only in the form of Death's silent protests. Reduced in volume, furious, he continues under the hero's mocking eye to walk up and down, with his scythe over his shoulder, inside the bottle–prison: *in that curious old bottle there is a little figure walking up and down with a scythe over his shoulder.*[63]

In the 'independent' versions of *The Spirit in the Bottle* (AT 331), unconnected with *Godfather Death*, whether the tale is from *The Thousand and One Nights*, Grimm's tale 99 or Perbosc's version (in Gascony) of *Punch and Ratapon*, the supernatural entity, imprisoned in the receptacle, begs, threatens and promises, in turn, while the hero–jailer jeers at him; or, alternatively, he weakens in the face of substantial promises granted, willingly or unwillingly, by the prisoner.

As far as we are concerned, it is obviously the dialogue contained in *Jean-de-trop* that is important, since this *Jean-de-trop* of 1885 can derive only from an eighteenth-century '*Jean-de-trop*' since lost (for want of a better name, I am giving this tale the code name in inverted commas); the '*Jean-de-trop*' of 1750 is also an ancestor of our *JLP* of 1756 and 1765.

In what, then, does the dialogue already mentioned between Death imprisoned in a gourd and Jean-de-trop, in the version of the tale that we possess (*JDT*, 1885), actually consist? I can see several elements in it: to begin with, logically enough, Death's demand to be set free. And then:

(1) a nominal address, made by the hero to godmother Death: he calls her by her title, in the form of the interjection *Godmother!* (Mairino!);

(2) an expression of gratitude for the past: 'You *have* made me happy';

(3) a negative judgement passed on godmother Death, at least in the relative, that amounts to: *I love you dearly, but I prefer my wife, and I am ready to keep you a prisoner as long as necessary*;

(4) lastly, a corollary of point (3), the hero asks godmother Death for a favour that will considerably extend the duration of his marriage: trapped as she is, the prisoner can hardly refuse such a request, and so she agrees.

One has only to consider paragraphs 66 to 69 of both Occitan versions of *JLP* (first and second) to find exactly the themes that I have just listed in *JDT*. Certainly, the hero does not converse with his grandmother – she is dead – and from the realistic, even hyper-realistic, point of view chosen by Fabre, a corpse has nothing to say: there is no way in which the dead woman can ask to be 'set free'. It is, then, a monologue, but certainly one addressed to the grandmother, for whom the hero, we should remember, has obligingly dug *a hole to pass*, not into a bottle, but *into paradise*. So it is to the grandmother's soul, which he has dispatched into the Beyond (either a true paradise or a 'Donkeys' Paradise', on earth, reserved for Huguenots), that the hero addresses his words.

(1) First he gives her a *title* and calls her (this is the first time that he has done so in his narrative) by the familiar interjection *Granetta*! ['Grandma']. Similarly, in the homologous sequence of the episode, Jean-de-trop 'interjected' a word to his godmother using the familiar title *Mairino* 'godmother'. We should remember that in Languedocian the word *mairino* also means 'grandmother'.[64] The loop is looped, therefore, from one tale to the other.

(2) J L P is later to express a certain affectionate gratitude towards his dead grandmother; this gratitude, of course, is situated in the semi-burlesque context that often characterizes the narrative: 'I mourned her, because she had left me something . . .' (The verb *plaindre* ['to mourn'] here means to utter a semi-ritual, semi-sincere lament in honour of a dead person, when one wishes to honour the dearly departed by evidence of retrospective affection.)

(3) J L P then makes, in turn, negative judgements on the old woman: *I did not mourn her . . . more than was reasonable . . . she was old, she could no longer walk, she no longer brought anything in . . . the damned glutton . . . to eat so much on the day of her burial . . .* [66, 67, first and second versions].

(4) He does not ask her for anything – that would be contrary to the realistic code, since she is dead – but as soon as he begins to discover the benefits, in other words, the treasure, which she has left

him, which will finance a possible marriage with Babeau, he immediately embarks on a dialogue that is at once imaginary and unquestionable, full of gratitude; it is still, of course, burlesque: *My dear little grandmother, what a good thing you did to die . . . Good! My dear grandmother! Requiem, my little grandmother, Requiem aeternum, may the good God protect you up there . . .* We see that in *JLP*, the hero's monologue culminates in redoubled gratitude; whereas in *JDT* and elsewhere the hero's dialogue with Death ends in a demand. For this reason, the dialogue between the hero and Death, in *JDT*, is limited to line E of Table 10 (left-hand column); by contrast, in *JLP*, this dialogue also begins in line E (right-hand column), but then spreads over lines F, G and H in such a way as to coincide, in the end, with the discovery of the treasure left by the dead grandmother.

To sum up, the hero's address to imprisoned Death (*JDT*) or to the buried grandmother Death (*JLP*) develops in the same way in both cases:

(1) invocation to this individual;

(2) feelings of gratitude towards her;

(3) negative judgements concerning her;

(4) requests for favours that will be immediately obtained (*JDT*), or thanks for favours that have already been obtained (*JLP*).

We now come to line F, or the sixth sequence of the episode (Table 10). The religious character of the situation is emphasized in a *serious* way (in *JDT*, left-hand column) or in a *burlesque* way (in *JLP*, right-hand column). Both narratives, *JDT* and *JLP*, are homologous through their derivation from a common source: it is important, therefore, to compare these two 'religious' sequences, in the left-hand and right-hand columns, on the same line (F). Taking the text of *JDT* (p. 193) first, we have: 'For eight days, death remained imprisoned in her little gourd; for eight days on earth, no one died. The devil was astonished to see no damned soul arrive. Our Lord (= Jesus or God) laughed when he saw all this. He knew that he would lose nothing by waiting. He loved Jean-de-trop dearly; he was a good, devout man [in Occitan, *que ero un ome brave e devoucieux*].' This 'religious' character of Jean-de-trop, the hero who has just neutralized Death, throws light, for the moment, on the negative, detestable aspects of the character of Death. In effect, the tale *JDT* accuses

Death of constantly producing damned souls, only to hand them over to the devil. To imprison Death is therefore to put the devil out of work. A good thing, too. God is delighted. He bursts out laughing. And JDT is regarded as a devout man. We have already met with the positive aspects of Death, who also produces, it should not be forgotten, saved souls for paradise. But we are not dealing with these for the moment: the narrator of *JDT*, in fact, suggests on this occasion that God, who has nothing to lose by waiting, will take charge of the saved souls, but a little later.

Jean-Baptiste Fabre, living when he did, must have been struck by the original paragraph of the (oral) tale, a tale that was an ancestor of the novella that he was writing; this same paragraph of 'religious judgement' was to re-emerge in the text of *JDT* of 1885, which I quoted a little earlier. In fact, the abbé has inserted, in the homologous point (line F of Table 10, right-hand column) of his narrative, a short text that is quite comparable to that of *JDT*. Of course, Fabre was operating, as so often in *JLP*, in a burlesque mode: the young man has just buried his dead grandmother (Table 10, lines C and D, right-hand column); and he has just begun a monologue addressed to her (line E, right-hand column).

But then he finds that there is nothing to eat in the old woman's house and declares: 'the damned glutton! But no, I don't think so, she was too devout [*era trop dévôta*] to eat so much on the day of her burial. On this last thought, which is perhaps the most Christian I've had in my life [*sus aquélla darniêira pénsada qu'és bélêou la pus chrétiénna*], I began my search again . . .' [67].

The two texts, deriving respectively from *JDT*, as a recent expression of an earlier version, and from *JLP*, show, once again, remarkable similarities. These become fully significant when one remembers that they concern the *same* sequence (line F) of the *same* episode (Table 10).

The use of the verb 'to be' in the third person of the imperfect indicative is to be found in both cases ('was' = *ero* or *era*, according to the Occitan pronunciation of the same word, which varied according to the regional origin of the authors). Above all, four adjectives, two of which are identical and two homologous, occur in crossed order (see Table 11). They are 'devout' in conjunction with 'good' (*JDT*), and 'devout' in conjunction with 'Christian' (*JLP*).

Because *JLP* operates according to a burlesque mode, unlike *JDT*, which is intended to be 'serious', even edifying, a devaluation takes place in *JLP* through the feminization of the adjectives ('dévôt*a*', 'chrétiénn*a*', instead of 'homme dévo*t* et brave'). Above all, the comic character of *JLP* implies a shift of the adjectives involved. It is no longer the excellent hero (JDT) who is sincerely presented as *dévot et brave*. It is JLP's grandmother who is derisively called *dévôta*, whereas this old Huguenot woman is, in fact, situated in a pejorative way (for Fabre) in the climate of religious antagonism that characterized the Vaunage in the 1750s. This elderly Protestant intervenes in an anti-Calvinist narrative written by a Catholic priest. The term *dévôta*, applied to her, can only, therefore, be grotesque: 'the damned glutton . . . she was too *devout* to eat so much on the day of her burial' [67].

Table 11	
JDT	*JLP*
Serious register (masculine adjectives)	Burlesque register (feminine adjectives)
Jean-de-trop was [*ero*] a good man	The grandmother was [*era*] too devout [*dévôta*]
and was a devout [[*dévot*]] man	this last thought, which is perhaps the most Christian I've had in my life

As for the words *this last thought, which is perhaps the most Christian I've had in my life*, the religious turn of phrase corresponds to a ritual formula in the Occitan and Catalan versions of AT 332, in which the hero describes himself as a good, devout Christian at the strategic point when he tricks Death.[65] This turn of phrase is also a way of declaring that JLP, in his usual outlook, is not particularly Christian; if indeed he was at the moment when this comic thought occurred to him.

Actually, there is nothing very Christian about our hero even if, from a strictly 'denominational' point of view, he belongs in principle among those Catholics who practise on only the great occasions of life: we have seen that he was not at vespers; however, he does marry in church, before a priest, his short-lived wife Judith Garouille, who is of Huguenot origin, if not a practising Protestant.

In any case, the undeniably *burlesque*[66] tendency of Fabre's work is not entirely original. It transmits, in its own comic way, which was perhaps enhanced by Fabre, an oral text that came to him from the story-tellers and that then reached us in the nineteenth century, still in oral form, in a version (*JDT*) which, on the contrary, is of a serious, even edifying kind.

Line G, or the seventh sequence, of Table 10: on the left (*JDT*), nothing of great importance takes place. Death is still locked up in the gourd; she is bored because she can no longer kill . . . 'After eight days, she was unhappy to see that her work was behind . . .' On the right, however, the same operation of locking, which could not be carried out in *JLP* at its canonical point (line D, right-hand column of Table 10), will now take place (line G, right-hand column). Indeed, the hero suspects that the chest that he has just discovered in the house of his dead and already buried grandmother might contain treasure . . . Then, 'before seeing what else there was in the blessed chest, *I double-locked my door*. I came back and pulled out two pieces of cambric . . .' [68].

Fabre's 'double-locking' is reminiscent of the double or triple precautions that are always taken in this situation by the hero of *Godfather Death* combined with *The Spirit in the Bottle*, or by the hero of *The Spirit in the Bottle* alone. When the various heroes of these tales have trapped the supernatural being in a receptacle, they, too, 'double-lock' it: 'Confine Death in the gourd with a tight cork' (*JDT*); 'shut the tap of the barrel in which Death is trapped and put back the peg in the vent' (GM, Corbières); 'prepare a cork which will stick in the neck and block the hole of the bottle properly' (Perbosc, *Punch and Ratapon*); 'the well-corked gourd' (Amades, tale 202, Catalonia); and, farther north, lock the well that contains Death with stones, earth and a stone lid (Flemish versions). But, of course, in *JLP* the operation of locking is shifted downwards, from line D, left-hand column (*JDT*) to line G, right-hand column (*JLP*) of Table 10. In *JDT* and in various southern (and other) versions of *Godfather* Death combined with *The Spirit in the Bottle*, it is a matter of protecting himself (line D, left-hand column) by this 'enclosure' against a possible *emergence* of Death; this character, in effect, had only just, in the previous line (C, left-hand column), been confined, still alive and still dangerous, in the receptacle. On the other hand, according to the realistic code of *JLP*, these precautions are not at all necessary in the corresponding line (D, right-hand column) of *JLP*: the recently buried grandmother Death was dead and would not come back to life. However, they are necessary lower down in line G (*JLP*), when the hero (who a little later will begin in line H the exploration of his treasure) has to lock his house from the inside; he has to lock his door against an external danger (the arrival of the police, neighbours, thieves . . .). Even in this case, nevertheless, the realistic code does not exhaust the problem: the treasure transports us quite clearly, as we shall see, into the world of the fairy-tale. In that world, grandmother Death might well, like Death jumping out of her gourd, leave her grave and come to disturb the hero by joining him *behind the door*. Jean-l'ont-pris, therefore, must lock his door against the outside (of his house), just as Jean-de-trop has to place a big cork against the inside (of his gourd). It should be remembered that a number of French and other versions of AT 332, several of them Occitan and Catalan, one Nivernais, one Venetian and one German, confirm that Death would be dangerous if *behind the door* (in the house), whereas Death is beneficent *in front of the door*, in other words, outside the house (see on this matter Chapter IX).

Lines H and I (right-hand column) of Table 10 concern respectively the giving of a treasure to the hero, by grandmother Death, which should confer greater advantages, marital and otherwise, on JLP (line H); and the return to circulation of a possibly lethal character, in one of the last sections of the novella (line I). These two 'lines' merge in the last section of Fabre's narrative; I shall therefore examine them together.

The treasure is the normal counterpart of the neutralization of grandmother Death (*JLP*) or of Death (A T 332). Under her pile of matches (the unlit lights or candles of life that she controlled), grandmother Death, now silenced and put away, has left a fortune, which the hero will avail himself of. In the episode 'Death in the bottle' of the Languedocian versions of A T 332, this 'treasure' is symbolic: two hundred years of extra life for the hero (A A) or the granting of the same length of life to the hero's wife (*JDT*); in the second case, it is a sort of interminable, two hundred-year cure of the hero's wife, who is also 'the rich man's daughter'. In the Narbonnais version of Gibert and Maugard, the confinement of Death in the wine barrel involves for the conquering hero, as an advantage granted by Death as part of the bargain, the cure of the hero's mother, who had previously been ill. In either case, then, the physician Death's godson gets, for himself, for his wife or for his mother, some kind of survival or cure. The symbolic treasure always amounts in this story to the restoration or the preservation of health, that of the doctor himself or that of a close relation. This is normal, since the hero has already been explicitly made a physician by Death. It should be added, as far as *JDT* is concerned, that this 'episode' ensures the continuation (for two hundred years!) of an already concluded marriage. In the isolated Occitan version (in other words, unconnected to A T 332) of *The Spirit in the Bottle*, Punch forces the devil Ratapon to hand over a treasure and to give him back a wife.

Generally speaking, the Occitan versions of the episode, which are more or less recent (collected in the nineteenth or early twentieth centuries) and which derive, more or less closely, from those that Fabre knew directly in the eighteenth century, end with the granting of three possible advantages to the hero:

(1) a true, material *treasure* (gold, money, etc.);

(2) a *wife* for the hero, if possible, a rich man's daughter;

(3) *health*, particularly for this wife.

It will be noted that *JLP*, in turn, conformed strictly to this triple requirement; the neutralization of grandmother Death brings three results.

(1) The hero receives treasure.

(2) Thanks to this treasure, he is able to negotiate an advantageous connection, and probably marry the powerful man's daughter. This treasure, referred to implicitly or explicitly, lies at the centre of all the negotiations carried out by J L P on this matter with the powerful man, and also with his daughter; in any case, the hero will physically possess the girl.

(3) Instead of restoring the health of the powerful man's daughter, as in *JDT*, a folklorico-oral homologue of *JLP*, Fabre's novella uses in a remarkably oblique way a motif that was, as far as I know, of the novelist's own invention, *no* equivalent of which is to be found in the many versions of AT 332 that are available: this motif may be described as 'undermining the health of the rival of the powerful man's daughter'! Instead of curing the heroine (*Babeau*, or Babelette [78]), her rival (Barbe-Garouille, also referred to as *Barbe* or Barbette or Garouillette [80]) is to be killed off by disease. It is a question not of 'curing Babette', but of 'killing Barbette'. This is the third blessing (after the treasure and after the possession of the powerful man's daughter) that will fall upon the hero, once he has neutralized grandmother Death. With *JLP* we remain, therefore, within the triple register of the relevant episode of AT 332 combined with AT 331 (*Godfather Death* combined with *The Spirit in the Bottle*). There is:

(1) granting of a treasure to the hero;

(2) granting of the powerful man's daughter to the hero;

(3) granting of health to the powerful man's daughter; or, by an inversion-twist that amounts to the same thing, granting of a fatal disease to the rival of the powerful man's daughter. This last process may be represented as in Table 12.

The 'advantages' that the tricked Death of AT 332 is forced to grant to the hero, the treasure that 'the spirit in the bottle' is forced to give up, belong, by definition, to the magical or miraculous procedures of the fairy-tale. How does this affect the treasure left by the dead grandmother in *JLP*? In principle, this treasure is simply the valuables that she fraudulently put aside from her son-in-law's thefts. However, the atmosphere of miracle, of magic, is very marked in this episode of Fabre's narrative. The treasure-chest at the beginning of the eighth sequence (line H, right-hand column of Table 10) is presented as a

Table 12		
NEGATION OF THE NEGATION		
The original model (AT 332), known in a great many versions and particularly in *JDT*	poses an affirmation: * save the health (= affirm the being)	of the powerful man's daughter.
The novel (*JLP*) that is based on it	replaces this affirmation by a double negation, which amounts to the same thing: kill the rival (= negate the negation)	of the powerful man's daughter.

To negate the negation is to affirm the being (and health) of the powerful man's daughter.

* The cure of the powerful man's daughter is a common theme in Occitan versions of AT 332: in *JDT*; in P. Bédat de Monlaur, *Le Meunier gascon* (1936) and *Les Contes du lézard* . . . (1943); in C. Joisten, *Contes populaires de l' Ariège* (1965), p. 63; in A. Ferrand, *Revue des traditions populaires* (1895), p. 594; in Brittany (Cadic, Luzel, etc.); and practically throughout Christian Europe and America, where versions of *Godfather Death* were collected. This theme of the cure of the powerful man's daughter often passed into the foreground; but originally it seems to have been secondary in relation to the more 'primitive' theme of the cure of the powerful man himself, which is to be found in the German versions prior to 1700; and, in France, in T. S. Gueullette, *Les Mille et Un Quarts d'heure* (1712) and in *JLP* itself: the 'cure' of Sestier is chronologically prior to the action concerning Babeau and Garouille. On the prognosis of death concerning the patient, as a source of wealth and happiness for the hero–physician/ Death's godson, see the Gascon version from the Landes of AT 332 collected by F. Arnaudin, *Contes populaires de la Grande-Lande* (1977), p. 558; and, above all, F. Caballero, *Cuentos populares andaluces coleccionados* . . . (1861), pp. 83–8; the Mexican versions of *Juan Holgado* collected by H. T. Wheeler, *Tales from Jalisco, Mexico* (1943); and, lastly, J. W. Wolf, *Deutsche Hausmärchen* (1851) – very important.

Noah's Ark [67]; it contains, therefore, in principle, all the wealth of creation (with, in addition, an implicit reference to the fact that the grandmother, like old Noah himself, was fond of the juice of the vine, whether fermented or not). Once the lid has been lifted, the wondering hero begins a prayer (*Rapiamus*) that belongs explicitly to 'the preface for Christmas'. After Noah, we have Noël; after the Old Testament, the New: Christmas [*Noël*] is the feast of treasure, which the Magi brought to the Infant Jesus. Later, continuing his search, the hero identifies himself with Christ on the Mount of Olives; he invokes and thanks the Holy Virgin, then heaven; lastly, St Anthony, himself the patron of lost articles and of prosperity of all kinds. To conclude, the fairy-tales themselves are evoked in the text of this sequence: indeed, Jean-l'ont-pris compares the benefits that are being showered upon him to those that surround the *Drapet* (a small Languedocian dragon, the dragon of fairy-tale, in a folkloric and southern version of a fairy-tale that has since been lost); he also compares these benefits to those that come to Cinderella at the end of her adventures. Never have we witnessed in Fabre's novella such a procession of supernatural references. This is a way of saying that, in fact, the treasure (and the novella as a whole) is not 'natural'.

Supernatural[67] *references to the treasure*
left by the dead grandmother

(1) Noah (Old Testament)
(2) Christmas [*Noël*] and the Infant Jesus (New Testament: God the Son)
(3) Christ in his Passion (New Testament: God the Son)
(4) the Virgin (marian cult)
(5) heaven and God (God the Father)
(6) St Anthony (cult of the saints)
(7) the *Drapet* (folklore)
(8) Cinderella (fairy-tale)

Once again one notices the skilful progression, full of subtle inter-weavings, that Fabre has worked out: from the Bible (Old and New Testaments) to the fairy-tale, invoking God the Father and God the Son, and those specifically Catholic forms of religious devotion, the cults of the Virgin and saints. What a range of miraculous references for treasure!

The reference to the fairy-tale (*Cinderella*) is crucial, since *JLP* derives from another fairy-tale (*Godfather Death*). By evoking

Cinderella, which he knew in the versions of Perrault and of Mme d'Aulnoy and through the vast oral tradition of the Midi, where this tale type was still current,[68] the abbé amused himself, at one and the same time, by providing a change and by putting us on the right track. I am not in the least claiming, quite the reverse, that as a whole the novella *Jean-l'ont-pris* derives from Perrault's *Cendrillon* or, more precisely, from Mme d'Aulnoy's *Finette-Cendron*. In fact, it can be proved in innumerable ways that *Jean-l'ont-pris* belongs to the cycle of *Death's Godson* (AT 332). But the two narratives, Mme d'Aulnoy's *Finette-Cendron*,[69] on the one hand, and *Jean-l'ont-pris* derived from *Death's Godson*, on the other, have in common certain linear developments: a young person (the cunning Finette-Cendron in the first case, JLP in the second) is unhappily afflicted by a stepmother, who, moreover, is ruined; fortunately, this young individual receives from the supernatural godmother (the fairy godmother in the first case, godmother Death or grandmother Death in the second) a chest full of textiles and jewels. This chest enables the young person to attract a prestigious individual of the opposite sex: the king's son in the case of Finette; the daughter of the powerful man (Babeau, daughter of the rich farmer) in the case of JLP.[70] Let us examine this comparison point by point, or, if I may call it that, this fragment of genetic thread, common to the two tales:

The child of a stepmother

(1) *Finette-Cendron (F-C)*: A royal couple is ruined. The mother/ cruel stepmother (the queen) gets rid of her daughter Finette by chasing her away.

(2) *Jean-l'ont-pris:* A recently enriched couple is ruined. The mother/cruel stepmother (Margot) gets rid of her son Jean-l'ont-pris by leaving him.

The supernatural godmother

(1) *F-C:* Fortunately, Finette has a supernatural godmother, the fairy Merluche, who befriends her.

(2) *JLP:* Fortunately, JLP has a grandmother, whom all our research identifies functionally as a supernatural being, the godmother

Death of the Occitan versions of AT 332. This grandmother/god-mother looks after JLP in a highly equivocal way, bordering on hostility.

The treasure-chest

(1) *F-C:* One day, the unhappy Finette is sitting by the blazing fireside in her home. The fairy godmother Merluche is conspicuous by her absence, and, indeed, she is not seen again physically in the narrative [*merluche = colin*, 'cod']. Finette, who has nothing to do, feels around in the gaps of the chimney; she finds a dirty *old* key that turns out to be made of gold; it opens a beautiful chest, in which there are clothes, diamonds, *lace, linen*, ribbons. Among these objects, there is a pair of *red velvet* slippers, embroidered with pearls.[71] The whole context shows that this chest is a present from the fairy godmother, though she is absent on that particular day: this is borne out by a comparison with other versions of Cinderella, such as that of Perrault.

(2) *JLP:* One day, the more or less orphaned JLP is alone at home. He has nothing to eat; his grandmother, a supernatural godmother, is absent (dead and recently buried). (We know that in the old versions of *Cinderella*, the supernatural being – mother or animal – who protects the young heroine is also buried, or at least dead, at the moment when her kindly action to Cinderella is revealed.)[72] Even the common fish of the southerners, the *arencâda* ['dry sardine'], the equivalent of the *merluche* ['cod'] of the northerners, is conspicuous by its absence in this house. JLP then discovers under a large heap of unused matches an old chest constructed of old bits of wood, in which are to be found valuable textiles (muslin and cambric), *lace*, jewels, gold coins, *clothes and linen*, such as handkerchiefs and silk stockings, silver cutlery and, finally, a large piece of *blue velvet on which are placed some twenty watches and gold snuff-boxes*. JLP has a new, strong chest made to hide his newly found treasure. It is clear that the old chest and its contents come from the grandmother.

Seduction of a prestigious individual of the opposite sex

(1) *F-C:* The contents of the treasure will enable Finette-Cendron

to adorn herself and so attract the attention of the king's son. It so happens that this king had benefited greatly from the rich estates of Finette's father, also a king, but now poor. Marriage solves everything; this will take place when the wealth, lost by Finette's father, is restored to her family by the king who is to become her father-in-law.

(2) *JLP:* The treasure discovered by J L P will enable him to marry the daughter of a powerful man. It so happens that this man (Sestier) had greatly exploited, even swindled [72], Truquette (the hero's father), who then lost everything and ended his career on the scaffold. The possible marriage of the two young people will return Sestier's illicit gains, extorted from Truquette, to the source.

The parallel course of the two narratives is impressive. Of course, Fabre goes his own way: his (hyper-realistic) tale is obviously harsher than Mme d'Aulnoy's fairy-tale. There are at least two deaths in Fabre's tale (Truquette and the grandmother), and even three, if one counts Barbe-Garouille; but there is none in *Finette-Cendron*. Then, there are certain shifts: the fire (and cinders) of Finette-Cendron's chimney are replaced by the pile of unlit matches in which J L P gropes around. These matches are there, of course, because they are among the essential objects of Fabre's tale. The dirty old key that turns out to be made of gold and opens a beautiful coffer for Finette-Cendron, disappears in the abbé's text.[73] But the 'oldness' of this key is transferred to the first chest that J L P discovers: it is an 'old' chest made up of bits of Noah's ark; the gold of the key is found again on many of the objects in J L P's chest (unlike Finette's coffer, which contains only pearls and diamonds, which, in the abbé's tale, become respectively gold coins and gold jewellery). Indeed, we note a striking resemblance and logical transformation: this movement of gold transforms Mme d'Aulnoy's *red velvet embroidered with pearls to be made into slippers* [*for the feet*] into *blue velvet covered with gold jewels* [*for the hands* – watches, snuff-boxes] found in J L P's chest. These alterations from one text to the other are not a matter of mere chance; they corroborate yet again the similarities, word for word, in the contents of the two chests: lace, linen, valuable textiles, ribbons in *Finette* and gold braid in *JLP*, etc. The order in which the objects in the chest are layered enables us to make another comparison between *Finette-Cendron* and *JLP:* this order is not indicated for

Finette's coffer itself, but in a previous episode in Mme d'Aulnoy's tale, Finette has a bag the precious contents of which (30 to 40 million diamonds) has explicitly come to her from her fairy godmother; this bag looks forward to the coffer that is to emerge a little later in Mme d'Aulnoy's tale. Moreover, the contents of these two receptacles are of the same kind. In Finette's coffer, they are '*clothes*, *diamonds*, *lace*, linen, and ribbons'. In Finette's bag, where – an important fact – the order of discovery of the objects is indicated, we find 'all the *lace* of the king and queen that serve to conceal Finette's fine *clothes* and the box of diamonds'. Let us compare, then, this order of discovery in Finette-Cendron's bag with that of the treasure in J L P's chest (see Table 13).

As we can see, the correspondences, line by line, in the two columns, between Finette's bag and coffer on the left and J L P's chest on the right, are remarkable. Taking into account the fact that *F-C* mentions pearls and diamonds, whereas *JLP* speaks of gold and silver, we have, by way of hiding the top of the bag or coffer, in the left-hand column *lace* and *ribbons*; in the right-hand column, under the layer of straw, 'braid' (*ribbons*) and, above all, the *lace* of great delicacy, which also appears in the reduced form of muslin and cambric. This first series constitutes what *hides* the rest. The second series consists of Finette's *fine* clothes, among which (in the coffer) are the celebrated *red velvet* slippers embroidered with pearls, and *linen*; these are echoed in the right-hand column (*JLP*) by the *blue velvet*, on which are placed gold snuff-boxes and watches, and *linen* (handkerchiefs and new silk stockings). Lastly, taking into account the passage from precious stones (*Finette*) to precious metals (*JLP*), the correspondence is perfect, in line 3 of Table 13, between the *box* of diamonds left by the fairy godmother at the bottom of Finette's bag (or coffer); and in *JLP*, in addition to the silver cutlery, the tiny casket, blest by St Anthony and placed at the bottom *left* of the chest, which contains fifty fine gold coins. Moreover, this line 3, in both columns, is filled with figures. The double reference, miraculous (St Anthony) and maleficent (the sinister *left* of the chest in *JLP* refers to the left side constantly chosen by grandmother Death and Quincarlot), stresses that this little coffer is to the highest degree the legacy, not of course of Finette's fairy godmother, but of J L P's grandmother/godmother Death. Lastly, the numbers correspond perfectly in line

Table 13

PRECIOUS OBJECTS IN *FINETTE-CENDRON*
AND *JLP*

Finette-Cendron	*JLP*
Contents of F–C's *bag*, in order of discovery from top to bottom (and simultaneous comparison with the contents of the girl's coffer)	Contents of JLP's *chest* in order of discovery from top to bottom
(1) *all the lace of the king and queen* . . . (homologous objects in Finette's coffer: lace, ribbons [= *braid*])	(1) 1 layer of straw 1 piece of muslin 2 pieces of cambric a small basket made of gold *braid* and about twenty packages of *lace* of unbelievable delicacy
(2) . . . *that serve to conceal Finette's fine clothes* . . . (homologous objects in Finette's coffer: *clothes*, including the *red slippers embroidered with pearls*; linen)	(2) a large piece of *blue velvet* on which are displayed some twenty gold watches and snuff-boxes handkerchiefs and silk stockings, all new
(3) and the *box* containing between 30 and 40 million diamonds provided by the fairy godmother (Mme d'Aulnoy, 1710, p. 120) (homologous objects in Finette's coffer: *diamonds*)	(3) and, lastly, at the bottom, two dozen silver spoons and forks; and to cap it all, in a *casket* blest by St Anthony, on the left [second version], 50 *jaunets* [gold coins], each worth 24 francs . . .
(4) total estimate: between 30 and 40 million (diamonds)	(4) '32,000 *livres*, not counting the value of the spoons and forks'; or again 'over 30,000 *livres*' [second version, 75, 77]

Finette-Cendron	*JLP*
In the lighted chimney	Under the pile of matches,
the dirty, old key,	the old, dilapidated chest,
implicitly left by the fairy godmother,	implicitly left by the grandmother/godmother,
opens	is then replaced
on the heroine's initiative	on the hero's initiative
the beautiful chest/coffer/ masterpiece	by the new, strong chest [70]
that contains treasure.	that will now contain the treasure.

4: 30 to 40 million diamonds in the 'box' in the left-hand column (*Finette*); 'over 30,000 *livres tournois*' in the 'chest' (*JLP*). We should add the remarkable concordance as far as origins are concerned: the contents of the heroine Finette's bag and coffer are gifts from her fairy godmother; they are also articles that were somewhat dishonestly 'borrowed' by the heroine from the king, her father (as in the case of the lace). The contents of JLP's treasure are a legacy from the grandmother/godmother, who herself obtained them somewhat dishonestly from the illicit gains of the hero's father, Truquette. One will also note the agile dialectic of old and new, of key and chests, in the two narratives, as they emerge respectively in the works of Mme d'Aulnoy and the abbé Fabre.

Again, this table did not emerge fully armed from the imagination of a commentator: it is Fabre himself who puts us on the scent by indicating the partial resemblance of a section of his narrative to the fairy-tale entitled *Céndrousétta-Bachassoun* or *Cendrillon-la-Souillon*, in this case *Finette-Cendron*.

With perverse and almost diabolical skill, Fabre has given his novella an additional and decisive clue: the contents of JLP's chest (gold and silver jewellery. precious textiles and linens) represent, in an exceptional way [75], the 'male contribution' of the young man towards his future marriage with Babeau. This *serious* male contribution corresponds in a homologous way to the burlesque contribution provided by Truquette (tin jewellery, cheap clothes, etc.) for his wedding with Margot. The Occitan word *finetta*, which refers to a particular textile, but which is also the exact Provençal transposition of the French *Finette* of *Finette-Cendron*, is specifically used of this first male contribution (that of the father, Truquette), which foreshadows the second male contribution (that of his son, J L P). In effect, Fabre's young hero tells how Truquette had given Margot a *vareuse de finette* ['flannelette jacket', 14]. The word *finessa* in the male contribution of the son (J L P) is a direct echo of the word *finetta* applied to the male contribution of the father (Truquette). The dead grandmother's chest found by her grandson contains, indeed, 'lace of indescribable delicacy [*finessa*]' [69]. In several ways, therefore, the word *Finette* forms the link, in the works of Mme d'Aulnoy and Fabre, between the clothes and lace of the hero's (or heroine's) parents and the clothes and lace of the hero himself (or heroine herself); this homologue is reinforced in Fabre's tale by the similar position of these effects, which is localized, for two successive generations, in the parallel framework of the 'male contribution' of a father and a son.

It is clear that it was no accident that Fabre should draw the homology between the suffixes *-ette* and *-on* in the terms he uses (Céndrou*sétta*-Bachas*soun*) and the same suffixes used by Mme d'Aulnoy (Fin*ette*-Cendr*on*).

Mme d'Aulnoy	Fin*ette*	Cendr*on*
Fabre	Cendrou*sette*	Bachas*soun*

The suffixes correspond, term by term, vertically. However, the same order of words and meanings is switched by Fabre in relation to those used by Mme d'Aulnoy: *Cendron* comes second in her work, but first in that of the abbé (*Céndrousétta*). The first word (*Finette*), which implies delicacy for Mme d'Aulnoy, refers to the second word (*Bachassoun*), which, for Fabre, implies dirt or soiling. Of course, the abbé, as usual, has bridged the gap between his educated culture, based on written literature (the work of Mme d'Aulnoy), and his oral culture as a folklore specialist who knows how to listen to people: a *Céndrousétta*, possibly possessing the additional name of Bachassoun, no doubt existed in Languedoc in Fabre's time; later, the collectors of oral traditions were to find in the following centuries a Cendrouillon-Patrouillon in Nivernais, a Cendrouse in Poitou, a Cendrouzette in Vendée, a Cendrasson in Ariège and a Pitcendras-Lharassas in Aude![74]

Of course, the abbé is careful to warn his reader: in his tale, Cinderella is not equivalent to the character one might expect. This charming young girl is not the grandmother, but, changing sex, she is identified specifically with Jean-l'ont-pris, the beneficiary, like Finette, of the gifts of his 'fairy godmother' (his grandmother). Furthermore, Fabre's novella does not derive, on the whole, from *Cinderella* (AT 510). It belongs to the cycle *Godfather Death* (AT 332). But the skilful use by Fabre of the structures of the narrative *Finette-Cendron*, in so far as they are compatible with those of his own narrative, provides us with a double advantage.

(1) It underlines or confirms in a general way that the novella *JLP* is not simply a flat description of real life in a Languedocian village, but quite definitely a fairy-tale containing elements of parody, parable and riddle, disguised as a hyper-realistic piece of fiction.

(2) It also confirms that the grandmother is her grandson's god-mother, and that she even functions as a supernatural godmother. However, we are confronted here with a particular and even aberrant case of the fairy godmother: indeed, J L P's grandmother is godmother Death; she is more dangerous than benevolent. She does not belong essentially to the *Cinderella* cycle; in fact, she belongs in every fibre of her being to the cycle of *Godfather Death*, transformed for us into godmother Death (AT 332).

(3) Cinderella or Finette-Cendron, like George Sand's Petite Fadette, is a heroine who succeeds in marrying the man she loves by the use of female dowry, in the form of treasure that she has previously obtained in a miraculous way. Faithful to the rules of the Occitan fiction of the *ancien régime*, which insist phallocratically on

the male contribution (see the first part of this book), Fabre has simply transformed this young female Finette-Cendron into the young male hero Jean-l'ont-pris.

Where, then, did the grandmother of the abbé's hero amass her treasure? J L P tells us: 'my grandmother had collected this store when times were good [when her son-in-law was making rich pickings as a swindler], and if Truquette and his comrades had not put it there, she must have done on her own account' [70]. In AT 332, the supernatural being (Death) teaches his protégé (*compère* or godson), here *compère* son-in-law (Truquette), how to amass a fortune as a physician or a swindler. However, are there cases in other versions of *Godfather Death* in which this supernatural being (Death) extracts his 'tithe' from the profits of his protégé, as the grandmother was to do in Fabre's novella at the expense of Truquette? The answer is yes. We know how close the Occitan and Catalan cultures were in the eighteenth century – geographically, linguistically and in many other ways. Culturally speaking, there were no Pyrenees. Now, in a Catalan version of AT 332,[75] Death deducts each night half the vast medical fees received during the day thanks to the diagnostic talents with which he has endowed his physician godson. It should be added that things turn out badly for the Catalan protégé of Death (as for Truquette); he, too, tries to cheat his patron. He kills him. Fabre may have invented the 'deduction' made by the grandmother or grandmother Death from the profits, precious textiles and stolen jewels that her son-in-law *compère* Truquette had amassed. But the abbé may just as easily have found this theme ready made in the oral versions of AT 332 circulating at that time between Languedoc and Catalonia. In any case, Fabre has emphasized by an evocation of the Dance of Death the fact that the dead grandmother, who had first deducted, then given, treasure, is a figure of Death: 'I would have danced the Dance of Death,' says J L P in the second version, re-membering the marvellous discoveries that he had made in his grand-mother's chest.

CHAPTER XII Death's Gifts

In any case, J L P is now [70–71] the master of his dead grandmother's treasure. What will he do with it?

On this question, a comparison arises with the first section of the second part of the tale *Jean-de-trop*, a Languedocian homologue of *JLP*. This second part concerns the life of the physician Death's godson (whereas the first part of *JDT* dealt with the brief biography of his parents, *compère* and *commère* of Death, themselves homologues of Truquette and Margot).

The second part of *JDT* is divided into two sections:

(1) *enjoying the gifts* given by Death to her physician godson – the ability to cure, seduce, marry and possess the daughter of a powerful man;

(2) *tricking Death* in order to wring from her, by force, a long extension of life for the hero's wife, the powerful man's daughter.

The second part of *JLP* (the biography of the young hero himself, the grandson of grandmother Death) is also constructed, seen from above, in two sections, but these are ordered in a way that is exactly the reverse of that of *JDT*. This construction, which is Fabre's own, proposes, in effect, the following actions, carried out by the hero J L P:

(1) *tricking the forces of death* and getting the better of grandmother Death in order to obtain gifts, such as the friendship of a powerful man and the granting of treasure; this treasure will in turn (later) enable the hero to win the body and possibly the hand and fortune of the powerful man's adorable daughter;

(2) *taking advantage of these gifts* from grandmother Death to:

(a) seduce the powerful man's daughter, the 'heroine';

(b) force this powerful man to give the hero his daughter's hand in marriage;

(c) 'counter-cure' the girl's rival, in other words, diagnose in advance, in the purest style of A T 332,[1] the death of this rival (which, by simple logical inversion, amounts to diagnosing the future good health of the heroine herself).

In other words, we have:

	SCHEMA OF THE SECOND PART	
	OF *JDT*	OF *JLP*
first section	Enjoying the gifts of Death	Tricking Death
second section	Tricking Death	Enjoying the gifts of Death

The reversal operated in the right-hand column (*JLP*) in relation to the left-hand column (*JDT*) proceeds from a specific and *literary* initiative on the abbé Fabre's part; this reversal is not met with as such in any known version of AT 332, whether from Languedoc, Catalonia, Germany or elsewhere. I shall later (in Chapter XIII) say something about the reasons for this reversal. For the moment, I shall confine myself to pointing out and uncovering its effects, as far as the second section of the second part of *JLP* is concerned.

Taking first the act of seducing the powerful man's daughter. Things are obviously very simple; the two young people find each other attractive: 'The daughter took a great liking to me,' says J L P [71].

Besides, the very fact that J L P now possesses a treasure constitutes for him, in relation to the heroine Babeau, and not only in relation to her father, an additional qualification of no mean sort.

The young man's task is to display the treasure (the male contribution to the marriage). The girl's rich father will thus be forced to give his consent to the marriage; this consent will derive from a 'suitability' or 'congruence', and will be drawn up *ipso facto* between:

(1) an attractive young man, hitherto poor, but who is now in possession of a large sum of money; and

(2) a beautiful girl, richly endowed by her father, with the additional expectation of a legacy.

We have, therefore, reached the ideal of social homogamy that is at the centre of all Occitan culture in the *ancien régime* (see the first part of this book). As Sestier more or less says to J L P: 'Our families are equal, Truquette's and mine; we both set out with nothing. *We have nothing to reproach ourselves with as far as virtue and honour are concerned* [*sic*]. Find 20,000 *livres* as a male contribution, and you will marry my daughter together with the 60,000 *livres* that you will get from me' [second version]. One is reminded of Adolphe's father, who also lived in the eighteenth century in the French-speaking and Franco-Provençal zone: 'It was a principle with my father that a young man must avoid contracting a lasting relationship with a young woman who was not his perfect equal in fortune, birth and outward advantages' (Benjamin Constant, *Adolphe*, Ch. II).

From this point of view, the matrimonial strategies in *JLP*, on the one hand, and those in various Occitan versions of AT 332, on the other, make an interesting comparison. Let us choose two versions in which, as in *JLP*, the hero is confronted with the daughter of a powerful man. These are *JDT* and the Gascon version collected by Bédat de Monlaur.

In *JDT*, the problem for the king (or the 'powerful man') is to persuade the hero Jean-de-trop to cure his daughter. The young man has, in effect, something to offer: his curative abilities (in fact, these are merely an ability to make a valid diagnosis, but the king does not look into the matter so closely). In exchange for this 'male contribution', the king, master of his own daughter and of her dowry, will decide on a 'female contribution' that will reward the contribution made by the young 'physician' by way of a 'cure': so the king offers Jean-de-trop a cartload of money, then (as the stakes rise) an entire province, then half of his crown, then, finally, his only daughter, which, once he is married, will make the young man heir presumptive to the throne.

In the version of AT 332 collected in Gascony by Bédat de Monlaur, an almost analogical situation is defined in considerable detail.

This version is particularly interesting; it has a number of archaic features: Death is a man, a *black lord*. This derives, of course, from an earlier form of the tale, preceding the feminization and Latinization of Death. Furthermore, the money in this Gascon text is counted in *livres tournois*; there is also mention of the intendant of the province of Languedoc and of the king of France, who is still creating marquises and who lives in the Louvre and not yet in Versailles! This version, despite the amphigoric style given it by its collector, bears the marks, therefore, of an early date – prior to 1789, of course, but also prior to 1750, if not to 1700. It derives, as does *Jean-de-trop*, from the vast oral corpus of versions of AT 332 that circulated in the Languedocian Midi, several of which came to Fabre's notice;[2] they were to be collected much later, from 1876 onwards, by Occitan folklore specialists, in forms that were slightly modified but always recognizable and structurally intact.

The physician–hero of Bédat de Monlaur's version functions, as is often the case in AT 332, as Death's *compère*[3] (and not as his godson); he is called to the sick-bed of the king's daughter. She does not marry the man who cures her (there is no question of such a marriage in Bédat de Monlaur's version); nevertheless, the king in this Gascon version, like the king in *Jean-de-trop*, offers the hero considerable rewards in order to persuade him to cure his daughter. And, in fact, the cure does take place. In the end, the king offers 20,000 *livres*; the hero accepts them; as he does so, he expels Death and the disease from the princess's bed by turning it around. The classic trick. The important thing for us is that the king in this Gascon version by Bédat de Monlaur has *stated* the exact price of his daughter's life; this price, which he agrees to pay, and does in fact pay, amounts to 20,000 *livres tournois*.

Let us now examine *Jean-l'ont-pris*. The contrary occurs, and yet it really amounts to the same thing. Here, the hero has nothing to offer the daughter of the powerful man by way of medical or, rather, in his case, paramedical talents. There is no question of his 'curing' Babeau, the daughter of the powerful man Sestier; she is in excellent health! JLP's paramedical talents and his ability to make a correct diagnosis or prognosis are certainly used, but in relation not to Babeau herself, but to Barbe-Garouille, Babeau's seriously sick rival. In these circumstances, the hero JLP, who has nothing to offer, is funda-mentally in the position of making a *request*: this difference separates him from his homologue Jean-de-trop and from the Gascon physician of Bédat de Monlaur. JLP desires the body of Sestier's daughter. He wants her hand, which is as charming as a Cupid's comb; he also wants to marry her for her money. And for that he will have to *pay*. Of course, he is in a position to do so, thanks to the 'fabulous treasure' that he has found under his dead grandmother's matches. This treasure constitutes, in fact, the typical male contribution to any possible future marriage: jewels, female garments, silver – in short, what a boy offers his betrothed in the form of male contribution in a

Languedocian notary's marriage contract. For her part the girl, or rather her father, prepares a dowry, by way of female contribution to the future household. The husband will have usufruct of this dowry.

That is precisely the point: Sestier will calculate the price that JLP will have to pay for his daughter; at the end of such a calculation, the powerful farmer receives exactly the same figure as that proposed by the king of France, in his Louvre, to the Gascon physician who treated and cured the princess in Bédat de Monlaur's version. The price *demanded* by Sestier (and *offered* by the king of France) is again 20,000 *livres tournois* [73] – the price *ne varietur* of the southern heroine of AT 332.

In other words:

(1) in the Languedocian and Gascon versions of AT 332, the king of France values the life of his daughter at a very large sum; he is ready to pay the physician 20,000 *livres* in the event of a cure, according to the old Gascon version of AT 332 (Bédat de Monlaur).

(2) in *JLP*, Sestier also values his daughter at 20,000 *livres*. But the situation in Fabre is reversed in relation to the other Occitan versions of AT 332. According to these versions, it is the powerful man who is obliged to ask and who pays the 20,000 *livres* to the physician in order to save the princess's life. In *JLP*, on the contrary, it is the hero who has to ask: he will have to find and display 20,000 *livres* if the rich farmer is to give him, in exchange, the hand of his daughter in marriage. These 20,000 *livres tournois* may also be compared with the twenty tons of gold that the king offers the hero who wishes to marry his daughter, in an Austro-baroque version of AT 332, which is closely related to our *Jean-de-trop*.[4]

So Fabre has worked on a corpus of oral versions of AT 332; they indicated a certain price to be placed on the powerful man's daughter: 20,000 *livres*, payable by the king to the physician–hero in the event of a cure. On the basis of this calculation, which he found ready made in a folklore that he knew very well, Fabre was content simply to turn the situation inside out: the 20,000 *livres* are still required, but the asker, now, is the hero, not the powerful man. It is therefore up to the hero to pay the 20,000 *livres* or at least to prove that he possesses them, as the counterpart required by folklore as the male contribution to the marriage.

In fact, JLP will have no difficulty finding the 20,000 *livres*, since his treasure, when sold, will bring him 25,000 to 32,000 *livres*; in these circumstances, the hero may allow himself to keep the gold and silver spoons that he had found in his grandmother's trunk – they will make a pleasant item in his household.[5]

Fabre, then, as in many versions of AT 332, has treated the theme of the hero's future marriage with the powerful man's daughter. But he has separated it from a context of curing the girl, and it is in this respect that his contribution is original. However, it is not *totally* original, since on this point Fabre was influenced by a fairly frequent motif in *Godfather Death*, in Occitan and other versions: that is, a prognosis of certain death, made by the hero, concerning an individual who is sick or who seems to be sick. This unpleasant prognosis, once verified, will in turn become for the hero a source of additional prestige and prosperity. Using such a motif, Fabre found it quite easy to replace the classic episode of AT 332 (*cure of the powerful man's daughter*, here Babeau) with an episode that is doubly negative and therefore strictly equivalent: *prognosis of death for the rival of the powerful man's daughter*[6] (this rival is Barbe-Garouille). We see that Fabre has not entirely dropped, far from it, the medical or paramedical side of the hero of AT 332. However, the abbé was confronted on this point with certain intrinsic difficulties that forced him to find a rather subtle solution.

Fabre the novelist has already, on the matter of Sestier's cure, indulged in almost acrobatic contortions.

For various reasons, he had decided that his hero would not be a proper physician. Indeed, the hyper-realistic convention that dominates his narrative forced the writer to effect a whole series of 'slippages'. The grandmother functioned as a Death who was not really one, since she was a real, living person who would eventually die. By the same token, her grandson and godson was no longer a physician but, at most, a paramedical figure. Sestier was no longer a king, but was reduced to the function of a rich farmer, a role more acceptable in terms of realistico-burlesque parody (moreover, there already existed certain equivalents of this role of 'kulak' in the earlier tradition of AT 332).[7] And, anyway, having refused to follow the advice of grandmother Death, Jean-l'ont-pris could hardly appear in an official capacity as the physician or 'educated man' that his grandmother had wished him to become.

For all these reasons, Fabre played about with the difficulties: in the business of Sestier's cure, he kept the three main ingredients of AT 332 (permutation of 180 degrees, prognosis of infallible survival, administration of a placebo of cold water), but he carefully reduced the character of the physician, since in any case the hero lacked the necessary substance on this point. JLP certainly played the role of nurse to Sestier after the attack that had knocked him senseless, but it was Sestier himself who made the prognosis of his own cure [60]. Again, JLP accompanied the 'sick' Sestier to his house, but it was a surgeon specially brought in who administered the placebo of cold water, etc.

Very often in the canonical cycle of AT 332, the hero, after treating the king or the powerful man, is taken to treat his daughter, the beautiful princess, who falls for the physician Death's godson. We find this theme in various Occitan versions of AT 332. It is also to be found, well beyond these, in Germany, where the tale originally developed; the superb German versions collected at a much later date by the brothers Grimm do possess this sequence: treating the king, then treating the king's daughter. The Flemish, Spanish, etc., versions also follow the same pattern.

Working on the Occitan, oral corpus of AT 332 in order to elaborate his novella, Fabre also came up against the classic sequence: treatment of the powerful man (Sestier); then treatment of the powerful man's daughter (Babeau). Would the abbé reduce his physician a second time? To assume so would be to underestimate the inexhaustible inventiveness of a good Languedocian writer. Instead of reducing the physician, the abbé reduces the patient. Babeau, Babette or Babelette remains healthy. But Barbe, Barbeau or Barbette (-Garouillette) will die. She will provide, therefore, the perfect occasion for a fatal prognosis by the team formed in AT 332 by Death and her 'physician protégé', just as she does for the specific team formed, in Fabre's narrative, by Quincarlot-the-gibbet and JLP, the latter becoming for the occasion the protégé of the former. This team of two persons – Quincarlot leading and Jean-l'ont-pris following – will therefore make it possible to formulate the fatal diagnosis in the case of Barbe-Garouille or Barbette-Garouillette,[8] the mephitic double and contra-type of the beautiful Babeau Sestier or Babette Sestier.

Can there be any doubt of the antithesis between these two women, in the most perfect, inverted symmetry? One has only to compare the two bodies, as described in Fabre's text. Moving from head to toe:

Babeau/Babette/Babelette	Barbe/Barbette/Garouillette
face that dazzles the eye eyes that reduce to ashes the coldest heart peach-coloured cheeks	short-sighted eyes
teeth as white as curdled milk arms as smooth as glass	scurvy that leads to loss of teeth scabies that make the skin shiny to the fingernails
hands like Cupid's comb	bumps like fungi all over the body
breasts to make you cry out for help	a weak chest
a waist and bearing to set one aflame	decaying lungs
virginity (temporary) of the 'Holy Virgin'	eight-month pregnancy (with twins)
feet such that the queen would buy for herself at the Paris meat-market	gangrened leg: 'a leg endowed with twenty sores in which gangrene has spread like a blessing'
a soul that is probably Catholic, at least non-Protestant	a Protestant soul

These contrasted correspondences are clear; they also lead one to compare the nicknames, first names and surnames of the two women:

Nicknames	Babeau, Babette, Babelette	Barbe, Barbeau, Barbette
First names	Elizabeth	Judith
Surnames	Sestier	Garouille

First names: Elizabeth is a first name taken from the New Testament, to which *Catholics* refer so readily. Elizabeth, in fact, is the mother of John the Baptist and cousin of the Virgin.

Judith is a first name taken from the Old Testament, to which the *Huguenots* tended to refer. In the Bible she is a girl who has killed her lover (Holofernes), just as Garouille would kill hers at a distance of a hundred paces, simply by her foul breath.

Surnames: Garouille signifies in Occitan not only a dirty woman, but also the fever-laden, plague-ridden, malarial marshes, a source of death; it is applied, for example, to the marshes of Camargue to the *south* of Solorgues. This name is contrasted, therefore, with Sestier or *Setier*, the good, old measure of wheat, typical of fertile, drained land; it originated in the fine wheatfields to the *north* of Solorgues (at Langlade), Monsieur Sestier's home country. In short, Garouille in opposition to Sestier is mortality against fecundity.

Indeed, in his novella, Fabre developed in a highly interesting way the theme of fecundity, in terms of pregnancy, swelling, a kind of 'fattening up' or rounding. Four persons and four series of texts are considered from this point of view.

(1) Babeau made pregnant by J L P became 'as round *as a tennis ball*' [86].

(2) Barbe-Garouille became 'big' [*grôssa*] with Sestier's child. 'Two months later, she gave birth to two kinds of water-rat . . . yesterday she died with them in the hospital at Sommières' [83]; or, as the second version has it, 'she could not deliver her cargo [*pacotille*] without dying [*sans en crever*, literally, 'without bursting from them'] . . . in the end, she gave birth to a couple of dead gentlemen who looked like water-rats . . . she dragged on for four or five days more . . . the day before yesterday, so that she would be better served than at Solorgues, I took her on a cart to the hospital at Sommières where she died on arrival'. This text, which is of an almost unbearable cruelty, is typical in this respect of fairy-tales; one has only to think of the ogre in *Tom Thumb* devouring his seven little daughters without blinking an eyelid.

(3) Third swelling: that of the grandmother. The lady so stuffs herself with grapes and other fruit that she bursts (dies). She leaves her grandson what the narrator specifically calls a cargo [*pacotille*], in other words, treasure. The same word (*pacotille*) is also used in the

novella about Barbe-Garouille's stillborn twins. The disappearance of both mother and children will leave the field free to the JLP–Babeau couple, thus bringing the hero happiness.

(4) The fourth episode of 'fattening up' has nothing tragic about it; JLP, having become a vineyard-keeper, also devours fruit, like his grandmother. But instead of dying from it, like she, he simply gets 'as fat as a capon' (a castrated rooster) [65].

These four phenomena may be arranged in a table:

	A	B	C
	THE ROLES	ON THE SIDE OF DEATH (given or received)	ON THE SIDE OF LIFE (lived or transmitted)
1	*Active roles:* Jean-l'ont-pris's lineage	Grandmother Death, stuffed with grapes, *dies*, leaving a *cargo* (treasure) that will bring JLP happiness.	Jean-l'ont-pris, stuffed with grapes, swells up like a capon (sterile fat).
2	*Passive roles:* Jean-l'ont-pris's two wives	Barbe-Garouille, doomed to die and pregnant, *dies*, giving birth to a *cargo* (the stillborn twins) that will bring JLP happiness.	Babeau, pregnant by JLP and round as a tennis ball, enjoys a fecund pregnancy.

Babeau/fecundity (C2) is defined as such, in opposition to Garouille/sterility (B2). In the central column of the table (column B) – the side of death – the active force of death (the grandmother in B1) and the passive victim of death (Barbe-Garouille in B2) are capable in the end of only 'bursting' (dying); they will then leave the hero *pacotilles* ['cargoes'] more dead than alive that will form the foundation of his future prosperity and happiness. On the right (in C1), JLP, being a male, can by definition accumulate only a sterile fat that suggests that of a capon (an 'infertile' bird). Fecundity triumphs only in the bottom right-hand corner (C2) with the fecund Babeau: J L P has made her pregnant with a foetus that promises the sweetest hopes. Babeau Sestier embodies fecundity, the forces of life, to the maximum.

Let us return to Barbe-Garouille: the prognosis of a death (of this unfortunate creature, for example) occurs frequently in our Occitan, Catalan, Castilian and other versions of A T 332. One does not have to be a great physician to make such a macabre prediction. As always in the tale type A T 332, there will be a dichotomy: one character will embody death, in the absence of the dead grandmother (Quincarlot, in this instance), while a second character, the hero, informed as he must be by this Quincarlot/Death, will be able to make without any risk of error the diagnosis of imminent death, concerning Garouille. Indeed, this diagnosis will be the source of a profitable operation,[9] as always in A T 332; J L P, informed by Quincarlot, can now allow himself to marry the dying woman and thus foil Sestier's traps. The hero rapidly becomes a widower. With the treasure from his dead grandmother, he can now entertain a serious hope of marrying Babeau; he begins by making her pregnant, sensibly enough.

We should also remember the equivalence mentioned above: Babeau's rival is Barbe-Garouille. Sestier has thrown this frightful creature at J L P's legs, in the hope of preventing a marriage between his daughter and the hero.

Now, a double negation equals an affirmation. I have shown that the classic task of the hero (J D T, for example) in numerous versions (southern French and others) of A T 332, a task that amounts to making *the infallible diagnosis that the health of the powerful man's daughter will be restored*, is carried out in *JLP* in a way that is both different and homologous: the hero J L P, tipped off by Quincarlot-the-gibbet, will himself make *the infallible diagnosis of the imminent death of the rival of the powerful man's daughter*. Two negations (*the imminent death* of the daughter's *rival*) equal an affirmation (*the restoration to health* of the *girl*). The tale is thus put back on its feet; or, to be more precise, through this pirouette, Fabre's novella falls back 'on the feet' of the tale that was its ancestor and that originally inspired it. By correctly prognosticating Barbe-Garouille's death, J L P carries out, in a paradoxical way, one of the essential functions of the hero–physician Death's godson, as generally encountered in AT 332 – in particular, in *Jean-de-trop*.

In its classic form, this function consists, in a simple way, of diagnosing the return to health of the powerful man's daughter. In both cases, JDT, by this 'affirmative' method, and JLP, by the oblique means of the 'double negation', arrive at exactly the same result. They both seduce the powerful man's daughter: the young princess, in the case of JDT; young Babeau, in the case of JLP.

In doing so, JLP also settles a conflict with Sestier. This may come as a surprise, but we should not forget that in AT 332 (French and other versions), the relations between the hero and the powerful man (heroine's father) are often strained, even if the two men later find themselves connected when the first becomes the son-in-law of the second.

Let us consider, for example, in the publications of the two great folklore specialists,[10] the oldest French version of AT 332, collected in France by Jacob Grimm in person (he died in 1863). The king (homologue of our Sestier) threatens to cut off the head of the physician Death's godson if he does not agree to treat 'His Majesty'. However, the two men are reconciled; after tricking Death, the hero ends his career comfortably as the son-in-law of a powerful man and as the king's heir. This is a version that possesses certain very ancient features. I am not saying this simply because it was the first to be collected in France by a (German) folklore specialist, even before that of Mistral (1876); in this respect it was preceded by that of the French writer Gueullette (published in 1712). In fact, the archaism of the *ancien régime* also appears in this *French* version of Grimm's in a number of ways: the threat to decapitate the hero by an executioner armed with a sword (this very old form of capital punishment is also to be found in the 'Swiss tale'); the presence on the shoulders of a lady (who is, unsuccessfully, a candidate for the role of godmother to the poor baby) of the cloak of the Virgin of Mercy, as in *JLP* ... Now it is striking to observe that in this *French* version of *Godfather Death* collected by Jacob Grimm, which in other respects is perfectly canonical, the relations between the powerful man and the hero, between, let us say, 'Sestier' and 'Jean-l'ont-pris', are very strained, though later they become more relaxed. The tension between Sestier and JLP seems to derive, therefore, from the very tradition of the tale from which our narrative is derived.[11]

In Fabre's narrative, in fact, JLP and Sestier are doubly in conflict: the powerful man Sestier refuses his daughter's hand to the hero (JLP); and the hero, for his part, categorically refuses, in an earlier stage, to marry Barbe-Garouille, the powerful man's abominable old mistress, whom the powerful man is trying to pass on to the hero. Moreover, this 'good riddance', if Sestier could carry it off, would kill two birds with one stone. A marriage between the frightful woman and the hero would enable the powerful man to prevent the hero from marrying his daughter; it would also relieve Sestier of a tie with an ugly mistress and the probability of a child by her – two phenomena that are highly inconvenient for this powerful man. In fact, Sestier achieves only one of his objectives: Garouille's death, judiciously foreseen by JLP, thanks to Quincarlot, will rid the rich farmer of a cumbersome connection. But he may also have to accept as his son-in-law (against his will) the young man who is to make him a grandfather.

However, one 'technical' problem remains: who, in the absence of the dead grandmother Death, will be able to make the diagnosis of the imminent death of Barbe-Garouille in order to enlighten Jean-l'ont-pris? The answer is easy . . . Fabre finds it in the original tale, but he also uses his sovereign rights as a writer – he has more than one trick up his sleeve. Death is dead. Long live Death! The grandmother is dead. Long live Quincarlot!

The problem of the 'survival of Death' is presented, in effect, for the realistic or hyper-realistic author that Fabre is, in different terms from those that confronted the oral story-tellers of *Godfather Death*. For this kind of popular story-teller, Death is a fantastic character who dominates the tale from beginning to end: he never dies, even if, of his own free will, he becomes as small as a cricket; even if he is enclosed for a long period in a hermetically sealed bottle. But the problems that faced Fabre were very special ones: this author parodies the supernatural in the real; or, rather, he drapes the surreal in the hyper-real. Once he has buried grandmother Death, he cannot bring her back to life. He has, therefore, to find someone else to carry out the same functions.

In this search for a substitute character, Fabre was stimulated by

the available corpus of oral versions of A T 332 then circulating in the
Occitan region and in France as a whole: we should not forget that
under the *ancien régime*, as in the nineteenth century, versions travelled
from north to south and vice versa, as part of the commercial, cultural
and religious links between the two regions.

Should we remember the famous map of the diffusion of the
Great Fear in 1789, spread in a few weeks by word of mouth? There,
no doubt, lies the virtue of an eighteenth century that is at once
traditional in folklore, *innovative* in literary transformations and *mobile*
in the propagation of stories.

The division into two of the character of Death, or the use in his
place of other characters, had already been done in the 'Swiss tale',
which was one of the origins, in *JLP*, of the life of Truquette.
Among the three candidates for the role of supernatural godfather
offered by the classic versions (heirs of the eighteenth century) of A T
332 (God, the devil dressed as a hunter[12] and Death), the 'Swiss
tale', contrary to the usual practice, chose not the third but the
second. Indeed, the devil, who is at once protective, enriching and
dangerous, makes a very good job of his role as godfather. He slipped,
with his usual agility, into the canonical structures of A T 332, though
they had been designed, in principle, with godfather Death in mind,
and not for a godfather devil. However, one difficulty did arise at the
end of this German-Swiss tale. Who was going to kill the unfortunate
cobbler of the 'Swiss tale', the cobbler who had become a victim of
the diabolical, supernatural entity, after having first been protected
by him? The devil is not a professional killer; he is not suited to
that role. The Swiss story-teller, therefore, brought back Death,
who had been ignored at the beginning of the narrative, planting
him at the conclusion of his text in the form of a recognizable
executioner; this executioner decapitates the hero in the most archaic
possible way, with a sword.[13] Thus the cobbler ended his days on
the block. Thus the supernatural entity was divided into two: first
the devil; then Death. The recipe was then used for Truquette,
whose biography was partially, but strongly, inspired by an Occitanized version of the 'Swiss tale', since lost (whereas the 'Swiss tale' was
to survive in a Swiss canton until it was collected in the 1920s).
Truquette had first been protected, then betrayed, by his mother-
in-law Death; he dies at the hands of the executioner at Nîmes,

observed by the sneering, one-eyed sheriff's officer, Quincarlot-the-gibbet.

JLP apart, the oldest known French version of AT 332 (after Gueullette's of 1712) was collected in France by the competent Jacob Grimm in the early nineteenth century. It, too, uses, with considerable virtuosity, the device of dividing Death into two:[14] the usual poor man, looking for a godmother for his newborn child, rejects the Virgin, despite the fact that she is wearing the Cloak of Mercy; he then accepts Death as the child's godmother. When this child, Death's godson, grows up, he becomes the classic physician who knows how to locate the 'correct' position of Death in relation to the sick-bed, and who also knows how to trick Death by turning the bed, etc. So the godson runs through the classic curriculum, accompanied as always by a trick played on Death; he treats a rich man and marries a rich man's daughter. Things get more complicated when the physician is called to the king's sick-bed: this king is himself the result of a division into two, since he emerges in the narrative *after* the treatment given a previous powerful man, whose daughter the physician will soon marry (in other French versions, the physician *immediately* marries the king's daughter, whom he has treated). In this French version collected by Jacob Grimm, Death is in turn somewhat duplicated by the Virgin Mary, whose Cloak of Mercy is sometimes evoked in *JLP*, in a burlesque way, in relation to grandmother Death herself (see Chapter XI). In Jacob Grimm's French version, these 'divisions' are at their height at the king's bedside: Death is present at the head of the royal bed; she therefore poses a threat to the sick man. But, sitting at the bedside is also our old friend from AT 332, the executioner, in full costume, ready *to decapitate the hero with his sword*; other characters, servants and guards (who are 'forces of death', like our vineyard-keepers), also await the king's orders to hand over the physician to the executioner, who will cut off his head if he does not agree to turn the bed round and trick Death . . . In these circumstances, the physician has no alternative but to carry out his task; indeed, he succeeds and becomes the king's heir. In this way he benefits by a double trick played on a Death who is so divided, into Death and executioner, that in the end she works against herself. What virtuosity in the telling! J L P's situation is certainly different; but how can we fail to be reminded of the young man who treats a rich farmer (Sestier) and who then seduces his daughter, and of the scene in which Sestier obtains the services of Quincarlot-the-gibbet and a few constables, ruffians and vineyard-keepers, in order to force the hero to follow his wishes.

I shall also have occasion to refer in the next chapter to Vernaleken's so-called Austro-baroque version of AT 332, which is so close to our *Jean-de-trop*; so much so that the two tales in the rococo region that extended in the seventeenth and eighteenth centuries from Languedoc to Austria, via the Alps and Lombardy, could not fail to have a precise and similar source within the more general cycle of AT 332 to which they both belong. Here, too, in this Vernaleken version, which was to be collected in the 1860s,[15] the supernatural entity of AT 332 is divided into two and even into three: first, there is the monkey; then Death ('Old Bones'), against whom the hero turned the patient's bed; and, lastly, the devil, who has to be shut up in a hermetically sealed receptacle – bottle, gourd or vase – to prevent him from harming the hero's wife, and powerful man's daughter, threatened by the infernal intentions of this devil.

It might be said that none of this really concerns, certainly not directly, the Occitan region. The sceptics have only to consult the Gascon version of AT 332, collected by Bédat de Monlaur. I have already had occasion to point out, beyond the unfortunately rather florid style of the collector, the archaic and authenticating features of this interesting version. In it Death appears as a male character, the *black lord*, who is none other than the *compère* Death [*Gavatter Tod*] of Sachs and Grimm. There is no question yet of turning him into a woman, a feminized, Latinized godmother. Furthermore, this Death is divided into two, since he has in his service a major-domo, or steward, who is also dressed in black, who summons for him those who are about to die and who remains in contact, at the end of the tale, with the physician–hero. Unfortunately, Bédat de Monlaur made a mediocre French translation of the tale and did not even give the original Gascon version, as he collected it. We are reduced, therefore, to seeing the word 'major-domo', used by Bédat de Monlaur, as the equivalent of 'usher' [*huissier*, in French; *huché*, in Occitan], used by Fabre to describe the official functions, in particular as the herald of death, carried out by Quincarlot [79–80].

In any case, the murderous, macabre, satanic aspects of Quincarlot, as a sub-division of grandmother Death, are perfectly clear.

First, let us remember that this character was one of three swindlers described by Fabre as thieves but whose names soon come to be associated with death or murder.

In the first version, they are called Crouquet, Jacquet and Quincarlot. The first name means 'hook'; the second is simply a diminutive of Jacques; and the third means 'cockroach'.[16] The second version complicates matters: Crouquet has lost his original name and is now called Renâouvi, which in Occitan means a 'widower who has married a widow'. In short, Death squared. This particular hook is certainly not for catching small fry. He attends to only the larger catches. Jacquet has also changed identity; or rather, like Truquette,[17] he has dropped his harmless pilgrim's Christian name and is now called Carcanas ('buzzard'], a bird of prey that devours the carcasses of dead animals. It is said of him [32, second version] that he is *as clever as Cartouche* [*scavant coûma Cartatoucha*]. The real Cartouche (who died in 1721), a famous swindler, was not excessively blood-thirsty. However, the rather fanciful redoubling in the Occitan name Cartatoucha of the sound *ta-to*, with four sounded syllables, instead of the two in French, suggests the *tartarassa*, a devourer of poultry, which crops up in other works of Fabre[18] and is again a synonym—homonym of *Carcanas*, a bird of prey. This is, moreover, a way of bringing out the first syllable *Car* of *Car*tatoucha, *Car*canas and the second syllable *car* of Quin*car*lot. This is quite simply the Occitan word *car*, meaning 'flesh', living or dead, bloody or decaying, on which the bird feeds. At the end of the narrative, Fabre stresses the importance of this *car* [*chair*, in French] [85]. Indeed, the abbé indulges in a number of puns, of which Philippe Gardy has provided an excellent analysis, on *car* (a French and Occitan conjunction that means 'in effect' or 'because') and on *car*, the Occitan word for 'flesh'. In this case, the reference is to the succulent flesh of Babeau, made pregnant by Jean-l'ont-pris; the flesh of this young woman was spared, however, by Quincarlot, who predestined for death only the rotten flesh of Barbe-Garouille. But in the case of the triptych formed by Crouquet/Renâouvi, or 'hook-widower of a widow'; *Car*canas/ *Car*tatoucha, the bandit Cartouche carcass-eating bird; and one-eyed Quin*car*lot, or the one-eyed Cockroach who soon will become Satan-the-gibbet, this thrice repeated, stressed *car* ['flesh'] can only refer to 'meat', which the carnivores – whether they are hooks, birds or insects [19] – want to kill or eat. I have already stressed in a preceding paragraph the macabre significance of a missing right eye and a surviving left eye, both applicable to Quincarlot: the evil eye, the sign of a corpse that is not really dead and that therefore becomes dangerous. Moreover, so that there should be no doubt on the matter, Quincarlot also wears his purse on the left [32]. Grandmother Death, who is officially a member of Quincarlot's 'partnership', also emphasizes all this: she is on the left, terribly on the left, in the sinister sense of the term. She is fond of hiding her right eye with her combustible hat of matches; she plays, like Quincarlot, at being one-eyed; she conceives her daughter 'on the left'; her treasure, like Quincarlot's purse, is found on the left; and she leaves it to her grandson on the left side [70].

The grandmother and Quincarlot/Satan-the-gibbet follow each other in the same functions of death, or herald of death, throughout the development of the narrative. Yet these two characters remain distinct from each other: in AT 322 Death is an ambivalent character. He arrives from above, from heaven: he is 'from God' at the beginning of the canonical narrative of the tale; then he gradually descends towards the lower, 'infernal' regions, towards the subterranean depths of his cave or cellar, where, beneath his castle, destined to burn out, are the candles of life. The story-tellers of *Godfather Death* have marked this descent of Death in many ways: descent from a tree; from a carriage, coach or cart; from heaven; from a dominant position; or from an attic or a loft at the very beginning of the narrative. There is then a gradual descent towards the cellar or cave at the end. In *Jean-de-trop*, Death, perched at the beginning on her carriage or coach, is still an intimate of Our Lord *God*. By the end of *JDT*, everything has changed. 'Our Lord' is delighted to learn that she is shut up in a hermetically sealed receptacle; in this way, she can no longer send damned souls to the *devil*. In *Jean-l'ont-pris*, from the attic from which she descends in haste [22], to the grave in which she is buried, from the comic comparison with the Virgin of Mercy, to the final descent into the Huguenots' burial pit, the grandmother also follows, in the burlesque mode of Fabre's novella, a descending trajectory. In any case, even if at moments there is a whiff of sulphur about her (her matches), she is not Satan. On the contrary, Quincarlot, the one-eyed bearer of misfortune, is presented to us as a Satan, a Beelzebub, a walking gibbet. He is from hell, and he takes to hell his unfortunate victim, Barbe-Garouille. He is close, on this point, to the devil (first the protector, then the destroyer of the hero) who is directly substituted for Death in the 'Swiss tale'; close also to the devil who, following the character of Death, animates the last part of the Austro-baroque version of AT 322, a close relation of our *Jean-de-trop*, collected by Vernaleken in 1864.

It is true that Quincarlot has grown into his role during the development of Fabre's novella. For a long time, indeed, Quincarlot is merely one personality among others within the forces of death surrounding the astute grandmother. These forces also include the *consul*, the riff-raff and the men in blue from Solorgues who arrest Truquette and take him to his death, at the hands of the executioner of Nîmes. In a more general way, the forces of death comprise the Huguenot community of Solorgues, that cursed Babylon, that manure pit, run by its corrupt municipality. Among these 'municipal' employees of ill omen, we also find the vineyard-keepers . . .

The grandmother dies; from then on, Quincarlot assumes his independence, his individual identity as an autonomous force of death or, at any rate, as herald of death.[20] He had already been present at Truquette's execution, and not as a condemned man. For the good cobbler, loyal and guileless, the faithful friend that he had always been, had never for a moment thought of implicating, that is to say, denouncing, Quincarlot. Quincarlot, witness of the hanging of his ex-accomplice, functioned, in short, as a kind of moral assistant to the executioner, as a pseudo-chaplain reciting with the victim, not without inner pleasure, the prayers for the dying [80]. The picture is made clearer when Quincarlot appears before JLP to inform him of the Garouille affair. From then on, the one-eyed man is characterized by the young man, quite explicitly, as a Satan–scaffold, a walking gibbet[21] [79–81].

We should add that this Quincarlot, as Marcel Barral observed, acquired the distinction of a Lucifer. He becomes a sort of gentleman, a diabolical lord of death who begins to speak more and more in French, or to mix French words with his native Occitan.[22] Then, as the grandmother had before, Quincarlot now surrounds himself with forces of death: he uses the lying evidence of the vineyard-keepers; he walks around with an escort of henchmen of his own kind [80]. He was only one of Death's assistants. By acting as the hero's *godfather*,[23] he becomes, in this last part of the novella, the unquestionable leader of death, until he is in turn supplanted by another, more distinguished leader, the baron. As Death's herald, Quincarlot is the first to announce Truquette's death on the scaffold [79]. Then, after this *a posteriori* information, comes the prediction of Garouille's imminent death and the actual death of the unfortunate woman; this prediction followed by its effect will be the exact, but inverted counterpart of what had been the announcement of Sestier's cure [60]. It will be recalled that this same announcement, concerning the powerful man's tribulations, had been preceded by a fight and followed by a complete cure. One must also remember that during this episode of the initial fight, J L P had first been seriously attacked by the hair. Then, thanks to the celebrated permutation of 180 degrees ($\frac{\pi}{2}$), he had completely tricked the forces of death. The rest followed logically enough: the rest, that is to say, the vineyard-keepers' attack on Sestier, then the announcement of the imminent success of the treatment and, lastly, the powerful man's complete recovery. In short, things had temporarily begun badly (for J L P) and had ended well (for Sestier).

This time, in the Quincarlot–J L P–Garouille episode, the opposite is the case; things begin well (for J L P) and end badly (for Garouille). It is true that one is in a situation that is the reverse of the preceding one: announcing death (for Garouille), rather than announcing cure (for Sestier).

J L P's *first* arrest, carried out by the antagonistic vineyard-keepers, who pull him by the hair, was a drama that might have turned out tragically – the hero could not have got out of it except by a trick. His *second* arrest, by Quincarlot, is a pleasant enough comedy that turns into farce.

Certainly, this 'second episode', that of 'putting the hero under arrest', does not begin in too promising a way. The chief warder, Quincarlot/Satan/Beelzebub, reminds the hero of a 'gibbet' and an 'executioner' [79–81]. His henchmen seize J L P by the *scruff of the neck*, as the vineyard-keepers had once done, and tie his arms behind him. But this inauspicious impression does not last. The reader is soon reassured. Quincarlot tries to appease the hero's fears. We breathe a sigh of relief. It should be stressed that the forces of death that surround and include Quincarlot, and that obey him, behave, in this instance, in a non-violent way. They do not attack the head, as they did in their earlier fight (see Chapter X). We remember that Truquette, Jean-l'ont-pris and Sestier had always been attacked, previously, at the *top* of the body, that is, at the head. The lowest blows, during the decisive struggle, did not descend below the navel: a stone thrown at Sestier's stomach [59]. And it is only during the first skirmish that J L P received 'seven or eight hundred blows on [the] shins' [54]. When things really did get serious, the vineyard-keepers grabbed him by the hair. So much so that as a reaction to these 'anti-head' practices, Truquette and Jean-l'ont-pris, both quite unconnected with the forces of death, tended to attack their opponents' bellies or backs. It comes, therefore, as some relief that the warders, led by Quincarlot-the-gibbet, attack, not J L P's head, nor even his chest, but, instead, cut the cord that held up his trousers [80], which fall grotesquely around his ankles. The very fact that the warders in question are called *coupe-jarrets* ['cut-throats', literally 'ham-stringers'] is significant. According to the classic encoding of A T 332/ *Godfather Death*, the meaning is quite clear: Death is no longer situated at the victim's *head*, the position in which, canonically, he is at his most dangerous; dangerous also because he is planning at this point to strangle him, twist his neck, cut off his head, etc. Death now stands at the young man's *feet*, like a well-behaved dog; around his ankles; his legs are ridiculously bared, but that is not serious. In this way J L P succeeds in doing what so many godson physicians in versions of A T 332 had such difficulty in achieving when they had to switch not only the patient's bed, but, later, their own bed, in order to put Death at their feet, thus protecting themselves from Death's attacks.[24] When he *himself* occupies this strategic position, at the patient's feet, Death indicates *ipso facto* that he is no longer lethal; he indicates in this way that he is sparing the life of the individual who, at another time, might have been his victim. In this instance it is Jean-l'ont-pris who is involved. Should we say that, once more, the permutation of 180 degrees has been carried out?

It is, in fact, carried out, but in a very different way from that of the previous occasion. During the vineyard-keeper's earlier attack, Jean-l'ont-pris had his arms tied behind his back, as he does now at the hands of Quincarlot; but he had also been immobilized, tied to the peach-tree or torture post. He had been viciously attacked on the head and on the hair. He owed his salvation only to the fact that, by a classic trick, he had changed places with the son of his persecutor, thus performing a permutation of 180 degrees on the *horizontal* plane – adopting the precise course of the godson physician tricking Death, when the latter turns his own bed around. In addition to this, he had whistled a few times in his young adversary's ears, thus using the magical 'mouth instrument' that, according to a version of AT 332 from central France, accompanies the obligatory panoply of the perfect hero who tricks Death.[25]

The forces of death, ridiculed and neutralized, had now been proved powerless to kill not only the hero, but even Monsieur Sestier. Apparently knocked senseless by them, this powerful man was soon on his feet again, even before being subjected, for form's sake, to the obligatory 'treatment' of a placebo of cold water.

This time, on the hero's second arrest, the situation is quite different. It is Death himself who, with the best will in the world, is to carry out a permutation of 180 degrees on the *vertical* plane, from the hero's head to his feet.[26] This is almost unprecedented in the long international list of versions of AT 332, where there is virtually no instance of a spontaneous conversion of Death to harmlessness (at this stage of the narrative) or of a *vertical* permutation of 180 degrees. But it should be said that the inversion-twist to the classic schema of AT 332 that Fabre has carried out in the second part of *JLP* is so new (finally putting back on its feet the canonical structures of the tale, which for some time the abbé had left upside-down) that it justified this kind of radical audacity (see the end of this chapter).

In any case, Death viciously attacked the hero's head during his first arrest. During the second arrest, he attacks only the lower parts of his body, feet and legs. Indeed, the word 'attack' is perhaps rather exaggerated in this case. There are no blows, merely a pitiful, humorous strip-tease. It is as though Death himself is giving the hero a present of his life. We are no longer at the stage of *Death's attacks*, but at the quite different stage of *Death's gifts*; having been transformed from grandmother into Quincarlot, from vineyard-keepers into ruffians, Death has taken on a decidedly kinder face.

Once again, in this second part of the novella (*JLP* in the strict sense, after the story of Truquette), we are faced with an absolutely total inversion of the classic schema, as outlined by Bolte and Polivka and then by Aarne and Thompson.

Table 14

FIRST SKETCH OF THE 'INVERSION'

(A) 'Classic schema' of AT 332/*Godfather Death* (development of the plot from top to bottom)

   (1) Death becomes godfather (phase a)
   (2) Death's gifts (phase b)
   (3) Death tricked (phase c)
   (4) revenge attack by Death (phase d)

(B) Schema (reverse of previous one) of the second part of Fabre's novella (J L P's autobiography, or *JLP 2*) (development of the plot from top to bottom)

   (1) attack by Death (phase d)
   (2) Death tricked (phase c)
   (3) Death's gifts (phase b)
   (4) return of godfather Death (phase a)

Moreover, Death, whose functions (after the grandmother's death) have been taken over by Quincarlot, will now present Jean-l'ont-pris with the most splendid of presents (apart from his life and the treasure), though in doing so he remains Death: he will present to the hero, 'on a silver platter', the life or rather the death of Barbe-Garouille. In other words, he will kill Barbe-Garouille, thus providing the young couple, Jean-l'ont-pris and Babeau, with well-founded hopes of happiness, marriage and wealth. At a stroke, all the young man's difficulties will be resolved; the hero will pocket the 100 pistoles that constitute the 'silver platter' which Monsieur Sestier, as a good prince, has offered as the prize to the brave young man who will rid him of his old mistress Garouille by marrying her. Certain of Garouille's imminent death, J L P marries her and remains her hus-

band for only a few weeks; then, having been made a widower, he
will marry, or so he hopes, the powerful man's daughter, whom he
has made pregnant. In this way he will increase his 'treasure' of over
20,000 *livres*, secretly 'inherited' from the grandmother; they will be
added to the 60,000 *livres* that he hopes to inherit through Babeau.
Killing three birds with one stone, the hero, in another area, even gets
the support of Quincarlot-the-gibbet, who is now kinder than ever;
he thus lays the stepping-stones for a future reconciliation with
Sestier. Sestier will have been relieved, thanks to JLP, of a cumbersome, unappetizing mistress; the hero will therefore have everything
to gain, after this woman's death, by getting back into the good graces
of the man whose son-in-law he ought in principle to become. Indeed,
this imminent son-in-law will prove simultaneously to be rich, the
father-to-be of a descendant for the powerful man, who will thus be
made a grandfather, and heir presumptive to this powerful man's
'kingdom', or, rather, to his large estate.

The trick of 'death inflicted by Death on a third person', to the
great advantage of the physician–hero of AT 332, has a long ancestry
in *Godfather Death*. We meet it,[27] in various Occitan, Andalusian and
Germanic versions of AT 332. In these versions, the hero is, of course,
advised by Death, who is invisible to everybody but him. He has only
to establish the infallibility of his diagnosis, which will then bring
him fat fees, by declaring the imminent death of some individual; in
fact, the hero knows, from a reliable source, that this individual will
die. The fatal event proves the doctor–hero's diagnosis to be correct,
to the astonishment of all. In this way he can pursue a profitable
medical career, without the recognition of the Faculty. It is simply
that in the classic 'four-part' versions of AT 332, this episode occurs
at the beginning of the second stage (b) of the tale,[28] followed by a
third and a fourth stage (c and d); this second stage (b) concerns
'Death's gifts'. However, in JLP's autobiography, an inverted (because literary and encoded) version of the fairy-tale, such an episode
occurs at the end of the penultimate stage of the plot, this stage itself
being devoted to 'Death's gifts'.[29]

Such a shift of stage 2 (paragraph A, Table 14) to stage 3
(paragraph B, Table 14), which derives from an inversion, belongs
to the general structures of the autobiography of JLP himself, an
autobiography that in the novel comes after the life of Truquette,

previously recounted by his son. This inversion requires some explanation. I shall come back to it.

In any case, Quincarlot, in his short speech to J L P [83], proceeds unquestionably to the announcement of a death, that of Barbe-Garouille. By acting in this way, this herald follows A T 332, in which the prediction, by Death, of the death of a patient who may bring 'treasure' to the hero [83] plays an absolutely central role.

However, the novelist comes up against certain technical difficulties here. Normally, in A T 332, this act of prediction must take place at the patient's bedside, Death placing himself (usually) at the patient's head. He is seen there by only the godson physician, remaining invisible to everyone else around the bed. He indicates the diagnosis by the position that he occupies in relation to the patient.

The head–foot dialectic, with its initial permutation of 180 degrees, has been fully employed, as we have seen, in relation to J L P. Sestier, too, experiments personally on two occasions with the prone position of an individual threatened by Death: the forces of death strike the rich farmer on the head and lay him out on the ground; Sestier then revives, stands up and wanders off, only to find himself once more horizontally on a bed, so that the indispensable placebo of cold water can be administered to him.[30]

With Barbe-Garouille, things are not so easy. Certainly, she is seriously ill and will soon have to take to her bed. It is 'feet first' (how could it be otherwise?) that J L P has her taken on a cart to the hospital at Sommières, where she dies almost on arrival. Sommières, a Protestant town, a town of misfortune, had certainly spelled *ill fortune* for Truquette, who had brought from that town, on carts or donkeys [31], the stolen goods that were to bring about his downfall; conversely, in so far as J L P is an anti-Truquette, Sommières brings him *good fortune*, since he is able to take on a cart the body of his short-lived wife, Garouille, and thus rid himself of her.

During Garouille's lifetime, however, Jean-l'ont-pris has sworn never to come within two hundred paces of that 'horrible beast', whose very smell is unbearable [83]. He tolerates an exception to this rule only during the few moments it takes a priest to bless his brief marriage to her [83, second version]. There is no question for J L P of going anywhere near his wife's bed after their wedding, and with good reason. In fact, the hero has no need of a bed, as he learns well enough. We have seen that Barbette-Garouille is in reality a frightful double, or to be more precise a 'division', of that dear Babette or Babeau, who functions, as far as the hero is concerned, as the ultimate prize. Now it is with Babeau, not with Garouille, that JLP will go to bed (secretly) – not in order to treat Babeau, since she is in perfect health, but in order to make her pregnant.

With Barbette-Garouille, therefore, there is no question of a 'bed'. The place has already been taken by Babette. The silent position of the Death of AT 332, who places himself without a word at the patient's head to signify his imminent death, will be replaced, therefore, in *JLP* by the words spoken by Quincarlot-the-gibbet to Jean-l'ont-pris, who does not even have to be a placebo-physician to carry out perfectly the simple role of typical hero of *Godfather Death* – the hero whom Death informs of a fatal prognosis concerning a third person, and who has made up his mind to benefit from this strategic information. Quincarlot's speech contains the announcement of Garouille's death in the form of a long, detailed, convincing list of the unfortunate woman's diseases. For good measure, however, Fabre will transpose once more into his realistic code what, in the classic version of AT 332 as known to him, appeared at the level of the fantastic code.[31] The usual character of Death in AT 332, at the patient's bedside, is (magically) seen by only the physician. Similarly, when Quincarlot-the-gibbet makes his announcement of Garouille's imminent death, he is careful to move away from the ruffians who accompany him; at the moment he must be seen by only JLP, for whom his message is intended [80].

Quincarlot emphasizes this distinctiveness and chosen isolation by using on this occasion a somewhat castrated, even French-based language.[32] As the herald of death, Quincarlot is identified, in this episode, with the lord of Death to be found, in this same role, in a southern French version of AT 332.[33] We are a long way from the time when this one-eyed individual, in Truquette's lifetime, in the first part of the novella, was merely the first of a trio of swindlers – macabre, certainly, perhaps even sinister. In this second part of the narrative devoted to the autobiography of JLP himself, Quincarlot/Cancrelas has grown in stature. It is just as well. As usher or chamberlain of Death, he has, by logical and successive steps, come to embody death directly. The grandmother had personified death for a long time. But she disappears well before the end of the novella; she therefore leaves a place to be occupied, and it is Quincarlot who takes it.

The announcement of Garouille's imminent death, spoken by Quincarlot, brings with it, before long, the conclusion of the narrative. Sestier's ex-mistress, having become the hero's wife for a brief period, does in fact die.

JLP will now be able to fulfil his finest dream and make the best of his widowerhood. He will soon marry, at least that is what the novelist leaves the reader to hope, the powerful man's daughter. Meanwhile, the young man has taken the wise precaution of making her pregnant. If all goes well and the wedding takes place, the hero's treasure and the inheritance left by Sestier will form a single fortune. It will lend respectability to the young man's rather suspect, ill-gotten treasure; in other words, the 'dirty' money that the grandmother had surreptitiously deducted from Truquette's swindling. JLP hopes one day to succeed, in insolent wealth, to 'his father-in-law the king', that is to say, to the rich farmer whose daughter he will (?) marry. All's well that seems to end well . . . Is it a happy ending? We cannot be entirely sure. At the very moment when JLP ends his story for the edification of the baron, Babeau is certainly pregnant. But she is not yet married. The wedding may well take place – but who will live to see it!

A general consideration now arises in relation to JLP's double narrative: that concerning his father, and his own. There is no problem about the first part (Truquette's biography). It canonically reproduces the classic structures of AT 332, as they are to be found in the other regional versions of this tale type, and especially in *Jean-de-trop*, the closest local homologue of *JLP*, not to mention the 'Swiss tale'. Things are not quite so clear in the case of the second part of Fabre's novella, that concerning the young hero's autobiography. Certainly, we have recognized in passing a number of motifs that are directly or closely linked to similar elements of AT 332/*Godfather Death*: predictions of cure or of death; a paramedical, if not medical hero; the placebo of cold water; grandmother Death as equivalent of godfather Death; the classic division of the character of Death, who is duplicated (as second-in-command) by the devil, which, in our narrative, makes Quincarlot succeed the grandmother; the use, in a coded or an adapted

form, apart from *Jean-le-sot*, of *The Spirit in the Bottle* (AT 331) –
this tale, in Brittany or the Midi, beginning with *Jean-de-trop*,
becomes closely associated with AT 332 (which does not prevent it
from being quite independent in other versions). However, the *general*
question of the structure occurs in the second part of the novella. Did
Fabre confine himself to constructing this part by dissecting the tale
type of *Godfather Death*, beginning with regional versions that he
knew, and then amusing himself by dotting JLP's autobiography
with these fragments, where they appear as disjointed limbs floating
about in some ambient liquid? Or can we also recognize in this second
part, as in the first, the legible structure, if reversed in this specific
case, of *Godfather Death*?

We have already had occasion to remark that Jean-l'ont-pris's
autobiography (the second part of the novella) is constructed in such
a way as to be exactly the reverse of the second (homologous) part
of *Jean-de-trop*.

This inversion is both reassuring and odd.

Jean-de-trop (second part)	*Jean-l'ont-pris* (second part)
(1) The hero takes advantage of *Death's gifts* to marry the powerful man's daughter.	(1) The hero *tricks the forces of death* and grandmother Death in particular; he gets treasure from her.
(2) The hero *tricks Death* and gets from her new advantages for his young wife.	(2) The hero uses this treasure as a *gift of Death* to seduce, make pregnant and possibly marry the powerful man's daughter.

It is *reassuring* because it confirms that the second part of *JLP*
(like the first, devoted to Truquette) derives from AT 332, itself
embodied in *Jean-de-trop* and in other regional, eighteenth-century
versions, these being the legitimate or putative ancestors of those
collected in the Occitan-speaking region from the 1870s onwards,
including *Jean-de-trop*.

However, it is also *odd*: never among the numerous Occitan versions, certainly, but also never among the Nivernais, Breton, Catalan, Italian, Mexican, German, Jewish, Irish, Greek, Bulgarian or Turkish versions that I have consulted,[34] have I met such an inversion of the structure of the myth.[35] In this matter, the abbé Fabre made full use of his rights as a literary creator; they allowed him to depart from the folkloric raw material that he had used as his initial source of inspiration. But how far, in this matter, do insolence in freedom and survival in fidelity go? Before answering, perhaps we should examine in greater detail the structure of AT 332 itself; it, too, should be considered in its relations with the Occitan versions of the tale, and with that 'literary', and therefore peculiar, version of it – *JLP*.

Bolte and Polivka in 1913, and then Aarne and Thompson in 1928 and 1961, revealed the four successive phases that characterize the recurrent structure of *Godfather Death*. The first two authors, in 1913, based their comments on more than 120 versions of AT 332, which were then known, written down, published or collected; this corpus extended over 600 years – from 1300 to 1900 – from Gibraltar to the Urals, and from the Baltic to Palestine, via the Occitan-speaking regions (*Jean-de-trop* included). Aarne and Thompson, in 1928 and again in 1961, added still further to this corpus hundreds of additional versions of the tale type; these had been collected in the meantime in the Christian world (and even in Jewish and Turkish regions) of Europe and the Near East, and in America (Quebec, Latin America, among the Irish, Armenian, Lithuanian immigrants in the United States, etc.), which had become Christian. I shall later analyse this schema, then, by comparing it with the Occitan versions that are most relevant in this matter: *Jean-de-trop*, of course; but also the Provençal versions collected by Mistral; the many fine versions from Ariège collected by Mir and Delample, Joisten, the *Almanach de l'Ariège* of 1895, Perbosc and Cézerac, and Adelin Moulis; the Gascon version of Bédat de Monlaur; Arnaudin's version from the Landes; Dezeuze's version from Cévennes-Montpellier (geographically so close to our *JLP*); Dujardin's version from Limousin (1911); Auguste Ferrand's version from Dauphiné; the Catalan versions of Amades and Maspons; Caseponce's version from Roussillon; Dardy's version from Agen; Marie-Aimée Méraville's version from the Auvergne ... All these versions possess their letters patent of nobility; several, and not the least of them, were collected in the last quarter of the nineteenth century. I shall, therefore, try to cover as much as possible of the region that I shall call, very generally, 'Occitan' (Gascon, Catalan, Provençal, Franco-Provençal . . .). However, I shall keep one eye on other French and foreign versions and on *Jean-l'ont-pris*, and the other eye, so to speak, on Bolte and Polivka and on Aarne and Thompson.

The title of AT 332, according to Aarne and Thompson (1928 or 1961), is '*Godfather Death*; man as doctor. Death at the patient's feet. The bed or the patient himself is swung round at an angle of 180 degrees on the horizontal plane'.

I. FIRST PHASE: *Death as godfather* (or often, in the Latin countries, *godmother*). A poor man chooses Death as godfather (or as godmother) because he regards him (her) as more just, more equitable, than any other figure of like importance – more equitable than, for example, 'the good God', 'Our Lord', 'the devil', the Virgin, St Peter, the king, etc. (Joisten, Gibert and Maugard, Dezeuze, *Almanach de l'Ariège*, Mistral, Bédat de Monlaur, etc.).

II. SECOND PHASE: *Death's gifts*. Death gives the poor man himself, Death's *compère* (Bédat de Monlaur, Mistral), or his son, Death's godson (Joisten, Gibert and Maugard, *Almanach de l'Ariège*, Dezeuze), the power to see Death at the head or foot of the patient's bed; Death also gives him the ability to make a diagnosis, fatal or not, as to the outcome of the disease from which the patient is suffering. These gifts bring prosperity in the form of fat medical fees to Death's *compère* or godson. In some versions (*Jean-de-trop*), the gifts in question are simply prosperity for Death's *compère*, but precise and canonical medical diagnosis only for Death's *godson*.

III. THIRD PHASE: *Death is tricked*. The physician tricks his protector (Death) in many ways, but particularly by swinging round the patient's bed (Bédat de Monlaur, etc.), at the end of which Death was standing in a position that spelled death for the patient (this position generally being at the patient's head or occasionally, in certain versions, at his feet). The French versions, from the Midi and elsewhere, and also Catalan, Flemish, Austrian and Quebec versions also used, as a ruse to deceive Death, a trick that consists in shutting Death up, temporarily at least, in a receptacle (Gibert and Maugard, *Jean-de-trop*, *Almanach de l'Ariège*). In six versions – two of them French

(Nivernais and Quebec), one Irish, one Scottish, one Lithuanian and one situated on the edge of the German baroque region (Austria) – these two tricks (swinging round of the patient's bed, then shutting Death up in a bottle) are used successively by the same hero, in the same narrative, against Death or against the supernatural entity (the devil) who is related to death.[36] In every case, this trickery leads to considerable benefits for the physician (cure of a powerful man); such benefits are often followed by an advantageous marriage to the daughter of this powerful man, who herself may have been cured by the hero. The benefits in question may also consist of a period of survival, temporary at least, conferred on the doctor himself; otherwise, he would be threatened with imminent death.

IV. FOURTH PHASE: *Death takes his revenge and attacks the hero.* Is he not furious at being tricked? With a view to this attack, he takes the physician down into the cave or cellar of lights: this is a kind of cavernous, even infernal, Beyond, situated underground – for example, under Death's castle. He kills the hero by extinguishing his light, his 'candle of life', which hitherto had kept him alive. This is what takes place in Mistral, Bédat de Monlaur, etc. In other cases (*Almanach de l'Ariège*), Death kills the physician quite simply when she suddenly emerges from her 'bottle', the receptacle–trap in which the hero had shut her up, having finally succeeded in one way or another in getting free. In several versions (*JDT 1* and *JDT 2*, for example),[37] the final disappearance of the hero, who is unquestionably doomed to die and is therefore a victim (like everybody else) of an act of revenge or of an attack by Death, is simply hinted at or postponed for a while, but it is not, for all that, annulled.

One of these four phases may be missing. Thus in the Provençal version collected by Mistral in 1876, phase III (*Death tricked*) does not appear. We pass directly from the first phase (*Death as godfather*), followed by the second (*Death's gifts*) to the fourth (*Death takes his revenge*), short-circuiting the third phase (*Death tricked*), which is missing. We should note that in this 'Mistral version', Death does not have to 'take revenge' in phase IV, since he has not been previously tricked in phase III. In such a case, the fourth phase will be called simply *Death attacks and kills the physician* (after taking him to the cellar of the lights of life). According to this hypothesis, he kills him not in a spirit of revenge, but simply by carrying out Death's natural functions, namely, to kill all living beings.

If we apply this same four-part schema of Bolte and Polivka and of Aarne and Thompson, concerning AT 332, to the two successive parts of the tale *Jean-de-trop* (homologue of *JLP*) and to the *first part* of *Jean-l'ont-pris* itself (in other words, to the biography of Truquette) what do we get? In fact, we know that this four-part schema applies perfectly to the three texts: its canonical order is still respected, even if one of the four phases of the schema may be missing in one or another of the three narratives – that is, *JDT 1* (life of Jean-de-trop's father), *JDT 2* (life of Jean-de-trop himself) and *JLP 1* (life of Truquette, Jean-l'ont-pris's father). I am ignoring for the moment the case of *JLP 2* (Jean-l'ont-pris's autobiography). Let us see, therefore, how the four-part schema is adjusted to the first three texts mentioned (see Table 15).

Of course, the comparison between columns B and D of Table 15 merely provides an overall glimpse of the homology between the life of Truquette (column D, or *JLP 1*) and the life of Jean-de-trop's father (column B, or *JDT 1*). The detailed demonstration, which alone can decide the validity of this homology, is to be found in Chapter IX (life of Truquette). I simply wanted to recall here, very briefly, how the four-part structure of AT 332/*Godfather Death* informs respectively three narratives: that is, the two successive parts of *Jean-de-trop* (*JDT 1* and *JDT 2*) and the first part of *Jean-l'ont-pris* (*JLP 1*, or the life of Truquette, which is homologous with the first part of *JDT*, or *JDT 1*).

Can the second part of *JLP* (or *JLP 2*), in other words, the autobiography of the hero JLP himself after the disappearance of his father, also be related, in a decisive way, to this four-part structure? The detailed study that I have carried out of the motifs contained in this strictly autobiographical second part already lead one to believe that it can. But only an overall view, yet to be defined, can carry conviction in such a field.

In the circumstances, we should remember the abbé Fabre's starting-point. He wanted to make the character of Jean-l'ont-pris an 'anti-Truquette'. Or, at least, he depicted the son (the hero) as the inverted, quasi-triumphant replica of his father. Truquette certainly enjoys a brief moment of insolent prosperity. But this Capitol is for

Table 15

APPLICATION OF THE FOUR-PART SCHEMA OF *GODFATHER/DEATH*

A	B	C	D
According to Bolte and Polivka and to Aarne and Thompson: *four-part structure of the tale* AT 332/*Godfather Death*	*JDT 1* (first part of *JDT*: life of hero's father)	*JDT 2* (second part of *JDT*: life of hero himself)	*JLP 1* (first part of *JLP*: life of Truquette) homologue of *JDT 1*, itself localized here in column B.
A1	B1	C1	D1
Death as godfather (or godmother)	A poor man (JDT's father) chooses Death as godmother for his child and therefore as his own *commère*.	The child (JDT) of a poor man becomes, through his baptism, Death's godson (= reference to B1).	A poor man (Truquette) makes the daughter of a certain old woman pregnant. This old woman occupies the strategic position of the Death of AT 332, and she functions as the child's grandmother/godmother and therefore simultaneously as Truquette's mother-in-law *commère*.

A2	B2	C2	D2
Death's gifts	Death brings prosperity to the poor man and his family.	Death gives JDT the gift of seeing Death at the foot of the patient's bed; thanks to this infallible diagnostic ability, JDT marries the king's daughter and becomes rich.	The mother-in-law *commère* brings prosperity to the poor man Truquette (whom she turns into a swindler) and to his family.
A3	**B3**	**C3**	**D3**
Death tricked	Nothing.	The hero tricks Death (by shutting her up in a gourd); in this way he gets an additional favour from her.	Nothing.
A4	**B4**	**C4**	**D4**
Death takes revenge and kills the hero (or simply attacks and kills him)	The poor man (and his wife) quietly disappear from the story.	The hero is supposed to live for two hundred years. Death will take him only after the official end of the tale.	The poor man dies, executed by hanging, at the hands of the hangman of Nîmes, an agent of the forces of death.

him only two steps away from the Tarpeian Rock. In the end, the unfortunate fellow seems, in his final moments on the scaffold, to be the victim of the System – of the *hangman* of Nîmes. In short, he is the anti-hero *par excellence*.

In contrast with this father, born only to die a loser, the gradually or, at least, temporarily victorious vocation of the hero Jean-l'ont-pris emerges in the first lines of his autobiography. And this occurs at the decisive moment when, unlike his father, he has rejected the bewitching teaching of grandmother Death. From this moment on, the whole of Truquette's biography is to begin again in the person of his son, but this time, *in reverse*, upside-down.

In other words, Fabre used, in this matter, the sovereign rights that belonged to the writer as a literary creator. He has done what no story-teller or transmitter of oral traditions of the hundreds of known versions of AT 332, what no author[38] working on *Godfather Death*, either dared, wished or was able to accomplish. In this sense the abbé acted as a true writer, and not simply as a traditional story-teller or as a mere adapter.

To be specific: Fabre has radically reversed in the second part of his novella (*JLP* 2, or 'J L P's autobiography') the classic structure of AT 332. His narrative as a whole, in its two parts – *JLP 1* and *JLP 2*, in other words 'Truquette' and 'J L P' – must therefore be read, in Table 16, in the following way: the central column B, the 'outward journey' (Truquette), from top to bottom; the right-hand column C, the 'return journey' (Jean-l'ont-pris), from bottom to top, following the arrow that indicates both the outward and the return journeys, vertically, like a capital U. That is why I have spoken of the game of snakes and ladders (simplified, of course).

Columns A and B of Table 16, read from top to bottom, take up again the data of columns A and D of Table 15. The problem is to see how Jean-l'ont-pris, in column C of Table 16, read from *bottom to top*, mounts in the opposite direction, like a salmon, the torrential collapse suffered by Truquette, a character who had descended or rushed *down* catastrophically *from top to bottom* column B of Table 16. Let us, therefore, follow the arrow in its rising trajectory, on the right in column C; it symbolizes in Table 16 the 'ascending' autobiography of J L P. Let us refer for the details to the preceding chapters (Chapters X, XI, XII). This autobiography was examined closely in the following way.

Table 16

TRUQUETTE AND JEAN-L'ONT-PRIS, OR THE GAME
OF SNAKES AND LADDERS

A From top to bottom: general structure of AT 332		B From top to bottom: story of Truquette (*JLP 1*)		C From bottom to top: story of JLP himself (*JLP 2*)	
(1) Death becomes the hero's godfather or godmother (and therefore *compère* or *commère* of the hero's originally impoverished father)	1	The poor man Truquette becomes the old woman's son-in-law and *compère*.		Hero's return to 'square 1', where his father's adventure had begun (B1).	8
(2) Death's gifts as source of prosperity for the hero	2	Truquette is showered with prosperity thanks to the old woman.		JLP seems to be showered with prosperity by the forces of death (by Quincarlot).	7
(3) Death tricked	3	Nothing (Truquette is certainly too inept to trick the forces of death).		JLP tricks the forces of death, including grandmother/Death.	6
(4) Death takes revenge on, or attacks, the hero	4	Truquette is arrested and hanged.		The old woman (grandmother Death) and the forces of death attack JLP.	5

(1) Line C5, bottom right-hand corner of Table 16: *Attacks on the Hero JLP.*

This is the beginning of J L P's own career: from the outset, he rejects grandmother Death's teaching. However, he knows that this teaching brings an initial apparent prosperity; but it is followed, like a time bomb, by ultimate catastrophe, as the sad fate of Truquette showed. J L P was at first to pay dear for this audacious rejection. He is to begin where Truquette ended. It is a risk that he dares and prefers to take. He will be proved right. The hero, then, is exposed, from this line C5, which constitutes the *first* phase of his autobiography, to the tribulations that usually constitute the final and fourth stage of A T 332. The forces of death try to take revenge on him. To intimidate him, to attack him, even to eliminate him. Various borrowings from the folklore cycle of *Jean-le-sot* allow the abbé to modulate the first stages of this attack. First the hero falls from the top of a tree. He is attacked by grandmother Death's donkey, and then has his head shaved by the old woman herself. The forces of death, as represented by the vineyard-keepers, then attack his hair and tie him to the fatal torture post or peach-tree.

(2) Line C6, right-hand column of Table 16 (from bottom to top): *Death Tricked.*

The cunning hero will get the upper hand all the same. He borrows from the third phase of A T 332, which thus becomes, through the complete inversion effected by Fabre, the second phase of his own story, the classic methods used to trick Death. Truquette had not even considered tricking his 'protectress' (see the 'Nothing' of square B3 of Table 16); J L P, who is much more cunning and audacious, uses the 'permutation of 180 degrees', which ensures his own safety and the cure of a powerful man, who *ipso facto* gives his (ambivalent) 'friendship' to J L P. The young man, engaged in this campaign of trickery, in the end neutralizes his grandmother Death. In order to do so he uses methods that are reminiscent, at the same strategic point of A T 332 and especially in *Jean-de-trop*, of the episode of 'Death imprisoned in a receptacle'. Thanks to this trick, which proves fatal to his grandmother, J L P gets hold of the old woman's treasure. Fabre was able to reckon here on a temporary similarity of plot, or of 'genetic code', between two fairy-tales: he made use, in passing, of

Mme d'Aulnoy's *Finette-Cendron*, mentioned by him as *Céndrousétta-Bachassoun* ['Cinderella the scullery maid', in Occitan].

(3) Line C7, right-hand column of Table 16 (from bottom to top): *Death's Gifts*.

The hero, wriggling like a salmon climbing one by one the successive steps of the dam, continues to mount, in the opposite direction to the normal itinerary, the squares of the structure of AT 332. Here he is in square C7 of this game of snakes and ladders, which, generally speaking, constitutes the novella *JLP*; this square C7 corresponds, line by line, to the second phase (*Death's gifts*) of the canonical structure of AT 332 (left-hand column, A2) and to the third movement of the young man's career (right-hand column, C7): after the *attack submitted to* and *Death tricked*, here we have *Death's gifts*, thanks to which the hero possesses the 'king's daughter' (thanks to which, in this modest peasant fiction, JLP confines himself to 'seducing and making pregnant the powerful man's daughter with a view, later, to contracting a lawful marriage with her'). Indeed, the forces of death, hitherto tamed by the trickery to which they were subjected through their own stupidity in the preceding phase, now react only half-heartedly. One might even say that they have gone over, temporarily – lock, stock and barrel – to the camp of the hero, against whom they do little more than produce a pseudo-attack, as an exercise in saving face. Now represented by Quincarlot-the-gibbet and by his henchmen, they confine their attack to the hero's feet, and not to his vulnerable head; to his trousers, and not to his hair. We have moved from the tragedy of Truquette to the comedy of Jean-l'ont-pris. The forces of death, represented by Quincarlot, have become, in fact, favourable to the young man, offering him the opportune prediction of the imminent death of Barbe-Garouille, Sestier's erstwhile mistress and mother-to-be of his children, whom the rich farmer had tried to palm off on the hero. Jean-l'ont-pris is thus able to benefit from this highly useful information: he will turn to his own advantage a marriage with Garouille, quickly followed by his widowerhood; meanwhile, he seduces Babeau, who will become pregnant as a result, and thus made available for a future marriage with JLP that is now both urgent and realizable. Will Jean-l'ont-pris in these circumstances really be able to achieve his dearest dream? Will he be able to marry

Babeau, the powerful man's daughter? Will the child to be born
of this pre-marital union emerge alive from its mother's womb,
thus enabling the newborn child to accumulate in its cradle all the
gifts of Fortune: the treasure recently discovered by its young father
JLP and the hopes of inheriting Sestier's fortune, which has
accumulated on the head of Babeau, who is the powerful man's
daughter, soon in all likelihood to be the hero's wife and before long
mother of the child? These happy solutions are quite conceivable.
Once they have been achieved, they will complete the phase of
Death's gifts, which in the second part of Fabre's novella remains
'open' and problematic. We do not know, in fact, whether the happy
outcome, the happy ending, will or will not take place. On this matter,
the reader is left unsatisfied. In any case, we now see that the comparison between *JLP 2* and *JDT 2*, in other words, between the
personal biography of Jean-l'ont-pris and the personal biography of
Jean-de-trop, each localized in the respective second parts of the two
overall narratives, yields its full significance. At first sight, we were
faced with what seemed like a simple inversion, involving two phases
of the story.

	Biography of Jean-de-trop (*JDT 2*)	Autobiography of Jean-l'ont-pris (*JLP 2*)
PHASE A (= phase 2 of AT 332, *Death's gifts*)	JDT benefits from Death's *gifts* and marries the king's daughter.	JLP *tricks* the forces of death and obtains a treasure from them.
PHASE B (= phase 3 of AT 332, *Death tricked*)	JDT *tricks* Death and wins new benefits from her.	JLP thus benefits from the *gifts* of the forces of death and places himself in a position to marry the powerful man's daughter.

In fact, this inversion concerns at least *three* phases in the canonical
structure of AT 332. Does the very incompletion of the hero's career,
the story of which seems to be left in suspense, make it impossible

for such a confrontation to be pursued to the final stage (fourth phase) of this career? We shall come back to this. The situation may be summarized, in any case, for the moment in Table 17, which briefly takes up four lines from Table 16.

Table 17

THE GENERAL STRUCTURE OF AT 332 AND
JLP'S AUTOBIOGRAPHY

From top to bottom:
canonical schema of
AT 332

From bottom to top:
JLP 2

DIRECTION OF NARRATIVE DEVELOPMENT

From top to bottom: canonical schema of AT 332	From bottom to top: JLP 2	
1 Death as hero's godfather or godmother	Final arrival of the hero JLP in what would usually be the 'starting square'* of the initially poor hero of AT 332	4
2 Death's gifts to the hero	Gifts of the forces of death to the hero JLP	3
3 Death is tricked by the hero	The forces of death are tricked by the hero JLP	2
4 The hero's godfather Death or godmother Death takes revenge on him and attacks him	The forces of death, including the grandmother acting as godmother, attack the hero JLP in a spirit of revenge	1
	JLP's autobiography	

* See Chapter XIII.

The fact that the hostilities between Death and the hero (*attack* carried out by her on him, and *trickery*, by way of reprisals, carried out by the hero on her) precede in *JLP 2* the receipt of *Death's gifts*, instead of following it as in the four-part canonical schema, Occitan and other, of AT 332, may help us to understand the fleeting use made by Fabre of *Cinderella* or Mme d'Aulnoy's *Finette-Cendron* (see Chapter XI). Indeed, in *Finette-Cendron*, too,[39] the attacks on the heroine *precede* the granting of wonderful benefits, such as the gifts of rich clothes, the meeting with the prince, the recognition of the heroine's identity by the prince by means of the velvet slipper. In the *normal* schema of *Godfather Death*, on the other hand, these attacks on the hero *follow* the granting of benefits. There is a difference, however: in *Finette-Cendron*, the maleficent force (the heroine's mother) and the beneficent force (the fairy godmother) are represented by two quite different characters. In *JLP*, they are the same person (Death grandmother/godmother), who plays successively the role of the maleficent force (attacking the hero directly or through others) and the role of the beneficent force (leaving the hero, on her death, a chest filled with treasure).

Elsewhere, this same fact, already stated (by which, contrary to the canonical schema of AT 332, the *hostilities of Death* precede in *JLP 2* the receipt of *Death's gifts*), has consequences for the very structure of our Languedocian novella: it reverberates in general and in detail on certain characteristic episodes of the narrative. In the first affair (Sestier), the (*dangerous*) attack by the vineyard-keepers on the hero precedes the (*innocuous*) medical prognosis by which Sestier is declared to be cured. In the Quincarlot–Garouille affair, the (*innocuous*) 'attack' by the one-eyed individual on the hero precedes the (tragic and *dangerous*) medical prognosis that announces Barbe-Garouille's imminent death. In the first case, during the phase of the 'Death against the hero' conflict, the tragedy (for the hero) precedes the comedy (for the sick Sestier). In the second case, the reverse is true: during the 'hero showered with Death's gifts' phase, the comedy (for the hero) precedes the tragedy (fatal to the sick Garouille; rewarding for the prognosticating hero). But, in both cases, the *attack* (serious or innocuous) of the forces of death on the hero precedes the deployment of the powers of prognosis (fatal or not) that will characterize *Death's gifts*. In a canonical AT 332 tale, however, the *attack* (in general very serious) by the forces of death on the hero always follows the hero's deployment of the powers of medical prognosis, which were the fruits of *Death's gifts*. By reversing the canonical schema, Fabre has therefore also reversed, on these precise points, the usual order of the factors.

It goes without saying that by constructing the second part of his narrative in this way, Fabre did not actually say to himself, 'I am going to switch, from end to end, in the second part of my novella, the four-part structure of the tale type AT 332, with which I had previously constructed, in accordance with the normal and canonical orientation, my first part, devoted to Truquette.' Fabre had never heard of Aarne and Thompson! It was simply that the abbé knew this four-part schema intuitively through the various regional versions of AT 332 that reached him. He was, we should not forget, a story-teller and a preacher. He then propagated these versions himself. But the abbé was interested, as the rest of his work (especially the plays) shows, in the not always easy or soluble problem of the construction of successful marriages, which must reconcile in principle love and money. This theme was typical of the Midi (see our first part). The abbé wanted, therefore, in the register of marital success (or at least in the register of a semi-marital semi-success, which looked like ending in marriage), to make his hero Jean-l'ont-pris the exact counterpart of what Truquette, JLP's father, had been, in the register of failure. In order to obtain the contra-proof, in other words 'JLP as the reverse of Truquette', in all its purity, the writer Fabre certainly proved bolder than the popular story-tellers, whose specific role was more a matter of transmitting and conserving than of innovating. The abbé wanted to parody *Godfather Death*, known to him hitherto (until 1756) in the form of oral Languedocian versions; with this in view, he wanted to encode, on the basis of the said *Godfather Death*, a cryptic tale that would be both *riddle* and *parable* [2, 45]. He always had a strong leaning to parody, as his burlesque *Aeneid* and *Odyssey*, written in the Occitan language with characters from the Midi, show. He loved the fairy-tales that circulated in his native region, and elsewhere, in the form of orally transmitted versions. One has only to think of his *Trésor de Substancion* and, above all, of his *Soirées de la Vaunage*, now unhappily lost, and his *Contes de Zima*. With these diverse, yet convergent preoccupations in mind, the abbé was led, in the second part of *JLP*, to reverse the basic scenario of AT 332, which he had followed in the first part ('Truquette') of

Jean-l'ont-pris. This scenario of AT 332 had also served as a repetitive model, as such, on two occasions – in the two successive parts of *Jean-de-trop*, a homologue of *Jean-l'ont-pris*. We have seen, and we shall see again in Chapter XIV, that in writing *Jean-l'ont-pris* Fabre had had to use an old version of this *JDT* that has not survived; he also used other regional versions of AT 332, the ancestors of those that were to be collected (*JDT* and others) in the Midi and elsewhere in the nineteenth century.

A simplistic view of Fabre's novella might lead one to suppose that the loop is looped: it would seem that Truquette's unfortunate adventure had now to be 'compensated' for, in terms of a U-turn in the narrative (see Table 16). This favourable compensation would then be effected to the advantage of JLP, the victim's son: he would triumph at the expense of the forces of death.

But such an interpretation of the facts would lack subtlety. In this case, Fabre did not wish to write a sentimental piece of fiction or a comedy of patronage, as so many Occitan plays are, including those of the abbé himself, in which the hero and heroine marry in the fifth act, watched over by their fond parents, neighbours and friends, eyes brimming with tears. *Jean-l'ont-pris* is a hard, uncompromising story. Moreover, as a general rule, AT 332/*Godfather Death*, the initial model of our novella, necessarily ends *badly*, with the victory of Death; this pessimistic end runs counter to the optimism with which the overwhelming majority of fairy-tales end: *they married and lived happily ever after*.[40] As we have seen, the concluding statements of the hero narrator, in *JLP*, are much more prudent in implication: *Jean-l'ont-pris and Babeau may get married and they may have a baby if Babeau's pre-marital pregnancy continues and is concluded normally*. Generally speaking, the 'unhappy' end (in other words, the automatic death of the hero, strangled by Death) characterizes the overwhelming majority of the oral versions of *Godfather Death*. The most that one can expect is that the hero's death will be considerably delayed (by two hundred years in the case of Jean-de-trop!). In certain versions of AT 332, the hero (or the hero's father) corresponds to a maleficent or unfortunate character who, by definition, is immortal: this may be *Bonhomme Misère* (France) or *Père-la-Disette* (Quebec versions) or Hatred and Envy (Italian tale of 1550, or more recent Flemish version). According to this hypothesis, the character with the negative or fearsome name who is thus presented in the plot is victorious over Death at the end of the version of AT 332 in question. However, it is poor consolation to know that Penury, Dearth, Hatred and Envy will accompany mankind forever. This survival has really nothing of a happy ending about it! The impression of pessimism is not therefore averted. On this question, let us turn to Fabre's novella: we see that it does not really have a happy ending. Square 3 of Table 17 (right-hand column) or square C7 of Table 16 represents the phase in which the hero benefits, and seems likely to benefit still further in the future, from Death's gifts. Now this square, 'Death's gifts', the last but one in the four-part schema of *JLP 2*, remains, to say the least, largely unfinished. What, in fact, does the hero *really* have at his disposal at the strategic point that he has reached in this square? He possesses a treasure, but he has not yet been able to invest it in a definite marriage which, among other uses, will serve as a 'screen' for this ill-gotten booty; in fact, this booty might well be scattered to the four winds. Besides, the hero, who is not yet married (contrary to the canonical happy ending of every self-respecting fairy-tale), is not yet even sure that he will get the child that would seal his marriage. Does not Babeau's pregnancy run the risk of arriving prematurely, before the marital union that would ensure the hero's fortune and happiness is concluded? If such a failure occurs, he can say goodbye to both his marriage and his treasure! Moreover, the authorities might well poke their noses into the young man's suspicious activities. In this great game of snakes and ladders, in which the hero seems to come back to the square 'Death's gifts' (which had been occupied by his father before misfortune struck), Fabre has offered only a mitigated happy ending, subject to the hazards of suspense.

In any case, we have arrived at only the third square[41] of JLP's 'ascent'. We have seen, in effect (Table 16, column C), that JLP 'rises' like a salmon in the opposite direction to the canonical structure of AT 332, which Truquette (column B) had lamentably and very normally descended. Truquette had passed

(1) through the 'godfather stage'; that is, from the realistic point of view from which the novella is written, alliance with a woman who

becomes his mother-in-law *commère* and, at the same time, the grand-mother/godmother of his newborn son, the future JLP. Then:

(2) Truquette passed through the stage of Death's gifts (the prosperity that came from the alliance with the old woman). Then:

(3) Truquette leaped over the 'Death tricked' square, incapable as he was (the poor fellow!) of seriously tricking an individual of substance like his mother-in-law. Lastly:

(4) Truquette landed in the square that we have called 'Death's attack on the hero' or, as here, 'on the hero's father',[42] a square in which he loses everything – including his life. Taking up the flame, JLP, impelled by Fabre, refused to repeat his father's mistakes, as many a hero of AT 332, beginning with Jean-de-trop, had done. So JLP reverses the structure. Rejecting his grandmother's teaching, he first comes up against the attacks of the forces of death (first square in his own career, and square C5 of Table 16, right-hand column). He reacts by tricking the forces of death in his own way (second square in his own career, and square C6 of Table 16); in the next square, it seems that he ought to be able to enjoy Death's gifts, that is, his grandmother's treasure and possession of the powerful man's daughter (third square in his own career, and square C7 of Table 16). Lastly, he ends his career in the fourth and last square of his ascent (square C8 of Table 16); this final square of Jean-l'ont-pris's ascent is homologous at the top of the ladder with the first square of Truquette's descent (square B1 of Table 16).

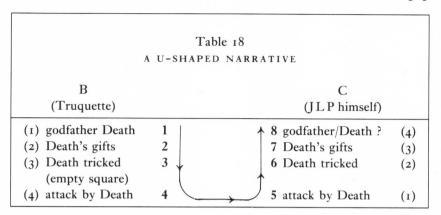

Table 18

A U-SHAPED NARRATIVE

B (Truquette)			C (JLP himself)	
(1) godfather Death	1	8 godfather/Death ?	(4)
(2) Death's gifts	2	7 Death's gifts	(3)
(3) Death tricked (empty square)	3	6 Death tricked	(2)
(4) attack by Death	4	5 attack by Death	(1)

N.B.: The numbers 1, 2, 3, 4 at the far left and the far right of the table correspond, in accordance with the four-part structure of AT 332, to the successive stages of Truquette's descending career and JLP's ascending career. In the middle, the numbers 1 to 8 around the U-shaped arrow mark the steps of this double career spread over the whole length of the novella.

Let us now turn to that square 8 (in Table 18) of the novel, which, at the same time, is square 4 of Jean-l'ont-pris's own career. In short, the hero has to return to square 1, to return, in any case, to the level or to the very position, *by going back*, from which Truquette, the hero's father, had *set out* on his *outward* journey. In other words, it is a question of *taking leave* of godfather Death, here the baron Death, in square 8, after *making contact* (and being contractually bound) through the father with godfather Death (in this case, grandmother Death) in square 1. The starting square, or square 1, at the level of the initial Truquette was that of *Death as godfather* or, quite simply, of 'god-fatherhood': in other words, in the realistic code of the novella, a poor man (Truquette) meets a strong personality (the old woman), who gives this poor man a wife (her daughter), who, in turn, gives him a child (JLP); moreover, the old woman becomes a *de facto commère* (for Truquette) and a *de facto* godmother (for JLP). We then have the move to the following squares: *getting rich* (in square 2, Truquette ceases to be poor); then, leaping over square 3 (*Death tricked*), we come to the *final catastrophe* (square 4). All this takes place as we move from top to bottom.

For Jean-l'ont-pris, the procedure is exactly the reverse: returning from bottom to top, he finally arrives at square 8, after crossing squares 5 (attack on him), 6 (the trickery organized by him) and 7 (getting rich). If one wants the loop to be looped and a snake to eat its own tail, Jean-l'ont-pris, in square 8, must confront a situation at the end of which a supernatural being (in terms of the tale type) or a naturalized being (according to Fabre's realistic code), a being, in any case, who functions as a godfather Death (the very same who through several incarnations has activated the novella from the beginning), will enable him to complete the process by which JLP will take leave of this 'being' himself. This final 'degodfatherization' ought to bring JLP from riches (square 7) to poverty (suggested by square 8). In this case, indeed, Jean-l'ont-pris would return at last, or tend to return through the mediation of that supernatural being (or 'natural-ized' being in the pseudo-realistic framework of the novella), to the initial situation of poverty in which his father, Truquette, found himself in square 1, before Death appeared as godparent of his child.

The loop would indeed be looped. There would indeed be 'a return to square 1'.

Let us now look at what actually takes place in this final square 8 of J L P's itinerary.

The hero seems to have generally benefited in the immediately preceding period (square 7) from 'Death's gifts' (his dead grandmother's treasure; the providential death of a frightful first wife; the hope of marrying Babeau, cleverly made pregnant). Now the hero, at the beginning of square 8, has just met an important individual about whom we do not know much more than that he is a 'lord' or 'baron' in the Vaunage. J L P has told him his whole story, which ends, in fact, with a reference to the various kinds of good fortune that seem to have befallen J L P, or that seem about to befall him. We then arrive, logically, into the middle of square 8, in the conclusion or, at least, the prospective conclusion of J L P's adventure. And what does this baron say?

First, he behaves towards the hero just like the grandmother, and even more like Quincarlot, as a herald of death (here, conditional). The baron seriously threatens the deceiver J L P with the scaffold, as a punishment for the illicit gains pocketed by the young man. These gains, it should be remembered, came to J L P in the form of treasure, which was itself accumulated through his father's and grandmother's swindling; they also came to the young man in the form of a deposit, represented by Babeau's pregnancy, of which he is the author. The scaffold might also punish the young man's complicity with Sestier, the rich and dishonest farmer who had started with nothing. 'Born of bad parents, you seem very likely to end up no better than they. Your alliance with that Sestier of Langlade, together with your own wretched inclinations, are very likely *to lead you to the gibbet* if you do not take care' [89]. For the third time in the novella, we feel a shudder at the reference to the scaffold: the first time, the grandmother had marked Truquette with her awl; then she had started him on the dishonest course that was to bring him to the scaffold. On the second occasion, Quincarlot had risen up before J L P like a living gibbet, only to turn his lethal attack on to the unfortunate Garouille. The third time, the baron . . .

By threatening in this way, the baron is not actually trying to get Jean-l'ont-pris hanged. Moreover, Quincarlot-the-gibbet was not, in fact, trying to get the young man hanged either. What the noble, mysterious baron wants is simply to manifest his own particular nature; he thus presents himself as a herald of death, the third to appear since the beginning of the novella, after the grandmother and the one-eyed Quincarlot. This third herald, as it happens, is conditional.

In fact, the baron's true 'aim' at this particular point in the plot is to move the young man from square 7 to square 8 in Table 18; from the more or less real 'wealth' which is characteristic of the 'Death's gifts' phase, to the desirable return to paternal poverty.[1] This return will satisfy both the imperatives of Christian morality dear to the abbé Fabre (restore the ill-gotten goods to their source) and the logic of the novella (loop the loop, and bring the son, after a long journey, back to the starting-point, from which he had thrust his initially poor father, in the first paragraphs of the narrative).

The baron, it should be noted, is quite clear on the matter. His aim is only to urge JLP to *make the leap* that will bring him from his dishonest pseudo-prosperity to honest poverty, of the original paternal type, that will be the correlative of the restoration of the stolen goods: 'Believe me, my child, change your ways and live as an honest man. Work, you were created for that. Seek out those to whom what you possess belongs and give it back to them. If you keep it, the least that can happen to you is that you will be unhappy and eaten up by remorse for the rest of your days' [89].

The recurrent character of godfather Death is crucial in square 1 of Truquette's career, and also in square 8 (the homologue of this square 1) of JLP's career. In these circumstances, we have a clearer understanding why this character cannot be played (in the final episode of Jean-l'ont-pris's fictional career) by the beings who took charge of it during the earlier stages of the narrative. The grandmother, the first protagonist of the role, is in any case dead and buried. Quincarlot-the-gibbet certainly has a point in common with the baron, that of being a (conditional) herald of the gibbet and death. But, as far as he personally is concerned, Quincarlot is essentially an evil genius, associated with dishonesty; his task is to enable the hero, in square 7 of Table 18, to make the 'leap' in the direction of illicit wealth and seduction, with an unpleasant marriage and widowerhood to cap it all. The whole of this strategy, which also involves making

Babeau pregnant, would end, if everything went according to plan, by one day acquiring Sestier's inheritance. In square 8 of Table 18, on the other hand, the baron advises J L P to make a 'leap' from ill-gotten wealth to honourable poverty: in this sense, the great lord rediscovers in himself the vocation of godfather Death as an equit-able, fundamentally just entity; as even a saviour of souls, or benefi-cent companion of Jesus Christ, as indeed we meet him at the be-ginning of the tale, in stage 1, among the various versions of A T 332 (for example, in the Occitan region, in the opening paragraphs of *Jean-de-trop*). After all, Fabre is a 'Catholic novelist'.

It will also be noted that the baron clearly presents himself as a *protector* of Jean-l'ont-pris: he calls him in turn, at the beginning of the tale, *friend*, *my friend*, *my child*. He thus combines the two charac-teristics, friendship and a certain paternalism, of every godfather: he is not necessarily a *relation*; he is often, at the outset, merely a *friend*; but as soon as he is a *godfather*, he in fact becomes *paternal* towards the *child* who is now in his charge.[2] But a question arises: how will J L P receive this 'appeal' to return to square 8 (Table 18), to the original paternal poverty of Truquette's beginnings in square 1, this appeal being made by a godfather Death represented, in realistic terms, by the baron from the Vaunage? *A priori*, the young man's reaction might seem rather negative towards this somewhat unattractive prospect, which involves, after all, at the end of his journey, a return to square 1. J L P's joking retort that peasants' remorse and conscience have caught a cold might well reinforce this negative impression.

In fact, J L P's real behaviour does not necessarily prove the baron wrong. The scarcely Occitanized refrain hummed by the young man, *La bônna avantûra, ô gué* ['Good luck come my way! Hey! Nonny-nonny!'], is the refrain of a song that was very popular at the time in France, including the Midi; it was known, in any case, by Fabre through Molière's *Le Misanthrope* (I, 2). For J L P, the most import-ant thing is that he has seduced Babeau.[3] The prospect of a vast fortune might, after all, leave him cold.[4] Moreover, the refrain sung by J L P, *La bônna avantûra, ô gué*, has a double meaning. If J L P does not make amends, Death or the gibbet will await him round the corner. Heedless as he is, his conscience having caught a cold, the hero is not very aware of the dangers that threaten him; but the baron, who returns laughing to his funereal castle, knows that

Death would lose nothing by waiting if JLP does not restore the stolen goods. To the tune of *la bonne aventure, ô gué*, a highly popular song was sung in France in Fabre's day; and our abbé, as his plays prove, knew many a French song of his time; he also, like Margot and Truquette, was very fond of *cansounéttas dé Paris* [9]. No doubt he also knew the 'popular song', composed by Collé in 1753 and hummed everywhere, in which a certain Cadet loses his beloved Babet to another man, her seducer.[5]

In this case, Babet might quite simply be our Babeau. And Cadet is also the name of one of the favourite heroes in Fabre's fiction and drama; in the abbé's plays, Cadet takes the role of a poor boy who seduces, as does JLP, the heart of a certain Babet/Babeau. The 'thief', or seducer, of the song, who might catch and punish the delinquent couple, Cadet (or JLP) and Babet (or Babeau), is not far away. If the hero of Fabre's novella does not willingly or under duress restore the ill-gotten goods, and does not return to the original poverty of his father, he will be taken by the scruff of the neck and hanged. Even the term *gueux* ['ragamuffin'; *gusas*, in Occitan], which is contemptuously applied to JLP in the last lines of the narrative, scarcely leaves any illusions as to the young man's real chances of wealth or social advancement. Moreover, Sestier himself is no better, having become rich dishonestly; his fortune is itself fragile. The baron is not wrong to return to his castle *laughing* [93]. He is very likely to win his bet and to have rightly foreseen the final return of the young man to the 'starting square'; for JLP, this is square 8 of Table 18, but it was square 1 in the introduction to the novella, where it referred to Truquette's initial poverty. This initial poverty was regarded as more honest than the various acquisitions of wealth that follow. Is not the very image of Jean-l'ont-pris in the final 'segment' of the book, as a ragamuffin who continues on his way, the very image in reverse of his father, a Rouergat ragamuffin: indeed, he continues on his way in the first lines of the narrative to Solorgues, a locality where he is unfortunate enough to plant his pilgrim's staff; it is from there that he joins the opulent, but funereal game of snakes and ladders to which Margot's mother invites him. Sedentariness and wealth ruined Truquette; poverty rediscovered at journey's end may save his son, Jean-l'ont-pris. Is there no point, then, in the novella? Has it been no more than a long dream, intercut by quasi-miraculous episodes, moving from one form of wretchedness to another? The wheel turns. Or again, to paraphrase Fabre's Occitan, *the bobbin turns*;[6] it comes back to its starting-point from square 8 to square 1 – from the final ragamuffin, J L P, to the initial ragamuffin, Truquette.

It is true that the last two squares, 7 and 8, of Table 18 are treated in chiaroscuro, purposely, by Fabre. The return to square 1 is suggested, rather than demonstrated. In square 7, the hero seemed to be moving inevitably towards a rich marriage. In square 8, he might, thanks to the baron's preaching, return to his father's poverty. The tendency, at least, seems clear. Fabre has written a novella in chiaroscuro, but not a fairy-tale, in which anything is acceptable, even a miracle. We know enough, when we think about it, to conclude that the novella ends in match drawn: 'You will be hanged if you do not repent,' says the baron to the hero. 'I wouldn't mind dying if I knew what remorse was,' the young man replies [89].

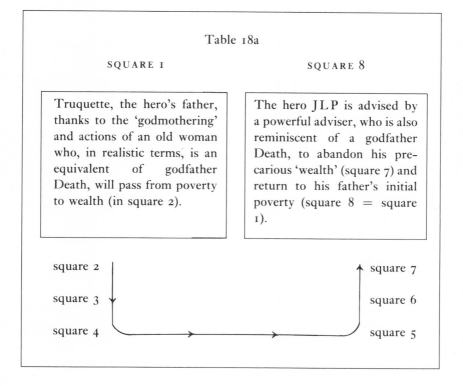

Table 18a

SQUARE I

SQUARE 8

Truquette, the hero's father, thanks to the 'godmothering' and actions of an old woman who, in realistic terms, is an equivalent of godfather Death, will pass from poverty to wealth (in square 2).

The hero J L P is advised by a powerful adviser, who is also reminiscent of a godfather Death, to abandon his precarious 'wealth' (square 7) and return to his father's initial poverty (square 8 = square 1).

square 2

square 3

square 4

square 7

square 6

square 5

In short, the respective paths of the father, the hero and Death *meet at the beginning of the narrative*; then, as far as the hero is now concerned, they *part at the end of the narrative*. Contact at the outset; leave-taking at the end.

The very composition of the novella, in this respect, is illuminating. J L P's narrative, concerning first the life of his father, then his own, is set within a first-degree plot, which gives the text as a whole its introduction and its conclusion. First the hero (J L P) meets a lord of the Vaunage, to whom he then relates a double story (Truquette's and his own); in the end, after he has told his story, this lord gives him a severe dressing down, in an attempt to get the peasant to reform his life. No one, among the various commentators of Fabre's work, has really taken any interest in this mysterious *seigneur de Vaunage*. Yet he has something to tell us about the intimate texture of the narrative.

First let me deal with a secondary question.

The noble baron of the Vaunage is not J L P's own lord. The hero's 'direct' lord, in the novella at least, is the lord of La Boissière, whose judge, clerk of the court, gamekeeper and official hunter are in charge of the everyday life of the Solorgues community, dominated in the last resort by the lord of La Boissière himself. He, personally, is an absentee land-owner; but he is potentially present in the narrative through his 'seigneurial officers'.

If the baron is *not* J L P's *direct* lord, what, essentially, is his function? The answer is that he is also, fundamentally, like the grandmother and like Quincarlot, a herald of death. The grandmother occupied in the narrative exactly the place occupied by Death in A T 332: she had marked her son-in-law Truquette with the awl. This Death was later to take the ultimate form of the scaffold. Quincarlot, who then takes over from grandmother Death, who was first tricked and who then disappeared, presents himself before Truquette's son as a walking gibbet, as a tangible promise of the scaffold.

It is true that at the moment of Quincarlot's unpleasant appearance, the hero has already trapped the forces of death and thus put them at his disposal. As a result, he no longer runs any risk, for the moment. Nevertheless the threat of the gibbet is precisely formulated by Quincarlot, and it continues to hang over him like a dark cloud: it is harmless enough for the moment, but it is dangerous for the future destiny of the young man, who has not forgotten his father's tragic fate. *My memory of Truquette was still green*, he says [75]. The threats of hanging, conditional as they may be, re-emerge at the end of the narrative, or rather at the end of the 'narrative of the narrative', outside the structure, that is to say, outside the 'structures as such' of the double biography of Truquette and J L P, recounted by the hero himself. This final reappearance or threatening announcement occurs when the baron says to the hero: 'Your alliance with that Sestier of Langlade, together with your own wretched inclinations, are very likely to lead you to the *gibbet* if you do not take care' [89]. It is a conditional scaffold, then. In fact, the baron, even if he represents death, suggests that the hero should return to poverty. The gibbet is not inevitable; it would only be a punishment for a refusal, if the hero rejected the logic of the tale, which leads him inexorably back to square 1, that is to say, to his father's poverty, beyond the final annulment of a godfatherhood.

As the conditional herald for J L P of a future strangling on the gibbet, in the good old tradition of godfather Death, the baron functions at least, like Quincarlot, as a chamberlain of Death. He belongs, in the foreground, to the vast gallery of forces who are manipulated by Death and who manipulate Death. I have called them, to simplify matters, 'forces of death': Fabre, careful to preserve his hyper-realism, could not leave to a single character, who, in such a case, would become a fantastic figure of fairy-tale, the task of appearing at the beginning of the tale, then of prognosticating for the hero's benefit a particular death or survival, then entering a bottle, then reappearing, then strangling with his own hands the hero's father or pulling out the hair of the hero himself, etc. The abbé had to distribute these various tasks and their authors in order to make them more credible in terms of narrative 'realism'.

What Fabre has done, therefore, is to follow certain versions of A T 332, regional variants of which were known to him. I am thinking of the version a Gascon descendant of which was later collected by Bédat de Monlaur; I am also thinking of versions that were later to be collected by folklore specialists in the form of the 'Swiss tale', and also in the form of the oldest *French* version of A T 332, collected by Jacob Grimm before 1863; lastly, I am referring to the Austro-baroque version by Vernaleken (1864), which is so close to our

Languedocian *Jean-de-trop*. According to these versions, the classic Death of AT 332 is split into two characters (a *black lord* and a *chamberlain of Death* in Bédat de Monlaur's version; *devil* and *executioner* in the 'Swiss tale'; and *Death* and *executioner* in Jacob Grimm's old French version). This split may even give rise to three characters (*monkey*, *devil* and *Death* in Vernaleken's version). Fabre has distributed his character of Death over three successive roles or poles: the tragico-burlesque figure of the grandmother; the diabolical Quincarlot; the worthy baron. Furthermore, these three characters are capable of manipulating certain subsidiary forces of death: in principle, they are not dependent upon them; but for their own specific and lethal ends, they make widespread use of them.

In the forefront of the three great incarnations of death stands the grandmother. She is the local, topical, functional representative of the AT 332 character of godmother Death. She is assisted by her daughter, Margot, a duplication or division of her mother. Even before the old woman, this Margot is quite capable of 'marking' the cobbler Truquette with a thrust of the awl between the ribs. We know that he will perish on the scaffold, as punishment for his thefts; yet they had been committed at the instigation of his mother-in-law and with the complicity of his wife, who manages to steer clear of any retribution. She quite simply runs off with her former suitor, the knife-grinder. He will know how to sharpen the edge of his wife's fearsome collection of knives; she is, indeed, as 'cutting' as the woman with the basil in Boccaccio's tale. Another modest, but indubitable assistant of the forces of death is the grandmother's donkey, which very nearly kills [*crever*] the young J L P by practically sitting on him.

After the grandmother, Quincarlot is the second of the great roles that embody death in *JLP*. From the outset, however, even before he acts on his own account, he functioned as a subordinate, under the old woman's direction, with the other two swindlers, who bore names redolent of death. Truquette, indeed, was bewitched by his mother-in-law, who transformed him into a swindler; he then immediately decided to form a partnership with these three criminals. Later, it is as a result of their intriguing, as the narrator specifically points out [36], that Truquette is arrested and hanged. This is as much as to say that they are responsible, partially at least, for his death. Moreover,

Quincarlot attended his execution, as a moral assistant to the executioner, far more than an accomplice of the condemned man. Lastly,
Quincarlot functions after the disappearance of the grandmother as
herald of death (that of Truquette in the past, then that of Garouille
in the future) and as Death/Satan/gibbet. He then uses, in order to
carry out his own task, two similar cut-throats and the evidence of
the corrupt vineyard-keepers.

Previously, even during the grandmother's lifetime, the forces of
death manipulated, in order to achieve their murderous ends, those in
charge of the municipal community of Solorgues, which, indeed, was
depicted, in anything but flattering terms, as Huguenot, a Babylon, a
manure pit. Among these local notables are the actual leaders of the
community (*consul* and farrier) and also the ordinary municipal officers, such as the 'men in blue', who make arrests, and the vineyard-
keepers, who carry out the same job. Lastly, in the background,
stands the executioner of Nîmes, who is to hang Truquette.

The vineyard-keepers, as we know, belong to the municipality of
Solorgues. However, they deserve particular attention among the
attackers manipulated by the forces of death. The role of these vineyard-keepers is a violent one, during the crucial attacks they make on
Jean-l'ont-pris and Sestier.

Lastly, as the third great incarnation of death, there is the baron
himself.

But who, therefore, in the novella does not belong wholly and
entirely to the forces of death, nor is manipulated by them to their
murderous ends? There are, in all, six individuals or institutions,
which I shall enumerate in roman figures from I to VI. They are
Truquette (I), of course, who is a victim and not an executioner; his
son, Jean-l'ont-pris (II), who for quite a long time thwarts the homicidal attacks directed at him, and finally overcomes them; Sestier
(III) may have been, for a time, an accomplice of the dishonest
activities of Truquette and his gang, but, more important, he occupies
in the narrative the classic position of the king or powerful man of A T
332. This situation is, therefore, very different from that of the
characters who embody death in this tale type, which does not mean,
of course, that there are not, later, temporary dissensions between the
hero of A T 332 and this powerful man, or that certain temporary
associations cannot be formed between him and Death (in Fabre's

tale, between Sestier and Quincarlot). But these associations are of a superficial kind. Fundamentally, Sestier and his daughter, Babeau (IV), are irreducible to the forces of death. Babeau, a force of fecundity, is *par excellence* an anti-Death. The unfortunate Barbe-Garouille (V), like Truquette, is not an accomplice of the forces of death, but rather their victim; her poor damned soul is thrown down into hell.

Lastly, a *seigneurie*, not to be confused with that of the baron from the Vaunage, loyally fights the fight against the forces of death, outside which, by this very fact, it is situated: this is the *seigneurie-châtellenie* of La Boissière (VI); its gamekeeper, judge and clerk of the court form an alliance with Sestier and JLP against the tentacular grip of what must be called, in Solorgues and around Solorgues, the alliance for Death.

To come back to the baron: he appears in the novella, after the grandmother and after Quincarlot, as the third herald or marker of the gibbet. The various allusions to him in the text make it possible to delineate his character.

The commoner Jean-l'ont-pris, in a way that is hardly respectful, remarks to this gentleman that he might, aristocrat though he be, behave like a vulgar thief, comparable to the most contemptible of Quincarlots: 'Quincarlot . . . was blind in the right eye . . .' JLP tells the baron, 'but, good heavens!, fine gentleman that you are, your lordship would find it difficult *to relieve him of what he had in the purse on his left side without his knowing*' [32]. This vexing allusion to the possibility that the baron might become a thief like Quincarlot is all the more pertinent in that it leads to a comparison of this lord with a character (Quincarlot) who is:

(1) a swindler;

(2) a member of a group whose members bear names associated with killing;

(3) an increasingly clear incarnation of diabolical Death, as the narrative develops.

Moreover, a few pages later, Fabre takes up again this comparison between the baron and Quincarlot-the-gibbet; indeed, the narrator considers (without actually doing so) subjecting this gentleman and Quincarlot to exactly the same treatment: hurling a stone at their faces [48, 81], hitting them either in the eyes or on the jaw. The nobleman and Quincarlot-the-gibbet are certainly tarred with the same brush. We should add that at the moment when the baron is threatened in this way [48], he is implicitly identified with a character in *Jean-le-sot*, from which Fabre makes a number of borrowings in passing.[7] This character is a supernatural being, the statue of a saint, which Jean-le-sot (with whom Jean-l'ont-pris temporarily identifies himself at this precise stage in the episode) smashes to pieces in order to steal the gold coins contained in its alms-box. JLP might also want to smash open the baron's skull. The hero's relationship with the baron, as with Quincarlot, at first, is therefore somewhat tense. Indeed, it becomes even more tense at the end of the narrative when the hero, taken off guard by the threat of the scaffold and by the lessons in morality to which the baron–horseman treats him, expresses regret that he has confided in him [88].

The continuity that leads from Quincarlot-the-gibbet to the baron, herald of death, is maintained in yet another way: Quincarlot, who is also capable of predicting death, deliberately uses French terms in his speeches to JLP, pretentiously mixing in his sentences words from northern and southern France.[8] Thus he stands out, at the end of his final emergence in the text, as an infinitely more distinguished character than the vulgar swindler he had been during Truquette's lifetime. Quincarlot has to some extent become a lord (of Death), since in Languedoc, too, to be seigneurial under the *ancien régime* was to have the privilege, unlike the ordinary, Occitan-speaking people, of knowing and speaking French. From this point of view, Quincarlot, who tries to speak French as much as possible, portends the formidable explosion of French that is to accompany the baron's speeches at the end of the novella, just as it had those at the beginning. They were such that they commanded respect at first from JLP himself, who mixed French words in his own conversation with the baron.[9] Quincarlot was already a quasi-lord of Death. The baron is to fill that lordly, and therefore French-speaking, role completely.

Compared implicitly and in various ways with the fatal Quincarlot, the baron also provides a subtle, but very clear parallel with Margot, the daughter and lethal accomplice of grandmother Death. *It would not be a miracle*, JLP tells the baron, *to see you drowned head over heels* [17]; in this way he stresses that this noble personage might ruin himself, making all due allowances for their difference in station, if he gave a feast comparable to that arranged for the marriage of

J L P's parents. Now, a few sentences earlier, Fabre had cited a similar sentence, spoken by the young men of Solorgues, discountenanced by the forthcoming wedding of Truquette and Margot: *Heavens! What a pity that Margot should go and lose her head with Truquette first!* [12] (or, more literally, *should go and drown herself like a great beast* in Truquette). There is, of course, a pun here: since Truquette means *chopine*, Margot is threatened with drowning herself in a *chopine*. However, it would be useless to stress the fact that if there is to be a symbolic drowning, it would involve for Margot drowning herself in marriage *par le cul* ['head over heels', but literally, 'through the ass', having been possessed by Truquette]; and this because of the marriage in which the young men imagined that she would be victim of the irremediable poverty of the cobbler who is to share her bed. In fact, the reverse happens: Margot, accomplice of her mother Death, was not 'drowned' by Truquette. It was she who, under the old woman's direction, contributed metaphorically to the 'drowning' of the unfortunate young man (in fact, to his arrest, followed by hanging). Why not apply these reflections on 'he who really gets drowned' to the relationship itself, tricking and tricked, which is formed, then looks like being broken off, between J L P and the baron? The young man threatens the aristocrat with drowning; in fact, it is the baron, a herald of death, who could well drown Jean-l'ont-pris.

Another way, for Fabre, of establishing certain relations between the baron and Margot: the notions of *freshness* [*fraîcheur*] and of *gaiety* [*gaillardise*], which play a very important role in the definition of three characters in the novella – Margot, Babeau and the baron.

(1) First, Margot. This girl is, in the first version, *the prettiest, most buxom* [*gaillarde*] *wench* [6]. In the second version, this beauty disappears, and Margot simply becomes '*the most buxom* [*gaillarde*] wench'. The notion of *gaillardise* is essential, therefore, to the character of Margot; the narrator stresses it again when he indicates that this girl, in flirting with the cobbler, did *whatever she could to arouse my father's good humour* [*gaillardise*] [9]. Margot's *gaillardise* is so virulent as to be contagious.

Furthermore, Margot has *a certain freshness*. In fact she is, to use the Occitan word, *fréscâssa*, that is, 'fresh' in the diminutive, 'really fresh' [8].

(2) Babeau also possesses, though to a lesser degree, these two

Table 19

ON CERTAIN 'DROWNINGS'

Relationships between characters	Words spoken	The actions
MARGOT AND TRUQUETTE	Margot is threatened with being *drowned* [*par le cul*] as a result of her adventure, followed by marriage, with Truquette.	In fact, Margot risks nothing. It is Truquette who is 'drowned', thanks to the attentions of Margot and her mother, both forces of death.
THE BARON AND JEAN-L'ONT-PRIS	The baron is threatened with being *drowned head over heels* [*par le cul*], if JLP is to be believed.	In fact, the baron risks nothing. It is JLP who might be 'drowned' one day, according to the prediction of the baron, a herald of death.

qualities; she is *fresh, buxom and good-natured* [71]. The notions (made comic here) of *gaillardise* and *fraîcheur* are certainly those that were selected by the author as a common denominator between Margot and Babeau.

(3) But things are to become more complicated! The baron in turn is presented as fresh and spirited [88, first and second versions]. The two relevant texts are as follows.

'Here is your castle, farewell!' JLP says to the baron. 'God keep you . . .'

first version . . . *frés* ['cool'] in summer and *câoudét* ['warm'] in winter' [88]

second version . . . *câoudét et gaillard*' [88]

We see that, by a different procedure from the preceding ones, it is *câoudét* ['warm'] on these two lines that is the common denominator with the two *essential* adjectives, which are common to the baron and to the two girls (Margot and Babeau), namely, as far as the baron is concerned, the two adjectives *frés* [first version] and *gaillard* [second version].

The other adjectives, *câoudét* (in relation to the baron), *poulida* ('pretty', in relation to the two girls), *âïmablassa* ('good-natured', in relation to Babeau), are marginal and do not concern the terms common to the three characters taken together.

It may be objected, in the case of the baron, that I am forcing the text somewhat. But we have only to turn to paragraph 3 [first version] and especially to the corresponding paragraph in the second version of the text: 'My lord, your cheek is fresh, you are very spirited [*gaillard*].' The baron's horse is also spoken of as 'spirited' [*gaillard*] and 'like a hobgoblin' [*foulêt*, 77].

What have Margot and Babeau in common? The key, it seems to me, is provided by Margot. On the one hand, deriving as she does from her mother and collaborating closely with her, she is a force of death. On the other hand, as a desirable young woman, made pregnant before marriage by Truquette, as Babeau was later to be in the same circumstances by Truquette's son, she embodies femininity, seductiveness, fecundity. On this point, Fabre has considerably innovated and enriched his text in relation to AT 332, in which the character of the hero's wife or mistress is treated in only a purely allusive manner and appears in little more than a functional way.

Table 20

		Feminity–Fecundity
Forces of death	The baron is *frés et gaillard*	Margot is *fréscâssa* and the more *gaillarde*
		Babeau is *fréscâssa* and *gaillardâssa*

Horizontally, at the top, under the heading of death, the baron and Margot stand out; he is *frés et gaillard*; she is *fréscâssa* ('fresh', plus the diminutive, that is, less seriously than he), but most *gaillarde* (more than he). These two modalities – less serious (with the diminutive) and superlative (the most) – compensate each other. Let us say that the baron and Margot both possess, as forces of death, the same overall quantity of, on the one hand, *fraîcheur* and, on the other hand, *gaillardise* (the vigour of Death, who strangles someone or scalps him). Vertically, on the right, under femininity, whose *fraîcheur* and *gaillardise*, in a different sense of the words, are indubitable attributes, Babeau (*fréscâssa* and *gaillardâssa*, with the diminutives) is certainly desirable, though a degree less attractive than Margot (*fréscâssa*, but the more *gaillarde*).

In Table 20, Death (whether called grandmother, Quincarlot or baron) enters horizontally into a relationship of *similarity* with Margot (who shares, through her mother, the very essence of the forces of death); Death enters vertically into a relationship of *exteriority* with the successive femininity of the three young women in the narrative – Margot, Barbe-Garouille and Babeau. Indeed, it will be noted that the three successive incarnations of death, the grandmother, Quincarlot and the baron, begin their relationships in the narrative with these three women at three comparable moments. The grandmother intervenes actively in the narrative only at the moment when Margot (her daughter), nearing the end of her pregnancy, is about to marry and give birth to Jean-l'ont-pris. Quincarlot intervenes personally in the text when Barbe-Garouille, also nearing the end of her pregnancy, is about to give birth to the twins, who are to die with her. Lastly, the baron makes himself known to J L P when his mistress, Babeau, is also well advanced in pregnancy, to the point of being 'as round as a tennis ball'. We recognize here, repeated three times, one of the oldest traditions of A T 332: the tradition according to which Death, destined to be a child's godfather, makes himself known to the father of the child even before his wife gives birth to the child in question.[10] Another tradition is to be found above all in recent versions, collected *after* the writing of *JLP*: according to this new tradition, the father sets out in search of a godfather only after the birth of the child; the father's meeting with Death, in these circumstances, takes place after the birth.

In any case, the baron is close, in a number of ways, to those forces of death that were embodied, before him, in Quincarlot and even earlier still in the person of Margot, as filial double of grandmother

Death. This aristocrat is also involved, as if in passing, with those direct instruments of the forces of death represented by the vineyard-keepers. It will be noticed, indeed, in support of this assertion, that the baron is the only nobleman mentioned as such in the narrative. The other 'possible' nobleman, the lord of La Boissière, does not appear personally in the text, but only through his 'officers' (judge, clerk of the court, gamekeeper, etc.). The baron is present from beginning to end of the narrative, since he introduces and closes the novella and since, while sitting on his horse, he listens to Jean-l'ont-pris's long confession in its entirety. Because he is the only nobleman in the text and the only listener to the narration, the baron feels necessarily concerned, indeed, personally affronted, when Jean-l'ont-pris attacks the nobles, or a noble in general, without further details. For example, Jean-l'ont-pris indicates that Sestier responds vigorously to the attacks of the agents of the forces of death represented by the vineyard-keepers; in order to do so, the farmer shakes them *like a gentleman's tapestry* [59]. Once again, the only gentleman in the narrative is associated with those forces of death embodied, as we have seen, by the vineyard-keepers.

The various clues gradually converge to form the macabre identity of the baron. Fabre quite clearly is tempted to define him as a *soul of silex* [second version, 76] or, literally, as a soul of 'cold stone'; this designation certainly suits a character whose role after the grand-mother and Quincarlot is to embody (without saying so specifically, the whole strange secret of Fabre's novella is there) the character of Death at the end of the narrative.[11]

The first person to represent Death in the novella was the grand-mother. From the beginning of the story, the narrator J L P had noted that his grandmother, in her youth, had been impregnated with the seminal fluid of a surgeon from the township of Calvisson; this locality was Huguenot, and therefore of ill-repute (at least from the point of view of Fabre and his 'Catholic' novella). This 'impregnation' gave rise to a pregnancy that nine months later culminated in the birth of Margot, the narrator's mother. There is no question, of course, of impregnating the baron, a male character, just as, originally at least, the lord of Death was male (Gascon version of AT 332) and just as the godfather Death of AT 332 is male in general. Yet the narrator's very last words correspond exactly to his first: the baron will become impregnated with the liquor of the Huguenot township of Calvisson, in other words, with *clairette*, or local white wine [93], which the grandson of the surgeon of Calvisson (J L P) will offer him; the grandson of the same surgeon who, two generations earlier, had impregnated the grandmother.

| Table 21 | | |
| THE FLUIDS OF CALVISSON | | |
A Lineage of human beings who do not belong to the forces of death, but who may come into contact with them	B The fluids of Calvisson	C Figures of Death
The grandfather, the surgeon of Calvisson	with a seminal fluid from Calvisson will impregnate ⟶	the woman who will become the hero's *vaunageole* grandmother.
The 'paramedical' grandson of this surgeon	with a 'fluid' from Calvisson (*clairette*) will impregnate ⟶	the baron from the Vaunage.

The seminal fluid that impregnated the hero's future grandmother issued from a sexual 'encounter' between that young lady and the surgeon of Calvisson. What is more, Jean-l'ont-pris insists [93] on the cheering and enlivening virtues of a drop of Calvisson *clairette*, a local white wine that turns all heads and will not fail to 'stimulate' the conscience of the baron from the Vaunage.

Herald of conditional death in the best tradition of A T 332, the baron has been drawn by Fabre with light touches, taken from all the characters belonging to the forces of death with whom he is successively compared: Quincarlot, grandmother Death, Margot, the vineyard-keepers.

The *lordship of Death* exercised by the baron is antagonistic to the *lordship of life* affirmed against him by the other aristocratic pole referred to in the novella. This is the *seigneurie* of La Boissière, whose agents dismiss the criminal vineyard-keepers, who are executants of the forces of death, and whose official gamekeeper is resolutely opposed to the hunter of La Boissière, who, on the contrary, was kind enough to provide the wild game for grandmother Death's table.

It should be added that Death is fond of surprising the hero of AT 332 in the vicinity of a cemetery (Catalan version, by Maspons, 1952), or again when the hero has been particularly successful in his use of the supernatural powers of diagnosis given him by Death.[12] This is exactly what the baron does: he surprises J L P in full triumph at the moment when, following his optimistic prognosis, he has just taken his wife to the cemetery and is able at last to marry the powerful man's daughter.

Perched *on his horse, one evening, at the end of the story*, the baron *looks down on* his possible victim, who is none other than *the hero who has just come from the cemetery*: this is entirely in line with the constant tradition of AT 332; Death physically dominates the hero at night. In Maspons's Catalan version, for example, geographically and structurally close to *JLP*, Death is *accompanied by a horse, at night*, during the scene of his *last meeting with the hero in the cemetery*. There is, however, a difference: in this Catalan version, which has the 'normal' ending of AT 332, Death gets the hero to mount his fantastic horse and takes him at full speed to the place of extinction of his light of life, where his head is cut off with a scythe. In *JLP* (in which the hero confines himself to ending not his life, but simply his career, by a return to square 1, to the precise spot where his ragamuffin of a father had begun), however, baron Death, on his fantastic [*foulêt*] horse, and the hero on foot leave each other with a few friendly, ironic words:[13] they simply imply a relatively distant threat concerning the hero's head, which might, if not actually cut off with a scythe, be hung up, with the rest of the body of its owner, at the end of a rope.

Incidentally, the Catalan version of AT 332 by Maspons authenticates still further the identity of the baron as one of the three principal figures of Death in *JLP*. One has only to look at the details common to both texts concerning the final meeting between the hero and

Death: it is night or evening [1, 3]; the story is told in or near a cemetery; there is a horse, belonging either to Death or to the baron.

Furthermore, in both cases, there is specific mention of a wild horse that can run like a mad sprite: in fact, this horse is called *foulêt* in Occitan [77][14] and *boig* ['mad'] in Catalan (Maspons, 1952, p. 119). Certainly, the two tales, for reasons of structure that I have pointed out, have different, even opposite endings from each other: in the Catalan versions of AT 332 collected by Maspons and by Caseponce (see Chapter XV), the hero is taken by Death on horseback to Death's field, where the extinguishable lights of life burn (Maspons, 1952, p. 119); or he is taken to Death's castle, in which, similarly, the lights of life burn (Caseponce, in D. Blanc, 1979, pp. 90–92). It is there that the hero will finally be attacked by Death. In *JLP*, however, baron Death *leaves* the hero, after making vague threats that the young man's head might well end on a scaffold. Then the baron returns *alone* on horseback to his classic *castle*. This contrast produces a remarkable opposition in relation to the final episode of 'forgiveness-remorse', which, nevertheless, is basically common in both cases. In Maspons (1952, pp. 119–20), the hero knows that he is going to die; so he asks Death's *forgiveness*, this request being motivated by remorse for having tricked Death during an earlier phase. In *JLP*, on the other hand, it is baron Death who takes the initiative in this final episode; he asks the young man (whom he will let escape) to feel *remorse*, since Jean-l'ont-pris has also made his fortune through swindling the forces of death [81–91].

But JLP finds himself in a position of relative strength: he will take leave of baron Death instead of being imprisoned, then decapitated by Death; in the circumstances, he refuses to feel the remorse demanded of him. On the contrary, he makes fun of the whole idea. Maspons's hero, however, was obsessed by remorse and himself asked for Death's 'forgiveness'.[15]

Let us return for a moment to the positions of Death in AT 332 when he wishes to be dominant: he may look down on the hero from above, as he kneels at his feet (Maspons, 1952, p. 119); he may be perched on a coach (*JDT*) or on a cabriolet (Nivernais) or on a cart (Brittany) or on a carriage (Germany);[16] he may fall from the top of a tree on to the hero (Andalusian version); or he may look down on him from a high seat (Icelandic version, the oldest of all) or look down on him from on high with the appearance of a gibbet (Quincarlot) or look down on him from the distance that separates a first-floor room from a cellar (the grandmother in 'Truquette'). Much may be said about the reasons for the high positions adopted by Death, whose characteristic trajectory in the tale moves from the heavens to the infernal depths of the cave of lights; [17] but for me the essential point is that this fact of 'altitude', in the case of the baron sitting on his horse, is so clearly stated at the beginning of *JLP*. The baron is also fascinated, at the beginning of the novella, by the *head* of the possible victim, to whom he promises a possible end on the gibbet. Indeed, much is said (in the first lines of Fabre's text) about the hero's jaw (he sings *à pleine mâchoire*, literally, 'with full jaw', that is, at the top of his voice), about his hair, about his hat pulled down over the back of his head, about the mourning band hanging from his hat, all seen through the dominant eye of the lord of the Vaunage . . . The treatment given, in the course of the novella, to the hair, nape of the neck and various parts of the faces of J L P and Sestier, showered with blows, combined with the fact that the Death of A T 332, when he is in an aggressive mood, attacks the head, should lead us to take these clues very seriously.

In *Jean-l'ont-pris*, as in other versions, the lord of Death owns a castle. The southern versions (and others) of A T 332 were to preserve on this point, on their collection in the nineteenth and twentieth centuries, the (*ancien régime*) traditions of this tale type, which had taken root in the Occitan region. It is to Death's castle, at the end of the plot, that Death takes the hero: this is the case in the version of A T 332 from Ariège (Perbosc and Cézerac manuscripts, end of tale 39; Mir and Delample, *idem*); the Gascon version of Bédat de Monlaur; the southern version of Albret (Dardy, 1891, p. 148); the Breton version by Luzel, one of the oldest of A T 332 to be collected in France (Luzel, 1881, p. 341); and, of course, the German versions (Wolf, 1851; Kühnau, 1911, p. 526). In the versions from Roussillon and Catalonia by Amades (tale 99, p. 245) and Caseponce (p. 91), Death's castle becomes a palace or even a *huge palace*. In certain Occitan versions, on the other hand, this 'castle' is mentioned, at the end of the tale, only as 'the residence or house of Death', beneath which the cellar with the candles is to be found (Moulis, Ariège, 1976, p. 110; *Lemouzi*, 1911; Méraville, Auvergne).

The figure of the baron, therefore, is linked in every way to the forces of death that appear in Fabre's novella. This character makes a conditionally fatal diagnosis in the best style of A T 332: *if you continue with your wicked behaviour, you will be strangled.* He is close in many ways to such forces of death in the story as the grandmother, Margot, the vineyard-keepers, Quincarlot; this is true even if the nobleman does not have the burlesque element of the old woman, or the diabolical aspects of Quincarlot. In fact, the Holy Trinity of Death in Fabre's story (grandmother, Quincarlot, baron) makes it possible for us to synthesize these three aspects of Death – the burlesque, the diabolical and the serious. The baron has a soul of silex; he haunts the vicinity of cemeteries; mounted on his spirit–horse, he threatens Death's godson, travelling on foot along the very path that might lead him to the lord's funereal castle. The third 'realistic' embodiment of godfather Death in the narrative, after the grandmother and Quincarlot, the baron is in this sense the mediator entrusted with the task of bringing the hero back to square 1, just as the old woman was the mediator who launched J L P's father, from this starting square, on the career that was to prove fatal to Truquette. The old woman initiated the godfatherhood granted by Death. In the opposite direction, with the baron, this godfatherhood is ultimately foreclosed. The hero certainly runs the risk of finding himself once again as a ragamuffin in his father's starting square. The path followed by the young man and by Death diverge: in paragraph 77, the spirited horse of the macabre baron seems to sense this inevitable divergence. In a style that is scarcely premature, the horse tries to achieve this separation by running off; so much so that its master has to bridle it and temporarily hold it back.[18]

In short, Fabre has preserved everything and displaced everything in relation to the original schema of A T 332, or rather in relation to the Languedocian versions of the tale type (the ancestors of our more recent southern versions of *Godfather Death*), which served as his model. These displacements carried out by the abbé concern the general structure of the model tale, while transferring 'laterally' its principal points of insertion: Jean-l'ont-pris is not a physician, as is the hero of A T 332, but simply a paramedical. He does not become the son-in-law of a king, of a 'king of Paris'. Our hero will simply be, if everything goes well for him, the son-in-law of a rich farmer, and husband of a pretty, rather well-endowed girl. In fact, this very outcome is by no means certain: it seems that at the end of the story, according to the baron's predictions (which, given the logic, respectively direct or inverted, of AT 332, must be regarded as true), the hero has above all a choice between the gibbet that ended his father's career and the poverty with which it began.

There are other lateral displacements: Sestier is not a king, but simply a big farmer, a self-made man; furthermore, he was a swindler. The grandmother is not the embodiment of death in the full sense of the term, but a miniature grandmother Death, not immortal as Death should be, but doomed to die like everyone else. This is why, following certain versions of AT 332, older prototypes of which were not unknown to Fabre, our abbé had to reincarnate his godfather Death a second, then a third time in the figures of Quincarlot and the baron.

Most remarkable of all is that this general operation of transference and displacement succeeded. Fabre was more or less to fail in a similar enterprise with his burlesque parodies of the *Aeneid* and the *Odyssey*, in which the Latin and Greek heroes are transformed into more or less comic figures from the Midi. It is not always easy to metamorphose, as the abbé specifically wished, 'Antiope' into a 'slut'. But the parody worked so well with *JLP* that it became invisible, and the abbé was accused of writing pure burlesque,[19] when in fact he was writing a burlesque of transposition, derived from a fairy-tale. Hence the unquestionable effects of strangeness to which the reader does not remain insensitive. Without wishing to – or because he wished to – Fabre has succeeded in making generations of admirers and scholars believe that he wrote a realistic novel about life in a Languedocian village long ago. In fact, there are certain realistic elements in his story, but essentially Fabre adopts, adapts, then inverts in hyper-realistic and caricatural terms a late medieval myth that later became a fairy-tale of the baroque period, which was still flourishing in the eighteenth century. Moreover, in the nineteenth century, this fairy-tale was to spread still farther. In the person of the abbé Fabre, Grimm disguised himself as Balzac. The mask stuck to the face.

So far I have considered the question of the 'sources' of *JLP* only in 'profile'. It is now time to confront them head on. In other words, in the first part of this book, I have assumed that *JLP* followed, very broadly, the models of Occitan fiction in the classical age; these models, thanks to the existence of a regional corpus that was manageable enough for a single researcher to work on, are readily accessible, but of course they also existed in the seventeenth and eighteenth centuries outside the Occitan region. In the second part of my study, I have 'focused' the approach still more. I attack the particular problem of the real origins and foundations of Fabre's novella. Generally speaking, I have linked these to folklore and oral literature, as it circulated in Languedoc during our author's time, and more precisely to the fairy-tales, possibly of an edifying character, recounted in the long dark evenings and disseminated by merchants, migrants, preachers, etc.

In any case, we know that Fabre was very interested in these tales: he was the author of a collection, since lost, entitled *Soirées de la Vaunage*. He spent his childhood in the Vaunage, and continued to live and work there as a priest. But this particular priest was not only listened to; he was also a good listener. No one objected if Fabre parodied, in the form of a burlesque, hyper-realistic, caricatural parable, one or several fairy-tales. Later, the abbé was to spend his life parodying the *Aeneid* and the *Odyssey*, disguising Homer's and Virgil's characters as typical Languedocian peasants. In *JLP*, he turned the godfather Death of AT 332 into a grandmother/godmother; the king or powerful man into a Monsieur Sestier, son of the people and determined not to fall back among them; the poor father and poor son (the *compère* and godson of Death in AT 332) into two villagers called Truquette and Jean-l'ont-pris, respectively son-in-law and grandson, but also *compère* and godson of the grandmother/godmother.

I was also led to locate five sources in folklore and fairy-tale, four of which at least are oral, used by the abbé Fabre for his *JLP*. These are respectively:

(1) Essential: the tale *Jean-de-trop*, one of the Languedocian versions of the cycle of AT 332/*Godfather Death*. This *Jean-de-trop* is crucial if we wish to understand the structure of the two parts of

JLP. The first ('Truquette', or *JLP 1*) may be deciphered, in comparison with *JDT 1*, in the very order in which the various episodes of the narrative are arranged. The second (life of J L P himself, or *JLP 2*) is arranged in the reverse order of its model, in other words, in the reverse order of the second part of *JDT*, or, more generally, in the reverse order of the four-part cycle of A T 332; when it follows this procedure, it returns faithfully, from the end to the beginning, along the canonical chain of *Godfather Death*, from which it sprang.

(2) Also important, from the point of view mentioned above, are the various Occitan and Catalan versions of A T 332 (those from Aude, Ariège, Gascony, the Landes, Roussillon, etc.); a knowledge of these texts of oral literature is of great assistance if one wishes to understand the sources, not lost, of Fabre's novella, which are also, in terms of lineage and relationship, sources of those versions collected later.

(3) Very important: a Swiss tale, also belonging to the cycle of A T 332/*Godfather Death* (see Chapter IX). Remarkable similarities, linked from end to end in the successive order of the sequences, connect the structure and the details of this tale to the 'life of Truquette'; so much so that one has to admit that a version of this 'Swiss tale', orally translated into Occitan, of course, circulated between the Gardons and Durance before or during the period in which Fabre was writing his own text. This assertion is necessary, and indeed there is nothing shocking about it, given the innumerable, long-standing links that had linked (via the Rhône) German-speaking Switzerland with eastern Languedoc since the Middle Ages and even more so since the sixteenth century of the Reformation and Counter-Reformation. We should not forget that the valley of the great river, that immense opening for all kinds of contact, begins in German-speaking Switzerland and ends in the Camargue, very close to our Occitan Vaunage. I set aside, of course, the hypothesis that Fabre knew German and travelled in Switzerland: there is everything to indicate that there is no truth in it.[1]

(4) A secondary source: the *Cinderella* cycle in the form of oral and local versions of the Occitan *Céndrousétta*, known to Fabre, and also in the form of written and widely published texts. I am thinking of Perrault's *Cendrillon* and, of course, of Mme d'Aulnoy's *Finette-Cendron* (first published in 1710).

(5) Another secondary source, and one that accounts for a par-

ticular episode in the novella: the cycle of *Jean-le-sot*, itself linked in various ways to the cycle of AT 332.

Let us set aside the problem of *Finette-Cendron* at once. It goes without saying that a man of Fabre's education had access to various aristocratic and ecclesiastical libraries, including his own; he had no difficulty in obtaining the widely distributed book by Mme d'Aulnoy that contained the *Finette-Cendron* that he used. There remains, if we set aside the somewhat insignificant problem of *Jean-le-sot*,[2] the big question: that of the cycle of AT 332/*Godfather Death*, or rather, those 'incarnations' of this cycle that are crucial or at least relevant from our point of view (*Jean-de-trop*, the 'Swiss tale', the various Occitan versions of *Death's Godson*, etc.).

To begin with, we must picture for ourselves a branching, even tree-like structure:

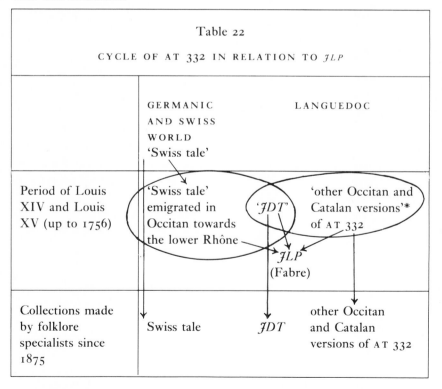

Table 22

CYCLE OF AT 332 IN RELATION TO *JLP*

* Among these is the very important tale that was later to be collected in Roussillon under the name *Galdric* (see Chapter XV).

In other words, in the relationship with AT 332 that Fabre had developed from his youth, he had not come across the Swiss tale, *JDT* and the Occitan and Catalan versions of *Godfather Death* in the state in which the collectors found them 120 years later (around 1875). What he did know, it goes without saying, was an earlier state of these tales, as they were disseminated orally around 1750 in Languedoc, the only region in which the abbé ever lived. That is why, from now on, when I am referring to this 'earlier state', dating at the latest from the first half or second quarter of the eighteenth century, I shall use inverted commas: '*JDT*', 'Swiss tale', 'Occitan and Catalan versions', etc. Furthermore, it is quite possible that these tales, in the forms in which they existed, were closer to one another, more interpenetrated, than were their more divergent nineteenth- and twentieth-century 'descendants', owing to inevitable processes of division. The present-day Occitan or Catalan versions of AT 332 and *JDT*, not to mention the Swiss tale, which was to survive in Switzerland, but whose oral, Languedocian ramifications seem to have disappeared, were able to form among themselves about 1750 complex ensembles from which Fabre drew his inspiration; they were to survive in the much later collections of folklore specialists only as separate offshoots. That is why in Table 22, when I refer to their 'earlier state', typical of the eighteenth century, I have linked them in hypothetical 'bubbles':

'Swiss tale'   '*JDT*'   'Occitan and Catalan versions' of AT 332

We should remember this point, even if we can do no more than suggest hypotheses. In any case, the fact that certain of these versions had more or less coagulated by Fabre's time, or were already divorced from one another, in no way changes their necessary reality, as a source of inspiration for Fabre and as the only overall explanation for the novella, in terms both of structure and of detail.

There remains the objection that springs from a radical scepticism. The Occitan and Catalan versions of AT 332 (including *JDT*) are (an extreme opponent might say) creations of the nineteenth century, collected if not invented by the folklore specialists of the 1880s, and are evidence, therefore, not of an earlier period, but simply of their own time. Such an objection has already been made to me on the subject of the (folkloric) *Candlemas bear*, broadly described by Van Gennep in Dauphiné in the nineteenth century, and whose existence in the same region in 1580 I deduced from a text that specifically attests the *symbolic* value of this disguise as a bear in the first few days of February. Have we any right to jump in this way from the nineteenth century to the end of the sixteenth century, a critic, a folklore specialist from the Dauphiné, asked me. Of course, one certainly has this right, since the Candlemas bear has been specifically recorded in classical France in a *seventeenth-century* proverb, which is evidence, like any old saying, of an even earlier existence.[3]

As far as our problem is concerned, it is not a question of 'jumping', as I am accused of doing, 'from the nineteenth century to the Renaissance'; it is simply a question of effecting a brief transition backwards from the oral literatures collected considerably later in France between 1860 and 1880 (even, in the case of Gueullette, in 1712) to those that Fabre knew, mainly through verbal transmission, in the mid-1750s when he was writing the first version of his novella. My resort to regressive history is limited, therefore, to a century; in the case of Gueullette (1712), it is not even regressive at all, it is canonically 'progressive'. Let me add, before justifying this approach, that if one rejects the 'bridge' that unites in this way two successive generations of an oral literature that remains remarkably constant (the generations around 1750 and 1860), one is condemned to understanding nothing at all about the overall and detailed structures of *Jean-l'ont-pris*; these become wonderfully clear, however, as soon as they are compared with the Occitan versions of AT 332 that I have examined.

And, to begin with, what is AT 332/*Godfather Death* in general? The answer is unequivocal: it is a tale that took root in the Christian world; it spread throughout the whole of Christendom, wherever the Christian institutions of baptism and godfatherhood existed. This tale type is to be found, in fact, in the German-speaking countries, where, according to some authors, it took root as a result of a pun on the words *Tod* ['death'] and *Tod* (a Franconian dialect word meaning

'godfather').[4] The tale has been widely identified in the
Scandinavian and Baltic countries, and among the Slavic nations as
far as Russia. The Orthodox Churches and Christian peoples of the
Balkans and those of the Asiatic parts of the former Turkish empire
also produced versions of this story (as in Romania, Bulgaria,
Yugoslavia, Albania, Armenia and the Christian populations of
Syria and Palestine). The whole of the Latin Catholic world,
whether in northern or southern France, in French-speaking or
Celtic-speaking Brittany, or in Italy, Spain or Portugal, has produced innumerable versions of AT 332. The British Isles have a
version of the tale (in Latin), introduced no doubt by preachers
in the middle of the fifteenth century. But Protestantism of
the puritan or puritanical Anglo-Saxon type almost entirely
wiped it out: it is true that AT 332 depicted, often with a religious
or moral aim, a character who is not directly theological (Death)
and miraculous acts that are both superstitious and papist (granting of medical gifts, which are simultaneously profane and
miraculous, etc.). Moreover, the institution of godfatherhood is
not widespread in the English world. *Godfather Death* is not,
therefore, to be found among the fairy-tales of England and
Wales. A single version has been collected in Scotland.[5] Catholic
Ireland, logically enough, has produced dozens of versions. The
same contrast is to be found between Flanders, with its traditional
papism, where there are many versions of AT 332, and Wallonia,
whose 'Jansenized', 'purified' Catholicism is resolutely resistant to
Godfather Death (no version has been identified among the
Walloons).

Of course, the tale emigrated to America with the European colo-
nists: the Anglo-Saxon Protestants, for reasons already mentioned,
ignored it. But Catholic Latin America produced a great many versions: in Mexico, in Central America, in Brazil, in the Caribbean and
even (in the eastern Atlantic) in the Cape Verde Islands. *Godfather
Death* arrived in the United States with the Catholic immigrants:
versions of the tale are to be found, therefore, in New Mexico, Texas
and Arizona (among the old surviving nuclei of the Mexican settle-
ments, which function as conservatories of Spanish culture in the
western states of the United States); versions are also to be found in
the suburbs of Detroit and Chicago (Lithuanian and Armenian

versions), as well as among the descendants of the Irish. Lastly, Quebec is of particular importance for us because it has preserved versions that were brought by the French immigrants before 1763, when Canada lost its direct ties with France. In their cultural isolation, these versions have preserved, often better than in Europe, many of the features of the French early eighteenth century, a period when *Godfather Death* in its French (and Occitan) forms reached Fabre's ears from the French Atlantic coast.

As a result of inevitable overlappings and cultural contacts, the tale spilled over slightly into non-Christian areas. But it did not go far beyond its natural frontiers, dictated as they were by the presence or absence of the Christian institution of godfatherhood. We do find, however, a sort of AT 332, a Death 'of the godfather type', but of course not really a godfather, in the Jewish world of Europe (Austro-German) and among the Jews of Morocco and Palestine. As far as Islam is concerned, the tale scarcely touched it. The Muslims of Turkey, certainly influenced by the Orthodox Christians who once co-existed with them in Asia Minor, knew of a tale that had taken root in their country: it concerns the angel of Death and his position in relation to the sick-bed. This Turkish tale corresponds more or less, minus the godfatherhood theme, to our AT 332. Apart from this, however, there is nothing. One would seek in vain for AT 332 in China, in primitive or Muslim Africa, in India.

Of course, AT 332 was able to incorporate certain pre-Christian elements. The cave or cellar of the lights of life, to which godfather Death finally dragged his victim, is reminiscent, according to certain scholars, of Meleager's firebrands, in ancient Greek legend.[6] Comparisons with this or that Indian myth have also been suggested. However, in its canonical structure, this tale was able to crystallize in a definitive way only in a specifically Christian environment, in which the institutions of baptism and godfatherhood function.

When did this crystallization take place?

It occurred gradually between the fourteenth and seventeenth centuries. Written or published literature has its own value, of course;

at the same time it serves as evidence of more secret, rather older processes; these took place in the submerged part of the iceberg, at the deeper level of oral transmission. The two phenomena, written and spoken, react upon each other. In any case, we are dealing with what one might call a 'best seller' of oral tradition; it gave rise, between the fourteenth and twentieth centuries, to numerous incursions into literature, in the full sense of the term, from the German medieval poet Hugo von Trimberg (about 1300) to an author of Westerns, the American of German origin B. Traven,[7] with the abbé Fabre occurring about half way. On the level of strictly oral literature, this flowering of the A T 332 type gave rise, in the nineteenth and twentieth centuries, to the collection of at least 350 versions of the tale in more than 30 different nations or peoples, in Europe, America and the Near East. Supposing that one did not have at one's disposal versions dating from the medieval or baroque periods, could one really maintain that this extraordinary international flowering (which took a considerable time to take root through slow transmission by word of mouth) was merely the product of the nineteenth century? Could one, in good faith, reject, on this arbitrary basis, any comparison of this tale with an Occitan novel dating from 1756? Obviously not! It is clear that what we are dealing with is oral literature that has developed over a *long period*.

In fact, there is an already impressive number of written versions dating from well before the eighteenth and nineteenth centuries. This first emergence of the tale type (still incomplete, it is true) dates from about 1300: the German poet Hugo von Trimberg, of Franconia, tells the story of Death, who becomes a child's godfather. It was based at first, certain scholars tell us, on a typically Franconian pun: *Tod*, the German word for 'death', is also the dialect word in that province, to the north of Bavaria, for 'godfather'. However, von Trimberg diverts the godfather Death of his poem not to the canonical plot of A T 332 (the physician Death's godson), but towards another tale, which was also to become a classic of fairy-tale: this is the type known as *Death's Messengers* (Grimm number 117 and A T 335). Von Trimberg's godfather Death sends these messengers to his *compère* to thank him for his loyal services and to announce – his death.[8]

This original change of direction is not unique: the motif of Death *as godfather* will serve once again as a prelude to another type of tale; in the German poem *The Story of Sanctus* (about 1570), the godfather Death motif introduces the story of *the little tailor who climbs up to the sky*, which is later to be found (without godfather Death) in Grimm's tale number 35.[9]

In fact, another, essential portion of our tale AT 332 emerged well before 1750, indeed not long after Hugo von Trimberg's work. What we have here is not godfather Death, but Death as protector of the young physician on whom he confers the gifts of infallible diagnosis, based on Death's position in relation to the sick-bed. This theme is developed for the first time in an Icelandic manuscript written by Bishop Jon Haldorfson (died in 1339). He had probably collected this story while travelling in a more southern country (Germany?) or from some clerical, Latin source; in this text, written in Icelandic, Death is called by the *Latin* name *Mors*. Here is a summary of Haldorfson's story:

A king's son withdraws from the world for three years, under a vow of silence, accompanied by only an old sage called *Mors* ['Death']. This isolation takes place in the middle of a forest belonging to the castle of Death. The young prince is sitting at the feet of this master, who himself, sitting on a very high seat, dominates his disciple; Mors is wearing a felt hat. After three years of silence, Mors teaches the young man a secret. If he sees him at the foot of a sick person's bed, the patient will die. If he sees him at the head of the bed, the patient will survive. (This schema is the reverse of that to be found in the majority of the later versions of AT 332.) With such a gift, the prince finds no difficulty in becoming a rich physician; in time he succeeds his father as king. After a hundred years Mors comes to kill him. The king tricks Mors by asking his permission to say a last *Pater Noster*, which he never finishes. Mors departs, tricked. After another hundred years, which make him more prosperous than ever, the physician–king, tired of life, ends his life, ends his *Pater Noster*. Mors comes to fetch him. He dies.

AT 332 is already there, almost complete. All that is missing is the motif of Death specifically designated *as a godfather*. The four-part structure is already in place: (1) Death as *protector* of a young man; (2) *Death's gifts* to his protégé, namely the gift of infallible diagnosis;

(3) *Death tricked*; (4) *Death's final triumph over the hero*, who in this particular narrative is quite happy to die.[10]

Furthermore, certain unvarying details that are to be found during the whole history of the tale, right up to the eighteenth, nineteenth and twentieth centuries, are already there, and, what is more, in their canonical positions in the structural chain of the narrative: Death is a being of the forest, in which he organizes his 'meetings' with the young man; he occupies a high, dominant position in relation to his protégé, before taking him down into the earth.

Two basic ingredients of AT 332 are already present, therefore, separately, about 1300 to 1340; 'Death as godfather' is present in von Trimberg; independently of this precise motif, the already four-part structure of AT 332 is present in the Icelandic manuscript dating from the first third of the fourteenth century. The synthesis between these two 'ingredients' or elements seems to have taken place some time between 1340 and 1450. Indeed, it appears in complete form in the middle of the fifteenth century. This observation represents a minor 'discovery' on my part; it derives from the reading of a manuscript dating from this period, preserved in the British Museum,[11] a reading that I am proposing here for the first time, with the assistance of Marie-Jeanne Tits.

This text, in Latin, forms part of a series of sermons intended to be 'spoken' in England, probably on the feast-days between Advent and Palm Sunday. The content of this text is as follows.

A man has only one son, whom he wants to call *False* (liar), and who is supposed to remain motionless (this 'stability' corresponds to the idea that lying and falsehood must remain forever on the earth). This man refuses to take as godfathers St Peter and St Paul, for they are 'unstable'; and he also rejects Jesus Christ as a possible godfather (for the son of God sends certain souls to hell). Lastly, the father meets a character called 'Death', and he agrees to accept him as the godfather for his son. Death enables the man to turn his son into a rich physician who sees Death at the patient's feet (the sign of imminent cure) or at his head (the sign of imminent death). It is the reverse of Haldorfson's Icelandic schema, mentioned above. The *chassé-croisé* formed by feet–head/life–death, *or the opposite*, which is to last for centuries in the story of AT 332 has already begun! The time comes when the rich physician must himself die: but he is too

cunning; he does not finish his *Pater Noster*, and thus becomes immortal. Falsehood will, therefore, always be in this world. End of the
sermon: dearly beloved, let us practise truth and confess our sins.

The four-part structure of this sermon based on a tale used as an
example (*exemplum*) integrates, naturally enough, the four elements
of the classic schema of AT 332.

(1) For the first time *in* AT 332 *itself*, one finds *Death as godfather*,
which von Trimberg had used *independently* of our tale type, itself
first recorded by Bishop Haldorfson. It should be noted that we are
dealing with the Germanic tradition of a male Death and therefore a
godfather [*der Tod*], although the Latin word *Mors* used in this text is
theoretically a feminine term. We also find in this version, for the
first time, the elimination in turn of a number of holy individuals
(Peter, Paul, Christ); they would have been quite willing to serve as
godfather, but they are rejected, for various reasons, by the hero's
father.

(2) There then emerges, in its correct place, the incident of *Death's
gifts*: as so often, this takes the form of the granting of the gift of
infallible diagnosis based on the position of Death at the foot or head
of the bed.

(3) *Death is tricked*, for the hero uses, against him, the *trick* of the
unfinished *Pater Noster*.

(4) This, however, is followed by the *revenge-attack* made by Death
thwarted: one of the aims of the tale, in the mind of the preacher
telling it, is, indeed, to show that an entity, Falsehood, which by
definition will always be present, will live forever. A little later in
Italy (about 1550), then in Flanders, this entity will become *Hatred*
and *Envy*; in France and elsewhere, *Penury* (*Bonhomme Misère*); in
Quebec, *Dearth*, a variant of 'Penury'.[12]

In any case, the tale of *Godfather Death* certainly assumed its
canonical form between 1300 and 1450, during a period that was also
a great epoch of the macabre, of the plague and of an omnipresent
death. The context – preaching – is also of crucial importance: from
the fifteenth century to the baroque period, the theme of godfather
Death was widely used by preachers, pious playwrights and Christian
iconography, because of its edifying possibilities.[13] These sermons,
delivered before huge audiences, and the plays, performed in the
same conditions, facilitated the diffusion of the tale among the

popular story-tellers and other transmitters of oral literature. Fabre, we must remember, was also a preacher. In his pulpit, his speech, like that of other preachers of his day, would be highly coloured, quite capable, with the help of terrifying 'examples', of making women weep.[14]

The theme of an eternal entity (Penury, Falsehood, etc.) introduced as a result of the action of godfather Death is identified for the first time about 1450 in the British Museum manuscript; it emerges again as such in Florence around 1550 in a novella by Giovanni Forteguerri. This very important text is, in fact, the first emergence of the tale in a Latin, and even Mediterranean, country.

Forteguerri's narrative takes place in urban Tuscany, during the plague. 'Signor' *Hatred* marries 'Signora' *Envy*. They have a child called *Scandal*, to whom they give Death as *godmother* (the feminization and Latinization has already occurred). Death offered her services herself, for reasons of her own; labouring all day long because of the local plague, she needs to find suitable accommodation nearby and uses the house of *Hatred* and *Envy*. Grateful for being accommodated in this way, Death gives *Hatred* the usual ability to make accurate diagnoses, which is fully characteristic of AT 332: if you see me at the foot of the sick-bed, the patient will live; at the head, he will die. *Hatred* becomes very rich, but he does not wish to die himself. So he persuades Jupiter and Mercury to decree that whoever climbs the fig-tree in his garden in order to eat the fruit will not be able to come down again except on the conditions imposed by *Hatred*. Death, gluttonous as ever, climbs the fig-tree and is caught in the trap: she is allowed down only on condition that she give immortality to *Hatred* and *Envy*. These two entities are thus doomed to remain forever on earth.[15]

Forteguerri has achieved for the first time, at least in the written and published literature, a synthesis that was to survive elsewhere in the oral tradition of the Latin countries – a synthesis between AT 332 (*Godfather Death*) and AT 330 (*Bonhomme Misère*, who obtains immortality by temporarily trapping Death in a fig-tree or pear-tree).[16]

Furthermore, by introducing into the narrative pagan antiquity (Jupiter and Mercury) during a period of plague, Forteguerri's novella stresses another ambiguity about the character of Death in our classical culture. This character came into his own during the medieval period of the macabre and of the great plagues, but the Graeco-Roman Renaissance gave him a new lease of life, since Thanatos (Death) in Greek mythology was not without importance.[17]

However, the royal road of AT 332 (at least in the written, and therefore known, literature) no longer passed in the sixteenth century through Italy and the Latin countries. It flourished in Catholic Germany, where it was to develop according to the successive directions of the Renaissance and the baroque. A German poem by Hans Sachs (1547) gives for the first time in its totality the four-part schema (which was more or less in use from the fourteenth and fifteenth centuries).

(1) A poor peasant refuses to take God as godfather for his child, for God is unjust, making some rich and others poor. The peasant, therefore, will choose Death as the child's godfather.

(2) Death showers gifts on this peasant: he gives him the usual ability to diagnose illness (Death near the bed, at the head or the foot, guarantees death or survival respectively). He thus becomes a rich physician. In particular, he treats a rich farmer (a 'Sestier', as we would say).

(3) The peasant–physician Death's *compère* tricks his *compère* Death and thus obtains a deferment for himself thanks to the trick of the 'unfinished *Pater Noster*' (see the texts from Iceland and the British Museum, above).

(4) Death takes his revenge a little later; he kills his deceiving *compère* by twisting his neck.[18] The general (four-part) schema is therefore absolutely complete; moreover, two motifs appear in the narrative that are later to be found in many versions of the tale, including that special version, *JLP*. These concern the treatment given a rich peasant, the local equivalent of our 'Sestier', and the fact that Death attacks the hero's neck when he is about to kill him. Attacks on the neck or head are to be a constant in the oldest French and German versions of AT 332. In Fabre's version, too, Truquette is finally hanged, and Jean-l'ont-pris is several times threatened in that part of his body. Of course, this in no way means that Fabre had read Hans Sachs, far from it. It is simply that the French and especially southern French versions that reached Fabre were to affect, through a cascade of intermediary transmitters, those structures and details

that certainly seem to have first been developed beyond the Rhine (possibly one hundred or two hundred years before).

The carnival play by the German playwright Jacob Ayrer (died in 1605) entitled *The Peasant with his Compère Death* uses the same four-part schema as Sachs. Ayrer, however, leaves a blank in place of 'paragraph 3'. This produces the following succession: (1) godfather Death; (2) gift to the peasant *compère* (the 'Truquette' character) of the ability to diagnose death or cure of a patient according to the position of Death in relation to the bed; (3) *no* attempt on the peasant's part to trick Death (this is the 'blank' mentioned above; the same 'blank' occurs at the same strategic point in the Swiss tale and in the 'life of Truquette'); (4) Death attacks the peasant by twisting his neck and killing him.

Ayrer's play also contains various details which, placed at the correct strategic point, are of considerable interest to us: the peasant *compère* of Death, like Truquette, has a child conceived well before marriage, a not very Catholic act that is condemned by the pious playwright. This carnival play has very papist resonances (as does *Jean-l'ont-pris*, written by a priest whose Roman Catholic prejudices are well in evidence); lastly, Death is presented by Ayrer as a rather diabolical character and as a brother of the devil, who himself appears on the stage. Another parallel with Sachs, and later with *JLP*: Ayrer's physician, Death's protégé, treats not kings, but peasants, 'Sestiers'. A placebo appears at the usual place in the narrative: neither a root nor cold water, as in so many later versions and in *JLP*, but two apple pips. There is even a 'Garouille', an unfortunate peasant woman whom the physician–hero knows and declares to be doomed to die, because Death stands at the wrong end of her bed. Lastly, we see the re-emergence in Ayrer of a macabre theme from the late Middle Ages: Death drags the peasant–physician (whom he is going to kill) into a *Dance of Death*.[19]

The unfinished German fable by Praetorius (1669) contains only the first two 'acts' of the four-part schema: (1) Death as godfather; (2) Death's gifts. It stops there and has nothing to say of the last two acts, which would be: [(3) Death tricked; (4) Death is revenged]. However, it closes with various elements that had not hitherto been developed in the written and literary versions of AT 332 published before 1669. These are:

(1) A thought with general implications: 'Death is a source of wealth; *funus itaque foenus fuit.*' This is the result of reflection on the second sequence, 'Death's gifts', which will yield, in *JLP*, the grand-mother's treasure.

(2) The prescription of a placebo-root. This enables the physician to cure, or rather to pretend to cure, those whom Death has indicated will survive in any case, since, seen by only the doctor, he stands at the patient's feet, the position in which Death is not threatening (the situation would be the reverse if the feet, as in various versions, were the dangerous position, and not the head). In this case, the placebo consists of a root; it is not yet the bottle of cold water (with or without the addition of liquorice) to be found, in competition with the root, in later versions of A T 332 (including *JDT* and *JLP*).

(3) A crucial fact: for the first time, this fable uses (as in the case of J D T or of J L P, Truquette's son, and as in many other versions of A T 332) not Death's *compère*, whose role in Praetorius is merely initial and episodic, but the son of this *compère*, in other words, Death's godson, who will become (as will J D T later) a physician, trained by his godfather in infallible diagnosis. As the son of Truquette, himself the son-in-law and *compère* of grandmother Death, J L P will also be 'objectively' her godson, and a paramedical.[20] Praetorius's fable is the first in the centuries-old cycle of A T 332 that is decidedly bigenerational, as *JLP* and *JDT* are later to be (but not *Galdric*, which remains monogenerational; see Chapter XV).

(4) This 'fable' compares the behaviour of the forces of death with the 'detestable' practices of the Jews.[21] Fabre, regrettably, does the same.

Finally, in 1691, an innovation of genius takes place at the level of the written literature (preceded, presumably, by the oral). This is the idea of *turning the bed round*.

This discovery emerges for the first time in 1691, again in Germany, in the *Biblisches Bilderbanquet* and in the work of the Catholic priest Andreas Strobl. This work is not only a fairy-tale, but also, explicitly, a theme of baroque preaching. This explains, again, the very rapid diffusion of this new 'mutation' of the tale. Moreover, the compilers of 1691, including Strobl, did not necessarily invent it. They may well have collected it from the 'oral' literature. Their text:

(1) *Godfather Death*: A poor peasant is looking for a godfather for

his child, who will be born in three weeks' time. The peasant first refuses Jesus as the child's godfather, for he considers himself too poor for such an honour. He then rejects the devil, dressed as a huntsman. Lastly, he meets Death, whom he accepts.

(2) *Death's gifts*: A grateful Death gives the poor peasant the gift of infallible diagnosis. (But it is the reverse of the usual form – the patient will die if Death stands at his feet, and survive, with the use of a non-specified placebo, if Death is at his head.) The new physician becomes rich.

(3) *Death tricked*: The physician sees Death at the foot of the bed of a rich merchant, doomed, therefore, to die. The physician is promised a rich reward if he cures him. The physician takes the rich man's pulse, then turns the bed round. The patient is saved.

(4) *Death 'takes his revenge'*: In fact, he does no more than threaten the physician after this exploit.

It is a remarkable version. You will note its Catholic inspiration: it is explicitly a theme for preachers. The physician's first two encounters, with God and with the devil disguised as a huntsman, are exactly the same as those of the cobbler in the 'Swiss tale' (originally German, then Occitanized), whose importance for our 'Truquette' has already been analysed. But in the 'Swiss tale', the cobbler does not expect the arrival of a third character, Death, in order to choose him as godfather for his child and as a future benefactor. He stops at the devil huntsman; he directly takes him as a substitute for Death (in this case) and as the contractual giver who will become his child's godfather, according to the classic structure of AT 332.

As later in *JLP*, where this point is stressed three times, the encounter with the future godfather Death, in Strobl, takes place shortly *before* the birth of the child. Similarly, the character of the 'rich merchant', whom the physician undertakes to cure, is a 'Sestier' (a powerful commoner), not a 'king', as is the case in a large number of later versions.

The important point is the fact of turning the bed round. This innovation probably dates from the seventeenth century, certainly not after 1690. Indeed, in a version of 1643, that of H. M. Moscherosch (*Geschichte Philanders von Sittewald*),[22] the trickery practised on Death is always obtained by the method that remained classic from the fourteenth century: the hero begins a *Pater Noster* and does not finish it for a hundred years or so. (This theme of the unfinished *Pater Noster* entered the French cycle of A T 332 in competition with the other traps laid for Death, such as imprisoning him in a bottle or turning the bed round. We even meet this *Pater Noster* in a version of *Godfather Death* from the Vaunage and Cévennes, collected by Dezeuze, and geographically very close to our *JLP*.)

The trick of the turned bed is supremely skilful. It was no doubt concocted in the seventeenth century, between 1643 and 1690 at the latest; it was then identified by the collections of numerous written and, later, oral versions. It consists of using the strategies of Death himself, who, depending on his intentions, stands at the head or at the foot of the bed; this strategy is then turned against Death by turning the bed round. It is remarkable that a rather learned physician should have been the first to have thought of this 'turning of the bed' in written literature, which implies the trajectory of a semi-circumference of 180 degrees, and sometimes (in certain versions) the constuction of a pulley under the bed to facilitate the operation. However, this method of 'swinging' the sick-bed round was to be highly successful: mentioned for the first time in Germany in 1691, it emerges in France from 1712 (in Gueullette's tale *Mort, et médecin protégé par la Mort*); it was not long before it colonized whole areas of the international cycle of A T 332.

One may well see it as a typical invention of the baroque age, in its Germano-Catholic, seventeenth-century forms; the tale owes its definitive construction, with its four parts, to the baroque period, a debt almost as considerable as that to the macabre age of the fourteenth and fifteenth centuries, when the first, no doubt essential, foundations of the narrative were laid.

In the century of Louis XIV, Death, in the baroque regions of Western civilization, remained a character of the greatest importance: from about 1650 to 1710 (as in the middle of the fifteenth century, a more death-obsessed period than the seventeenth century was to be) Death made some very remarkable literary appearances. On this question see Saint-Simon's *Mémoires* and the researches of Michel Vovelle.[23]

From the late seventeenth or early eighteenth century, *Godfather Death* became something of an (unofficial) best-seller in the oral literature of fairy-tale in the German language. The long career that it had already enjoyed from the fourteenth century, marked by its many emergences in written literature, follows closely the versions that were to be collected on the other side of the Rhine in the nineteenth century, beginning with the collections of the brothers Grimm, who set the example. They commenced their work in 1812, collecting and publishing at once a superb version taken from oral sources whose 'roots' lay in the eighteenth century.[24]

Perhaps we should say a few words about this version. Its salient features are also highly relevant to our purposes.

(1) *Godfather Death*: A poor man has a thirteenth child. He rejects God as an (unjust) godfather, then rejects the devil on the grounds that he is a deceiver; in the end, he chooses Death because he is egalitarian. The baptism takes place on a Sunday.

(2) *Death's gifts*: The child grows up. His godfather takes him into a forest, tells him that he will make him into a physician and explains to him how he will know whether the patient will live (Death at his head) or die (Death at his feet). The placebo-potion given to a patient who is to survive is a herb (tale 44); or, in the case of Grimm's tale 42 (*The Lord Compère*), the beginning of which at least is very close to our tale 44, a small glass of water.[25] The physician becomes rich.

(3) *Death tricked*: This physician tricks Death, first while curing the sick king, by turning the bed round. (*Death will turn a blind eye*, the physician reassures himself; by this phrase, which also notes an important detail about Death's 'one-eyed tendencies', the physician means that Death will not object, or so he hopes.) The hero again tricks Death, in the same way, while curing the king's daughter, for he is attracted to her, and he is happy to be able to bring back the natural colour to the cheeks of this princess, whom he hopes to marry.

(4) *Death is revenged*: Furious at being tricked a second time, Death takes his revenge. He takes his godson down into a subterranean cellar filled with lighted candles; he puts out the candle that is equivalent to his godson's life. He dies.

The structure of this version is, of course, the same as that of the French or Languedocian AT 332; taking into account certain transformations introduced by Fabre that I have studied in Chapter XII, it also corresponds to the structure of *JLP*. In it we find the usual four-part schema and also, in their correct canonical places, certain essential developments: ignored by the written versions of the sixteenth and seventeenth centuries, these are common to Grimm, to *JLP* and to the oral, eighteenth-century cycle (German, French and international) of A T 332. Thus the 'treatment' or diagnosis is applied first to the powerful man ('Sestier'), then to the powerful man's daughter (the princess or 'Babeau'), who is later to marry the hero. (We have seen how Fabre, with quite ecclesiastical cunning, but in a way that really changes nothing essential, has simply taken the initiative of replacing the affirmation 'treatment or favourable diagnosis for the powerful man's daughter' by the double negation 'diagnosis of death for the rival of the powerful man's daughter'.) Similarly, in Grimm and in *JLP*, the day of the baptism is fixed for a Sunday; I would stress the fact that Death *turns a blind eye* (Grimm) or that grandmother Death hides her right eye (*JLP*), when his or her relationship with the hero has not yet deteriorated too much or when it is still good. I would also stress the attractive beauty of the princess's cheeks (reminiscent of Babeau's peach-coloured cheeks [72]). Lastly, I would stress the importance (and here I come back to the central problems of the tale's structure) of the functions of the paternal *hero's son*: this son is to become, in fact, the principal hero, as Death's godson and as the homologue of *Jean-l'ont-pris*; this young man will be more decisive from now on in the economy of the narration than was his father, in other words, Death's *compère* or 'Truquette'.

One should also note a certain loss of vitality in the tale as collected in the 1810s, as compared with the vigorous German and French models collected between the sixteenth and eighteenth centuries (including *JLP*). There is no longer any question in Grimm's version of a pre-nuptial conception of the child who, when baptized, will become Death's godson: in Ayrer's play and in *JLP*, by contrast, this child was conceived in an act of fornication that took place before marriage. Similarly, the physician–hero in Grimm's version no longer treats a wealthy peasant or rich farmer ('Sestier'), as in the German version of the seventeenth century, in Fabre and in a more recent version from the Landes;[26] instead, the patients become a 'king' and a 'princess' in the tale of 1812. The brothers Grimm or their informants, even those from the countryside, have ceded, therefore, to the debilitating, prettifying tradition of the fairy-tales of the seventeenth and eighteenth centuries. We know that the French authors Perrault, d'Aulnoy and Mme Leprince de Beaumont were to carry this monarchizing tendency even further. In Grimm, Death is also less cruel and less crude; in 1811 he kills in a more elegant way than he did in 1550 or 1750; in our old versions (Sachs, Ayrer, etc.) and in *JLP*, he strangled his victim, had him hanged or twisted his neck. Grimm, however, tells how Death *seizes his godson with his icy hand*; but he does not stress, as did the older, more violent versions, from Hans Sachs to *JLP*, that it was the victim's neck that he seized; he does no more than suggest a potential threat to the victim's neck.

These various observations are important for our subject: Fabre parodied and encoded the narrative in his own way; even in the framework of this practice, he was able to preserve or restore, in *JLP*, those *hard*, *strong* characteristics of the tale that an already decadent oral tradition was later to weaken on both sides of the Rhine after 1800. Among these strong characteristics are pre-marital sex, practised by the hero's father or by the hero himself; the location of the narrative in an authentically popular environment of peasants or village people, poor or rich, and not in some Fairyland court; a strong stress on the processes of strangling, etc. Did Fabre restore, on his own initiative, as a result of his own hyper-realistic temperament, certain of these early characteristics of the tale; or, given that he had access to various oral versions of AT 332, circulating in large numbers in Languedoc during the first half of the eighteenth century, must we assume that these versions remained close, 'fairy-tale'-like as they were in principle, to a certain peasant crudity and asperity, characteristic also of the oldest German versions (sixteenth and seventeenth centuries)? The already late versions collected after 1810, from Grimm to the German and Occitan collectors of the 1880s, tend to sweeten that asperity, either by means of an inevitable weakening of the old vitality, due to the 'better' education of the popular story-tellers; or because the collectors themselves eliminated certain details thought to be too realistic or too crude, a sort of castration to which the abbé Fabre, who had fear neither of words nor of things, had the wisdom not to practise.

We now have the first point of a crucial demonstration: a whole cycle, Christian in tendency and already internationalized, of AT 332 certainly flourished before the time of the abbé Fabre. The written literatures of the fifteenth, sixteenth and seventeenth centuries, in Latin, Italian and German, produced the tale in all its structural completeness and in its popular vitality. They are, moreover, the visible part of a vast iceberg of oral tradition, spread by word of mouth and even more by the preaching first of the macabre, then of the baroque age.

Latin, the international language of the little world of preachers, facilitated the travels of the tale from Germany (its country of origin?) to France and the other Mediterranean countries. The importance of the oral versions was to become self-evident when they were collected by folklore specialists, for the most part between 1812 and 1900. Meanwhile, the eighteenth century was the great period for *Godfather Death*; that century serves as a bridge between the written literatures of oral origin of the sixteenth and seventeenth centuries (from Sachs and Forteguerri, about 1550, to Strobl and Gueullette about 1690 to 1712) and the oral literatures, which were to pass into writing thanks to the collectors (beginning with Grimm in 1812). It is therefore hardly surprising, in view of the fact that our demonstration must be carried further still into the strictly French domain, that Fabre should have gathered together in this already widely available cycle the elements and structure of his narrative, reshaping both without altering them. The 'Swiss tale', in particular, in its 'earlier state' in the mid-eighteenth century, derived directly from the old German versions of AT 332, identified in the written literature of the seventeenth century (Strobl's version). The 'Swiss' story-teller confined himself to substituting for character number 3 (Death), encountered by the child's father, who needs a godfather, character number 2 (the devil disguised as a huntsman), previously encountered in the same circumstances. This character number 2 carries out in the 'Swiss tale' all the functions that in most other versions are carried out by character number 3. That this 'Swiss tale', securely rooted in the old German tradition, should have spread ever closer, by oral transmission, along the valley of the Rhône (a German river at the outset, becoming Languedocian in the end); that it thus should have reached, in Occitan translation, the ears of Fabre in his Vaunage, presents no difficulty, no conceptual impossibility. And it accounts for a whole series of crucial features in the biography of Truquette, from the detailed structure of the narrative to the name of the principal character (*Schöpplein* = *chopine*-Truquette).

But the question that concerns me here is a wider one: was Fabre inspired not only by the 'Swiss tale', but also by already specifically French versions, especially Occitan-Catalan, of AT 332? That these versions originated in Germany, as eminent specialists believe, is highly conceivable, even probable. But what concerns us is to determine the actual or highly probable presence about 1750 to 1755 of one or several of these hitherto French versions of AT 332, circulating in France, including the Occitan region. To be more precise, was a sort of '*Jean-de-trop*', ancestor or precursor of the tale collected in the 1880s, already alive in France, on the market of oral transmission about 1750? The answer is necessarily positive, in principle, given the close kinship, to the point of homology, that unites *JLP* and *JDT*. It is *Jean-l'ont-pris* that represents a literary version of AT 332, based on an old prototype of '*JDT*', or on a close prototype of that tale:[27] this 'prototype' served as an intermediary for Fabre's novella. The theoretical affiliation runs from '*JDT*' (itself accompanied by an environment of sister versions) to *JLP*. We now have to determine how that theoretical affiliation was able to become embodied in the reality of a process of engendering, in which Fabre's talent, of course, played a great part.

The first known version of AT 332 in France is that of Gueullette (1712). This (as in the case of Fabre's tale) was not a literal transcription of an oral source, but a parody of the tale (obtained from an oral source): it was transposed into a comic 'Orient'. It was a transparent parody, however; Fabre's, on the other hand, is so encoded that it soon becomes hermetic for non-initiates, that is to say, after 1800, for everybody.

Second version: this was to be collected during the first half of the nineteenth century, *in France*, but in an indeterminate province, by Jacob Grimm (1785–1863). It was found in his papers after his death and published in German in the *Anmerkungen* (1913) by Bolte and Polivka (the paragraph concerning tale 44 of the brothers Grimm is on p. 383).

Then comes the Provençal version of AT 332, collected by Mistral in 1876, and our Languedocian *Jean-de-trop*, published in 1885. Other versions from the Midi and Dauphiné were collected and published from 1890 onwards. The latest, published in the 1950s, are not the least interesting, collected as they were from rural story-tellers who had been active since 1910 or 1920. In Brittany, the first known collections were those of Luzel and Sébillot, from 1880. In Nivernais (Millien and Delarue), the collection also dates from 1880. In Anjou, the first publication took place in 1898.

It will be noticed that almost all the versions at our disposal come from the Midi or from Brittany: in short, the most outlying and, essentially, dialectal parts of the country. Or, again, these versions come from regions that are closest to the outlying ones: Nivernais, which borders southern Auvergne; Anjou, which borders Brittany. Northern France neglected tale A T 332 from a relatively early date. First macabre, then baroque Catholicism, which sustains *Godfather Death* almost everywhere, became weak in the strictly French-speaking regions, where the influence of a more modern, austere, Jansenist Christianity penetrated at an early date; thus 'superstitions', so necessary to the baroque fairy-tale, disappeared to a greater or lesser degree. These 'superstitions' were preserved, however, in the best possible conditions, among the more traditional, non-French-speaking regions of the Midi and the west; those linguistic fortresses played the role of 'museums of popular traditions'. From this point of view, *Jean-l'ont-pris* was written in an Occitan environment that was to prove most favourable to the local conservation (up to the twentieth century) of the tale type that had served as the framework for Fabre's novella. We have noted a similar contrast in Belgium: Flanders, with its picturesque papism, conservative and old-fashioned, abounded in versions of A T 332; Wallonia, on the other hand, first Jansenized, then rationalized by the anti-folkloric universalism of French culture, proved to be unfavourable to the preservation of the tale. The same contrast exists between Ireland and England.

Whatever may have happened later to the distribution, above all in the Midi, Brittany or Flanders, of its areas of refuge or survival, the tale *Godfather Death and His Physician Godson* was certainly known in the France of the *ancien régime* where, from the beginning of the eighteenth century, the 'marvellous' was so much in demand. This is clear in the version published by Gueullette in 1712, in which the writer[28] employed a comic orientalism that never fooled his critics and biographers: a comfort-loving bourgeois of a retiring disposition, Gueullette had scarcely ever been outside Paris or Choisy-le-Roi. But he gave his fairy-tale king a name that he might have found in a bazaar: the Great Iskender. He dressed up the plots of his tale in turbans and babouches; these plots he borrowed from novelists or from *local*, oral (northern French) tradition, which he knew well and had a great taste for.[29] Convinced, quite wrongly, of the Turkish origin of his own family, which in fact came from northern France, he saw himself as Molière's Mamamouchi. His plot is as follows.

A poor woodcutter intends to drown his newborn child in a river, then hang himself. Death stops him; he tells him to take the child back to his cottage; he teaches him about a few medicinal plants. Above all, he tells him how he can make an infallible diagnosis, which, in this tale, is as follows: Death at the foot of the bed = the patient will be cured; Death at the head = certain death. The woodcutter thus becomes a physician, protected by Death. But he betrays his protector and saves the mortally ill sovereign (the 'Great Iskender') from Death, who is standing at his head; in order to do this, he swings the royal bed around on the horizontal plane, back to front. Four strong fellows are employed to carry out this 'turning round of the bed'.

Again, the 'oriental' setting should not mislead us: if we set aside the very general structure of AT 332, common in East and West to all versions of the cycle, Gueullette's pseudo-exotic narrative has nothing at all to do with the few Turco-Muslim versions of the same tale in our possession; they are, however, apart from the Jewish versions, the only ones known to us that are not in fact Christian and that are situated to the east of Graeco-Slav Orthodoxy, in a country that we may describe as 'Tartar'.

Let us examine this more closely: the Turkish version, the only one available to us, published by Boratav in 1953, concerns a poor man, accompanied by Azraïl, angel of Death. This version knows nothing of the technique of turning the bed round. It mentions as a guarantee of health only the absence of Azraïl/Death, in relation to the sick-bed; this version ends with the granting of forty years' extra life to the poor man, who meanwhile has become a physician (Eberhard and Boratav, 1953, tale 112). The Turks borrowed this tale from their Orthodox Christian compatriots. They simply de-Christianized and

Islamicized it in their own fashion. The character of the angel of Death certainly seems to come, in any case, from the Orthodox tradition. Indeed, in the Greek countries, A T 332 is animated not by the Western-type 'Death', with a few touches from pagan antiquity, but by the supernatural character whose specific task it is to transport the souls of the dead, and who is none other than the archangel Michael (Dawkins, 1953).

These *turqueries* (if we set aside the extremely general, world-wide common structure of A T 332) have nothing to do with Gueullette's tale. Death, as seen by this narrator from Choisy-le-Roi, is a classic character of Western Christian folklore; he is certainly not an 'angel', Greek, Turkish or Tartar, even if he has a habit in the Western versions of A T 332 of descending 'from on high' towards the infernal 'below'. As for Gueullette's hero, a woodcutter by trade, he seems to me by this fact to be an absolutely typical character of *Godfather Death* of an already French type. Indeed, in Germany, where the tale originated, the hero is a master weaver, a tailor, sometimes even a broom-maker or a cobbler (Mackensen, 1934, p. 617). Never, on the other side of the Rhine, is this character said to be a woodcutter. From this point of view, the French versions belong to a national tradition that is wider than the cycle of A T 332 itself (see La Fontaine's *Death and the Woodcutter*); they certainly favour the trade of woodcutting as far as the poor hero of *Godfather Death* is concerned. This is the case in Gascony, in Languedoc, in Roussillon, in Limousin and in Albret. In Brittany, the hero is in the wood trade, but he is a carpenter, not a woodcutter.[30] The narrators of these French versions in which the hero is a woodcutter never had any contact, even by intermediary transmission, with Gueullette's text, which was to remain confidential and is much less exhaustive than theirs: indeed, there is lacking in the pseudo-orientalist text of 1712 many of the Christian practices (baptism, godfatherhood, etc.), and also the fourth act of the four-part schema of the tale (*Death takes his revenge*). This act, on the other hand, is canonically present in the oral and French versions, mentioned above, which are complete. If these oral texts do not derive from Gueullette and if, however, they have in common with it the typical characterstic of the *French* version of A T 332, namely, the trade of woodcutter for the hero Death's *compère*, one must admit for this and for many other reasons that there already existed in France before 1712 one or more oral versions of AT 332: they inspired, on the one hand, Gueullette himself, who mutilated, orientalized or 'Mamamouchized' them in his own way, and, on the other, by continuous filiation over two hundred years (and well beyond our abbé Fabre), the versions that were to survive until they were collected between 1876 and 1900 in the environment of the Midi, which, however, was not unaware of *Godfather Death* in Gueullette's time.

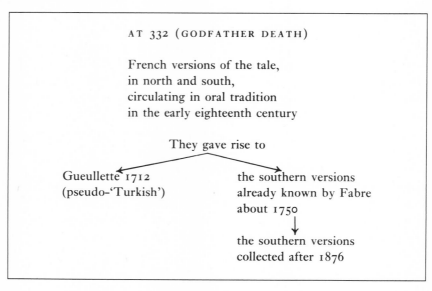

AT 332 (GODFATHER DEATH)

French versions of the tale,
in north and south,
circulating in oral tradition
in the early eighteenth century

They gave rise to

Gueullette 1712
(pseudo-'Turkish')

the southern versions
already known by Fabre
about 1750

the southern versions
collected after 1876

It may be objected that Gueullette would have been able to derive the plot of his tale of 1712 from a direct reading of the German work of 1691 by Andreas Strobl, which contained the raw material of such a narrative. (This 'raw material' included Death's gifts to the future physician and the tricking of Death, above all the theme of turning the bed round, which emerged in the written literature only in 1691 in Germany.) This objection does not hold: Gueullette, like Fabre, was ignorant of all German culture. Furthermore, the German reference books (the *Biblisches Bilderbanquet* and the works of Andreas Strobl about 1691), already rare on the other side of the Rhine, were unavailable in France at the period, judging at least by the contemporary catalogues of our libraries, where they are desperately lacking. They were to become (relatively) accessible in France only through the scholarly re-editions of the nineteenth and twentieth centuries, but that is another story. As far as AT 332 is concerned, we can see, therefore, only the *oral* (which was already flourishing at the time not only in Germany, but also in France) as the possible source for Gueullette's tale of 1712.

Gueullette's version of AT 332, the first to be published in France and one of the first in Europe, is also remarkable for other reasons: it mentions, for example, the celebrated placebo of medicinal herbs already used by the German Praetorius in 1669, and even by the Icelandic bishop at some time between 1300 and 1339. The placebo of cold water, which was to be substituted for the herbs in many more recent versions of AT 332, appears for the first time in the international cycle of *Godfather Death* only with *JLP* (1756) and with Grimm in 1812 (tale no. 42: *The Lord Compère*).

The Gueullette version, moreover, possesses two innovations. The theme of turning the bed round first appeared in the written literature in the German texts of the 1690s. At the moment immediately preceding the trick, Death was fatal at the patient's head, harmless at his feet. The second appearance of this turning, in Gueullette, proceeds in reverse order: Death is fatal when he is at the feet, and vice versa at the head. This is a frequent variation in AT 332, in both the oral and the written forms.

Above all, Gueullette innovates by 'monarchizing' his tale. His physician treats an emperor, the Great Iskender. All the earlier German versions (up to 1691 inclusive) and Fabre's novella of 1756, and certain of our southern versions from the nineteenth century, simply take a rich peasant as the character of the 'powerful man'. The 'royalization' of the powerful invalid inaugurated by Gueullette, following oral models unavailable to us, was to continue in the German, French, etc., versions in the forms in which they were collected after 1800, which owe absolutely nothing to Gueullette. It would seem then that one may discern, from the 1700s, a divergence at the level of the oral versions. Certain of these (which were to influence Fabre and survive him) do not keep to the traditional theme of the AT 332 of the seventeenth century, and make the powerful invalid a mere rich farmer, a 'Sestier'. Others, which influenced Gueullette and which were to prevail later in the majority of the oral versions collected, embellish this powerful invalid and make him, *à la*

Gueullette or *à la* Grimm, into an emperor or a king. By the same token, the daughter of this powerful man, our 'Babeau', becomes a princess!

Working on AT 332, Gueullette orientalized and Islamicized in an artificial way the oral, Christian version, which had already become naturalized in France and which had come to his knowledge. He was, therefore, embarrassed by a problem of religious institutions: Death, in his version, could not be either a godfather or a godmother, since godfatherhood and baptism were Christian institutions; they were inapplicable in the so-called Islamic and 'Tartar' setting in which Gueullette's *Mille et Un Quarts d'heure* takes place. So this author found an elegant solution to the problem: the poor man was certainly the father of a newborn child, as in every Christian version of AT 332 (whereas in the *true* Turkish version, that of Boratav, there is no question of any child at all). But Gueullette's pseudo-'Tartar' woodcutter, unable to take the child for a brief immersion in the baptismal font, takes him with him to drown him in the river. As for Death, instead of envisaging for himself a godfatherhood in relation to the child and a *compérage* in relation to the father (obviously unthinkable in even an imaginary Islamic country), he simply tells the woodcutter to take the child back to his cottage, and that from then on all will go well for father and son. The space of the baptism is therefore well marked, but *in absentia*, in Gueullette's 'Turkish' novella.

All this is another way of saying that Gueullette certainly worked from a 'Christian' version of AT 332, which he then rewrote in a 'Turkish' mode. This version was no doubt of distant German origin, but in the absence of any possible contact between the writer and the German book itself, it must have reached Gueullette's ears through an oral tradition that was *already implanted* in France.

One thing, in any case, is certain: AT 332 circulated and had already taken root in France in the 1700s, and during the first half of the eighteenth century; from this point of view, Gueullette simply represents the emerging symptom of an oral circulation, and not the active factor of an additional diffusion, beginning with the very modest written version he left us.

In AT 332 (Christian) [baptism]	In Gueullette (pseudo-Turkish) [non-baptism]
Father and son leave their house, with a view to an immersion (baptismal) of the son.	Father and son leave their house, with a view to an immersion (drowning) of the son.
Contact with Death (godfather) and (baptismal) immersion.	Contact with Death (unofficially godfather) and non-immersion.
Return to house.	Return to house.

An additional proof of the oral life of the tale in France in the time of Louis XIV and Louis XV is to be found in the Quebec tales.[31] Unquestionably, and whatever their development in Canada from 1763 to our day, they reflect an earlier state of our French folklore, as it survived in the memories of those who set out for Canada between the beginning of the seventeenth century and 1763, when Quebec was annexed by England, thus marking the end of an important French-speaking immigration. The fairy-tales that came from France were then to be preserved in the best possible way in that relatively enclosed cultural environment of the French-speaking people of Quebec, protected as it was from external influences by its French Catholic irredentism; as far as AT 332 is concerned, this tale type in Quebec was hardly contaminated by Protestant, English versions from Ontario, which no longer exist, nor by the Irish versions, which are in fact very different from the Quebec ones, if one subtracts the general features of the narrative structure common to the entire international cycle of the tale.

We have then some ten Quebec versions of AT 332; their roots lie deep in the French eighteenth century, which is essentially before 1763 and therefore largely prior to *JLP* (1756). In Quebec, the following themes and motifs emerge in the usual four-part schema.

(1) *Godfather Death*: A poor man meets Death, who becomes the *godfather* of his child.

(2) *Death's gifts*: Death gives the poor man the ability to make medical diagnoses as follows:

$$\frac{\text{Death}}{\text{Cure}} = \frac{\text{Death at the head of the patient's bed}}{\text{Death at the foot of the patient's bed}}$$

or the reverse (the two terms being reversed in the first part of the equation).

He also gives him a placebo in the form of a phial containing some inefficacious liquid, which he will administer in the case of a favourable diagnosis.

(3) *Death tricked*: The physician treats a king, often at a great distance away (the king of France), whom he has to go and see by ship. The physician sees Death near the king's bed in the fatal position (at the head or at the foot, depending on the version); in order to protect the king, he has the bed turned round by four strong men.

In certain versions, the physician–hero then uses an additional trick: Death, furious at this 'turning round', is tricked by the hero into making himself as small as a fly, and being shut up in a bottle.

(4) *Death takes his revenge*: Someone frees Death by mistake from this bottle, and he immediately kills the physician. However, when the hero is called *Penury* [*Misère*] or, according to a Canadian innovation, *Dearth* [*Disette*], he manages, before being killed by Death, to ask Death permission to eat another apple, and of course he gets only half way through it. Death must therefore allow him to go on living. That is why, as we might have suspected, penury and dearth will always be among us.

The four-part structure of these tales from Quebec is classic, as far as AT 332 is concerned; there is not a lot to be said about them. However, certain details, suitably placed at the strategic point (of the tale) where one should in fact find them, are of the utmost importance.

(1) The liquid placebo, placed in a phial, plays an important role (in competition with the medicinal herbs in other versions) among the many French versions of AT 332, including *Jean-de-trop* and *Jean-l'ont-pris*. Now, of course, this liquid placebo was already in place in

the Quebec tales that derive directly from the backward-looking *ancien régime* of the eighteenth century, prior for the most part to 1760.

(2) Four men – no more, no less – to turn the king's bed round is exactly the same number, for the same operation, as indicated by Gueullette in 1712. In later versions collected after 1880, however, the number of these men may vary or not be mentioned at all. So one is therefore, once again, in Quebec, on the well-marked terrain of the versions of the first half of the French eighteenth century.

(3) The 'royalization' of the character of the powerful invalid appears already well under way in these Quebec versions, backward-looking as they are. From this point of view, they contrast sharply with the German versions of the seventeenth century, which are even older; they also contrast with *JLP* and with other versions that remained more 'populist' and more original, in which the powerful man is simply a rich peasant.

(4) The *double* trick used by JLP – (a) tricking Death by turning round; (b) neutralizing her by 'imprisoning' her – has already been identified, in its two stages, in one of the Quebec versions.[32]

(5) The final trick of the apple only half eaten by the hero is common in Quebec; it is, however, unknown or forgotten in the French versions, apart from *a single* version from the Landes coast, collected by Arnaudin.[33] This version from the Landes seems to have preserved an archaic feature which was lost in all other French versions, but was exported to Quebec and preserved there. This provides a further certificate of antiquity to Arnaudin's Landes version, which I have already used for topical comparisons with *JLP*.

In short: Quebec, that marvellous cultural island that was for so long, before its present-day modernization, evidence of a French Catholic eighteenth century that refused to die, such a Quebec validates the idea of a *Godfather Death* that had already forgotten its German roots, and, exploring the possible variants, spread throughout the France of the old Louis XIV and the young Louis XV. In these circumstances, there was nothing to prevent it from serving as raw material, already predigested, for the abbé Fabre.

An additional, but not superfluous, argument along the same lines derives from certain fundamental archaisms contained in versions of AT 332 collected by folklore specialists in the Midi and in Brittany between 1880 and 1920. A Breton version, for example, collected by Guériff, is obviously set in the eighteenth, or even the sixteenth century. The setting of the Gascon version published by Bédat de Monlaur suggests certain institutions of the *ancien régime*: the *provincial intendant* plays the role of 'powerful man' whose wife is ill; the sums of money are calculated in *livres tournois*; the king resides in the *Louvre* (still not at Versailles!). A hypercriticism or simply a legitimate criticism might accuse these 'features' of being recent interpolations of the story-teller or collector. But here is a fact that, in my opinion, is even more convincing. In the original Occitan version of *Jean-de-trop*, the Occitan word *carrosso* ['coach'; *carrosse*, in French] is used three times (twice of Death's coach; once of the king's coach, the vehicle that takes the physician JDT to the palace). Now, on two occasions, L. Lambert, who was the conscientious collector of this tale in its original version and in French translation, inadvertently translated this word *carrosso* by the French word *voiture* ['carriage'] – *la voiture de la Mort, la voiture du roi*. Lambert used the correct translation *carrosse* only once. This is a precise and important fact: it was not Lambert who, in 1885, introduced the word *carrosso* into the tale. It was the narrator himself (the peasant story-teller of the Narbonne region who 'dictated' his story to our collector). This villager used the word *carrosso* in the 1880s, at a time when these vehicles no longer existed in France. This use reproduced an older version, probably dating from the eighteenth century at least; dating in any case from an already distant period when story-tellers naturally had their rich travellers moving around in coaches. Perrault also introduced these vehicles into his stories either because he was repeating what his informant story-teller had told him, or because he was conforming quite simply to the reality of the life of the people of quality under Louis XIV.

Very interesting, too, is the expression used by the Narbonnais story-teller of *JDT* about Jean-de-trop's father: *poor as a church rat*, an old expression that is to be found in d'Alembert and, above all, in the Duc de Saint-Simon, but hardly at all in the nineteenth century. We meet it on two occasions at least among the Occitan versions of AT 332, in the introduction to the tale, and in the characterization of the poor man: once in *Jean-de-trop*, and again in a version of *Godfather Death* collected in Limousin and published in 1911 (*Lemouzi*).

Let us stop here. Too many clues are now piling up: an immense *geographical* proliferation of versions of A T 332 spread over four continents (in western Asia, in North Africa, above all in Europe and America), which would have taken many years; the *historical* antiquity (from the fourteenth century to the eighteenth and to our own day) of the international (German, Italian, English, Latin, then French) cycle of *Godfather Death*; the existence of a specifically French version (Gueullette) in 1712; the antiquity of various Quebec versions, which function as an authentic past in the present; the precise archaism, too, of our southern versions, miraculously preserved in the linguistic conservatories of Occitania and Roussillon. These clues come together and lead us to the conclusion that A T 332 certainly circulated in France, in both north and south, about 1755 and 1756 when Fabre was writing his novella. The abbé could, indeed must, have drawn his inspiration from this tale, which was so readily available to him.

Of course, it might be said that in 1812 Grimm was collecting or at least inventing a story of godfather Death that did not exist before his collection or not long before. But a mere inspection of the monuments of German and European literature that, on the subject of A T 332, reveal from 1300 the popular–oral or learned–oral in written literature shows that Grimm was collecting from his rural informant a story that, in fact, was almost five hundred years old and went back to the years 1300 to 1450. The same applies in France: the first collections of the French A T 332 were made by Jacob Grimm (no doubt in 1805 or 1813, during his visits to France; in any case before his death, which occurred in 1863); Grimm's work was then continued by Mistral and by other collectors from 1876 to 1880. What they revealed was not 'recent stuff'. In fact, they brought to light stories that were already widespread in northern and southern France from about 1712 to 1755, the strategic time for Fabre's work, assisted in advance by that of Gueullette. Furthermore, I repeat, if one rejects such an affirmation, supported by data of all kinds, one is condemned to understanding almost nothing at all about Fabre's novella.

I have already referred to the archaisms of *Jean-de-trop*, which are all the more interesting because they were noted down by the bourgeois collector from the peasant story-teller, even without the collector being aware of it. This tale, *JDT*, whose ancestor '*JDT*' was one of the most important matrices of Fabre's novella, is of crucial importance to us. Indeed, *JDT*, as a 'sub-type' of tale type AT 332, is not simply a little Narbonne tale collected by some worthy local folklore specialist in the 1880s. It seems, in fact, to have circulated quite widely and for a long time (compare its archaisms, already mentioned), throughout the Catholic baroque region, both within France and beyond it. This is the region where AT 332 has been preserved *par excellence*.

Ankou's Godson, a Breton tale collected and published in 1908 by the excellent collector the abbé Cadic (Cadic, 1908, pp. 8–10), is particularly interesting in this respect.[34]

Here is a summary of it, with, in brackets, the parallel progression, segment by segment, of *Jean-de-trop*.

(1) A poor man has many children and is looking for a godfather for his latest born [*JDT*: same situation].

(2) He meets Ankou (the Breton personification of death) perched on a cart, wearing a shroud that fails to hide his fleshless bones [*JDT*: Death, riding in a coach, exposes her bones, which she later covers with a cloak when she goes to the baptism].

(3) Ankou, still perched on his cart, declares that he will be the child's godfather and protector [*JDT*: Death, still in her coach, is made the child's godmother; immediately afterwards, she presents herself as protectress and source of prosperity for the child and his family].

(4) The baptism is the occasion for a great meal. A wealth of victuals provided by the godfather are served to all the neighbours. Everyone eats and drinks to excess [*JDT*: a large meal, provided by the supernatural powers, including the godmother; consumption of innumerable victuals; all the neighbours and friends are lavishly entertained].

(5) During this meal, Ankou renews his promises of prosperity for his godson while sowing terror among the guests, who view with apprehension the broad smile on his toothless mouth [*JDT*: Death mingles in the same way hot and cold; she causes terror among the guests by showing them her fleshless bones, and repeats her promises of prosperity for her godson].

(6) The family of the Breton godson live more or less normally during the boy's childhood [*JDT*: the family of the Languedocian godson live in prosperity during the godson's childhood].

(7) Seven years after his first appearance, Ankou returns to see this family. He then takes over the education of his godson; later, he informs the godson, who has just reached the age of eighteen, that he will teach him to become a physician: Death visible at the head of the patient's bed = death; at the foot = cure [*JDT*: Death returns and teaches her godson, now eighteen years of age, how to make medical diagnoses; this is exactly the same procedure as in the Breton tale: Death at the patient's head = death; Death at his feet = cure].

(8) Ankou's godson makes a fortune in his medical profession [*JDT*: *idem*].

(9) The young man is summoned to the royal palace to cure the king's daughter, who is seriously ill. The king himself goes to fetch the physician [*JDT*, *idem*: summons to the royal palace to cure the king's daughter, who is seriously ill;[35] the king sends his own coach to bring the physician to court].

(10) The king offers the physician 'half his kingdom', then his daughter herself in marriage, in order to obtain her cure [*JDT*: the king offers the physician 'half his crown', then his daughter in marriage, in order to obtain her cure].

(11) The physician tricks Death by swinging the princess's bed round; he therefore cures her, then plans to marry her [*JDT*: the physician cures the princess, marries her, then tricks Death in order to obtain an extension of the life of the princess, whom he has already married].

(12) Death kills the princess on the wedding-night, then kills the physician by taking him down into the cellar of lights [*JDT*: happy ending – the hero and his wife survive for two hundred years].

Of these two 'stories', one was told to Lambert by a peasant in the Narbonne region, the other was related to the abbé Cadic by a Breton tailor. The endings of the two tales are different. But their respective development over the first ten or eleven homologous segments (out of twelve segments in all) is remarkably parallel and even similar, both in general and in detail.

Similarly, *Hans-with-the-Goitre* [*Hans-der-Kröpfige*] within the vast family of AT 332 belongs to the more specific lineage of *JDT*; in short, this Austrian character is close to the Languedocian hero JDT. Once more, one has to consider a multinational region, Catholic and west European, in this case Austria, Switzerland, Occitania, Brittany; the narratives of oral literature travelled throughout that area by means of story-tellers and preachers, even if it is not easy or even necessary for us to specify the plot's place of origin.

Hans-with-the-goitre (whose 'tale' was collected from popular story-tellers by Theodor Vernaleken in Austria, about 1860)[36] is a boy who leads a poor, wandering life, after being thrown out of his home by his father. He meets in turn, in a wood, three supernatural beings: a monkey, the devil and Death (the last being a male character, called *Bones* or *Skeleton*). These three bring Hans certain adventures and various treasures. Skeleton, in particular, promises Hans that he will enable him to cure the king's daughter and marry her, while warning him that if he, Skeleton, stands at the head of the princess's bed, she will surely die. Skeleton adds that if Hans does not manage to beat him at the great game of who will be the cleverer of the two, Hans's head will fall under the executioner's axe. Skeleton suggests that in such an event the devil (who is thus seen as a close accomplice of Skeleton) will drag Hans's soul down into hell. (In any case, the devil had promised, after his first meeting with him, to come back to see Hans at the end of seven years.) So Hans goes to the princess's bedside, at the head of which, alas!, stands Death. The monkey is fortunately kind enough to turn the bed the other way about. The princess is cured, and her father gives her in marriage to the hero. Some time later, the devil reappears in the guise of a 'horrible Jew' (we know that AT 332 in Germany and even in Languedoc is often infected with anti-Semitism). This devil, who frequents the cemetery and carries off souls, is trying to bring about the couple's death in order to take the souls of the hero and his wife. Furious, Hans manages to shut up this diabolical being in a vase, which he seals tightly and throws into a precipice. From then on, husband and wife live in wealth and happiness.

On the subject of this tale, let us note first a fact that is quite exceptional in the *Germanic* cycle of AT 332: the hero bears the name *Hans* (the German equivalent of Jean ['John']). Usually, the heroes of this cycle in the German-speaking countries are called Claus, Michael or *Death*, a homonym of, but not to be confused with, their godfather. Or, quite simply, they remain anonymous. This Christian name, 'Hans-der-Kröpfige', or 'Hans-with-the-goitre', certainly confirms the particular place of this Austrian hero within the 'subtype' of AT 332, in close proximity to his homologue, Jean-de-trop; and also in close proximity to Jean-l'entrepris, or 'the stupid' (Jean *l'emprès* or *Jean-l'ont-près* or Jean-l'ont-pris), and to Juan Holgado ['the lazy'], the hero of the Franco-Occitan and Spanish cycle of AT 332. The characteristic (goitre, laziness, stupidity, etc.) after the Christian name Jean (Hans or Juan) is always negative and mocking, except that the hero in fact mocks his mockers. There again, this is no more than a presumption, though one certainly finds in both narratives (*Jean-de-trop* and *Hans-with-the-Goitre*) a succession of similar segments placed in the same order.

Let us note these two parallel sequences, shown in Table 32.

To simplify matters, let us call '*Jean-de-trop*' the master text of the oral literature from which our three narratives diverged (they separated at an unknown geographical source, but one that we can locate somewhere in the Catholic, baroque Europe of the *ancien régime*). These three narratives are *Hans-with-the-Goitre* from Austria, *Jean-de-trop* from Languedoc and *Ankou's Godson* from Brittany. Collected or rather published after collection in 1864, 1885 and 1908 respectively, quite independently of one another, the three texts refer, of course, to a clearly older period during which the divergence from which they sprang occurred. This divergence occupied enough time for the three tales (especially the Austrian and the Languedocian ones) to become substantially different from one another. However, this divergence has not effaced the undeniable kinship of structure between the three texts. Taking into account the fact that the earliest published of the three was collected about 1860 from a story-teller who had therefore learned it some time before 1850, it seems reasonable to suggest a hypothetical chronology for the master '*JDT*' ('master' relatively speaking, of course, in other words, 'previous to and pre-existing' the divergence in question). Let us say that this 'earlier state' of '*JDT*' flourished *before 1800*, in short, during the eighteenth century at the latest.

In passing, let us note a remarkable procedure on the part of the

	Table 23	
	A	B
	Hans-with-the-Goitre	*Jean-de-trop*
1	A young, poor hero hopes for and receives advantages and treasure from supernatural beings who are allied, namely, Death and the devil.	A young, poor hero hopes for and receives advantages and wealth from Death.
2	Death (*Skeleton*) teaches him how Death standing at the patient's head indicates death, at his feet, a cure.	Death gives the same type of teaching to Jean-de-trop (see square 2 opposite).
3	Called to the bedside of the king's daughter, Hans cures her by having the bed turned round (Death was at her head).	Called to the bedside of the king's daughter, Jean cures her without turning the bed round (Death was at her feet).
4	Hans marries the princess.	Jean marries the princess.
5	The supernatural being allied to Death (the devil) wishes to take the life of the king's daughter.	The supernatural being (Death) refuses to extend the life of the king's daughter.
6	The hero defeats this intention by enclosing the supernatural being in a vase, which he carefully blocks up.	The hero defeats this refusal by enclosing Death in a gourd, which he carefully corks.
7	Happy ending: the hero and the princess, his wife, live happily ever after.	Same happy ending as in square 7 opposite.

story-teller of *Hans-with-the-Goitre*; in order to achieve the ends of godfather Death, he has recourse successively to *several* supernatural entities: the monkey and, above all, the devil and Death. Similarly, in *JLP*, Fabre incarnates successively his forces of death in the semi-

burlesque grandmother, in the diabolical Quincarlot and in the grave
baron. This similarity would possess no other interest if we did not
know, for other reasons, the kinship, whose historico-chronological
background we must now analyse, between *Hans-with-the-Goitre*,
Jean-de-trop and *Jean-l'ont-pris*.

The chain is now completed. In the second part of this book, I worked
out a model that is not 100 per cent historically descriptive (how could it
be?), but that is *heuristic*, *explanatory* and *operational*, as to the sources
of inspiration from which *Jean-l'ont-pris* (1756) derived. First I
showed that this tale was linked, geographically and structurally, to
the Languedocian, Occitan, Catalan and Roussillonnais versions of
the cycle A T 332/*Godfather Death*; it is particularly closely related to
those 'sub-types' of A T 332, the Languedocian *Jean-de-trop* and the
'Swiss tale' (which, it has to be admitted, once migrated orally and
dialectally as far as the lower Rhône). I then showed that this
'relationship' was not miraculous: A T 332/*Godfather Death*, to which
Fabre's novella is attached through skilful encoding, was already
circulating in France and in Languedoc before 1756, the date of the
abbé's first draft. This earlier circulation is obviously of crucial
importance. Lastly, I showed, incidentally, that the sub-type of A T
332 that is closest to our *Jean-l'ont-pris*, namely, the Languedocian
Jean-de-trop, also derives from an 'oral text' that would be known
in the eighteenth century to a writer like Fabre, since Fabre
himself was a great lover of popular traditions and fairy-tales. In
these circumstances, it is the whole structure of *Jean-l'ont-pris*, in its
entirety and in detail, that we must now elucidate; it is explained
legitimately once it is compared with the different versions of the
fairy-tale whose ancestors Fabre used to 'encode' his narrative.
Moreover, we know, thanks to German, French, Italian and Anglo-
Latin literature, a number of ancestors of these ancestors. Our knowledge proceeds, therefore, simultaneously forwards (the nineteenth-
century versions of A T 332 collected after 1812) and backwards (the
north European, German, Latin, Italian and French versions existing
between 1300 and 1712). Fabre's novella is thus caught in a 'fork' of
which the 'backward' branch ends in 1712 (Gueullette) and the 'forward' branch begins in 1812 (Grimm, followed by Lambert and the
other collectors, in the Midi and throughout the world).

*

A last point, however: is it possible to rediscover in some relatively recent version of AT 332, collected about 1880 in southern or central France, close to our Languedoc, something of that freshness that makes Fabre's novella so valuable and which could also derive from its oral sources?

Often, alas!, the story-tellers or collectors of the nineteenth century, possessing rather too much education, lost that original, invaluable freshness.

In one case, however, it seems to me that such a freshness was preserved: I am thinking of a Nivernais version of AT 332/*Godfather Death*, collected by Millien and Delarue about 1880.[37] Here is my own summary of this version.

A poor couple has twelve children. The carnival arrives. They go to bed. Will they, won't they? They make love. Nine months pass. A baby is born. The father goes to the woods. He accepts Death as godfather. The child will be called, by association of ideas, *Death*. Godfather Death provides for the needs of the parents and the child, and gives them materials to build a house. After seven years, godfather Death takes over the education of the child, with a view to making him a physician. Godfather Death gives him the secret of correct diagnosis: Death at the head = health for the patient, and vice versa. Furthermore, godfather Death gives the new doctor a tiny instrument to place on his own tongue, which will aid him in his 'treatment'. The young man treats the sick king, and places the instrument on his own tongue. The king is cured. The physician then cures the king's daughter and wants to marry her. He tricks Death in order to cure the princess's sick brother. He goes to revisit his godfather Death at his house in the wood and dies in the room with the candles, following the extinction of his own candle.

One has only to look at this version attentively to see that it remains faithful to the schema of *Jean-de-trop*; faithful, too, to the schema of *Jean-l'ont-pris*, taking into account certain literary twists, which are perfectly acceptable in terms of the permanence of the structure, made by Fabre in the writing of his novella: the couple make love in unequivocal terms (for example, Truquette and Margot); god-fatherhood by Death; the child is called Death.[38] In *Jean-l'ont-pris*, this name is 'they have taken him' [*ils l'ont pris*], for Death has *taken* his father, now hanged. In *Jean-de-trop*, it is 'too much' [*de trop*].

The hero is too *de trop* to survive; he is on the side of Death. Indeed, he will skilfully manipulate Death in order to remain alive. The prosperity of the parental couple in the short Nivernais version is expressed, as in Truquette's case, by the giving of a house. The education of the son, of the Nivernais son who is the equivalent of Jean-de-trop and of Jean-l'ont-pris, is carried out by Death, in the usual way, after several years. In this Nivernais tale, the period of time is exactly *seven years*; this figure has disappeared from *Jean-de-trop*, but it is also to be found, with the same function in the narrative, in the two versions, Breton and Austrian (*Ankou's Godson* and *Hans-with-the-Goitre*), that are extremely close to *Jean-de-trop*. They have preserved certain features lost by the latter during the long history of oral transmission in the eighteenth and nineteenth centuries.

Next comes the episode of Death's gifts, given to the young man (and not only to his parents). These presents take the form of the classic medical techniques of A T 332: Death at the foot of the bed = death, etc. The medical hero of the Nivernais tale also uses an 'instrument on the tongue' at the moment when he manipulates the forces of death, just as Jean-l'ont-pris uses the whistle (and Truquette, his whistling) at the same point in the narrative. The Nivernais hero treats the king (just as Jean-l'ont-pris treats Sestier). But he also treats, as in *Jean-de-trop*, the king's daughter. (In *Jean-l'ont-pris*, Fabre has transformed this treatment into an 'anti-treatment' of the powerful man's 'anti-daughter', namely, Barbe-Garouille.) The tricking of Death, as in *Jean-de-trop*, takes place on the occasion of the treatment given by the hero to preserve or extend the life of the king's child (in Nivernais, his son; in *Jean-de-trop*, his daughter). In *Jean-l'ont-pris*, for various reasons, including the inversions of the narrative that I have analysed, the tricking of Death occurs in the first, paramedical act in which the hero is concerned with the health or temporarily threatened life of the king, or rather with that of the powerful man (Sestier). Lastly, we come to the final reckoning with Death: here the Nivernais tale ends with the death of the hero. *Jean-de-trop*, on the other hand, ends with a rather insipid happy ending. As for Fabre's narrative, it remains (because of the specific, 'inverted' structure that characterizes its second part) in expectation, but not certainty, of a happy ending.

The short Nivernais narrative does not have the force of detail of

Jean-l'ont-pris or the poetic charm of *Jean-de-trop*. But it, too, derives from a 'common trunk' that gave rise to these two texts; in other words, that gave rise to Fabre's unsentimental narrative in the eighteenth century, and to the over-worked, ornamented narrative of the nineteenth-century Narbonnais story-teller. This Nivernais version managed – this is one of its merits – to preserve something of the fresh crudeness of an original that has since been lost, long ago diffused into several 'examples', oral and variable, in diverse regions of southern and western Europe, and more particularly in southern, central and western France. Fabre was a great lover of oral literature; he loved this original version, a joy for the writer that he was, a pleasure for the abbé's listeners or readers that we are.

At the end of this chapter, I shall propose a genealogy of the narratives that I have examined, including *Jean-l'ont-pris* itself. Let us call, using a highly arbitrary term, the 'older *Jean-de-trop*' (in inverted commas, to differentiate it from the later *Jean-de-trop* version that was collected and published in 1885) the 'original' tale (this origin being not absolute, which would be quite meaningless here, but relative only to our subject, in relation to which this 'older *Jean-de-trop*' enjoys a simple situation of pre-existing anteriority). This 'older *Jean-de-trop*' would thus appear to be situated in the much broader, more general framework at the A T 332 cycle – the Germanic, French, Occitan and southern European cycle of *Godfather Death*. The 'older *Jean-de-trop*', with its location and multinational circulation, gave birth, by virtue of its anteriority, to the strictly literary, yet nevertheless folkloric creation, in 1756, of Fabre's *Jean-l'ont-pris*. This 'older *Jean-de-trop*' was to survive, moreover, in the nineteenth century in the form of at least four versions: Austrian, Narbonnais, Breton and Nivernais, the first three being more detailed and, one might say, more poetic, the last being crude and short, and remaining closer, by virtue of a certain native freshness, to the 'original'.

It is obviously difficult to pronounce on the place, even approximately, of the first blossoming of this 'older *Jean-de-trop*', which was to become in Languedoc one of the important matrices of our *Jean-l'ont-pris*. It represents one of the green offshoots of that multiple, living and broader root-stock, A T 332/*Godfather Death* in general, from the Middle Ages, the Renaissance and the baroque period. Let us note first that Death, in three of the four versions derived from this 'older *Jean-de-trop*' that were collected between 1864 and 1908, is a *godfather* [*der Tod*] and not a godmother. (This feminization and Latinization occurs only in Languedoc. I am referring on this point to the grandmother who acts as godmother in *Jean-l'ont-pris* and to the godmother in *Jean-de-trop*. We should also note in the literary, but nevertheless very old version, *Jean-l'ont-pris*, the occurrence of two male characters among the forces of death, that is, Quincarlot and the baron.) We should also remember the epicentre, generally thought to be German, of AT 332/*Godfather Death*, and the clearly German origin of the 'Swiss tale', which, after its oral migration through Provence and the lower Rhône, was also to become one of the matrices of *Jean-l'ont-pris*. These different data incline me to the view that this 'older *Jean-de-trop*' also travelled, during the baroque age, from the German-speaking, Austro-Swiss world in which it crystallized, through southern France (the Languedoc of *Jean-l'ont-pris* and *Jean-de-trop*), through central France (the Nivernais tale of *Death*) and to Celtic western France (the Brittany of *Ankou's Godson*). I might add in passing that I do not mean to deny the Celtic nature of Ankou, but to suggest that under his sinister cloak-shroud, this Breton character was quite capable of sheltering a number of importations from the east. Table 24 will conclude this point.

The folkloric comparisons carried out in this book are, of course, of limited scope. Let us set them, in all lucidity and therefore in all modesty, against two far more ambitious undertakings: that of Dumézil, who traces, over a span of three thousand or four thousand years, the Indo-European myths, which brought trifunctionality, from India to Scandinavia, and from Ireland to Iran; and that of Lévi-Strauss, including and deducing from one another tales or myths by the hundred, over an area extending from the Amazon Basin to the Rocky Mountains, to reveal the deepest structures of the human mind, as it has been formed over hundreds of thousands of years. In comparison, the dimensions of the work I am presenting here appear small, decidedly provincial. Beginning with a Languedocian text, I have attempted to explore, for purposes of comparison, the purely regional sector of the Occitan fiction of the *ancien régime*. I then considered the cycle of *a single* tale type (AT 332/*Godfather Death*). While still keeping one eye on Fabre's narrative, I have tried to

Table 24

THE 'OLDER *JEAN-DE-TROP*', SUB-TYPE OF AT 332/*GODFATHER DEATH*, IDENTIFIED IN SOUTHERN AND FAR-WESTERN EUROPE (AUSTRIA, OCCITANIA, BRITTANY.)

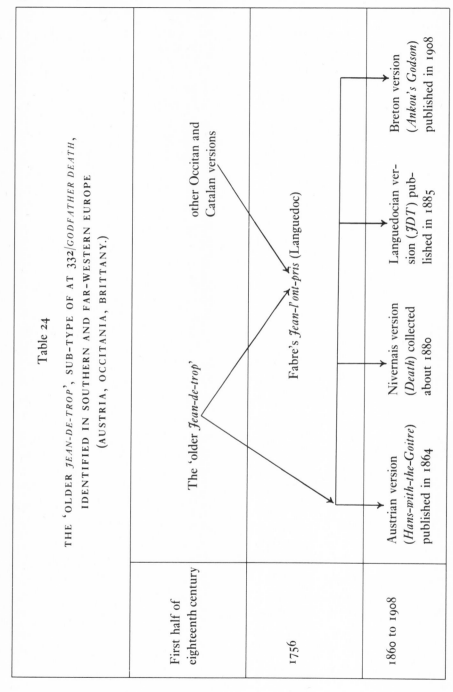

First half of eighteenth century	The 'older *Jean-de-trop*'		other Occitan and Catalan versions
1756		Fabre's *Jean-l'ont-pris* (Languedoc)	
1860 to 1908	Austrian version (*Hans-with-the-Goitre*) published in 1864	Nivernais version (*Death*) collected about 1880	Languedocian version (*JDT*) published in 1885 / Breton version (*Ankou's Godson*) published in 1908

follow the various versions of this tale over four hundred years and in several countries (Germany, mainly southern France, Catalonia, etc.). The diffusion of the themes studied, which migrated a short distance over the Rhine–Rhône or Alps–Cévennes axes, does not present the enormous problems involved in a cultural transference from the Himalayas to Sweden (or vice versa). The contacts among the western European countries referred to here were constant: they took place by means of roads, rivers, exchanges of all kinds; story-tellers, itinerant or sedentary; wandering preachers, who knew Latin. On the frontiers they were bilingual in two vulgar tongues, Germanic and Romance; the oral transmission, during the hundred years before and after 1756, in a period of major flowering in non-written literature, would meet no insurmountable obstacles – on the contrary. One will forgive, then, the rural researcher that I am for broaching a problem in popular culture whose narrow scope certainly did not require the encyclopedic knowledge of a historian of religions who reads forty languages, or the genius of one of the greatest anthropologists of our time. To conclude this point, I hope I will be allowed to quote an opinion of some authority; it summarizes the spirit of the comparative enquiry that I have undertaken concerning *Jean-l'ont-pris* and *Godfather Death*: 'The only demonstrations to which we may lay claim,' declares Lévi-Strauss, 'are those that enable us to explain more than one could before ... They clear the ground for other demonstrations that will come later and explain still more, and so on, *ad infinitum*.'[39] Indeed, it seems to me that in view of my interpretation, one can now explain 'more than one could before' about *Jean-l'ont-pris*. This interpretation reveals, as Fabre himself says, 'riddles';[40] it gives Fabre's novella a certain internal coherence, in its entirety and its details; this internal coherence was totally lacking as long as one confined oneself to seeing this narrative as simply 'village realism'.

Originating in a fairy-tale, *JLP*, thanks to the master sources of *Godfather Death*, has repercussions on a more general conception of the fairy-tale itself. On this point, I shall make use of the fine work of the anthropologist Nicole Belmont, which owes much to the work of V. Propp. Nicole Belmont has worked out a model that accounts for the structure of a fairly large number of tale types, including, in fact, *Godfather/Death*. At the centre of these narratives, according to Nicole Belmont, lies a phenomenon of supernatural initiation of the young man or hero. This initiation is reminiscent of that undergone by boys among the peoples of Africa or among the South American Indians: 'The initiation phase in these countries consists for the boy of being extricated from the influence of his mother (or of his father, or of his environment), in order to be integrated (after this phase), through marriage, into the society of truly adult men . . . The young men of the Ojibwa Indians move away from their families . . . until such time as a supernatural character appears to them who is called their guardian spirit.'[41] Among the peoples of Indo-European origin, which include those of northern and southern France, 'this initiation has disappeared from rituals, supposing these to have ever existed, but it remains present in the Imaginary, in the myths on which fairy-tales are based.' The hero of such tales is also striving, during this initiation stage, to break the Oedipal links that have bound him to his parents during childhood and adolescence. His task is to prepare himself for the possession of a wife; she is born of a king or of a rich man, since we are in a fairy-tale world; the wedding will mark the young man's final severance from childhood and youth.

The hero who undergoes such an initiation must in the course of it bind himself, for a time, to supernatural entities who facilitate the transition. These may be embodied by the forces of death or by Death in person. These have their roots, in any case, in the Beyond or in the land of the dead, which is quite alien to our everyday world.

This general model applies to tales that have many different versions, such as *The Love of Three Oranges* (AT 408) or *The Voyage into the Other World* (AT 471). Such a model also covers AT 332/*Godfather Death*, a tale derived from a myth. Lastly, through AT 332, the 'Belmont model' operates at a deep level in *Jean-l'ont-pris*, a novella derived from a tale. Thanks to the intercessions of grandmother Death, transposed from the supernatural into the hyper-realistic, Truquette makes a final break with his native Rouergue; he becomes the son-in-law and *compère* of Death; he marries the attractive and dangerous Margot; the marriage turns out to be disastrous. Similarly, the successive intercessions of those strange characters, also naturalized from the Beyond – grandmother Death, again, the diabolical

Quincarlot and the mysterious baron – take Jean-l'ont-pris through the macabre stages of a necessary initiation: in due course they will enable him to obtain treasure, and to enjoy the body of the adorable Babeau, the rich man's daughter.

Is there ready to hand any 'other demonstration', of the type proposed by Lévi-Strauss in the quotation in Chapter XIV, that will take us still further? It seems to me, in any case, that the theory which I have proposed throughout the second part of this book ought to be tested, confirmed or 'refuted' by independent evidence. Is *Jean-l'ont-pris* really an adaptation, encoded by the abbé Fabre, of a *Godfather Death* that had already spread in oral versions through Occitania during the writer's youth? If so, the traditional thesis of the flat 'village realism' of *JLP* would appear inadequate, to say the least. In any case, the moment has come to put my own theory (now expounded in detail) to the test.

This test will take the form of a version from Roussillon or northern Catalonia of *Godfather Death*, which I have deliberately kept until the end. It comes from Vallespir, the tiny cultural conservatory in the valley of the Tech in the eastern Pyrenees, which, from the folkloric, linguistic and geographical point of view, are so close to the Narbonnais Languedoc of *JDT* and to the Nîmois-Montpellierian Languedoc of *JLP*. This Roussillonnais version was published in Catalan by the abbé Estève Caseponce,[1] a remarkable local collector of fairy-tales, in his *Contes Vallespirenchs replegats per En Mir y Nontoquis*.[2] The text collected by Estève Caseponce, in Catalan, is called *The Coal-merchant–Physician* [*El Metge carboner*]. The excellent version produced by the Roussillonnais priest, from oral sources, fully confirms the conclusions that I have drawn in the second part of this work concerning the close kinship between *JLP* and A T 332/*Godfather Death*, and concerning the even closer affinity that specifically links *JLP* with the particular cycle of *Jean-de-trop* and related versions from Languedoc and Roussillon. Here is a summary of the *Coal-merchant–Physician*, a narrative that I shall call, from now on, *Galdric*, the name of the 'coal-merchant–physician' in the tale.

First part of the tale: Galdric and Rosetot

PHASE A: *Death as godfather.* The poor coal-merchant Galdric, husband of the young lady Rosetot (a diminutive of Rosette), is standing

at the roadside when a man passes by, a just man, worthy to become
the godfather of his newborn child; he already has half a dozen
children. The poor coal-merchant, who has failed to find a godfather
for this child among his relations, friends and acquaintances, has
then rejected various characters for this role, including a cobbler and
other craftsmen belonging to different guilds (seven in number),
then St Peter, then Our Lord himself. The coal-merchant is losing
patience, when at last he sees an individual (Death), wrapped in
a cloak, whose bones rattle like bits of wood [brocs de llenya]. Seeing
him, the coal-merchant–hero feels a shiver down his back [esquena].
Overcoming his fear, he nevertheless accepts Death as godfather
(male), because he is just. (It will be noted that this version of the tale
belongs, by virtue of this fact and also for a number of other reasons,
to a well-preserved stratum: Death is not a *godmother*, and has not
therefore undergone the usual feminization of the role that often
occurred in the Latin countries. He remains a godfather, as in the
original A T 332 from the Germanic countries, *Gevatter Tod* in the
masculine, in other words, *compère* Death or godfather Death. This
authenticating archaism does not, in fact, prevent the introduction,
later in this Catalan version of the tale, of certain anachronisms
dating from between 1780 and 1850, concerning, for example, the use
of potatoes and the cholera epidemic.)

In any case, Galdric takes Death to his house [casa], to the great
scandal of the 'neighbours and acquaintances', who are panic-
stricken.

Death goes into the coal-merchant's hovel [casota]. He says to
Rosetot, Galdric's wife: *Do not be afraid.* Indeed, a little later, Death
adds: *I am your friend.* He then promises future prosperity to the
couple. He goes off to the church for the child's baptism, accompanied by the nursemaid, who holds the baby; an old neighbour, who
has agreed to be godmother; the father, who is holding his last but
one child in his arms; and all the rest of the brood. The baby is
wearing special swaddling-clothes and a richly coloured shawl. The
ceremony takes place on Sunday, since the villagers are just leaving
church when the baptismal procession arrives.

This ceremonial, macabre arrival causes a new scandal: everybody
flees at the sight of Death and his entourage. Even the children do
not pick up the sweetmeats which, according to custom, have been

distributed. The baptism takes place, despite the priest's terror. The baby behaves perfectly and appears not to mind the splashes of baptismal water. The 'creature'[3] (that is, the infant), having become a Christian, is then wrapped in the multicoloured shawl, and the procession returns to the house, as the church bells ring out a somewhat sinister peel. The story-teller adds in passing that this event takes place in a small village [*poblet*] and that the story was told to him by his own godmother.

When they (the baptismal procession) are about to reach the house, the guests [*convidats*] distribute several dozen small cakes and a couple of quarter handfuls of chestnuts [*jittar, per relleu, qualques dotzenas de neules i un parell de cosses de castanyons*]. Then they have a little feast with a few almonds, a mountain cheese with a thousand scents, a golden rye cake and a jug of resinous wine.

When the 'feast' is over, Death takes his leave, again promising wealth to the coal-merchant's family; then, after passing the door (*in front of the door*, outside), he announces to the coal-merchant Galdric that he is going to pay him for the *honour* that has been given him, that is, the 'honour' of being offered the godfatherhood and feasted. 'You did not flee from me like all the others,' says Death. 'You honoured me. I am going to reward you, not by giving you money (I do not have any), but by changing your trade.' The coal-merchant retorts that, despite his poverty, he has always managed to provide his family with bread on the table and soup in the pot; and although his hands and face are black, his heart is always white.

Death then explains to him that he will make him into a physician. He will know in advance that his patient will soon die if he sees Death crouching at the patient's head; conversely, if Death is not at his head, the patient will recover. Death promises the future physician that, armed with this infallible diagnosis, he will gather money by the spadeful [*a paladas*].

All he needs now is to obtain clothes suitable for a gentleman, in keeping with his new profession. So Death advises a somewhat worried Galdric to sell the now unfashionable earrings that he had given to Rosetot as a wedding present.[4] 'With that,' Death concludes, 'you will be able to buy your gentleman's clothes and support your family until your work as a physician begins to make you rich.'

Second part of the tale: Galdric as physician

PHASE B: *Death's gifts*. The coal-merchant and his wife accept Death's 'generous' propositions. Galdric and Rosetot are delighted at the idea of becoming respectively a 'gentleman' and a 'lady'.

Galdric arrives in town with thirty coins [*douros*], which he has obtained from the sale of his wife's earrings. With this sum he buys (in particular) a silver snuff-box and, of course, a doctor's coat, shoes with silver buckles and a doctor's tall hat, or toque.

When he gets to the city, Galdric learns that the king's son is sick, and he goes to the royal palace to see him. He observes that Death is not sitting at the head of the sick-bed, and he is therefore able to predict infallibly the prince's cure. He also correctly predicts the imminent death of the son of the king's gardener, who is also sick, but almost recovered, at whose head he sees Death crouching. On each of his 'medical visits', either to the king's son or to the gardener's son, Galdric takes great care to take the patient's pulse in order to display his great competence.[5]

At the sight of this double prediction by Galdric, the king, very impressed, gives a dinner for the physician, and sets before him such exquisite sweetmeats that the former coal-merchant thinks for a moment that he will gorge himself so much that he will burst.

Galdric is then installed in a room, with a bed enclosed in silk and lace draperies; as a result, he imagines that he is being put in a chapel [*capella*] and is thought to be a 'saint'.

Galdric is tired from walking all morning from his old hovel to the royal city. He falls asleep in his new, luxurious room. During the next eight days, the coal-merchant continues to eat 'better and better' and to sleep 'like a caterpillar in a cocoon'.

After eight days, the king's son has recovered, and the gardener's son has died. After the burial of the gardener's son, the king gives Galdric 1,000 *douros* as a reward for his skill and care. The coal-merchant–physician, delighted, thinks he has 'caught the hare napping'; in no time at all, the poor coal-merchant has become a great gentleman. He dresses his wife and children like princes, and has a palatial castle built on the site of his former shack. There he gives feasts: rare birds of every plumage are eaten there, and bread as white as a lily, wines and liqueurs of every colour, fruit from every land.

The coal-merchant is truly happy. The wind may blow, poor men [*Ronge-oignons*] may shiver, but all is well.

PHASE C: *Death tricked*. Death invites Galdric to visit his palace. The hero is afraid and has gooseflesh, on hearing the cry of the shades of those whom Death has touched with his scythe. In hall after hall Death shows the hero men's lights of life. Death is going to kill the coal-merchant, but the latter tricks him by promising to say a *Pater Noster*, which he does not recite. He says of this trick, a little later, *I am a good Christian, but . . .*

PHASE D: *Death takes his revenge and attacks the hero*. In the end, Death tricks Galdric into saying his *Pater Noster*. Then he is able to seize the hero, who dies. And *cric crac*, concludes the story-teller, the tale is over.

This version of AT 332 from Roussillon, which I have called *Galdric*, is very close geographically and structurally to our *Jean-de-trop* from Aude, not to mention *Jean-l'ont-pris* from the Vaunage. Of course, there is an important difference. *JLP* and *JDT* are bigenerational: first the adventures of Truquette (or of JDT's poor parents); then those of JLP (or of JDT, as physician). Galdric, on the other hand, covers both parts: he is monogenerational; he is first a poor man like JDT's father, then a physician like JDT himself. The four-part cycle of AT 332 occurs twice, at the level of the father, then of the son, in *JDT* (and similarly in *JLP*) but only once in *Galdric*.

In any case, one finds in *Galdric* (abbreviated to *G*) a similar concatenation of sequences homologous to those found in *JDT*: at the beginning, a poor family; 'half a dozen' children; lack of relations or friends willing (*JDT*, p. 184) or able (*Galdric*, p. 38) to be godfather to the child. The same word for 'relations' [*parents*, in Occitan and in Catalan] is used in both texts at this precise point. A succession of characters is then paraded before us: Jesus Christ is accepted (*JDT*) or refused (*G*) as godfather; immediately afterwards, Death is accepted as godmother (*JDT*) or accepted as godfather (*G*). Then Death causes a scandal with his or her appearance before the baptismal feast (*G*) or during it (*JDT*). The child's *elder brother* is referred to in both tales: (1) he fetches two women invited to the baptism, namely, the nursemaid and an old neighbour who agrees to become godfather

Death's *commère* (the baby's godmother) in the Roussillonnais version (*Galdric*, p. 46); (2) he turns two capons on the spit for the baptismal meal (*JDT*, p. 187). On two successive occasions in both tales, during or around the baptism, Death promises prosperity. The instructions given by Death to the hero are followed by 'miraculous cures' (Death being at the patient's feet, in fact, and therefore harmless) in the king's family. The hero has previously gone to the town (Paris in *JDT*, some indeterminate city in *Galdric*; in any case, it is the city where the king lives). Galdric treats the king's son, just as JDT treats the king's daughter; in the end the hero tricks Death, temporarily in *JDT*, and temporarily, too, in *Galdric*. This trick is the occasion of another strategic and tactical concordance between *Galdric* and *JDT*: during phase 3 (*Death tricked*), in the course of which the Roussillonnais Death is outwitted by the hero Galdric, Death is afraid of being out of work (p. 63), and that 'no one will die' [*moriria pas mingù*] in Catalan. This is exactly what takes place in phase 3 (*Death tricked*) of the second part of *JDT* (p. 193); during the period in which JDT manages to confine Death, 'no one dies' [*digus non mouriguet*, in Occitan]. It should be added that the last words are the same in both tales: *cric crac, the tale is over*.[6] Later, in a comparison between *Galdric* and *JLP*, I shall bring out other similarities, even in detail, between *Galdric* and *JDT*. Furthermore, we are dealing with two oral versions of the same tale type (AT 332), narrated in two neighbouring regions in languages (Occitan and Catalan) that are very close to each other. It does not go without saying, but it is perfectly legitimate to believe, that these two versions are closely related, in overall structure and in detail.

More interesting, of course, are the comparisons that may be made between *Galdric* and *JLP*, since this time we are dealing with the interpretation of an important literary work. The parallel that emerges as a result of these comparisons can in no way derive from an act of plagiarism committed by the abbé Caseponce (1907) at the expense of the abbé Fabre (1756). This parallel derives from a kinship between the two tales that goes back to a common model prior to both of them; this model represents in turn one of the local incarnations that took root in Languedoc and in Catalonia of the master structures of AT 332, which were originally (well before 1756) imported from more easterly regions.

Let us begin with an episode that appears as a veritable 'signature', definitely linking the JLP from Languedoc, through a common 'ancestor', to the coal-merchant–physician from Roussillon. This is the distribution of 'sweetmeats', on entering and leaving the church for the baptism, in the tale from Roussillon; it is paralleled by the similar incident when the guests enter and leave the church during the wedding of Truquette and Margot in *JLP*. I have shown in Chapter IX that these two festive ceremonies (baptismal and nuptial) are homologous. To be more precise, Fabre has transferred to the festivities of *marriage* itself, which, because of Margot's already well-advanced pregnancy, precedes the birth and baptism of J L P by only a few days, what in the classic version of AT 332, in Languedoc, Catalonia, etc., concerns the festivities of baptism: these may include the distribution of sweetmeats in the street, which occurs just before the banquet itself, whether it is nuptial or baptismal. In the case of *JLP*, these 'sweetmeats' (and others) are thrown to the crowd of bystanders by Truquette, Margot and the grandmother (Margot's mother); in *Galdric*, it is the guests themselves [*convidats*][7] who carry out this 'general aspersion'.

The difference is easily explained: in *JLP*, Truquette and Margot have their hands free and can therefore fling handfuls of hazelnuts and hackberries into the roadway. In the Roussillonnais tale, on the other hand, it is a baptism and not a wedding: the wife, who has only just given birth, stays in bed and does not go to the baptism; the husband has his hands full, carrying the last but one child, who is already heavy; it is therefore quite logical that it should be the guests who throw the sweetmeats to the crowd.

Jean-l'ont-pris and the Catalan tale present, on the subject of these distributions of sweetmeats, the following acts (see Table 25).

Squares A, B and E of Table 25 concern respectively the places, times and final outcome of the episode in question. They present no problem since they are similar in both columns, left and right, except that we are dealing with a baptismal ceremony on the left, and with an immediately pre-baptismal nuptial ceremony on the right. Lines C and D reinforce this impression of very close kinship between the Catalan tale and *JLP* (or, once more, between the locally Roussillonnais AT 332 and the Languedocian *JLP*), since we are dealing, in effect, with a traditional distribution of sweetmeats,

Table 25

DISTRIBUTION OF SWEETMEATS DURING THE FESTIVITIES

	Roussillonnais tale (pp. 46–8)	*JLP* [15–16]
A. Places of this distribution	A1: on the path leading from the house to the church, then from the church to the house (return journey)	A2: same locations (exactly) as in A1
B. Times of this distribution	B1: before and after the baptism of the child of Galdric and Rosetot	B2: before and after the wedding of Truquette and Margot, which precedes by some days the baptism of their child, JLP
C. Food given not to the guests, but thrown to the on-lookers	C1: 'several *dozen* small cakes [*neules*]' are thrown	C2: '*four* pounds of hazelnuts, which my father threw. . .' [15]
D. Food distributed	D1: 'a couple (*parell*) of quarter handfuls [*cosses*] of chestnuts' are also thrown	D2: 'all the handfuls of hackberries that my mother threw to left and right as she raised her leg' [15]
E. Final meal (baptismal or nuptial)	E1: final meal (after the baptism)	E2: final meal (after the wedding) [homologous meal to that in E1]

appearing in both columns at the same strategic point of the episode. Even more interesting is the homology between the two *successive* distributions of sweetmeats, which occur on the left and right respectively. In both cases, there is a decline from one distribution to the next. The Roussillonnais version (on the left) confines itself to recording the agricultural products involved. Moreover, these products were either baked or smoked: in the first distribution (C1) of Table 25 the sweetmeats consist of *neules* (small, compact, delicious cakes, made of Eucharistic dough, baked in the oven); then in D1 the distribution consists of *châtaignons* ['smoked chestnuts', in other words, the poor man's bread].

The corresponding sub-episode of *JLP* (on the right) is confined to wild or uncooked food, in contrast with the cooked sweetmeats of *Galdric*. At the first distribution, the small cakes of the Roussillonnais tale are replaced, logically enough, in Fabre, by hazelnuts, which are also compact and succulent; at the second distribution, the plebeian *châtaignons* are replaced by hackberries, which grow wild and are more vulgar and less edible still.

LINES C AND D IN TABLE 25 (detail)

	Galdric	*JLP*
First distribution	small cakes ↓	hazelnuts ↓
Second distribution	chestnuts	hackberries

The ways of enumerating and measuring the foodstuffs distributed on both occasions are also strikingly parallel.

In the first distribution, the items thrown are enumerated in fours or in multiples of four, in other words, dozens. 'Several *dozen* small cakes' (*Galdric*) or '*four* pounds of hazelnuts' (*JLP*).

In these two cases, we do not yet find the measurements of *volume* that are systematically employed in the second distribution: we find only a measure of weight, the *pound* (four *pounds* of hazelnuts in *JLP*); or no measure at all, but simply an enumeration (several dozen small cakes in *Galdric*).

During the second distribution, the throwing of food among the crowd of onlookers is introduced, in Roussillon as in *JLP*, by the indefinite article or number 'one'. *A* couple [*parell*] of quarter handfuls [*cosses*] of chestnuts (Roussillon), and '*a quartaud* of hackberries' [*JLP*, second version] or '*a* handful of hackberries' [*JLP*, first version]. Moreover, the measurements used are of exactly the same kind: in both cases they are measurements of volume. In *JLP*, they are the *pugnère* ['handful'] and the *quartaud*[8] (which is itself the quarter of a measurement of volume), these two terms, *pugnère* and *quartaud*, being widely used in Languedoc and Catalonia. One also finds these two terms, fused together, in the word *cosse*, which is used, in the same line D of Table 25, by the Roussillonnais version. *Cosse*, in Catalan or in Occitan, actually means 'fraction of a handful', or, to be more precise, 'a quarter handful'.[9]

SECOND DISTRIBUTION OF SWEETMEATS	
Volumetric measurement used	
JLP	Roussillonnais version
[second version] *quartaud* ['quarter'] ————————→	*cosse*, in other words quarter
[first version] handful ————————→	of a handful

After these sweetmeats, we go into the kitchen–dining-room of the house and observe in the register of poverty, on both left and right, the profound similarity of the two meals that accompany respectively the baptism in Roussillon and the immediately pre-baptismal wedding in *JLP*.

Very noticeable are the often pejorative and ironic expressions used opposite each other in the left-hand and right-hand columns: in F1, the almonds are 'cadged'; in F2, Truquette's wild fruits add up to a ridiculous list for a wedding meal. In G1, the cake is not wheaten, but rye; in G2, the cereals form not bread, but a sort of peasant boiled pudding called *farinette*. The mountain cheese in H1 refers back to

Table 26

MENUS OF THE TWO MEALS

	The 'little feast' of the Roussillonnais version	The poverty-stricken meal in *JLP*
F. Fruit	F1: a few almonds cadged from Arenys	F2: chestnuts, sloes, cornel-berries, arbutus-berries, mulberries [17]
G. Cereal-based food	G1: a cake made of golden rye	G2: two large pots of girdle-cakes
H. Animal produce	H1: a mountain cheese with a thousand scents	H2: *garrigue* fox, frogs, *roussette*, magpies [17]
J. Wine	J1: a pitcher of resinous wine	J2: a four-*setier* barrel of wine

the *garrigue* fox of H2: a double reference to wild or semi-wild nature. Lastly, the pitcher of 'resinous wine' in J1 corresponds, unit for unit, to the barrel of J2.

If these two homologous meals remain at the level of a certain poverty characteristic of *JLP*, the following dinners given by Galdric, now rich or about to be, will suggest, on the other hand, the splendid baptismal feast given for Jean-de-trop. *Galdric* thus forms a bridge between the poverty of *JLP* and the 'purely' fairy-tale atmosphere of *JDT*.

There can be no doubt that *Galdric* is closely related to both *JLP* and *JDT*, which are themselves closely related to each other. The common, original denominator is one or several old versions of a sub-type of AT 332, long native to Languedoc and Roussillon; one should stress among these versions, particularly but not exclusively, the presence of this archaic version, necessarily prior to 1756, which I have called, for lack of a better name, the 'older *Jean-de-trop*'.

Once *JLP* is securely linked in this way to *Galdric* and vice versa, a whole series of similar, additional details help to form many more links between the two narratives.

Table 27

COMPARISON OF GALDRIC AND JDT

JDT's baptismal meal (p. 187)	The two meals that will later be described at the baptism of Galdric's son (pp. 49 and 59 of the Catalan–Roussillonnais text published by Caseponce, 1907)
K1: 'on the table' [*taulo*, in Occitan] . . .	K2: 'on the table' [*taula*, in Catalan] . . .
L1: a large pot for the soup . . .	L2: soup in a pot . . .
M1: a turkey and two capons . . .	M2: rare birds of every plumage . . .
N1: large bottles of old wine . . .	N2: wines and liqueurs of every colour . . .
O1: fruit of every kind . . .	O2: fruit from every land . . .
P1: a *white* table-cloth, *snow-white* bread; creams . . .	P2: *bread as white as a lily* . . . Though the hands of the master of the house are black his heart is ever *white* . . .

We should note first the remarkable homology in the names, at the level of the parental couple, in both cases.

These two couples occupy the same functional position in both narratives. It is therefore interesting to observe that the names of the two women are composed in exactly the same way: a word that designates a flower (*Rose* or *Rosette*, and *Marguerite*) followed by the diminutive suffix -*ot*. The flower 'rose' is simply 'extended' into *Rosetot*; the flower 'marguerite' is 'contracted' into *Margot*.[10] The

Table 28	
The husbands' *names*	
Roussillonnais version	*Galdric* is *Rosetot*'s husband.
JLP	*Truquette* is *Margot*'s husband.

names of the two men, on the other hand, are very different semantically; Truquette, in Occitan, means 'pint pot' and Galdric, who, as we shall see later, is more interested in tobacco than in wine, bears a name of Catalono-Visigothic origin. These two male names, however, are both characterized by a veritable forest of consonants (five in each case): they are rich in noisy assonances of the *dric-truc*, *cric-crac* or *triqua-traqua* kind, in other words:

GaLDRIC

TRUQueTTe

Let us return now to the shared motifs, located at homologous points, which will finally establish the close kinship between *JLP* and AT 332/*Galdric*. First motif: the character of Death is wrapped in a 'coloured cloak' [*manta de color*] at his first appearance *at the beginning* of *Galdric*; now, logically, in the course of a rather later link in the basic narrative, when Death or grandmother Death causes a scandal, it is the fact that she is now without this necessarily pre-existing cloak, the fact that she is naked or in her night-dress, that fully characterizes this later episode in *JDT* and in *JLP* [22].

In the Roussillonnais version, Death's bones at the beginning of the narrative make a sinister noise like 'bits of wood' [*brocs de llenya*]. In *JLP*, grandmother Death, at the beginning of the narrative, specializes in the manufacture of bits of wood [*brocs* or *brouquéttas*], in other words, matches; we have seen how Fabre gives these matches [*allumettes*, in French] the role carried out by the lights of life in the classic versions of AT 332. Similarly, in *JLP*, the young men of

Solorgues who are courting Margot look down on the other girls in the village as though they were 'bits of wood' [*flocs de bôï*] or 'bats' [8]. Later, it is Margot, now monopolized by her lover Truquette, who is in turn abandoned, for good or ill, by her lovers [12]: she is now treated by them as a 'bit of wood' (comparable to her mother's sinister bones) or as a bat (bird of ill-omen).

A little later, the preparations for the feast (nuptial and pre-baptismal in *JLP*, baptismal in *JDT* and in *Galdric*) attract *friends and relations* in *JLP* [15], *relations, friends and neighbours* in *JDT* (pp. 184 and 186), *neighbours and acquaintances* in *Galdric* (pp. 45 and 46). The coal-merchant Galdric and his Rosetot live in a hovel [*casota*, p. 46] in their native Vallespir; at the beginning of their married life, Truquette and his Margot live in a cellar [*crôtta*, 19], which serves both as a bedroom and as a cobbler's workshop. The village of Solorgues is a 'hole' [*cros*], so small that it does not even have a resident priest; the village in which Galdric lives is also a tiny locality [*poblet*, p. 47].

In *JLP*, *JDT* and *Galdric*, one finds the same promises of prosperity made by Death (or grandmother Death) to the parental couple and baby during the same ceremonial, scandalous festivities; these three narratives (see Chapter X) also mention the scandalous effect produced by the appearance of the macabre character of Death or grandmother Death on the couple's neighbours. The *bell* is tolled, on *Sunday*, for the journey to the church (explicitly or implicitly for the baptism), in *Galdric* and in *JLP*. The child of Truquette and Margot and the child of Galdric and Rosetot are both compared to a *creature* who is becoming 'Christian', and who wishes to be Christian and even 'a good Christian' or 'most Christian' (*Galdric*, pp. 38 and 47; *JLP* [67] and, second version [69]). *Galdric* is similar on this point both to Fabre's work [67] and to other Catalan versions from farther south ('I'm a good Christian,' says the hero of AT 332 in the text collected by Amades).

The words used by Death after the feast and the scandalous scene caused by his or her appearance, when Death promises prosperity to the godson and his family, are substantially, if not exactly, the same in both narratives: 'Down-and-outs like us,' says grandmother Death, 'are ladies and gentlemen compared with lousy tramps like you; my son-in-law and daughter have [*sount rîchés*] over 100 francs of their own, not to mention what they'll have from me' [*JLP*, 26]. In *Galdric*, there is a similar idea at the same strategic point (farewell to hunger and suffering, welcome wealth), and the same words, at this very point, right down to the finest detail: 'Death took leave of Galdric's family, assuring them that they had done with suffering and would now be rich [*serien rics*]' (p. 48).

Following the great tradition of the Spanish, Venetian, German and, above all, Occitan (*JLP* and *JDT* included, see Chapter X) versions of A T 332, Death in *Galdric* distributes his gifts and promises of great prosperity *in front of the door*, that is to say, once he has passed the threshold of the hero's house, *going out* (p. 48). Conversely, he becomes dangerous once again when he is behind the door (behind the door of his own palace and inside it [*Galdric*, p. 59 and above all p. 60]. The significance of being *in front of* and *behind the door* is exactly the same as in *JLP* and *JDT*. The wedding meal (*JLP*) or baptismal meal (*Galdric*) is compared in both cases to an *honour* paid by the hero to his guests, including Death (*JLP* [14]; *Galdric*, p. 48). The Roussillonnais Death remarks that everybody flees from him, except Galdric (p. 48); similarly, Truquette, after eliminating all his competitors, stands at the same strategic point in the narrative as the only character who has succeeded in becoming intimate with grandmother Death and her daughter, Margot [12]. The end of the pathetic banquet (nuptial or baptismal) is marked in both texts, Languedocian and Roussillonnais (and also in another Catalan version, that collected by Amades), by the same words: 'After the feast . . .' [*Aprés la fêsta . . .*, *JLP*, 18]; 'When the feast was over . . .' [*El festill acabat . . .*, *Galdric*, p. 48]. These two phrases, in both cases, come immediately after the lists of food provided at the two banquets, analysed in Table 26.

One should also note a remarkably similar transition in *Galdric* and in *JLP*. Indeed, these two narratives depict (1) scandalous scenes: the terrifying appearance of Death, banquet, disturbance (*JLP*) or general terror (*Galdric*). These scenes are followed after a 'transition' by the beginning (2) of the phase of prosperity. This transition from (1) to (2) is marked in *JLP* [26–27] by the following sentence: *Each went his own way*. This 'each' refers to the people who, taking part outside [*défôra*, 23] in the scandalous disturbance, are not part of Truquette's family; and *peace was restored to our house* [*ét la paix sé réstabliguêt jusquas dins l'oustâou*]. *My father and mother were still in love . . . They ate their meal in peace, then went to bed as though nothing had happened.* Next morning

Truquette and his wife decide to follow grandmother Death's advice; they turn to prosperity, which is both miraculous and short-lived.

In *Galdric*, more briefly (p. 51), things happen in a similar way: at the same transitional and strategic point in the narrative, just after the scandalous scene and the banquet, and just before the couple's decision concerning their future prosperity, 'the coal-merchant went back into his *house* [*a casa*] . . . When the guests had gone *outside* [*fora*] and when the children of the house [*mainadeta*] had gone to *sleep*, Galdric said to his wife . . .' There follows a conversation that is said by the narrator to be confiding (p. 52) and long (p. 53). The three essential ingredients for a similar transition are therefore present in both tales: the strangers leave, go *outside* [*fora*]; the couple return to their loving intimacy in the *house* [*ostal, casa, mainada*], as they go to *sleep*, and just before taking the final decision as to their future prosperity.

The Roussillonnais godfather Death and grandmother Death of *JLP* announce to the hero in exactly the same way and at the same moment that he must change his trade [*mestié* of cobbler, in Occitan; *ofici* of coal-merchant, in Catalan] in order to become rich (*JLP* [29]; *Galdric*, p. 49). Then Death informs Galdric that once he has become rich in this way, by changing his trade, he will be able to get money 'by the spadeful' [*a paladas*, p. 50]. At the previous stage, Truquette, while still poor [*JLP*, 3], did not have 'a spadeful of earth' [*una palada*] of his own. Later, when Truquette is temporarily rich [35], the money certainly does not come to him in spadefuls, but 'like a downpour of rain' – 'in bucketfuls', as we would now say.[11] Before the hero gets rich, Death (or grandmother Death) plans his attack: he wants to turn Galdric (or Truquette) into a 'gentleman' and Rosetot (or Margot) into a 'lady'.[12] These two titles of 'gentleman' and 'lady' are used in both tales at exactly the same point. And, in fact, Galdric, at the height of his prosperity, dresses his wife and children *like princes* (p. 57). While Truquette, weighed down by his recently acquired bags of crowns, dresses his family so well [35] that his son might be taken 'for the son of the king of Majorca' [second version, 35], in other words, for a prince. This allusion to Majorca in *JLP* might also suggest certain Catalan roots or kinships, as far as the oral version of AT 332 used by the abbé Fabre as raw material for his tale is concerned. We know that the Balearic Islands, which include Majorca, and Roussillon belonged to Catalonia.

At the height of their fortune, Truquette and Galdric both go into 'property': the former cobbler, J L P's father, buys himself 'the finest house *in the neighbourhood*' (Solorgues) [34], while the former coal-merchant has a castle built *on the very site of his old shack* (p. 58). There, too, the strategic and tactical similarity is remarkable. The new palatial building is situated in both cases on the same site as the old, wretched home.

One may also follow the same detail from one tale to the other. For example, Truquette, *before he acquires his great fortune*, buys mere *tin buckles* [14] for his wedding. Galdric, *once he begins to make his fortune*, acquires *silver buckles* for his shoes (p. 53).

A remarkable similarity of a strategic and tactical kind concerns the sale of the young wife's clothes and wedding trousseau [in Fabre's Occitan, *fardas*]: Truquette had bought these wedding *fardas*, these rather ridiculous clothes and tin jewellery, for his wife the day before the wedding [14]. He then sells them, some days after the wedding, in order to buy food for his penniless family, now increased by a new-born child [19]. With the money obtained from this sale, Truquette also buys for himself, explicitly, cheap wine [*vinét*] and, implicitly, tobacco. Or at least this is what emerges from the insults showered upon him by his wife [19]: immediately afterwards, she calls him a drunkard and a *tabateur* (that is, someone who abuses tobacco).

Now, in an exactly homologous way, Galdric sells the gold earrings (now unfashionable) which he had given to his future wife just before their wedding; they form part of the *joyas*, jewels or trousseau that he had given her. The Catalan word *joyas* is the equivalent, in this respect, of the Occitan word *fardas* ['trousseau'], which also means old clothes. On this subject, see pages 51 and 52 of *Galdric*, and the words *enjoyar* and *joyas* as synonym of *fardas* in the *Diccionari de la llengua catalana* of Labernia y Esteller.

With the money that he has obtained, like Truquette, from the sale of his wife's trousseau, Galdric buys, again like Truquette, food for his wife and children. He also buys *for himself* a silver snuff-box. At this precise point in the development of the narrative (according to Margot's insults), Truquette sinks into drunkenness, as does the hero of the 'Swiss tale'. But he also takes to tobacco, as does his homologue Galdric. Here, as elsewhere, AT 332, in its Languedocian and Roussillonnais forms, has exercised a powerful influence over Fabre's novella. Tobacco, dear to Truquette, and the silver snuff-box, dear to Galdric, are acquired at exactly the same moment in the same way; these ingredients are to mark the beginning of the respective rise to fortune of these two heroes, from now on recipients of *Death's gifts*.

Galdric does not confine himself to selling Rosetot's *joyas*; Truquette is not content to sell all of Margot's *fardas*. The Roussillonnais hero, encouraged by Death's advice, and with his wife's agreement, also sells all he possesses in his coal-merchant's cabin [*tot lo que tenet per aqui*, p. 52]; in short, everything that is not strictly indispensable to the survival of his family. From this he gets a little money: 30 *douros*, which he takes to the town, tied in a handkerchief, and with which he buys the clothes that are to enable him to embark on his brilliant medical career. Truquette behaves in exactly the same way throughout the homologous episode; the ex-cobbler is encouraged by the advice of grandmother Death, and this time he is not opposed

Table 29	
SALE, MONEY, TOWN	
A 'Truquette' (Occitan)	B *Galdric* (Catalan)
A1: Grandmother Death advises Truquette to set himself up in commerce.	A2: Death advises Galdric to set himself up in medicine.
B1: In the future, grandmother Death will contribute to the prosperity of Truquette's household.	B2: In the future, Death will contribute (by his position in relation to the sick-bed) to the prosperity of Galdric's medical career.
C1: In view of this wealth to come, Truquette first sells his cobbler's equipment.	C2: In view of this wealth to come, Galdric first sells everything in his coal-merchant's house.
D1: He gets 10 crowns.	D2: He gets 30 *douros*.
E1: He goes to town (Sommières) with this money.	E2: He goes to town (unnamed) with this money.
F1: He buys fine textiles for his new career in commerce.	F2: He buys fine clothes for his new career in medicine.

by his wife Margot: *he sold everything he had in the shop for a total of 10 crowns and, next day, set out for the fair at Sommières* (the most important town in the immediate vicinity of Solorgues) [31]. There, with this money and, what is more, using fraudulent methods, he buys goods, which turn out to be mainly textiles: stuffs, muslin, wool.

Here, the parallel, in general and in detail, between Truquette and Galdric is extraordinary. For the general similarities see Table 29.

As for the detailed parallels, the phases that correspond to the various lines of Table 29 often correspond word for word in both texts. Here is an example, limited to a single sub-episode:

Galdric (p. 53): *a fortnight later, the coal-merchant went off* [*anava*] *to the town with 30 douros* (derived from the sale of his tools, etc.).

'Truquette' [31]: from the sale of the tools of his trade, the cobbler obtained *a total of 10 crowns and, next day, set out* [*anêt*] *for the fair at Sommières*.

These two sentences, which relate to lines C and D of Table 29, each comprise the same four items of information:

(1) the amount of money (in tens of the monetary unit, derived from the sale of the tools);

(2) information as to the time ('a fortnight later', or 'next day');

(3) the hero goes off (use of the verb 'to go' [*anar*, in Catalan; *ana*, in Occitan]);

(4) the purpose of this journey is to go to the town (it is not named in *Galdric*; for Truquette it is Sommières).

Truquette and Galdric both end their careers in a remarkably similar way, seized by Death, in the same sequences.

First, in 'Truquette' [34–36]:

(1) Business is highly successful: the ex-cobbler buys the finest house in the neighbourhood [34], in his own village (Solorgues).

(2) Money falls in buckets into Truquette's coffers, and this hero has all the signs of prosperity (fine clothes, a large stock of stuffs, etc. [35–36]).

(3) The spit is turning, and Truquette is about to sit down for dinner with his family in a comfortable atmosphere of relaxation and calm [36].

(4) The forces of death from Solorgues (*consul*, men in blue, etc.) come to arrest Truquette and hand him over to that other incarnation of death, the executioner of Nîmes. Under heavy guard, Truquette

completes the journey from Solorgues to Nîmes, where Death will seize him and strangle him (by hanging).

In *Galdric* (p. 59):

(1) Business is highly successful: Galdric has a castle-like palace built, on the very site of his former modest home.

(2) The former coal-merchant is surrounded by all the external signs of wealth: gold, silver, porcelain, mirrors.

(3) He gives an excellent dinner, which begins with delectable poultry of all kinds (in principle, this poultry is roasted on a spit).

(4) Death leaves the dinner; he takes the coal-merchant with him on a long journey to his macabre residence. After being tricked in the meantime, Death finally seizes [*agafar*] the coal-merchant and kills him.

It is easy to see that these four sequences – (1) the castle; (2) wealth; (3) the dinner; (4) the hero's last, fatal journey, accompanied by Death and the forces of death – correspond exactly in both tales.

We have established, therefore, the perfect parallel between the careers of Galdric and Truquette; we can now go back over them, in order to pick out certain relevant and revealing details. Take the series of incidents in which Death creates a scandal: in *JLP*, these incidents occur some days after the wedding and after the birth that follows a few days later. They take place, presumably, on the Sunday of the baptism, the same day Margot and her child go out for the first time. A *scandalous* disturbance is caused by grandmother Death and her daughter Margot as they leave the house; these ladies ought in principle to be going to the church. During this disturbance [second version, 25] the mother [*maire*] of a boy who has lost a third of his hair in the fight *pulls her son by the sleeve* in an attempt to get him to leave the field of battle. Now, at the moment of godfather Death's *scandalous* arrival at the church, during the moment preceding the baptism of the baby Galdric (pp. 46–7), the children are so terrified *that they cling to the skirts* of their mother [*mare*] in order to flee all the faster. The skirt of one, the sleeve of the other. The same gesture of flight is inverted, but it is ultimately symmetrical and comparable (son–clothes–mother):

(1) the mother pulls her son by the sleeve ('Truquette');

(2) the son clings to his mother's skirt (*Galdric*).

Moreover, in both cases, the parents tell their children, small and defenceless as they are, to keep away from Death: 'move away, let him pass' (*Galdric*, p. 47); 'Come on! Get out of there! Let them settle it among themselves!' [*JLP*, 25].

During this scandalous scene, and on several other occasions in Fabre's novella, grandmother Death is compared to the Virgin Mary, to the 'Mother of God' or *Viergette*, who is, of course, dangerous, even deadly. This identification of Death with 'Macabre Mary' is also suggested, at the same point, in the Roussillonnais tale (p. 63).

During the disturbance that immediately precedes the scandalous scene, grandmother Death pricks her son-in-law's skin with an awl; and Margot, worthy daughter of this deadly mother, had already amused herself, in a rather premonitory way, with pricking Truquette's skin with this same awl. I have already compared Fabre's awl with other pricking or cutting instruments with which the Death of A T 332 arms himself in versions that are geographically, structurally and chronologically very close to *JLP*. I am thinking of the *needle* held by godfather Death in Mistral's Provençal version; of the *arrow* in Strobl's valuable, archaic version (1691); of the *scythe* that pierces the hero's heart at the end of Cadic's Breton version (1908), which is so similar to our Languedocian *JDT*. All these sharp instruments are held by Death in person. It is interesting, therefore, to learn that the scythe with which Death is armed, and with which he fatally *touches* human beings, is mentioned three times in *Galdric* (pp. 60, 61, 63) and in other Catalan versions of A T 332 (see that of Maspons, 1952, p. 120).

Another feature common to Fabre's text and the tale as collected by Caseponce: in that same scandalous disturbance and, earlier, too, during the festivities marking the wedding and baptism ('Truquette') or simply the baptism (*Galdric*), a similarly sharp distinction is drawn between the ordinary onlookers, who pick up the sweetmeats (or fishbones) in the street and who are the horrified witnesses or participants in the scandal caused by Death, and the guests themselves, who are allowed into the house, into the room where the feast takes place. Moreover, the same word [*convidats*, in Catalan; *couvidats*, in Occitan] is used in both texts to designate the second, privileged category of 'guests'.

Lastly, if we go back to the very beginnings of the three narratives (*Galdric*, *JLP*, *JDT*), one notes the close kinship, made up of both similarities and logical transformations, that characterizes the beginnings of these texts: the coal-merchant Galdric wants to find a godfather for his child; in fact, he is to meet Death. He begins by setting out [*m'en vaig su'l caminal*, p. 39; use of the verb 'to go']. Then he waits at the wayside for the approach of the future godfather, who, as it happens, after several fruitless meetings, turns out to be Death. This canonical beginning is to be found in many versions of AT 332 in various countries. Similarly, the cobbler Truquette sets out with his pilgrim's staff from his native Rouergue [19 and 77] for Solorgues, where he 'will plant his pilgrim's staff' [second version, 6]; there he meets the woman who is to become his son's grandmother/godmother Death, and his own mother-in-law *commère* Death. In *Jean-de-trop*, the father also sets out in search of a godfather and godmother for the child JDT; this journey is also referred to, as in *Galdric*, by the verb 'to go': so the man went off to visit all his relations . . . , all his friends, etc., to find a godfather [*l'ome va . . . l'ome s'en va . . .* , p. 185].

Lastly, a few words about the (male) companion of the (female) grandmother Death in *JLP*, and about the two (female) companions of the (male) godfather Death in *Galdric*. There is a total symmetry here, between *JLP* and *Galdric*, in the inversion.

JLP's grandmother/godmother Death, being a female character, is accompanied by a male companion who is none other than the surgeon of Calvisson, her *lover*. He is at once the lover and *compère* of grandmother Death, the natural father of her daughter Margot and the grandfather, on the left hand, objectively godfather of JLP, who is himself the grandson of grandmother Death. (The grandfather indeed – see Chapter IX – is *ipso facto* godfather of his grandson, just as the grandmother is godmother, and they are therefore mutually *compère* and *commère*.) How does *Galdric* fit in with this? It goes without saying that Death (a male character) is joined in *Galdric* by a *commère* companion, just as Death (a female character) is accompanied in *JLP* by a *compère* companion, in the person of the surgeon of Calvisson. In fact, the tale of *Galdric* actually goes one better, and Death (male) has two (female) companions! Just before the baptism (p. 46), Galdric's eldest son 'went to fetch the nursemaid and an old neighbour, who agreed to be the *commère* of this strange godfather Death; indeed, the eyes of this old woman were very weak, and she took him [godfather Death] to be a young man, proud of bearing and fresh of skin. Once the baby was dressed in his festive swaddling-clothes, the godfather went to the church flanked by the godmother [the godfather's old *commère*] and the nursemaid (who carried the baby).'

Let us now try to present this simple (or double) character who

	C	D	E
	Tale	Death's sex	Identity of Death's companion *compère* or companion *commère*
A	*JLP*	female	surgeon of Calvisson (*male*)
B	*Galdric*	male	double *female* character (1) nursemaid (2) the old woman chosen as the child's godmother and Death's *commère*

Table 30
DEATH'S COMPANIONS

N.B. Columns D and E always imply, respectively, characters of the opposite sex.

thus functions (in relation to Death) as companion *compère* or companion *commère* in these two versions of A T 332.

How can we define, in terms of this table, the character in column E of Table 30, who 'accompanies' Death? There are two things to be said about him or her.

(1) His or her relationship with Death is one of affection, and even of physical attraction (of a somewhat morbid kind?). This is clear as far as the old *commère* in *Galdric* is concerned: almost blind, she imagines her *compère*, the frightful character Death with the fleshless skull, as 'a young man, proud of bearing and fresh of skin' (p. 46). In *JLP*, it is even simpler: the surgeon of Calvisson is the *lover* of his *commère* Death, which implies a minimum of sexual attraction towards her.

(2) In *JLP* and in *Galdric*, the character who 'accompanies' Death is also paramedical: in short, Death not only kills; he or she may also cure, at least through an intermediary. The lover of grandmother Death in *JLP* is therefore a surgeon. Symmetrical with this surgeon, one of Death's two companions in *Galdric* is the nursemaid (whose task it is to look after women in labour and their newborn children).

Once again, then, and on a precise point, there is a remarkable symmetry (by antithesis) between *JLP* and *Galdric*.

	Table 31 SEX AND FUNCTIONS OF DEATH'S COMPANION(S)		
Tale	Opposite sex to that of Death	Paramedical function	Physical attraction for Death
JLP	Grandmother Death's male companion and *compère* is ⟶	→ *surgeon* at Calvisson ⟶	→ *lover* of the woman who later, as an old woman, becomes 'grand-mother Death'.
Galdric (1)	Godfather Death's first female companion ⟶	→ is a *nursemaid* (for women in childbirth and their babies).	
Galdric (2)	Godfather Death's second female companion or *commère*	⟶	regards Death (amorously) as 'a young man, proud of bearing and fresh of skin'.

Lastly, we should note that the lists of trades in *Galdric* and in 'Truquette' provide an interesting comparison. At the beginning of the Roussillonnais tale, a woodman in the great tradition of AT 332, in other words, a *coal-merchant* (Galdric), chooses among several candidates for his child's godfather, including first a *cobbler*, then *Death*. In *JLP*, we skip the first stage (the coal-merchant). We come, therefore, directly to a *cobbler* (Truquette), who chooses Death as mother-in-law/*commère* for himself and grandmother/godmother for his child.

The homology between *Galdric* and 'Truquette' is thus established from beginning to end: we find it, indeed, at the level of the overall structure and also in the common features that make the two tales resemble each other in one episode after another. I have mentioned, on this matter, the distribution of sweetmeats, the respective menus

of the two festive banquets, the names of the husbands, the dress
or state of undress of Death, the pieces of wood, the invitations to
the festivities, the sounds that accompany the scandalous Sunday
outing, the characterization of the hero, the precise promise 'to be
rich', the significance of the place of Death in front of or behind
the door, the end of the banquet, the hero's change of trade, the
references to spadefuls of money (or of earth), the splendid dress
of the hero's family, the fact that the hero builds a magnificent
residence on the site of his former poor home, the tin buckles
(which then become silver ones) for the hero's shoes, the sale of
the wife's clothes and wedding jewellery, the hero's addiction to
tobacco, the sale of all the equipment in the shop followed by a
journey into town and the buying of textiles, the identical way in
which the heroes end their careers, the way the little boys cling to
their mothers during the scandalous scene, the comparison between
Death and the Virgin Mary, the piercing tools used by Death, the
clear distinction between onlookers and guests at the first feast, the
characteristics of 'Death's companion' and the initial choice of the
hero's trade. In all, twenty-six similar actions or situations may be
located in the two tales, at the strategic points determined by their
common chronology; some of these actions may be broken down in
turn into a series of sub-episodes, which are themselves comparable
with each other in their individuality and sequence.

The comparison between *Galdric* and *JLP* may be carried even
further; it will go beyond the life of Truquette to the biography of
Jean-l'ont-pris himself. However, before we examine this 'overflow',
an overall structural comparison among *JLP*, *JDT* and *Galdric* is
called for.

One might start with the *names*. To sum up: *JLP* is a quadrinominal
narrative (at least). We have the two names of the earlier generation;
these are at the outset the functional equivalents of Jean-de-trop's
parents, and also the functional equivalents of those other two parents,
Galdric and Rosetot. (In *JLP*, the names of the parents are *Truquette*
and *Margot*.) In addition, we have the two names of the young, as yet
illegitimate couple belonging to the next generation (*Jean-l'ont-pris*
and *Babeau*), not to mention various other more or less comical names,
such as *Sestier, Garouille, Quincarlot/Cancrelas*, etc.

Galdric is a binominal narrative: we have the names of the older couple, *Galdric* and *Rosetot*; but their child remains anonymous, as do the other characters in the tale.

Lastly, *JDT* is a mononominal narrative. A single name is mentioned: that of the hero Jean-de-trop, the functional equivalent of Jean-l'ont-pris. The other characters of *JDT* all have roles, but none has a name.

In fact, these three descriptions (of *JLP* as 'quadrinominal', *Galdric* as 'binominal' and *JDT* as 'mononominal') tell us very little about the structure of the three narratives. They tell us rather about a certain state of historical wear and tear: *JLP*, adapted by the talented abbé Fabre from one or several oral versions that proved to be extremely rich, is literally stuffed with details and proper names. *Galdric*, too, is filled with details that derive from the very distant past; this proof of antiquity derives particularly from the systematic comparison between this *Galdric* and *JLP*, a comparison that will be continued later. The ancient richness of the Roussillonnais tale is also to be deduced by the still binominal character of *Galdric*. Lastly, *JDT* is as worn as a pebble: the erosion of this tale over centuries, in an already urbanized Narbonnais environment, proved stronger than the cultural conservatories of the Vallespir, which kept *Galdric* in use. This intense erosion eliminated many of the details in *JDT*; it also brought about the *mononominal* character of this narrative, in which only one proper noun (Jean-de-trop) managed to survive.

Having said this, erosion may well destroy the onomastic, thematic and other asperities; it respects, nevertheless, the basic structure, especially in the case of *JDT*: this tale is polished like a pebble with the wear of centuries. It remains, however, more structurally complex than *Galdric*. In effect, *JDT* is bigenerational (like *JLP*). *Galdric* is only monogenerational. In *JDT* and in *JLP*, the four-part schema of AT 332/*Godfather Death* is played out *twice in succession*, first at the level of the parents, then at the level of the children. It is played out only once in *Galdric*. It should be remembered that this four-part schema breaks down canonically in the following way: (a) godfather Death; (b) Death's gifts; (c) Death tricked; (d) Death is revenged and attacks the hero.

Table 32 is clear: in a single generation Galdric follows the course taken in two generations by Truquette the father and JLP the son, or, again, by JDT's father and JDT himself. That is why, mainly for the first phase (a) of the four-part schema of *Galdric*, in square

Table 32

STRUCTURES OF THREE TALES COMPARED

	A	B	C
1	JLP: bigenerational structure (see Table 14, p. 362) The four-part schema of AT 332 will be played out twice	JDT: bigenerational structure (see Table 15, p. 372–3) The four-part schema of AT 332 will be played out twice	Galdric: monogenerational structure The four-part schema of AT 332 will be played out only once
2	first part: life of Truquette The four-part schema is played out once in the normal direction (a) grandmother/godmother Death (b) Death's gifts to Truquette (c) (Death tricked) (d) Death attacks Truquette, who disappears spectacularly from the narrative	first part: life of JDT's parents The four-part schema is played out once in the normal direction (a) godmother Death (b) Death's gifts to JDT's parents (c) (Death tricked) (d) JDT's parents disappear discreetly from the narrative	first part: beginnings of Galdric's career This part comprises only the first phase (a) of the four-part schema (a) godfather Death takes Galdric under his protection
3	second part: life of JLP, son of Truquette and paramedical The four-part schema is played out for a second time, but in reverse order. This is the 'return to square 1' (see Tables 14 and 16) (d) the forces of death attack JLP (c) they are tricked by JLP (b) he benefits from Death's gifts (a) farewell to godfather Death	second part: life of JDT, 'physician' The four-part schema is played out for a second time in the normal direction (see Table 15) (a) JDT's godmother Death (b) Death's gifts to JDT, 'physician' (c) Death tricked by JDT (d) JDT will disappear only two hundred years after the happy ending	second part: life of Galdric, 'physician' This second part comprises the following three phases (b, c and d) of the four-part schema: (b) Death's gifts to Galdric, 'physician' (c) Death tricked by Galdric (d) Death takes revenge and kills Galdric

C2 of Table 32, there is a definite homology between *Galdric* and 'Truquette' (a comparison that has already been made). But let us look at the second (lower) part of the right-hand column of Table 32, square C3: there we see that there is *also* a homology between the life of Galdric (in the last three phases [b, c, and d] of this four-part schema) and the biography of J L P himself (in the second part of column A, square A3). So we shall now examine, without claiming completeness, just a few of the elements in this new comparison. After the 'Galdric–Truquette' comparison, let us now turn to the 'Galdric–J L P' comparison.

Before the respective heroes of the two tales are showered with gifts, the curing (and 'non-curing') operations in which they both take part are very remarkable. Following the schema of A T 332, Jean-l'ont-pris is a participant in the various stages in the *cure* of the powerful man (Sestier); he is then associated, through Quincarlot-the-gibbet, with the diagnosis of *certain death* in relation to the frightful Barbe-Garouille, the daughter of a farmer called Master Garouille. This woman, moreover, is the unattractive former mistress of the powerful man, Sestier.

Galdric, too, takes part in the diagnosis and cure of a *powerful man's* son (the *king's* son). Then, in the same way, assisted by Death, he makes a diagnosis of inevitable and imminent death in the case of the young son of the king's gardener.

It will be noticed that, for each of the two heroes, the various actions of cure and of non-cure may be arranged in a perfectly legible table, consisting of four squares. Horizontally, we have the question of age; vertically, we have the question of social status, and of the powerful man's more or less immediate entourage.

Let us read this table.

Horizontally: (1) J L P works on adults of 'parental' age: that is, Sestier, *father* of a girl, whom he will later cure (square C1); Garouille, soon to be *mother* of stillborn twins, and who will soon die (square D1). (2) Galdric works on young males who are 'sons of someone': the king's son, who will recover; the gardener's son, who will die (C2 and D2).

Vertically: once this horizontal shift from the generation of the 'parents' (line 1) to that of the sons (line 2) has been observed, we realize that the prognoses of cure (column C) and of death (column

Table 33			
PROGNOSES OF CURE AND OF CERTAIN DEATH			
A	B	C	D
Narrative	Generation	Cure is certain ↓	Death is certain ↓
Name of hero who participates in cure or non-cure ↓	Persons about whom the prognosis is made ↓	Persons of high social status ↓	Persons of low rank dependent on the superior persons of column C ↓
1 JLP →	JLP works on adults of parental age (Sestier and Garouille).	JLP takes part in the cure (after a favourable prognosis) of the powerful man Sestier.	JLP makes a prognosis of certain death for Garouille, ex-mistress of the powerful man Sestier and daughter of a farmer.
2 Galdric →	Galdric works on young males who are 'sons' (king's son and gardener's son).	Galdric makes a prognosis of cure for the king's son.	Galdric makes a prognosis of certain death for the son of the king's gardener.

D) conform respectively to two strict and distinct models; this applies as much to *Galdric* as to *JLP*.

In column C, the prognosis of cure always applies to a character of high social status (the rich and powerful Sestier in *JLP*) or even very high (the king's son in *Galdric*).

In column D, the prognosis of imminent death applies to a character in a far more humble position, and who, moreover, is dependent on the powerful man previously referred to in column C. Let us look first at square D1: in *JLP*, the character condemned to death is the unattractive former mistress (not even legitimate wife!) of the powerful man; she is the daughter of a poor farmer, and her name (Garouille) suggests both dirt and swamps.

In *Galdric* (square D2) the character doomed to die is the son of the king's gardener; this young gardener [*hortolanet*] is also a humble dependant of the powerful man (the king). Like Barbe-Garouille, his feet sink into well-watered ground, not, of course, swampy ground [*marécage*], but ground for *maraîchage* ['land irrigated for market gardening'].

The same details of these homologous processes of cure or non–cure correspond perfectly from one text to the other. Let us begin with the episode of a *diagnosis of imminent death*, concerning Barbe-Garouille (*JLP*) and the son of the king's gardener (*Galdric*). In *Galdric*, the physician, informed by Death, has correctly predicted the young gardener's death; as a result, he immediately receives 1,000 *douros* from the king, just after the burial [*enterro*] of the unfortunate boy. He sets out, 'very pleased with himself', with the 1,000 *douros* in his pocket (p. 57), which do not weigh heavily because he is so delighted.

In *JLP*, the scene is exactly and substantially the same: J L P has correctly predicted Barbe-Garouille's death. Once she is buried [*énterrâda*], he sets off for home, very pleased with himself: 'Now I am going off with a quiet heart, I care about nothing' [85]. He has 1,000 *livres* [80], in other words, 100 pistoles more in his purse, which also come to him from the powerful man (Monsieur Sestier). It is true that the circuit of these '1,000 francs' has been rather more complicated than that of the 1,000 *douros* given to Galdric. Monsieur Sestier referred to them in order to encourage J L P to marry Garouille, who previously received them as a dowry. But Garouille's death makes it possible to complete the trajectory of these 1,000 *livres*, of which J L P becomes *ipso facto* the heir, as the dead woman's widower and legatee. The operation is ultimately the same in both cases. Moreover, in one of the versions of *JLP*, Fabre specifically states that the 1,000 francs will be *accredited in advance* to the hero [second version, 83]; Barbe-Garouille, while still alive, did not catch so much as a glimpse of them: in which case, the similarity between *JLP* and *Galdric* becomes *total*.

The comparison, then, is as follows.

(1) *Galdric:* After the death (cleverly predicted by the hero) of the

gardener's son, a dependant of the powerful king, the hero Galdric receives 1,000 *douros*, which originally come from the powerful king and which make him very pleased with himself, as he walks home after the young gardener's burial.

(2) *JLP:* After the death (cleverly predicted by the hero) of the humble Barbe-Garouille, a dependant of the powerful man Sestier, the hero J L P receives 1,000 *livres*, which originally come from the powerful man Sestier. After the burial of Garouille, he goes off 'with a quiet heart', with not a care in the world.

With these *douros* and *livres*, one also notes the historical and local roots of these two tales, which merely emphasize still further their mutual kinship. A Catalan and Roussillonnais, member of a province that had not long ago (1659) been annexed by the French crown, the hero Galdric continues to count in *douros*, in Spanish currency. The hero J L P, a Languedocian and therefore a traditional subject of the king of France, naturally uses French currency: *livres, écus,* pistoles.

After these phenomena of death or of non-cure, let us now examine the processes of predicted and successful cure: that of the powerful man Sestier in *JLP* and that of the powerful king's son in *Galdric*.

In both cases, these cures take place in a similar way, in three distinct, successive stages.

First stage: correct diagnosis
Galdric: The hero Galdric makes the correct diagnosis of the imminent cure of the powerful king's son (p. 55), who is seriously ill.

JLP: The powerful man himself, together with the hero J L P, makes the diagnosis of his own cure, after the attack that has been made upon him [60].

Second stage: the dinner
Galdric: The powerful king, delighted with his son's cure, gives a dinner for the hero, the coal-merchant or 'woodman' [*boscarol*, p. 57], who so stuffs himself with good things that he is ready to burst (p. 56).

JLP: The powerful man Sestier, delighted with his own cure, gives a dinner for the hero and a third person; they dine 'like three pit-sawyers', that is, like three woodmen, or workers in wood [63].

Third stage: the final cure

Galdric: The powerful man's son, cured of his illness, finally rises from his sick-bed (p. 57).

JLP: The powerful man Sestier, cured from the attack made upon him, finally rises from his bed [63].

In both narratives, in Catalan and in Occitan, emphasis is placed on the ultimately evanescent, almost fictitious character of the disease or wounds sustained by the individual who is now cured. In the shorter *Galdric*, this is expressed very quickly: 'the king's son was once more up and about, his complexion rosy and fresh *as if there had never been anything the matter with him* [*com si mai havia tingut res*].' In *JLP*, a whole rhetorical passage follows, but it begins literally with the same words: '*It was nothing* [*aco's pas rés*], Monsieur Sestier was a former shepherd, his skin was hard, he did not feel the blows, etc.'

In the three-stage episode thus described, only one of the initial actions is displaced from one narrative to the other, that by which the hero goes to the powerful man's residence to take part in the treatment during which this powerful man, or his son, will be cured. This residence of the powerful man is the royal city (in *Galdric*) or Langlade, Sestier's village (in *JLP*).

In *Galdric*, the hero's journey from his native village to the town (p. 53), *through steep mountain paths* (p. 47), takes place before the first stage, which itself is devoted to the prognosis of cure in relation to the powerful man. In *JLP*, the hero's journey from Solorgues to Langlade [62], *through bad paths* [second version, 62], takes place after the same prognosis.

When we compare the 'cures' effected by Jean-l'ont-pris and by Galdric, we remember that grandmother Death, in her comic sermon to her grandson, lays great stress on the robe and tall pointed hat that JLP will one day have to wear [41], when he becomes 'the skilful man'. Similarly, in the Roussillonnais tale, after deliberating at length with godfather Death, the hero does not waste much time in changing his clothes; he soon procures the outward signs of his new status as a doctor, which are, similarly, 'a gentleman's coat' and a tall toque [13] (pp. 50–51 and 53).

Another, highly logical concordance: at the beginning of his

Table 34 CURE OF THE POWERFUL MAN	
Galdric	*JLP*
Hero goes to the powerful man's residence	1. Prognosis of cure in favour of the powerful man
1. Prognosis of cure in favour of the powerful man's son	Hero goes to the powerful man's residence
2. Celebratory dinner to which the hero is invited	2. Celebratory dinner to which the hero is invited
3. Complete cure of the powerful man's son, who rises from his bed	3. Complete cure of the powerful man, who rises from his bed

adventure, the hero JLP is punished for rejecting his grandmother Death's tempting (and dangerous) teaching. He is not therefore showered with *Death's gifts* (which he will enjoy much later). In this situation of *lack*, JLP is incapable of catching hares [51]. He does not even have the opportunity of catching one for three months on end. However, he would like to imitate those shepherds who break the front legs of a hare with a stick, those shepherds who succeed in life and become, later, as rich as the former shepherd Monsieur Sestier. It is a pointless wish, alas. At least for the moment . . .

The hero Galdric, on the other hand, once he receives Death's gifts, is so happy that he feels he has *caught the hare napping* (p. 57); in Catalan, he has caught the hare in the *jas*: this word *jas* in Occitan and Catalan means 'bed' or 'litter'. It is hardly surprising, then, that JLP a little later [67], when he is at last receiving Death's gifts, discovers fortune under a *jas*, or straw bed; he had expected to find food there, just as Galdric metaphorically catches the hare in the *jas*. But it is quite simply the grandmother's treasure that lies under this straw *jas* in the chest that Jean-l'ont-pris has just opened. Between Fabre's novella and *Galdric*, there is, therefore, a veritable *chassé-croisé* of highly correlated images and realities, around the hare's *jas* or litter (or the absence of the hare), food, treasure and the absence or presence of Death's gifts.

There is another incident of the same type: some moments before receiving Death's gifts (the grandmother's treasure), J L P, who is still a ragamuffin, does not even find an onion [*ceba*] to eat [67]. Galdric, however, at the height of his career, will have Death's gifts showered upon him. He will eat his fill: the wind may still 'make *Ronge-oignons* [*Rosegacebès*] shiver, but Galdric won't give a fig' (p. 59). It is a logical correlation: before receiving Death's gifts, J L P was so poor and so *lowly* situated that he did not even rise to the level of a modest *Ronge-oignons*. After receiving Death's gifts his homologue Galdric will be so rich that he will look down on all the *Ronge-oignons* of the earth.

The *fears* of Galdric, on the one hand, and of J L P, on the other, at the sight of Death as a character, or on contact with the forces of death, are also comparable in terms of both situations and words: when Galdric sees Death for the first time (p. 44), he feels a cold shiver down his spine [*esquena*, in Catalan]. When J L P confronts for the first time those forces of death represented by the vineyard-keepers [second version, 54], he gets at least nine hundred blows from a stick on his back [*sus mas esquînas*, in Occitan]. Similarly, when J L P, in the last part of the novella, catches a glimpse of that other incarnation of death represented by the diabolical Quincarlot, who takes him prisoner [79, 80 and especially 80 in the second version], he refers several times to his fear; at the same moment, his beloved Babeau, who is also impressed by this scene, 'weeps and clucks like a hen who is having her chicks taken from her' [second version, 80]. These two elements, real and metaphoric ('fear' and the 'hen'), are to be found together again in the fear felt by Galdric (p. 61) when he visits Death's palace: 'hardly had they passed the door than the coal-merchant heard behind him a *terrifying* cry that gave him *gooseflesh* [*carn de gallina*]'. As for the coal-merchant's wife, who is the functional equivalent of Babeau, J L P's mistress, she is so 'terrified by Death' that she 'fears that the milk will curdle in her' (p. 52). She is more than a 'mother-hen', she is a 'mother-nurse'.

The theme of the lights of life in *Galdric* and in *JLP* also call for comparison. In the Roussillonnais tale, Death shows the hero his light [*lluminária*, p. 60], in other words, men's candles of life. Fabre has transformed these lights of life into *allumettes* ['matches'], a French word with the same root and a similar sound. Fabre, who knew the northern French word very well, chose, for his Occitan text, the Provençal term *brouquéttas*.

At the end of the tale of *Galdric*, Death refers to his palace (p. 59), where he will finally take the hero. I have already noted the parallel between this *palace* of Death, which is to be found in a large number of versions of AT 332, southern French, German, etc., and the baron's *castle*, at the end of *JLP* [93]; this is made especially relevant in view of my demonstration that the baron in *JLP* represents the third incarnation of death, after the grandmother and Quincarlot.

Galdric (monogenerational) is the homologue first of Truquette, then of Jean-l'ont-pris himself, in the bigenerational tale *JLP*.

As far as the hero's 'swaddling-clothes' are concerned, the same images flourish in terms both of Galdric and his child, on the one hand, and of Truquette and his child (who will grow up), on the other. At the time when, at the outset of his career, Galdric is still the homologue of Truquette, Galdric's child is still the homologue of the child J L P. Galdric's child turns out at first to be perfectly behaved [*sage comme un ange*]; he is splendidly dressed (wrapped in a *trousseau de gala*), topped by a multicoloured shawl.

Then Galdric himself enters the second part of the tale that concerns him and the second phase of his four-part cycle (the so-called phase of *Death's gifts*). We have seen how Galdric becomes at this point the functional homologue of J L P himself, and not, as earlier, the homologue of Truquette. One will not be surprised, therefore, to see this Galdric (who is from now on showered with Death's gifts) installed in a room 'in the midst of pieces of silk and lace' (p. 56). 'There he slept like a caterpillar, so much so that he might have been taken for a saint [*Sant*], and thought that he had been put into a chapel [*capella*].' JLP is certainly not the 'greatest saint in the Litanies' [75], but his grandmother [30] sees him as a 'little lamb . . . in a priest's chasuble [*capélan*]'. Elsewhere, J L P is cocooned in such a wealth of ribbons and lace that he might be taken for a bobbin [35].

The images of the hero as a small or big baby, angel or lamb, saint, bobbin or caterpillar smothered in lace in a *capélan-capella*, certainly echo from one text to the other.

During the preceding, and homologous phase, in both narratives, the close kinship between the tale *Galdric* and the tale *JLP* (in general), and between the hero Galdric and the hero JLP (in particular), becomes particularly clear in the form of a bifurcation characteristic of Death's speech: 'Well, well,' Death says to the coal-merchant (p. 49),[14] 'I know that you have always been a good, honest man. So I don't want to make you one of those rich men who think of nothing but wasting the money earned by others, and who lead poor, unhappy souls away from the straight and narrow path. If I make you rich, and you will become so, it will be by working honestly. I want to make you a physician . . . I'll explain everything to you, you'll see how easy it is.'

Nothing could be more strategic in effect than the bifurcation brought about by this speech: at the precise point in the tale *Galdric*, Death is confronted with a choice. *Either* he makes his protégé into a dishonest man, a swindler, a Truquette, like the cobbler–hero of the first part of *Jean-l'ont-pris*, and like the cobbler–hero, also a criminal (but a murderer, not a swindler), of the 'Swiss tale' (see Chapter IX), *or* he chooses the solution of the Roussillonnais Death, who deliberately rejects the first possibility. This being the case, Death has only to jump a generation: he will make Galdric into a physician, like Jean-de-trop, son of Death's protégé, who will become a medical hero; and like Jean-l'ont-pris, son of grandmother Death's protégé, who will become a paramedical hero.

Let us summarize in a schema this tree of possibilities open to the Roussillonnais Death of AT 332, and note among these possibilities the selection that is finally made (this final selection is placed in the two lower squares, in the right-hand column, of Table 35).

The educational speech of the Roussillonnais Death bifurcates, therefore, from the outset, from the first moment (Table 35, bottom right-hand square), towards the medical career which makes Galdric, in a *serious* way, a pious, honest worker. The educational speech of grandmother Death in *JLP* bifurcates only at a second stage towards the paramedical speech which will make Jean-l'ont-pris in the second

Table 35

OPTIONS OFFERED TO THE ROUSSILLONNAIS DEATH OF AT 332/*GALDRIC* AND THE SOLUTION CHOSEN BY HIM

In the context of the possibilities offered by the classic plot of AT 332 (monogenerational from the fourteenth century and possibly bigenerational from 1669 [see Chapter XIV]) the Roussillonnais Death might make of the hero Galdric —

— whom he protects

— A delinquent who might be

TYPE OF HERO	(An insignificant / prosperous character)	A delinquent who might be		whom he protects
THE HERO, DELINQUENT (OR NOT) (first generation)	An *insignificant*, but prosperous *character*, like JDT's father.	A *murderer* (like the cobbler–hero of the 'Swiss tale'), whose child will not be the hero of the rest of the tale. This is the *monogenerational* solution adopted by the 'Swiss tale', versions of which once existed in the Midi (see Chapter IX).	A *swindler*, like Truquette, cobbler–thief–hero of the first part of *JLP*.	*In fact*, the Roussillonnais Death will immediately make of the hero whom he protects (Galdric) an honest man, who will himself become, by the deliberate choice of Death, the classic medical hero of AT 332. Galdric, who synthesizes in himself two generations (Truquette and JLP), is therefore the functional equivalent of Truquette until his perversions; he then becomes the equivalent of JLP.
THE MEDICAL OR PARA-MEDICAL HERO (second generation, in principle)	This insignificant character has a son, JDT, who is to become the true (*medical*) hero of this Languedocian version (*JDT*) of AT 332.		This swindler, Truquette, will have a son (JLP), who will become the second and in fact principal (*para-medical*) hero of Fabre's tale.	
TYPES OF SOLUTION CHOSEN: BIGENERATIONAL OR MONOGENERATIONAL	The bigenerational solution is chosen by the tale *JDT*.	The monogenerational solution is chosen by the 'Swiss tale'.	The bigenerational solution is chosen by Fabre's *JLP*.	*The monogenerational solution is chosen by the tale* Galdric.

generation, in a burlesque way, a worker blest by God. This double articulation is perfectly borne out by our texts.

A few words on the notion of 'worker'. The advice given by the Roussillonnais godfather Death stresses the fact that Galdric, following the godfather's advice, will behave in a pious, *hardworking* way. *You will not lead poor, unhappy souls away from the straight and narrow path*, concludes Death (p. 49) to Galdric. *If I make you rich, and you will become so, it will be by working honestly* [*travaillant honestament*]. Jean-de-trop also becomes rich in similar circumstances; the tale *JDT* (p. 193) stresses in religious terms that this young man is *good and pious*. In the case of *JLP*, the terms used are even closer to those used by *Galdric*; but, as always with Fabre, they are used in a burlesque way. We have already analysed in detail the paramedical career of JLP, which is based and encoded (if inverted) on the schema of AT 332, as are, in the normal way, the careers of Galdric and JDT. Furthermore, JLP, once he has discovered grandmother Death's treasure, declares [75] that he wants to 'rise slowly like a man who works [*travâilla*] hard and is blest by God'. It is easy to recognize here, transformed into the comic style, the two aims that the Roussillonnais Death, concluding his educational, medical speech, had proposed, seriously, to his protégé Galdric: keep your soul on the straight and narrow path and 'work honestly' [*travaillar* or *treballar*].

The 'bifurcation' that gives *Galdric* its *monogenerational* structure and *JLP* its *bigenerational* structure is to be found in a number of 'key' details in the tales. Such a key detail will be singular in *Galdric*, but divided into two, because 'bifurcated', in *JLP*. I shall take the example of the 'narrator's little phrase', which assumes the following form in *Galdric* (p. 52): 'The coal-merchant went to recount [*contar*] to his wife *by thread* and by needle all that Death had told him.' This sentence is to be found with its circumstances and its characteristic words, but *divided into two*, in *JLP*, in the two successive and respective parts of Fabre's novella, that concerning the life of Truquette and that concerning the autobiography of JLP (see Table 36).

The narrative metaphors used by the hero are indeed, as we have seen, similar in both tales. At the beginning of the narrative, Galdric

Table 36	
THE NARRATOR'S LITTLE PHRASE	
I The tale *Galdric*	II The tale *Jean-l'ont-pris*
A. At the beginning of the single four-part cycle (of AT 332), which forms the tale *Galdric* as a whole, the hero called Galdric recounts to his wife, Rosetot (docile executant of Death),* before she goes to *sleep*, what Death has told him: 'The coal-merchant went to recount [*contar*] to his wife *by thread* and by needle *all that Death had told him* [*le havia dit*]' (p. 52).	B. At the beginning [5, 7] of the *first* four-part cycle (of AT 332), which forms the first part ('Truquette') of the tale *JLP*, the hero recounts to the baron (who is one of the three figures of Death in the tale) the story of his father Truquette, which contains what grandmother Death had said to Truquette: 'follow things *by their thread*', J L P says to the baron after deciding to recount [*contar*] his story.
	C. At the beginning [45] of the second four-part cycle (of AT 332), which forms the second part (*JLP*, in the strict sense) of the tale *JLP*, the narrator–hero recounts to the same baron (apologizing for running the risk of sending him to *sleep*, and before the baron in fact goes to sleep) what his grandmother Death had told him, in other words, '*all* the wonderful things my grandmother *told* [*disié*] me'.

* The tale *Galdric* specifically stresses, in fact (see D. Blanc, *Récits et Contes populaires de Catalogne* [1979], p. 80), that Rosetot is 'trusting in the power that Death must have [*confiant amb el poder que devia tenir la Mort*]'. In *Galdric*, Rosetot is the homologue of Margot who, in *JLP*, functions as a double of her mother Death (see Chapter IX). 'Trusting in Death', Rosetot also occupies, therefore, if less brilliantly than Margot, a role as Death's assistant. The additional homology between Rosetot in *Galdric* and the baron in *JLP* (compare columns I and II above) confirms, together with many other clues, that the baron is also one of the figures of Death (see Chapter XIII).

starts to tell of his meeting with Death: he describes this episode therefore 'by thread and by needle' [*per fil et per agulla*, p. 52]. At the beginning of his entire narrative, Jean-l'ont-pris has just summarized his father's meeting with grandmother Death and her family; as he does so, he says: 'Let us take things as they fell out' [literally, by their thread, *pér soun fîou*, in Occitan, 7].

At the end of a meticulous comparison based on an entire structural ensemble and on dozens of homologous details, which I have certainly not exhausted, there can be no possible doubt: within the large family of A T 332, and in the more restricted context of the versions of *Godfather Death* that are specifically Occitan and Catalan, *Galdric* and *JLP* behave not only as cousins, but as brothers or at least as half-brothers, closely related to each other, and closely related to other brothers or half-brothers. This 'Languedoc–Roussillon' fraternity throws an even brighter light on the now resolved problem of the origins and structure of the novella *Jean-l'ont-pris*.

CHAPTER XVI On a Few Grains of Salt

In order to understand Fabre's text, it has also been necessary to leave the Occitan or Roussillonnais world and even France itself. Reference to the 'Swiss tale', to the Austrian *Hans-with-the-Goitre*, to innumerable versions of the tale type – in Catalonia, Andalusia, Quebec, Germany and elsewhere – have provided certain keys to the mythical biographies, which seemed at first to be purely Languedocian, of Truquette, Jean-l'ont-pris and his homologue Jean-detrop. From the seventeenth century, at the earliest, a common market of *Godfather Death* had been established from its distant origins in late medieval Germany. Between the two sides of the Rhine, and probably on those of the Rhône, cultural contacts were always close during the baroque age. The various versions of AT 332, Germanic or Latin, were always errant, as was Margot, Truquette's ex-wife, who travelled the world with her lover, the knife-grinder. Sailing closer, armed with the increasing international evidence that this book has provided, I shall now explore, for the purposes of my research, a German version of AT 332, which I have so far only touched on. It throws light on certain still obscure aspects of Fabre's text. This is *Death's Castle*;[1] it took root long ago, was collected in the 1840s and was published in 1851 by J. W. Wolf.[2] Here is a summary of the plot.

A poor man accepts Death as godfather for his son. When this son is older, Death comes to see him and launches into the usual educational, medical speech of AT 332, with, however, certain original features. 'I shall make you a great physician,' he tells the child. 'When I'm at the head of the bed, the patient's plight will be quite hopeless; but when I am at the patient's feet, he will be curable. You will then place three grains of salt in sweetened milk, and this drink will cure the patient in three days.'

The boy obeys these precepts and becomes a rich physician. He cures the king's daughter and is given as a reward as much gold as a horse can carry;[3] he then foresees the imminent death of the queen, which greatly pleases the king (who wanted to get rid of the lady). The king at once gives the physician double the previous reward, and eight days later marries another woman!

Death then strongly advises the godson physician (who does not follow this advice) to take a path *on the left*, which will bring him happiness. However, Death absolutely refuses to kill his godson and does all he can to help him to live. In the end, when the normal hour of death arrives for him, the physician sees Death at the head of his bed; he knows he is doomed. He quickly moves his body 180 degrees in the bed on the horizontal plane. Death is now at his feet. Death runs immediately to his head. He responds at once by swinging his body in the opposite direction. This constant movement goes on all night. In the end Death admits defeat by this trick and by another (that of the unfinished *Pater Noster*); so he gives the hero fifty more years of life.

One detail stands out: the medical prescription of the placebo proposed by Death in his usual educational speech is original in relation to the usual placebo of AT 332, which consists of a herb, a phial of water or a mixture of the two (herb tea), administered to the patient by the physician. Here the placebo consists of three grains of salt in sweetened milk; this mixture cured in three days the patient whom Death had previously declared to be curable by standing at her feet. Now this is close, in a very suggestive way, to the advice given by grandmother Death to her godson and grandson Jean-l'ont-pris in the educational speech that she gives him, at the exact point occupied by Death's speech in the Occitan, German and other versions of AT 332 (including those of Wolf and Fabre). *If you are invited to a castle*, the old woman says to Fabre's young hero [44], [and] *there are ladies present, don't forget to pinch their thighs and slap their knees, then drink their health, clink their glasses, put your five fingers cleanly into the salt and sprinkle their food with it. In this way you will be considered a well-brought-up young man* ... The second version of *JLP* [44] takes up exactly the same text; moreover, it mentions that the ladies in question are at table, but instead of 'your five fingers', the grandmother tells JLP to use 'two fingers like this'.

Grains of salt in tasteless meat, drinking the health of a lady with appetizing thighs with whom one clinks glasses while drinking her health; grains of salt in sweet milk, in the form of a drink to bring back to health a desirable young lady ... Is this simply a superficial resemblance, in two examples of Death's speech to his or her godson (in Wolf, 1851, and in *JLP*)? Or does this detail, carefully placed at the same strategic point, betray once more profound kinships and provide more keys? These kinships derive from a common, specific version (of a more general A T 332) that once circulated between Germans and French, from east to west, and helped to build Wolf's version, on the one hand, and *JLP*, on the other.

Let us now compare Wolf's version of oral origin and Fabre's written version in *JLP*. From the 'common trunk' formed by Death's educational speech to his or her godson, which possesses a remarkably similar 'motif' in each case (the placebo of salt), these two tales develop in a way that is both inverted and homologous.

Table 37

ON A FEW GRAINS OF SALT

Wolf version	Personal autobiography of J L P
I Usual genesis of godfather Death through the biography of the hero's father, Death's *compère*	I Transposed genesis of god-father Death through the bio-graphy of Truquette, the hero's father, and the childhood of the young J L P
II Death's (serious) educational speech to the hero, notably about the grains of salt in the milk used to restore health	II The grandmother's (burlesque) educational speech to the hero, notably about the grains of salt on the meat 'to bring health'
III Development of the plot from top to bottom	III Development of the plot from top to bottom (reverse structure of that to be found opposite)
A1: *Death's gifts* the hero foresees the cure of the king's daughter and is duly rewarded	D2: *Death tricked* to escape the forces of death, J L P effects, *with his own body* remaining upright,* a turn of 180 degrees (Chapter X)
B1: *Death's gifts* (a) the hero foresees the actual death of the king's wife, who has become an encumbrance on her husband, and he is duly rewarded*	C2: *Death's gifts* (b) grand-mother Death leaves the hero treasure 'on the left-hand side' of a chest (Chapter XI)

C1: *Death's gifts* (b) Death promises great wealth to the physician if he takes a left-hand fork	B2: *Death's gifts* (a) the hero foresees the actual death of Garouille, the powerful man Sestier's mistress, who had become an encumbrance on her lover; the hero expects to get rich as a result, this taking the form of marriage to a rich girl
D1: *Death tricked* to escape Death, the physician effects, *with his own body* remaining horizontal, a turn of 180 degrees	A2: *Death's gifts* (double of square B2) The hero foresees the actual death of Garouille, rival of the powerful man's daughter, and expects to get rich as a result (we have shown [Chapter XII] how *to foresee the death of the rival of the powerful man's daughter* is equivalent, as a double negative (death *and* rival), to the affirmation, *to cure the rich man's daughter*)

* We should remember that there is a logical and canonical succession here (if only in an inverted direction) of motifs which, in Wolf and in *JLP*, prove to be original *within the general cycle of* AT 332; this justifies a *specific* comparison between *JLP* and Wolf's version. These original motifs include the prediction of *the death of the king's wife* (or of Garouille, the powerful man's mistress), and the 'turning round' of the hero's own body and not (as in most versions) of the patient's body. These two facts constitute two quite particular events, which isolate Wolf's version and *JLP* within the overall cycle of *Godfather Death*; they justify, in view of the general structural similarity between the two narratives, which is also specific, the precise comparison that I am making here.

We should take into account, of course, in reading Table 37, how much the plot of J L P's personal autobiography (*JLP 2*) is an inverted form of the classic plot of AT 332 (see Table 18, column C, at the end of Chapter XII). We should take into account in particular that there is a permutation from one to the other of two essential segments of the four-part cycle of AT 332, namely, *Death's gifts* and *Death tricked*. The latter occurs after the former in AT 332, but the other way round in *JLP*, because of the overall inversion of the four phases of the four-part cycle in J L P's personal autobiography, in relation to their normal development in all the usual versions of AT 332. In these circumstances, we see that, for the whole of paragraph III of Table 37, the right-hand column (*JLP*) is precisely the inverted image of the left-hand column (Wolf).

BRIEF SUMMARY OF PARAGRAPH III OF TABLE 37

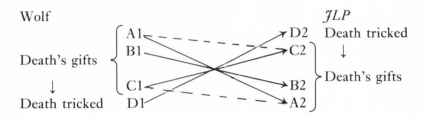

This close kinship through strict inversion (itself typical of the particular construction of the personal autobiography of Jean-l'ont-pris [end of Chapter XII and Chapter XIII]), a kinship too in terms of the detail of the most relevant motifs, is not the result of some miraculous coincidence linking the Wolf version and the Fabre version. In fact, we must make an effort to imagine the extremely rich folkloric space of the eighteenth century, in which circulated, in the Occitan region, the imported versions of AT 332 that were still close, simply by virtue of their origins, to those collected in the nineteenth century in the Germanic world by Müller in Switzerland, Grimm and Wolf in Germany, Vernaleken in Austria. Some of these versions, which were Occitanized long ago, were collected, much later, on the French side of the Rhine, by Mistral, Lambert, etc., from about 1876 to 1880. Others must have disappeared from the Midi in the meantime; they survive today in the collective memory only through Swiss and German collections made in the country of origin, or in the literary adaptation (in fact half inverted) made by the abbé Fabre in the country which at the time was an importer of these tales. Of course, I am deducing the past *existence* of the southern versions, while readily admitting that they may well have lived in the eighteenth century in a state of interpenetration or anastomosis in relation to one another, including those that were later to be their descendants, themselves collected by collectors who were to work in the Midi from 1876 onwards.

*

In any case, the comparison between *JLP* and the Wolf version throws a new light on the grandmother's educational speech to her grandson [41–44]; this speech gains in coherence; it takes root and is seen more than ever to share the strict logic of AT 332. But first let us remember what we learned in Chapter X: the grandmother's speech is aimed at a certain supernatural, even maleficent, initiation. The hero, subjected to his grandmother's teaching, must learn to conceal his right eye under his pointed hat, formed by a tripod of sulphur-tipped matches, as his grandmother shows him. He must show only his left eye, 'the evil eye' (like Quincarlot's), which would portend (if the hero agreed to proceed in this way) suspect prosperity, followed by eventual catastrophe *à la* Truquette.

Second, grandmother Death always has an eye to social advancement, or to frequenting the upper classes, which are from the outset easily accessible to Death, who by definition dines and sleeps with everybody, great persons included [45]. She will therefore try (in vain) to urge her grandson to frequent such people.

The hero is urged by his grandmother to keep, and if possible to exalt, his rank, which is not inconsiderable. This preoccupation with honour, pride and rich connections characterizes, as we have seen, not only *JLP*, but many versions of AT 332 from the Midi, which, in their opening paragraphs, were models for the abbé Fabre. So the hero must not take off his hat before anybody; nor must he wipe his nose on his robe, because such a robe signifies respectability. He must raise it, in order to wipe his nose more easily – on his undershirt. Lastly, when he decides to greet someone, he must not lower his dignity by raising his hat; he will simply perform small bows, blowing [*péter*, literally 'farting'] [4] kisses into his hand and scratching with his foot like a hen.

But JLP takes care not to practise the bows advocated by his grandmother; in a spirit of contrariness, he takes up pirouettes, in order to make fun of his grandmother and of the schoolmaster who is to be her devoted accomplice [47]. We should add, at last, that the grandmother's speech is crypto-medical, and therefore is attached, in a disguised, but no less secure way, to the godfather Death of AT 332. On this matter, I have already indicated (beginning of Chapter X) that the grandmother recommends her grandson to wear a robe and a pointed hat, which, in fact, are both rejected by JLP. Now the robe and pointed hat (like the tripod model made of matches, which the grandmother erects slantwise on her head) are the very insignia of the medical profession. In the Occitan versions of AT 332 that have come down to us, the hero is specifically advised by Death to wear these two 'medical insignia'.[5]

Furthermore, the overall homology (even, indeed especially, when in Fabre it is inverted) between JLP's personal autobiography and Wolf's version (Table 37) stresses the importance of that part of the grandmother's speech concerning the 'grains of salt'.

Wolf's version of 1851 emerged in Germany, through successive generations, from an old oral story that was also, at the end of the cultural migration westward, one of the sources of the personal autobiography of JLP. In any case, one of the motifs of that version (that of the grains of salt), placed at its canonical point, namely, Death's *educational speech* to the hero, certainly seems to have travelled, circulated among the far-flung collectors of AT 332. In this Wolf version, indeed, Death explains to the hero, who is soon to become a physician, that when he (Death) is at the patient's feet, he has only to give the patient lying on her sick-bed a drink, which he will make up himself, consisting of sweetened milk and three grains of salt; the patient will then recover *ipso facto* in the three days. (In fact, in the Wolf version, the patient is always a woman: a queen or a princess.)

The grandmother's speech has nothing, in principle, to do with medicine. There is, therefore, no question of a sick-bed or a patient. However, as in Wolf, there is mention of consorting with distinguished ladies: the queen and princess for whom the physician must formulate a fatal or a favourable prognosis, in Wolf; the ladies of the manor in the grandmother's burlesque speech; lastly, the powerful man's mistress and daughter in the equally burlesque context of the hero JLP's relations with Sestier. This hero, if the grandmother is to be believed, is not to *cure* these ladies, but to *bring them health* by drinking with them at table [44], after surreptitiously palpating their legs. The hero cannot perceive Death at the ladies' feet (the canonical position of Death at the patient's feet, the position in which in principle the hero has permission according to Wolf to administer the salt-placebo), since the ladies in Fabre's story are sitting, their feet concealed under the table. But the hero, unable to see the ladies' feet, and therefore whether Death is placed there, does not deprive himself of the pleasure of feeling their knees and thighs. (What we have here, as so often in *JLP*, is a burlesque equivocation between apparent vulgarity and, at a deeper level, the exploration of a possible position of Death.) Lastly, in both cases, once the exploration of the legs is completed, the placebo is of exactly the same kind. In Wolf, we have the three grains of salt in the sweetened milk (milk = *ipso facto* unsalted), which is consumed in the form of a drink by the lady in question. The detail is both alimentary (salt, milk) and numerical (*three* grains of salt, for a cure in *three* days). In Fabre, we have the salt taken between *five* fingers [first version] or between *two* fingers [second version] which the hero then puts on the plate piled with meat (initially unsalted), which the lady in question eats, while clinking glasses and drinking with the hero. The details given by Fabre are certainly numerical (*five* fingers or *two* fingers, instead of *three* grains of salt that cure in *three* days, as in Wolf); they are similarly alimentary: salt is sprinkled in both cases over food deriving from cattle (milk in Wolf, meat in Fabre). The table in the aristocratic lady's dining-room (in *JLP*) has replaced the bed in the sick princess's bedroom (in Wolf's version of AT 332).

This may be summarized as in Table 38.

The speech of J L P's grandmother is certainly crypto-medical, or in other words 'medical', but concealed. It corresponds point by point to the educational speech made by Death to the hero, in the canonical first part of the four-part cycle of AT 332. At the same time, the medical import of this speech is concealed for Fabre's average reader: it is quite possible that some of the abbé's listeners, during a possible public reading of the text made by the author in some drawing-room one evening about 1760, might have known the oral versions of AT 332 that were then circulating in Languedoc; it is therefore possible that they understood the burlesque import of *JLP* in general, and of the grandmother's speech in particular. We, too, can elucidate this burlesque import, overall and in detail, since we now know, with a view to comparison, the complete panoply of versions of AT 332 from the Midi, Catalonia, northern France, Germany, etc. Nevertheless, for the 'average reader', in the nineteenth and even in the twentieth century, the grandmother's rhetoric and the novella of *JLP* as a whole represent a text of which we had temporarily lost the key. This text had become both strange and obscure, and therefore fascinating; it was forgotten that

Table 38

ON A FEW GRAINS OF SALT
(IN THE SEQUENTIAL ORDER OF THE TEXTS)

Wolf, 1851	*JLP* [44] first and second versions
The physician–hero visits a lady on her sick-bed.	The hero visits a lady who is at table [44, second version].
He examines her legs and sees Death at her feet.	He slaps her leg (knee and thigh), with apparently erotic intent.
He makes a prognosis that the lady will be restored to *health*.	He drinks to the lady's *health*.
He gets her to drink a potion.	He 'clinks glasses' with her, after which she drinks.
This potion, which he has made up, consists of *three* grains of salt * in a product of animal origin (sweetened milk, that is, un-salted).	He prepares food for the lady, consisting of salt sprinkled with *two*, or *five*, fingers on a product of animal origin (unsalted meat).
From now on he is regarded as an eminent 'society' physician.	From now on he is regarded as 'a well-brought-up young man who knows how to behave in society'.

* These three grains of salt in sweetened milk (Wolf, 1851) or the grains of salt sprinkled (with two or five fingers) over meat (Fabre, 1756) are related to the other placebos of a similar type referred to in certain older versions of AT 332, one of which at least (German) has been preserved: in that of Ayrer (died in 1605), the placebo consists of 'two apple pits in bread'. Salt, however, is a commodity that, in fairy-tales, serves as a prophylactic, or protection against illness, evil, etc. (S. Thompson, *Motif Index of Folk-Literature* [1933], vol. VI, p. 699; vol. III, pp. 78–9; vol. V, p. 559; etc.).

it was a hyper-realistic version of a whole family of oral versions of a folk-tale which clearly belonged to the world of the supernatural.

*

To complete this explanation of the educational speech given by grandmother Death to her grandson Jean-l'ont-pris, I shall return, briefly, to the Roussillonnais tale, *Galdric*. Death's educational and directly medical speech to the hero Galdric, who is the functional equivalent of the hero Jean-l'ont-pris, contains a rather curious sentence: *When I have explained it all to you*, says Death to the Roussillonnais coal-merchant, *you will see that it is as easy as blowing* [*bufar*] *and moving your fingers* (p. 69). In fact, the Occitan-Catalan word *bufar* ['to blow hard' or 'to breath in deeply'] and the fact of moving the fingers are regarded by Death as the ('easy') equivalent of 'the thing'; this medical 'thing' consists (according to the Roussillonnais Death) of locating the position of Death at the head of the patient (or not) and of thus diagnosing the imminent death (or not) of the patient.

In *JLP*, the grandmother's educational speech to the young hero is *crypto*-medical. Instead of clearly explaining these problems of Death's position in relation to the patient's head or feet, Fabre launches into a long speech about *breathing* and *fingers*, which were passed over very quickly in the homologous speech made by Death to Galdric. These actions are precisely, in *Galdric*, the burlesque 'equivalent' of the classic and medical techniques of AT 332; moreover, these techniques would be fully explained by the grandmother if her speech were *directly* medical, which it is not.

(1) First, what is there about *breathing* in grandmother Death's educational speech to JLP?

(a) *Breathing out* corresponds to the advice given to the hero to wipe his nose on his shirt, by a noisy sniffing [*nifflarés*]: this action expels the mucus in the most effective way.

(b) *Breathing in* (for the hero who wishes to greet someone who is worth bothering with) is a matter of making 'a loud kiss [*poutou*] in the hollow of your hand' [43].

It is useless to labour the point that when blowing one's nose, one necessarily expels air, and while kissing, one breathes air in. Indeed, this is the double meaning of the verb *bufar* ['to breathe in and out'] used in *Galdric*; it is also the double use to be found in Fabre and no doubt in the oral versions on which his tale is based.

(2) Second, the fact of *moving one's fingers*.

This action is referred to only briefly in Death's speech to Galdric.

Grandmother Death, on the other hand, develops this 'moving of the fingers' at some length in her lecture to J L P, referring in the first place not to the fingers [*doigts*] themselves, but to the toes [*doigts de pied*], active and bare, like a hen's claws: just after kissing the hollow of his hand, the hero, when greeting an important person [43], must 'step back, bow, scraping the ground with both feet like a hen'.

But, quite clearly, the hero also has occasion *to move his fingers*. 'If you are invited to a castle,' grandmother Death tells the hero in the same speech [44], 'don't forget to *pinch* their thighs and *slap* their knees [that is, with the fingers in both cases] . . . put your *five fingers* cleanly into the salt and sprinkle their food with it.' The second version [44] simply replaces the 'five fingers' with the 'two fingers like this'. The fingers of Fabre's hero must *move* in order to pinch the lady's thigh, to slap her knee and above all to pick up the salt-placebo and sprinkle it over the meat.

The whole programme of 'breathing and moving the hero's fingers', identified at precisely the same strategic and tactical point, advocated by the Roussillonnais godfather Death (*Galdric*) and the Languedocian grandmother Death (*JLP*) is, therefore, summarized in *Galdric* but fully deployed in *JLP*. These *movements with the fingers*, accompanied by *breathing*, to which *Galdric* refers only briefly, are detailed at length in Fabre's novella. Furthermore, they make it possible to introduce the motif of the grains of salt, of which another version of A T 332, Wolf's, has provided us with an explanation, at the same precise point in Death's educational speech. By means of a detailed comparison between *JLP*, on the one hand, and *Godfather Death*, whether regional or general, on the other, we have succeeded in completely deciphering grandmother Death's strange educational speech, as it is delivered at the beginning of Jean-l'ont-pris's personal autobiography. The speech is at once crypto-medical (administering a placebo including salt), sociological (frequenting the great), gestural, symbolic and perhaps magical ('breathing and moving the fingers'). All this, of course, is situated in the order of the bur-lesque deliberately chosen by Fabre in order to introduce the magical into the real. Moreover, the abbé had loyally warned his readers: the grandmother's speech is not a lot of nonsense, but a series of *parables* [45]. In other words, it is symbolic from beginning to end.

Conclusion

I began this work as a simple local monograph, based on the elements of village realism to be found, according to the specialists,[1] in Fabre's novella. During several years of research, I have followed, therefore, the example set in this field by the historian E.-G. Léonard. At the outset, I wanted to relate *Jean-l'ont-pris* to the social reality of the Vaunage in the eighteenth century. We know something of this reality from, among other sources, the *Chronologiette*, or intimate journal, of Pierre Prion, cellarman at the Château d'Aubais-en-Vaunage from 1740 to 1760. In fact, Prion was a fellow-citizen, contemporary and friend of Fabre. I had an opportunity of rediscovering the manuscript of this *Chronologiette*[2] and of testing in a positive way the factual accuracy of certain references to be found in the abbé's tale. This first undertaking, which I devoted to the study of a certain kind of realism, was not therefore without foundation. *Jean-l'ont-pris* contains many elements that speak of the 'everyday life of the village' or hamlet in the Vaunage of the eighteenth century, whether that community is called Aubais or Solorgues. Certainly, Fabre's tale seems realistic enough. The world of the Rouergat immigrants, rural craftsmen and groups of rustic youth is brilliantly evoked in Fabre's text. The Huguenots of that region, like J L P's grandmother, really were buried 'in a hole in open countryside', outside the official Catholic cemeteries. The wig of the *parvenu*, so dear to Monsieur Sestier, was certainly regarded as an outward sign of social standing in the countryside, however recently acquired it may have been. The vineyard-keepers, so easily bribed [54], were indeed, as our Languedocian archives show, important characters in the communal life of the agrarian world described by the abbé-novelist.[3] Each *seigneurie* in the Vaunage, like that of La Boissière, employs, Pierre Prion tells us, a huntsman. The absence of a physician in *JLP* is also explained by the fact that in the Vaunage, according to Prion, the lower classes resorted to surgeons and quacks, rather than to qualified doctors.

A close study of the surviving archives of the villages of Nages-et-Solorgues (the native district of the principal heroes in the novella) and of Langlade (that of Monsieur Sestier) enables us to specify the ultimately rather narrow limits of this 'realism'. The land around Langlade and above all around Solorgues (which was in full demographic expansion between 1730 and 1760) had been turned, about 1750, by the largely Protestant owners into intensely and efficiently run olive-groves, vineyards and orchards. This makes it all the more understandable, following Fabre's text, that a Capuchin friar should come collecting tithes on olive oil at Solorgues, and that the vineyard-keepers or peach-orchards should play such a central role in the narrative. Having said this, we have to admit that, in the mid-eighteenth century, and more generally from 1650 to 1780, not a single proper name of the abbé's fictional characters (Sestier at Langlade; Truquette, Garouille, Carcanas, Crouquet, Renâouvi, Quincarlot at Solorgues) is to be found on the lists of *real* names belonging to the inhabitants of these localities, as they appear in legal documents, cadastral surveys, assessment books or records of municipal meetings. Only the baron of La Boissière, to whose *seigneurie* Solorgues belongs (in Fabre's novella), appears among the assessment books of Nages-et-Solorgues in the years between 1730 and 1750; he is certainly the greatest land-owner and the only considerable aristocratic taxpayer in this twin community. This lord does not appear personally in *Jean-l'ont-pris*, of course; he is evoked only indirectly through his subordinates – the gamekeeper, the professional hunter, the clerk of the court, etc. The other characters of the novella form a gallery of imaginary individuals: their names correspond to no local onomastics, but to macabre functions (Carcanas, Renâouvi . . .) or to names from folklore, even pejorative ones (Truquette, Garouille . . .). Two characters at least, who embody death, namely, the grandmother and the anonymous baron from the Vaunage, do not have names: indeed, they suggest the unspeakable essence of Death.[4] Quincarlot/Cancrelas, a diabolico-macabre incarnation, is simply named by the term (*Quincarlot*) that designates a repugnant insect [*cancrelas*, 'cockroach'].

This examination of the archives brings the historian back to the text of the narrative itself, which certainly contains its share of oddities: who is this 'young peasant', Jean-l'ont-pris, who never touches a pick handle and who never harvests a grain of wheat, even as a worker on someone else's land? In terms of rural activities, this boy does no more than maim donkeys, steal fruit and guard vineyards.

Beyond what it describes as village life, Fabre's story, one has to admit, also contains a large element of *fantasy*.

A dogmatic researcher would no doubt preserve in a rigid way the 'problematic' that he had originally brought to his subject. I certainly believe that documentation provides answers, but it also raises new questions in the course of research. I have therefore gone beyond the 'realistic' hypothesis; it is correct, but inadequate. I have embarked on an examination of the Occitan fiction of the *ancien régime*, in its relations with Fabre's story, and of the relevant cycle of a fairy-tale. At the end of my research it seemed to me that *Jean-l'ont-pris*, studied as a whole and in its smallest detail, was situated at the intersection of two larger cultural groups.

Horizontally, *Jean-l'ont-pris* belongs to the general model that underpins Fabre's dramatic work and Occitan literature as a whole. In this instance, it is more particularly a question of Occitan drama between 1580 and 1789. The central problem lying at the heart of this model may be formulated thus: *how can he marry her?* More specifically, how can an often poor and usually gifted young man find the money, land or capital (property, status, etc.) necessary to win a girl's hand in marriage, and, more important, the consent of the girl's father or family? Second, how is he to eliminate a possible rival? How is he to use, for such purposes, his capital, if he happens to have any already? This problem is not peculiar to the culture of the Midi, but this culture did strive to resolve it with single-minded obstinacy, obsessional concentration and a variety of approach that win respect, interest, even admiration from the scholar. Let us call this first problem *Love and Money*.

Our Languedocian novella also belongs to a second model or cultural group; it is smaller than the previous one, in terms of content, but it is more lasting in the long run. *Jean-l'ont-pris* belongs, in effect, to the tale type called *Godfather Death* or *Death's Godson* (Aarne and Thompson, 332). Let us call this second problem *Death, Money, Love*. In other words, how will the hero, using a pact with a certain supernatural being, in this instance, Death, allied perhaps with the devil, manage to obtain the capital that will enable him to resolve problem number 1, which, of course, amounts to obtaining the capital necessary to persuade a father or a mother to give up a daughter? At the outset, Fabre certainly used a local version (*Jean-de-*

Solorgues?) and several regional versions of *Godfather Death*. The sub-title of the second version of his novella, 'deriving from the archives of Solorgues', no doubt refers to this use. He could be referring, in fact, to only the *oral* archives, since the *written* municipal archives of 'Solorgues' were preserved at the (very modest) town hall of Nages, from which the double community of 'Nages-et-Solorgues' was adminis-tered. Furthermore, these written archives contain none of the names (which in fact are imaginary) of the characters of the abbé's story.

The history of tale type A T 332/*Godfather Death* flows (vertically) as a linear flow from its (known) origins about 1300 to 1340 to its general diffusion throughout the Christian world in the eighteenth and nineteenth centuries; this diffusion is then followed by a gradual extinction of the oral tradition from 1950 onwards. Occitan fiction, based on the economic and amatory problems of marriage, spread like a synchrony of the *ancien régime* over some sixty works of imaginative literature, in the seventeenth and eighteenth centuries. Written in 1756, *Jean-l'ont-pris* is situated at the meeting of these two currents, or axes, vertical and horizontal. It was this intersection that made Fabre's achievement possible.

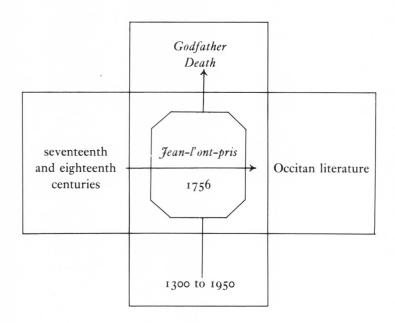

For a historian of the communities of ordinary people under the *ancien régime*, all this forms part of the broader problematic of what the anthropologist George M. Foster has called 'the theory of *limited good*'.[5] In a traditional society like that of rural Languedoc in the eighteenth century, a young man wants to 'advance himself': with this end in view, he has to make an honourable and profitable marriage; to do this he must possess in advance, in his own family or in his expectations of inheritance, certain capital in the form of status, money and land; or he must, in one way or another, obtain such capital. Since the rural economy was stagnant or (in the case of eighteenth-century Languedoc) of slow growth, offset by demographic expansion, it is difficult for this young man to accumulate his capital through his own work and savings; it is extremely difficult for him to rise in this way as 'a man who works hard and is blest by God' [75]. Indeed, the total land wealth at the disposal of the community is limited, if only by the boundaries of the locality. The theatre of Marseille, where maritime commerce made possible the rapid acquisition of fortunes, and therefore rapid changes of fortune in a suitor's prospects, is exceptional in this regard. Elsewhere, the stereotypes of Occitan culture suggest that one cannot become rich without at the same time making someone else poor. Such at least is the tendency of an ideology that survived for some two hundred years. In these circumstances, the young man will have to obtain, by force or by trickery, the capital he needs from some other source – his own family, his rival, the family of his future wife or the very girl he hopes to marry.

Furthermore, the 'non-élitist' mentality of the eighteenth century has not yet suffered the attacks of rationalism; it still has a taste for the magical and the marvellous. In order to undermine completely the implacable theory of 'limited good', it can turn only to sources of wealth that are outside the community: in the absence of vast prospects deriving from an endless growth of 'raw materials', the hero must find a treasure, some source of hitherto unexploited wealth; or he must get rich through his own family's dishonesty;[6] or he must turn to some supernatural power (the devil,[7] Death); or, lastly, like our Jean-l'ont-pris, he must combine all three solutions. So Death will provide the treasure for the hero only on certain dangerous conditions. It is in this way that the physician Death's godson in the tale type *Godfather Death* operates.

In *Jean-l'ont-pris*, Fabre explored these various possibilities. The pact with Death always turns out badly. Occitan drama always ends well. The abbé, at the intersection of these two requirements, ended his tale with a 'draw'. The hero will end his career, it seems, where his father had begun, in poverty – but not in tragedy. Fabre has also escaped, with *JLP*, the happy ending of the Occitan theatre. This happy ending was too frequent in his works and in those of others: one has only to look at the Occitan drama of the *ancien régime* (1580–1790). A century before Frédéric Mistral and Eugène Le Roy, the abbé Fabre had exorcised the sentimental plot with which, throughout the eighteenth century, so many writers in the Midi had been content. By avoiding any direct reference to the supernatural, be encoding the fantastic beings (Death) as everyday, and sometimes burlesque villagers (Quincarlot and the grandmother), Fabre passed from the register of the supernatural to that of the merely strange. He took an incidental part in that process of secularization or elimination of the baroque Death that Michel Vovelle[8] sees as one of the principal cultural phenomena of the French Midi under the *ancien régime*. One inside the other, Fabre made, in his novella, a *summum* of Occitan culture and literature in the seventeenth and eighteenth centuries. He transcended these, moving in the direction of a still unknown future. This future was to become embodied later, in various ways, in the tales of Grimm, in the rural 'realism' of a Balzac or a Zola and in the great poems of the Félibrige. Occitan drama and fairy-tale have, meanwhile, given us access to the structures and secret mechanisms of a story of imagination: *Jean-l'ont-pris* provides the key to the literature of the classical Midi. *Godfather Death* provides the key to *Jean-l'ont-pris* itself. In its own way, Fabre's novella describes both stages of the infraculture[9] of the Enlightenment: a ground floor, occupied by the dialect writers of the provinces; and a basement, crossed, as if by cables, by the oral networks of folk-tale transmission.

Notes

Preface

1. On the highly debatable 'realism' of *Jean-l'ont-pris*, see J. Troubat (1877), p. xi, and J.-B. Noulet, *Essai sur l'histoire littéraire des patois du midi de la France* . . . (1877), especially the chapter devoted to the priest–writers of the eighteenth century: 'Fabre depicts according to nature the life of the countryside in the last century.' See also, more subtly argued, C. Camproux, *Histoire de la littérature occitane* (1971), p. 128; M. Barral, *Jean-Baptiste Favre, sa vie, son œuvre* . . . (1971), p. 184 and *Jean-l'ont-pris*, p. 13; Y. Rouquette (1967); and, somewhat hasty as to Fabre's completely rural, so-called realism, M. Coulon (1929), p. 47. On the unquestionable character of this 'masterpiece', see, for example, C. Camproux (1971); R. Lafont and C. Anatole, *Nouvelle Histoire de la littérature occitane* (1970), vol. II, p. 476; and M. Coulon (1929), who sees Fabre as 'the greatest Occitan writer between the Troubadors and Le Félibrige'.

2. In this English version of the book, the two versions of *Jean-l'ont-pris* (1756 and 1765), together with Philippe Gardy's French translation, which were printed in the 1980 French edition, have been omitted. Instead, there is an English translation based on the French [Tr.].

Jean-l'ont-pris

1. During his argument with Margot, Truquette gets so excited that he lapses into the Occitan of his native Rouergue and not that of the Vaunage, which he learned later. The sound of him speaking Gavach, which would sound odd and coarse to the inhabitants of the 'lowlands', excited Margot's anger even more.

2. *Crouquet*, that is to say, *crochet* ['hook'].

3. *Quincarlot* suggests *quincarlat*, the Occitan equivalent of the French *cancrelat* ['cockroach'].

4. Occitan corruption of *ecce homo* (the words spoken by Pontius Pilate at Christ's appearance after the scourging).

Chapter I

1. M. Barral, *Jean-Baptiste Favre, sa vie, son œuvre* . . . (1971). I have retained the original spelling of the name – Fa*b*re.

2. A franc of 20 sous, minted at Tours [Tr.].

3. M. Barral (1971), p. 182. The many references to Mahon in *JLP* are to Port Mahon (Balearic Islands), made famous by its siege (1756).

4. This absorption of the folk culture of the region, in the course of Fabre's various and generous social activity, emerges very clearly in the *Chronologiette* by Pierre Prion, a contemporary and friend of the abbé at Aubais, and in the writing, by Fabre, of the *Soirées de la Vaunage*, a work now lost. See also E.-G. Léonard, *Mon village sous Louis XV* (1941).

5. On the antagonism between the academic movement (provincial and French-speaking) of the eighteenth century and the earlier baroque world of Occitan literature, see the thesis by D. Roche, *Le Siècle des lumières en province . . .* (1978), p. 20.

6. I have used the following abbreviations: *JLP* for Fabre's novella *Jean-l'ont-pris*; J L P for the hero of that novella. '*JLP*' and 'J L P' (in inverted commas) for the same story and hero, but in the oral form of the folk-tale that came to Fabre's notice and that he used for his novella (on this subject, see the second part of this book). The same system is employed for *Jean-de-trop*, presented in my book as *JDT* and J D T (for the version published in 1885), '*JDT*' and 'J D T' (for the earlier version, which existed before 1756).

7. Barbe-Garouille, Garouille, Garouillette: three slightly different names for the same character in the abbé Fabre's novella.

8. I have not included in this list a few plays which, because they are not primarily concerned with marriage, are outside the scope of my subject: one might mention *Les Fourberies du siècle* (1684) by Palamède Tronc de Codolet, who *adapts* (very well) the French *Pathelin*, and, again, *Monsieur Lambert* (1757) by Antoine Clet, of Puy, which depicts only half of what is to become our 'marriage square', etc.

9. See C. D. Brenner, *A Bibliographical List of Plays in the French Language (1700–1789)* (1967). I should point out that I have not used in my study the seventeenth- and eighteenth-century religious drama of the Languedoc because, though full of vitality, it is not relevant to my concerns here. See C. Camproux, *Histoire de la littérature occitane* (1971), pp. 114–15. Nor, for the same reason, have I made use of a number of tragedies, in the strict sense of the term, that the Occitan theatre produced.

10. This also applies to the carnivalesque and semi-Occitan play by J.-B. Masse, a Freemason from Marseille: *Le Protée*, performed in that city at the carnival of 1759 (ms. Bibliothèque Arbaud, Aix, 2652 A–1).

11. Uncle: Fescais de La Tour, *Le Faux Ami* (ms. Bibliothèque Arbaud,

Aix, MQ 155). Guardian: *Le Tuteur jaloux*, by Gravelle (Marseille-Avignon, 1759). Older brother: *Daphnis et Alcimadure* by Cassanea de Mondonville. About these plays, and those cited later, see the Bibliography.

12. These two plays, published at Marseille in 1781 and 1782, are to be found in the municipal libraries of Aix and Marseille.

13. See *L'Opéra de Frontignan* by N. Fizes. The Provençal Fescais de La Tour, in two manuscript plays of the eighteenth century (*Les Insulaires* and *Le Rival généreux*), also 'substituted' a mother for the 'daughter's father', as far as deciding on the young heroine's marriage is concerned (Bibliothèque Arbaud, Aix, 2652 A–1; see also Bibliography).

14. See C. Lévi-Strauss, *The Elementary Structures of Kinship* (1969), pp. 108, 454–61, and *Structural Anthropology* (1968).

15. *Comédie de Seigne Peyre et Seigne Joan*, a play acted by two peasants from Montélimar (1580). (See the Bibliography.) Only the young hero's father and the young heroine's father appear in it.

16. See the character of the manservant in Rousset's *Le Jaloux attrapé*.

Chapter II

1. J.-J. Cassanea de Mondonville, *Daphnis et Alcimadure* (1754). The 'gift of the beloved's goods', a gift imposed on a timid hero by a waiting-maid, is also the mainspring of Agricol Lapierre-Chateauneuf's play *Le Faux-Seing ou l'adroite soubrette*, performed at Marseille and Avignon in 1787 (marriage square: the *rival*, the *hero*, the *heroine* and her *mother*).

2. J.-B. Noulet, *Essai sur l'histoire littéraire des patois du midi de la France . . .* (1877), the part devoted to the seventeenth century.

3. *Ibid.*, pp. 120ff.

4. On this subject, see the thesis by H. Michel, 'Pratique notariale . . . à Montpellier' (1979), on Montpellier in the eighteenth century.

5. Occitan text in P. Pansier, *Théâtre provençal d'Avignon au XVIIᵉ siècle* (1832), pp. 63–135.

6. This play is to be found in *Théâtre populaire de Béziers* (see the Bibliography).

7. Text in Provençal, from the late sixteenth century; (1843), vol. I, pp. 19ff.

8. Reference in the Bibliography. Attribution to J. Calhol is to be found

516 LOVE, DEATH AND MONEY IN THE PAYS D'OC

in particular in P. Gardy, *Langue et Société en Provence au début du XIXe siècle* . . . (1978), p. 59.

9. Mss. J.-B. C. Fabre or Favre, 'Œuvres de Saint-Castor', vol. IV (Bibl. municipale de Montpellier).

10. Performed at Marseille in 1777 for the entry of Monsieur, the king's brother. Published at Avignon in 1777.

11. Bibliothèque nationale, pièces originales 100, contrat Fargeon, 5 July 1720; ADH II E 60/116/F° 174 (7 April 1729). Documents kindly provided by H. Michel, professor of history at the University of Montpellier.

12. This play is included in works by F. de Cortète (*c.* 1586–1667), published in the *Recueil des travaux de la Société d'agriculture, sciences et arts d'Agen*, XVII (or XVIII), 2nd series (1915). See also R. Lafont, *Francès de Corteta* (1968).

13. Another reference to the search for female capital for the dowry of a girl who wants to get married, or whose lineage is trying to marry her off, is to be found in *Les caquets de l'accouchée*, a text dating from the *ancien régime*, also from northern France (see the Bibliography).

14. Other 'blind spots' or 'censorings' practised by the Occitan theatre in the seventeenth and eighteenth centuries: it never depicts a bastard son or a bastard daughter of a lay parent, still less of a priest. In this respect, Fabre's *Jean-l'ont-pris* is unusual.

15. P. Lamaison, 'Parentée, patrimonie et stratégie matrimoniales sur ordinateur . . .' (1978), p. 41.

16. M. Barral, *Jean-Baptiste Favre, sa vie, son œuvre* . . . (1971), p. 249.

17. According to Expilly, Caderousse had 800 'fires', or households (about 3,600 inhabitants), in the second half of the eighteenth century, after a period which, in principle, was one of demographic expansion.

18. There are a number of editions of this work, including that of Placide Cappeau (J.-B. Favre, *Le Siège de Caderousse* [1876]). It has the advantage of also containing the printed account of the real episode.

19. Boiardo (1441–94) is the Italian author of an epic (*Orlando Innamorato*) which mixes the Carolingian cycle and the Breton cycle; he is a precursor of Ariosto. Pantaloon is a character of Venetian comedy from the seventeenth century onwards (he is a retired merchant). Octave (as in Molière's *Les Fourberies de Scapin*) is a 'juvenile lead in comedy, frivolous, impulsive, amorous'.

20. In the second version of *Jean-l'ont-pris*, the hero's treasure is also

constituted, after being converted into cash, by the resulting sum of money and two dozen silver spoons and forks.

21. This is the procedure used in two Marseillais plays dating from the reign of Louis XV. In Audibert's *Le fortuné Marseillais* (in French, with parts in Provençal, 1736), the 'marriage square' consists of (A) the hero's two rivals; (B) the hero, who benefits from an inheritance; (C) the heroine; and (D) her mother. In M. de Gravelle's *La Marseillaise* (1760), the square consists of the rival, Captain Louragan; the hero (a merchant's clerk, later an heir); the heroine; and her father, a merchant. The Marseillais plays, in a city in which commerce flourished in the eighteenth century, often use the sudden arrival of a bill of exchange to transform the hero's finances in the right direction.

22. *Bulletin de la Société archéologique, scientifique et littéraire de Béziers*, VI (1847–57), 119ff.

23. On the extremely gradual transition from Provençal to Franco-Provençal, through 'progressive interferences', see the remarkable thesis by J.-C. Bouvier, *Les Parlers provençaux de la Drôme* (1976), pp. 469–71. There certainly is a cultural unity formed by Dauphiné–Provence–Languedoc. The Dauphinois intellectuals were well aware of the fact from the late sixteenth century onwards. See, in this respect, my *Carnival in Romans* (1980), Ch. XIV.

24. P. Lamaison (1978), p. 134. See also A. Collomp (1977), p. 462.

25. See *Les Mariages rhabillés*. On the non-Occitan pastoral, see I. Gerhardt, 'Essais d'analyse littéraire de la pastorale dans les littératures italienne, espagnole et française' (1950). Apart from the great texts cited by Racan, Mairet and Tasso, see, for a later period, Fontenelle's *Poésies pastorales* (1688); their highly idyllic inspiration has nothing to do with our southern intrigues, which are based on the transfer, from male to female, of money and goods. See also (an idyllic tendency similar to Fontenelle's) Ollenix du Mont-sacré (abbé Nicolas de Monteux), 'Cinq histoires comiques' in *Le Premier Livre des bergeries de Juliette* (1588).

26. *Théâtre populaire de Béziers*, vol. 1.

27. This is the central theme of *Jammetto* (see the Bibliography), an authentically rural comedy in Occitan, in a cultural eighteenth century that no longer exists, written by a priest and performed about 1730 at Carcassonne. It had immense success among both the urban and the rural public; whole fragments of the play were preserved for a long time, for a century or two, in the Occitan tradition of these regions, and later collected by scholars. (This preservation, which is proved both by the eighteenth-century manuscripts and by publication in the twentieth century, constitutes, incidentally, a

weighty argument to prove the transmission of such oral literature as *JLP/JDT*, from the eighteenth to the nineteenth century.) The plot of *Jammetto*: the peasant Antony is on the point of ruining himself and selling his house in order to win a court case against Guilhem, another peasant; the latter's daughter Jammetto loves Ramoun, Antony's son, and he loves her. A conciliator succeeds in saving Antony's house and fortune, threatened by the immense and ridiculous expenses of the case; in fact, he manages to obtain the consent of Ramoun's irascible father to the marriage of the hero and heroine. The father of the charming Jammetto also gives in. The two households will henceforth be one. The wedding with which the play ends is therefore motivated both by the love of the young couple and by economic considerations: Ramoun can guarantee happiness, administered in the form of interminable kisses laid on his future wife; he can also guarantee prosperity for the extended family that he, his wife, his parents and parents-in-law will henceforth form:

the obstacle: the case	Guilhem, Jammetto's father
Ramoun, Antony's son	Jammetto, his daughter

the marriage saves the hero's expectations of an inheritance, threatened by the case; these expectations also guarantee the young couple's future prosperity

28. In G. Zerbin, *La perlo dey Muses et Coumedies provensalos* (1655).

29. J. Jasmin, *Papillottos* (1842), vol. II.

30. This assimilation of the Huguenots to Satan was accepted in the Occitan popular literature of this time. See J.-B. Noulet (1877), p. 76 (on the complicity between Satan and Calvin), in the text *La Métamorphose des huguenots en escargots dans la vallée de Lectoure*. The Huguenot/serpent/devil is also cited in R. Sauzet, *Contre-Réforme et Réforme catholique en Bas-Languedoc, Le diocèse de Nîmes au XVIIᵉ siècle* (1979), p. 352.

31. Toulouse, 1604. Reprinted at Saint-Gaudens, 1932.

32. G. Zerbin (1655).

33. *Ibid.*

34. J. de Cabannes (1653–1717), *Marra ou lou fouil fu sagi*, comedy in five acts, manuscript in the Bibliothèque Méjanes, Aix. I am indebted to Philippe Gardy for a complete transcription.

35. Fescais de La Tour, *Le Bon Père* (1783; ms. Bibliothèque Arbaud, Aix). (See the Bibliography.)

36. Bibliothèque nationale, ms. français, ancien suppl. français (12508).

37. P. Lamaison (1978), p. 136: the case of Baptiste Souchon (February 1766).

38. On these hypotheses, see A. Collomp (1977), pp. 450–52. A brief investigation into notaries' records at Aubais (the village in Gard where the abbé Fabre wrote and lived) and also in those at Lodève (Hérault) provide a number of examples relating to these various possibilities:

(1) Examples in which a future husband is sole heir to the wealth and particularly the house of his parents. Once married, he will, in principle, live with them, enjoying usufruct of their wealth. On this basis he will obtain for himself a girl and a dowry: see ADG II E 13–132 (notary of Aubais), marriage contracts of 14 November, 30 November, 7 December, 8 December, 11 December 1744, and 3 January, 13 January, 24 January, 23 February, 22 March and 2 September 1745.

(2) Examples of considerable male contribution to the marriage contract: ADG II E 13–132 (22 October 1744); ADH II E 40–247, notary of Lodève (3 February 1737 and 14 February 1737).

(3) Male contribution approximately equal to that of the woman: ADH II E 81–50, notary of Saint-Martin-de-Londres (marriage of Guillaume Amalou and Marguerite Vals); see also *ibid.*, 9 February and 9 March 1755; ADG II E 13–132 (28 February 1745, 3 April, 19 September and 28 September 1745, 26 October 1746).

(4) Male contribution that appears to be less than that of the woman (but taking into account the husband's expected inheritance, the female contribution in the long term is probably lower): ADG II E 13–132 (19 May and 26 October 1744); ADH II E 40–247, notary of Lodève (9 February 1737).

(5) The husband's probable inheritance explicitly indicated, in addition to his immediate contribution: ADG II E 13–132 (6 December and 7 December 1744).

(6) Gift (with a view to a future marriage) from a son who is not a potential heir, put into a *will*: ADG II E 13–132 (11 September 1746).

(7) Wealth of late husband (Sieur Jean Gruvel) much greater than the dowry of his late wife (Marie Delort): ADG II E 13–132 (1 March 1747).

(8) Role of the brother in the giving away of his sister (see *Daphnis et Alcimadure*): ADH II I 40–247 (notary of Lodève), 26 February 1737.

39. This does not mean, of course, that the dowry, in terms of statistical history, is very representative (whether it is large or small) of the wealth, high or low, of the family of the endowed girl (see P. Lamaison [1978], p. 74; J.

Nicolas and R. Nicolas, *La vie quotidienne en Savoie au XVIIIe siècle* [1979], pp. 779, 911; and, finally, A. Daumard and F. Furet, *Structures et Relations sociales à Paris au XVIIIe siècle* [1961]).

40. A. Collomp (1977), p. 476. However, the notaries' records show isolated cases of a 'free and major' daughter marrying according to her own wishes (ADG II E 13–132, notary of Aubais, 23 November 1746).

Chapter III

1. J. Lacroix, *Récits et Contes populaires du Languedoc* (1978), vol. I, p. 119 (according to *Revue des langues romanes*, III [1872], 410–13). Isaac Despuech, a seventeenth-century writer from Montpellier, alludes in his *Folies du sage* to the legend of the 'rock that opens' at Substancion.

2. Republished at Sarlat in 1839.

3. Ms. Bibliothèque Arbaud, Aix, MQ 152–153.

4. N. Fizes, *L'Opéra de Frontignan* (1679), p. 11.

5. Morizot, *Pierre et Perrette*, Marseille, 1758 (Bibliothèque nationale, Res.); M. Poulhariez, *Le Taciturne*, originally performed at Marseille (published in Paris in 1778).

6. There are a number of examples of this practice among the notaries of the Languedoc: ADG II E 13–132 (notary of Aubais): 19 April 1745; 23 May, 28 September, 8 October 1745; 13 January, 24 September 1746.

7. On payment of the dowry 'on the table' to the husband, see, for example, ADH II E 40–247 (notary of Lodève): 26 January 1737 and 4 March 1737. For the remainder of the dowry paid in instalments *to the husband*, even by the wife, after the marriage, see also: ADG II E 13–132 (8 November 1744; 6 September 1746; 18 September 1746; 25 September 1746; 14 November 1746).

8. Gifts from the woman's uncle to assist her marriage: ADG II E 13–132 (2 November 1744 and 15 April 1746).

Chapter IV

1. Y. Castan, *Honnêteté et Relations sociales en Languedoc* (1974).

2. Occitan text published in *Bulletin de la Société archéologique, scientifique et littéraire de Béziers*, V (1844–6), 217ff.

3. This play was republished in *Recueil de pièces rares et facétieuses anciennes et modernes* (1873), vol. III (Bibliothèque nationale, Res., ZP 1744 [3]).

4. This complex play also contains another plot, already analysed in Chapter II.

5. Bibliothèque nationale, ms. français, ancien suppl. français (12508) (mss. of Jean de Cabannes).

6. J.-L. Flandrin, *Les Amours paysannes* (1970), p. 239, and P. Lamaison, 'Parenté, patrimonie et stratégie matrimoniales sur ordinateur . . .' (1978), p. 89.

Chapter V

1. *Bulletin de la Société archéologique, scientifique et littéraire de Béziers*, VI (1847–57), 75ff.

2. This meaning is given by the registers of capitations for villages in the Languedoc in the eighteenth century.

3. Fescais de La Tour, *Le Rival officieux* (ms. Bibliothèque Arbaud, Aix, MQ 152–153).

4. Jacques Calhol, *Moussu Jus* (in Occitan; performed at Marseille in 1784; published in 1804, 1823, etc.).

5. Fescais de La Tour, *Le Faux Ami* (ms. Bibliothèque Arbaud, Aix, MQ 155); J.-B. Masse, *Le Protée* (Marseille, carnival, 1759). The 'marriage square': the rival, the hero, the heroine and the heroine's father.

6. These two plays are *Les Insulaires* (a Turkish-style piece) and *Le Rival généreux* (1783). Both are in manuscript form in the Bibliothèque Arbaud, Aix-en-Provence (dossier MQ 152–153).

7. In legal practice, certain cases of this kind, in which a seducer or his accomplices try to 'lay the blame' for an illegitimate pregnancy on another man who is, in fact, innocent, are to be found in M. Garden, *Lyon au XVIIIe siècle, Les Belles Lettres* (1970), p. 424.

8. Francis Sabie, *Pan's Pipe, Three Pastoral Eclogues* (1595), published in *Modern Philology*, VII (April 1910). I am indebted to Mme Dorangeon, of the University of Rheims, for this information, which I quote.

9. R. Lafont, *Francès de Corteta* (1968), pp. 12–13.

10. Published by P. Pansier, *Théâtre provençal d'Avignon au XVIIe siècle* (1932).

11. See, for example, ADH II E 40–247 (notary of Lodève): 4 March 1737; ADG II E 13–132; 10 January and 13 February 1745.

12. On the relative importance of Satanism, which hardly survived in the Languedoc after 1600, see R. Sauzet, *Contre-Réforme et Réforme catholique en Bas-Languedoc, Le diocèse de Nîmes au XVIIᵉ siècle* (1979), vol. I, p. 255.

13. See an article on the *aiguillette* in my *Territoire de l'historien* (1978), vol. II, pp. 144–9. One of the popular plays (seventeenth century) from Avignon, published by Pansier (1932), deals in highly bawdy terms with an impotent husband who was supposedly a victim of the *aiguillette*. According to Alfred Soman, the eminent specialist on the archives of the Parlement de Paris from 1500 to 1650, the *aiguillette* was frequently used in sorcery between 1600 and 1650; it was always practised by a man.

14. E. Ladurie (1978), p. 147.

15. Bibliothèque nationale, ms. français, ancien suppl. français (12508).

16. A. Greimas and J. Courtes, *Sémiotique, Dictionnaire . . .* (1979), p. 61.

17. See, on this subject, P. Lamaison, 'Parenté, patrimonie et stratégie matrimoniales sur ordinateur . . . (1978), on eighteenth-century Lozère.

Chapter VI

1. See, on this subject, R. Nelli, *L'Érotique des troubadours* (1974), vol. I, p. 240. On the life of Bernart de Ventadour, see, for example, the *Dictionnaire biographique des auteurs* (1956), vol. I.

2. *Félix et Thomas Platter à Montpellier* (1892).

3. See also the very rural *Jammetto* from Carcassonne, again from the eighteenth century (see Chapter II).

4. It will be noted that in this very 'primitive' play the 'love square' is reduced, most unusually, to a triangle. The place of the rival, top left, is vacant. In a certain play (in Occitan and French) by Antoine Clet, *Monsieur Lambert* (Le Puy-en-Velay, 1757), the whole left part of the square, rival and hero, has entirely disappeared! Only the girl, the French-speaking (endowed, therefore, in the eyes of the period, with a substantial cultural capital) Friquetta, remains, dominated by her father, Monsieur Lambert, a magistrate at Le Puy and purely Occitan-speaking. The plot of the play, therefore, is no longer about love, but is an attack on the magistrature of Le Puy.

5. *Scatabronda*, by the abbé Fabre de Thémines (of Cahors), published at 'Rotterdam' (?) in 1697. According to Patrick Ferté, of the University of Cahors, a seventeenth-century specialist, Fabre de Thémines never existed, and the author of *Scatabronda* is some as yet unidentified writer from the Cahors region.

6. In fact, a great deal of research, including the recent and very remarkable work of Patrick Ferté (whom I would like to thank), shows that *Scatabronda* is a faithful account of a real event that took place at Cahors! According to the play, the true Romiguière in fact marries the true Jeanneton: but this time it is extremely difficult to make the father-in-law Scatabronda/Berrié conform to the rules of the Occitan 'love square'. Indeed, simply by abuse of power, professor Berrié will set up his new son-in-law Romiguière first as a graduate and doctor in law, then as a pseudo-*agrégé*, which will then confer on this incompetent young man the social status of 'symbolic capital' that will make him worthy, retrospectively, of marrying Jeanneton. (P. Ferté, 'Une agrégation frauduleuse à la Faculté de droit de Cahors en 1699', *Fédération des Sociétés académiques et savantes, Languedoc, Pyrénées, Gascogne*, 32nd congress, Cahors, June 1977, pp. 51–9.)

7. This remark particularly applies to *Jacquou*. In other interesting, but more conventional novels from the Périgord (*Le Moulin de Frau*, for example), E. Le Roy remains faithful to the classic model handed down to him by literary and social traditions.

Chapter VII

1. Étienne Souriau, *Les Deux cents mille Situations dramatiques*, p. 87.

2. On this play of oppositions, see A. Greimas, *Sémantique structurale* (1966), pp. 175–80, and E. Souriau, pp. 83–112.

3. See *L'Opéra d'Aubais* by the abbé Fabre.

4. See L. Mair, *Marriage* (1971), Ch. 4.

5. *Ibid.*, p. 74.

6. Bourdieu, *Annales* (1972), 1106–25.

7. P. Lamaison, 'Parenté, patrimonie et stratégie matrimoniales sur ordinateur . . .' (1978), pp. 99ff. In what follows, I quote this remarkable work at some length. See also A. Collomp (1977), p. 469.

8. All this passage, with the exception of the sentences in brackets, is a continuation of the long quotation taken from Lamaison (1978).

9. A comparison with Brittany: at Hédé (Ille-et-Vilaine), 46 per cent of marriages were made within the same occupational group (Régine Dalnoky, *Hédé* [1979]). See also D. Richet, 'Comportement familial des élites à Paris au XVIe siècle', pp. 5–6, and Heinrich Rüthing, 'Unterschichten in Spätmittelalterlichen Städten' (on class endogamy in a town of the Weser in the sixteenth century). These two as yet unpublished works were presented in

typescript to the Colloquium on the Family (Centre de recherches historiques, École des hautes études), 1 October 1979.

10. P. Lamaison (1978), pp. 245–6.

11. I have borrowed these terms from the anthropologist C. Geertz.

12. A. Molinier, *Sérignan* (1968), p. 188; G. Delbos, 'Faycelles-en-Quercy' (1969); J. Sentou, *Fortunes et Groupes sociaux à Toulouse sous la Révolution* (1969); A. Collomp (1977), p. 448; G. Durand, *Vin, vigne et vignerons en Lyonnais et Beaujolais (XVIᵉ–XVIIIᵉ siècle)* (1979), p. 351; C. Carrière, *Négociants marseillais au XVIIIᵉ siècle* (1973), vol. I, p. 291. Of the Marseille merchants, 9.3 per cent married into the nobility, 71.1 per cent into merchants' families and 19.6 per cent into other social categories. There are in this group (so frequently described by the Marseillais drama between 1730 and 1790) socio-occupational homogamy and class endogamy.

13. J. Sentou (1969), p. 58. This need for male contribution proportional to the female dowry is demonstrated statistically from the fifteenth century (cadastral survey of 1437), in the Provençal and Languedocian lower Rhône, by the computerized study in which L. Stouff, 'Arles à la fin du Moyen Age' (1979), vol. III, graph 86, correlates male wealth and female dowries, at the level of married couples. The same, very high correlation between male contribution and female contribution, at various levels of the social hierarchy, existed in the rural Beaujolais studied by G. Durand (1979), pp. 352, 370. See the graphs by Stouff and Durand reproduced in this book on pp. 146–7.

14. Comte C. de Villeneuve, *Mœurs des Provençaux ...* (1826; 1972), pp. 146ff.

15. J. Nicolas and R. Nicolas, *La Vie quotidienne en Savoie au XVIIIᵉ siècle* (1979), Ch. 1.

16. N. Salomon, *Recherches sur le thème paysans dans la 'comedia' au temps de Lope de Vega* (1965), pp. 688–9.

17. Unpublished information kindly provided by Henri Michel.

18. Text of 22 August 1036 (in Bigorre) kindly given to the author by Mme Mussot-Goulart. On the male *augment de dot* in the Middle Ages, see the lectures given by G. Duby (*Medieval Marriage* [1978], pp. 5–6, 38) at Johns Hopkins University (Baltimore).

19. E. Boserup, *Woman's Role in Economic Development* (1970), p. 50, quoted by J. Goody and S. J. Tambiah, *Bridewealth and Dowry* (1973), p. 45.

20. According to Élizabeth Claverie, who has studied rural crime in Lozère in the nineteenth century, the criminality of young men seeking to obtain

capital in order to be able to marry according to their wishes remained high in this department well after 1789.

21. The female dowry was recorded for the first time in lower Languedoc in 1078 (in an aristocratic family). It was already the corollary of the exclusion of women from patrimonial succession (M.-T. Gramain, 'Les Paysans de la région de Béziers au Moyen Age' [1979], p. 219).

22. J. Yver, *Essai de géographie coutumière* (1966), pp. 167–74 (on testamentary arbitrariness, based on Roman law, in Burgundian custom). On testamentary arbitrariness in Languedoc itself, represented by the *institution of heir*, see any Languedocian notary's records, between the sixteenth century and the Revolution. For example: ADG II E 13–132; 2 May, 20 May 1744; 20 August, 18 September, 20 September 1744; 6 May 1746; 15 May, 2 September, 29 September, 30 October, 2 November 1746; 12 January 1747 (three wills); 13 January and 24 April 1747.

23. N. Rétif, texts placed at the end of G. Rouger's edition of *La Vie de mon père* (1970), pp. 200–214. P. Lamaison, in his thesis on eighteenth-century Lozère or Gévaudan, notes the relevance of Rétif's texts to this problem (1978, p. 174).

24. See L. Stouff (1979), vol. III, graph 86.

25. According to the information provided by Louis Henry and by INED, at a seminar held in 1978 at the Hautes Études with Jacques Dupaquier on birth control, ultimate descendants, for 1,000 women, in a comparison between couples married between 1740 and 1769 and those married between 1790 and 1819, fell by 30.2 per cent; the region thus considered corresponds to the south-east and south-west quarters of France (an average drawn up by myself on information provided by Louis Henry, concerning a female sample divided into four age groups at marriage).

Chapter VIII

1. I am thinking of his *Soirées de la Vaunage* (now lost), his *Contes de Zima* ('Œuvres de Saint-Castor', Bibliothèque municipale de Montpellier, vol. VII) and his *Le Trésor de Substancion*.

2. J. Lacroix, *Récits et Contes populaires de Languedoc* (1978), vol. I, p. 37, which reproduces J. Thérond's version (*Revue des langues romanes*, XLIX [1901], 551–71).

3. *JLP* [41]: 'So much for you, Jean de Paris.' There were a number of editions, in 'blue' and popular literature, of *Jean de Paris* between 1714 and

1748 (see Bibliothèque nationale, under 'Anonymous'). I have also consulted an early-sixteenth-century edition in the Bibliothèque Méjane, Aix-en-Provence.

4. J. Guilaine, *Récits et Contes populaires du Languedoc* (1978), vol. II, p. 37.

5. A. Aarne and S. Thompson (1961), tale 570.

6. J. Guilaine (1978), vol. II, p. 37.

7. On these questions, see C. Joisten, *Contes populaires du Dauphiné* (1971), vol. I, p. 87; P. Delarue and M.-L. Tenèze, *Le Conte populaire français* (1957–76), vol. I, pp. 275ff.; and A. Aarne and S. Thompson (1961), pp. 284–90.

8. Local oral tradition collected by G. Delbos, 'Faycelles-en-Quercy' (1969), Ch. V.

9. Parable [45]; riddles [second version].

Chapter IX

1. L. Lambert, 'Lou filhol de la Mort', *Revue des langues romanes*, XXVII (1885), p. 186. This version, published in Occitan with a French translation, was collected about 1880 in the Narbonne region by the excellent Languedocian folklore specialist, L. Lambert, from an Occitan-speaking story-teller. In Chapter XV I shall analyse a version from Roussillon of AT 332, which I shall call *Galdric* and which is also very close to *JLP*.

2. An old expression: 'poor as a church rat' (Duc de Saint-Simon, *Mémoires*, vol. I, p. 45).

3. We recognize here an old view of medical art, according to which, the technical means of cure being very limited, the main object is to manage to produce a good diagnosis, or more directly still, a valid prognosis, whether it be fatal or favourable.

4. Let us immediately set to one side the hypothesis according to which the tale *Jean-de-trop* derives from the tale *Jean-l'ont-pris*. Among Fabre's works known before 1880, the text of *Jean-l'ont-pris* was much less widespread than *Le Sermon de Sistre* or *Le Siège de Caderousse*. Indeed, Lambert collected *JDT* from a story-teller from Narbonne working in the oral tradition; he faithfully reproduced what he heard, without always fully understanding it. *JDT*, as J. Bolte and J. Polivka, *Anmerkungen zu den Kindern-Hausmärchen der Brüder Grimm* (1913–18) (commentaries on Grimm's tale 44) certainly felt, is a pure product of the ancient cycle of *Godfather Death*. *JLP* is a literary ramification deriving from the cycle, through a common 'ancestor' of

JDT and of *JLP*, as a structural study carried out not merely on the surface, but in depth, shows. On the other hand, it is intellectually impossible to 'deduce' *JDT* from *JLP*. Similarly, in the scale of evolution, the 'reptiles' (*JLP*) are situated after the 'fish' (*JDT*), and not the reverse. And this is so when one finds the fossil of a fish (*JDT*) in geological strata that are subsequent to those in which one has found the fossil of the reptile (*JLP*), this 'delayed' occurrence deriving from the fact that this particular fish lived after this particular reptile, without prejudicing the fact that the first is zoologically the 'ancestor' of the second.

5. The numbers in square brackets refer to the numbering made by Philippe Gardy to the text of *JLP*, here reproduced in an English translation.

6. See the scene in which his wife Margot makes fun of his Rouergat accent and expressions [20].

7. J. Ayrer, *Dramen* (1618; 1865), p. 2467. See also the seventeenth-century version of H. Wolff, 'Der Gevatter Tod' (1644) in J. Bolte, 'Das Märchen vom Gevatter Tod', *Zeitschrift des Vereins für Volkskunde* (1894), p. 39.

8. Father Andreas Strobl, who published one of the oldest versions of AT 332 (in the 1690s), lays great stress on the fact that the peasant–hero of the tale is a 'great sinner', unworthy of God (A. Strobl, in E. Moser-Rathe, *Predigtmärlein der Barockzeit* [1964], p. 273).

9. On the antiquity of the institution of baptismal godfatherhood in Christianity (before the eighth century), see A. Vacant, *Dictionnaire de théologie catholique* (*1935*), *vol. XI, article on Parenté* (*spirituelle*). See also M. J. Bennet, 'Spiritual Kinship . . . in Traditional Society', *Social History Society Newsletter*, IV, No. 1 (1979), p. 3.

10. L. Dardy, *Anthologie populaire de l'Albret* (1891), p. 143, a version of AT 332, and P. Sébillot, *Contes des landes et des grèves* (1900), p. 246, a Breton version of the same tale.

11. The German version of AT 332, collected by H. Pröhle, *Kinder- und Volksmärchen* (1853), stresses this idea of 'choice': Death (according to this version, which on this point goes very far) is automatically the godfather of *all* the children, but in the case of the hero of the tale, he is chosen by the baby's father.

12. W. Liungman, *Die schwedischen Volksmärchen* (1961), pp. 73–4.

13. Godfather Death in France: P. Sébillot, 'La Mort en voyage', *Archivio . . .* IV (1885); certain manuscript versions by A. Millien and P. Delarue (Nevers); F. Mistral, *Prose d'Almanach* (1926), p. 24. Death, as both godfather and godmother: C. Joisten, *Contes populaires de l'Ariège* (1965), p. 62. A masculine

Death's male major-domo: P. Bédat de Monlaur, *Le Meunier gascon* (1936). Godmother death: G. Maugard, *Contes de Pyrénées* (1955), p. 116.

14. 'Setting out, in search of a godfather': at the beginning of the second version of the tale, Truquette sticks his 'pilgrim's staff' into the ground at Solorgues before meeting grandmother Death/*commère*/godmother; the same goes for the version of AT 332 from Roussillon (E. Caseponce, in D. Blanc, *Récits et Contes populaires de Catalogne* [1979], p. 71). This waiting for godfather Death by the hero's father, on the edge or at the end of a road, after having picked up a traveller's staff, is also to be found in the German versions of AT 332 (N. L. Bechstein, *Deutsches Märchenbuch* [1846], p. 40; A. Birlinger, *Aus Schwaben, Sagen, Legenden* ... [1874], pp. 372–3; etc.), in Flemish versions of AT 332 (P. de Mont and A. de Cock, *Dit zÿn Vlaamsche Wondersprookjes* [1896], p. 182, etc.), among others.

15. See the Occitan dictionaries of F. Mistral, *Lou Trésor dou Félibrige* ... (1932), and L. Alibert, *Dictionnaire occitan–français* (1966) under the word *pepin, pepi*. There are two mentions of the word in *L'Almanach de l'Ariège* (1895), p. 55.

16. This tradition of the grandmother/godmother (when she survived long enough, she could perform the additional function) had already been well attested in seventeenth-century France. See on this question A. N. Galpern's fine contribution in C. Trinkaus and H. Oberman, *The Pursuit of Holiness in Late Medieval and Renaissance Religion* (1974), p. 154. See also comte C. de Villeneuve, *Mœurs des Provençaux* ... (1826), vol. III, p. 253, reflecting the practice of the *ancien régime* and of the Empire, in the area of the southern Rhône: 'the grandfather and the grandmother are by right godfather and godmother.' But, of course, if they are dead, younger people may be substituted for them. See AD Bouches-du-Rhône (Aix), notaries of the Bouches-du-Rhône 202–E–255 (Cannat): baptisms of 23 September 1745, 13 January 1746, 13 February 1746; of 21 July 1746, 21 November 1745 (compare 8 February 1745); of 28 November 1745 at Aix-en-Provence. Parish registers, parish of Sainte-Madeleine: compare f° 14, f° 19V° (J.-J.-H. Aillaud's godmother [= grandmother]), f° 15 and 21V°; the same goes for Mad. Arquiest; *ibid.*, 4 January 1742 (grandmother/godmother); *ibid.*, parish Saint-Esprit: 2 April 1768 (baptism: grandmother = godmother). The low survival rate of grandparents does not make these cases much of a majority, but the stereotype is clearly marked. See also on this question of the grandmother automatically becoming her first grandson's godmother, Françoise Zonabend's long article in *Annales* (May–June 1978), 666: the maternal grandmother is the godmother (if possible automatically) of the first child. See also Y. Verdier in the journal *Le Débat*, No. 3 (July 1980), 43: the *meirineta* of the Dauphiné as grandmother/godmother.

17. See F. Mistral (1932), vol. II, article on *meirino*.

18. L. Lallement, *Folklore argonnais* (1914), p. 23.

19. E. Le Roy, *Moulin du Frau* (1979), p. 36, and G. Rocal, *Le Vieux Périgord* (1927), p. 50.

20. According to the abbé P. Duffard, *L'Armagnac noir* (1901 and 1902), whom I quote from A. Van Gennep, *Manuel du folklore français contemporain* (1943–58), vol. I–1, p. 128, Duffard's book being unobtainable at the Bibliothèque nationale. On Savoie, see A. Van Gennep, 'En Savoie', in vol. I–1, pp. 38–9, and J. Nicolas and R. Nicolas, *La Vie quotidienne en Savoie au XVIIIᵉ siècle* (1979), p. 109. Jean-l'ont-pris's grandmother is all the more qualified to be his godmother because she is finally (mother and father apart) his closest relation (but not susceptible to incest with him) in the village. Indeed, Truquette, an immigrant from Rouergue, has no relations in the locality.

21. On the educative role of grandparents in the countryside under the *ancien régime*, see M. Bloch, *Les Caractères originaux de l'histoire rurale française* (1952). It should also be noted that in certain versions of AT 332 in which Death is not officially the godfather or the godmother, other solutions of substitution have been found: thus in the Flemish version published by V. de Meyen, *De Vlaamsche Vertelselschar* (1927), Death is the hero's adoptive father. In the Jewish tales of the German-speaking countries inspired by AT 332 and quoted by G. Meyer, *Essays und Studien zur Sprachgeschichte und Volkskunde* (1885), Death, unable to be godfather since the (Christian) institution of godfatherhood does not exist among the Jews, becomes the hero's father. In the Turkish tales (W. Eberhard and P. N. Boratav, *Typen Türkischer Volksmärchen* [1953]), the angel of Death of AT 332 is simply the hero's protector.

22. A useful reminder: *JDT*, abbreviation for the narrative *Jean-de-trop*; JDT, abbreviation for the character Jean-de-trop. The same system is used for the abbreviations *JLP* and JLP.

23. These thirteen years, taking into account the period of pregnancy and suckling, and of the ageing of Jean-de-trop's mother, correspond to the six births, including the most recent one, that marked the marital life of JDT's parents.

24. The theme of the 'two capons [castrated cocks] and turkey' (in *Jean-de-trop*), which become a pair of crows and half a dozen magpies at the structurally similar point in the banquet in *JLP*, will be used again later, but this time as such by the abbé Fabre, who is careful to reinvest what is left over to make

maximum use of the materials provided for him by his (oral) sources. This is a new clue, among so many others, of the kinship between *JDT* and *JLP*. Indeed, these birds reappear in a later part of the narrative of *JLP*, during the fight between the two vineyard-keepers, on the one hand, and Monsieur Sestier, on the other: *the two of them advanced boldly in the direction of Monsieur Sestier, like two Mahon cocks* [not castrated this time] *confronting a turkey* [59]. The theme of the *two against one* is taken up again later in the next few sentences, but in the opposite direction, as if to stress the importance of these two cocks and this turkey: '*A* well-directed blow fell straight on Monsieur Sestier's skull, to which he responded subtly with *two* blows about his adversary's ears.'

25. Again, on the subject of these similarities, one should note the common recurrence of the numbers 'two' and 'four' in this culinary and gastronomic sub-episode, which is, strategically and tactically, homologous in each case, within the twin tales *JLP* and *JDT*. That is, in *JDT* (p. 187): '*two* capons on the spit, which was turned by the oldest of the *four* children.' In the second version of *JLP*: '*two* crows turning on the spit . . . *two* large pots of flour, *two* fine cooked cod'; and, again, in the first version of Fabre's tale at the same place: '*two* large pots of girdle-cakes . . . *four* panfuls of chestnuts . . . plus a *four-setier* butt of wine' [17].

26. By 'turning' [*virer*, in French; *vira*, in Occitan] the tamis sieve [18]. So this verb is found again here and also a little later: 'luck turned' [36], only to culminate in the ruin of Truquette's family. One thus sees, again, the verb 'to turn', which in the form of the turning spit was already common to *JDT* and *JLP*. In a more general way, the spit and the turning sieve symbolize fortune, still favourable at the point of the wedding banquet of J L P's parents, but which had become disastrous when the riff-raff of Solorgues, participating in the forces of death, come to arrest Truquette: then fortune will 'turn' against him, at the point when the spit in Truquette's kitchen 'turns' and when the riff-raff 'turn' the infant J L P like a *bobbin* [36]. See also [35]: J L P is already compared to a *bobbin*. The link between the turning spit in the kitchen, the 'turning tamis sieve' and the 'bobbin', a link attested, at the homologous point, in both *JDT* and *JLP*, is therefore very strong; it is not only factual, but philosophical, since it represents the 'turning' of fortune's wheel.

27. A description of the eighteenth-century tamis sieve is to be found in L. Ligier, *La Nouvelle Maison rustique* (1740), vol. I, p. 638 (reference provided by Mme C. Beutler).

28. In the second version, the association, at the poverty-stricken banquet,

of the half dozen *magpies* and the *fox* (as food) is repeated, in a figurative sense, shortly afterwards in the 'half dozen curtsies' made to 'an old fox' (that is, an old woman).

29. Version of A T 332 from mid-Ariège: M. Mir and F. Delample, *Histoires et Récits du pays occitan* (1948), p. 108. Version by A. Perbosc and S. Cézerac, tales 38 and 39.

30. On the hunter as the mediator with wild nature, in the culture of the West, see J. Le Goff and P. Vidal-Naquet, 'Lévi-Strauss en Brocéliande' (1979), p. 284.

31. On the wooded, or at least wild environment (of a non-agricultural nature), of the godfather Death of A T 332, which is mentioned always at the beginning and often at the end of his career, see (apart from the beginning of the 'Icelandic' version prior to 1339, reproduced in H. Gering, *Islendzk Aeventyri . . .* [1882]) the German versions by J. Grimm, tale 44; J. W. Wolf, *Deutsche Hausmärchen* (1851); H. Pröhle (1853); T. Vernaleken, *Œsterreiche Kinder- und Hausmärchen* (1864) (the relation of the hero so close to our J D T, with the supernatural entities in the forest, including Death, is referred to three times); L. Aurbacher, *Ein Volksbüchlein* (1879); P. Zaundet, 'Wom armne Weber, wie er einen Gevattern gesucht' (1926); W. von Schulenburg, *Wendisches Volkstum in Sage, Brauch, und Sitte* (1934); a brief synthesis of this woodland problem of A T 332 in L. Mackensen, *Handwörterbuch des deutschen Märchens* (1934–40), vol. II, p. 617. In France: F.-M. Luzel, *Légendes chrétiennes de la Basse-Bretagne* (1881), pp. 341, 351. In Occitania: M.-A. Méraville, *Contes populaires de l'Auvergne* (1970), p. 101. This version of A T 332 from the Auvergne, collected by Méraville, is particularly interesting for us since it stresses the woodland environment of Death, accepted as godmother; furthermore, the fox is rejected as godfather since animals can no longer speak. Fabre stresses the woodland character of the menu of the feast of grandmother Death, in which the fox appears not as a godfather, but as a choice of food. See also in the French versions, including the oldest (Th.-S. Gueulette, *Les Mille et Un Quarts d'heure* [1712]), the importance of the trade of *woodcutter* (= woodland, again) for the hero of A T 332 (on this particular speciality of the hero or the hero's father of the French version of A T 332, see Chapter XIV).

32. The second version is definite on this point: it is quite clear from the context that 'in front of the door' is situated outside the house.

33. L. Alibert (1966), and F. Maspons, *Contes populars catalans* (1952), p. 119. An Italian version of A T 332 from the Abruzzi also uses the local dialect

term *lumette* ['small lights']: 'Novelle populari abruzzesi', *Archivio* . . . V (1886), p. 204.

34. F. Arnaudin, *Contes populaires de la Grande-Lande* (1977), p. 587, tale 101.

35. The initial gift of two candles or lights of life by Death to the hero, one foretelling a death, the other a survival: J. B. Rael, *Cuentos españoles de Colorado y Nuevo Mexico*, p. 634, tale 83 and tales 84 and 86 (these are various 'Castilian' versions of AT 332 from the United States). This motif has travelled well beyond the territory of the Romance languages: in the Armenian version of AT 332 collected by F. Macler, *Contes, légendes et épopées populaires d'Arménie* (1928), the angel of Death gives two lights of life (two candles) to the hero for his wedding.

36. F. Gueriff, *Contes populaires du pays de Guérande* (1974), p. 89.

37. It should be added that at the very moment when she sets about once again making *brouquéttas* ['matches'] [39], the grandmother refers expressly to the hero's *brôca* ['stick' or 'log', 41] when she calls him 'my darling [*ma queque*], my log [*brôca*], my soul, my prince, my king, my emperor'. These terms are all to be used again for others and by other characters in the novella (*king* for JLP, Truquette or Sestier; *darling* [*queque*] for the grandmother's ass [51]); only the log, that is to say the *brouquétta*, seems to be specific to the relationship between the grandmother/godmother and her grandson/godson. In this matter, the hero certainly has at his disposal in his relationship with his grandmother his own log or light of life that is characteristic of the southern (and other) versions of AT 332. Hans Andersen, in a way quite independent of Fabre, took up the idea of the match as a 'light of life' (or of death, when it goes out) in his famous story *The Little Match Girl*.

38. The Venetian version was collected by G. Widter, A. Wolf and R. Köhler, 'Volksmärchen aus Venetien', *Jahrbuch für roman, und englisch literatur*, VII (1886), pp. 17–18. The German (Silesian) version was collected by R. Kühnau, *Schlesische Sagen* (1911), p. 525. It is very close on this point to *Jean-de-trop* and *Death's Godson*, which I analyse at the end of Chapter XIV: Death arrives in a fine carriage (*JDT*, in a coach) *in front of the door* of his future godson's father. There follows the classic scene of sponsorship and baptism. Later, the hero, thus protected by Death, treats a princess (in view of the favourable position of Death in relation to the bed) with a placebo of cold water; with his fat fees, he buys a magnificent house for himself, etc. The Catalan version is that of F. Maspons (1952).

39. Moreover, it will be noted that, later, the grandmother Death does not live *in the same house* as her son-in-law. She lives opposite [22], on the other

side of the street. When the son-in-law is arrested, soon to be followed by his hanging, the grandmother, this time, is *in* Truquette's house [36–38]. While on the theme of 'in front of the door or behind the door', it might be noted that J L P [47] remains carefully *in front of the door* of the school, when he tries to avoid the dangerous aggression of the forces of death emanating from the grandmother, the municipality, the school, etc., which infest the locality of Solorgues. However, it is *behind the door* of his own house that Truquette is the victim of dangerous acts that foreshadow his final death and disappearance, and that are unleashed against him by his wife and mother-in-law [20]: '. . . said Truquette, moving towards the door'.

40. E. Caseponce, *Contes Vallespirenchs replegats per En Mir y Nontoquis* (1907), p. 48: Death was first inside the house behind the door; it is not until he has crossed the threshold and is outside the house (in front of the door) that he promises the doctor that he will make his fortune.

41. In the Millien and Delarue manuscripts (version A of A T 332), Death travels in a carriage and pair. In a Catalan version of A T 332 (F. Maspons [1952], p. 119), Death is on horseback (see also Albrecht Dürer, *The Horseman, the Devil and Death*, which also shows the latter on horseback). In Brittany, the Ankou (Death) of A T 332 travels on horseback or in a cart.

42. Millien and Delarue manuscripts, in one of the versions from Nevers; R. Kühnau (1911); F. Cadic, *La Paroisse bretonne de Paris* (1908), p. 8.

43. F. Caballero, *Cuentos populares andaluces colleccionados* (1861); L. Lambert (1885); Millien and Delarue, version A; H. Gering (1882), Icelandic version of A T 332 (see Chapter XIV); T. Vernaleken, 'Der Fährmann und der Tod', *Germania* . . . XXIX (XVII) (1884), p. 415. In the last two references, Death appears at the beginning of the tale as an enormous being; this is also the case in Dauphiné, culturally and geographically so close to lower Languedoc (A. Ferrand, 'Le filleul de la Mort' [1895], p. 594, reproduced in C. Joisten, *Contes populaires du Dauphiné* [1971], vol. I, p. 168). The size of the Death woman from Dauphiné of A T 332 is mentioned in this text. See also A. M. Espinosa, *Cuentos populares de Castilla, recogidos de la tradición oral* (n.d.), p. 83. The dominant position and size of Death in relation to the hero is symbolized by the fact that she dominates him from above, hanging from a tree; then, when she is no longer hanging, having returned to her pseudo-death, she marches on the hero with 'gigantic' steps to kill him. The version from the Abruzzi ('Novelle populari abruzzesi', *Archivio* . . . V [1886], p. 204) explains this idea of height: Death comes from God and descends from heaven to meet the hero; she will then take him into the infernal depths of the cellar with lights.

44. Same intervention, hysterical in this case, of the 'bell-ringing', at the

same stage, at once ceremonial and scandalous, of the narrative, in the Catalano-Roussillonnais version (of AT 332) of E. Caseponce (1907), p. 47, so close in other ways to *JLP* and *JDT*.

45. F. Mistral (1926), pp. 24–5; in the very old and authentic Strobl version (used for preaching) of AT 332 dating from the 1690s (in Germany), godfather Death carries an arrow. In the Breton version of AT 332 collected by F. Cadic (1908), pp. 6–8, which is so close, in general and in detail (see Chapter XIV), to our *JDT* (itself very close to *JLP*), Ankou (Death) kills the hero at the end of the tale (shortly after his marriage) with a blow from the *tip* of the scythe, at the young man's *heart*. In Fabre's second version, when the grandmother, shortly after the fight, calls her son-in-law Truquette 'my heart, my leather', she is inevitably referring by a double meaning to the leather (skin) of the cobbler Truquette, which she has marked and pierced with an awl in the immediately preceding episode; it cannot be said that she wishes a great deal of good to this man's heart, which she might very well pierce in the same way as Ankou (in fact, Truquette is later to be hanged).

46. Two women are *commères* when one is the godmother of the other's child.

47. Truquette did not take this poking seriously, as he should have done: *My father . . . did not take any of this seriously . . .* [9]. Objectively, nevertheless, the cobbler functioned as the antithesis and designated victim of his wife: she 'pricked' her husband's skin with an awl; he blocked up the holes in his future wife's shoes. As often with Fabre, a sexual insinuation (blocking holes) accompanies and masks an infinitely more important opposition.

48. It is of course Margot [beginning of paragraph 9] who comes to Truquette's cellar-shop, at the beginning of their courtship, and cuts the matches and tips them with sulphur. But Fabre had (grammatically) so arranged matters, in this paragraph 9, that it is impossible to say, strictly speaking, whether it is a question of the mother (JLP's future grandmother) or the daughter (Margot). They are, in this way, cleverly merged.

49. H. Sachs, *Sämtliche Fabeln und Schwänke* (1547); J. Grimm and W. Grimm, *Kinder- und Häusmarchen* (1812), tale 44: *so geht's dir an den Kragen*; P. J. Cornelissen and J. P. Vervliet, *Vlaamsche Volksvertelsels en Kindersprookjes* (1900), p. 80, Flemish version; Millien and Delarue (Nevers) version A, at the end Death suffocates his godson.

50. C. Joisten, *Contes folkloriques des Hautes-Alpes* (1955), pp. 17, 40, and G. Massignon, *Contes corses* (1963), pp. 38–9. See also D. P. Rotunda, *Motif Index of the Italian Novella in Prose* (1942), p. 263.

51. Fabre had indeed read Boccaccio. He wrote a series of tales, supposedly

inspired by *The Thousand and One Nights* (in fact, very close to T.-S. Gueulette's *Mille et Un Quarts d'heure* [1712]), which he called *Les Visites de Zima* (J.-B. C. Fabre or Favre, 'Œuvres de Saint-Castor', manuscripts of the Bibliothèque municipale, Montpellier, vol. VII). Now *Zima* ('the magnificent') is actually a character in the fifth novella of the third day (Elisa) of Boccaccio's *Decameron*.

52. This valuable version in *German* translation is very little known in France, from which it originated (in it, Death is *godmother*, as she should be, as a Latin feminine noun, and not godfather, as in the Germanic, masculine form, which confirms Jacob Grimm's claim as to the French character of the text). It is reproduced, in a version taken from J. Grimm's papers, in J. Bolte and J. Polivka (1913–18), pp. 383–5, commentaries on Grimm's tale 44.

53. Grimm, tale 44: *Künftigen Sonntag ist die Taufe*. See also N. L. Bechstein (1889), p. 88. In E. Caseponce (1907), p. 46 (version from Roussillon), the baptism occurs just after the village mass, and therefore on a Sunday. In the Alps, even today, baptism almost invariably takes place on Sunday after the mass.

54. For example, F. Arnaudin (1977), p. 578 (in the Occitan zone), and P. Zaunert (1926), p. 195 (in the German epicentre).

55. R. Sauzet, *Contre-Réforme et Réforme catholique en Bas-Languedoc, Le diocèse de Nîmes au XVIIᵉ siècle* (1979), p. 684.

56. Fabre stresses that when Margot, the daughter of a Protestant, drops the other boys (also Protestants) of the Huguenot village of Solorgues, and takes up with the Catholic Rouergat Truquette, she becomes *prouder and more unyielding than the housekeeper of the curé of Bezouces*. This is an allusion which would be understood by contemporary natives of the region: Bezouces (R. Sauzet [1979], pp. 147, 238, 375, 448) was indeed a profoundly and heroically Catholic village in a Protestant environment. By taking up with Truquette, Margot also flirts with the Catholicism of the '*curé* of Bezouces'; she finally adopts the 'papist' religion when she is married in the Church.

57. *Régalats-vous à vostre aise* (*JDT*, p. 188). The narrator of *JDT* uses the verb *se régaler* only for this extension (the usual eating up of what is left) of the post-nuptial, pre-baptismal banquet. *JLP*, inspired by an older version, had used this verb at the banquet itself: 'tell me if there wasn't enough to feast [*pèr régala*] all the friends and relations' [15].

58. Concerning this *bobbin*, see note 26 above.

59. A. Perbosc and S. Cézerac (1954), tale 39: the hero of AT 332, at the moment of his magical enrichment, becomes the owner of two *métairies*.

F. Arnaudin (1977), p. 590 (Landes): at the same point the hero has 'a fine house' built. The buying of the fine house by the hero is also to be found in the Breton version of AT 332 collected by F.-M. Luzel (1881), p. 355, at the same strategic point in the narrative. See also R. Kühnau (1911), p. 526 (German AT 332): same detail. And, of course, the Roussillon version of *Galdric*, so close to *JDT* and *JLP* (see Chapter XV).

60. M. Barral, *JLP*, p. 76.

61. A. Le Braz, *La Légende de la Mort chez les Bretons armoricains* (1902), vol. I, p. 182. Brittany is not, in my opinion, separated by the so-called Celtic Iron Curtain from the rest of French culture, whether of north or south. The Celtic character of Brittany is, of course, of crucial importance; but eighteenth-century France was not the immense Amerindian America, in which stories travelled slowly and with difficulty. The very example of AT 332, which spread in similar forms throughout the French hexagon, with Brittany and Languedoc in the forefront (not to mention the rest of Europe), stresses the ease of exchanges of all kinds, cultural and otherwise, in the France of this period. Perhaps I will be allowed here to force a door that is already open: the theme of the 'evil eye' is not peculiar to Brittany! See, on this question, the innumerable references collected in Europe and throughout the world by S. Seligmann, *Der böse Blick* (1910), a synthesis that has not yet been superseded: in particular, in vol. I, pp. 66, 78, 82, 194, 217 (the dangerous character of one-eyed individuals throughout the Mediterranean basin, Italy, Spain and even as far as Ireland); and in vol. II, pp. 220, 226, 227, 289 (the 'left', as both an indication of the evil eye and a protection against it).

62. See the references given on this matter by J. Le Goff and P. Vidal-Naquet (1979), p. 291, on medieval and traditional culture.

63. M. Barral, *Jean-Baptiste Favre, sa vie, son œuvre* ... (1971), p. 120; quotation taken from a text by Fabre entitled *Le Deuil de l'amitié*.

64. In F. Dezeuze, *Contes d'un pêcheur de lune* (1953), p. 71 (Languedocian version of AT 332) there is also a father's death, as for Truquette. It is from the seventeenth century that the successive versions of *Godfather Death*, beginning with the German ones, ceased to be interested only in Death's *compère*, and also developed a biography of his godson (see Chapter XIV). The Languedocian version collected by Dezeuze is all the more important for us since it takes place at Carnas, a locality very close to Solorgues.

65. G. Forteguerri, *Novelle edite ed inedite* (1550), published in 1882.

66. *Ils l'ont pris* or *la Mort l'a pris*. JLP has, therefore, a name that evokes the action of Death. In a German version of AT 332 (H. Pröhle [1853], p. 56) and in a version from Nevers collected by Millien and Delarue (version B),

the hero Death's godson is quite simply, by metonymy, himself called Death, or Doctor Death, from the name of his godfather or godmother. Or again he is called Just (in C. Joisten's version from Ariège, *Contes populaires de l'Ariège* [1965], p. 62, collected in 1953), because his godfather or godmother (Death) is just. The name 'Jean-de-trop' also indicates a certain nominal 'marking' by Death: the child who bears this name is usually *de trop* and is not therefore fated to live.

67. The territory of the Franco-Provençal languages corresponds particularly to Dauphiné and Savoie.

68. Text taken from J. Müller (parish priest of Altdorf and collector of popular tales), *Sagen aus Uri* (1943–5), pp. 106–7, tale 1199. This is a translation and summary from the German text. I would like to thank Mme C. Beutler, who helped me in the translation of certain paragraphs in dialect.

69. Tale told to Joseph Müller by Hans Aschwenden, aged fifty, in the 1920s at Igental.

70. K. Ranke, *Schleswig-holsteinische Volksmärchen* (1955), pp. 12, 265.

71. For example, in that of A. Orain, *Contes de l'Ille-et-Vilaine* (1901) (Brittany) and of T. Vernaleken (1864) (Austria). In the old versions of A T 332 (see that of Ayrer, who died in 1605), Death is regarded as a brother of the devil. The abbé Fabre himself, with the characters of the grandmother, Quincarlot and the baron, slips skilfully from Death to the devil and back to Death again, depending on his sources and his own creativity (see Chapters XII and XIII).

72. In paragraph [6] of the tale.

73. F. Mistral (1932), vol. II, under the word *Truqueto*; M. Barral, *JLP*, p. 68; L. Roumieux (1890). F. Mistral stresses the Gardois character of this word *truquette*; moreover, he translates *boire truquette* as *boire chopine*.

74. See my *Paysans de Languedoc* (1966), vol. I, p. 209 (according to the testimony of the German-Swiss Platter), and J.-P. Henry, *Jean-Pierre* ... (1978), p. 117.

75. Among the many Languedocian texts (Catholic ones, *à la* Fabre) that give a maleficent and even diabolical image of the Protestantism of the seventeenth and eighteenth centuries, see those quoted by R. Sauzet (1979), p. 741.

76. A good example is to be found in the illuminated manuscripts of Boccaccio's *Decameron*, composed in the fifteenth century for the Duke of Burgundy, which has been reproduced recently (p. 48) in an edition published

by Seghers in 1978. Also see, in Joseph Bédier's edition of *Tristan et Yseut*, the beheading of Guenelon by Gorvenal's sword. More recently, an engraving from the period of Louis XIII, no doubt contemporary with the genesis of our 'Swiss tale', represents in 1615 the Maréchal d'Ancre beheaded by the sword in 1704 (Saint-Simon, *Mémoires*, vol. II, p. 297).

77. J. Bolte and J. Polivka (1913–18), p. 383, commentaries on Grimm's tale 44.

78. See in this chapter and in Chapter X.

79. See R. Sauzet (1979).

80. In this chapter, I have strongly linked *Jean-l'ont-pris* to two master versions of AT 332/*Godfather Death*, namely, *Jean-de-trop* (Languedocian) and the 'Swiss tale' (which was necessarily Occitanized in Fabre's period or before). In Chapter XV an additional linking of *JLP* to the southern cycle of *Godfather Death* will be made, by means of a careful comparison between Fabre's tale and *Galdric*, the Catalano-Roussillonnais version of AT 332 collected by the abbé Caseponce.

81. F. Mistral (1932), vol. II, under *Margot*: the word *Margot* is the equivalent of a tamed magpie, and of death. It is also worth mentioning that Truquette ate magpies [17] at his funereal wedding, and that JLP nearly killed himself trying to get hatched magpies from their nests [50].

Chapter X

1. See Chapter XIV.

2. J. Bolte and J. Polivka, *Anmerkungen zu den Kindern-Hausmärchen der Brüder Grimm* (1913–18), p. 377, commentaries on Grimm's tale 44; see also A. Aarne and S. Thompson, 'The Types of the Folktale', *Folklore Fellows Communications*, XXV, No. 74 (1928), tale type 332, and the new complete edition of this crucially important work (1961), under tale 332, *Godfather Death*.

3. One will also notice here a contrasting homology; the versions of AT 332 may be divided (on one precise point) into two groups: those in which the physician–hero uses (in his treatment) a vegetable substance (a herb or a root), and those in which he uses a liquid (a placebo of cold water, a phial of some liquid). The 'Swiss tale' belongs to the first category (the use of a root by means of which the cobbler puts his wife back on her feet, after she has given birth). *JLP* belongs to the second category, that of 'liquids': hence the use of a placebo of cold water when an attempt is made to cure Sestier (see Chapter XI), in which JLP takes part; and the use of soup or broth, also

liquids, in the earlier medical action, when Truquette helps his young wife, who has just given birth, to recover.

4. J. W. Wolf, *Deutsche Hausmärchen* (1851), pp. 367–8, and L. Aurbacher, *Ein Volksbüchlein* (1879), p. 121: the doctor turns his own body at an angle of 180 degrees on the horizontal plane in his sick-bed, in order to escape Death, who had come to inform him of his death.

5. This is the method used at the end of the oldest known version of AT 332, noted down by an Icelandic bishop (died in 1339); see, on this matter, H. Gering, *Islendzk Aeventyri* . . . (1882), vol. I, p. 148. One finds the same technique in many different places, and among the southern French versions of AT 332 in Albret (L. Dardy, *Anthologie populaire de l'Albret* [1891], p. 149), in the region around Nîmes and Montpellier (*Jean de Carnas*, by F. Dezeuze, *Contes d'un pêcheur de lune* [1953]), in the Landes (F. Arnaudin, *Contes populaires de la Grande-Lande* [1977], p. 580).

6. See Chapter IX.

7. On Penury as hero of AT 332, see, for example, F. Arnaudin (1977), tale 101; on the fine 'mixture' of the tale of Penury, who gets Death to climb the fig-tree, and AT 332, see the version from the Cape Verde Islands published by E. Clews Parsons, *Folklore from the Cape Verde Islands* (1923), pp. 182, 185; on the Anglo-Latin Falsehood, see the British Museum manuscript (about 1450), which I analyse with M. J. Tits in Chapter XIV; on Dearth, see the manuscript versions from Quebec, kindly provided by Mme Maranda; on Hate and Envy, see G. Forteguerri, *Novelle edite ed inedite* (1550), and the Flemish versions of V. de Meyen, *De Vlaamsche Vertelselschar* (1927), pp. 182–4, and of A. Nameoc, *Volk en Taal* (1891), p. 259. Penury is fundamentally a character of AT 330 D (P. Delarue and M.-L. Tenèze, *Le Conte populaire français* [1957–76], vol. I; A. Aarne and S. Thompson [1961], paragraph 330 D).

8. See, on this subject, C. Lévi-Strauss, in R. Bellour, *Le Livre des autres, entretiens* (1978), pp. 404–6.

9. This Truquette–JLP antithesis is a fundamental one: for example, the *envious* were responsible for Truquette's downfall [36]; JLP so arranges matters that the *envious* [75] do not bring about his downfall and are not jealous of his strategy with Barbe-Garouille [80]. Similarly, Truquette is a weak character, a constant loser; he finds himself at the end of his career of illusory prosperity 'with nothing more than what's in the palm of your hand' [36], or in the words recorded by F. Mistral in his *Lou Trésor dóu Félibrige* . . . (1932) under the entry *Truqueto*, 'clean as Truquette' (clean as an empty *chopine*). JLP, however, is a 'winner'. A final example: it is the goods dis-

honestly *imported* from Sommières, in *carts*, that bring about Truquette's final downfall. But it is by *exporting* in a *cart* his dying wife to a hospital at *Sommières* that J L P guarantees his triumph and gains access to his treasure [31, 83].

10. See, for example, *JDT*, p. 188; C. Joisten, *Contes populaires de l'Ariège* (1965), p. 62; and, outside southern France, F. Cadic, *La Paroisse bretonne de Paris* (1908), p. 6, generally very close to *JDT*. When the hero does go to school, it is to primary school, and no further: in A T 332, whether in versions from Languedoc (*JDT*, p. 189), Andalusia (F. Caballero, *Cuentos populares andaluces colleccionados* [1861], p. 84) or Castille (A. M. Espinosa, *Cuentos populares de Castilla, recogidos de la tradición oral* [n.d.], p. 79) he tells Death that he knows neither Greek nor Latin nor medicine.

11. See C. d'Aigrefeuille, *Histoire de Montpellier* (1875), vol. I. The chapter on the annexation of Montpellier by France.

12. J.-N. Biraben, *Les Hommes de la Peste* (1976), pp. 130–41.

13. J. W. Wolf (1851), pp. 365–8.

14. Grimm, tale 44: *Death will shut one eye*, the doctor says to himself while concocting the first *successful* deception, which will not yet bring with it the reprisals practised on him by Death. In the Flemish version of A T 332 collected by A. Nameoc (1891), p. 259, Death in his educational phase makes it quite clear that when he shuts one eye the patient will get better, thus confirming the favourable diagnosis of the future doctor, Death's godson.

15. The theme of *Death on the left* ('sinister') is taken up again by Fabre, on the subject of the discovery of the treasure (see Chapter XII). Two other versions of A T 332 (P. Zaunert, 'Wom armen Weber, wie er einen Gevattern gesucht' [1926], and J. W. Wolf [1851]) also used this left–right opposition: 'when Death is on the right of the sick-bed, the patient will be cured; on the left he will die' (P. Zaunert [1926]: a version of A T 332 collected in a German-speaking region of the Danube). To begin with, at least, the left, which is certainly dangerous in the long term, favours the hero of A T 332, during the period when *Death showers gifts upon him*: the dead grandmother's treasure, which comes as a blessing to Jean-l'ont-pris, is specifically placed *on the left*. In the versions of P. Zaunert (1926) and of J. W. Wolf (1851), 'Death on the left' provides the physician–hero with the opportunity of lucid, and therefore profitable diagnoses, even if they are hopeless from the point of view of the patient; or it provides him with the possibility of a temporarily happy outcome for himself.

16. F. Arnaudin (1977), p. 578: Death's *compère*, having become a rich doctor, wears a hat (version of A T 332 from the Landes). The same occurs in

the Gascon version collected by P. Bédat de Monlaur, *Le Meunier gascon* (1936) and *Les contes du Lézard, contes du pays de Gascogne* (1943), with its high, pointed hat (similar, from this point of view, to the tripod advocated by the grandmother), and also with the three costumes that the future doctor must wear, according to Death's educational speech. On the future doctor's robe and hat, see also *Galdric* (AT 332 from Roussillon, very close to *JLP*) (1907), pp. 51, 53.

17. J.-P. Henry, *Jean-Pierre* . . . (1978), p. 85.

18. F. Mistral (1932), article under *Jan-l'Emprès*; M. Barral, *Jean-Baptiste Favre, sa vie, son œuvre* . . . (1971), p. 184; and the same author's *JLP*, p. 78 (Jean l'emprès = Jean the senseless). See also *JLP* itself [59]: 'Monsieur Sestier . . . as though he had been knocked senseless.'

19. According to Donatien Laurent, who has kindly provided this information, the character of Ankou was recorded in Brittany for the first time in the ninth century in a gloss on the intersigns of Death. But its incorporation in the European cycle of AT 332 is the result of a synthesis that is not of Celtic origin and that, in any case, took place after the ninth century.

20. F.-M. Luzel, *Légendes chrétiennes de la Basse-Bretagne* (1881), pp. 335 ff., 346ff.

21. P. Sébillot, *Littérature orale de la Haute-Bretagne* (1881), p. 135.

22. Second version and in a (burlesque) reference to this theme of the 'pilgrim of St James of Compostella' in reference to Truquette, JLP's father [77]. This motif of Truquette as a character twice referred to as a pilgrim allows Fabre to trace a rather remarkable connection. We have seen and will further demonstrate that Truquette's three accomplices – Quincarlot/Cancrelas (= Satan, gibbet and evil eye), Crouquet/Renâouvi (= hook, widower who marries a widow) and Jacquet/Carcanas (= buzzard, eater of dead flesh) – obviously belong to the forces of death, dominated by the grandmother. However, they are also associated with the hero's father, Truquette, whose accomplices they are. This second, subsidiary link is marked by the fact that Jacquet [32] is identified (as is Truquette) with a pilgrim and, of course, with a pilgrim to the shrine of St James of Compostella (as his Christian name suggests).

23. I wish to thank Mme Maranda, who is in charge of the folklore archives at Laval University, Quebec, and who confirmed, with supporting evidence, this crucial point.

24. J.-F. Bladé, *Contes populaires de la Gascogne* (1886), pp. 123ff.

25. Manuscript version of *Jean-lou-pec*, kindly lent to the author by Daniel Fabre.

26. The equivalence between eye and anus (the eye that does not see) is stated in the version of AT 332 from Roussillon called *Galdric*: at the sight of godfather Death, the choirboys attending the baptism of Death's godson are so terrified that 'not a grain of maze could have entered them through the eye that does not see' (E. Caseponce, *Contes Vallespirenchs replegats per En Mir y Nontoquis* [1907], p. 47).

27. This is practically always the case in the French versions of the tale, whether from the north or the south, Basque, Occitan-speaking or French-speaking (except in Bladé's *Jean-lou-pec*, in which the hero really does die). See the references to these various versions in the next few notes and in the Bibliography.

28. F.-M. Luzel (1881), p. 355.

29. On the antiquity of the tale *Jean-le-sot*, I would recall the 'proof by Quebec' (that it existed before 1763), which I have already referred to; I would also point out that the first important versions were not collected in France itself until the 1880s.

30. See these versions of *Jean-le-sot* in P. Sénéquier, 'Blason populaire provençal', *Revue des traditions populaires*, XII (1897), p. 75 (Provence); P. Sébillot (1896), p. 443 (Brittany); J. Vinson, *Le Folklore du Pays basque* (1883), pp. 93ff. (the Basque country). To these references, which will be completed below, I would add at this stage A. Millien and P. Delarue (1953), p. 293, tale 24 (contains an exhaustive bibliography), and three manuscript versions of *The Farting Donkey*, in the Millien papers at the Musée des Arts and Traditions Populaires (texts kindly lent by Mme A. Tenèze). Outside France, see also A. Aarne and S. Thompson (1961), tale type 1240 (the man sitting on the branch that he cuts), and S. Thompson, *Motif Index of Folk-Literature* (1933), motif J 2311–1 (a fool is told that he will die on his mount's third fart).

31. J. Vinson (1883); P. Sébillot (1894), p. 338 and (1896), pp. 442, 443 (a fortune-telling witch); J.-F. Bladé (1886); D. Fabre (1968); C. Beauquier, *Blason populaire de la Franche-Comté* (1897), pp. 133–40; *L'Almanach de Barbizier* (journal from Franche-Comté) (1949), p. 265 (Pafoi's donkey).

32. L. Beuve, *Œuvres choisies* (1950), pp. 61ff.

33. P. Sénéquier (1897), p. 75, and C. Beauquier (1897), pp. 133ff.

34. A. Millien and P. Delarue (1953).

35. C. Beauquier (1897), pp. 135ff.

36. C. Robert and M. Valière, *Récits et Contes populaires de Poitou* (1979), pp. 63, 103–4.

37. J. Vinson (1883), pp. 93–8.

38. W. Webster, *Basque Legends* (1879), p. 67.

39. *Ibid.*

40. In particular, the Breton versions by F. Cadic (1908), pp. 6–8, so close to *JDT*, and of F.-M. Luzel (1881), p. 351 (king of France or of Paris). We should note that as far as *Jean-de-trop* is concerned, Paris is presented as the seat of the king of France (Versailles is ignored) and as the great capital that dominates the northern horizon, political and geographical, of Languedoc. Similarly Langlade, Monsieur Sestier's residence, is the first large village situated immediately to the north (north-north-east) of Solorgues (see map).

41. A thorough investigation that I have carried out in the communal archives of Langlade and of Nages-et-Solorgues (preserved in the departmental archives of Gard) shows that the proper names of the novel, Sestier and Garouille (at Langlade) and Truquette (at Solorgues), not to mention, of course, Jean-l'ont-pris, are a pure invention on the part of Fabre, and do not belong, according to the evidence of innumerable documents that have survived from the eighteenth century (parish registers, assessment books, cadastral surveys, etc.), to the real onomastic stock of these various localities.

42. All the German versions of tale 332 that are earlier than 1700 (in fact, earlier than Grimm, published in 1812) refer to the notable as a rich, but simple villager (see Chapter XIV). It was Grimm (1811–12) in Germany and Gueullette (1712) in France who were the first to discover an oral tradition, more recent than the preceding one, in which the notable tends to be identified with the king. Is this a Perrault-type monarchization of the tale?

43. Bédat de Monlaur (1936 and 1943); A. Moulis, *Contes merveilleux des Pyrénées* (1976), p. 107; and M. Mir and F. Delample, *Histoires et Récits du pays occitan* (1948), p. 109.

44. D. S. MacIntosh, 'Blacksmith and Death', *Midwest Folklore*, I (1951), p. 53 (Irish version of AT 332 from Illinois), and J. Frank Dobie, *Puro Mexicano* (1935), pp. 174ff. (Mexican version of AT 332 from Texas).

45. In actual fact, in eighteenth-century Languedoc, this was the municipality of Nages-et-Solorgues, to which the 'sub-community' of Solorgues delegated a *consul* ['magistrate'] of its own (see, for example, on this subject, R. Sauzet, *Contre-Réforme et Réforme catholique en Bas-Languedoc, Le diocèse de Nîmes au XVIIe siècle* (1979), and the communal archives of Nages-et-

Solorgues for the years 1730 to 1760, sub-series BB, CC and GG in the departmental archives of Gard).

46. Solorgues, and more generally the double community of Nages-et-Solorgues; see on this subject the many statistical tables used by R. Sauzet in his thesis (1979), and which give 90 per cent and more Protestants or 'new converts' at Nages-et-Solorgues in the seventeenth and eighteenth centuries. The oral establishment of tale AT 332 in the hamlet of Solorgues must, therefore, have taken place after the 'Protestantization' of this locality around 1560.

47. *Inci homme*: Occitan deformation of the Latin *Ecce homo*; M. Barral, *JLP*, p. 84. These were the words spoken by Pontius Pilate when he pointed to Christ after the scourging: *Ecce homo* ['This is the man'].

48. Fabre, however, is not hostile to the peasants in general, but to those he calls, speaking of J L P, 'peasants of his kind', those who are accomplices, in varying degrees, of the forces of evil [87].

49. On Fabre's profound piety, see his *Lettres à son neveu . . .* , published by M. Barral (1960). On the almost complete Protestantism of the confederated communities of Nages-et-Solorgues in the eighteenth century, see R. Sauzet (1979), pp. 588, 748, 763.

50. On the strong Catholicism of the village of Bezouces, see R. Sauzet (1979), under the many references listed in the index, in particular, pp. 147, 375, 448; I have listed in an earlier note the same references in the pagination of the edition of this book deposited at Lille III, 1979.

51. See Chapter II.

52. R. Sauzet (1979), p. 395; J.-B. Fabre, *JLP*, in the early paragraphs relating to Solorgues.

53. See the very old, and therefore authenticating version (1547) of H. Sachs, *Sämtliche Fabeln und Schwänke* (1903), p. 317, and J. Grimm and W. Grimm, *Kinder- und Hausmärchen* (1812), tale 44, *Godfather Death*: *it would cost you your neck*, says Death to the hero, when the latter begins to betray him, and before Death seizes him with his icy hand. The final suffocation of the hero is also to be found in the Nivernais version of Millien and Delarue (1953), version A.

54. The version of AT 332 from the Landes collected by F. Arnaudin (1977), p. 578, also handles the 'scalping' theme, but in another way: the physician–hero, at the point at which he is struggling with Death, takes off his hat (lays bare his head). Usually, this doctor wears a spectacular hat, as a sign of his high functions as a 'curer'.

55. This Occitan word corresponds to the French *pelé* [literally 'baldpate'], used in the expression *un pelé, un tondu* [a 'nobody']. Following Gardy's rendering of *pelé* into French as *vaurien*, I have translated the term into English as 'good-for-nothing' [Tr.].

56. According to L. Alibert, *Dictionnaire occitan–français* (1966).

57. See also on the subject of the hair as a symbol of strength and vitality, B. Lincoln, 'Treatment of Hair . . .', *History of Religions*, XVI (1977).

58. The affair involving J L P, the peach-tree, the vineyard-keepers and Sestier takes place specifically on a Sunday, the day of vespers [57]. It should be remembered that Sunday was also the day when Margot went out for the first time [19], probably for the baptism of her child, but also because it was the canonical day for the baptism of A T 332 (see Chapter IX, and Grimm, tale 44: *The baptism takes place next Sunday*, says the poor man, the father of Grimm's hero, to Death, who becomes the child's godfather).

59. It is remarkable, apart from the Mahon cocks [59], that the allusions to the king of Majorca (Truquette) and to Margot-la-*Mahona* are situated in the same paragraph (relating to the prosperity of Truquette and of the baby J L P [second version]). These texts on Mahon (Port Mahon) were no doubt suggested by the recent memory of the siege of Port Mahon by the French in 1756, which was a considerable event in the popular mind, especially in Languedoc (see the manuscript of P. Prion's *Chronologiette*, from Aubais, [1744–59], p. 242, 29 April 1756). This dates the first version of *JLP* to the years 1756 to 1760. Port Mahon belonged to the English. Again, this is a Protestant (British) coding, which places Margot, born a Huguenot, and the vineyard-keepers of the Huguenot Solorgues, on the side of evil; whereas Truquette (Margot's victim) and J L P, both of Rouergat, and therefore Catholic, descent, and Sestier, the victor (together with J L P) over the vineyard-keepers, are on the side of good (the Catholic side); they are defeated in the first part of the tale, victorious in the second, just as the French 'papists' were finally victorious at Port Mahon over the English Protestants in 1756.

60. See E.-G. Léonard, *Mon village sous Louis XV* (1914), pp. 91–2, and P. Prion, manuscript of the *Chronologiette* (1744–59).

61. I have taken this term from the Occitano-Gascon version of A T 332 collected by P. Bédat de Monlaur (1936 and 1943). It offers most interesting points of comparison with *JDT* and *JLP*.

62. See Chapter XIV.

63. I use here the version published by F. Caballero (1861), pp. 83–8; see also R. H. Busk, *Patrañas or Spanish Stories* (1870), pp. 122–30.

64. On this placebo of water, which recurs in a large number of versions of AT 332, see Chapter XI.

65. *Bat*, then *screech-owl* (bird of ill-omen), then *dog:* in his *JLP*, the abbé Fabre also alludes, literally or metaphorically, during Truquette's biography, to animals that portend the hero's death – *bats* [8], *magpies* [17], *dogs* [21]. On each occasion they are animals that are linked to Margot's biography, and therefore bode ill for Truquette: it is, in fact, the other girls of the maleficent Solorgues, Margot's competitors, who are compared to *bats* [8]; the *magpies*, and other wild animals from the natural habitat of Death (see Chapter IX), are consumed during Margot's wedding feast [17]; lastly, it is Margot herself, who is compared to a young *dog* who gets a beating for its dinner [21], during the fight in which Truquette has already had his skin pricked and made to bleed by grandmother Death (his mother-in-law Death). But, in *Juan Holgado*, the three animals arrive on the scene at the end of the tale, during the hero's final decline. In *JLP*, where Truquette's fatal decline is very swift, the portents of death arrive in the first part of the narrative.

66. J. Bolte and J. Polivka (1913–18), vol. III, pp. 293–7. See also S. Thompson, *The Folktale* (1951), p. 47, and G. Widter, A. Wolf and R. Köhler, 'Volksmärchen aus Venetien', *Jahrbuch für roman. und englisch liter-atur*, VII (1886), p. 19. Lastly, see A. Aarne and S. Thompson (1961), tale type 335.

67. J. B. Rael, *Cuentos españoles de Colorado y Nuevo Mexico*, p. 144, tale 86, *La Comadre Sebastiana*; S. Robe, *Index of Mexican Folktales* (1975), pp. 65–6 (Mexico, Central America and Hispanic United States) (AT 332 and AT 332 B: Vc and Ve); and L. Da Camara Casardo, *Contes traditionnels du Brésil* (1978), p. 246, *Le camarade de la Mort*.

68. Greek tale published by B. Schmidt, *Griechische Märchen* . . . (1877).

69. Indeed, the second version of the tale states that the fight in which this episode occurs is an *estignassada générala* ['general seizure of hair'].

70. In this episode the dangerous Margot actually *burns* her husband. This 'burning' role was suggested by small touches in two earlier passages in the novella, concerning Margot's apparently innocent flirtation with Truquette: Fabre suggested [11] that she took fire at her man's first fart. Previously, well before she threw the *hot wax* at his face, she had gently stroked him [9] with a ball of *wax* (not heated).

71. There is an exception: *Hans-with-the-Goitre*, in Austria (T. Vernaleken, *Œsterreiche Kinder- und Hausmärchen* [1864]); the history of this hero of an Austro-baroque *Godfather Death* is very close to those of *Jean-de-trop*, *JLP* and the hero of the Breton version of AT 332 collected by F. Cadic (1908),

pp. 6–10. See also a German hero of AT 332 called *Michael Death* (not Hans, the synonym of Jean), in the version of K. Simrock, *Handbuch der deutschen Mythologie* (1887), p. 275.

Chapter XI

1. I shall come back to the problems of the Nocturne, strictly speaking, in *JLP*. We should take note how generally important, in this novella, are the evening and night hours, where the encounters of both heroes (Truquette and J L P) with the forces of death are concerned: there is the encounter with the baron [1, in the evening]; the evening meal with the three thieves, grandmother Death's accomplices [32, second version]; Truquette's acts of robbery committed at night [31]; Truquette is made a prisoner (with, for him, fatal consequences) by the municipal representatives of Solorgues, in the evening [36, second version]; the dangerous attack by the grandmother's donkey on J L P takes place in the evening [51]; J L P's capture by the vineyard-keepers takes place in the evening [57, second version]; lastly, Sestier's miraculous cure takes place at night [63].

2. T. Vernaleken, 'Der Fahrmann und der Tod', *Germania* . . . XXIX (XVII) (1884).

3. H. Sachs, *Sämtliche Fabeln und Schwänke* (1547; 1893 and 1903); J. Ayrer, *Dramen* (1618); and A. Strobl (1691).

4. It will be noticed that Jean-l'ont-pris lays great stress [62, second version] on this distance and, above all, on the difficulty of the journey, by bad roads, between Solorgues and Langlade, a village situated to the north of Solorgues. Similarly, the Occitan, Roussillonnais and Breton versions of AT 332 stress the distance, length and, above all, tiring character (E. Caseponce, *Contes Vallespirenchs replegats per En Mir y Nontoquis* [1907], pp. 53, 56 [Roussillon]) of the journey from the Languedocian, Roussillonnais or Breton village of the physician–hero to 'Paris' or 'the Louvre', or whatever other royal residence this physician visits in order to treat the king (Versailles is never mentioned). See *JDT*, p. 190; P. Bédat de Monlaur, *Le Meunier gascon* (1936) and *Les Contes du Lézard, contes du pays de Gascogne* (1943); F.-M. Luzel, *Légendes chrétiennes de la Basse-Bretagne* (1881), p. 355; F. Cadic, *La Paroisse bretonne de Paris* (1908), pp. 8–10. In *JLP*, the 'nurse'–hero travels with the powerful man whom he has helped to cure [62, second version]. The same solution occurs in F. Cadic (1908), which is so close to our *JDT*. In *JDT*, the hero travels in the same coach as the king.

5. Versions by H. Sachs (1547); J. Ayrer (late sixteenth century); and A. Strobl (1691).

6. See, on this matter, the fine entries on *drac, dragas, dragon*, etc., in F. Mistral, *Lou Tresor dou Félibrige* (1932).

7. J. Duvernoy, *Le Registre d'inquisition de Jacques Fournier . . . 1318–1325* (1965), vol. III, under the words in question in the word index (end of the volume).

8. Sestier's ravenous appetite is clearly indicated at the hero's first meeting with him [62 and 63], and by the rich man's mouth, 'agape a rod wide' [72]. This may be compared with the king of *Jean-de-trop*, which, in other ways, too, is so close our *JLP*. Indeed, it is the king of France's *cook* who goes to fetch Jean-de-trop when the princess is ill. In both cases, the hero's first meeting with the powerful man is placed under the sign of 'cooking'.

9. See F. Mistral (1932), under *Diantre, Diauco*, etc.

10. In [80], Quincarlot stresses that he is a *relation* of J L P and was Truquette's *best friend*. His relationship with the young hero is not on the side of Truquette, a Rouergat with no relations in the Gard, and who was simply his friend. It must therefore be located on Margot's side, which relates Quincarlot, by blood or by marriage, to grandmother Death.

11. On the *cross* and the *sign of the cross* as a *strictly Catholic* and *anti-Protestant* symbol in the Nîmes region in the eighteenth century, see R. Sauzet, *Contre-Réforme at Réforme catholique en Bas-Languedoc, Le diocèse de Nîmes au XVIIᵉ siecle* (1979). The *Cadets de la Croix*, in early-eighteenth-century Cévenne, were anti-Camisard guerrillas. The Catholic Rouergat Truquette gives a brass cross [14] to Margot (daughter of a Huguenot mother), whom he will marry in the Roman Church, by way of Catholicizing their marriage and Catholicizing the bride herself all the more.

12. On two occasions, J L P also identifies himself, discreetly enough, with a lamb or childish *agnelet*; this animal is rather reminiscent, through the 'pascal lamb', of the burlesque 'Christic' pretensions of the hero, who is also compared in passing, on the same occasion, to a priest wearing his chasuble [30 and 70, second version].

13. J. Bolte and J. Polivka, *Anmerkungen zu den Kindern-Hausmärchen der Brüder Grimm* (1913–18), pp. 383–5.

14. See, on this matter, Luke 22: 47–8.

15. Bibliography on the Virgin of Mercy: Louis Réau, *Iconographie de l'Art chrétien* (1955), t. II, vol. 2, pp. 112–20; P. Perdrizet, *La Vierge de Miséricorde* (1908); Père Alexandre d'Arles (Capuchin), *Histoire de la fondation du Monastère de la Miséricorde d'Arles* (1705), in particular pp. 39–40; P. Grosez (S J), *Vie de Marie-Madeleine de la Trinité* (1696), mystical eroticism; A.

Piny, *Vie de Marie-Madeleine de la Trinité* (1697), first chapters; H. Brémond, *La Provence mystique au XVIIe siècle* (1908), Chs. Xff.

16. *The Catholic Encyclopedia* (1907), article under 'Candlemas'.

17. See my *Montaillou* (1978). For the nineteenth century see D. Fabre and J. Lacroix, *Vie quotidienne des pays de Languedoc au XIXe siècle* (1973), p. 207, and A. Van Gennep, *Folklore du Dauphiné* (1946), vol. I, under the paragraph devoted to Candlemas [*la Chandeleur*].

18. J. W. Wolf, *Deutsche Hausmärchen* (1851), p. 367. I shall return again to this version by Wolf, who throws light on several important points in *JLP*. Moreover, it is not usual for the 'king' of AT 332 (our Sestier here) to die at the end of the tale. This death is reserved for the hero himself, and even then, not always.

19. J. Bolte and J. Polivka (1913–18), p. 383. It should be stressed that this version collected by Jacob Grimm is a French one from well inland, and not, for example, an Alsatian one; indeed, in it Death is a godmother, in the Latin mode, and not a godfather, in the German style.

20. 'Our Sister Death', the expression was used by St Francis of Assisi himself.

21. Quoted by M. Barral, *Jean-Baptiste Favre, sa vie, son œuvre* . . . (1971), p. 54. On the two images of the character of Death – as mother (of divine essence) and as stepmother (of diabolical essence) – see C. Martineau-Genieys, *La Thème de la mort dans la poésie française de 1450 à 1550* (1978), pp. 48–9, 54–5, 86 and, above all, 87; and C. Thiry, 'De la mort marâtre à la mort vaincue' (1979).

22. In the versions of AT 332 from the western German region (Palatinate and Switzerland), the Green Man, a diabolical character, is sometimes the *direct* stand-in for Death, in his role as dangerous godfather–protector (the case of the 'Swiss tale': see end of Chapter IX); sometimes, more usually, this same Green Man/devil is simply, after God, the character who is rejected by the paternal hero as godfather of his child, and who therefore gives place shortly afterwards to Death, who is himself finally accepted as godfather (K. Winkler, *Oberpfälzische Sagen, Legenden, Märchen* . . . [1935], pp. 264–5).

23. Another marker, both English and Protestant, concerns the grandmother, whom we know, explicitly, to be Huguenot: she presents herself and her family as the group of 'milords' [ladies and gentlemen, 26], an English word, popular in France, indicating wealth and respectability.

24. Quincarlot/Satan/Death is 'Jewish' in Fabre; the supernatural being of AT 332 (the devil) is also 'Jewish' in the Austrian version of T. Vernaleken,

Œsterreiche Kinder- und Hausmärchen (1864), p. 23, which is very close to *JDT*.

25. The ill fate shared by Truquette and Garouille is also marked by their identification with the 'animal' state: Truquette is called a *bestiassa* [12, second version]; Garouille is a *malabestia* ['horrible animal', 83].

26. Predestination, see book 9 of vol. III of Jansenius, *Augustinus*.

27. On the symbolism, which is ultra-Catholic and anti-Protestant, of the Cross in the Nîmes region, see R. Sauzet (1979).

28. M. Barral, *JLP*, p. 86, has quite rightly noted on this matter that the theme of Protestant Holland as the enemy of Catholic France was well known in France (including Occitania, which provided Louis XIV with a large number of soldiers from the Dutch wars of 1672 onwards). See the words of the song 'Auprès de ma blonde', which go back to this period: *Il est dans la Hollande, les Hollandais l'ont pris.*

29. For example, the version of A. Orain, *Contes de l'Ille-et-Vilaine* (1901) (Brittany); that of T. Vernaleken (1864); and, of course, very close to our *JLP*, the 'Swiss tale'.

30. On the 'descent' of Death from heaven on God's orders, to drag the hero below, towards the infernal cave of lights, see the Sicilian version of AT 332, which is particularly telling in this instance, collected by L. Gonzenbach, *Sizilianische Märchen aus dem Volksmund gesammelt* (1870), pp. 123–4, tale 79.

31. Apart from the diocese of Vabre, the town of Millau, which were often Calvinist, there were practically no Protestants among the Rouergats, especially among the poorer inhabitants of that region, who had moved in the eighteenth century from the Catholic mountain areas of Aveyron towards the Languedoc. See, on this matter, my *Territoire de l'historien* (1978), vol. II, pp. 309ff.

32. J. W. Wolf (1851), pp. 367–8, and L. Aurbacher, *Ein Volksbüchlein* (1879), p. 121.

33. Written and printed version: T. S. Gueullette, *Les Mille et Un Quarts d'heure* (1712); then the oral versions, which the Quebec version proved to have existed before 1763. On Gueullette himself, see Chapter XIV; on the fact that Fabre probably had read Gueullette, see the decisive comments by M. Barral (1971), p. 119, n. 6.

34. See, on this matter, the more general thoughts of J. Starobinski, *1789* (1979), pp. 165–6.

35. The hero of AT 332 *fights with Death*: A. Millien and P. Delarue mss., version C (collected in Nivernais about 1886).

36. Millien and Delarue mss., tale 332, version B; of course, the magic use of the whistle is not confined to tale AT 332 (it is to be found in other tale types): see, for example, P. Bédat de Monlaur (1943), Ch. XXIX. As far as *JLP* is concerned, this whistle as used by the hero is first the careful reply to that used by the vineyard-keepers. The vineyard-keeper's son then tries, in vain, to recover the whistle, which remains the property and magic talisman of the hero JLP. I have constantly stressed, in my analysis, that the vineyard-keepers and their children belong to the forces of death; that amounts to saying that JLP has stolen this effective whistle from the forces of death, and that he is determined that they will not get it back.

37. On the relation between the *chopine* and the medical or surgical hero of AT 332 see Chapter IX.

38. The placebo of *water* or other liquid in AT 332 in the Occitan-speaking regions: *JLP* [63]; *JDT*; F. Mistral, *Prose d'Almanach* (1926), pp. 26–7 (jug of cold water). Outside the Occitan-speaking regions: F.-M. Luzel (1881), pp. 348, 355; H. Greville, 'L'homme qui cherchait un parrain juste', *Revue des traditions populaires* XIII (1898), pp. 644ff. (Brittany and Anjou); J. Grimm and W. Grimm, *Kinder- und Hausmärchen* (1812), tale 42; P. Zaunert, 'Wom armen Weber, wie er einen Gevattern gesucht' (1926). Placebo of water and meat (= *herb tea* or *broth*): M. Mir and F. Delample, *Histoires et Récits du pays occitan* (1948); A. Perbosc and S. Cézerac mss., tale 39; F. Arnaudin, *Contes populaires de la Grande-Lande* (1977), p. 588 (broth); *JLP* [19] (broth or meat *soupettes* given by Truquette to his wife, homologous but very different from the root given by the hero of the 'Swiss tale' to his wife, which had been given to him, in turn, by the Green Man to cure her). Outside the Occitan-speaking regions: T. Vernaleken (1884), p. 414. Placebo made of *herbs* or roots, in general outside the Occitan-speaking region: notably Grimm, tale 44; the 'Swiss tale'; L. Aurbacher (1879); A. de Llano Roza de Ampudia, *Cuentos asturianos recogidos de la tradición oral* (1925), p. 70 (Asturias).

39. Maranda file, item 51, recorded 5 January 1966.

40. *Almanach de l'Ariège* (*Almanach patoues de l'Ariejo*) (1895), p. 55.

41. The bottle of *brandy* is also to be found in the same sequence of AT 332, in a Breton version (P. Sébillot, 'La Mort en voyage', *Archivio* . . . IV (1885), p. 428.

42. Unpublished Occitan version collected in the Corbières around Aude by U. Gibert, in 1925, from a villager in his fifties. French translation by G.

Maugard, *Contes de Pyrénées* (1955), pp. 116–20. I wish to thank U. Gibert, who lent me a copy of his original manuscript in Occitan.

43. Nivernais: Millien and Delarue mss., versions A and D. Brittany: P. Sébillot (1885), pp. 427, 429. Scandinavia: R. T. Christiansen, *Studies in Irish and Scandinavian Folktales* (1959), p. 207. Catalonia: J. Amades, *Folklore de Catalunya, Rondallistica; Rondalles* (1950), p. 492. Quebec: Maranda file, recording No. 1859 (1954) and item 51 (1966).

44. A. Perbosc, *Contes de Gascogne* (1954), p. 103.

45. J. Bolte and J. Polivka (1913–18), vol. II, p. 414, commentary on Grimm's tale 99.

46. Indeed, it will be noted that the agents of this municipality, on Truquette's arrest [36], treated the cobbler most harshly; they were already less violent with Margot (stripped down to her night-dress); they hardly did anything to the grandmother other than not showing her the respect that would normally be her due.

47. See on this subject my *Paysans de Languedoc* (1966), vol. I, p. 28. The universal municipal institution of vineyard-keepers or *bandiers* in Languedoc and Provence goes back at least to the Middle Ages, even to the twelfth century; consult on this subject the recent thesis by M.-T. Gramain, 'Les Paysans de la région de Béziers au Moyan Age' (1979), pp. 859, 945, and L. Stouff, 'Arles à la fin du Moyen Age' (1979), p. 504, on the regions of Béziers and Arles in the medieval period.

48. M. Mir and F. Delample (1948), beginning of the tale, and F. Dezeuze, *Contes d'un pêcheur de lune* (1953), p. 20, also at the beginning of the tale (in both cases we have a bad meal given by the man who is to become Death's *compère*, and who at the time has only an *arencâda* or dried sardine to eat, until the arrival of the prosperity that is about to be showered upon him; this prosperity will immediately take the canonical form of 'Death's gifts').

49. A new, rather subtle parallel between these homologous stages of the respective biographies of father and son. One will also note the similar occurrence of an episode involving wine in the phase that immediately precedes 'Death's gifts', in the stories of Truquette and JLP: Truquette [*chopine*] drinks wine at his wedding meal, then buys cheap wine for himself, then is called a drunkard by his wife during the ensuing row [19–21], just before the grandmother takes over and showers her son-in-law with her dangerous advice as to how to get rich (we have seen how this episode involving wine, in Truquette's case, is also close to a similar theme in the 'Swiss tale'). Similarly, in JLP's biography, just before the discovery of the treasure that symbolizes for the hero the entry into the lucky phase of 'Death's gifts', we see Sestier

invite his saviours to come and have a drink [*boire traqua*, 60; Truquette is the diminutive of *Truqua*]; Sestier and his guests get drunk (except J L P). Then the grandmother dies of an excess of grapes. Truquette had stupidly allowed himself to be in the middle of this dangerous episode involving wine, whereas J L P, very wisely, remains a spectator. He leaves it to his 'counterpart', the surgeon, to drink a few glasses of wine in his place, at the resuscitated Sestier's bedside [63].

50. I am paraphrasing here J. Starobinski (1979), p. 166.

51. G. Maugard (1955), p. 118.

52. Maranda file, item 51 (1966).

53. P. Sébillot (1885), p. 429, and *Contes des landes et des grèves* (1900), pp. 251–2.

54. Collection Lacourcière, recording no. 1859, recorded in 1954.

55. In the Roussillonnais-Catalan version of A T 332 that I call *Galdric*, the passing through a hole does not take place, since Death is trapped, not in a bottle, but by an unfinished prayer, the *Pater Noster*. However, the narrator, careful not to lose anything, uses this theme at the end of the tale: 'And *cric! crac!*/the tale is finished/thereupon there was a rat, which, *passing through a hole*, etc.' (E. Caseponce [1907], p. 65).

56. Version collected in Occitan from a villager of Crabies (*Almanach de l'Ariège* [1895], p. 56): 'pass through the eye of a needle'.

57. Millien and Delarue mss., version A.

58. V. Chauvin, *Bibliographie des ouvrages arabes . . .* (1902), vol. VI, p. 24; D. S. MacIntosh, 'Blacksmith and Death', *Midwest Folklore*, I (1951), p. 53 (Irish version of A T 332, collected in Illinois in 1950 from the granddaughter of a story-teller active in the 1890s); J. Russel-Reaver, 'Four Lithuanian-American Folktales', *Southern Folklore Quarterly*, XII, No. 4 (1948), p. 262 (Lithuanian version in the United States); Quebec: recording No. 7, 1859, collected in 1954; A. Perbosc (1954), p. 104 (Gascony).

59. A. de Cock, 'Compeere de Dood', *Volkskunde*, VII (1894), pp. 35–9.

60. A. de Cock, 'De Dood als Doopvader', *Volkskunde*, V (1892), pp. 184–8, and P. de Mont and A. de Cock, *Dit zÿn Vlaamsche Wondersprookjes* (1896), pp. 182–7.

61. The grandmother was the *original* inspiration behind the team formed by Truquette and his three accomplices, including Quincarlot [28–32]. Indeed, she remained more or less surreptitiously one of them [70].

62. In certain versions of A T 332, notably those preserved in those

'conservatories' of traditional Spanish culture in the Spanish-Mexican enclaves of the state of New Mexico in the United States, the hero, like J L P, kills Death. However, since, unlike Fabre's tale, it is a fairy-tale *in the full sense of the term*, Death rises again and kills him (S. L. Robe, *Hispanic Folktales from New Mexico* [1977], tale 38).

63. Maranda file, recording no. 1859, collected in 1954.

64. F. Mistral (1932), vol. II, p. 311, entry under *meirino*.

65. 'Devout': *JDT*; see also J. Amades (1950), p. 493: *jo sóc molt bon cristià* ['I am a very good Christian'], declares the hero as he tricks Death by the Catholic method of the unfinished *Pater Noster*.

66. See, on this subject, the fine book by M. Barral on the abbé Fabre (1971).

67. All the references listed are to be found in paragraphs 67, 68, 69 and 70 of the first version of *JLP*, and in the same paragraphs, with additional references, notably on *Cinderella*, in the second version.

68. P. Delarue and M.-L. Tenèze, *Le Conte populaire français* (1957–76), vol. II, under tale 510 A, in their commentaries on *Cinderella*.

69. Mme d'Aulnoy, *Les Contes de Fées* (1710), pp. 110–47.

70. It will be noted that in the case of *Cinderella* and *JLP* in particular, and *Death's Godson* in general, the abbé Fabre used a method similar *in both cases*: in effect, he used his profound knowledge of the Languedocian folklore of the period (represented in this case by *Céndrousétta-Bachassoun*, whose name is a local one, and which he refers to in paragraph [70] of the second version), together with his reading of French written literature (Mme d'Aulnoy's *Finette-Cendron*). Similarly, as far as *Death's Godson* (AT 332) is concerned, he used the oral Occitan versions of *Godfather Death* that he had heard, while remembering his French readings of, for example, the *Godfather Death* of Gueullette (1712), an author whom he seems to have known (M. Barral [1971], p. 119). But in the first case (*Finette-Cendron*), the abbé used more of the written version; in the second case (*Death's Godson*), he relied more on oral tradition.

71. Mme d'Aulnoy's slipper corresponds, of course, to the famous *glass slipper* in Perrault's *Cendrillon*.

72. Bruno Bettelheim, 'Cinderella', in *The Uses of Enchantment* (1976); see also Grimm's *Cinderella* and M.-F. Orsini-Marzoppi, *Récits et Contes populaires de Corse* (1978), p. 77, *Cinnarella*.

73. Indeed, Fabre actually used the golden key and the coffer as talismanic

objects that made it possible to reach the heart and body of a girl, enclosed in a harem: see his *Visites de Zima*, in the style of *The Thousand and One Nights* ('Œuvres de Saint-Castor' [abbé J.-B. C. Fabre]), vol. VII, in the manuscripts of the Bibliothèque Municipale de Montpellier.

74. P. Delarue and M.-L. Tenèze (1957–76), vol. II, pp. 250ff. (see their commentaries on tale type 510 A, *Cinderella*). Note also that Truquette, J L P's father, occupies in the abbé's novella, in terms of family situation, a position homologous with that of the king, Finette-Cendron's father. This is an additional reason to attribute to Truquette 'the heart of a king' [72].

75. Version published by F. Maspons, *Contes populars catalans* (1952), p. 118.

Chapter XII

1. Prediction of someone's death as a source of wealth for the hero of A T 332: Occitan versions of the tale by F. Arnaudin, *Contes populaires de la Grande-Lande* (1977), p. 588; A. Moulis, *Contes merveilleux des Pyrénées* (1976), p. 107; A. Perbosc and S. Cézerac mss. (A T 332, death of the lord of Peirestortes). See also F. Caballero, *Cuentos populares andaluces colleccionados* (1861) (Andalusia); J. W. Wolf, *Deutsche Hausmärchen* (1851) (Germany); and, above all, E. Caseponce, *Contes Vallespirenchs replegats per En Mir y Nontoquis* (1907), pp. 55–7 (Roussillon) – on this version, see Chapter XV.

2. See also in *JLP* [second version, 40] the hero's own comparison of himself with a king popularly referred to as *Quatorze* and who is none other than Louis XIV. Was this an archaism, dating from the Louis XIV period, of the oral version known to Fabre about 1750, and which was the source of his text?

3. *Compère* of godfather Death = father of godfather Death's godson.

4. T. Vernaleken, *Œsterreiche Kinder- und Hausmärchen* (1864), p. 225. On this version, see Chapter XIV. See also the Hanseatic version of A T 332 by R. H. Bünker, *Schwanke, Sagen, und Märchen in heanzischer Mundart* (1906): the physician–hero is given 20,000 florins for curing a countess by turning the bed around.

5. Sestier's demand of 20,000 *livres tournois* from the hero, who is asking for his daughter's hand in marriage, occurs in the first version [73]. The various contractual estimates of J L P's treasure, all above this figure of 20,000 *livres*, are to be found in paragraphs [77, etc.] of the first and second versions (see Table 13).

6. This 'prognosis of death for the *rival* (A) of the powerful man's daughter' is at the same time a 'prognosis of death for the powerful man's encumbering wife or [here] frightful *mistress* (B), whom the powerful man wishes to get rid of' (Barbe-Garouille plays both roles at once, A and B). Fabre was able to use an already existing version as far as the prognosis of type B is concerned, since it also appears in the German version of AT 332 collected by J. W. Wolf and published by him in 1851. This version has very interesting similarities, in overall structure as well as in detail, with *JLP* (see Chapter XVI).

7. See Chapter XI and Chapter XIV.

8. Barbetta or Barbette and Garouillette [second version, 80].

9. See the references provided in note 67 of Chapter XI.

10. J. Bolte and J. Polivka, *Anmerkungen zu den Kindern-Hausmärchen der Brüder Grimm* (1913–18), pp. 383–4, commentaries on Grimm's tale 44.

11. In *Galdric*, too (version of AT 332 from Roussillon, which is very close to *JLP*, as I shall show later in Chapter XV), the king turns out to be very threatening towards the hero if he is unfortunate enough to make an incorrect diagnosis (E. Caseponce [1907], p. 55).

12. Grimm, tale 44; on the devil disguised as a huntsman, turning up as a candidate for the role of godfather in AT 332, see the Strobl version (late seventeenth century) and the 'Swiss tale'; see also F. Dezeuze, *Jean de Carnas* in *Contes d'un pêcheur de lune* (1953), pp. 69–70, in which the king, dressed as a hunter, is refused as a candidate for the role of godfather.

13. A still earlier example of this decapitation by an executioner's *sword*: Bibliothèque de l'Arsenal, ms. 5070 (fifteenth century), a miniature illustrating the fifth tale of the fourth day of Boccaccio's *Decameron*. See also *Tristan et Yseut*, edited by Joseph Bédier, Chapter II, concerning the Morholt whose sword cuts off people's heads. And the engraving, made between 1615 and 1620, already quoted in this book (Chapter IX), depicting the decapitation of the Maréchale d'Ancre.

14. Text in J. Bolte and J. Polivka (1913–18), in the commentaries concerning *Godfather Death* (Grimm's tale 44).

15. T. Vernaleken (1864); see Chapter XIV.

16. See F. Mistral, *Lou Trésor dou Felibrige* (1932), under the entries for *Quincarlat* and *Quincarlot*.

17. See Chapter X, note 22 and this chapter, note 19.

18. See J.-B. Fabre, *Le Siège de Caderousse* (1876), p. 220: *la tartarassa sus d'anedas . . .*, in other words: 'the buzzard on the ducks like wolves on sheep'.

In view of this image offered elsewhere by Fabre, Carcanas, Quincarlot's accomplice, is implicitly compared to a (devouring) wolf. As far as the form *Cartatoucha* for Cartouche is concerned, it was not invented by Fabre but borrowed by him from Languedocian and more generally Occitan usage (see, in the eighteenth century, the Languedocian or Cévenol dictionary of the abbé de Sauvages under the entry *Cartatoucho,* and F. Mistral (1932), under *Cartatoucho*).

19. Truquette's three 'accomplices' are essentially bound up with Death and the forces of death, and possibly bound up (as far as Quincarlot is concerned) with diabolism: this is indicated by the various names and comparisons (Carcanas, Cartatoucha, Crouquet, Renâouvi, Quincarlot, Satan-the-gibbet, etc.) with which he is associated. Their very slight links with Truquette, who is not a force of death, but a victim of Death, is marked, however, by a single light touch, through the name or nickname of one of them, Jacquet, and this only in the first version. Indeed, Truquette, following the initially itinerant vocation of the father of Death's future godson in A T 332, is twice compared to a pilgrim carrying a staff, at the canonical beginning of the narrative [second version, 6] and specifically to a pilgrim of St James of Compostella [77]. Hence this link, which is certainly tenuous, between this pilgrim of St James (Jacques) and *Jacquet,* one of the three accomplices, who is to become *Carcanas* in the second version.

20. It should be noted that Quincarlot performs the role of herald of death three times: he explicitly announces Truquette's death (which took place several years previously), the future death of Garouille and possible death (symbolized by the image of the gibbet) for J L P himself.

21. Apart from the 'Swiss tale', the substitution of the devil for Death as representing the supernatural entity of A T 332 is also practised in A. Orain, *Contes de l'Ille-et-Vilaine* (1901), pp. 208ff. (Brittany), and P. J. Cornelissen and J. B. Vervliet, *Vlaamsche Volksvertelsels en Kindersprookjes* (1900) (Flanders).

22. M. Barral (*JLP*), in his analysis of the last paragraph of *JLP,* at the end of the book. It should also be noted that the grandmother, the representative of Death, adopts a great many French terms in her long speech to her son-in-law [29]. On the French-speaking baron Death, see Chapter XIII; see also the end of the novella *JLP* itself.

23. On Quincarlot's *godfatherhood* of J L P, paragraph [80] of the first version is crucial: in it Quincarlot insists first on the friendship and kinship that bind him to the young man's father and mother. After these protestations of friendship, he calls J L P *my son,* then *my child* [see also second version,

80]. In a burlesque way, as always in Fabre, Quincarlot has everything of the godfather about him: kinship, friendship and artificial paternity in relation to his 'godson' JLP. The same could be said of the baron (see Chapter XIII).

24. J. W. Wolf (1851).

25. Nivernais version of AT 332 (A. Millien and P. Delarue, ms. B).

26. More specifically still: during the first attack on Jean-l'ont-pris, accompanied by arrest, the vineyard-keepers, who first confined their attacks to the hero's shins [54], later, when things become more serious, get hold of him by the nape of the neck, his head and his hair [57, first and second versions]. During the second attack, also accompanied by arrest, one of them takes him by the scruff of the neck [80], but very soon the attack, which in fact is harmless enough, *descends* to the buttocks and the lower parts – his trousers are dropped around his ankles – instead of *rising* dangerously towards his head, as was the case in the preceding attack. Besides, during the first arrest, the hero was immobilized, tied to the peach-tree, the torture post [57]. During the second attack, his hands are tied behind his back, but he continues to walk; he remains *mobile*, in the company of Quincarlot and his henchmen [second version, 80].

27. See the beginning of this chapter.

28. See Table 14, paragraph A, line 2 (b).

29. See Table 14, paragraph B, line 3 (b).

30. On the position of JLP himself, at the moment of the 'permutation of 180 degrees carried out on the horizontal plane', during the attack by the vineyard-keepers, see Chapter XI.

31. See, for example, T.-S. Gueullette, *Les Mille et Un Quarts d'heure* (1712; 1753), p. 288, on the invisibility of Death, except to the physician–hero, at the patient's bedside.

32. M. Barral, *JLP*, pp. 94–5.

33. P. Bédat de Monlaur, *Le Meunier gascon* (1936) and *Les Contes du lézard, contes du pays de Gascogne* (1943).

34. On these versions (which number 168 in all), one will find a list in the Bibliography, in alphabetical order of the authors or collectors, or, in the case of anonymous authors, under the title.

35. There is, however, one exception: in a Catholic country, the Lithuanian version, also reversed, collected by H. Gering, *Islendzk Aeventyri* (1883). One cannot, therefore, totally exclude the hypothesis that the abbé Fabre found the structural inversion (which characterizes *JLP 2*) already in existence in

one of the oral, Occitan versions of AT 332, which guided him in writing *JLP*, and *JLP 2* in particular.

36. Nivernais: Millien and Delarue mss., version D (AT 332); Quebec: Maranda file, item 51 (recorded 5 January 1966); Austria: T. Vernaleken (1864); Ireland: D. S. MacIntosh, 'Blacksmith and Death', *Midwest Folklore*, I (1951), pp. 52–3 (an Irish version collected in Illinois); Lithuania: J. Russel-Reaver, 'Four Lithuanian-American Folktales', *Southern Folklore Quarterly*, XII, No. 4 (1948), p. 262; Scotland: J. MacDougall, *Folktales and Fairy Lore* (1910).

37. *JDT 1*: life of JDT's father (and mother); *JDT 2*: life of JDT himself. The second narrative follows the first in the same tale *JDT* (see beginning of Chapter IX).

38. There are a number of literary, theatrical and other adaptations of *Godfather Death*, dating from the sixteenth and seventeenth centuries (Sachs, Ayrer, etc.) and up to the nineteenth and twentieth centuries. See, on this subject, *Zeitschrift des Vereins für Volkskunde* (1896), p. 62, paragraph 19. See also B. Traven, *Macario* in *The Night Visitor and Other Stories* (1966), a rather flat, fictional adaptation of a Mexican version of AT 332. See also J. Bolte, 'Das Märchen vom Gevatter Tod', *Zeitschrift des Vereins für Volkskunde* (1894), pp. 34–5. On the possibly Lithuanian exception, see note 35.

39. See, on this subject, the decisive analysis by A. Aarne and S. Thompson (1961), pp. 175–9, under the commentaries concerning tale type 510 (*Cinderella*).

40. There exist in fact (in addition to *JDT*) some versions of AT 332 that are almost purely optimistic: T. Vernaleken (1864), and D. S. MacIntosh (1951), p. 53 (Irish version of AT 332 collected in Illinois).

41. Square C7 of the right-hand column of Table 16; square 3, moving upwards in the right-hand column of Table 17.

42. We should remember that in various versions of AT 332 (including *JDT*), Death's gifts go first to the hero's father (Death's *compère*, or 'Truquette'), then to the hero himself (Death's godson, or 'JLP'). In other words, the four-part schema is played out twice, once in terms of the father, again (at greater length) in terms of the son. In *JLP*, JLP's own autobiography is twice as long as the biography of his father Truquette. In *JDT*, the life of the son, Jean-de-trop, is also rather longer than that of his parents.

Chapter XIII

1. On Truquette's initial poverty, see *JLP* [1–20].

2. It will be noted that from 'friend' to 'son', the gradation of terms used by the baron to JLP is exactly the same as that used by Quincarlot; both of these characters, following the grandmother, embody successively the role of godfather Death to the young hero. They begin, therefore, by referring to their friendship for JLP, then they call him 'my son' and 'my child' (see Chapter XII, note 23).

3. On this stereotype, see also La Fontaine's fable 'Les deux pigeons' (book IX, fable 2), and *Tristan et Yseut* (ed. Joseph Bédier), Ch. IX: rather love than a kingdom.

4. *Jean de Paris* (late medieval novel that passed into popular literature in the eighteenth century) is the type of the rich seducer.

5. J. Monnet, *Anthologie françoise, ou chansons choisies depuis le XIIIe siècle jusqu'à présent* (1765), vol. II, p. 157. According to F. Girard, this song was written by Charles Collé and dates from 1753, three years before the first version of *JLP* (see Bibliography, under Collé, Charles).

6. *JLP* [35] and, above all, [second version, 36]. On the symbolism (referring to fortune's wheel), in Fabre and in *JDT*, of the *tamis sieve*, the *spit* and the *bobbin* which turn or spin, see Chapter IX.

7. See Chapter X.

8. M. Barral, *JLP*, pp. 94–5.

9. 'Je vous souhaite *lou* bonsoir,' says JLP to the baron [3], in more or less pure French.

10. A. Strobl (1691).

11. The baron may have a soul of silex, literally a soul of 'cold stone', which refers us to the fundamental role of freshness and cold, linked to *gaillardise* (cold strength), in the definition of those two 'forces of death', the baron and Margot.

12. A fine example is the German version of AT 332 collected by H. Pröhle, *Kinder- und Volksmärchen* (1853): Death's godson emerges, very pleased with himself, from a cure that he has just made by tricking his protector – and he meets, as he makes his triumphant exit from the sick-room, Death, who drags him off to the cellar with lights, where he dies.

13. Catalan version (horse and cemetery): F. Maspons, *Contes populars catalans* (1952), p. 119. See also the Breton version, P. Sébillot, 'La Mort en

voyage', *Archivio* . . . IV (1885), p. 423. Also refer, incidentally, to Albrecht Dürer's engraving *The Horseman, the Devil and Death*.

14. F. Mistral, *Lou Trésor dou Félibrige* . . . (1932), vol. I, under the word *Foulèt* ('lively, busy, and mischievous sprite, like the *drac*, or devil, of folklore, in opposition to the satanic devil'). In the system of opposition of Table 8, the baron on his 'spirited horse' is a *dragas* of folklore, as was the grandmother, that other incarnation of death.

15. Also very suggestive is the 'final fall' of the story *Godfather Death* in Maspons's version (1952), p. 120: after the murder of the physician–hero by Death himself, the story-teller concludes: 'End of tale, amen Jesus/behind the door, there is a spindle.' As we have seen (Chapter IX), in *JLP* and in A T 332 in general, Death is classically beneficent when 'in front of the door' (of the house) and 'dangerous' *behind the door*. The presence of the spindle (classic symbol of accidental death, manipulated by the Fate Clotho) *behind the door* is not, therefore, without interest, immediately after the physician–hero has been put to death by Death in person.

16. For references to these various versions, related to *JDT*, see Chapter XIV.

17. On this question, see the Sicilian version of A T 332 collected by L. Gonzenbach, *Sizilianische Märchen aus dem Volksmund gesammelt* (1870).

18. The structural study of the tale *Galdric* (see Chapter XV) also allows us to locate Death in a very precise situation, in which he is the exact homologue of our baron.

19. See the title of M. Barral's thesis, *J.-B. Favre* . . ., *Essai sur le burlesque dans la littérature occitane*.

Chapter XIV

1. On the life, travels (over a very limited area) and reading of Fabre, see M. Barral, *Jean-Baptiste Favre, sa vie, son œuvre* . . . (1971).

2. The existence of a vast cycle of *Jean-le-sot* in Quebec, which has many similarities with its French homologue, is a weighty argument in favour of the existence of this cycle in France before 1763, when cultural (and other) links between Quebec and metropolitan France were broken. I would like to thank Mme Maranda, who provided me with a huge file on this subject (see Bibliography).

3. Robert Chanaud, in *Monde alpin et rhodanien*, 6th year (1978), 261. See

also G. Duby, *Le Monde*, 10 February 1979, and A. Van Gennep, article on 'La Chandeleur en Savoie', in *Revue d'ethnographie et des traditions populaires* (1924), 6, which quotes a French proverb to be found in seventeenth-century collections of proverbs (prior to 1678): 'If it is fine and sunny at Candlemas, the bear will hide for six weeks.' The complete references for this proverb and for several similar ones in the seventeenth and eighteenth centuries are to be found in A.-J.-V. Le Roux de Lincy (1842), vol. I, no. 3, p. 65. Chanaud's ignorance of Van Gennep's crucially important work concerning his own regional speciality is difficult to excuse. More unforgivable still is the fact that Chanaud should have erected this ignorance into a theoretical argument. As for the highly symbolic character of the bear disguise of 1580, as of all the disguises and clothes mentioned by Judge Guérin in 1580, see the text of this *Guérin*, perfectly edited, with my collaboration, in P. Venault *et al.*, *Un soulèvement populaire, Romans, 1580* (1979), pp. 38–100.

4. W. Liungman, *Die schwedischen Volksmärchen* (1961), p. 74.

5. See A. Aarne and S. Thompson (1961), under tale type 332, and J. MacDougall, *Folktales and Fairy Lore* (1910).

6. J. Grimm, *Deutsche Mythologie* (1844), p. 813. See, above all, J. Bolte and J. Polivka, *Anmerkungen zu den Kindern-Hausmärchen der Brüder Grimm* (1913–18), p. 388, tale 44, and W. Liungman (1961), pp. 74–5.

7. See the Bibliography, under this name.

8. H. von Trimberg, *Der Renner* (1909), vol. III, pp. 276–80, verses 23665 to 23785. See also W. Liungman (1961), pp. 73–5; J. Bolte, 'Das Märchen vom Gevatter Tod', *Zeitschrift des Vereins für Volkskunde* (1894), p. 34; J. Bolte and J. Polivka (1913–18), p. 379, commentaries on Grimm's tale 44; L. Mackensen, *Handwörterbuch des deutschen Märchens* (1934–40), vol. II, p. 615.

9. Poem published by J. Bolte in *Zeitschrift für Deutsche Philologie*, XXXII (1900), p. 349, verse 85. See J. Bolte and J. Polivka (1913–18), p. 379, and L. Mackensen (1934–40), vol. II, p. 615.

10. H. Gering, *Islendzk Aeventyri . . .* (1882), pp. 204ff. (Icelandic text and German translation), and A. Wesselski, *Märchen des Mittelalters* (1925), pp. 211–13, commentary.

11. See the Bibliography, under *British Museum*.

12. Very short reference to this Anglo-Latin text in J. A. Herbert, *Catalogue of Romances in the Department of Manuscripts in the British Museum* (1910), vol. III, pp. 675–6. The text itself is in manuscript (not yet published) in the British Museum, Royal Manuscript 8F, VI, fol. 1 v° (about 1450).

13. British Museum manuscript; *Biblisches Bilderbanquet*; and the statue of

Death as a godfather in the church of Landivisiau, according to A. Le Braz, *La Légende de la Mort chez les Bretons armoricains* (1902), vol. I, p. xxxiii. See also A. Strobl (1691), and the edifying play by J. Ayrer (before 1605).

14. M. Barral (1971), pp. 32–3; P. Prion, manuscript of the *Chronologiette* (1744–59), f° 174, v° 178, 202.

15. G. Forteguerri, *Novelle edite ed inedite* (1550), published in 1882, p. 14.

16. P. Delarue and M.-L. Tenèze, *Le Conte populaire français* (1957–76), under tale types A T 330 and 332. G. Bollème, *La Bibliothèque bleue* (1971), pp. 208ff., and E. Clews Parsons, *Folklore from the Cape Verde Islands* (1923), pp. 183ff. (A T 330 and A T 332 mixed, in the folklore of Portuguese origin of the Cape Verde Islands).

17. On its role in the myth of Sisyphus, see P. Delarue and M.-L. Tenèze (1957–76), concerning tale type 330, in relation to *Bonhomme Misère*.

18. J. Bolte and J. Polivka (1913–18), p. 379; H. Sachs's complete text in J. Bolte (1894), p. 37; H. Sachs, *Sämtliche Fabeln und Schwänke* (1893 and 1903), vol. I, pp. 290ff., and vol. IV, pp. 315ff.

19. J. Ayrer, *Ein Fassnachtspiel, der Baur mit seinem Gefatter Todt*, in *Dramen* (1865), vol. IV, pp. 2467ff. The poem by H. Wolff ('Der Gevatter Tod', February 1644), which is reproduced in J. Bolte (1894), p. 39, adds nothing original to Ayrer's play, on which Wolff's poem is based and of which it is a summary.

20. On this subject, see J. Praetorius, *Das Patengold machet reich*, in J. Bolte (1894), p. 38.

21. See Chapter XI.

22. H. M. Moscherosch, *Geschichte Philanders von Sittewald* (1643), p. 671, consulted by me in L. A. von Arnim, *Sämtliche Werke* (1842), vol. XI, pp. 165–6, and in the edition of F. Bobertag (1964), p. 306. The invention of the turned bed is to be found, for the first time in writing, in the *Biblisches Bilderbanquet* about 1691 (text reproduced in A. Birlinger, *Nimm mich mit* [1871], p. 271, and in the highly important book devoted to the tales used by preachers in the baroque period by E. Moser-Rath, *Predigtmärlein der Barockzeit* [1964], pp. 273, 470 – Moser-Rath reproduces Father Andreas Strobl's teaching version of the 1690s).

23. M. Vovelle, *Piété baroque et Déchristianisation en Provence au XVIIIe siècle* (1973).

24. Grimm, tale 44: *Der Gevatter Tod*.

25. Grimm, tale 42: *Der Herr Gevatter*.

26. See the version in F. Arnaudin, *Contes populaires de la Grande-Lande* (1977). The large number of surviving versions of A T 332, collected after 1876 in Provence, and above all in Languedoc, Ariège, Roussillon, Catalonia, and in Occitania in general, more numerous than in the rest of France (Brittany apart), certainly shows that in terms of antiquity, from the 1740s onwards, the Languedoc and the lower Rhône were the strongholds for the multiform circulation of the tale *Godfather Death*, which occasioned and considerably facilitated Fabre's work. It is true that the folklore of northern France, because it is totally French-speaking, was more eroded by the cultural modernization of the nineteenth and twentieth centuries than was that of the Occitan and Breton regions.

27. A plausible hypothesis would be that Fabre used a pre-existing popular and oral version of A T 332 which had taken root in the village of Nages-et-Solorgues: a sort of *Jean-de-Solorgues* or *Jean-l'ont-pris de Solorgues*, and similar in principle to the *Jean de Carnas* (another local version of A T 332), which Dezeuze was to collect not far from there, much later, about 1920 to 1940. Carnas is indeed geographically quite close to Solorgues (F. Dezeuze, *Contes d'un pêcheur de lune* [1953]).

28. R. Laufer, *Lesage* (1971), pp. 113, 200, 227; M.-L. Dufrénoy, *L'Orient romanesque en France (1704–1789)* (1946–7), vols. I and II, p. 135 and index; J.-E. Gueullette (descendant and biographer of the writer), *Thomas-Simon Gueullette* (1938); and, of course, T.-S. Gueullette, *Les Mille et Un Quarts d'heure* (1712).

29. See J.-E. Gueullette (1938), the opening chapter on the origins of the writer Gueullette.

30. P. Bédat de Monlaur, *Le Meunier gascon* (1936); F. Dezeuze (1953); *Lemouzi* (1911); L. Dardy, *Anthologie populaire de l'Albret* (1891); F. Cadic, *La Paroisse bretonne de Paris* (1908); E. Caseponce, *Contes Vallespirenchs replegats per En Mir y Nontoquis* (1907), as published in D. Blanc, *Récits et Contes populaires de Catalogne* (1979), p. 70.

31. See the Bibliography, under *Quebec*.

32. Maranda file, item 51 (1966).

33. F. Arnaudin (1977), p. 580.

34. I would like to thank Donatien Laurent, the eminent Breton folklore specialist, who provided me with this valuable version.

35. The journey of the physician–hero from Languedoc to Paris (*JDT*) or from Solorgues to Langlade [*JLP*, 62] is a journey towards victory on the part of the hero, who is to treat and cure the powerful man. Conversely, and

logically, the return of the hero J L P from Langlade to Solorgues is temporarily seen as a disaster [80].

36. T. Vernaleken, *Œsterreiche Kinder- und Hausmärchen* (1864), pp. 234ff.

37. A. Millien and P. Delarue mss., version B (AT 332).

38. In C. Joisten, *Contes populaires de l'Ariège* (1965) (the version of AT 332 from Ariège), the hero is called Just, like Death.

39. C. Lévi-Strauss, in R. Bellour and C. Clément, *Claude Lévi-Strauss* (1979), p. 164.

40. *JLP* [2].

41. I am freely paraphrasing here Nicole Belmont's text, from her article 'Contes populaires et mythes', in *Dictionnaire des mythologies* (1980).

Chapter XV

1. On this author, see the interesting work by D. Blanc, *Récits et Contes populaires de Catalogne* (1979), p. 183.

2. E. Caseponce, *Contes Vallespirenchs replegats per En Mir y Nontoquis* (1907), pp. 38–65.

3. The word 'creature(s)' is used twice by the story-teller, once about the child that is about to be baptized, and again about his brothers and sisters, born before him (E. Caseponce [1907], pp. 47, 53).

4. The coal-merchant (E. Caseponce, in D. Blanc [1979], pp. 78, 82) certainly sold his wife's unfashionable earrings, which he had given her as part of the *fardas* or *joyas* (jewellery and clothes that a future husband usually gives his future wife on the eve of the wedding). See D. Labernia y Esteller, *Diccionari de la llengua catalana* (n.d.), under *enjoyar* and *joyas*.

5. The taking of the pulse is seldom noted among the activities of the physician–hero of AT 332 at the bedside of his 'patients'. Previous to this Roussillonais version, I have met it only in A. Strobl's version of German origin (1691), which, in fact, marks a very important stage in the final form assumed by the classic schema of AT 332; Strobl's version inserts for the first time in phase 3 (*Death tricked*) of the tale the motif of 'turning the bed round'; it therefore represents an essential stage reached by the tales on their collection.

6. The term *cric crac* at the end of the tales is often used in Roussillon and in Narbonnais. Further east, among the story-tellers of the Vaunage and Camargue, it becomes *per trîqua ou pér trâqua*. These two words are still

employed in eastern Languedoc, according to Philippe Gardy; they were already to be found in *JLP* ['by hook or by crook', 73]. This is yet another way of saying that *JLP* is also a fairy-tale.

7. The same word, *convidats* or *couvidats* ['guests'], is used in Occitan, and in *Galdric* in Catalan (p. 48), in reference to the guests at Truquette's wedding.

8. See F. Mistral, *Lou Trésor dou Felibrige* (1932), under the word *quartau(d)*.

9. On the meaning of the words *neule* or *neula*, *parell*, and *cosse* or *cossa*, see, under these words, D. Labernia y Esteller (n.d.); L. Alibert, *Dictionnaire occitan–français* (1966); and, above all, F. Mistral (1932).

10. In *JLP*, Margot is a simple (lethal) double of her mother Death. Rosetot is clearly more independent (of Death); however, she too chose a certain allegiance to Death: she 'trusts in the power that Death must have' (E. Caseponce [1907], p. 52) and acts accordingly.

11. By comparing *JLP* and *Galdric*, one may follow the respective progression of the comparison concerning the 'spadeful' and 'rain': the hero of AT 332 was first poor and did not have a 'single' spadeful of earth of his own (*JLP*). Then, having become rich, he earns money by the 'spadeful' (*Galdric*). When he was poor, he had to be content with 'eating turnips as though it rained them' [*JLP*, second version, 17]; when he becomes rich, 'money poured in', like rain [*JLP*, 35].

12. There are many references in *Galdric* (1907), pp. 51, 53, 57; similarly, see *JLP* [30 and 77].

13. When JLP has been showered with Death's gifts (see Chapter XII), he can at last permit himself, for the first time in his life, to wear a hat, the sign of his new, semi-medical or simply semi-bourgeois respectability [45]. Similarly, Truquette, when he too has been showered with Death's gifts, bought himself a wig [35]. One will notice the complete parallel with *Galdric* and with many other versions, southern and other, of AT 332 (see P. Bédat de Monlaur, *Le Meunier gascon* [1936] and *Les Contes du lézard, contes du pays de Gascogne* [1943]). The sudden, miraculous enrichment of the hero is often symbolized by the buying of luxurious headgear.

14. Compare this introduction to the speech by the Roussillonnais Death with the introduction to grandmother Death's educational speech to her son-in-law *compère*, Truquette [*JLP*, 28–29ff.]. After a *Bé! Bé!* (*Bien! Bien!*, *Galdric*, p. 49), which corresponds exactly to the words of grandmother Death concerning the desirable well-being [*Ben*] of the family [*JLP*, 28], the Roussillonnais Death begins his chat: 'I know', he says to Galdric, '*that you have always been a good strong* [*vaillant*] *man*' (p. 49). Grandmother Death

opens her speech to Truquette in a similar vein [30]: 'You're a big, strong, sharp-witted fellow ...' But these two homologous introductions are to be followed by two different opinions in the two tales, and these correspond respectively to the two possible branches of the alternative previously expounded by the Roussillonnais Death: swindling *à la* Truquette or medicine *à la* Galdric – even *à la* Jean-l'ont-pris, who himself, in the second part of the tale, becomes in effect 'paramedical'. Compare also another Catalan version of AT 332, that of F. Maspons, *Contes populars catalans* (1952), p. 117, in which Death also says to the hero: 'You are a good, brave [*vaillant*] man ... I shall make you rich.'

Chapter XVI

1. On Death's castle (in which Death resides when he is not travelling, according to the end of Wolf's tale), see the end of Chapter XIII (for the southern equivalent of Death's castle, including *JLP*).

2. J. W. Wolf, *Deutsche Hausmärchen* (1851), pp. 365–8.

3. It will be noticed, as far as this version of Wolf's is concerned, that there is a precise comparison with the *JLP/JDT* cycle, that this reward for curing the king's daughter, at the same strategic point in the tale, is homologous with that received in *Jean-de-trop* (p. 191) for curing the king's daughter: 'A cartful of money' (*JDT*); 'a horse laden with as much gold as it could carry' (J. W. Wolf [1851]).

4. The whistle or the act of whistling plays a role in the strategy (in love, in society or in life) of the two heroes, father and son, in Fabre's novella (see Chapter XI); this role is under the control of the forces of death or operates against them. The fart, whether real [11] or metaphoric [43], forms part of this strategy in a secondary way.

5. P. Bédat de Monlaur, *Le Meunier gascon* (1936), p. 59; F. Arnaudin, *Contes populaires de la Grande-Lande* (1977), p. 578; and H. Pourrat, *Trésor des contes au village* (1979), pp. 243–4.

Conclusion

1. J. Rouquette, *La Littérature d'oc* (1968), p. 74; '*Jean-l'ont-pris* ... tableau véridique des mœurs villageoises'.

2. See the Bibliography, under Prion, Pierre.

3. See my *Paysans de Languedoc* (1968), vol. II, p. 918.

4. On this village onomastics, or rather this absence of true onomastics, see (in the Bibliography) the numbers of the village archives that I have consulted.

5. See the Bibliography, under Foster, George M.

6. This belief in *limited good* (the impossibility of getting rich without stealing from one's neighbour or 'finding treasure' outside the economic ensembles in question) is also present, on a broader scale, at the level of the European states of the *ancien régime*. It is to be found, for example, in the thinking of Colbert. 'That minister believed,' wrote Ernest Lavisse (*Histoire de France* [1911] vol. VII–1, p. 170), that there is *'only the same quantity of money circulating throughout Europe, augmented from time to time by money coming from the West Indies'* (Peru and Mexico); he believed that the quantity of trade is constant and cannot be increased *'as long as the peoples are always equal in number in all states and consumption is similarly always equal'*. An increase may come about only through the discovery of new trade, *'but it is not permissible to reason on something so improbable'*. Therefore, *'the number of 20,000 vessels (15,500 Dutch, 4,000 English, 500 French) with which the entire trade of Europe is conducted cannot be increased'*. This is, said Colbert, unquestionable. Thus, *'one can increase the money* [circulating in the kingdom] *only if at the same time one takes the same quantity from neighbouring states . . . English and French can increase their trade and the number of their vessels only at the expense of the total of 20,000 vessels, and consequently from the 15,000 or 16,000 Dutch . . . Trade is a war of money against all the states of Europe.'*

7. According to M. Traussig, professor of anthropology at the University of Michigan, the tradition according to which one takes the devil as godfather of a child (and as one's own *compère*–protector) still survives among the common people of certain Andean countries in South America.

8. M. Vovelle, *Piété baroque et Déchristianisation en Provence au XVIIIᵉ siècle* (1973).

9. In this case the term 'infraculture' is in no way pejorative, any more than that of 'infrastructure'. What is meant by this word, in the cultural sphere, is simply the culture existing at the provincial, even plebeian level, in contrast with the higher level, that of the 'Enlightenment', which dominates the entire landscape. A subterranean ethnography of the eighteenth century seems, from this point of view, perfectly conceivable, despite the contrary opinion of K. Pomian (see his highly interesting text in *Le Débat*, No. 3 [July–August 1980], 117).

Bibliography

The following list comprises (among others) all the works of Occitan literature of the period 1570 to 1790 that are relevant to my purposes, and all the versions of AT 332/*Godfather Death* published (or occasionally in manuscript), with the single exception of those that are accessible only in the Slav, Baltic or Scandinavian languages. This list contains, with many other titles, references to 65 Occitan or southern French works of the seventeenth and eighteenth centuries, to be found in 49 collections, as well as references to 168 versions of *Godfather Death*.

Aarne, A., and Thompson, S. 'The Types of the Folktale', *Folklore Fellows Communications*, XXV, No. 74 (1928), 59. Tale 332: *Godfather Death*. See also the new edition of this crucially important work (*Folklore Fellows Communications*, No. 184 [1961], 123–4), considerably extended, under tale 332.

Aigrefeuille, Charles d'. *Histoire de Montpellier*. Montpellier, 1875.

Albania: the *Essays* by Gustav Meyer (see under this name) contain on p. 246 an interesting Albanian version of AT 332, which is very close to the Italian one used by the dramatist Ricci, about 1835 (see under this name).

Alibert, Louis. *Dictionnaire occitan–français*. Toulouse, 1966.

Almanac patoues de l'Ariejo (*Almanach de l'Ariège*) 1895, pp. 55–7. *La Morte e le Medeci*.

Amades, Joan. *Folklore de Catalunya, Rondallistica; Rondalles*. Vol. I: *Rondalles meravelloses*. Barcelona, 1950, pp. 243, 492, 493, 494. Tales 99, 202, 203, 204.

Ambard, Robert. *La Comédie en Provence au XVIIIᵉ siècle*. Aix-en-Provence, 1957.

L'Amoureux et sa fille. Lost play, performed at Toulon in 1495 (Arch. dep. du Var, E 645, f° 25, reg. du notaire Honoré Paves), according to Vieu, E., and Petit, J.-M., 1973, p. 19 (perhaps one of the oldest examples of our Occitan 'love square').

Andersen, Hans. *The Little Match Girl*.

Andrade, Manuel J. *Folklore de la República dominicana*. Ciudad Trujillo, 1948, pp. 370–71. AT 332: *La Comadre Muerte*, etc. As in *JDT* and *Hans-with-the-Goitre*, the king offers half his kingdom to the hero if he cures his daughter.

Âne de Pafoi, L', see Barbizier.

Archivio per lo studio delle Tradizioni populari, XXIII (1906–7), 212–14. AT 332, from Sicily: *La Morti*.

Armengaud, André, and Lafont, Robert. *Histoire d'Occitanie*. Paris, 1979. In particular, Chs. IV and V, pp. 412–636.

Arnaud, Marie-Hélène. 'Las fonccions dramaticas dins las pastorales et tragi-comédias de Béziers'. *Obradors*, Centre d'études occitanes, Univ. de Montpellier III, No. 5 (1971), 34–74.

———. *Les Techniques de l'écriture dramatique dans le théâtre de Béziers*. Diss. Montpellier, 1971. (I arrived at the conclusions contained in the first part of my book independently of the fine work by Marie-Hélène Arnaud, whom I did not know at the time, but who preceded me in this field by several years.)

Arnaudin, Félix. *Contes populaires de la Grande-Lande*. New ed. Sabres, 1977. Tales 100 and 101: two versions of AT 332 from the Landes, collected respectively in 1878 and 1903 (Gascon text and French translation).

Arnim, Ludwig Achim von, see Moscherosch, Hanss Michael.

Audibert. *Le Fortuné Marseillais*. Performed at Marseille in 1735, published in 'Amsterdam' in 1736 and in Marseille in 1775.

Aulbe, le comte d', see Bonet du Lac, Claude.

Aulnoy, Madame d'. *Les Contes de fées*. Paris, 1710 (BN Y2–8796), pp. 110–47. *Finette-Cendron* (and numerous later editions). On this tale, see also Aarne, A., and Thompson, S., 1961, tale 510, and Delarue, Paul, and Tenèze, Marie-Louise, vol. II, tale 510.

Aurbacher, Ludwig. *Ein Volksbüchlein*. 3rd ed. Leipzig, 1879, pp. 119–21. Tale 51: *Gevatter Tod*.

Ayrer, Jacob (*c*.1543–1605). *Dramen*. Published by A. von Keller, from the edition of 1618, Stuttgart, 1865. Vol. IV, pp. 2467–89. Play 36: *Ein Fassnachtspiel, der Baur mit seinem Gefatter Todt*.

Bakhtine, Mikhaïl. *L'Œuvre de François Rabelais* . . . Paris, 1970. See, in particular, p. 101 (on parody, *à la* Fabre; compare also the Matamore, mentioned in this book, with Féau's Captain Fricasse, 1665).

Barbizier. *Almanach populaire comtois*. 1949, pp. 265–6. Tale 3: *L'âne de Pafoi* (a Comtois version of *Jean-le-sot*), in 'Douze contes recueillis à Lantenne-Vertière, by Validan'.

Barral, Marcel, see Fabre, Jean-Baptiste Castor, *Lettres* . . .

——. *Jean-Baptiste Favre* [Fabre], *sa vie, son œuvre* . . . Montpellier, 1971. Of crucial importance.

Baughmann, E. W. *Types and Motif Index of the Folktales of England and North America*. Indiana University Folklore Series, No. 20. The Hague, 1966, p. 9. North American references, minus Quebec, of tale A T 332.

Beauquier, Charles. *Blason populaire de la Franche-Comté* . . . pp. 133–40. A Comtois version of *Jean-le-sot*.

Bechstein, N. L. *Deutsches Märchenbuch*. Leipzig, 1846, pp. 90–93 (1889, pp. 64–71). *Gevatter Tod*.

Bédat de Monlaur, P. *Le Meunier gascon*. Paris, 1936, pp. 35–44. *Le bûcheron médecin*. The same 'Gascon' version of A T 332 is to be found in the same author's *Les Contes du lézard, contes du pays de Gascogne*. Paris, 1943, pp. 57–68.

Bellour, Raymond. *Le Livre des autres, entretiens*. Paris, 1978. In particular, p. 216 (with R. Barthes) and pp. 403–6, interview with C. Lévi-Strauss.

——, and Clément, Catherine, eds. *Claude Lévi-Strauss*. Paris, 1979.

Belmont, Nicole. 'Contes populaires et mythes'. In *Dictionnaire des mythologies*. Paris, 1980.

Bennett, Michael J. 'Spiritual Kinship . . . in Traditional Society'. *Social History Society Newsletter*, IV, No. 1 (Spring 1979), 2–3. On the importance of godfatherhood in the medieval and late medieval period.

Benoet du Lac, see Bonet du Lac, Claude.

Bernoni, Domenico G. *Tradizioni popolari Veneziani*. Venice, 1875. Vol. I, p. 6. A T 332: *El giusto*. See also Crane, Thomas Frederick.

Beuve, Louis. *Œuvres choisies*. Saint-Lô, 1950, pp. 61ff. *Jean-le-sot* or *Jean Bart* [*sic*] from Normandy.

Béziers . . ., see *Théâtre populaire de Béziers*.

Biblisches Bilderbanquet (1691), version of A T 332, reproduced by Birlinger, A. *Nimm mich mit*. 1871, p. 271; and by Moser-Rath, Elfriede, 1964 (see under this name), which also gives, through Andreas Strobl, the same version of A T 332.

Biraben, Jean-Noël. *Les Hommes et la Peste*. Paris, 1976.

Birlinger, Anton. *Aus Schwaben, Sagen, Legenden* . . . Vol. II: *Sitten* . . . 1874, pp. 372–3, paragraph 27. A T 332: *Der Gevattersman*. Placebo of water; bed mounted on casters to trick Death. See also Birlinger above, reference to *Biblisches Bilderbanquet*.

Bladé, Jean-François. *Contes populaires de la Gascogne*. Paris, 1886. Vol. III, pp. 123–9. *Jean-lou-pec*, or 'Jean the Fool'.

Blanc, Dominique, see Caseponce, Estève.

Blanc-Gilli, Mathieu. *La Bienfaisance de Louis XVI vo leis festos de la Pax* . . . Marseille, 1783.

Bloch, M. *Les Caractères originaux de l'histoire rurale française*. Paris, 1952. Bloch, Maurice. 'Marriage Among Equals . . .' *Man*, XIII, pp. 21–33. Anthropology of homogamy.

Boccaccio. *The Decameron*. Fifth tale of the fourth day: *The Pot of Basil*.

Boggs, Ralph S. 'Index of Spanish Folktales'. *Folklore Fellows Communications*, No. 90 (1930), 50–51. References to the Spanish A T 332.

Bollème, Geneviève. *La Bibliothèque bleue*. Paris, 1971. About *Bonhomme Misère*, in the eighteenth century.

Bolte, Johannes. 'Das Märchen vom Gevatter Tod'. *Zeitschrift des Vereins für Volkskunde*, 4th year (1894), 34–41. Important.

———. 'Bemerkung zu Gonzenbach'. *Zeitschrift des Vereins für Volkskunde*, 6th year (1896), 67–8. Under paragraph 19: bibliography on the tale *Gevatter Tod*, about the Sicilian tales, collected by Laura Gonzenbach.

———. 'Zu den Schwankstoffen in Meisterliede'. *Zeitschrift für Vergleichende Litteraturgeschichte*, XI (1897), 66. Bibliography on *Gevatter Tod*.

———. *Historia von Sancto* (*History of Sanctus*, sixteenth century). *Zeitschrift für Deutsche Philologie*, XXXII (1900), 349–71. See p. 349, verse 85.

———. *Handwörterbuch des Deutschen Märchens*. Berlin, 1930. Vol. I, p. 332. Right-hand column (on A T 332 in Hungary).

———, and Polivka, Jiřj. *Anmerkungen zu den Kindern-Hausmärchen der Brüder Grimm*. 3 vols. Leipzig, 1913–18. The commentary concerning the tale *Godfather Death* (A T 332 or Grimm 44) is to be found, in addition to a valuable French version (p. 383), in vol. I, pp. 377–88; see also vol. II, pp. 414ff.: *The Spirit in the Bottle*.

Bonet du Lac, Claude. *La Tasse* (sixteenth-century play). In *Recueil de pièces rares et facétieuses anciennes et modernes*. Paris, 1873. Vol. III (Bibliothèque nationale, anonymes, Res., ZP 1744 [3]).

Bonnet-Bonneville, B. *Ce que espavarian pas, ou Jean-Pierre vengu de Brest; Jean-Pierre venu de Mahon ou le train du Pharo*. Marseille, 1781 and 1782. These plays may be consulted in the municipal libraries of Aix and Marseille.

———. *Les Vœux satisfaits ou lou Roumavagi*, Aix, 1788.

Boratav, Pertev N., see Eberhard, Wolfram, and Boratav, Pertev N.

Bossy, John. 'Padrini e Madrine'. *Quaderni storici*, May–August 1979.

Bouvier, Jean-Claude. *Les Parlers provençaux de la Drôme*. Paris, 1976. On the geographical continuity between Occitan and Franco-Provençal.

Brémond, Claude. 'Les bons récompensés et les méchants punis'. In Chabrol, Claude. *Sémiotique narrative et textuelle*. Paris, 1973.

Brenner, C. D. *A Bibliographical List of Plays in the French Language (1700–1789)*. Berkeley, 1967. List of 11,662 titles.

Briggs, K. M. *A Dictionary of British Folktales*. Bloomington, 1970. Part A, vol. I, p. 39. No AT 332/*Godfather Death* in the collection of folktales from Great Britain; a very different situation from that in Ireland.

British Museum, British Library, Royal Manuscript 8f, VI, fol. v°C (about 1450). Anglo-Latin manuscript of AT 332 in a collection of sermons (unpublished).

Brueis or Brueys, Claude (1570–c. 1640). *Jardin deys musos provensalos*. Aix, 1628. Rpt. Marseille, 1843. Contains nine works, most of them plays. Not to be confused with the *Jardin des muses provençales*, published in 1665 (see *Jardin deys musos provençalos*).

Bulletin de la Société archéologique, scientifique et littéraire de Béziers . . ., see *Théâtre populaire de Béziers*.

Bünker, R. H. *Schwänke, Sagen, und Märchen in heanzischer Mundart*. Leipzig, 1906, pp. 146–9. Tale 63: *Tat als G'vatta*. Hanseatic version of AT 332, dialectal and classical. The 'doctor' hero is promised 20,000 florins to cure a countess (cure obtained by turning the bed around).

Busk, R. H. *Patrañas or Spanish Stories*. London, 1870. See, especially, p. 123.

Caballero, Fernan. *Cuentos populares andaluces colleccionados . . .* Leipzig, 1861, pp. 83–8. *Juan Holgado y la Muerte*.

Cabannes, Jean de (1653–1717). *Liseto amouroso, Marra . . ., lou Jugi avare, le Paysan astrologue*. Manuscript plays preserved in the Bibliothèque nationale (ms français ancien suppl. français, 12508), and at the Bibliothèque Méjane d'Aix (ms 162 [624-R. 256], 4 plays), 'Leis pouesios provençalos de Moussu de Cabano gentillomé de la villa d'Aix'.

Cabrol, F., and Leclerc, H. 'Parrain et marrain'. In *Dictionnaire d'archéologie chrétienne et de liturgie*. Paris, 1938. Vol. XIII.

Cadic, l'abbé F. *Le filleul de l'Ankou* (Breton tale collected from a master tailor at Mebrand, and from an inhabitant of Plumélian). *La Paroisse bretonne de Paris.* September 1908, pp. 8–10 (photocopy kindly lent by Donatien Laurent).

Calhol, Jacques. *Moussu Jus.* Marseille, performed in 1784; published notably in Marseille, 1804.

——. *Le Marché de Marseille vo lei doues Coumaires.* Marseille, 1785; Avignon, Year VII.

Campbell, Marie. *Tales from the Cloud Walking Country.* Bloomington, 1958, pp. 185–6. *The doctor . . . with Death,* Irish tale from Kentucky. Classic AT 332, in which Godfather Death merges at the end with the devil.

Camproux, Charles. *Histoire de la littérature occitane.* Paris, 1971. See, especially, pp. 113–28, 154, for Camproux's important commentary on the *unity* of the Occitan theatre from the sixteenth to the eighteenth century, and its perpetuation of the conventions of Latin comedy.

Capiote or *pastorale limousine* (I have used the Bordeaux edition of 1684).

Les Caquets de l'accouchée. Paris, 1855.

Carrière, Charles. *Négociants marseillais au XVIIIe siècle.* 2 vols. Marseille, 1973.

Caseponce, l'abbé Estève. *Contes Vallespirenchs replegats per En Mir y Nontoquis.* Perpignan, 1907, pp. 38–65. *El Metge Carboner* (*Galdric,* the coal-merchant–physician). Very important. A valuable, but incomplete, edition of this tale is also to be found in Blanc, Dominique. *Récits et Contes populaires de Catalogne.* Paris, 1979, pp. 70ff.

Cassanea de Mondonville, see Mondonville, J.-J. Cassanea de.

Castan, Yves. *Honnêteté et Relations sociales en Languedoc.* Paris, 1974.

Cerquand, M. *Légendes et Récits du Pays basque.* Paris, 1875. Vol. II, p. 10. A Basque version of *Jean-le-sot.*

Chartier, Roger. 'Les arts de mourir, 1450–1600'. *Annales* (January 1976), 51–76 (a special number of the journal *Annales* on 'Death').

Chaunu, Pierre. *La Mort à Paris.* Paris, 1978. On Death in the classical period.

Chauvin, Victor. *Bibliographie des ouvrages arabes . . .* Vol. VI (on *The Thousand and One Nights*). Liège, 1902, pp. 24–5. Tale 195: *Le génie et le pêcheur* (about *The Spirit in the Bottle*).

Chocheyras, Jacques. *Théâtre religieux en Savoie et en Dauphiné.* Geneva, 1971 and 1975. On the origins of the theatre of the Midi.

Christiansen, Reidar T. *Danske Studies*, II (1915). On AT 332, in Danish; important bibliography for AT 332.

———. 'The Norwegian Fairy-tales'. *Folklore Fellows Communications*, No. 46 (1922), 10. For the tale AT 332: *Death and the Doctor*.

———. *Studies in Irish and Scandinavian Folktales*. Copenhagen, 1959, Ch. V, pp. 207–11. On AT 332 in Ireland and in Scandinavia: comparative study.

Chronologiette . . ., see Prion, Pierre.

Clark, M., Kemper, R. W. and Nelson, C. 'The Image of Limited Good'. *Essays in Honor of George Foster*. The Kroeber Anthropological Society Papers, Nos. 55 and 56. Berkeley, 1979.

Clément, Catherine, see Bellour, Raymond, and Clément, Catherine.

Clet, Antoine (eighteenth-century playwright from Velay). *Monsieur Lambert*. Le Puy-en-Velay, 1757.

Clews Parsons, Elsie. *Folklore from the Cape Verde Islands*. Part I, pp. 182–6 (*Compadre Death*). Memoirs of the American Folklore Society, vol. XV. 1923. Part I.

Cock, A. de. 'De Dood als Doopvader'. *Volkskunde*, V (1892), 184–8. Classic version of the Flemish AT 332; Death gives the physician–hero treasure of gold and silver.

———. 'Compeere de Dood'. *Volkskunde*, VII (1894), 35–9.

Coelho, F. Adolpho. *Contos populares portugueses*. Lisbon, 1879, pp. 56–8. *Comadre Morte*.

Cointat, Michel. *Tresques en Languedoc*. Paris, 1979. Village monograph; see, in particular, pp. 209–11, on paternal and masculine omnipotence in Languedoc.

Collé, Charles. *Chansons nouvelles et gaillardes*. Oudot, 1753 (Bibliothèque nationale, Rés. Enfer 300). This booklet contains (pp. 11–12) the song 'Un soir revenait Cadet . . .' mentioned at the beginning of my Chapter XIII, and composed between 1750 and 1753 (according to François Girard, of Lyon).

Collomp, A. 'Maison . . ., famille, en Haute-Provence aux XVIIᵉ et XVIIIᵉ siècles'. *Ethnologie française*, VIII, No. 4 (1978), 301–20. See also an article by the same author on this subject in *Annales* (1977), p. 469.

Collot d'Herbois, J.-M. *Le Nouveau Nostradamus, ou les fêtes provençales*, Avignon, 1977.

Comédie de Seigne Peyre et Seigne Joan, 'jouée à Montélimar en 1576 par deux paysans'. Lyons, 1580 (Benoist Rigaud) and Paris, 1832 (Bibliothèque nationale, Rés. anon. ye 3255).

Corblet, l'abbé J. 'Parrains et marraines, étude liturgico-historique'. *Revue de l'art chrétien*, XIV (1881), 336–51, and XV, 26ff. About the antiquity, late medieval at least, of the institution of godfatherhood.

Cornelissen, P. J., and Vervliet, J. B. *Vlaamsche Volksvertelsels en Kindersprookjes*. Lierre, 1900, pp. 77–80. Tale 18: AT 332.

Cortète or Courtète, François de (*c.* 1586–1667). *La Miramoundo* and *Ramounet*. Plays published in the seventeenth century, and republished, in particular, in the *Recueil des travaux de la Société d'agriculture, sciences et arts d'Agen*, XVII, 2nd series (1915).

Cosquin, Emmanuel G. *Contes populaires de Lorraine*. Paris, n.d. Vol. II, pp. 234–40. Motif of the 'lights of life', but outside the context of AT 332.

Coulon, M., see Fabre, Jean-Baptiste Castor, *Istoria* . . .

Coye, J.-B. (1711–77). *Lou Novy parat*. 1743. Various editions, at 'Cracow' (?), 1743; Arles, 1829; etc.

Crane, Thomas Frederick, trans. *Italian Popular Tales*. By D. G. Bernoni. Boston and London, 1885.

Da Camara Casardo, Luis. *Contes traditionnels du Brésil*. Paris, 1978, p. 246. AT 332: *Le Camarade de la Mort*.

Dardy, l'abbé Léopold. *Anthologie populaire de l'Albret*. Vol. II: folk-tales. Agen, 1891, pp. 143–9. Tale 43: *La Mort et Bernard*.

Daumard, Adeline, and Furet, François. *Structures et Relations sociales à Paris au XVIIIᵉ siècle*. Paris, 1961. On social homogamy.

Dawkins, R. M. *Modern Greek Folktales*. Oxford, 1953, pp. 466–8. Tale 80: *A Just Man for a Godfather*. Classic version of AT 332. The role of Death is played by the archangel Michael, who carries off the souls of the dead (see the Breton Ankou). The physician–hero uses a placebo of sweetened water.

Delarue, Paul, and Tenèze, Marie-Louise. *Le Conte populaire français*. Paris, 1957–76. Notably in vol. I, *La Mort-parrain* (AT 332), and in vol. II, pp. 250ff., *Cendrillon* (AT 510 A).

Delbos, George. 'Faycelles-en-Quercy'. Diss. Toulouse, Faculté des lettres, 1969.

Deulin, Charlemagne. *Contes d'un buveur de bière*. Paris, 1893. Contains a literary version of Belgian origin of AT 332/*Godfather Death*.

Dezeuze, François. *Contes d'un pêcheur de lune*. Montpellier, 1953, pp. 69–72. *Jean de Carnas*. Version of AT 332, geographically very close to *JLP* and collected by a scholar from Montpellier (Carnas is a locality in the Sommières region).

Dictionnaire d'archéologie chrétienne . . ., see Cabrol, F., and Leclerc, H.

Dobie, J. F., see Frank Dobie, James.

Dottin, Georges. *Contes et Légendes d'Irlande, traduits du gaélique*. Le Havre, 1901, pp. 168–70. Tale 26: *Le Trépas et le médecin*. Classic version of AT 332, collected from a dialect-speaker in the county of Cork. Turning round of the bed by four men as in Gueullette (1712), and as in the Quebec version of AT 332.

Drouin, Simon. *Catalogue des documents occitans de la collection Rondel*. Béziers, 1978.

Duby, Georges. *Medieval Marriage*. Baltimore, 1978, p. 56 (on the male dowry and patrimony) and pp. 13–21 (on the ideals of the troubadours).

Duffard, l'abbé Paul. *L'Armagnac noir*. Angers et Auch, 1901 and 1902, p. 145 (on grandparents as godfather and godmother).

Dufrénoy, Marie-Louise. *L'Orient romanesque en France (1704–1789)*. 2 vols. Montreal, 1946–7. In particular, vol. II, p. 135, on Gueullette.

Dujardin, A. 'À la recherche d'un homme juste'. *Lemouzi*, 19th year (1911), 179–80. Limousin version of AT 332.

Durand, Georges. *Vin, vigne et vignerons en Lyonnais et Beaujolais (XVIᵉ–XVIIIᵉ siècle)*. Lyon, 1979. In particular on social homogamy; a fine graph, p. 353.

Dutil, Léon. *L'État économique du Languedoc à la fin de l'Ancien Régime*. Paris, 1911, pp. 593–4. On the craftsmen of Nages-et-Solorgues in the eighteenth century.

Duvernoy, J. *Le Registre d'inquisition de Jacques Fournier . . . 1318–1325*. 3 vols. Toulouse, 1965. In particular, a fine index of Occitan words.

Eberhard, Wolfram. 'Typen Chinesischer Volksmärchen'. *Folklore Fellows Communication*, No. 120 (1937). Absence, and for very good reason, of AT 332 in the repertoire of Chinese tales.

——, and Boratav, Pertev N. *Typen Türkischer Volksmärchen*. Wiesbaden, 1953, p. 133. Type 112 of the classification of Turkish tales (AT 332): *Vierzig Jahre Leben*, Islamicized, simplified, but recognizable version of AT 332, from Turkey via Orthodox Christianity.

Éliard, Aurore. 'La société paysanne et le Bien limité'. *Annales de l'université de Toulouse-le-Mirail*, IX, fasc. 3 (1973), 49–61. On the theory of George M. Foster, see under this name.

Espinosa, Aurelio M. *Cuentos populares de Castilla, recogidos de la tradición oral*. Buenos Aires–Mexico, n.d., p. 78. Tale 33: *El médico y la Muerte*. In this version, which is typical of *Godfather Death*, the cobbler–hero sells all the equipment in his shop to get food, as also do the cobbler Truquette and Caseponce's hero Galdric (1907).

Ettner, Johann Christoph von. *Dess getreuen Eckharts Unwürdiger Doctor* . . . Augsburg and Leipzig, 1697, p. 190. Old allusion to AT 332.

Fabre, abbé ('Fabre de Thémines', de Cahors). *Scatabronda* . . . 'Rotterdam', 1697. Fabre de Thémines is the imaginary name of an unknown author.

Fabre, Daniel. *Jean-le-sot*, unpublished version collected in Minervois (Hérault) in April 1968, and lent to the author in manuscript form.

——, and Fabre, Claudine, see Lambert, L.

——, and Lacroix, Jacques. *Vie quotidienne des pays de Languedoc au XIXe siècle*. Paris, 1973. See, in particular, p. 207, on the Candlemas candles.

Fabre, abbé Jean-Baptiste Castor. Works in Occitan: *L'Opéra d'Aubais, Le Trésor de Substancion, Le Siège de Caderousse* (see also the edition of 1876). Works in French: *Le Galimatias* and *Les Visites de Zima*, manuscript in the Montpellier municipal library (under 'Œuvres de Saint-Castor', [J.-B. C. Fabre]), etc.

——. *Istoria de Joan l'an près* [*Jean-l'ont-pris*]. Editions of J. Troubat (Paris, 1877), L. Roumieux (Montpellier, 1890), M. Coulon (Paris, 1929), Y. Rouquette (Libre Occitan, 1967), and P. Gardy (Paris, 1980).

——. *Lettres à son neveu, le chevalier de Saint-Castor*. Montpellier, 1960.

Féau, Charles, see *Jardin deys musos provençalos*.

Ferrand, Auguste. 'Le filleul de la Mort'. *Revue des traditions populaires* (1895), 594. Version from Dauphiné of AT 332: *Le filleul de la Mort*. Text reproduced by Charles Joisten, 1971 (see under this name).

Fescais de la Tour, Provençal playwright. Plays written about 1780 to 1783, unpublished and preserved in manuscript in the Bibliothèque Arbaud, Aix-en-Provence, MQ 152–155. In particular *Le Bon Père, Le Rival officieux, Le Loup-Garou, Le Faux Ami, Les Insulaire*, and *Le Rival généreux*. Fescais de La Tour is also, which is unusual in the literature of the Midi, the author of two tragedies, *Titus* and *Marseille sauvée* (about the tribulations of Marseille in the sixteenth century). These tragedies do not concern the subject of this book.

Fizes, Nicolas (1646–1716). *L'Opéra de Frontignan*. 1679. Montpellier, 1873.

Flandrin, J.-L. *Les Amours paysannes*. Paris, 1970.

Forteguerri, ser Giovanni. *Novelle edite ed inedite*. 1550. Bologna, 1882, pp. 14–41. *Novella prima*. This is the first known Italian version of AT 332.

Foster, George M. Articles on the theory of 'limited good' in *Journal of American Folklore*, LXXVII (1944), 39–44, and in *American Anthropologist*, LXVII, No. 2 (1965), 293–315. See also Éliard, A.; and Clark, M., Kemper, R. W. and Nelson, C.

Fox, Nikolaus. *Märchen und Tiergeschichten in den Landschaften der Westmark*... Saarlautern, 1943, pp. 98–9. AT 332: *Der Tod als Pate*.

Frank Dobie, James. *Puro Mexicano*. Austin, 1935, pp. 76–7. *La Madrina Muerte*.

——. *Tongues of the Monte*. Boston, 1935 and 1955, pp. 169–78. Hispano–American version, from Texas, of AT 332: *Death in the Forest*.

Furet, François, see Daumard, Adeline, and Furet, François.

Galdric, see Caseponce, Estève.

Garden, M. *Lyon au XVIIIe siècle, Les Belles Lettres*. Paris, 1970.

Gardy, Philippe. 'Benoet du Lac (Claude Bonet), comte d'Aulbe, aux dernières années du XVIe siècle'. In *Mélanges de philologie romane, langue et littérature occitanes, offerts à Charles Camproux*. Montpellier, 1978, pp. 509–30.

——. *Langue et Société en Provence au début du XIXe siècle: le théâtre de Carvin*. Paris, 1978. Text and important bibliography.

Garnett, Lucy M. J. *The Women of Turkey and their Folklore (The Christian Women)*. London, 1890, pp. 185–91. *The Just One*. Absolutely classic version of AT 332, from the Greek Christians of the Turkish empire. A dominant Death, looking down from above, at the sitting physician–hero.

Gerhardt, Irène. 'Essai d'analyse littéraire de la pastorale dans les littératures italienne, espagnole et française'. Diss. Leyden, 1950.

Gering, Hugo. *Islendzk Aeventyri, islandische Legenden, Novellen, und Märchen*. Halle, 1882. Vol. I, pp. 143–52, 204–11. Tale 78. Icelandic text and German translation of the first historically identified version – it is 'Icelandic', but influenced by the Latin culture of the clergy – of AT 332, in 1339. Important bibliography, pp. 149–52.

——. *Islendzk Aeventyri*. Halle, 1883. Vol. II, pp. 395–6. Very interesting

Lithuanian version (German translation) of A T 332. Death, who is dangerous *behind the door*, when he has gone through the keyhole, is shut up by a *farmboy* in a small *cask*. In order to get out, he must grant the boy the usual medical gifts of A T 332. He again tricks Death. As in *JLP*, *Death's gifts* comes after *Death tricked*; many other similarities in this narrative show that the sub-type (within the general type of A T 332) from which *JLP* and *JDT* emerged was itself widespread in *Catholic* culture throughout Europe (including Lithuania).

Gibert, Urbain. 'Lo filhol de la Mort'. Manuscript kindly lent to the author by Urbain Gibert, who collected this version of A T 332 in Aude from M. Denarnaud (aged fifty), of Montferrand (Corbières audoises) in 1925. This is the version (later translated by Gaston Maugard, see under this name) which I sometimes call 'Gibert and Maugard', or G M.

Girard, François. 'La Chanson française au XVIIIᵉ siècle'. Diss. Univ. de Paris IV, 1979.

Gonzenbach, Laura. *Sizilianische Märchen aus dem Volksmund gesammelt*. Leipzig, 1870. Part I, pp. 123–4. Tale 19: *Gevatter Tod*. Classic version of A T 332; like that from the Abruzzi (see 'Novelle populari abruzzesi'), it stresses Death's *descent* from God's heavenly home, at the beginning, to the underground cave of lights at the end.

Goody, Jack, and Tambiah, S. J., *Bridewealth and Dowry*. Cambridge, 1973. See, in particular, pp. 45ff.

Goubert, Jean-Pierre. 'Médicalisation de la société française à la fin de l'Ancien Régime'. *Annales de Bretagne*, LXXXVI, No. 3 (1979), 221–9. On the low social status of surgeons – important in *JLP* – in relation to physicians.

Goulemot, J.-M. 'Démons, merveilles . . . et philosophie à l'âge classique'. *Annales* (1980). On popular peasant culture.

Gramain, M.-T. 'Les Paysans de la région de Béziers au Moyen Age'. Diss. Univ. de Paris I, 1979.

Gravelle, M. de. *Le Tuteur jaloux*. Marseille–Avignon, 1759; *La Marseillaise*. Avignon, 1760. Examples in Marseille Municipal Library.

Greimas, A. *Sémantique structurale*. Paris, 1966, pp. 175–80.

——. 'Les actants, les acteurs, les figures'. In Chabrol, Claude. *Sémiotique narrative et textuelle*. Paris, 1973.

——, and Courtes, J. *Sémiotique, Dictionnaire* . . . Paris, 1979. See, in particular, p. 61.

Greville, Henri. 'L'homme qui cherchait un parrain juste'. *Revue des traditions populaires*, XIII (January 1898), 664–5. A T 332 from Anjou: the hero takes his staff and sets out in search of a just godfather; it follows the classic cycle of *Godfather Death*.

Grimm, Jacob. *Deutsche Mythologie*. Göttingen, 1844. Vol. II, Ch. XXVII (*Tod*), pp. 812–13 (lights of life).

———. See the valuable version of A T 332 which he collected in France, reproduced in Bolte, Johannes, and Polivka, Jiřj. *Anmerkungen . . .* under tale 44, p. 383.

———, and Grimm, Wilhelm. *Kinder- und Hausmärchen*. 1812. Tale 44: *Der Gevatter Tod* and, incidentally, tale 42: *Der Herr Gevatter* and tale 177: *Die Boten des Todes*. I have used, among others, the Zurich edition (1974), vol. I, pp. 195–8.

Gueriff, Fernand. *Contes populaires du pays de Guérande*. La Baule, pp. 88–91. *Le filleul de l'Ankou*.

Gueullette, J.-E. *Thomas-Simon Gueullette*. Paris, 1938.

Gueullette, Thomas-S. *Les Mille et Un Quarts d'heure*. 1712. I have used the Paris edition of 1753, vol. II, pp. 281–90. *Aventure d'Iskender . . .*: that is, two successive texts, including *A Woodcutter and Death*; particularly relevant is tale 73. On Gueullette, 'the indefatigable *pasticheur*', disguising European tales, in particular *Hans the Piper*, in oriental dress, see Delarue, Paul, and Tenèze, Marie-Louise, vol. I, pp. 25–6.

Guilaine, J. *Récits et Contes populaires du Languedoc*. Paris, 1978. Vol. II.

Guilcher, J.-M., see Serreau, J.-M. and G.

Guillaume, P. 'Les actes du mariage, source d'histoire sociale . . .' *Bull. du Centre d'histoire régionale*, No. 2 (1978), 16. On socio-occupational homogamy.

Hanauer, J. E. *Folklore of the Holy Land*. London, 1907, pp. 176–81. Tale 5: *The Angel of Death*. Islamicized (Palestinian) version, which remains nonetheless the classic A T 332 of Christian origin. The angel of Death is the hero's *father*, in the absence of godfatherhood in Islam.

Hansen, Terence Leslie. *The Types of the Folktale in Cuba, Puerto Rico, the Dominican Republic, and Spanish South America*. Univ. of California Folklore Studies, No. 8. Berkeley, 1957.

Hawkes, Terence. *Structuralism and Semiotics*. Berkeley, 1977. pp. 91–4. On the 'actants'.

Henry, J.-P. *Jean-Pierre . . .* [a child's memories, 1814–35]. Lausanne, 1978. See, in particular, p. 237, on the hierarchical society.

Henssen, Gottfried. *Der Volk erzählt, Münsterländische Sagen und Märchen.* Munster, 1935, pp. 151–2. Tale 127: *Der Dot als Päten.* Westphalian version of A T 332, dialectal and classic. The king, who is sick, promises the 'doctor'–hero half his kingdom if he cures him. The physician, in order to turn the king round in his bed, gets hold of him by his trousers.

Herbert, J. A. *Catalogue of Romances in the Department of Manuscripts in the British Museum.* London, 1910. Vol. III, pp. 675–6. Inventory of the Royal Manuscript 8f, VI, fol. I v° (A T 332, in Latin, *c.* 1450, see *British Museum*).

Hoogasian-Villa, Susie. *One Hundred Armenian Tales, and Their Folkloristic Relevance.* Detroit, 1966, pp. 323–7. Tale 45: *The Soul-Taking Angel.* Pages 437 and 515 contain an important bibliography. Classic version of A T 332, collected in the Armenian community in Detroit: Death represented by the angel Gabriel, the 'soul taker'.

Hungary: inventory of Hungarian fairy-tales, including A T 332; see *Folklore Fellows Communications*, XXV–XXVIII (1928–9).

Hyde, Douglas. *Legends of Saints and Sinners.* Dublin, n.d. [late nineteenth century], pp. 154–62. *Shaun the Tinker.* The end of this Irish tale corresponds to the schema of A T 332.

Ipolyi, Arnold von. 'Beitr. zur deutschen Mythologie a. Ungarn'. *Zeitschrift für deutsche Mythologie und Sittenkunde herausgegeben von J. W. Wolf.* Göttingen, 1853. Vol. I, pp. 262–4. Slavic version of A T 332 from the Hungarian territories of Austria-Hungary. Classic schema. At the end, Death breaks the hero's neck.

Jahn, Ulrich. *Volkssagen aus Pommern und Rügen.* 2nd ed. Berlin, 1889, pp. 33–6. Tale 43: *Der Tod . . .* and tale 46: *Lebenslicht . . .* Two versions of A T 332: hero a worker in wood; theme of *two* lights of life, etc.

———. *Volkssagen aus Pommern . . .* Completed ed. Leipzig, 1891, pp. 61–3. *Das Patenkind des Todes.* Classic Pomeranian version of A T 332: turning round of the bed by four servants as in Gueullette (1712) and in the Quebec versions (see my Chapter XIV); Death is first dangerous, then lethal, on two occasions explicitly *behind the door* (inside the hero's house, then in Death's own house).

Jahrbuch für roman. und englisch literatur, VII (1866), 19. On *Juan Holgado* (see Caballero, Fernan) and Grimm's tale 177: *Death's Messengers.*

Jammetto. Occitan play performed about 1750 at Carcassonne (mss. Bibliothèque nationale, papiers Grégoire, Nouv. acqu. françaises, 2798, f° 102, no. 33, 'collections patoises', file kindly lent by Henri Giordan).

Large fragments of this play were also preserved in Aude, by purely oral tradition, up to the twentieth century, which confirms the survival of oral Occitan culture from the time of the abbé Fabre to the Third Republic. Extracts from *Jammetto*, collected from oral tradition, were published in the *Revue des langues romanes*, XXXV (1891), 287–90, and in *Folklore* (Aude), nos. 7–8 (July–August 1939), 245–62.

Jardin deys musos provençalos. Collection of plays, 1665 (contains plays by Féau and Brueys).

Jasmin, Jacques. *Françounette*. In his *Papillottos*. Agen, 1842. Vol. II.

Jean de Carnas, see Dezeuze, François.

Jean (or 'Jehan') *de Paris*. Medieval tale, fine sixteenth-century edition in the Bibliothèque Méjanes, Aix-en-Provence; popular eighteenth-century editions in the Bibliothèque nationale (see the Bibliothèque nationale file under 'Anonymes').

Jean-de-trop, see Lambert, L.

Jean-le-sot, see Aarne, A., and Thompson, S., 1961, tale 1240 and Thompson, Stith, 1933, motif J–2311–1.

Jeanroy, A. *Histoire sommaire de la poésie occitane des origines à la fin du XVIIIᵉ siècle*. Toulouse, 1945. See p. 161, on the abbé Fabre.

Jegerlehner, J. *Sagen aus dem Unterwallis*. 1909, p. 191. Tale 42: *Search for a Just Man* (AT 332).

Joisten, Charles. *Contes folkloriques des Hautes-Alpes*. Folklore des Alpes, No. 2. Ed. Erasme. Paris, 1955. See, above all, pp. 17 and 40. *The Girl with the Pot of Basil* as representing Death.

——. *Contes populaires de l'Ariège*. Paris, 1965, pp. 61–3. Tale 5: *La Mort-parrain*, collected by Joisten in 1953 from Angèle Canal, farmer's wife, aged seventy.

——. *Contes populaires du Dauphiné*. Grenoble, 1971. Vol. I, p. 168. Tale 22: *La Mort-parrain, le filleul de la Mort*. See also vol. I, p. 87. *The Platinum Flower*.

Juan Holgado, see Caballero, Fernan.

Kemminghausen, see Schulte-Kemminghausen, Karl.

Kohler, Reinhold. *Kleinere Schriften zur Märchenforschung*. Weimar, 1898. Vol. I, pp. 291–2, para. 3. Interesting bibliographical and other information on the tale *Der Gevatter Tod*.

Krauss, Friedrich S. *Sagen und Märchen der Sudslaven*. Leipzig, 1884. Vol. II, pp. 119–20. Tale 67. Yugoslav AT 332. Death dominant (perched on the hero's shoulders); encountered in the *wildness* of a village of mad dogs; correct prediction of a death as a source of wealth for the hero.

Kühnau, Richard. *Schlesische Sagen*. Vol. II: *Elfen, Dämonen, und Teufel-Sagen*. Leipzig, 1911, pp. 524–30. Tales 1156 and 1162. Two classic versions of A T 332: woodcutter hero; Death who winks and rides in a carriage; the hero becomes a physician, gets rich and buys a fine house.

Labernia y Esteller, D. Pere. *Diccionari de la llengua catalana*. 2 vols. Barcelona, n.d.

Lacave, Michel. 'Typologie sociale des systèmes juridiques méridionaux'. In *Confluence des droits savants et des pratiques . . .* Colloque de Montpellier. Ed. Giuffre. Milan, 1977, pp. 71–90. Especially on paternal absolutism in the Midi.

Lacroix, Jacques. *Récits et Contes populaires du Languedoc*. Paris, 1978. Vol. I, especially p. 37.

Lafont, Robert. *Francès de Corteta*. Lo Libro occitan. Lavit (Tarn-et-Garonne), 1968. See also the unfortunate A. Armengaud.

——, and Anatole, Christian. *Nouvelle Histoire de la littérature occitane*. 2 vols. Paris, 1970. See particularly vol. II, pp. 474ff.

Lallement, l'abbé Louis. *Folklore argonnais. Almanach Matot-Braine*. Vol. LVI, p. 23. Reims, 1914.

Lamaison, P. 'Parenté, patrimoine et stratégie matrimoniales sur ordinateur; une paroisse du Haut-Gevauden [Ribennes] du XVIIᵉ au debut du XIXᵉ siècle'. Diss. Univ. de Paris V-Sorbonne, 1978.

Lambert, L. *Lou filhol de la Mort [Jean-de-trop]*, in Occitan and in French. *Revue des langues romanes*, XXVII (1885), 184–93. Very important. This text has been reproduced (in French only) in Fabre, Daniel and Fabre, Claudine. *Récits et Contes populaires du Languedoc*. Paris, 1978. Vol. III, pp. 31–7.

Lapierre-Chateauneuf, Agricol. *Le Faux-Seing ou l'adroite soubrette*. Marseille–Avignon, 1783.

Laport, G. Numbered index of the 'Contes populaires wallons'. *Folklore Fellows Communications*, C I (1932). No A T 332!

Larade, Bertrand. *La Margalide gasconne* (Collection of poems in Occitan). Toulouse, 1604. Rpt. Saint-Gaudens, 1932.

Laufer, Roger. *Lesage*. Paris, 1971, pp. 113, 200, 227. On the pseudo-oriental character of Gueullette's works.

Le Braz, Anatole. *La Légende de la Mort chez les Bretons armoricains*. Paris,

1902. Especially vol. I, p. xxxiii. Statue of a godfather Death at Landivisiau (Brittany).

Le Goff, Jacques, and Vidal-Naquet, P. 'Lévi-Strauss en Brocéliande', see Bellour, Raymond, and Clément, Catherine.

Lejeune, Rita. 'La femme dans la littérature . . . occitane, XIᵉ–XIIIᵉ siècles'. *Cahiers de civilisation médiévale*, XX (1977), 201–18. Possible comparison with the not very 'feminist' Occitania of the sixteenth and seventeenth centuries.

Lemouzi, 1911, see Dujardin, A.

Léonard, Émile-G., *Mon village sous Louis XV*. Paris, 1941.

Le Roux de Lincy, Antoine-Jean-Victor. *Le Livre des proverbes français*. Paris, 1842. Vol. I, no. 3, p. 65, quoting *Le Calendrier des bons laboureurs pour 1678* (see Le Roux, *ibid.*, bibliography, p. cxvii) on the Candlemas Bear.

Le Roy, Eugène. *Moulin du Frau*. Paris, 1979.

———. *Jacquou le Croquant*. Paris, 1900.

Le Roy Ladurie, Emmanuel. *Les Paysans de Languedoc*. Paris, 1966.
———. *Territoire de l'historien*. Paris, 1978.
———. *Carnival in Romans*. London, 1980 (New York, 1979).

Lévi-Strauss, C. *Structural Anthropology*. Trans. C. Jacobson and B. Grundfestschorpf. London, 1968.

———. *The Elementary Structures of Kinship*. Trans. J. H. Bell, J. R. Von Sturmer and R. Needham. London and Boston, 1969.

Lincoln, Bruce. 'Treatment of Hair . . .' *History of Religions*, XVI (May 1977), 351–9. On hair as a symbol of vitality.

Liungman, Waldemar. 'Das warscheinliche Alter des Volksmärchens in Schweden'. *Folklore Fellows Communications*, No. 156 (1955), 11 (AT 332) and 37–40 (in general).

———. *Die schwedischen Volksmärchen*. Berlin, 1961, pp. 73–5. AT 332: *Gevatter Tod*. Excellent historical account of the tale, in spite of a mistake concerning Gueullette (1712), who is presented as being authentically 'Tartar'.

Llano Roza de Ampudia, Aurelio de. *Cuentos asturianos recogidos de la tradición oral*. Madrid, 1925, pp. 69ff. Tale 20: *El médico y la Muerte* (AT 332).

Longeon, Claude. *Une province française à la Renaissance*. Saint-Étienne, 1975, pp. 187–218, 472–83. Intellectual life in Forez, sixteenth century.

Luzel, F.-M. *Légendes chrétiennes de la Basse-Bretagne*. Paris, 1881. Vol. I, pp. 335–57.

MacCurdy, Raymond R., Jr. 'Spanish Folklore from St Bernard, Louisiana'. *Southern Folklore Quarterly*, XVI, No. 4 (1952), 232–3. Tale 2: *El Cuento de la Muerte*. The physician on his deathbed; 'turning round' not of the bed, but of Death.

MacDougall, James. *Folktales and Fairy Lore*. Edinburgh, 1910, pp. 69–73. *Donald of the Burthens* is the Scottish version in Gaelic (with English translation) of A T 332. Classical schema of the tale: woodcutter who becomes a physician; the trick of the turned-round bed; followed by the tricks of the unfinished prayer and Death imprisoned in a bottle.

MacIntosh, David S. 'Blacksmith and Death'. *Midwest Folklore*, I (April 1951), 51–3. Irish tale collected in Illinois. Godfather Death and Death trapped in a bottle.

Mackensen, Lutz. *Handwörterbuch des deutschen Märchens*. Berlin, 1934–40. Vol. II, pp. 615–20.

Macler, Frédéric. *Contes, légendes et épopées populaires d'Arménie*. Vol. I: *Contes* (translated from the Armenian). Paris, 1928, pp. 142–9. *Gabriel or the Soul-carrying Angel*, from H. Haïrapetian (in Armenian). *Burakn*, XIII, No. 6 (1900), 359–61. In this A T 332, Gabriel, the angel of Death, gives the hero, on the day of his wedding, the two lights of life or two candles that are often to be found in other versions (Occitan, Spanish . . .), including Truquette's wedding in *JLP* (see my Chapter IX).

MacManus, Seamus. *Tales That Were Told*. Dublin, 1960, p. 84. *Tinker of Tamlacht*. After an incident in which the devil is shut up in a sack, there follows a classic A T 332 (Irish here). The sick king threatens to have the physician–hero killed if he does not cure him (see the old *French* version of Grimm); the bed is turned round by four strong fellows, as in Gueullette (1712), and as in the Quebec A T 332.

Mair, Lucy. *Marriage*. Harmondsworth, 1971.

Maranda, Elli K., see *Quebec*.

Martineau-Genieys, C. *La Thème de la mort dans la poésie française de 1450* [in fact from 1150] *à 1550*. Paris, 1978.

Maspons y Labros, Francesco. *Contes populars catalans*. Barcelona, 1952, pp. 117–20. An important local version of A T 332.

Masse, J.-B. *Le Protée*, with passages in Provençal. Play performed at Marseille at the carnival of 1759 (ms. Bibliothèque Arbaud, Aix, 2652 A–1).

Massignon, Geneviève. *Contes corses*. Aix-en-Provence, 1963, pp. 37–40. Tale 18: *Lesta* (*Girl with the Basil*, especially p. 38).

Maugard, Gaston. *Contes de Pyrénées*. Paris, 1955, pp. 116–19. *Le filleul de la Mort*. This is an excellent French translation, but with some small variants, of the Occitan version collected by Urbain Gibert (see under this name).

Mayer, M. *Lou Retour doou Martegaou*. Play performed and published at Marseille in 1775.

Megas, Georgios A. *Folktales of Greece*. Chicago, 1970, pp. 46–8. Tale 23: *The Shepherd* . . . (AT 332 in Greece).

Méraville, Marie-Aimée. *Contes populaires de l'Auvergne*. Paris, 1970, pp. 101–5. Tale 13: *La marraine et son filleul* (AT 332 of Auvergne).

Meyen, Victor de. *De Vlaamsche Vertelselschar*. Antwerp, 1927. Vol. II, pp. 182–4. Tale 124: *Doctor Hatt en Nijd*. The physician–hero of AT 332 is called Hatred-and-Envy, as in the story by G. Forteguerri, about 1550.

Meyer, Gustav. *Essays und Studien zur Sprachgeschichte und Volkskunde*. Berlin, 1885, pp. 242–76. *Der Pathe des Todes*. Contains (unfortunately without precise references) important analyses of European Jewish and Lithuanian versions of AT 332, as well as an interesting Albanian version (see *Albania*).

Meyer, Maurits de. 'Les contes populaires de la Flandre'. *Folklore Fellows Communications*, XXXVII (1921), 34–5, 46 (for AT 332); *Folklore Fellows Communications*, CCIII (1968), 16–20, 50 (for AT 332). Inventory of Flemish versions, in Belgium, of fairy-tales.

Michalhe or Michaille, playwright from Béziers, early seventeenth century, see his plays under *Théâtre populaire de Béziers*.

Michel, H. 'Pratique notariale . . . a Montpellier [*c.* 1680]'. In *Les Actes notariés*. Strasbourg, 1979, pp. 163–71.

Michel, Henri. 'La Civilisation populaire en Languedoc à l'époque moderne'. Diss. Univ. de Montpellier.

Millet, Jean. *Pastorale et Tragi-comédie de Janin*. Grenoble, 1633; *La Pastorale de la constance de Philin et Margoton*. Grenoble, 1635; *La Bourgeoisie de Grenoble*. Grenoble, 1665.

Millien, Achille, and Delarue, Paul. Manuscripts in the Musée des Arts et Traditions Populaires. They contain collections of Nivernais tales made in the 1880s. Five versions of AT 332 kindly provided by Mme Tenèze, and catalogued from *A* to *E*; four versions of *Jean-le-sot* or *L'Âne qui pète* (AT 1240 and 1313).

——. *Contes du Nivernais et du Morvan*. Paris, 1953, pp. 293–4. Tale 24 belongs to the cycle of *Jean-le-sot*. Important bibliography. It also refers to tale type AT 1240 and 1313, and to motif J 2311–1 of Stith Thompson, *Motif Index of Folk-Literature* (see under this name).

Mir, Mathilde, and Delample, Fernande. *Histoires et Récits du pays occitan*. Angoulême, 1948, pp. 108–11. *Misère et la Mort*. Version of AT 332 collected by the authors in mid-Ariège, from two elderly peasant women.

Mistral, Frédéric. *Prose d'Almanach*. Paris, 1926, pp. 20–31. *L'ome juste*. Reproduction in Provençal and in French of a Provençal version of AT 332, first published by Mistral in 1876.

——. *Lous Trésor dou Félibrige* (French–Provençal dictionary). 2 vols. Paris, 1932.

Molinier, A. *Sérignan* (Hérault). Montpellier, 1968.

Mondonville, J.-J. Cassanea de. *Daphnis et Alcimadure*. Paris, 1754. Languedocian pastoral.

Monnet, Jean. *Anthologie françoise, ou chansons choisies depuis le XIIIᵉ siècle jusqu' à présent*. 3 vols. Paris, 1765. See also Collé, Charles.

Mont, P. de. 'Vragen en Aanteekeningen'. *Volkskunde*, I (1888), 56–7. Devil, then Death, in a Flemish AT 332.

——, and Cock, A. de. *Dit zÿn Vlaamsche Wonderssprookjes*. Ghent, 1896, pp. 182–7. Tale 24: *Van Doopvader Dood*.

Morizot. *Pierre et Perrette ou le galant jardinier*. Marseille, 1758 (Bibliothèque nationale, Rés.).

La Mort au Moyen Age. Proceedings of a conference of the Association des historiens médiévistes français. 1975. Strasbourg, 1977.

Moscherosch, Hanss Michael. *Geschichte Philanders von Sittewald*. Published by Felix Bobertag from the original text of 1643, Darmstadt, 1964. See also Arnim, Ludwig Achim von. *Sämtliche Werke*. Leipzig, 1842. Vol. XI, pp. 165–6. Publication of this same text.

Moser-Rath, Elfriede. *Deutsche Volksmärchen*. Berlin, 1964, pp. 118–19. Tale 28: *Gevatter Tod*.

——. *Predigtmärlein der Barockzeit*. Berlin, 1964, pp. 213–14 (Andreas Strobl), 273–5 (Strobl's version of AT 332 of 1691) and 470 (AT 332, tale 121).

Moulis, Adelin. *Contes merveilleux des Pyrénées*. Verniolle (Ariège), 1976, pp. 105–11. *Misère*. Version from Ariège of AT 332, collected by Moulis in 1948.

Müller, Joseph. *Sagen aus Uri*. Vol. III. *Schriften der schweizerische Gesellschaft für Volkskunde*. Vol. XXVIII. Ed. Robert Wildhaber. Basel, 1943–5, pp. 106–7. Tale 119: 'Swiss tale'.

Nameoc, A., see *Volk en Taal*.

Nelli, René. *L'Érotique des troubadours*. Paris, 1974.

Nicolas, Jean, and Nicolas, Renée. *La Vie quotidienne en Savoie au XVIIIe siècle*. Paris, 1979.

Noulet, J.-B. *Essai sur l'histoire littéraire des patois du midi de la France au XVIIIe siècle*. Paris, 1877. Rpt. Geneva, 1971.

'Novelle populari abruzzesi'. *Archivio per lo studio delle Tradizioni populari*, V, 4th series (1886), 203. Tale 1: *Miseria*. AT 332, in which Death falls from the sky.

Olsvanger, I. *Aus der Volksliteratur der Ostjuden, Schwänke, Erzählungen* . . . Basel, 1920. *The Son of the Angel of Death* (in Yiddish, kindly translated by Jean Baumgarten). Classic (Jewish) version of AT 332 mixed with 'Belphégor'. Placebo of water mixed with liquorice, as in *JDT*. Conflict between the hero and powerful man, as in *JLP*.

Orain, Adolphe. *Contes de l'Ille-et-Vilaine*. Paris, 1901, pp. 207–15. *Le médecin de Fougeray*.

Orsini-Marzoppi, Marie-France. *Récits et Contes populaires de Corse*. Paris, 1978. Vol. I, pp. 77–9. *Cinnarrella*, version collected in 1978 in Corsica.

Pansier, P. *Théâtre provençal d'Avignon au XVIIe siècle*. Avignon, 1932. Plays, in particular by Séguin.

Parsons, E. Clews, see Clews Parsons, Elsie.

Pauzer, Friedrich. *Die Kinder- und Hausmärchen der Brüder Grimm*. Wiesbaden, 1947, pp. 304–5. The commentaries on tales 42 and 44.

Pélabon, Étienne (1745–1808). *Maniclo vo lou Groulié bel esprit*. Avignon, 1790.

Perbosc, Antonin. *Contes de Gascogne*. Coll. Suzanne Cézerac. Paris, 1954, pp. 102–6. *Polichinelle et Ratapon*. Occitan version of *The Spirit in the Bottle*, collected at Loze in 1902.

——, and Cézerac, Suzanne. Manuscripts of Occitan stories, collected from oral versions and preserved in the Musée des Arts et Traditions Populaires, tales 38 and 39 (texts and French translations).

Petit, J.-M., see Vieu, E., and Petit, J.-M.

Pitré, Giuseppe. *Fiabe, Novelle e Racconti popolari Siciliani*. Palermo, 1875. Vol. II, p. 399. Tale 109: *La Morti e só figghiozu*.

Platter. *Félix et Thomas Platter à Montpellier* (1552–99). Montpellier, 1892.

Poulhariez, M. *Le Taciturne*. Originally performed at Marseille. Paris, 1778.

Pourrat, Henri. Series of *Trésor des contes au village*. Paris, 1979, pp. 236–47. Two versions of AT 332 from Puy-de-Dôme; they are situated at the crossroads of other versions from the Midi (Occitan and Roussillonnais) as are *JDT*, *JLP*, Bédat de Monlaur and *Galdric*. They deserve a study of their own.

Praetorius, Johann. *Das abenteuerliche Glückestopf.* 1669, pp. 147ff. *Das Patengeld machet reich.* Old version of AT 332, reproduced in Bolte, Johannes, 1894, p. 38 (see under this name).

Prion, Pierre. Manuscript of the *Chronologiette* from the village of Aubais (Gard), from 1744 to 1759, a photocopy of which was kindly lent to me by Gérard Jean, of Aubais.

Pröhle, Heinrich. *Kinder- und Volksmärchen*. Leipzig, 1853, pp. 54–9.

Prym, E., and Socin, A. *Syrische Sagen und Märchen, aus dem Volksmunde gesammelt*. Göttingen, 1881, p. 299. Syrian-Christian version of AT 332: Death as an angel of Death makes a pact of deferment with the hero, who escapes death for a long time, thanks to the trick of the unfinished *Pater Noster*.

Quebec: I am grateful to Mme E. Maranda for lending me a file comprising six Quebec versions, five of which are not published, of *Godfather Death*, as well as sixteen Quebec versions of the tale *Jean-le-sot* (the file belongs to the folklore archives of the Laval University, Quebec).

Rael, Juan B. *Cuentos españoles de Colorado y Nuevo Mexico*. Stanford, pp. 141–4, 634. Tales 84, 85, 86, 83. Death gives the hero of AT 332 two candles or lights of life; the hero is shaved and finally killed by Death.

Ranke, Kurt. *Schleswig-holsteinische Volksmärchen*. Kiel, 1955, pp. 11–14, 265. Valuable bibliography on AT 332.

Reed, Evelyn. *Woman's Revolution: From Matriarchal Clan to Patriarchal Family*. New York, 1975. See, especially, Ch. X, pp. 224, 234ff.

Ricci, Luigi, and Ricci, Francesco. *Crispino e la comare*. Milan, n.d. [*c.* 1840]. Rather literary, but typical dramatic version of AT 332, whose hero, like Truquette, is a cobbler.

Robe, Stanley L. *Mexican Tales and Legends from Vera Cruz*. Folklore Studies, No. 23. Berkeley, 1971. Tale 6 (at the end, Death takes the shaven hero) and tale 8.

———. *Index of Mexican Folktales*. Folklore Studies, No. 26. Berkeley, 1975, pp. 65–7. Tale 332. Crucially important references to the Spanish (later Mexican) versions of A T 332: the woodcutter hero; Death dangerous *behind the door*; shaving of the hero's head; attracting Death instead of tricking her; etc.

———. *Hispanic Folktales from New Mexico*. Berkeley, 1977, pp. 76–9. Tales 38 and 39. The hero hides *behind the door*, but Death catches him! He appears to kill Death, who revives.

Robert, Catherine, and Valière, Michel. *Récits et Contes populaires du Poitou*. Paris, 1979. Vol. I, pp. 63, 103–4, 175, 178. Cycle from Poitou of *Jean-le-sot*, collected in the 1970s.

Rocal, l'abbé Georges. *Le Vieux Périgord*. Paris and Toulouse, 1927, p. 50.

Roche, Daniel. 'La Mort au XVIIIᵉ siècle'. *Annales* (1976), 76–120.

———. *Le Siècle des lumières en province: Académies et académiciens provinciaux*. Paris and The Hague, 1978.

Rond den heerd. VIII (1873), 341–2. *Van Pieter . . . die de dood zocht*.

Rotunda, D. P. *Motif Index of the Italian Novella in Prose*. Bloomington, 1942, p. 263.

Rouger, G. *La Vie de mon père*. Paris, 1970.

Roumieux, L. See Fabre, Jean-Baptiste Castor, *Istoria* . . .

Rouquette, Jean. *La Littérature d'oc*. Paris, 1968. See, in particular, pp. 72–5.

Rouquette, Y. See Fabre, Jean-Baptiste Castor, *Istoria* . . .

Rousset, Pierre. *Lou Jaloux otropat*. Written about 1645; various editions at Sarlat, 1676, 1694, 1839, etc.

Routtier or Routié, Alexandre. *Lou Mariagi de Margarido*. Marseille, 1781.

Russel-Reaver, J. 'Four Lithuanian-American Folktales'. *Southern Folklore Quarterly*, XII, No. 4 (1948), 261–2. *God and Death. The Spirit in the Bottle* (here in a sack) and *Godfather Death*.

Saal, G., see Stier, G.

Sachs, Hans. *Sämtliche Fabeln und Schwänke*. Ed. E. Goetz and K. Drescher. Halle, 1893 and 1903. Vols. I and IV, pp. 290, 315. Poems 99 and 448. 'Der Pawer mit dem Dot', 1547.

Salomon, Noël. *Recherches sur le thème paysans dans la 'comedia' au temps de Lope de Vega*. Bordeaux, 1965.

Sanctus, History of, see Bolte, Johannes, 1900.

Sauzet, Robert, *Contre-Réforme et Réforme catholique en Bas-Languedoc, Le diocèse de Nîmes au XVIIe siècle*. Diss. Univ. de Lille III. Paris and Louvain, 1979.

Scatabronda, see 'Fabre de Thémines'.

Schischmanoff, Lydia. *Légendes religieuses bulgares*. Paris, 1896, pp. 174–94. Tales 72, 73, 75. Three fine classic versions of AT 332. Death represented by the archangel Michael, taker of souls. Placebo of water. Death in a dominant position and residing in a forest.

Schmidt, Bernard. *Griechische Märchen* . . . Leipzig, 1877, pp. 177, 235. *Gevatter Charos*. Versions of AT 332 from the West and collected in Greece at Mitylene. Godfather Charos. Placebo of coloured water; the hero turns the bed round in order to escape Death/Charos/godfather, who then takes him by the hair, and finally kills him (despite the fact that he had tried to disguise himself by shaving his beard).

Schönwerth, F. *Aus der Oberpfalz, Sitten und Sagen*. Augsburg, 1859. Vol. III, pp. 12–15. Tale 3: the physician–hero of AT 332 first cures a rich peasant.

Schulenburg, Willibald von. *Wendisches Volkstum in Sage, Brauch, und Sitte*. 2nd ed. Leipzig, 1934. Rpt. Lichtenstein, 1968, pp. 54–5. *Der Tod als Gevatter*.

Schullerus, Adolf. 'Verzeichnis der Rumänischen Märchen'. *Folklore Fellows Communications*, No. 78, p. 37. Inventory of Romanian versions of the tale AT 332.

Schulte-Kemminghausen, Karl. *Die niederdeutschen Märchen der Brüder Grimm*. Veröffentlichungen der Volkskundlichen Kommission des Prov. Insiti. für Westfal. Landes- und Volkskunde, Heft 1. Münster-in-Westfalen, 1932, pp. 73–5. Tale 17: *Gevatter Tod*.

Sébillot, Paul. *Littérature orale de la Haute-Bretagne*. Paris, 1881, pp. 135ff., 137ff. The priest's fart, etc.

———. 'La Mort en voyage'. *Archivio per lo studio delle Tradizioni popolari*, IV (1885), 422–9. Three versions of AT 332 which Sébillot was later to republish in *Contes des landes* . . ., 1900.

———. Various Breton versions of *Jean-le-sot* or *The Farting Donkey*. *Revue des traditions populaires*, IX (1894), 388–9; and XI (1896), 442–4.

———. *Contes des landes et des grèves*. Rennes, 1900, pp. 245–58. Three Breton versions of AT 332, collected by Sébillot in 1882 and 1883.

———. *Les Joyeuses Histoires de Bretagne*. Paris, 1910, pp. 142ff. On the 'donkey's fart'; see also Sébillot, Paul, 1896, p. 442.

Séguin, see Pansier, P.

Seigne Peyre . . ., see *Comédie de Seigne Peyre . . .*

Seligmann, S. *Der böse Blick.* 2 vols. Berlin, 1910.

Sénéquier, P. 'Blason populaire provençal'. *Revue des traditions populaires*, XII (1897), 75. On 'le Sot' or 'le Niais' in Provence.

Sentou, Jean. *Fortunes et Groupes sociaux à Toulouse sous la Révolution.* Toulouse, 1969.

Serreau, J.-M. and G. *Veillées aux quatre coins de France.* Paris, 1943, pp. 135–9. *Le filleul de l'Ankou.* Classic Breton version of A T 332, collected by J.-M. Guilcher. The turning round of the sick-bed on pulleys. Death = character from the wild Landes.

Simrock, Karl. *Handbuch der deutschen Mythologie.* Bonn, 1887, p. 275.

Staes, G. 'Compeere de Dood'. *Volkskunde* (1894), 35–9. *Godfather Death* combined with *Death Trapped in the Bottle.*

Starobinski, Jean. *1789.* Paris, 1979.

Stier, G. *Ungarische Volksmärchen* [from the text of G. Saal]. Pest, 1857, pp. 30ff. *Der Arme und der Tod.* Classic (Hungarian) version of A T 332. Baptism on a *Sunday*, with *festivities.*

Storch, Karl. *Deutsche Märchen aus Westböhmen.* Marienbad, 1937, pp. 29–30. Version of A T 332 from the Sudetenland.

Stouff, Louis, 'Arles à la fin du Moyen Age.' Diss. Univ. d'Aix-en-Provence, 1979. Apart from the data on social homogamy, this dissertation clearly shows the possibilities of social ascent for a shepherd who becomes a big farmer (pp. 604–5) in the manner of Monsieur Sestier in *JLP.*

Strobl, Father Andreas (*c.* 1691), see Moser-Rath, Elfriede, 1964.

Suilleabhain, Sean O., and Christiansen, Reider T. 'The Types of the Irish Folktale', *Folklore Fellows Communications*, No. 188 (1963), 84–5. Inventory of the many Irish versions of A T 332.

Sveinsson, E. O. 'Verzeichnis isländisher Märchenvarianten'. *Folklore Fellows Communications*, No. 83 (1928), 32. Old and more recent Icelandic versions of A T 332.

'Swiss tale', see Müller, Joseph.

Théâtre populaire de Béziers (1616–57, plays performed on Ascension Day), in the *Bulletin de la Société archéologique de Béziers*, V (1844–8) and VI (1855) (the whole of vol. V and half of vol. VI).
    Histoire du valet Guilhaumes et de la Chambrieiro Antoigne.

Pastorale du berger Célidor et de Florimonde sa bergère (1629).

Histoire du mauvais traitement fait par ceux de Villeneuve à la ville de Béziers pendant la contagion (1632).

La Fausse Magie découverte, histoire tragi-comique où après plusieurs Combats et Duels est accompli le mariage de Crisante avec Olimpe (1635).

Pastorale del bergé Silvestre ambé la bergeyro Esquibo (1650).

Les Mariages rabillez (1647).

Las amours de Damon et de Lucresso (1657).

Histoire Pastorale [de Sirene, Diane, Riolan] (1633).

Thiry, Claude. 'La Plainte funèbre'. *In Typologie des sources du Moyen Age occidental*. Brepols, 1978, fasc. 30.

——. 'De la mort marâtre à la mort vaincue'. The 9th international colloquium of Louvain. *La Mort au Moyen Age*. Louvain, May 1979.

Thompson, Stith. *Motif Index of Folk-Literature*. Bloomington, 1933. In particular, vol. II, pp. 431–2 (the 'lights of life'); vol. IV, pp. 339–40 (tricking Death by turning the bed round: motif K 606). See also, motifs J 486, D 1724, D 1825, D 1851–2, Z 111 (and also F 384–1–2: salt makes the food harmless; see my Chapter XVI).

——. *The Folktale*. New York, 1951, pp. 46–7. On *Godfather Death*, *The Spirit in the Bottle*, *Death's Messengers*.

Todorov, Tzvetan. *Introduction à la littérature fantastique*. Paris, 1976.

Toschi, Paolo. *Le Origini del teatro italiano*. Turin, 1955.

Traven, B. *The Night Visitor and Other Stories*. New York, 1966, pp. 193–235. *Macario*, a literary development of a version of A T 332 of Spanish American origin. A Death from a forest, standing over the hero, at the beginning of the tale, etc.

Trimberg, Hugo von. *Der Renner*. Published by G. Ehrismann, Tübingen, 1909. Vol. III, pp. 277ff. *Von dem Tode*.

Trinkaus C., and Oberman, H. A. *The Pursuit of Holiness in Late Medieval and Renaissance Religion*. Leyden, 1974.

Tronc de Codolet, Palamede. *Lei fourbaries dau siècle . . .* 'Cologne', 1757. The first edition dates from 1684.

Troubat, Jules, see Fabre, Jean-Baptiste Castor, *Istoria . . .*

Vandorpe, A. *Volksvertellingen* [in Flemish]. 1905. Rpt. about 1920. Vol. I, pp. 50–71. A T 332: *Hop, in mijnen Zak*.

Van Gennep, A. *Manuel du folklore français contemporain*. Paris, 1943–58. Vol. I–1, p. 128. *Du berceau à la tombe*. On grandparents as godfather and godmother.

Veckenstedt, E. *Wendische Sagen.* Graz, 1800, p. 341. *Der Tod.*

Vellote ou le mariage à la mode, 1716. Languedocian play (at Gignac). Analysed by J.-B. Noulet, 1877 (see under this name), p. 105. Four characters: the daughter, the widowed mother, the lover, the soldier.

Venault, P., et al. *Un soulèvement populaire, Romans, 1580.* Paris, 1979.

Vernaleken, Theodor. *Œsterreiche Kinder- und Hausmärchen.* Vienna, 1864, pp. 223–32. Tale 42: *Der Kröpfige* ['with the goitre']. Apart from its remarkable homology with *JDT*, this tale combines the motif of the turning round of the bed with that of enclosing Death in a bottle, as does version D of A T 332 in the Millien and Delarue manuscripts, and a Quebec and a Scottish version.

———. *In the Land of Marvels, Folktales from Austria and Bohemia.* London, 1883, pp. 232–40. *Hans-with-the-Goitre.* English translation of the original German version of 1864.

———. 'Der Fährmann und der Tod'. *Germania, Vierteljahrsschrift für deutsche Alterthumskunde,* XXIX (XVII of the new series) (1884), 414– 16. Tale 5. This other version of A T 332, less important for us than the previous one (that of Vernaleken, 1864), has nevertheless preserved the macabre, plague-laden atmosphere in which the tale originally developed between 1300 and 1500.

Vervliet, J. B. *Ons Volksleven* (in Flemish). 1889. Vol. I, pp. 23–5. *The Man Who Sought Justice.*

Vidal-Naquet, P., see Le Goff, Jacques, and Vidal-Naquet, P.

Vieu, E., and Petit, J.-M. *Repertori del teatre d'oc.* Montpellier, 1973.

Villeneuve, comte Christophe de Villeneuve-Bargemont. *Mœurs des Provençaux . . .* 1826. Rpt. 1972.

Vinson, J. *Le Folklore du Pays basque.* Paris, 1883, pp. 93–8. A *Jean-le-sot* from the Basque country.

Volk en Taal, 3rd year, fasc. 11 (1891), 259. *Haat en Nijd . . .* A T 332: *Hatred-and-Envy,* tale collected by A. Nameoc; see Meyen, Victor de.

Volkskunde, XV (1903), 40–41. *Van den Zieken man die den Dood fopte.*

Vovelle, Michel. *Piété baroque et Déchristianisation en Provence au XVIIIᵉ siècle.* Paris, 1973.

———. 'L'histoire au miroir de la Mort'. Montpellier, 1979 (photocopy).

Waldburg, R. O. 'Zwei Märchen aus der Bukowina'. *Zeitschrift für Deutsche Mythol. herausgeg. von J. W. Wolf.* Göttingen, 1853. Vol. I, pp. 358–60.

Gevatter Tod, in Bukovina. The physician–hero of AT 332 makes for himself (in vain) a gyratory bed in order to escape Death.

Webster, W. *Basque Legends*. London, 1879, p. 67. *Jean-le-sot*.

Weitz, Margaret C. 'François de Belleforest's la Pyrénée'. *Renaissance Quarterly*, XXXI, No. 3 (Autumn 1978), 322–31. On the first Gascon and French pastoral novel (1571).

Wesselki, Albert. *Märchen des Mittelalters*. Berlin, 1925, pp. 211–13. On the first identified [Icelandic] version of AT 332.

Wheeler, Howard T. *Tales from Jalisco, Mexico*. Philadelphia, 1943. Tale 152: A Spanish-American version of *Juan Holgado*. Tales 154, 155 (pp. 443–53), in particular tale 154: the role of the devil, together with Death, as an indicator of fatal diagnosis, for the benefit of the physician–hero of AT 332.

Widter, G., Wolf, A. and Köhler, R. 'Volksmärchen aus Venetien'. *Jahrbush für roman und englisch literatur*, VII (1866), 16–19. *Der Gevatter Tod*. This classic Venetian version of AT 332 also contains the important motif of Death being dangerous 'behind the door'.

Winkler, Karl. *Oberpfälzische Sagen, Legenden, Märchen* . . . Kallmünz, 1935, pp. 264–5. *Der Tod als Gevatter*. This version of AT 332 is closely related to the 'Swiss tale' (see Joseph Müller), itself a brother or father of our 'Truquette'.

Wlislocki, Heinrich von. *Märchen und Sägen der Transsilvanien Zigeuner*. Berlin, 1886, pp. 94–6. Tale 38: *Der Tod als Pate*. Classic, bigenerational version of AT 332 from an Orthodox Christian gypsy environment. Death dangerous *behind the door* (inside his underground residence).

Wolf, J. W. *Deutsche Hausmärchen*. Göttingen and Leipzig, 1851, pp. 365–8. *Der Schloss des Todes*.

Wolff, Heinrich. 'Der Gevatter Tod'. Reproduced in Bolte, Johannes, 1894, p. 39 (see under this name). Poem of February 1644.

Yver, J. *Essai de géographie coutumière*. Paris, 1966.

Zaunert, Paul. 'Wom armen Weber, wie er einen Gevattern gesucht'. In *Deutsche Märchen an dem Donaulande*. Jena, 1926, pp. 194–7.

Zender, Mathias. *Volksmärchen und Schwänke aus der Westeifel*. Bonn, 1935, pp. 16, 155. Tale 11: *Der Tod als Pate*.

Zerbin, Gaspard. *La perlo dey Muses et Coumedies provensalos*. Aix, 1655 and 1872.

Zingerle. *Sitten, Braüche und Meinungen des tiroler Volkes*. 2nd ed. 1871, p.

160. After Bolte, Johannes, 1896 (see under this name). *Godmother Death*, who is usually the feminized incarnation, in the Latin countries, of the male godfather Death, is reused as such (by cultural importation from the south?) in a Tyrolean version of A T 332.

Zonabend, Françoise. 'La parenté baptismale à Minot (Côte-d'Or)'. *Annales* (1978), 656–76. See, in particular, pp. 666ff., on the maternal grandmother and godmother.

Index